Everyman's Thesaurus of
English Words and Phrases

Pan Reference Books

Everyman's Thesaurus of English Words and Phrases

revised from PETER ROGET

by D. C. Browning, MA (Glasgow),
BA, B Litt (Oxon)

Pan Books London and Sydney

Everyman edition first published 1952 by J. M. Dent and Sons Ltd
This edition published 1972 by Pan Books Ltd,
Cavaye Place, London SW10 9PG
9th printing 1978
All rights reserved
ISBN 0 330 02951 7
Printed and bound in Great Britain by
Hazell Watson & Viney Ltd, Aylesbury, Bucks

INTRODUCTION

It is just a hundred years since Roget's *Thesaurus of English Words and Phrases* was first published. In the course of that century of unprecedented development and change our language and vocabulary have undergone modifications and additions which have been dealt with from time to time in previous revisions of the work. But a new generation has grown up since the last recension, and the time seemed ripe for a more complete overhaul which would make it thoroughly up to date. Accordingly, the opportunity has been taken, in preparing this new single-volume edition, of giving the work as complete a revision as was possible, short of doing the whole compilation afresh. Every paragraph has been carefully reviewed, over 10,000 words and phrases have been added, and the articles have been 'tidied up' so that all additions follow the logical order which agrees with the original plan.

In the course of its century of use Roget's *Thesaurus* has come to be as widely accepted and as indispensable to writers as a dictionary, and its system and arrangement have become so familiar that any radical alteration of them would lessen the value of the book to those who know their way about it from constant use. For that reason no attempt has been made to modify the main scheme which Roget originally laid down, and except for a few very minor alterations of numbering where the order had become confused the arrangement is the same as in previous editions. Within this scheme the articles have been greatly amplified and expanded, some of the pages containing up to a hundred fresh insertions.

The list of contents at the beginning sets out the plan of classification, and indicates the general divisions of the book. Readers who are interested in the detailed subdivisions of the classification will find them in the different paragraph headings, and the general principles of the work are explained in Roget's original Introduction, now printed at the end of the volume.

Technical Terms.

In giving some account of the additions which have been made, it is natural to start off with those technical terms which have been coined to fit modern scientific, political, and cultural developments. The wide range of the subjects covered is shown by these typical examples taken at random: *air-condition, airgraph, allergy, antibiotic, Appleton layer, bathysphere, Dadaism, deviationist, diarchy, displaced person, electrolysis, existentialism, fifth column, Gallup poll, geriatrics, Heaviside layer, hydroponics, intercom, ionosphere, iron curtain, libido, liquidate, parapsychology, psychotherapist, quisling, radar, robot, rotor, stratosphere, surrealism, telekinesis, television, troposphere, weather station.*

Aviation.

Along with the previous section may be grouped the very numerous terms which deal with recent developments in aviation and aerial warfare. These represent new types of aircraft: *autogiro, flying fortress, flying wing, jet aircraft, stratocruiser, stratoliner*; new types of weapon: *atom bomb, buzz-bomb, doodlebug, flying bomb, guided missile, V1, V2*; new names for personnel: *group-captain, wing-commander, squadron-leader, flight-lieutenant*; and for their evolutions: *air lift, bunt*. Finally there are words for the yet untried adventure of interplanetary voyaging: *astronautics, spacecraft, space ship, space travel*.

Everyday Neologisms.

In addition to words marking scientific advance there are also, of course, many neologisms reflecting change or fashion in everyday affairs, such as *baby-sitter, bingle, blurb, bottle-neck, bottle party, bulldozer, cannibalize, cartophily, embus, exclosure, frogman, green belt, infrastructure, jive, lumberjacket, nylons, phillumenist, play-pen, plug* (repeat), *prefab, pullover, quiz, screen* (test), *stockpile, totalizator, zipper*.

Slang Terms.

New slang terms form a considerable proportion of our additions, and among them will be noted a large number of service, particularly Air Force Coinages; the newest arm seems to have eclipsed the Navy in fertility of etymological invention. A few of the more recent terms are: *blah, browned off, bunce, chokka, dippy, erk, flap* (fuss), *flat out, flicks* (cinema), *gen, good show, hush-hush, It, Joe Soap, loopy, mike* (microphone), *never-never system, oodles, popsy, scarper, scatty, shemozzle, smashing, sprog, toffee-nose, twerp, whodunit*, and such phrases as *get cracking, get weaving, gone for a Burton, in a spin, it's in the bag, a piece of cake, shoot down in flames, step on it, tear off a strip, couldn't care less*.

Americanisms.

So many of our slang and other new words are borrowed from across the Atlantic that they demand a separate paragraph. A number of the commoner Americanisms had already been incorporated in the work, but fresh additions include *attaboy, bobbysoxer, boloney, bonehead, bughouse, burp, calaboose, chipper, come-back, cutie, didoes, doll up, faze, floosy, 'fraid-cat, G-man, gander* (look), *goo, grip-sack, haywire, hick, high-hat, hoodlum, hooey, hophead, jeep, jinx, josh, juke box, mazuma, mortician, motel, oomph, once-over, pan* (face), *pep, pinch-hitter, punk, rube, scram, screwball, simoleons, simp, smog, snoop, soup-and-fish, spondulics, stand-in, stooge, stuffed shirt, teenager, tuxedo, upstage, wisecrack, wop, yegg*, along with phrases like *cut no ice, hit the hay, out of kilter, stick one's neck out, take a run-out powder, give the frozen mitt*.

Scotticisms.

The opportunity has also been taken to insert a few of the terms in most common use north of the Tweed or wherever there are colonies of

Scots. Only the most familiar words have been inserted, such as *ben,
brae, callant, canny, clachan, clarts, dander, dunt, fash, flyte, glaur, gowk,
havers, hoots, jalouse, kenspeckle, kittle, kyle, kyte, lum, ooss, pech, ploy,
quaich, scunner, shilpit, shoogle, siller, skelp, skirl, smeddum, smirr,
snowk, sonsy, speer, stot* (bounce), *stour, stramash, thole, thrapple, thowless, tirrivee, wean* (child), *wersh, wheesht.*

Nouns of Assemblage.

Among the more interesting old-fashioned additions may be men-
tioned the collection of nouns of assemblage in paragraph 72. In
addition to the familiar *flock, herd, drove, pack*, there are listed the
distinctive terms *sounder* (of swine), *skulk* (of foxes), *pride* (of lions),
charm (of finches), *flush* (of mallards), *gaggle* (of geese), and *wedge* (of
swans). To old patrons of the work this list should make up for the
omission of the tedious and pointless catalogue of different methods of
divination, from aeromancy to sciomancy, which was formerly given
as a footnote under *Prediction* (511).

Changes and Excisions.

Very few changes have been made in the original grouping. The
list of types of *tobacco-pipe* has been transferred from the *Air-pipe*
paragraph to the *Tobacco* section, where it will naturally be more in
keeping. The account of religious terms towards the end of the book
has been rearranged so that *dissenters* and *nonconformists* are no longer
grouped with *idolaters, fire-worshippers*, and other *heathens* under the
comprehensive but hardly explicit heading of *Heterodoxy*. A number
of foreign words and phrases have been omitted, particularly the more
out-of-the-way Latin phrases, which are no longer so popular as in the
days when Classics and culture were synonymous. Finally, many
words, like *caisson, chaperon, château*, which were formerly italicized
as foreign are now printed in ordinary characters, having been accepted
as English.

The Index.

A clear idea of the extent of the volume's expansion can be gathered
from the size of the index, which occupies 744 columns as against 608
somewhat shorter columns in the last Everyman edition. The opportunity has been taken of arranging the alphabetization of the references
according to the up-to-date 'nothing-before-something' system set out
in the pamphlet on Alphabetical Arrangement published by the British
Standards Institution. By this system phrases are inserted in order
after their initial word, and hyphened words are reckoned as two except
when the initial component is merely a prefix. Every attempt has
been made to render the index as complete as possible, and the process
of hunting the required word in the body of the work has been further
simplified by the insertion of numerous cross-references in those cases
where one paragraph is closely related to others.

1952   D. C. B.

NOTE

SINCE the first publication of the single-volume edition in Everyman's Reference Library in 1952 several reprints and a substantial revision in 1962 have taken account of recent developments in English vocabulary.

Two hundred words or meanings have been inserted in their appropriate places throughout the various sections, and corresponding references have been added to the index. In 1955 separate sections were allotted to *Aircraft, Cinema* and *Radio*. The revision of 1962 reflected progress in space travel, radio, transport and jazz music, with such words as *astronaut, lunik, orbital; newscast, teleprompter, transistor; clearway, speedway, traffic warden; bebop, rock-and-roll, skiffle*. Also included were examples of terms coined for types of pompous circumlocution (e.g. *officialese, gobbledygook*), and modern slang.

D. C. Browning having relinquished his editorship, the publishers' staff have continued the process of updating with numerous words in the same sections, and have added many more hitherto omitted from other sections. The present edition of the *Thesaurus* continues to record the neologisms of recent years in the *push-button* age, among them *bent, hippy, junkie, mini-, teach-in, whizz-kid* and everyday phrases such as *cliff-hanging, hive-off, industrial action, lean over backwards, steady as she goes*, and *at the end of the day*.

1971

CONTENTS

Everyman's Thesaurus of
English Words and Phrases

CLASS I

WORDS EXPRESSING ABSTRACT RELATIONS

1°. *Being in the Abstract*

1 EXISTENCE (*Substantives*), being, life, vital principle, entity, ens, essence, quiddity, subsistence; co-existence (120).

Reality, actuality, positiveness, absoluteness, fact, truth (494); actualization.

Presence; existence in space (186).

Science of existence, ontology; existentialism.

(*Phrases*) The sober reality; hard fact; matter of fact; the whole truth; no joke.

(*Verbs*) To be, to exist, have being, subsist, live, breathe, stand, abide, remain, stay, obtain, occur, prevail, be so, find itself, take place, eventuate, consist in, lie in; to vegetate, pass the time.

To come into existence, arise, come out, emerge, come forth, appear (448).

To bring into existence, produce, bring forth, discover (161), objectify.

(*Adjectives*) Existing, being, subsisting, subsistent, in being, in existence, extant, living, breathing, obtaining, prevailing, prevalent, current, afoot.

Real, actual, positive, absolute, essential, substantial, substantive, self-existing, self-existent; undestroyed, tangible, not ideal, not imagined, not supposititious, not potential, virtual, effective, unideal, true, authentic, genuine, mere, objective.

(*Adverbs*) Actually, really, absolutely, positively, etc., in fact, *de facto*, *ipso facto*.

(*Phrase*) *In esse*; *cogito ergo sum.*

2 INEXISTENCE (*Substantives*), non-existence, not-being, nonentity, *nihil*, nil, non-subsistence, nullity, vacuity, blank (4), negativeness, absence (187), removal (185).

Annihilation, abeyance, extinction (162); nirvana.

Philosophy of non-existence, nihilism.

(*Phrases*) No such thing; Mrs. Harris; 'men in buckram.'

(*Verbs*) Not to be, not to exist, etc.

To cease to be, pass away, perish, vanish, fade away, dissolve, melt away, disappear (449), to be annihilated, extinct, etc., to die (360), to die out.

(*Phrases*) To have no being; to have no existence; to be null and void; *non est*; to be no more; 'to leave not a rack behind'; to disappear into thin air; to be brought out of existence.

(*Adjectives*) Inexistent, non-existent, non-existing, etc., negative, blank, absent.

Unreal, potential, virtual, baseless, unsubstantial (4), imaginary, ideal, vain, fanciful, unpractical, shadowy, fabulous (515), supposititious (514).

Unborn, uncreated, unbegotten, unproduced, unmade.

Annihilated, destroyed, extinct, gone, lost, perished, melted, dissolved, faded, exhausted, vanished, missing, disappeared, departed, extinct, defunct (360).

(*Adverbs*) Negatively, virtually, etc.

(*Phrase*) *In nubibus.*

2°. Being in the Concrete

3 SUBSTANTIALITY (*Substantives*), hypostasis, person, thing, being, something, existence, entity, reification, corporeity, body, physique, substance, object, article, creature, matter, material, stuff (316), substratum, protoplasm.

Totality of existences, world (318), continuum, plenum.

(*Phrase*) Something or other.

(*Adjectives*) Substantive, substantial, personal, bodily, tangible, true, real, concrete, corporal, corporeal, material, objective, hypostatic.

(*Verbs*) Substantialize, actualize, materialize, reify, embody.

(*Adverbs*) Substantially, etc., essentially.

4 UNSUBSTANTIALITY (*Substantives*), insubstantiality, nothingness, nihility, nothing, naught, damn-all, *nihil*, nil, nix, love, zero, cipher, a duck, duck's-egg, pair of spectacles; nonentity, nobody, no one (187).

A shadow, phantom, phantasm, phantasmagoria, dream, mockery, air, thin air, idle dream, pipe dream, castle in Spain (515), idle talk, ignis fatuus, *fata morgana*, mirage.

Void, vacuum, vacuity, vacancy, voidness, vacuousness, inanity, emptiness, hollowness, blank, chasm, gap, hiatus (198); empty space, ether.

(*Phrases*) Nothing at all; nothing whatever; nothing on earth; nothing under the sun; not a particle.

A man of straw; *vox et praetera nihil*; 'such stuff as dreams are made on.'

(*Verbs*) To vanish, fade, dissolve, evaporate.

(*Adjectives*) Unsubstantial, immaterial, void, vacant, vacuous, blank, null, inane, idle, hollow, airy, visionary (515).

3°. Formal Existence

Internal Conditions

5 INTRINSICALITY (*Substantives*), inbeing, immanence, inherence, inhesion, essence; essentiality, essentialness, subjectiveness, subjectivity, essential part, soul, quintessence, quiddity, gist, pith, core, backbone, marrow, sap, lifeblood; incarnation.

Nature, constitution, character, type, quality (157), temperament, temper, manner, spirit, ethos, habit, humour, grain, endowment, capacity, capability, moods, declensions, features, aspects, specialities, peculiarities (79), particularities, idiosyncrasy, idiocrasy, diagnostics.

(*Verbs*) To be innate, inborn, etc.

External Conditions

6 EXTRINSICALITY (*Substantives*), extraneousness, objectiveness, objectivity, accident, superficiality, incident.

(*Adjectives*) Derived from without, objective, extrinsic, extrinsical, extraneous, modal, adventitious, adscititious, incidental, accidental, nonessential, outward (220).

Implanted, engrafted.

(*Adverb*) Extrinsically, etc.

(*Phrases*) To be in the blood; to be born like that.

(*Adjectives*) Derived from within, subjective, intrinsic, intrinsical, inherent, essential, natural, internal, implanted, inborn, innate, inbred, engrained, inherited, immanent, indwelling, radical, constitutional, congenital, connate, hereditary, instinctive, indigenous.

(*Phrases*) In the grain; in the blood; bred in the bone.

Characteristic, peculiar, qualitative, special, diagnostic (79), invariable.

(*Adverbs*) Intrinsically, subjectively, substantially, at bottom, *au fond*, at the core.

4°. *Modal Existence*

Absolute

7 STATE (*Substantives*), condition, category, class, kind, estate, lot, case, constitution, habitude, diathesis, mood, temper, morale.

Frame, fabric, structure, texture, contexture (329), conformation, organism.

Mode, modality, schesis, form, shape (240), figure, cut, cast, mould, stamp, set, fit, tone, tenor, trim, turn, guise, fashion, aspect, complexion, style, manner, character, kind, get-up, set-up, format, *genre*.

(*Verbs*) To be in a state, to be in condition, to be on a footing, etc.

To do, fare; to have, possess, enjoy, etc., a state, condition, etc.

To bring into a state, etc. (144).

(*Adjectives*) Conditional, modal, formal, structural, organic, textual.

(*Phrases*) As the matter stands; as things are; such being the case.

(*Adverb*) Conditionally, etc.

———

Relative

8 CIRCUMSTANCE (*Substantives*), situation, phase, position, posture, attitude, place, point, bearings, terms, fare, regime, footing, standing, status, predicament, contingency, occasion, juncture, conjuncture, emergency, exigence, exigency, crisis, pinch, impasse, pass, push, plight, fix.

(*Phrases*) How the land lies; how the wind blows; how the cat jumps.

(*Adjectives*) Circumstantial; given, conditional, provisional, modal, critical, contingent, incidental (6, 151), circumstanced, placed.

(*Verb Phrases*) To bow before the storm; to take things as they come; to cut one's coat according to the cloth.

(*Adverbs*) In or under the circumstances, conditions, etc.; thus, so; in such a case, contingency, etc.; accordingly, such being the case; since, sith, seeing that, as matters stand, as things go.

Conditionally, provided, if, an if, if so, if so be, if it be so, if it so prove, or turn out, or happen; in the event of, provisionally, unless, without.

(*Phrases*) According to circumstances; as it may happen, or turn out; as the case may be; *pro re nata*; wind and weather permitting; D.V.; rain or shine; sink or swim; at all events; other things being equal; *ceteris paribus*.

SECTION II—RELATION

1° *Absolute Relation*

9 RELATION (*Substantives*), relationship, bearing, reference, standing, concern, cognation, correlation (12), analogy, affinity, homology, alliance, homogeneity, connection, association, approximation, similarity (17), filiation, affiliation, etc. (11, 166), interest, habitude; relativity.

Relevancy, pertinency, fitness, etc. (646, 23).

Aspect, point of view, comparison (464); ratio, proportion.

Link, tie (45), homologue.

10 Want or absence of relation.

IRRELATION (*Substantives*), disconnection, dissociation, disassociation, misrelation, independence, isolation (44), multifariousness, disproportion; commensurability, irrelevancy; heterogeneity, irreconcilableness (24), impertinence.

(*Verbs*) To have no relation with, or to, to have nothing to do with, to have no business there, not to concern, not to admit of comparison.

(*Verbs*) To be related, have a relation, etc., to relate to, refer to, have reference to, bear upon, regard, concern, touch, affect, have to do with, pertain to, belong to, appertain to, answer to, interest.

To bring into relation with, correlate, associate, connect, affiliate, link (43), bring near (197), homologize; to bring to bear upon.

(*Phrase*) To draw a parallel with.

(*Adjectives*) Relative, correlative, cognate, relating to, relative to, relevant, in relation with, referable to, pertinent (23), germane, belonging to, pat, to the point, apposite, to the purpose, apropos, *ad rem*, just the thing, quite the thing; pertaining to, appertaining to, appurtenant, affiliated, allied, related, implicated, connected, associated, *en rapport*, in touch with, bound up with, homological, homologous.

Approximate, approximative, approximating, proportional, proportionate, proportionable, allusive, comparable, like, similar (17).

(*Adverbs*) Relatively, thereof, as to, about, connecting, concerning, touching, anent, as relates to, with relation to, relating to, as respects, with respect to, in respect of, respecting, as regards, with regard to, regarding, in the matter of, with reference to, according to, while speaking of, apropos of, in connection with, inasmuch as, whereas, in consideration of, in point of, as far as, on the part of, on the score of, under the head of, *in re*; pertinently, etc. (23).

To isolate, separate, detach, disconnect, segregate (44).

(*Adjectives*) Irrelative, irrespective, unrelated, without reference, etc., to, arbitrary, episodic, remote, far-fetched, forced, out of place, out of tune (414), inharmonious, malapropos, irrelevant, foreign to, alien, impertinent, inapposite, extraneous to, strange to, stranger to, independent, parenthetical, incidental, outlandish, exotic, unallied, unconnected, disconnected, unconcerned, adrift, detached, isolated, insular.

Not comparable, incommensurable, inapplicable (24), irreconcilable, heterogeneous (83), unconformable.

(*Phrases*) Foreign to the purpose; nothing to the purpose; having nothing to do with; *nihil ad rem*; neither here nor there; beside the mark; *à propos des bottes*; dragged in by the scruff of the neck.

(*Adverbs*) Parenthetically, by the way, by the by, *obiter dicta*, *en passant*, incidentally, irrespectively, irrelevantly, etc.

---

11 Relations of kindred.

CONSANGUINITY (*Substantives*), relationship, kindred, blood, parentage (166), filiation, affiliation, lineage, agnation, connection, alliance, family connection, family tie, nepotism.

A kinsman, kinswoman, kinsfolk, kith and kin, relation, relative, friend, sibling, one's people, clan, connection, one's own flesh and blood, brother, sister, father, mother, uncle, aunt, nephew, niece, stepfather, etc., brother-in-law, etc., guid-brother, etc., cousin, cousin-german; first, second cousin; cousin once, twice, etc., removed; grand- or great-grandfather, etc., great-uncle, etc., a near relation, a blood-relation, a distant relation or relative, congener, collateral.

Family, issue, fraternity, sisterhood, brotherhood, parentage, cousinhood, etc.; race, stock, generation, sept, clan, tribe, strain.

(*Verbs*) To be related, to have or claim relationship with.

(*Adjectives*) Related, akin, consanguineous, congeneric, family, kindred, affiliated, allied, collateral, sib, agnate, agnatic, fraternal, of the same blood, nearly or close related, remotely or distantly related.

(*Phrase*) Blood is thicker than water.

12 Double relation.

RECIPROCALNESS (*Substantives*), reciprocity, mutuality, correlation, correlativeness, interdependence, interchange, interaction, reciprocation, etc. (148), alternation (149), barter (794).

(*Verbs*) To reciprocate, alternate, interchange, interact, exchange, counterchange, interdepend.

(*Adjectives*) Reciprocal, mutual, common, correlative, alternate, alternative; interchangeable, interdependent, international.

(*Adverbs*) Reciprocally, mutually, etc.

(*Phrases*) *Mutatis mutandis*; each other; vice versa; turn and turn about.

---

13 IDENTITY (*Substantives*), sameness, oneness, coincidence, coalescence, convertibility; selfness, self, ego, oneself, number one; identification, monotony; equality (27), tautology (104).

Synonym; facsimile (21), counterpart (17).

(*Verbs*) To be identical, to be the same, etc., to coincide, to coalesce.

To render the same.

To recognize the identity of, to identify, recognize.

(*Adjectives*) Identical, identic, same, self, selfsame, very same, no other, ilk, one and the same, ditto, unaltered, coincident, coinciding, coessential, coalescing, coalescent, indistinguishable, tantamount, equivalent, equipollent, convertible, much the same.

(*Adverbs*) **All** one, all the same, *ibidem*, ibid, identically, likewise.

(*Phrases*) *Semper idem*; *toujours la même chose*; *alter ego*; on all fours; much of a muchness.

14 Non-coincidence.

CONTRARIETY (*Substantives*), contrast, foil, set-off, antithesis, contradiction, opposition, oppositeness, antagonism (179, 708), distinction (15).

Inversion, reversion (218).

The opposite, the reverse, inverse, converse, antonym, the antipodes (237).

(*Phrases*) The reverse of the medal; the other side of the shield; the tables being turned.

(*Verbs*) To be contrary, etc., to contrast with, contradict, contravene, oppose, negate, antagonize, invert, reverse, turn the tables, to militate against.

(*Adjectives*) Contrary, opposite, counter, converse, reverse, antithetical, opposed, antipodean, antagonistic, opposing, conflicting, inconsistent, contradictory, contrarious, contrariant, negative.

(*Phrases*) Differing *toto caelo*; diametrically opposite; as black to white; light to darkness; fire to water; worlds apart; poles asunder.

(*Adverbs*) Contrarily, contrariously, contrariwise, *per contra*, oppositely, *vice versa*, on the contrary, *tout au contraire*, quite the contrary, no such thing.

---

15 DIFFERENCE (*Substantives*), variance, variation, variety, diversity, modification, allotropy, shade of difference, nuance; deviation, divergence, divarication (291), disagreement (24), dissimilarity (18), disparity (28).

Distinction, contradistinction, differentiation, discrimination (465); a nice or fine or subtle distinction.

(*Phrases*) A very different thing; a *tertium quid*; a horse of a different colour; another pair of shoes.

(*Verbs*) To be different, etc., to differ, vary, mismatch, contrast, differ *toto caelo*.

To render different, etc., to vary, change, modify, varify, diversity, etc. (140).

To distinguish, differentiate, severalize (465), split hairs, discriminate.

(*Adjectives*) Different, differing, disparate, heterogeneous, heteromorphic, allotropic, varying, distinguishable, discriminative, varied, modified, diversified, deviating, diverging, devious, disagreeing (24), various, divers, all manner of, multifarious, multiform, variform (81), variegated (440), diacritical.

Other, another, other-guess, not the same.

Unmatched, widely apart, changed (140).

(*Phrase*) As different as chalk is from cheese.

(*Adverbs*) Differently, variously, otherwise.

2°. *Continuous Relation*

16 UNIFORMITY (*Substantives*), homogeneity, homogeneousness, consistency, connaturality, conformity (82), homology, accordance, agreement (23), regularity (58), routine, monotony, constancy.

(*Verbs*) To be uniform, etc., to accord with, harmonize with, hang together, go together.

16A Absence or want of uniformity. NON-UNIFORMITY (*Substantives*), variety, multiformity (81), diversity, unevenness, irregularity, unconformity (83).

(*Adjectives*) Multiform, multifarious, various (81), diversified, inconsistent, of various kinds.

To become uniform, conform with, fall in with, follow suit.

To render uniform, to assimilate, level, smooth (255).

(*Adjectives*) Uniform, homogeneous, homologous, of a piece, of a kind, consistent, connatural, monotonous, even, unvarying, flat, level, constant.

(*Adverbs*) Uniformly, uniformly with, conformably (82), consistently with, in unison with, in harmony with, in conformity with, according to (23).

Regularly, at regular intervals, invariably, constantly, always, without exception.

(*Phrases*) In a rut (or groove); *ab uno disce omnes*; 'forty feeding like one.'

3°. *Partial Relation*

17 SIMILARITY (*Substantives*), resemblance, likeness, similitude, affinity, semblance, approximation, parallelism (216), analogy, brotherhood, family likeness; alliteration, head-rhyme, pun, assonance, repetition (104), reproduction.

An analogue, copy (21), the like, facsimile, match, double, pendant, fellow, pair, mate, twin, *alter ego*, parallel, counterpart, brother, sister; simile, metaphor (521), resemblance, imitation (19).

(*Phrases*) One's second self; *Arcades ambo*; birds of a feather; *et hoc genus omne*; a chip of the old block; the very spit (and image) of.

(*Verbs*) To be similar, like, resembling, etc., to look like, resemble,

18 DISSIMILARITY (*Substantives*), unlikeness, dissimilitude, diversity, divergence, difference (15), novelty (123), originality (515), disparity (28).

(*Verbs*) To be unlike, etc., to vary (15, 20).

To render unlike, to diversify (140).

(*Phrase*) To strike out something new.

(*Adjectives*) Dissimilar, unlike, disparate, of a different kind, class, etc. (75); diversified, novel, new (123), unmatched, unique, unprecedented (83).

(*Phrases*) Nothing of the kind; far from it; cast in a different mould; as different as chalk is from cheese.

(*Adverb*) Otherwise.

bear resemblance, favour, approximate, parallel, match, imitate, take after (19), represent, simulate, personate, savour of, have a flavour of, favour, feature.

To render similar, assimilate, approximate, reproduce, bring near, copy, plagiarize.

(*Adjectives*) Similar, like, alike, resembling, twin, analogous, analogical, parallel, allied to, of a piece, such as, connatural, congener, matching, conformable, on all fours with.

Near, something like, suchlike, mock, pseudo, simulating, representing, approximating, a show of, a kind of, a sort of.

Exact, accurate, true, faithful, close, speaking, lifelike, breathing.

(*Phrases*) True to nature; to the life; for all the world like; like as two peas; *comme deux gouttes d'eau*; cast in the same mould; like father, like son.

(*Adverbs*) As if, so to speak, as it were, quasi, as if it were, just as, after, in the fashion or manner of, *à la*.

---

19 IMITATION (*Substantives*), assimilation, copying, transcription, transcribing, following, repetition (104), duplication, reduplication, quotation, reproduction.

Mockery, mocking, mimicry, mimicking, echoing, reflection, simulation, counterfeiting, plagiarism, forgery, fake, fakement, acting, personation, impersonation, representation (554), copy (21), parody, paraphrase, travesty, burlesque, semblance, mimesis.

An imitator, mimic, impersonator, echo, cuckoo, parrot, ape, monkey, mocking-bird.

Plagiary, plagiarist, forger, counterfeiter.

(*Phrase*) *O imitatores, servum pecus.*

(*Verbs*) To imitate, copy, plagiarize, forge, fake, reproduce, photograph, repeat (104), echo, re-echo, transcribe, match, parallel, emulate, do like, take off, hit off, reflect, mirror, model after (554).

To mock, mimic, ape, simulate, personate, impersonate (554), act, represent, adumbrate, counterfeit, parody, travesty, caricature, burlesque.

(*Phrases*) To take or catch a likeness; to take after; to follow or tread in the steps of, or in the footsteps of; to take a leaf out of another's book; to follow suit; to go with the stream; to be in the fashion.

(*Adjectives*) Imitated, copied, matched, repeated, paralleled, mock, mimic, parodied, etc., modelled after, moulded on, paraphrastic, imitative, mimetic, slavish, mechanical, synthetic, second-hand, imitable.

(*Adverbs*) Literally, verbatim, to the letter, *literatim, sic, totidem verbis*, so to speak, in so many words, word for word, *mot à mot* (562).

20 NON-IMITATION (*Substantives*), originality, inventiveness, novelty.

(*Adjectives*) Unimitated, uncopied, unmatched, unparalleled, inimitable, unique, original, novel.

(*Verb*) To originate.

VARIATION (*Substantives*), alteration, modification, difference (15), change (140), deviation (279), divergence (291); moods and tenses.

(*Verbs*) To vary, modify, change, alter, diversify (140).

(*Phrase*) To steer clear of.

(*Adjectives*) Varied, modified, diversified, etc.

(*Adverbs*) Variously, in all manner of ways.

---

21 Result of imitation.

COPY (*Substantives*), facsimile, counterpart, effigies, effigy, form, likeness, similitude, semblance, reflex,

22 Thing copied.

PROTOTYPE (*Substantives*), original, model, pattern, standard, type, scale, scantling, archetype, protoplast,

portrait, photograph (556), photo-stat, microfilm, enlargement, minia-ture, study, cast, autotype, electro-type, imitation, replica, representa-tion, adumbration.

Duplicate, transcript, transcrip-tion, repetition (104), réchauffé, reflection, shadow, record, recording.

Rough copy, fair copy, revise, car-bon copy, tracing, rubbing, squeeze, draft or draught, proof, pull, reprint.

antitype, module, exemplar, example, ensample, protoplast, paradigm, fugleman, lay figure.

Text, copy, design, plan, blue-print, keynote.

Mould, matrix, last, plasm, pro-plasm, mint, die, seal, stamp, nega-tive.

(*Verbs*) To set a copy, to set an example.

Counterfeit, parody, caricature, burlesque, travesty, paraphrase, forgery.

(*Phrases*) A second edition; a twice-told tale.

4°. *General Relation*

23 AGREEMENT (*Substantives*), accord, accordance, unison, uni-formity, harmony, union, concord, concert, concordance (714), cogna-tion, conformity, conformance (82), consonance, consentaneousness, con-sensus, consistency, congruity, con-gruence, congeniality, correspondence keeping, parallelism.

Fitness, pertinence, suitableness, adaptation, meetness, patness, rele-vancy, aptness, aptitude, coaptation, propriety, apposition, appositeness, reconcilableness, applicability, appli-cableness, admissibility, commensur-ability, compatibility, adaptability.

Adaptation, adjustment, gradua-tion, accommodation, reconciliation, reconcilement, concurrence (178), consent (488), co-operation (709).

(*Verbs*) To be accordant, to agree, accord (714), correspond, tally, jibe, respond, harmonize, match, suit, fit, befit, hit, fall in with, chime in with, quadrate with, square with, cancel with, comport with, assimilate, unite with.

To render accordant, to adapt, ac-commodate, adjust, reconcile, fadge, dovetail, dress, square, regulate, com-port, graduate, gradate, grade.

(*Phrases*) To become one; to fit like a glove; to suit one to a T.

(*Adjectives*) Agreeing, accordant, concordant, consonant, congruous, consentaneous, consentient, corre-sponding, correspondent, congenial,

24 DISAGREEMENT (*Substantives*), discord, discordance, dissonance, dis-harmony, dissidence, discrepancy, unconformity, disconformity, non-conformity, incongruity, incongru-ence, *mésalliance*, discongruity, jar-ring, clashing, jostling (713), incon-sistency, inconsonance, disparity, disproportion, disproportionateness, variance, divergence, jar, misfit.

Unfitness, repugnance, unsuitable-ness, unsuitability, unaptness, in-eptitude, inaptness, impropriety, inapplicability, inadmissibility, irre-concilableness, irreconcilability, in-commensurability, inconcinnity, in-compatability, inadaptability, inter-ference, intrusion, irrelation (10).

(*Verbs*) To disagree, belie, clash, jar, oppose (708), interfere, jostle (713), intrude.

(*Phrase*) To have no business there.

(*Adjectives*) Disagreeing, discordant, discrepant, jarring, clashing, repug-nant, incompatible, irreconcilable, intransigent, inconsistent with, un-conformable, incongruous, dispropor-tionate, disproportioned, unpropor-tioned, inharmonious, inconsonant, mismatched, misjoined, misjudged, unconsonant, incommensurable, in-commensurate, divergent (291).

Unapt, inapt, inept, inappropriate, improper, unsuited, unsuitable, in-apposite, inapplicable, irrelevant, not pertinent, impertinent, malapropos, ill-timed, intrusive, clumsy, unfit,

harmonizing, harmonious with, tallying with, conformable with, in accordance with, in harmony with, in unison with, in keeping with, squaring with, quadrating with, falling in with, of one mind, of a piece, consistent with, compatible, reconcilable with, commensurate.

Apt, apposite, pertinent, germane, relating to, pat, bearing upon (9), applicable, relevant, fit, fitting, suitable, happy, felicitous, proper, meet, appropriate, suiting, befitting, becoming, seasonable, deft, accommodating, topical.

(*Phrases*) The cap fits; to the point; to the purpose; *rem acu tetigisti*; at home; in one's element.

unfitting, unbefitting, unbecoming, misplaced, forced, unseasonable, far fetched, inadmissible, uncongenial, ill-assorted, ill-sorted, repugnant to, unaccommodating, irreducible.

(*Phrases*) Out of season; out of character; out of keeping; out of joint; out of tune; out of place; out of one's element; at odds; a fish out of water.

(*Adverbs*) Discordantly, etc.; at variance with, in defiance of, in contempt of, in spite of, despite.

———

Section III—Quantity

1°. *Simple Quantity*

25 Absolute quantity.
Quantity. (*Substantives*), magnitude (192), amplitude, size, mass, amount, volume, area, quantum, measure, substance.

Science of quantity, mathematics.

Definite or finite quantity, handful, mouthful, spoonful, bucketful, pailful, etc.; stock, batch, lot.

(*Adjective*) Quantitative.

(*Phrase*) To the tune of.

26 Relative quantity.
Degree (*Substantives*), grade, gradation, extent, measure, ratio, stint, standard, height, pitch, reach, sweep, radius, amplitude, magnitude, water, calibre, range, scope, shade, tenor, compass, sphere, rank, station, standing, rate, way, sort.

Point, mark, stage, step, position, slot, peg; term (71).

Intensity, might, fullness, strength (31), conversion (144), limit (233).

(*Adjectives*) Comparative, gradual, shading off.

(*Adverbs*) By degrees, gradually, *gradatim*, inasmuch, *pro tanto*, however, howsoever, step by step, rung by rung, bit by bit, little by little, by inches, inch by inch, by slow degrees, by little and little, in some degree, to some extent.

2°. *Comparative Quantity*

27 Sameness of quantity or degree.
Equality (*Substantives*), parity, co-extension, evenness, equipoise, level, balance, equivalence, equipollence, equilibrium, poise, equiponderance, par, quits.

Equalization, equation, equilibration, co-ordination, adjustment, symmetry.

28 Difference of quantity or degree.
Inequality (*Substantives*), disparity, imparity, imbalance, odds, handicap, bisque, difference (15), unevenness.

Preponderance, preponderation, inclination of the balance, advantage, prevalence, partiality.

Superiority (33), a casting vote; inferiority (34).

A drawn game or battle, a dead heat, a draw, a tie.

A match, peer, compeer, equal, mate, fellow, brother (17), equivalent, makeweight.

(*Phrases*) A distinction without a difference; a photo finish.

(*Verbs*) To be equal, etc., to equal, match, come up to, keep pace with; come to, amount to, balance, cope with.

To render equal, equalize, level, balance, equate, aequiparate, trim, dress, adjust, fit, accommodate, poise, square; to readjust, equipoise, equilibrate, set against.

(*Phrases*) To be or lie on a level with; to come to the same thing.

To strike a balance; to establish or restore equality; to stretch on the bed of Procrustes; to cry quits.

(*Verbs*) To be unequal, etc., to preponderate, outweigh, outbalance, overbalance, prevail, countervail, predominate, overmatch, outmatch (33).

To fall short of, to want (304), not to come up to.

(*Phrases*) To have or give the advantage; to turn the scale; to kick the beam; to topple over.

(*Adjectives*) Unequal, uneven, disparate, partial, unbalanced, overbalanced, top-heavy, lopsided, preponderating, outweighing, prevailing.

(*Phrases*) More than a match for, above par; below par; *haud passibus aequis.*

———

(*Adjectives*) Equal, even, quit, level, coequal, co-ordinate, equivalent, synonymous, tantamount, convertible, equipollent, equiponderant, equiponderous, square.

Rendered equal, equalized, equated, drawn, poised, levelled, balanced, symmetrical, trimmed, dressed.

(*Phrases*) On a par with; on a level with; much of a muchness; as broad as it is long; as good as; all the same; all one; six to one and half a dozen of the other; not a pin to choose between them; tarred with the same brush; diamond cut diamond.

(*Adverbs*) Pari passu, equally, symmetrically, *ad eundem*, practically, to all intents and purposes, neck and neck.

29 Mean (*Substantives*), medium, intermedium, compromise, average, norm, balance, middle (68), *via media, juste milieu.*

Neutrality, mediocrity, middle course, shuffling.

(*Phrases*) The golden mean; the average man; the man in the street.

(*Verbs*) To compromise, pair off, cancel out.

(*Phrases*) To sit on the fence; split the difference; strike a balance; take the average; reduce to a mean; to take a safe course.

(*Adjectives*) Mean, intermediate, middle, median, normal, average, mediocre, middling, ordinary (82), neutral.

(*Adverb phrases*) On an average; in the long run; half-way; taking the one with the other; taking all things together; in round numbers.

30 COMPENSATION (*Substantives*), equation, commutation, compromise (774), idemnification, neutralization, nullification, counteraction (179), recoil (277), atonement (952).

A set-off, offset, makeweight, counterpoise, ballast, indemnity, hush-money, amends, equivalent.

(*Phrases*) Measure for measure; give and take; *quid pro quo*; tit for tat.

(*Verbs*) To compensate, make up for, indemnify, countervail, counterpoise, balance, compromise, outbalance, overbalance, counterbalance, counteract, set off, hedge, redeem, neutralize (27), cover.

(*Phrases*) To make good; split the difference; fill up; make amends.

(*Adjectives*) Compensating, compensatory, countervailing, etc., equivalent, equipollent (27).

(*Phrase*) In the opposite scale.

(*Adverbs*) However, yet, but, still, all the same, for all that, nevertheless, none the less, notwithstanding, be that as it may, on the other hand, although, though, albeit, *per contra*.

(*Phrases*) As broad as it's long; taking one thing with another; it is an ill wind that blows nobody any good.

Quantity by Comparison with a Standard

31 GREATNESS (*Substantives*), largeness, magnitude, size (192), multitude (102), fullness, vastness, immensity, enormity, infinity (105), intensity (26), importance (642), strength.

A large quantity, deal, power, world, macrocosm, mass, heap (72), pile, sight, pot, volume, peck, bushel, load, stack, cart-load, wagon-load, truck-load, ship-load, cargo, lot, flood, spring tide, mobs, bags, oodles, abundance (639), wholesale, store (636).

The greater part (50).

(*Verbs*) To be great, etc., run high, soar, tower, transcend, rise, carry to a great height (305).

(*Phrases*) To know no bounds; to break the record.

(*Adjectives*) Great, gross, large, considerable, big, ample, above par, huge, full, saturated, plenary, deep, signal, extensive, sound, passing, goodly, famous, noteworthy, noble, heavy, precious, mighty (157), arch, sad, piteous, arrant, red-hot, downright, utter, uttermost, crass, lamentable, consummate, rank, thorough-paced, thorough-going, sovereign, unparalleled, matchless, unapproached, extraordinary, intense, extreme, pronounced, unsurpassed, unsurpassable.

Vast, immense, enormous, towering, inordinate, severe, excessive, monstrous, shocking, extravagant, exorbitant, outrageous, whacking, thumping, glaring, flagrant, preposterous, egregious, overgrown, stupendous, monumental, prodigious, marked, pointed, remarkable, astonishing, surprising (870), incredible, marvellous, transcendent,

32 SMALLNESS (*Substantives*), littleness, minuteness (193), tenuity, scantness, scantiness, slenderness, meanness, mediocrity, insignificance (643), paucity, fewness (103).

A small quantity, modicum, atom, particle, molecule, corpuscle, microcosm, jot, iota, dot, speck, mote, gleam, scintilla, spark, ace, minutiae, thought, idea, suspicion, *soupçon*, whit, tittle, shade, shadow, touch, cast, taste, grain, scruple, spice, sprinkling, drop, droplet, driblet, globule, minim, dash, smack, nip, sip, scantling, dole, scrap, mite, slip, snippet, tag, bit, morsel, crumb, paring, shaving (51), trifle, thimbleful, toothful, spoonful, cupful, mouthful, handful, fistful.

Finiteness, a finite quantity.

(*Phrases*) The shadow of a shade; a drop in a bucket or in the ocean.

(*Verbs*) To be small, etc., to run low, diminish, shrink, decrease (36), contract (195).

(*Phrases*) To lie in a nutshell; to pass muster.

(*Adjectives*) Small, little, wee, scant, inconsiderable, diminutive, minute (193), tiny, minikin, puny, petty, sorry, miserable, shabby, wretched, paltry (643), weak (160), slender, feeble, faint, slight, scrappy, fiddling, trivial, scanty, light, trifling, moderate, low, mean, mediocre, passable, passing, light, sparing.

Below par, below the mark, under the mark, at a low ebb, imperfect, unfinished, partial (651), inappreciable, evanescent, infinitesimal, atomic, homoeopathic.

Mere, simple, sheer, bare.

incomparable, tremendous, terrific, formidable, amazing, phenomenal, superhuman, titanic, immoderate.

Indefinite, boundless, unbounded, unlimited, incalculable, illimitable, immeasurable, infinite, unapproachable, unutterable, indescribable, unspeakable, inexpressible, beyond expression, swingeing, unconscionable, fabulous, uncommon, unusual (83).

Undiminished, unrestricted, unabated, unreduced, unmitigated, unredeemed, untempered.

Absolute, positive, decided, staring, unequivocal, serious, grave, essential, perfect, finished, completed, abundant (639).

(*Adverbs*) In a great degree, much, muckle, well, considerably, largely, grossly, greatly, very, very much, a deal, not a little, no end, pretty, pretty well, enough, richly, to a large extent, to a great extent, ever so, mainly, ever so much, on a large scale, insomuch, all lengths, wholesale, in a great measure.

In a positive degree, truly (494), positively, verily, really, indeed, actually, in fact, fairly, assuredly, decidedly, surely, clearly, obviously, unequivocally, purely, absolutely, seriously, essentially, fundamentally, radically, downright, in grain, altogether, entirely, completely.

In a comparative degree, comparatively, *pro tanto*, as good as, to say the least, above all, most, of all things, pre-eminently.

(*Adverbs*) In a small degree, on a small scale, to a small extent, a wee bit, something, somewhat, next to nothing, little, inconsiderably, slightly, so-so, minutely, faintly, feebly, lightly, imperfectly, scantily, shabbily, miserably, wretchedly, sparingly, weakly, slenderly, modestly.

In a limited degree, in a certain degree, to a certain degree or extent, partially, in part, some, somewhat, rather, in some degree, in some measure, something, simply, only, purely, merely, in a manner, at least, at most, ever so little, thus far, *pro tanto*, next to nothing.

Almost, nearly, well-nigh, all but, short of, not quite, close upon, near the mark.

In an uncertain degree, about, thereabouts, scarcely, hardly, barely, somewhere about, say, more or less, *à peu près*, there or thereabouts.

In no degree, noways, nowise, nohow, in no wise, by no means, not in the least, not at all, not a bit, not a bit of it, not a whit, not a jot, in no respect, by no manner of means, on no account.

(*Phrases*) As little as may be; after a fashion; in a way.

Within an ace of; on the brink of; next door to; a close shave (or call).

In a complete degree, completely (52), altogether, quite, entirely, wholly, totally, *in toto, toto coelo*, utterly, thoroughly, out and out, outright, out and away, fairly, clean, to the full, in every respect, *sous tous les rapports*, in all respects, on all accounts, nicely, perfectly, fully, amply, richly, wholesale, abundantly, consummately, widely, as . . . as . . . can be, every inch, *à fond, de fond*, far and wide, over head and ears, to the backbone, through and through, *ne plus ultra*.

In a greater degree, even, yea, *a fortiori*, still more.

In a high degree, highly, deeply, strongly, mighty, mightily, powerfully (157), profoundly, superlatively, ultra, in the extreme, extremely, exceedingly, excessively, consumedly, sorely, intensely, exquisitely, acutely, soundly, vastly, hugely, immensely, enormously, stupendously, passing, surpassing, supremely, beyond measure, immoderately, monstrously, inordinately, tremendously, over head and ears, extraordinarily, exorbitantly, indefinitely, immeasurably, unspeakably, inexpressibly, ineffably, unutterably, incalculably, infinitely, unsurpassably.

In a marked degree, particularly, remarkably, singularly, uncommonly, unusually, peculiarly, notably, *par excellence*, eminently, pre-eminently, superlatively, signally, famously, egregiously, prominently, glaringly, emphatically, strangely, wonderfully, amazingly, surprisingly, astonishingly, prodigiously, monstrously, incredibly, inconceivably, marvellously, awfully, stupendously.

In a violent degree, violently, severely, furiously, desperately, tremendously, outrageously, extravagantly, confoundedly, deucedly, devilishly, diabolically, with a vengeance, *à outrance*, like mad (173).

In a painful degree, sadly, grievously, woefully, wretchedly, piteously, sorely, lamentably, shockingly, frightfully, dreadfully, fearfully, terribly, horribly.

Quantity by Comparison with a Similar Object

33 SUPERIORITY (*Substantives*), majority, supremacy, primacy, advantage, preponderance, excess (641), prevalence, pre-eminence, championship.

Maximum, acme, climax, zenith, summit, utmost height, record, culminating point (210), the height of, lion's share, overweight.

(*Phrases*) A Triton among the minnows; cock of the walk; *ne plus ultra; summum bonum.*

(*Verbs*) To be superior, etc.; to exceed, surpass, excel, eclipse, transcend, top, overtop, o'ertop, cap, beat, cut out, outclass, override, outmatch, outbalance, overbalance, overweigh, overshadow, outdo; preponderate, predominate, prevail.

To render larger, magnify (194).

(*Phrases*) To have the advantage of; to have the upper hand; to bear the palm; to have one cold; to beat hollow; to take the shine out of; to throw into the shade; to be a cut above.

(*Adjectives*) Superior, greater, major, higher, surpassing, exceeding,

34 INFERIORITY (*Substantives*), minority, subordination, shortcoming (304); deficiency, minimum.

(*Verbs*) To be less, inferior, etc., to fall or come short of, not to pass (304); to want, be wanting.

To become smaller, to render smaller (195); to subordinate.

(*Phrases*) To be thrown into the shade; to hide one's diminished head; to give a person best; to play second fiddle.

(*Adjectives*) Inferior, deficient, smaller, minor, less, lesser, lower, sub, subordinate, subaltern, secondary, second-rate, second-best.

Least, smallest, wee-est, minutest, etc., lowest.

(*Phrases*) Weighed in the balance and found wanting; not fit to hold a candle to.

(*Adverbs*) Less, under or below the mark, below par, at the bottom of the scale, at a low ebb, short of, at a disadvantage.

———

excelling, passing, ultra, vaulting, transcending, transcendent, unequalled, unsurpassed, peerless, matchless, unparalleled, without parallel.

Supreme, greatest, utmost, paramount, pre-eminent, foremost, crowning, sovereign, culminating, superlative, topmost, top-hole, highest, first-rate, champion, A1, the last word, the limit.

(*Phrases*) *Facile princeps; nulli secundus; primus inter pares.*

(*Adverbs*) Beyond, more, over and above the mark, above par, over and above, at the top of the scale, at its height.

In a superior degree, eminently, pre-eminently, egregiously, prominently, superlatively, supremely, above all, of all things, principally, especially, particularly, peculiarly, *par excellence, a fortiori.*

Changes in Quantity

35 INCREASE (*Substantives*), augmentation, enlargement, extension, dilatation (194), increment, accretion, development, rise, growth, swell, swelling, expansion, aggrandizement, aggravation, rise, exacerbation, spread, climax, exaggeration, diffusion (73), flood-tide; accession (37).

(*Verbs*) To increase, augment, enlarge, amplify, extend, dilate, swell, wax, expand, grow, stretch, shoot up, mushroom, rise, run up, sprout, burgeon, advance, spread, gather head, aggrandize, add, superadd, raise, heighten, strengthen, greaten, exalt, enhance, magnify, redouble, aggravate, exaggerate, exasperate, exacerbate, escalate,

(*Phrases*) To add fuel to the flame; to pour oil on the flames.

(*Adjectives*) Increased, augmented, enlarged, etc., undiminished; cumulative; additional (37).

(*Adverb*) Crescendo.

36 NON-INCREASE.

DECREASE (*Substantives*) diminution, depreciation, lessening, reduction, abatement, bating, declension, falling off, dwindling, contraction (195), shrinking, attenuation, extenuation, anticlimax, abridgment, curtailment (201), coarctation, narrowing; deduction (38).

Subsidence, wane, ebb, decrement, (*Verbs*) To decrease, diminish, lessen, dwindle, decay, crumble, shrink, contract, shrivel, fall off, fall away, waste, wear, wane, ebb, subside, decline, languish, wear off, run low, grow downward.

To abridge, reduce, curtail, cut down, pare down, subtract, shorten, cut short, dock (201), bate, abate, fritter away, attenuate, extenuate, lower, weaken, dwarf; to mitigate (174), to throw in the shade.

(*Phrase*) To hide its diminished head.

(*Adjectives*) Decreased, diminished, lessened, etc., shorn, short by, decreasing, on the wane.

(*Adverbs*) *Diminuendo, decrescendo.*

3°. Conjunctive Quantity

37 ADDITION (*Substantives*) adjection, introduction, superinduction, annexation, superposition, superaddition, subjunction, supervention, increment, accession, superfetation, corollary, reinforcement, supplement, accompaniment (88), interposition (228), insertion (300).

(*Verbs*) To add, annex, affix, superadd, supplement, reinforce, subjoin, superpose, throw in, clap on, tack to, append, tag, engraft, saddle on, saddle with, superinduce, introduce, work in, interleave, extra-illustrate, grangerize.

To become added, to accrue, advene, supervene.

(*Phrase*) To swell the ranks of.

(*Adjectives*) Added, annexed, etc., additional, supplementary, supplemental, suppletory, subjunctive,

38 NON-ADDITION.

SUBDUCTION (*Substantives*), subtraction, abstraction, deduction, deducement, retrenchment, removal, elimination, ablation (789), purgation, curtailment, etc. (36), garbling, mutilation, truncation, abscission, excision, amputation, detruncation, sublation, castration, apocope.

Subtrahend, minuend; decrement, discount.

(*Verbs*) To subduct, exclude, deduct, subtract, abscind, retrench, remove, withdraw, eliminate, bate, detract, deduce, take away, deprive of, curtail (36), garble, truncate, mutilate, eviscerate, exenterate, detruncate, castrate, spay, geld, purge, amputate, cut off, excise, cut out, dock, lop, prune, pare, dress, clip, thin, shear, decimate, abrade (330).

adscititious, additive, accessory, cumulative.

(*Adverbs*) Additionally, in addition, more, *plus*, extra, and, also, likewise, too, furthermore, forby, item, and also, and eke, else, besides, to boot, etcetera, and so forth, into the bargain, over and above, moreover.

(*Adjectives*) Subtracted, deducted, etc., subtractive.

(*Adverbs*) In deduction, etc., less, *minus*, without, except, excepting, with the exception of, but for, barring, save, exclusive of, save and except (83).

With, together with, withal, along with, including, inclusive, as well as, not to mention, to say nothing of; jointly, conjointly (43).

39 Thing added.

ADJUNCT (*Substantives*), additament, addition, affix, appendage, annex, suffix, postfix, inflexion, augment, increment, augmentation, accessory, item, garnish, sauce, supplement, extra, bonus (810), adjective, addendum, complement, corollary, continuation, increment, reinforcement, pendant, apanage.

Sequel (65), postscript, codicil, envoy, rider, corollary, heel-piece, tag, tab, skirt, flap, lappet, trappings, tail, tailpiece (67), queue, train, suite, cortège, accompaniment (88).

(*Phrase*) More last words.

40 Thing remaining.

REMAINDER (*Substantives*), residue, remains, remnant, the rest, relics, leavings, heel-tap, odds and ends, cheese-parings, candle-ends, off-scourings, orts.

Residuum, *caput mortuum*, dregs, refuse (645), scum, recrement (653), ashes, dross, cinders, slag, sediment, silt, alluvium, stubble; slough, exuviae, result, educt.

Surplus, overplus, surplusage, superfluity, excess (641), balance, complement, fag-end, stump, butt, rump, wreck, wreckage, ruins, skeleton.

(*Verbs*) To remain, be left, be left behind, exceed, survive.

(*Adjectives*) Remaining, left, left behind, residual, exuvial, residuary, sedimentary, outstanding, net, cast off, odd, over, unconsumed, surviving, outlying.

Superfluous, over and above, exceeding, redundant (641), supernumerary.

41 Forming a whole without coherence.

MIXTURE (*Substantives*), admixture, commixture, commixtion, intermixture, alloyage, marriage, miscegenation.

Impregnation, infusion, infiltration, diffusion, suffusion, interspersion, transfusion, seasoning, sprinkling, interlarding, interpolation, interposition (228), intrusion; adulteration, sophistication.

Thing mixed, a touch, spice, tinge, tincture, dash, smack, sprinkling, seasoning, infusion, suspicion, *soupçon*, shade, bit, portion, dose.

Compound resulting from mixture, blend, alloy, amalgam, magma, *mélange*, half and half, hybrid, *tertium quid*, miscellany, medley,

42 Freedom from mixture.

SIMPLENESS (*Substantives*), singleness, purity, clearness, homogeneity.

Purification (652), elimination, sifting, winnowing.

(*Verbs*) To render simple, simplify, sift, winnow, bolt, screen, sort, eliminate; to separate, disjoin (44).

To purify (652).

(*Adjectives*) Simple, uniform, of a piece, homogeneous, single, pure, clear, sheer, blank, neat, absolute, elemental, elementary; unmixed, unmingled, untinged, unblended, uncombined, uncompounded, undecomposed, unadulterated, unsophisticated, undiluted, straight.

Free from, exempt from.

(*Phrase*) Pure and simple.

pastiche, pasticcio, patchwork, odds and ends; farrago, jumble (59), mess, salad, sauce, hash, hodge-podge or hotchpotch or hotchpot, mash, mish-mash, job lot, omnium gatherum, gallimaufry, olla podrida, olio, salmagundi, pot-pourri, Noah's ark, cauldron, marquetry, mosaic (440), complex.

A cross, hybrid, mongrel, half-breed, Eurasian, mulatto, quadroon, octoroon, sambo.

(*Phrases*) A mingled yarn; a scratch team.

(*Verbs*) To mix, commix, immix, intermix, associate, join (43), mingle, commingle, intermingle, bemingle, interlard, intersperse, interpose, interpolate (228); shuffle together, hash up, huddle together, deal, pound together, stir up, knead, brew, jumble (59); impregnate with.

To be mixed, to get among, to be entangled with.

To instil, imbue, infuse, infiltrate, dash, tinge, tincture, season, sprinkle, besprinkle, suffuse, transfuse, attemper, medicate, blend, alloy, amalgamate, compound (48), adulterate, sophisticate, infect, cross, intercross, interbreed, interblend.

(*Adjectives*) Mixed, mingled, intermixed, etc., motley, miscellaneous, promiscuous; complex, composite, mixed up with, half-and-half, linsey-woolsey, mongrel, heterogeneous; miscible.

43 JUNCTION (*Substantives*), joining, joinder, union, connection, connecting, hook-up, conjunction, conjugation, annexion, annexation, annexment, attachment, compagination, astriction, ligation, alligation, colligation, fastening, linking, accouplement, coupling, matrimony (903), grafting; infibulation, inosculation, symphysis, anastomosis, association (72), concatenation, communication, approach (197).

Joint, join, juncture, pivot, hinge, suture, articulation, commissure, mitre, seam, stitch, meeting, reunion, mortise.

Closeness, firmness, tightness, compactness, attachment, communication.

(*Verbs*) To join, conjoin, unite, connect, associate, put together, embody, re-embody, hold together, lump together, pack, fix together, attach, affix, saddle on, fasten, bind, secure, make fast, grapple, moor, clench (or clinch), catch, tie, pinion, strap, sew, lace, string, stitch, tack, knit, tat, crochet, knot, button, buckle, hitch, lash, truss, bandage, braid, splice, swathe, gird, tether, picket, harness, inspan, bridge over.

Chain, enchain, shackle, pinion, fetter, manacle, handcuff, lock, latch,

44 DISJUNCTION (*Substantives*), disconnection, disunity, disunion, disassociation, disengagement, abstraction, abstractedness, isolation, insularity, oasis, separateness, severalness, severality.

Separation, parting, detachment, divorce, sejunction, seposition, segregation, insulation, diduction, discerption, elision, caesura, division, subdivision, break, fracture, rupture, dismemberment, disintegration, dislocation, luxation, severance, disseverance, severing, fission, scission, rescission, abscission, laceration, dilaceration, wrenching, abruption, disruption, avulsion, divulsion, tearing asunder, section, cutting, resection, cleavage, fissure, breach, rent, split, crack, slit, tear, rip, dispersion (73), incision, dissection, vivisection anatomy.

Anatomist, prosector.

(*Phrase*) *Disjecta membra.*

(*Verbs*) To be disjoined, separated, etc., to come off, fall off, get loose, fall to pieces.

To disjoin, disconnect, disunite, part, dispart, detach, separate, space, space out, cut off, rescind, segregate, insulate, dissociate, isolate, disengage, set apart, liberate, loose, set free (750), unloose, unfasten, untie, unbind,

belay, brace, hook, clap together, leash, couple, link, yoke, bracket, hang together, pin, nail, bolt, hasp, clasp, clamp, screw, rivet, solder, weld, impact, wedge, rabbet, mortise, mitre, jam, dovetail, enchase, engraft, interlink, inosculate, entwine, enlace, interlace, intertwine, intertwist, interweave, interlock.

To be joined, etc., to hang or hold together, cohere (46).

(*Adjectives*) Joined, conjoined, coupled, etc., bound up together, conjunct, corporate, compact.

Firm, fast, close, tight, taut, secure, set, fixed, impacted, jammed, locked, etc., intervolved, intertwined, inseparable, indissoluble, inseverable, untearable.

(*Phrases*) Hand in hand; rolled into one.

(*Adverbs*) Conjointly, jointly, etc. With, along with, together with, in conjunction with.

Fast, firmly, closely, etc.

---

disband, unfix, unlace, unclasp, undo, unbutton, unbuckle, unchain, unfetter, untack, unharness, ungird, unpack, unbolt, unlatch, unlock, unlink, uncouple, unpin, unclinch, unscrew, unhook, unrivet, untwist, unshackle, unyoke, unknit, unsolder, ravel out, unravel, disentangle, unpick, unglue, switch off, shut off.

Sunder, divide, subdivide, divorce, sever, dissever, abscind, cut, scissor, incide, incise, snip, nib, cleave, rive, slit, split, split in twain, splinter, chip, crack, snap, burst, rend, break or tear asunder, shiver, crunch, chop, cut up, rip up, hack, hew, slash, whittle, haggle, hackle, discind, tear, lacerate, mangle, mince, gash, hash, knap.

Dissect, cut up, carve, slice, castrate, detruncate, anatomize; take, pull, or pick to pieces; unseam, tear to tatters, tear piecemeal, divellicate, disintegrate; dismember, disembowel, eviscerate, disbranch, dislocate, joint, disjoint, behead, mince, break up, crunch, gride, comminute (330), vivisect.

(*Phrase*) To tear limb from limb.

(*Adjectives*) Disjoined, disconnected, etc., snippety, disjointed, multipartite, abstract, disjunctive, isolated, insular, separate, discrete, apart, asunder, loose, free, liberated, disengaged, unattached, unannexed, distinct, unassociated, unconnected, adrift, straggling, dispersed, disbanded, segregated.

Cut off, rescinded, etc., rift, reft.

Capable of being cut, scissile, fissile, discerptible.

(*Adverbs*) Separately, etc., one by one, severally, apiece, apart, adrift, asunder; in the abstract, abstractedly.

45 Connecting medium.

VINCULUM (*Substantives*), link, connective, connection, junction (43), conjunction, copula, intermedium, hyphen, bridge, stepping-stone, isthmus, span, girder.

Bond, filament, fibre (205), hair, cordage, cord, thread, string, packthread, twine, twist, whipcord, tape, ferret, raffia, line, snood, ribbon, riband, rope, cable, hawser, painter, halyard, guy, guy-rope, wire, chain.

Fastening, tie, tendril, tendon, ligament, ligature, strap, tackle, rigging, traces, harness, yoke, band, withe, withy, brace, bandage, roller, fillet, thong, braid, inkle, girth, cinch, cestus, girdle, garter, halter, noose, lasso, lariat, surcingle, knot, running-knot, slip-knot, reef-knot, sailor's knot, granny-knot, etc.

Pin, corking-pin, safety-pin, nail, brad, tack, skewer, staple, clamp, vice, bracket, cramp, screw, button, buckle, brooch, clasp, slide, clip, hasp, hinge, hank, bolt, catch, latch, latchet, tag, hook, tooth, hook and eye, lock, locket, holdfast, padlock, rivet, anchor, grappling-iron, stake, post, gyve, shackle (752).

Cement, adhesive, mucilage, glue, gum, paste, size, goo, solder, lute, putty, bird-lime, mortar, stucco, plaster, grout.

46 COHERENCE (*Substantives*), cohesion, adherence, adhesion, accretion, concretion, agglutination, conglutination, aggregation, consolidation, set, cementation, soldering, welding, grouting.

Sticking, clinging, adhesiveness, stickiness, gumminess, gummosity, glutinosity (352), cohesiveness, density (321), inseparability, inseparableness, tenaciousness, tenacity.

Clot, concrete, cake, lump, conglomerate (321).

(*Verbs*) To cohere, adhere, stick, cling, cleave, hold, take hold of, hold fast, hug, grow or hang together, twine round.

To concrete, curdle, cake.

To glue, agglutinate, conglutinate, agglomerate, consolidate, solidify (321); cement, lute, paste, gum, grout, stick, solder, weld.

(*Phrases*) To stick like a leech; to stick like wax; to clink like ivy, like a bur, like a limpet.

47 Want of adhesion.

INCOHERENCE (*Substantives*), non-adhesion, immiscibility, looseness, laxity, slackness, relaxation, freedom, disjunction.

(*Phrases*) A rope of sand; *disjecta membra.*

(*Verbs*) To loosen, make loose, slacken, relax, unglue, unsolder, etc., detach, untwist, unravel, unroll (44, 313), to comminute (330).

(*Adjectives*) Incoherent, immiscible, detached, non-adhesive, loose, slack, lax, relaxed, baggy.

Segregated, flapping, streaming, dishevelled, unincorporated, unconsolidated, uncombined.

(*Phrase*) Like grains of sand.

(*Adjectives*) Cohesive, adhesive, cohering, tenacious, sticky, tacky, glutinous, gluey, gooey, gummy, viscous (352), agglutinatory.

United, unseparated, sessile, inseparable, inextricable, infrangible (321).

48 COMBINATION (*Substantives*), union, unification, synthesis, incorporation, amalgamation, coalescence, crasis, fusion, embodiment, conflation, absorption, blending, centralization; mixture (41).

Compound, composition, amalgam, impregnation, decompound, decomposite, resultant.

(*Verbs*) To combine, unite, unify, incorporate, amalgamate, synthesize, embody, unify, re-embody, blend, merge, fuse, absorb, melt into one, consolidate, coalesce, centralize; to impregnate, to put together, to lump together.

(*Adjectives*) Combined, compound, composite, coalescent, synthetic, synthetical, impregnated with, engrained.

49 DECOMPOSITION (*Substantives*), analysis, resolution, dissolution, disintegration, catalysis, electrolysis, corruption (653), dispersion (73), disjunction (44).

(*Verbs*) To decompose, rot, disembody, analyse, electrolyse, decompound, resolve, take to pieces, separate into its elements, dissect, unravel (313), break up.

(*Adjectives*) Decomposed, etc., catalytic, analytic, analytical, corrupted, dissolved.

4°. *Concrete Quantity*

50 WHOLE (*Substantives*), totality, integrity, integrality, allness, entireness, entirety, *ensemble*, collectiveness, individuality, unity (87), indivisibility, indiscerptibility, indissolubility; embodiment, integration.

All, the whole, total, aggregate, integer, gross amount, sum, sum total, *tout ensemble*, upshot, trunk, hull, skeleton, hulk, lump, heap (72).

The principal part, bulk, mass, tissue, staple, body, compages, the main, the greater part, major part.

(*Phrases*) The whole caboodle; the whole boiling.

(*Verbs*) To form or constitute a whole, to integrate, embody, aggregate, amass (72), to total, amount to, come to.

(*Adjectives*) Whole, total, integral, entire, one, unbroken, uncut, undivided, seamless, individual, unsevered, unclipped, uncropped, unshorn, undiminished, undemolished, undissolved, unbruised, undestroyed, indivisible, indissoluble, indissolvable, indiscerptible.

Wholesale, sweeping.

(*Adverbs*) Wholly, altogether, totally, entirely, all, all in all, as a whole, wholesale, in the aggregate, in the mass, *en masse*, in the lump, *en bloc*, on the whole, *in toto*, in the gross, *in extenso*, in the bulk, to the full, throughout, every inch.

(*Phrases*) The long and short of it; nearly or almost all; root and branch; lock, stock, and barrel; hook, line, and sinker; in the long run; in the main; neck and crop; from end to end; from beginning to end; from first to last; from head to foot; from top to toe; fore and aft; from alpha to omega.

51 PART (*Substantives*), portion, item, division, subdivision, section, chapter, verse, extract, passage, gobbet, sector, segment, fraction, fragment, frustum, detachment, piece, bit, lump, chunk, dollop, scrap, whit, swatch, morsel, mouthful, scantling, cantle, cantlet, slip, crumb (32), fritter, rag, tag, shred, tatter, splinter, snatch, cut, cutting, snip, snippet, snick, collop, slice, chip, chipping, shiver, sliver, matchwood, spillikin, smithereens, driblet, clipping, paring, shaving, debris, odds and ends, oddments, sundries, detritus, lamina, shadow, flotsam and jetsam, pickings.

Parcel, share, instalment, contingent, compartment, department, dividend, dose, particular, article, clause, paragraph.

Member, limb, lobe, lobule, arm, branch, scion, bough, joint, link, ramification (256), twig, bush, spray, sprig, offshoot, leaf, leaflet, stump, stub, butt, rump, torso.

(*Verbs*) To part, divide, subdivide, break (44); to partition, parcel out, portion, apportion (786), to ramify, branch, branch out.

(*Adjectives*) Part, fractional, fragmentary, scrappy, lobular, sectional, aliquot, divided, multifid, partitioned, isomeric.

(*Adverbs*) Partly, in part, partially, piecemeal, in detail, part by part, by driblets, bit by bit, little by little, by inches, inch by inch, foot by foot, drop by drop, in snatches, by fits and starts.

—

52 COMPLETENESS (*Substantives*), entirety, fullness, impletion, completion (729), perfection (650), solidity, stop-gap, makeweight, padding, filling up, integration, absoluteness, sufficiency; complement, supplement (39).

Fill, load, bumper, brimmer, bellyful, skinful.

53 INCOMPLETENESS (*Substantives*), deficiency, defectiveness, shortcoming (304), unreadiness, defalcation, failure, imperfection (651), hollowness, patchiness.

Part wanting, omission, defect, break, deficit, ullage, caret, lacuna, hiatus (198).

(*Verbs*) To be complete, etc., suffice (639).

To render complete or whole, to complete, exhaust, perfect, finish, make up, fill up, charge, load, replenish, make good, piece out, eke out.

(*Phrases*) To give the finishing touch; to supply deficiencies; to go to all lengths; to go the whole hog; to thrash out.

(*Adjectives*) Complete, entire, whole (50), absolute, perfect, full, plenary, solid, undivided, with all its parts, supplementary, adscititous, thorough, exhaustive, radical, sweeping, searching; consummate, thorough-paced, regular, sheer, unmitigated, unqualified.

(*Verbs*) To be incomplete, etc., to fail, fall short (304).

To dock, lop, mutilate, garble, truncate, castrate (38).

(*Adjectives*) Incomplete, unfinished, imperfect, defective, deficient, wanting, failing, short by, hollow, meagre, insufficient, half-baked, perfunctory, sketchy, scrappy, patchy.

Mutilated, garbled, docked, lopped, truncated; proceeding, in progress.

(*Phrase*) *Cetera desunt.*

Crammed, saturated, brimful, chock-full.

(*Adverbs*) Completely, entirely, to the full, outright, wholly, totally, thoroughly (31), *in toto, toto caelo,* in all respects.

(*Phrases*) To the top of one's bent; up to the ears; *à fond*; from first to last; from beginning to end; *ab ovo usque ad mala.*

---

54 Composition (*Substantives*), make-up, constitution, constituency, crasis.

Inclusion, admission, comprehension, reception.

(*Verbs*) To be composed of, to consist of, be made of, formed of, made up of, be resolved into.

To contain, include, hold, comprehend, take in, admit, embrace, involve, implicate.

To compose, constitute, form, make, make up, fill up, build up, put together, embody.

To enter into the composition of, to be or form part of (51), to merge in, be merged in.

(*Adjectives*) Comprehending, containing, including, comprising, etc.

Component, constituent, formative, forming, constituting, composing, etc., belonging to, appertaining to, inclusive.

55 Exclusion (*Substantives*), non-admission, omission, exception, rejection, proscription, repudiation, exile, banishment, excommunication.

Separation, segregation, elimination, seposition.

(*Verbs*) To be excluded from, etc., to be out of it.

To exclude, shut out, bar, leave out, omit, reject, repudiate, neglect, blackball; lay, put, or set apart or aside; segregate, pass over, throw overboard, slur over, neglect (460), excommunicate, banish, expatriate, extradite, deport, ostracize, relegate, rusticate, send down (297), rule out.

To eliminate, weed, winnow, screen, bar, separate (44), strike off.

(*Phrase*) 'Include me out.'

(*Adjectives*) Excluding, omitting, etc., exclusive.

Excluded, omitted, etc., unrecounted, inadmissible.

(*Adverbs*) Except, save, bar, barring, excepting.

---

56 Component (*Substantives*), component part, integral part, element, constituent, ingredient, member,

57 Extraneousness (*Substantives*), extrinsicality (5), exteriority (220).

limb (51), part and parcel, contents (190), appurtenance, feature, personnel.

A foreign body, alien, stranger, intruder, outsider, incomer, interloper, foreigner, dago, wop, *novus homo*, parvenu, immigrant, newcomer, new chum, pommy, greenhorn, tenderfoot.

(*Adjectives*) Extraneous, foreign, alien, tramontane, ultramontane, interloping.

(*Adverbs*) Abroad, in foreign parts, overseas.

Section IV—Order

1°. *Order in General*

58 ORDER (*Substantives*), regularity, orderliness, tidiness, uniformity, even tenor, symmetry.

Gradation, progression, pedigree, line, descent, subordination, course, series (69), array, routine.

Method, disposition, arrangement, system, economy, discipline, pattern, plan.

Rank, station, hierarchy, place, status, stand, scale, step, stage, period, term (71), footing; rank and file, pecking order.

(*Verbs*) To be or become in order, to form, fall in, arrange itself, place itself, range itself, fall into its place, fall into rank.

(*Adjectives*) Orderly, regular, in order, arranged, etc. (60), in its proper place, correct, tidy, shipshape, trim, *en règle*, well regulated, methodical, business-like, uniform, symmetrical, systematic, unconfused, undisturbed, untangled, unruffled, unravelled, still, etc. (265).

(*Phrases*) In apple-pie order; Bristol fashion.

(*Adverbs*) Systematically, methodically, etc., in turn, in its turn.

Step by step, by regular steps, gradations, stages, periods, or intervals, periodically (138).

At stated periods (138), *gradatim, seriatim*.

(*Phrase*) Like clockwork.

59 Absence, or want of Order, etc.

DISORDER (*Substantives*), irregularity, asymmetry, anomaly, confusion, confusedness, disarray, untidiness, jumble, huddle, litter, lumber, farrago, mess, hash, clutter, pie, muddle, mix-up, upset, hotchpotch, hugger-mugger, anarchy, anarchism, imbroglio, chaos, tohubohu, omnium gatherum (41), derangement (61).

Complexness, complexity, complication, intricacy, intricateness, implication, perplexity, involution, ravelling, tangle, entanglement, snarl, knot, coil, skein, sleave, network, labyrinth, Gordian knot, jungle.

Turmoil, *mêlée*, tumult, ferment, stew, fermentation, pudder, pother, riot, uproar, bobbery, rough-house, rumpus, scramble, fracas, vortex, whirlpool, maelstrom, hurly-burly, bear - garden, Babel, Saturnalia, Donnybrook, pandemonium.

Tumultuousness, riotousness, inquietude (173), derangement (61), topsyturvydom (218).

(*Phrases*) Wheels within wheels; confusion worse confounded; most admired disorder; *concordia discors*; hell broke loose.

A pretty kettle of fish; a fine state of things; a how-d'ye-do; the fat in the fire; a bull in a china shop; the devil to pay.

The cart before the horse; hysteron proteron.

(*Verbs*) To be out of order, irregular, disorderly, etc., to ferment.

To derange, put out of order (61).

(*Phrases*) To be at cross-purposes; to make hay of.

(*Adjectives*) Disorderly, orderless, out of order, disordered, misplaced, out of place, deranged, disarranged (61), irregular, desultory, anomalous, untidy, sloppy, slovenly, tousled, straggling, unarranged, immethodical, unsymmetrical, unsystematic, unmethodical, undigested, unsorted, unclassified, unclassed, asymmetrical.

Disjointed, out of joint, out of gear, out of kilter, confused, tangled, involved, intricate, complicated, inextricable, irreducible.

Mixed, scattered, promiscuous, indiscriminate, casual.

Tumultuous, turbulent, riotous, troublous, tumultuary (173), rough-and-tumble.

(*Adverbs*) Irregularly, etc., by fits and snatches, pell-mell; higgledy-piggledy, hugger-mugger; at sixes and sevens; helter-skelter, harum-scarum, anyhow.

60 Reduction to Order.

ARRANGEMENT (*Substantives*), disposal, disposition, collocation, allocation, distribution, sorting, assortment, allotment, apportionment, marshalling, alignment, taxis, taxonomy, gradation, organization, ordination; plan (626).

Analysis, sifting, screening, classification.

Result of arrangement, digest, synopsis, analysis, table, register (551).

Instrument for sorting, sieve, riddle, screen (260).

(*Verbs*) To order, reduce to order, bring into order, introduce order into.

To arrange, dispose, place, form; to put, set, place, etc., in order; to set out, collocate, pack, marshal, range, align (or aline), rank, group, parcel out, allot, distribute, assort, sort, sift, riddle.

To class, classify, categorize, file, string, thread, tabulate, pigeon-hole, catalogue, index, register, take stock.

To methodize, digest, regulate, size, grade, gradate, graduate, alphabetize, co-ordinate, systematize, organize, settle, fix, rearrange.

To unravel (246), disentangle, ravel, card, disembroil.

(*Phrases*) To put or set to rights; to assign places to.

(*Adjectives*) Arranged, methodical (58), embattled, in battle array.

(*Phrase*) A place for everything, and everything in its place.

61 Subversion of Order, bringing into disorder.

DERANGEMENT (*Substantives*), disarrangement, misarrangement, displacement, misplacement, dislocation, discomposure, disturbance, bedevilment, disorganization, perturbation, shuffling, rumpling, embroilment, corrugation (258), inversion (218), jumble, muddle, disorder (59).

(*Verbs*) To derange, disarrange, misarrange, misplace, mislay, discompose, disorder, embroil, unsettle, disturb, confuse, perturb, jumble, tumble, huddle, shuffle, muddle, toss, hustle, fumble; to bring, put, or throw into disorder, trouble, confusion, etc., break the ranks, upset.

To unhinge, put out of joint, dislocate, turn over, invert; turn topsy-turvy; turn inside out (218), bedevil, throw out of gear.

To complicate, involve, perplex, tangle, entangle, embrangle (or imbrangle), ravel, ruffle, tousle, rumple, dishevel, muss, litter, scatter, make a mess of, monkey with, make hay of.

(*Adjectives*) Deranged, etc., disordered (59).

2°. *Consecutive Order*

62 PRECEDENCE (*Substantives*), coming before, antecedence, antecedency, anteposition, priority (116), anteriority, the *pas*, the lead.

Superiority (33), precession (280).

(*Verbs*) To precede, come before, lead, introduce, usher in.

To place before; to prefix, affix, premise, prelude, preface, prologize.

(*Phrases*) To have the *pas*; to take the lead; to have the start; set the fashion; to open the ball.

(*Adjectives*) Preceding, precedent, antecedent, anterior, prior, previous, before, ahead of, leading.

Former, foregoing; coming or going before; precursory, precursive, prevenient, inaugural, prodromal, prodromic, preliminary, aforesaid, said, aforementioned, prefatory, introductory, prelusive, prelusory, proemial, preparatory, preambulatory.

(*Adverbs*) In advance, ahead, in front of, before, in the van (234).

---

64 PRECURSOR (*Substantives*), antecedent, precedent, predecessor, forerunner, pioneer, outrider, avant-courier, leader, bell-wether, herald, harbinger.

Prelude, preamble, preface, foreword, prologue, prodrome, protasis, prolusion, overture, premise, proem, prolepsis, prolegomena, prefix, introduction, heading, advertisement, frontispiece, groundwork (673).

(*Adjectives*) Precursory, prefatory (62).

---

66 BEGINNING (*Substantives*), commencement, opening, outset, incipience, inception, inchoation, initiative, overture, exordium, introduction (64), inauguration, début, onset, brunt, alpha.

Origin, source, rise, conception, birth, infancy, bud, embryo, germ, egg, rudiment, *incunabula*, start, cradle, starting-point, starting-post (293); dawn, morning (125).

63 SEQUENCE (*Substantives*), coming after, consecution, succession, posteriority (117), secondariness; following (281).

Continuation, order of succession, successiveness; alternation (138).

Subordination, inferiority (34).

(*Phrase*) *Proxime accessit.*

(*Verbs*) To succeed, come after, follow, come next, ensue, come on, tread close upon; to alternate.

To place after, to suffix, append.

(*Phrases*) To be in the wake or trail of; to tread on the heels of; to step into the shoes of; to assume the mantle of.

(*Adjectives*) Succeeding, coming after, following, subsequent, ensuing, sequent, sequacious, consequent, next; consecutive, amoebean, alternate (138).

Latter, posterior.

(*Adverbs*) After, subsequently, since, behind, in the wake of, in the train of, at the tail of, in the rear of (234).

---

65 SEQUEL (*Substantives*), afterpart, aftermath, suffix, successor, tail, runner-up, queue, train, wake, trail, rear, retinue, suite, appendix (39), postscript, epilogue, peroration, excursus, after-piece, tailpiece, tag, colophon, afterthought, second thoughts, *arrière pensée*, codicil, continuation, sequela, apodosis.

(*Phrases*) More last words; to be continued.

(*Adjectives*) Subsequent, ensuing (63).

---

67 END (*Substantives*), close, termination, desinence, conclusion, finish, finis, finale, period, term, terminus, limit, last, omega, extreme, extremity, butt-end, fag-end, stub, tail, nib, tip, after-part, rear (235), colophon, coda, tailpiece, tag, *cul-de-lampe*, peroration, swan-song.

Completion (729), winding-up, *dénouement*, catastrophe, consummation, expiration, expiry, finishing

Van, vanguard, title-page, heading, front (234), fore-part, head (210).

Opening, entrance, entry, inlet, orifice, porch, portal, portico, gateway, door, gate, postern, wicket, threshold, vestibule, mouth, *fauces*, lips.

Alphabet, A B C, rudiments, elements.

(*Phrase*) The rising of the curtain; the thin end of the wedge.

(*Verbs*) To begin, commence, inchoate, rise, arise, originate, initiate, open, dawn, set in, take its rise, enter upon, embark on, set out (293), recommence, undertake (676).

To usher in, lead off, lead the way, take the lead or the initiative; head, stand at the head, stand first; broach, set on foot, set a-going, set abroach, set up, handsel, institute, launch, strike up.

(*Phrases*) To make a beginning; to cross the Rubicon; to break ground; set the ball in motion; take the initiative; break the ice; fire away; open the ball; kick off; tee up; pipe up.

(*Adjectives*) Beginning, commencing, arising, initial, initiatory, initiative, inceptive, incipient, proemial, inaugural, inchoate, inchoative, embryonic, primigenial, aboriginal, rudimental, nascent, natal, opening, dawning, entering.

stroke, knock-out, K.O., death-blow, *coup de grâce*, upshot, issue, fate, doom, Day of Judgment, doomsday.

(*Phrases*) The *ne plus ultra*; the fall of the curtain; '*le commencement de la fin.*'

· (*Verbs*) To end, close, finish, expire, terminate, conclude; come or draw to an end, close or stop, be all over, pass away, give out, peter out, run its course; to say one's say, perorate, be through with.

To come last, bring up the rear.

To bring to an end, close, etc., to put a period, etc., to; to make an end of; to close, finish, seal, wind up, complete, achieve (729), crown, determine.

(*Phrases*) To cut the matter short; to shut up shop.

(*Adjectives*) Ending, closing, etc., final, terminal, eschatological, desistive, definitive, crowning.

Last, ultimate, penultimate, antepenultimate, hindermost, rear, caudal, conterminal, conterminous.

Ended, closed, terminated, etc., through.

Unbegun, fresh, uncommenced.

(*Adverbs*) Once for all, in fine, finally, at the end of the day, for good, for good and all.

———

First, foremost, leading, heading, maiden.

Begun, commenced, etc.

(*Adverbs*) At, or in the beginning, at first blush, first, in the first place, *imprimis*, first and foremost, *in limine*, in the bud, in embryo.

From the beginning, *ab initio, ab ovo.*

68 MIDDLE (*Substantives*), midst, mean, medium, happy medium, *via media*, middle term, centre (223), *mezzo termine, juste milieu*, half-way house, hub, nave, navel, omphalos, bull's-eye, nucleus.

Equidistance, equator, diaphragm, midriff; bisection (91).

Intervenience, interjacence, intervention (228), mid-course (628).

(*Adjectives*) Middle, medial, median, mesial, mean, mid, middlemost, midmost, mediate, intermediate (29), intervenient, interjacent (228), central (222), equidistant, embosomed, merged.

Mediterranean, equatorial.

(*Adverbs*) In the middle, amid, amidst, midway, amidships, midships, half-way.

(*Phrases*) In the thick of; *in medias res.*

69 Uninterrupted sequence.

CONTINUITY (*Substantives*), consecution, consecutiveness, succession, suite, progression, series, train, chain, catenation, concatenation, scale, gradation, course, procession, column, retinue, cortège, cavalcade, rank and file, line of battle, array, pedigree, genealogy, lineage, race.

File, queue, echelon, line, row, rank, range, tier, string, thread, team, tandem, randem, suit, flush, colonnade.

(*Verbs*) To follow in, form, a series, etc.; to fall in.

To arrange in a series, to marshal (60); to string together, file, thread, graduate, tabulate.

(*Adjectives*) Continuous, sequent, consecutive, progressive, serial, successive, continued, uninterrupted, unbroken, entire, linear, in a line, in a row, etc., gradual, constant, unremitting, unintermitting, evergreen (110).

(*Adverbs*) Continuously, consecutively, etc., *seriatim*; in a line, row, series, etc., in succession, etc., running, gradually, step by step; uninterruptedly, at a stretch, at one go.

(*Phrase*) In Indian file.

70 Interrupted sequence.

DISCONTINUITY (*Substantives*), interruption, pause, period, interregnum, break, interval, interlude, episode, lacuna, cut, gap, fracture, fault, chasm, hiatus (198), caesura, parenthesis, rhapsody, anacoluthon.

Intermission, alternation (138); a broken thread, broken melody.

(*Verbs*) To be discontinuous, etc.; to alternate, intermit.

To discontinue, pause, interrupt, break, interpose (228); to break in upon, disconnect (44); to break or snap the thread.

(*Adjectives*) Discontinuous, inconsecutive, broken, interrupted, unsuccessive, desultory, disconnected, unconnected, fitful, spasmodic, sporadic, scattered.

Alternate, every other, intermitting, alternating (138).

(*Phrase*) Few and far between.

(*Adverbs*) At intervals, by snatches, *per saltum*, by fits and starts, *longo intervallo*.

---

71 TERM (*Substantives*), rank, station, stage, step, rung, round, degree (26), remove, grade, link, place, peg, mark, point, *pas*, period, pitch, stand, standing, status, footing, range.

(*Verbs*) To hold, occupy, find, fall into a place, station.

3°. Collective Order

72 ASSEMBLAGE (*Substantives*), collection, dozen, collocation, compilation, levy, gathering, ingathering, muster, round-up, colligation, contesseration, *attroupement*, association, concourse, conflux, convergence, meeting, assembly, congregation, at home (892), levee, club, reunion, gaudy, soirée, conversazione, accumulation, cumulation, array, mobilization.

Congress, convocation, convention, *comitium*, committee, quorum, conclave, synod, caucus, conventicle, eisteddfod, mass-meeting.

73 NON-ASSEMBLAGE.

DISPERSION (*Substantives*), scattering, dissemination, diffusion, dissipation, spreading, casting, distribution, apportionment, sprinkling, respersion, circumfusion, interspersion, divergence (291), demobilization.

Odds and ends, waifs and strays, flotsam and jetsam.

(*Verbs*) To disperse, scatter, sow, disseminate, diffuse, shed, spread, overspread, dispense, disband, disembody, distribute, dispel, cast forth; strew, bestrew, sprinkle, sparge, issue, deal out, utter, resperse, intersperse,

Miscellany, olla podrida, museum, collectanea, menagerie (636), Noah's ark, anthológy, encyclopaedia, portfolio, file.

A multitude (102), crowd, throng, rabble, mob, press, crush, horde, posse, body, tribe, crew, gang, knot, band, party, swarm, school, shoal, bevy, galaxy, covey, flock, herd, drove, corps, troop, troupe, squad, squadron, phalanx, platoon, company, regiment, battalion, legion, host, army, division.

set abroach, circumfuse; to decentralize, demobilize; to hive-off.

(Phrases) To turn adrift; to scatter to the four winds; to sow broadcast; to spread like wildfire.

(Adjectives) Unassembled, uncollected, dispersed, scattered, diffused, sparse, spread, dispread, widespread, sporadic, cast, broadcast, epidemic, adrift.

(Adverbs) Sparsim, here and there, passim.

———

A sounder (of swine), skulk (of foxes), pride (of lions), charm (of finches), flush (of mallards), gaggle (of geese), wedge (of swans).

Clan, brotherhood, fraternity, sisterhood, party (712).

Volley, shower, storm, cloud, flood, deluge.

Group, cluster, clump, set, batch, battery, pencil, lot, pack, budget, assortment, bunch, parcel, packet, package, bundle, fascicle, fascicule, fasciculus, faggot, wisp, truss, tuft, rosette, shock, rick, fardel, stack, sheaf, stook, haycock.

Accumulation, congeries, heap, hoard, lump, pile, rouleau, tissue, mass, pyramid, bale, drift, snowball, acervation, cumulation, glomeration, agglomeration, conglobation, conglomeration, conglomerate, coacervation, coagmentation, aggregation, concentration (290), congestion, omnium gatherum.

Collector, tax-gatherer, whip, whipper-in.

(Verbs) To assemble, collect, muster, meet, unite, cluster, swarm, flock, herd, crowd, throng, associate, congregate, conglomerate, concentrate, congest, rendezvous, resort, flock together, get together, reassemble.

To bring, get or gather together, collect, draw together, group, convene, convoke, convocate, collocate, colligate, round up, scrape together, rake up, dredge, bring into a focus, amass, accumulate, heap up, pile, pack, do up, stack, truss, cram, pack together, congest, acervate, coagment, agglomerate, garner up, lump together, make a parcel of; to centralize; to mobilize.

(Phrases) To heap Pelion upon Ossa; to collect in a drag-net.

(Adjectives) Assembled, collected, etc., undispersed, met together, closely packed, dense, crowded, serried, huddled together, teeming, swarming, populous.

(Phrases) Packed like sardines; crowded to suffocation.

74 Place of meeting.

Focus (Substantives), point of convergence, corradiation, rendezvous, home, headquarters, club, centre (222), gathering-place, meeting-place, trysting-place, rallying-ground, haunt, howff, resort, museum, repository, depot (636).

4°. Distributive Order

75 CLASS (Substantives), division, category, predicament, head, order, section, department, domain, province.

Kind, sort, variety, type, genus, species, family, phylum, race, tribe, caste, sept, clan, gens, phratry, breed, kith, sect, set, assortment, feather, stripe, suit, range, run.

Gender, sex, kin, kidney, manner, nature, description, denomination, designation, character, stamp, stuff, *genre.*
(*Adjectives*) Generic, racial, tribal, etc.
(*Verbs*) To classify, catalogue (60).

76 INCLUSION (*Substantives*), comprehension under a class, reference to a class, admission, comprehension, reception, subsumption.

Inclusion in a compound, composition (54).

(*Verbs*) To be included in, to come under, to fall under, to range under; to belong, or pertain to, appertain; to range with, to merge in, to be of.

To include, comprise, comprehend, contain, admit, embrace, receive; to enumerate among, reckon among, reckon with, number among, refer to, place under, class with or among, arrange under or with, take into account, subsume.

(*Adjectives*) Including, inclusive, all-embracing, congener, congeneric, congenerous, *et hoc genus omne*, etcetera.
Included, merged, etc.
(*Phrase*) Birds of a feather.

77 EXCLUSION from a class (*Substantives*), rejection, proscription.

Exclusion from a compound (55).

(*Verbs*) To be excluded from, etc.; to exclude, proscribe, debar, rule out, set apart (55).

(*Phrase*) To shut the door upon.

(*Adjectives*) Exclusive, excluding, etc.

78 GENERALITY (*Substantives*), universality, catholicism, catholicity.

Every man, every one, everybody, all, all hands.

Miscellaneousness, miscellany, encyclopaedia, generalization, prevalence, drag-net.

(*Phrases*) The world and his wife; N or M.

(*Verbs*) To be general, common, or prevalent, to prevail.

To render general, to generalize.

(*Adjectives*) General, generic, collective, comprehensive, encyclopaedic, panoramic, bird's-eye, sweeping, radical, universal, world-wide, cosmopolitan, catholic, common, oecumenical, transcendental, prevalent, prevailing, all-pervading, epidemic, all-inclusive.

Unspecified, impersonal; every, all.

(*Adverbs*) Whatever, whatsoever, to a man; generally, universally, on the whole, for the most part.

79 SPECIALITY (*Substantives*), particularity, peculiarity, individuality, haecceity, thisness, personality, characteristic, mannerism, idiosyncrasy, trick, gimmick, specificness, specificity, eccentricity, singularity (83).

Version, reading (522).

Particulars, details, items, counts.

I, myself, self, I myself, *moi qui vous parle.*

(Phrases) *Argumentum ad hominem*; local colour.

(*Verbs*) To specify, particularize, individualize, realize, specialize, designate, determine.

(*Phrases*) To descend to particulars; to enter into detail.

(*Adjectives*) Special, particular, individual, specific, proper, appropriate, personal, private, respective, several, definite, determinate, especial, certain, esoteric, endemic, partial, party, peculiar, characteristic, distinctive, typical, unique, diagnostic, exlusive, *sui generis*, singular, exceptional (83).

This, that, yonder, yon, such and such.

(*Adverbs*) Specially, specifically, etc., in particular, respectively, personally, individually, *in propria persona.*

Each, apiece, one by one, severally, seriatim, namely, *videlicet*, viz., to wit.

5°. *Order as regards Categories*

80 RULE (*Substantives*), regularity, uniformity, constancy, standard, model, nature, principle, the order of things, routine, prevalence, practice, usage, custom, use, habit (613), regulation, precept (697), convention, *convenances.*

Form, formula, law, canon, principle, keynote, catchword.

Type, archetype, pattern, precedent, paradigm, the normal, natural, ordinary or model state or condition; norm, control.

81 MULTIFORMITY (*Substantives*), variety, diversity, multifariousness, allotropy, allotropism.

(*Adjectives*) Multiform, variform, polymorphic, multifold, manifold, multifarious, multigenerous, omnifarious, omnigenous, heterogeneous, motley, epicene, indiscriminate, desultory, irregular, diversified, allotropic; different (15).

(*Phrase*) Of all sorts and kinds.

(*Phrases*) A standing order; the bed of Procrustes; laws of the Medes and Persians.

(*Adjectives*) Regular, uniform, constant (82).

---

82 CONFORMITY (*Substantives*), conformance, observance, naturalization, harmony, convention (613).

Example, instance, specimen, sample, ensample, exemplar, exemplification, illustration, pattern (22), object lesson, case in point, quotation, the rule.

(*Phrases*) The order of the day; the common or ordinary run of things (23); a matter of course.

(*Verbs*) To conform to rule, be regular, orthodox, etc., to follow, observe, go by, bend to, obey rules; to be guided or regulated by, be wont, etc. (613), to comply or chime in with, to be in harmony with, follow suit; to standardize, naturalize.

To exemplify, illustrate, cite, quote, put a case, produce an instance, set an example.

(*Phrases*) To go with the crowd; to do in Rome as the Romans do; to follow the fashion; to swim with the stream; to keep one in countenance.

(*Adjectives*) Conformable to rule, regular, uniform, constant, steady, according to rule, *en règle, de rigueur*, normal, well regulated, formal, canonical, orthodox, conventional, strict, rigid, positive, uncompromising (23).

Ordinary, natural, usual, common, wonted, accustomed, habitual (613), household, average, everyday, current, rife, prevailing, prevalent, established,

83 UNCONFORMITY (*Substantives*), nonconformity, unconventionality, informality, arbitrariness, abnormity, abnormality, anomaly, anomalousness, lawlessness, peculiarity, exclusiveness; infraction, breach, violation, of law or rule; individuality, idiosyncracy, mannerism, eccentricity, aberration, irregularity, unevenness, variety, singularity, rarity, oddity, oddness, exemption, salvo.

Exception, nondescript, a character, original, nonesuch, monster, monstrosity, prodigy (872), *lusus naturae, rara avis*, freak, curiosity, crank, queer fish; half-caste, half-breed, cross-breed, mongrel, hybrid, mule, mulatto (41), *tertium quid*, hermaphrodite, sport.

Phoenix, chimera, hydra, sphinx, minotaur, griffin, centaur, hippocentaur, hippogriff, basilisk, cockatrice, tragelaph, kraken, dragon, wyvern, roc, sea-serpent, mermaid, merman, cyclops, unicorn.

(*Phrases*) Out of one's element; a fish out of water; neither one thing nor another; neither fish, flesh, nor fowl, nor good red herring; a law to oneself.

(*Verbs*) To be unconformable to rule, to be exceptional, etc.; to violate a law or custom, to stretch a point.

(*Phrases*) To have no business there; to beggar description.

(*Adjectives*) Unconformable, excep-

received, stereotyped, acknowledged, typical, accepted, recognized, representative, hackneyed, well-known, familiar, vernacular, commonplace, trite, banal, cut and dried, naturalized, orderly, shipshape, run of the mill.

Exemplary, illustrative, in point, of daily or everyday occurrence, in the order of things.

(*Phrases*) Regular as clockwork; according to Cocker (or Hoyle).

(*Adverbs*) Conformably, by rule, regularly, etc., agreeably to; in accordance, conformity, or keeping with.

Usually, generally, ordinarily, commonly, for the most part, as usual, *more solito*, *more suo*, *pro more*; of course, as a matter of course, *pro forma*.

Always, uniformly (16), invariably, without exception, never otherwise.

For example, for instance, *exempli gratia*, *inter alia*.

(*Phrases*) *Ab uno disce omnes*; *ex pede Herculem*; *ex ungue leonem*; birds of a feather.

tional, abnormal, anomalous, anomalistic, out of order, out of place, misplaced, irregular, unorthodox, uneven, arbitrary, informal, aberrant, stray, peculiar, funny, exclusive, unnatural, eccentric, unconventional, Bohemian, beatnik, hippy, yippy.

Unusual, unaccustomed, unwonted, uncommon, rare, singular, unique, curious, odd, extraordinary, strange, *outré*, out of the way, egregious, out of the ordinary, unheard of, queer, quaint, old-fashioned, unfashionable, nondescript, undescribed, unexampled, *sui generis*, unprecedented, unparalleled, unfamiliar, fantastic, newfangled, grotesque, bizarre, weird, eerie, outlandish, exotic, preternatural, unexampled, unrepresentative, uncanny, denaturalized.

Heterogeneous, heteroclite, amorphous, out of the pale of, mongrel, amphibious, epicene, half-blood, hybrid (41), androgynous, betwixt and between.

(*Phrases*) 'None but himself could be his parallel'; caviare to the general.

(*Adverbs*) Unconformably, etc.; except, unless, save, barring, beside, without, but for, save and except, let alone, to say nothing of; however, yet, but.

Section V—Number

1°. *Number in the Abstract*

84 NUMBER (*Substantives*), symbol, numeral, figure, cipher, digit, integer, counter, a round number, notation, a formula; series.

Sum, difference, subtrahend, complement, product, factorial, multiplicand, multiplier, multiplicator, coefficient, multiple, least common multiple, dividend, divisor, factor, highest common factor, greatest common measure, quotient, sub-multiple, fraction, vulgar fraction, mixed number, numerator, denominator, decimal, circulating decimal, recurring decimal, repetend, common measure, aliquot part, reciprocal, prime number; permutation, combination, election.

Ratio, proportion, progression (arithmetical, geometrical, harmonical), percentage.

Power, root, exponent, index, function, logarithm, antilogarithm; differential, integral, fluxion, fluent; incommensurable, surd.

(*Adjectives*) Numeral, complementary, divisible, aliquot, reciprocal, prime, fractional, decimal, factorial, fractional, mixed, incommensurable.

Proportional, exponential, logarithmic, logometric, differential, fluxional, integral.

Positive, negative, rational, irrational, surd, radical, real, imaginary, impossible.

85 NUMERATION (*Substantives*), numbering, counting, tale, telling, tally, calling over, recension, enumeration, summation, reckoning, computation, ciphering, calculation, calculus, algorism, dactylonomy, rhabdology.

Arithmetic, analysis, algebra, differential and integral calculus.

Statistics, dead reckoning, muster, poll, census, capitation, roll-call, muster-roll, account, score, recapitulation, demography.

Addition, subtraction, multiplication, division, proportion, rule of three, reduction, involution, evolution, practice, equations, extraction of roots, approximation, interpolation, differentiation, integration.

Abacus, logometer, ready-reckoner, slide-rule, sliding-rule, tallies, Napier's bones, calculating machine, tabulator, totalizator, totalizer, tote, cash-register.

(*Verbs*) To number, count, tell, tally, call over, take an account of, enumerate, muster, poll, run over, recite, recapitulate; sum, sum up, cast up, tell off, score, cipher, compute, calculate, reckon, estimate, figure up, tot up; add, subtract, multiply, divide; amount to.

Check, prove, demonstrate, balance, audit, overhaul, take stock.

(*Adjectives*) Numerical, arithmetical, logarithmic, numeral, analytic, algebraic, statistical, computable, calculable, commensurable, incommensurable, incommensurate.

86 LIST (*Substantives*), catalogue, inventory, schedule, register, census, return, statistics, record (551), account, registry, syllabus, roll, terrier, cadastre, cartulary, tally, file, muster-roll, roster, rota, bead-roll, panel, calendar, index, table, book, ledger, day-book, synopsis, bibliography, contents, invoice, bill of lading, bill of fare, menu, red book, peerage, baronetage, Almanach de Gotha, Debrett, Domesday Book, prospectus, programme, directory, gazetteer, who's who.

Registration, etc. (551).

2°. *Determinate Number*

87 UNITY (*Substantives*), unification, oneness, individuality, singleness, solitariness, solitude, isolation (893), abstraction; monism.

One, unit, ace, monad.

Someone, somebody, no other, none else, an individual; monist.

(*Verbs*) To be alone, etc.; to isolate (44), insulate, set apart.

To render one, unify.

(*Phrase*) To dine with Duke Humphrey.

(*Adjectives*) One, sole, single, individual, apart, alone, lone, isolated, solitary, lonely, lonesome, desolate, dreary, insular, insulated, disparate, discrete, detached; monistic.

Unaccompanied, unattended, *solus*, single-handed, singular, odd, unique, unrepeated, azygous.

Inseverable, irresolvable, indiscerptible, compact.

88 ACCOMPANIMENT (*Substantives*), coexistence, concomitance, company, association, companionship, partnership, collaboration, copartnership, co-efficiency.

Concomitant, adjunct, context, accessory (39), coefficient, companion, attendant, fellow, associate, consort, spouse, colleague, collaborator, partner, copartner, side-kick, buddy, satellite, escort, hanger-on, parasite, shadow; travelling tutor, chaperon, duenna.

(*Verbs*) To accompany, chaperon, coexist, attend, associate or be associated with, keep company with, collaborate with, hang on, shadow, wait on, to join, tie together.

(*Phrases*) To go hand in hand with; to be in the same boat.

(*Adjectives*) Accompanying, coexisting, attending, attendant, concomi-

(*Adverbs*) Singly, etc., alone, by itself, *per se*, only, apart, in the singular number, in the abstract, one by one; one at a time.

One and a half, sesqui-.

---

tant, fellow, twin, joint, associated with, accessory.

(*Adverbs*) With, withal, together with, along with, in company with, collectively, hand in hand, together, in a body, cheek by jowl, side by side; therewith, herewith, moreover, besides, also, and (37), not to mention.

89 DUALITY (*Substantives*), dualism, duplicity, twofoldness, doubleness, biformity; polarity.

Two, deuce, couple, brace, pair, dyad (or duad), twins, Siamese twins, Castor and Pollux, Damon and Pythias, fellows, gemini, yoke, span, file, conjugation, twosome; dualist.

(*Verbs*) To unite in pairs, to pair, pair off, couple, match, mate, bracket, yoke.

(*Adjectives*) Two, twain, dual, binary, dualistic, duplex (90), duplicate, dyadic, binomial, twin, tête-à-tête, Janus-headed, bilateral, bicentric, bifocal.

Coupled, bracketed, paired, etc., conjugate.

Both, both the one and the other.

90 DUPLICATION (*Substantives*), doubling, gemination, reduplication, ingemination, repetition, iteration (104), renewal.

(*Verbs*) To double, redouble, geminate, reduplicate, repeat, iterate, re-echo, renew (660).

(*Adjectives*) Double, doubled, redoubled, second.

Biform, bifarious, bifold, bilateral, bifacial, twofold, two-sided, two-faced, duplex, duplicate, ingeminate.

(*Adverbs*) Twice, once more, over again, *da capo*, *bis*, *encore*, anew, as much again, twofold (104, 136).

Secondly, in the second place, again.

---

91 Division into two parts.

BISECTION (*Substantives*), bipartition, dichotomy, halving, dimidiation, bifurcation, forking, branching, ramification, divarication, splitting, cleaving.

Fork, prong, fold, branch, Y.

Half, moiety, semi-, demi-, hemi-.

(*Verbs*) To bisect, halve, divide, split, cut in two, cleave, dimidiate, dichotomize.

To separate, fork, bifurcate, branch out, ramify.

(*Phrases*) To go halves; to go fifty-fifty; to split the difference.

(*Adjectives*) Bisected, halved, divided, etc., bipartite, bicuspid, bind, bifurcated, bifurcate, cloven, cleft, split, etc.

---

92 TRIALITY (*Substantives*), trinity.

Three, triad, triangle, triplet, trey, trio, tern, trinomial, leash, threesome, trefoil, triquetra, *terza rima*, trilogy.

Third power, cube.

(*Adjectives*) Three, triform, trine, trinal, trinary, ternary, ternal, ternate (93), trinomial, tertiary, tri-.

93 TRIPLICATION (*Substantives*), triplicity, trebleness, trine.

(*Verbs*) To treble, triple, triplicate, cube.

(*Adjectives*) Treble, triple, tern, ternary, ternate, triplicate, trigeminal, threefold, third.

(*Adverbs*) Three times, thrice, threefold, in the third place, thirdly.

---

94 Division into three parts.

TRISECTION (*Substantives*), tripartition, trichotomy; third part, third.

(*Verbs*) To trisect, divide into three parts.

(*Adjectives*) Trifid, trisected, tripartite, trichotomous, trisulcate, triform.

95 QUATERNITY (*Substantives*), four, tetrad, quadruplet, quad, quartet, quaternion, foursome, square, tetragon, tetrahedron, tessara, quadrature; tetralogy.

(*Verbs*) To reduce to a square, to square.

(*Adjectives*) Four, quaternary, quaternal, quadratic, quartile, tetractic, tetra-, quadri-.

96 QUADRUPLICATION.

(*Verbs*) To multiply by four, quadruplicate, biquadrate.

(*Adjectives*) Fourfold, quadruple, quadruplicate, fourth.

(*Adverbs*) Four times, in the fourth place, fourthly, to the fourth degree.

97 Division into four parts.

QUADRISECTION (*Substantives*), quadripartition, quartering, a fourth, a quarter.

(*Verbs*) To quarter, to divide into four parts.

(*Adjectives*) Quartered, etc., quadrifid, quadripartite.

98 FIVE (*Substantives*), cinque, cinqfoil, quint, quincunx, pentad, pentagon, pentahedron, quintuplet, quin, quintet.

(*Adjectives*) Five, quinary, quintuple, fivefold, fifth.

SIX, half a dozen, hexad, hexagon, hexahedron, sextet.

(*Adjectives*) Senary, sextuple, sixfold, sixth.

SEVEN, heptad, heptagon, heptahedron, septet.

(*Adjectives*) Septenary, septuple, sevenfold, seventh.

EIGHT, octad, octagon, octahedron, octet, ogdoad.

(*Adjectives*) Octonary, octonal, octuple, eightfold, eighth.

NINE, ennead, nonagon, enneagon, enneahedron, novena.

(*Adjectives*) Enneatic, ninefold, ninth.

TEN, decad, decagon, decahedron, decade.

(*Adjectives*) Decimal, denary, decuple, tenfold, tenth.

TWELVE, a dozen.

(*Adjectives*) Duodenary, duodecimal, twelfth.

THIRTEEN, a long dozen, a baker's dozen.

TWENTY, a score, icosahedron.

(*Adjectives*) Vigesimal, twentieth.

FORTY, twoscore.

(*Adjective*) Quadragesimal.

FIFTY, twoscore and ten.

(*Adjective*) Quinquagesimal.

SIXTY, threescore.

(*Adjectives*) Sexagesimal, sexagenary.

SEVENTY, threescore and ten.

EIGHTY, fourscore.

99 QUINQUESECTION, etc.

(*Adjectives*) Quinquefid, quinquarticular, quinquepartite.

Sexpartite.

Septempartite.

Octopartite.

DECIMATION, tithe.

(*Verb*) To decimate.

NINETY, fourscore and ten.

HUNDRED, centenary, hecatomb, century. One hundred and forty-four, a gross.

(*Verb*) To centuriate.

(*Adjectives*) Centesimal, centennial, centenary, centurial, centuple, centuplicate, hundredfold, hundredth.

THOUSAND, chiliad, millennium.

(*Adjective*) Millesimal.

MYRIAD, lac, crore.

MILLION, billion, trillion, etc.

3°. *Indeterminate Number*

100 More than one.

PLURALITY (*Substantives*), a number, a certain number, a few, a wheen, a round number.

(*Adjectives*) Plural, more than one, upwards of, some, a few, one or two, two or three, umpteen, certain.

(*Adverb*) Etcetera.

101 ZERO (*Substantives*), nothing (4), nought (or naught), cipher; nobody, *nemo*.

(*Adjectives*) None, not one, not any, not a soul.

———

102 MULTITUDE (*Substantives*), numerousness, numerosity, numerality, multiplicity, majority, profusion, legion, host, a great or large number, numbers, array, power, lot, sight, army, sea, galaxy, populousness (72), a hundred, thousand, myriad, million, etc.

A shoal, swarm, draught, bevy, flock, herd, drove, flight, covey, hive, brood, litter, mob, nest, crowd (72).

Increase of number, multiplication, multiple; greater number, majority.

(*Verbs*) To be numerous, etc., to swarm, teem, crowd, come thick upon, outnumber, multiply, to people.

(*Phrase*) To swarm like locusts or bees.

(*Adjectives*) Many, several, a wheen, sundry, divers, various, a great many, very many, full many, ever so many, no end of, numerous, profuse, manifold, multiplied, multitudinous, multiple, multinomial, endless (105), teeming, populous, peopled.

Frequent, repeated, reiterated, outnumbering, thick, crowding, crowded; galore.

(*Phrases*) Thick as hail; thick as leaves in Vallombrosa; plentiful as blackberries; in profusion; numerous as the sands on the seashore; their name is Legion.

103 FEWNESS (*Substantives*) paucity, a small number, handful, scantiness, rareness, rarity, thinness.

Diminution of number, reduction, weeding, elimination, thinning; smaller number, minority.

(*Verbs*) To be few, etc.

To render few, reduce, diminish in number, weed, weed out, prick off, eliminate, thin, thin out, decimate.

(*Adjectives*) Few, scanty, scant, rare, infrequent, sparse, scattered, hardly or scarcely any, reduced, thinned, etc.

(*Phrases*) Few and far between; you could count them on the fingers of one hand.

———

104 REPETITION (*Substantives*), iteration, reiteration, harping, recapitulation, run, recurrence (136), recrudescence, tautology, monotony; cuckoo-note, chimes, repetend, echo, burden of a song, refrain, jingle, renewal, rehearsal, réchauffé, rehash, reproduction (19).

Cuckoo, mocking-bird, mimic, imitator, parrot.

Periodicity (138), frequency (136).

(*Phrase*) A twice-told tale.

(*Verbs*) To repeat, iterate, reiterate, recapitulate, renew, reproduce, echo, re-echo, drum, hammer, harp on, plug, rehearse, redouble, recrudesce, reappear, recur, revert, recommence.

(*Phrases*) Do or say over again; ring the changes on; to harp on the same string; to din or drum in the ear; to go over the same ground; to begin again.

(*Adjectives*) Repeated, repetitional, repetitionary, repetitive, recurrent, recurring, reiterated, renewed, ever-recurring, thick-coming, monotonous, harping, sing-song, mocking, chiming; above-mentioned, said, aforesaid.

(*Phrases*) It's that man again; cut and come again; *crambe repetita.*

(*Adverbs*) Repeatedly, often (136), again, anew, over again, afresh, ditto, *encore, de novo, da capo, bis* (90).

(*Phrases*) *Toties quoties*; again and again; in quick succession, over and over again; ever and anon; time after time; year after year; times out of number; *ad nauseam.*

105 INFINITY (*Substantives*), infiniteness, infinitude.

(*Adjectives*) Infinite, numberless, innumerable, countless, sumless, untold, unnumbered, unsummed, incalculable, unlimited, limitless, illimitable, immeasurable, unmeasured, measureless, unbounded, boundless, endless, interminable, unfathomable, exhaustless, termless, indefinite, without number, without limit, without end, unending.

(*Adverbs*) Infinitely, etc., without measure, limit, etc., *ad infinitum*, world without end.

SECTION VI—TIME

1°. *Absolute Time*

106 DURATION (*Substantives*), time, period, term, space, span, spell, season, era, epoch, decade, century, chiliad, age, cycle, aeon.

Intermediate time, while, interval, interim, pendency, intervention, intermission, interregnum, interlude, recess, break, intermittence, respite (265).

Long duration (110).

(*Phrases*) The enemy; the whirligig of time.

(*Verbs*) To continue, last, endure, remain, go on; to take, take up, fill or occupy time, to persist, to intervene.

107 TIMELESSNESS (*Substantives*), neverness, absence of time, no time, *dies non.*

Short duration (111).

(*Adverbs*) Never, ne'er, at no time, on no occasion, at no period, nevermore, *sine die.*

(*Phrases*) On Tib's eve; at the Greek Calends; *jamais de ma vie*; 'jam every other day.'

To pass, pass away, spend, employ, while away or consume time, waste time.

(*Adjectives*) Continuing, lasting, enduring, remaining, persistent, perpetual, permanent (150).

(*Adverbs*) While, whilst, so long as, during, pending, till, until, up to, during the time or interval, the whole time or period, all the time or while, in the long run, all along, throughout, from beginning to end (52).

Pending, meantime, meanwhile, in the meantime, in the interim, *ad interim, pendente lite*, from day to day, for a time, for a season, for good, yet, up to this time.

108 Definite duration, or portion of time.

PERIOD (*Substantives*), second, minute, hour, day, week, fortnight, month, lunation, quarter, year, leap-year, lustrum, quinquennium, decade, lifetime, generation, century, age, millennium, *annus magnus.*

(*Adjectives*) Hourly, horary; daily, diurnal, quotidian; weekly, hebdomadal, menstrual, monthly, annual, secular, centennial, bicentennial, etc., bissextile, seasonal.

(*Adverbs*) From day to day, from hour to hour.

Once upon a time; Anno Domini, A.D.; Before Christ, B.C.

108A CONTINGENT DURATION.
During pleasure, during good behaviour, *quamdiu se bene gesserit.*

110 Long duration.

DIUTURNITY (*Substantives*), a long time, an age, a century, an eternity, aeon.

(*Phrases*) *Temporis longinquitas*; a month of Sundays.

Durableness, durability, persistence, lastingness, continuance, permanence (150), longevity, survival.

Distance of time, protraction, extension or prolongation of time, delay (133).

(*Verbs*) To last, endure, stand, remain, continue, abide, tarry, protract, prolong, outlast, outlive, survive; spin out, draw out, eke out, temporize, linger, loiter, lounge (275), wait.

(*Phrase*) To live to fight another day.

(*Adjectives*) Durable, of long duration, permanent, enduring, chronic, intransient, intransitive, intransmutable, lasting, abiding, persistent; livelong, longeval, long-lived, macrobiotic, diuturnal, evergreen, perennial, unintermitting, unremitting, perpetual (112).

Protracted, prolonged, spun out, long-winded, surviving, lingering.

(*Adverbs*) Long, a long time, permanently.

(*Phrases*) As the day is long; all the

109 Indefinite duration.

COURSE (*Substantives*), progress, process, succession, lapse, flow, flux, stream, tract, current, tide, march, step, flight, etc., of time.

Indefinite time, aorist.

(*Verbs*) To elapse, lapse, flow, run, proceed, roll on, advance, pass, slide, press on, flit, fly, slip, glide, run its course.

(*Adjectives*) Elapsing, passing, etc.; aoristic.

(*Adverbs*) In course of time, in due time of season, in process of time, in the fullness of time.

(*Phrase*) *Labuntur anni.*

——

111 Short duration.

TRANSIENTNESS (*Substantives*), transitoriness, impermanence, evanescence, transitiveness, fugitiveness, fugacity, fugaciousness, caducity, mortality, span, shortness, brevity.

Quickness, promptness (132), suddenness, abruptness.

A *coup de main*, bubble, Mayfly, nine days' wonder.

(*Verbs*) To be transient, etc., to flit, pass away, fly, gallop, vanish, fade, intromit.

(*Adjectives*) Transitory, transient, transitive, passing, impermanent, evanescent, fleeting, momentary, fugacious, fugitive, flitting, vanishing, shifting, flying, temporary, temporal, makeshift, provisional, provisory, rough and ready, cursory, galloping, short-lived, ephemeral, deciduous, meteoric.

Brief, sudden, quick, prompt, brisk, abrupt, extemporaneous, summary, hasty, precipitate.

(*Adverbs*) Temporarily, etc., *en passant, in transitu,* extempore.

In a short time, soon, at once, awhile, anon, by and by, briefly, presently, apace, eftsoons, straight, straightway, quickly, speedily, promptly, presto, slapdash, directly,

day long; all the year round; the live-long day; hour after hour; morning, noon, and night; for good; for many a long day.

---

112 PERPETUITY (*Substantives*), eternity, sempiternity, immortality, athanasy, everlastingness, perpetuation.

(*Verbs*) To last or endure for ever, to have no end: to eternize, perpetuate.

(*Adjectives*) Perpetual, eternal, everlasting, sempiternal, coeternal; endless, unending, ceaseless, incessant, unceasing, uninterrupted, interminable, having no end, unfading, evergreen, never-fading, amaranthine, ageless, deathless, immortal, undying, never-dying, imperishable, indestructible.

(*Adverbs*) Always, ever, evermore, aye, for ever, for aye, for evermore, still, perpetually, eternally, etc., in all ages, from age to age.

(*Phrases*) For ever and a day; *esto perpetua*; for ever and ever; world without end; time without end; *in secula seculorum*; to the end of time; till Doomsday; till hell freezes; to a cinder.

---

114 Estimation, measurement, and record of time.

CHRONOMETRY (*Substantives*), chronology, horology, horometry, registry, date, epoch, style, era.

Greenwich, standard, mean, local, solar, sidereal time; summer time, double summer time.

Almanac, calendar, ephemeris, chronicle, annals, register, journal, diary, chronogram, time-book.

Instruments for the measurement of time, clock, watch, stop-watch, repeater, chronograph, chronometer, sextant, timepiece, dial, sun-dial, horologe, pendulum, hour-glass, water-clock, clepsydra; time signal.

Chronographer, chronologer, chronologist, time-keeper, annalist.

(*Verbs*) To chronicle, to fix or mark the time, date, register, etc., to bear date, to measure time, to beat time, to make time, to time.

(*Adjectives*) Chronological, chronometrical, chronogrammatical.

(*Adverb*) O'clock.

113 Point of time.

INSTANTANEITY (*Substantives*), instantaneousness, moment, instant, second, split second, minute, twinkling, trice, flash, breath, span, jiffy, flash of lightning, suddenness (111).

(*Verbs*) To twinkle, flash, to be instantaneous.

(*Adjectives*) Instantaneous, push-button, sudden, momentary, extempore.

(*Phrases*) Quick as thought; quick as a flash; quick as lightning.

(*Adverbs*) Instantly, momentarily, *subito*, presto, instanter, suddenly, plump, slap, slapdash, in a moment, in an instant, in a second, in no time, in a trice, in a twinkling, at one jump, in a breath, extempore, *per saltum*, in a crack, out of hand.

(*Phrases*) Before one can say 'Jack Robinson'; in a brace of shakes; between the cup and the lip; on the spur of the moment; in the twinkling of an eye; in a jiffy; in two ticks; on the instant; in less than no time; at one fell swoop; no sooner said than done.

115 False estimate of time.

ANACHRONISM (*Substantives*), error in time, prolepsis, metachronism, prochronism, parachronism, anticipation. Disregard or neglect of time.

(*Verbs*) To anachronize, misdate, ante-date, postdate, overdate, anticipate.

(*Adjectives*) Anachronistic, anachronous, misdated, undated, overdue, postdated, antedated.

(*Phrases*) To take no note of time; to prophesy after the event.

immediately, incontinently, forthwith; suddenly, *per saltum*, at one bound.

(*Phrases*) At short notice; the time being up; before the ink is dry; here to-day and gone to-morrow (149); *sic transit gloria mundi*.

2°. *Relative Time*

I. TIME WITH REFERENCE TO SUCCESSION

116 PRIORITY (*Substantives*), antecedence, anteriority, precedence, pre-existence.

Precursor, predecessor, prelude, forerunner (64), harbinger, antecedent; the past (122).

(*Verbs*) To precede, come before, forerun, pre-exist, prelude, usher in, dawn, announce (511), foretell, anticipate, forestall.

(*Phrases*) To be beforehand; to steal a march upon.

(*Adjectives*) Prior, previous, preceding, precedent, anterior, antecedent, pre-existent, pre-existing, former, foregoing, aforesaid, said, above-mentioned, prehistoric, antediluvian, pre-Adamite.

Precursory, prelusive, prelusory, proemial, introductory, prefatory (62), prodromal, prodromic.

117 POSTERIORITY (*Substantives*), succession, sequence, subsequence, supervention, sequel, successor (65), postlude.

(*Verbs*) To follow, come or go after, succeed, supervene, ensue.

(*Phrases*) To tread on the heels of; to follow in the footsteps of.

(*Adjectives*) Subsequent, posterior, following, after, later, succeeding, post-glacial, post-diluvial, post-diluvian, puisne, posthumous, postprandial, post-classical.

(*Adverbs*) Subsequently, after, afterwards, since, later, later on, at a subsequent or later period, proximo, next, in the sequel, close upon, thereafter, thereupon, whereupon, upon which, eftsoons, below, *infra*.

(*Adverbs*) Before, prior to, previously, anteriorly, antecedently, aforetime, ere, ere now, erewhile, before now, heretofore, ultimo, yet, beforehand, above, *supra*.

(*Phrase*) Before the flood.

118 THE PRESENT TIME (*Substantives*), the existing time, the time being, the present moment, juncture, crisis, epoch, day, hour; the twentieth century.

Age, time of life.

(*Verb*) To strike while the iron is hot.

(*Adjectives*) Present, actual, current, existing, that is.

(*Adverbs*) At this time, moment, etc., now, at present, at this time of day, at the present time, day, etc., to-day, nowadays, instant, already, even now, but now, just now, upon which.

(*Phrases*) For the time being; for the nonce; *pro hac vice*; on the nail; on the spot; on the spur of the moment; now or never.

119 Time different from the present.

DIFFERENT TIME (*Substantives*), other time.

Indefinite time, aorist.

(*Adjective*) Aoristic.

(*Adverbs*) At that time, moment, etc., then, at which time, etc., on that occasion, upon, in those days.

When, whenever, whensoever, upon which, on which occasions, at another or a different time, etc., otherwhile, otherwhiles, at various times, ever and anon.

(*Phrases*) Once upon a time; one day; some other time; one of these days.

120 SYNCHRONISM (*Substantives*), synchronization, coinstantaneity, co-existence, coincidence, simultaneousness, coevality, contemporaneousness, contemporaneity, concurrence, concomitance.

Having equal times, isochronism.

A contemporary, coeval, coetanean.

(*Verbs*) To coexist, concur, accompany, synchronize.

(*Phrase*) To keep pace with.

(*Adjectives*) Synchronous, synchronal, synchronistic, simultaneous, co-existing, coincident, concomitant, concurrent, coeval, coetaneous, contemporary, contemporaneous, coeternal, isochronous.

(*Adverbs*) At the same time, simultaneously, etc., together, during the same time, etc., in the interim, in the same breath, in concert, *pari passu*; meantime, meanwhile (106), while, whilst.

121 Prospective time.

FUTURITY (*Substantives*), the future, futurition, the approaching time, hereafter, the time to come, posteriority (117), after time, after age, the coming time, the morrow, after days, hours, years, ages; after life, millennium, doomsday, the day of judgment, the crack of doom.

The approach of time, the process of time, advent, time drawing on, the womb of time.

Prospection, anticipation, prospect, perspective, expectation (507), horizon, outlook, look-out.

Heritage, heirs, progeny, issue, posterity, descendants, heir apparent, heir presumptive.

Future existence, future state, post-existence, after-life, beyond.

(*Verbs*) To look forward, anticipate, forestall (132), have in prospect, keep in view, expect (507).

To impend, hang over, lie over, approach, await, threaten, overhang, draw near, prepare.

(*Phrases*) Lie in wait for; bide one's time; to wait impatiently; kick one's heels.

To be in the wind; to be cooking; to loom in the future.

(*Adjectives*) Future, to come, coming, going to happen, approaching, impending, instant, at hand, about to be or happen, next, hanging, awaiting, forthcoming, near, near at hand, imminent, threatening, brewing, preparing, in store, eventual, ulterior, in view, in prospect, prospective, in perspective, in the offing, in the wind, on the cards, that will be, overhanging.

Unborn, in embryo, in the womb of time.

122 Retrospective time.

PRETERITION (*Substantives*), the past, past time, *status quo*, days of yore, time gone by, priority (116), former times, old times, the olden time, ancient times, antiquity, antiqueness, lang syne, time immemorial, prehistory.

Archaeology, palaeology, palaeontology, palaeography, archaism, retrospection, retrospect, looking back.

Archaeologist, antiquary, medievalist, palaeographer, palaeologist, Dr. Dryasdust.

Ancestry (166), pre-existence.

(*Phrases*) The good old days; the golden age; the rust of antiquity.

(*Verbs*) To pass, be past, lapse, go by, elapse, run out, expire, blow over; to look back, cast the eyes back, retrospect, trace back, dig up, exhume.

(*Phrases*) To have run its course; to have had its day.

(*Adjectives*) Past, gone, gone by, over, bygone, foregone, pristine, prehistoric, quondam, lapsed, elapsed, preterlapsed, expired, late, *ci-devant*, run out, blown over, that has been.

Former, foregoing, late, last, latter, recent, overnight, preterperfect, preterpluperfect, forgotten, irrecoverable, out of date.

Looking back, retrospective, retroactive, *ex post facto*; archaeological, etc.

Pre-existing, pre-existent.

(*Adverbs*) Formerly, of old, erst, whilom, erewhile, before now, time was, ago, over, in the olden time, anciently, in days of yore, long since, retrospectively, ere now, before now, till now, once, once upon a time, hitherto, heretofore, *ultimo*.

(Adverbs) Prospectively, hereafter, by and by, some fine day, one of these days, anon, in future, to-morrow, in course of time, in process of time, sooner or later, *proximo*, in after time.

On the eve of, ere long, at hand, near at hand, on the point of, beforehand, against the time.

After a time, from this time, henceforth, henceforwards, thence, thenceforth, thenceforward, whereupon, upon which.

(Phrases) All in good time; in the fullness of time.

The other day, yesterday, last night, week, month, year, etc.; just now, recently, lately, of late, latterly.

Long ago, a long while or time ago, some time ago.

(Phrases) Once upon a time; from time immemorial; in the memory of man; time out of mind.

Already, yet, at length, at last.

---

2. TIME WITH REFERENCE TO A PARTICULAR PERIOD

123 NEWNESS *(Substantives)*, novelty, recentness, recency, modernity, freshness, greenness, immaturity, youth (127), rawness.

Innovation, renovation (660), renewal.

Nouveau riche, parvenu, upstart, mushroom; latest fashion, *dernier cri.*

(Verbs) Renew, renovate, restore (660), modernize.

(Adjectives) New, novel, recent, fresh, green, evergreen, raw, immature, untrodden, advanced, twentieth-century, modern, modernistic, avant-garde, neoteric, new-born, nascent, new-fashioned, up-to-date, new-fangled, vernal, renovated, brand-new, split-new, virgin.

(Phrases) Fresh as a rose; fresh as a daisy; fresh as paint; just out; spick and span.

(Adverbs) Newly, recently, lately, afresh, anew.

124 OLDNESS *(Substantives)*, age (128), antiquity, eld, anciently, primitiveness, maturity, decline, decay, obsolescence; seniority, eldership, primogeniture.

Archaism, relic, antique, fossil, eolith; elder, doyen.

(Verbs) To be or become old, mature, mellow; to age, fade, decay.

(Adjectives) Old, ancient, antique, antiquated, out-of-date, of long standing, time-honoured, venerable, hoary, primitive, diluvian, antediluvian, fossil, palaeozoic, preglacial, palaeolithic, neolithic, primeval, primordial, prime, pre-Adamite, prehistoric, antemundane, archaic, classic, medieval.

Immemorial, inveterate, rooted, traditional.

Senior, elder, eldest, oldest, first-born (128).

Obsolete, obsolescent, out-of-date, stale, time-worn, faded, decayed, effete, declining, played-out, crumbling, decrepit (128), *passé.*

(Phrases) Nothing new under the sun; old as the hills; old as Methuselah; old as Adam; before the Flood; time out of mind; since the year one.

125 MORNING *(Substantives)*, morn, morrow, forenoon, a.m., prime, dawn, daybreak, dayspring, peep of day, break of day, matins, aurora, first blush of the morning, prime of the morning, twilight, crepuscule, sunrise, sun-up, cockcrow.

126 EVENING *(Substantives)*, eve, e'en, decline of day, close of day, eventide, nightfall, curfew, vespers, evensong, dusk, twilight, gloaming, eleventh hour, sunset, sundown, afternoon, p.m., bedtime, midnight; autumn, Indian summer, St. Martin's

Noon, midday, noontide, meridian, noonday, prime; spring, summer, midsummer.

(*Adjectives*) Matutinal, auroral, vernal, midsummer.

---

127 YOUTH (*Substantives*), infancy, babyhood, boyhood, juvenility, childhood, youthhood, juniority, juvenescence, adolescence (131), minority, nonage, teens, tender age, bloom, heyday, boyishness, girlishness.

Cradle, nursery, leading strings, pupilage, pupilship, puberty.

(*Phrases*) Prime or flower of life; the rising generation; salad days; schooldays.

(*Adjectives*) Young, youthful, juvenile, callow, sappy, beardless, under age, in one's teens, boyish, girlish, junior, younger.

(*Phrase*) In statu pupillari.

summer, St. Luke's summer, winter the fall.

(*Phrases*) The witching time of night; the dead of night; blind-man's holiday.

(*Adjectives*) Nocturnal, vespertine, autumnal, hiemal, brumal.

128 AGE (*Substantives*), old age, senility, senescence, oldness, longevity, years, anility, grey hairs, climacteric, decrepitude, hoary age, caducity, crow's feet, superannuation, dotage, anecdotage, seniority, green old age, eldership.

(*Phrases*) The vale of years; decline of life; the sere and yellow leaf; second childhood.

(*Adjectives*) Aged, old, elderly, senile, matronly, anile, in years, ripe, mellow, grey, grey-headed, hoary, hoar, venerable, timeworn, declining, antiquated, *passé*, rusty, effete, decrepit, superannuated.

Patriarchal, ancestral, primitive, older, elder, senior; eldest, oldest, first-born, bantling, firstling.

(*Phrases*) With one foot in the grave; marked with crow's feet; advanced in life, or in years; stricken in years; no chicken; long in the tooth; old as the hills.

---

129 INFANT (*Substantives*), babe, baby, nursling, suckling.

Child, bairn, wean, little one, brat, toddler, kid, chit, urchin, bantling, bratling, papoose, elf, piccaninny.

Youth, boy, lad, laddie, stripling, youngster, teenager, callant, younker, gossoon, nipper, whipster, whippersnapper, schoolboy, young hopeful, hobbledehoy, cadet, minor.

Girl, lass, lassie, wench, miss, colleen, flapper, bobbysoxer, damsel, maid, maiden, *jeune fille.*

Scion, sapling, seedling, tendril, mushroom, nestling, chicken, larva, chrysalis, tadpole, whelp, cub, pullet, fry, foetus, calf, lamb, lambkin, colt, filly, pup, puppy, foal, kitten.

130 VETERAN (*Substantives*), old man, seer, patriarch, greybeard, gaffer, grandsire, grandam, dowager, matron, crone, beldam, hag, sexagenarian, octogenarian, centenarian, oldster, old-timer, old stager, old buffer, fogy, geezer.

Methuselah, Nestor; elders, forefathers, forbears, fathers, ancestors, ancestry.

(*Adjectives*) Veteran, aged, old, grey-headed (128).

(*Adjectives*) Infantine, infantile, puerile, boyish, girlish (127), virginal, childish, baby, babyish, unfledged, new-fledged, kittenish, callow.

(*Phrases*) In leading-strings; at the breast; in arms; in one's teens; tied to mother's apron-strings.

131 ADOLESCENCE-(*Substantives*), puberty, pubescence, majority, adultness, maturity, ripeness, manhood, virility.

A man, adult (373), a woman, matron (374), *parti*; ephebe.

(*Phrases*) Prime of life; man's estate; flower of age; meridian of life; years of discretion; *toga virilis*.

(*Adjectives*) Adolescent, pubescent, of age, out of one's teens, grown up, mature, middle-aged, manly, virile, adult.

Womanly, matronly, nubile, marriageable, out.

3. TIME WITH REFERENCE TO AN EFFECT OR PURPOSE

132 EARLINESS (*Substantives*), timeliness, punctuality, readiness, promptness (682), promptitude, expedition, quickness, haste, acceleration, hastening, hurry, bustle, precipitation, anticipation, precociousness, precocity.

Suddenness, abruptness (111).

(*Phrases*) A stitch in time saves nine; the early bird catches the worm.

(*Verbs*) To be early, to be in time, keep time, be beforehand.

To anticipate, forestall, book, engage, bespeak, reserve.

To expedite, hasten, haste, quicken (274), press, dispatch, accelerate, precipitate, hurry, bustle (684).

(*Phrases*) To take time by the forelock; to steal a march upon; to be beforehand with; to be pressed for time.

(*Adjectives*) ¹Early, ¹prime, rathe, timely, timeous, punctual, matutinal, forward, ready, quick, expeditious, precipitate, summary, prompt, premature, precocious, prevenient, anticipatory, pre-emptive.

Sudden, abrupt, unexpected (508), subitaneous, extempore.

(*Adverbs*) Early, soon, anon, betimes, apace, eft, eftsoons, in time, ere long, presently, shortly, punctually, to the minute, on time, on the dot.

Beforehand, prematurely, before one's time, in anticipation.

Suddenly, abruptly, at once, extempore, instanter.

(*Phrases*) In good time; at sunrise; with the lark; early days.

On the point of; at short notice; on the spur of the moment; all at once; before you can say 'knife'; no sooner said than done.

133 LATENESS (*Substantives*), tardiness, slowness (275), delay, cunctation, procrastination, deferring, lingering, lagging, etc., postponement, dilatoriness, adjournment, shelving, prorogation, remand, moratorium.

Protraction, prolongation, leeway.

(*Phrase*) Fabian tactics.

(*Verbs*) To be late, etc., tarry, wait, stay, bide, take time, dally, dawdle, linger, loiter, lag, bide one's time, shuffle (275, 683).

To stand over, lie over, hang fire.

To put off, defer, delay, leave over, suspend, stave off, postpone, adjourn, carry over, shelve, procrastinate, temporize, stall, filibuster, prolong, protract, draw out, spin out, hold up, prorogue.

(*Phrases*) To tide it over; to bide one's time; to let the matter stand over; to sleep on it; to kick (or cool) one's heels.

(*Adjectives*) Late, tardy, slow, dilatory (275), posthumous, backward, unpunctual, procrastinatory, behindhand, belated, overdue.

Delayed, etc., suspended, pending, in abeyance.

(*Adverbs*) Late, after time, too late, behind time; at length, at last.

Slowly, leisurely, deliberately.

(*Phrases*) Late in the day; a day after the fair; at the eleventh hour; after death, the doctor.

134 OCCASION (*Substantives*), opportunity, chance, opening, break, show, room, suitable or proper time or season, high time, opportuneness, tempestivity, seasonableness, crisis, turn, juncture, conjuncture.

Spare time, leisure, holiday (685), spare moments, hours, etc., time on one's hands.

(*Phrases*) Golden (or favourable) opportunity; the nick of time;

(*Verbs*) To use, make use of, employ, profit by, avail oneself of, lay hold of, embrace, catch, seize, snatch, clutch, pounce upon, grasp, etc., the opportunity.

To give, offer, present, afford, etc., the opportunity.

To time well; to spend or consume time.

(*Phrases*) To turn the occasion to account; to seize the occasion; to strike the iron while it is hot; to make hay while the sun shines; *carpe diem*; to take the tide at the flood; to furnish a handle for.

(*Adjectives*) Opportune, timely, well-timed, timeful, timeous, seasonable, happy, lucky, providential, fortunate, favourable, propitious, auspicious, critical.

(*Adverbs*) Opportunely, etc., on the spot, in proper or due time or season, high time, for the nonce.

By the way, by the by, *en passant*, *à propos*, parenthetically.

(*Phrases*) In the nick of time; on the spur of the moment (612); now or never; at the eleventh hour; time and tide wait for no man.

135 INTEMPESTIVITY (*Substantives*), untimeliness, unsuitable time, improper time, unseasonableness, inopportuneness, evil hour.

Hitch, impediment (706), check, *contretemps*.

(*Verbs*) To be ill-timed, etc., to mistime, intrude, come amiss.

To lose, omit, let slip, let go, neglect, pretermit, allow, or suffer the opportunity or occasion to pass, slip, go by, escape, lapse; to lose time, to fritter away time (683).

(*Phrase*) To let slip through the fingers; to lock the stable door when the steed is stolen.

(*Adjectives*) Ill-timed, untimely, untimeous, mistimed, unseasonable, out of season, unpunctual, inopportune, untoward, intrusive, too late (133), too early (132), malapropos, unlucky, inauspicious, unpropitious, unfortunate, unfavourable, unsuited, unsuitable.

(*Adverb*) Inopportunely, etc.

(*Phrases*) As ill luck would have it; in evil hour; after meat, mustard; a day before (or after) the fair.

3°. Recurrent Time

136 FREQUENCY (*Substantives*), oftness, recurrence, repetition (104), recrudescence, reiteration, iteration, run, reappearance, renewal, *ritornello*, *ritournelle*, burden.

Frequenter, *habitué*, fan, client.

(*Verbs*) To recur, revert, return, repeat, reiterate, reappear, renew, reword.

To frequent, resort to, visit, attend, haunt, infest.

(*Adjectives*) Frequent, common, not rare, repeated, reiterated, thick-coming, recurring, recurrent, incessant, everlasting, perpetual, rife; habitual (613).

137 INFREQUENCY (*Substantives*), rareness, rarity, uncommonness, scarcity, fewness (103), seldomness.

(*Verb*) To be rare, etc.

(*Adjectives*) Infrequent, rare, scarce, unfrequent, uncommon, unprecedented, unheard-of.

(*Phrase*) In short supply.

(*Adverbs*) Seldom, rarely, scarcely, hardly, scarcely ever, ever, hardly ever, not often unfrequently.

Once, once for all, once in a way.

(*Phrases*) Once in a blue moon; angels' visits.

(*Adverbs*) Often, oft, oft-times, not infrequently, frequently, often-times, many times, several times, repeatedly.

Again, anew, afresh, *de novo*, ditto, over again, *da capo*, again and again, over and over, ever and anon, many times over, time after time, time and again, repeatedly (104).

Perpetually, continually, constantly, incessantly, everlastingly, without ceasing.

Sometimes, occasionally, at times, now and then, now and again, from time to time, at intervals, between whiles, once in a while, there are times when.

Most often, for the most part, generally, usually, commonly, most frequently, as often as not.

(*Phrases*) A number of times; many a time (and oft); times out of number.

138 REGULARITY of recurrence, punctuality.

PERIODICITY (*Substantives*), inter-mittence, beat, ictus, pulse, pulsation, rhythm, lilt, swing, alternation, alter-nateness, bout, round, revolution, rotation, turn.

Anniversary, jubilee; silver, golden, wedding; centenary, bicentenary, tercentenary, etc.; feast, festival, birthday.

139 IRREGULARITY of recurrence uncertainty, unpunctuality, fitfulness.

(*Adjectives*) Irregular, uncertain, unpunctual, capricious, desultory, unrhythmic, unrhythmical, fitful, spasmodic, flickering, casual.

(*Adverbs*) Irregularly, etc., by snatches, by fits and starts, skip-pingly, now and then, occasionally.

Regularity of return, rota, cycle, period, stated time, routine.

(*Phrase*) The swing of the pendulum.

(*Verbs*) To recur in regular order or succession, to come round, return, revolve, alternate, come in its turn, beat, pulsate, intermit; to regularize.

(*Adjectives*) Periodic, periodical, recurrent, cyclical, revolving, inter-mittent, remittent, alternate, every other, alternating, rhythmic, rhythmical, steady, punctual.

Hourly, daily, diurnal, tertian, quotidian, weekly, hebdomadal, fortnightly, bi-monthly, monthly, biannual, annual, yearly, biennial, triennial, centennial.

(*Phrase*) Regular as clockwork.

(*Adverbs*) Periodically, at regular intervals, at stated times, at fixed periods, punctually, from day to day.

By turns, in turn, in rotation, alternately, in shifts, off and on, ride and tie, hitch and hike.

SECTION VII—CHANGE

1°. *Simple Change*

140 Difference at different times.

CHANGE (*Substantives*), alteration, mutation, permutation, variation, modification, modulation, inflexion, mood, qualification, innovation, meta-stasis, metabolism, deviation, turn, diversion, inversion, reversion, re-versal, eversion, subversion (162),

141 Absence of change.

PERMANENCE (*Substantives*), per-sistence, endurance, *status quo*; main-tenance, preservation, conservation, conservatism, *laissez-faire*, rest, sleep, establishment, truce, suspension, settledness (265), perdurability, stability (150).

bouleversement, upset, organic change, revolution (146), substitution (147), transposition (148), transit, transition.

Transformation, transmutation, transfiguration, metamorphosis, transmigration, transubstantiation, transmogrification, metempsychosis, avatar.

Vicissitude, flux, unrest (149); change of mind, tergiversation (607).

(*Phrase*) The wheel of fortune.

(*Verbs*) To change, alter, vary, modify, modulate, diversify, qualify, tamper with, edit, turn, shift, veer, tack, chop, shuffle, swerve, warp, deviate, turn aside, turn topsy-turvy, upset, invert, reverse, introvert, subvert, evert, turn inside out.

Form, fashion, mould, model, vamp, warp, work a change, superinduce, resume, disturb (61), innovate, reform, remodel, refound, new-model, modernize, revolutionize.

Transform, transume, transmute, transfigure, transmogrify, metamorphose, pass to, leap to, transfer.

(*Phrases*) To ring the changes; to turn over a new leaf; to introduce new blood; to shuffle the cards; to turn the corner; to wax and wane; to ebb and flow; *tempora mutantur; nous avons changé tout cela.*

(*Adjectives*) Changed, altered, new-fangled, warped, etc.; transitional, metamorphic, metabolic, metastatic.

(*Adverb*) *Mutatis mutandis.*

---

142 Change from action to rest.

CESSATION (*Substantives*), discontinuance, desistance, quiescence.

Intermission, remission, suspension, interruption, suspense, stand, halt, closure, stop, stoppage, pause, rest, lull, breathing-space, respite, truce, drop, interregnum, abeyance.

Comma, colon, semicolon, period, full stop.

(*Verbs*) To discontinue, cease, desist, break off, leave off, hold, stop, pause, rest, drop, lay aside, give up, have done with, stick, hang fire, pull up, give over, shut down, knock off, relinquish (624), surcease.

To come to a stand, or standstill, suspend, cut short, cast off,

(*Phrase*) The law of the Medes and Persians.

(*Verbs*) To remain, stay, stop, persist, tarry, hold, last, endure, continue, dwell, bide, abide, maintain, keep, hold on, stand, subsist, live, stand still, outlive, survive.

To let alone, let be.

(*Phrases*) To keep one's footing; to hold one's ground; to stick to one's guns; to stand fast.

(*Adjectives*) Persisting, etc., permanent, established, unchanged, unmodified, unrenewed, unaltered, fixed, settled, unvaried, intact, inviolate, persistent, stagnant, rooted, monotonous, unreversed, conservative, unprogressive, undestroyed, unrepelled, unsuppressed, unfailing, stationary (265), stereotyped, perdurable.

(*Adverbs*) *In statu quo,* for good, finally, at a stand, at a standstill, *uti possidetis.*

(*Phrases*) *J'y suis, j'y reste ; plus cela change, plus cela est la même chose ; esto perpetua.*

---

143 CONTINUANCE in action (*Substantives*), continuation, perseverance, repetition (104), persistence, run.

(*Verbs*) To continue, persist, go on, keep on, abide, keep, pursue, hold on, run on, follow on, carry on, keep up, uphold, sustain, perpetuate, persevere, keep it up, stick it, peg away, maintain, maintain one's ground, harp upon, repeat (104), take root.

(*Phrases*) To keep the pot boiling; to keep the ball rolling.

(*Adjectives*) Continual, continuous, continuing, etc., uninterrupted, inconvertible, unintermitting, unreversed, unstopped, unrevoked, unvaried, unshifting, perpetual (112).

go out, be at an end; intromit, interrupt, arrest, intermit, remit; put
an end or stop to.

To pass away, go off, pass off, blow over, die away, wear away, wear
off (122).

(*Phrases*) To shut up shop; to stay one's hand; to rest on one's oars;
to rest on one's laurels.

(*Interjections*) Hold! hold on! stop! enough! avast! *basta !* have done!
a truce to! stop it! drop it! cheese it! chuck it! stow it! cut it out!

144 Gradual change to something different.

CONVERSION (*Substantives*), reduction, transmutation, resolution, assimilation; chemistry, alchemy; growth, lapse, progress, becoming; naturalization.

Passage, transit, transition, transmigration, flux, shifting, sliding, running
into, etc.; phase, conjugations; convertibility.

Laboratory, alembic, crucible (691).

Convert, pervert, vert, turncoat, renegade, apostate.

(*Verbs*) To be converted into; to become, get, wax, come to turn to,
turn into, assume the form of, pass into, slide into, glide into, lapse, shift,
run into, fall into, merge into, melt, grow, grow into, open into, resolve itself
into, settle into, mature, mellow; assume the form, shape, state, nature,
character, etc., of; illapse.

To convert into; to make, render, form, mould, reduce, resolve into;
transume (140), fashion, model, remodel, reorganize, shape, modify, transmogrify; assimilate to; reduce to, bring to; refound, re-form, reshape.

(*Adjectives*) Converted into, become, etc., convertible, transitional.

(*Adverbs*) Gradually, *gradatim*, by degrees, step by step, by inches, inch
by inch, by little and little, by slow degrees, consecutively, seriatim, *in
transitu*.

145 REVERSION (*Substantives*), return, reconversion, relapse (661), recidivism, atavism, throwback, reaction, recoil (277), backlash, rebound,
ricochet, revulsion, alternation (138), inversion, regression (283).

Reinstatement, re-establishment (660).

(*Phrases*) The turning-point; the turn of the tide; *status quo ante bellum.*

(*Verbs*) To revert, turn back, return to, relapse, recoil, rebound, react; to
restore (660), to undo, unmake.

(*Phrase*) To turn the tables (719).

(*Adjectives*) Reverting, etc., restored, etc., regressive, retrogressive, atavistic,
revulsive, reactionary.

(*Interjection*) As you were!

146 Sudden or violent change.

REVOLUTION (*Substantives*), counter-revolution, revolt, rebellion (742),
transilience, jump, leap, plunge, jerk, start, spasm, convulsion, throe, storm,
earthquake, catastrophe, cataclysm (173).

Legerdemain, conjuration, sleight of hand, hocus-pocus (545), harlequinade,
witchcraft (992).

A revolutionary, revolutionist, counter-revolutionist, deviationist; the red
flag.

(*Verbs*) To revolutionize, remodel, recast, refashion, reconstruct.

(*Adjectives*) Revolutionary, radical, extreme, intransigent, catastrophic,
cataclysmic.

(*Adverbs*) Root and branch.

147 Change of one thing for another.

SUBSTITUTION (*Substantives*), commutation, supplanting, replacement, supersession, enallage, metonymy, synecdoche, antonomasia.

Thing substituted, substitute (634), succedaneum, makeshift, shift, apology, stand-in, pinch-hitter, locumtenens, representative, proxy; understudy, deputy (759), vice, double, dummy, changeling, scapegoat, stooge; stop-gap, jury-mast, palimpsest, metaphor (521).

(*Phrase*) Borrowing of or robbing Peter to pay Paul.

(*Verbs*) To substitute, put in place of, commute, supplant, cut out, change for, supersede, take over from.

To give place to; to replace.

(*Phrases*) To serve as a substitute, etc.; to do duty for; to stand in the shoes of; to take the place of.

(*Adjectives*) Substituted, etc., vicarious, subdititious, makeshift, provisional.

(*Adverbs*) Instead, in place of, in lieu of, in the room of, *faute de mieux*.

148 Double and mutual change.

INTERCHANGE (*Substantives*), exchange, commutation, intermutation, reciprocation, transposition, permutation, shuffling, castling (at chess), hocus-pocus, interchangeableness, interchangeability.

Reciprocity (12), retaliation (718), barter (794).

(*Phrases*) A Roland for an Oliver; tit for tat; *quid pro quo*.

(*Verbs*) To interchange, exchange, bandy, transpose, shuffle, change hands, swap, dicker, permute, reciprocate, commute, counterchange.

(*Phrases*) To play at puss in the corner; to play musical chairs; to return the compliment; to give and take; you scratch my back and I'll scratch yours.

(*Adjectives*) Interchanged, etc., reciprocal, mutual, commutative, interchangeable, intercurrent.

(*Adverbs*) In exchange, vice versa.

2°. *Complex Changes*

149 MUTABILITY (*Substantives*), changeableness, changeability, inconstancy, variableness, mobility, instability, unsteadiness, vacillation, unrest, restlessness, slipperiness, impermanence, fragility, fluctuation, vicissitude, alternation, vibration, oscillation (314), flux, ebbing and flowing, ebbs and flows, ups and downs, fidgets, fidgetiness, fugitiveness, disquiet, disquietude.

A Proteus, chameleon, quicksilver, weathercock, kaleidoscope, harlequin; the moon.

(*Phrases*) April showers; shifting sands; the wheel of fortune; the Cynthia of the minute.

(*Verbs*) To fluctuate, vary, waver, flounder, vibrate, flicker, flit, flitter, shift, shuffle, shake, totter, tremble, vacillate, ebb and flow, turn and turn about, change and change about.

150 IMMUTABILITY (*Substantives*), stability, unchangeableness, unchangeability, constancy, permanence, persistence (106), invariableness, durability, steadiness (604), immobility, fixedness, stableness, settledness, stabiliment, firmness, stiffness, anchylosis, solidity, aplomb, ballast, incommutability, insusceptibility, irrevocableness.

Rock, pillar, tower, foundation, fixture.

(*Phrase*) The law of the Medes and Persians.

(*Verbs*) To be permanent, etc. (265), to stand, stand fast, stand pat, remain.

To settle, establish, stablish, perpetuate, fix, set, stabilitate, retain, keep, hold, make sure, nail, clinch, rivet, fasten (43), settle down, set on its legs.

(*Phrases*) To build one's house on a rock; to weather the storm.

To fade, pass away like a cloud, shadow, or dream.

(*Adjectives*) Mutable, changeable, variable, ever-changing, inconstant, impermanent, unsteady, unstable, protean, proteiform, unfixed, fluctuating, vacillating, shifting, versatile, fickle, wavering, flickering, flitting, restless, erratic, unsettled, mobile, fluttering, oscillating, vibratory, vagrant, wayward, desultory, afloat, alternating, plastic, disquiet, alterable, casual, unballasted, volatile, capricious (608).

Frail, tottering, shaking, shaky, trembling, fugitive, ephemeral, transient (111), fading, fragile, deciduous, slippery, unsettled, irresolute (605), rocky, groggy.

Kaleidoscopic, prismatic, iridescent, opalescent, shot.

(*Phrases*) Unstable as water; changeable as the moon, or as a weathercock ; *sic transit gloria mundi*; here to-day and gone to-morrow.

Present events

151 EVENTUALITY (*Substantives*), event, happening, occurrence, incident, affair, transaction, proceeding, fact, matter of fact, phenomenon, advent.

Business, concern, circumstance, particular, casualty, accident, adventure, passage, crisis, episode, pass, emergency, contingency, consequence (154).

The world, life, things, doings, course of things, the course, tide, stream, current, run, etc., of events.

(*Phrases*) Stirring events; the ups and downs of life; a chapter of accidents; the cast of the dice (156).

(*Verbs*) To happen, occur, take place, take effect, come, come of, become of, come about, come off, pass, come to pass, fall, fall out, run, be on foot, fall in, befall, betide, bechance, turn out, go off, prove, eventuate, draw on, turn up, crop up, supervene, survene, issue, arrive, ensue, arise, spring, start, come into existence, fall to one's lot.

(*Adjectives*) Immutable, incommutable, unchangeable, unaltered, unalterable, not to be changed, constant, permanent, invariable, undeviating, stable, durable (265), perennial (110), valid.

Fixed, steadfast, firm, fast, steady, confirmed, immovable, irremovable, rooted, riveted, stablished, established, incontrovertible, stereotyped, indeclinable, settled, stationary, stagnant.

Moored, anchored, at anchor, on a rock, firmly seated, deep-rooted, ineradicable.

Stranded, aground, stuck fast, high and dry.

Indefeasible, irretrievable, intransmutable, irresoluble, irrevocable, irreversible, inextinguishable, irreducible, indissoluble, indissolvable, indestructible, undying, imperishable, indelible, indeciduous, insusceptible of change.

(*Phrases*) *J'y suis, j'y reste*; *stet* ; can the Ethiopian change his skin, or the leopard his spots?

Future events

152 DESTINY (*Substantives*), fatality, fate, doom, destination, lot, fortune, star, planet, preordination, predestination, fatalism, inevitableness, kismet, karma, necessity (601), after life, futurity (121).

(*Phrases*) The decrees of fate; the wheel of fortune.

(*Verbs*) To impend, hang over, overhang, be in store, loom, threaten, await, come on, approach, stare one in the face, foreordain, preordain, predestine, doom, must be.

(*Phrase*) To dree one's weird.

(*Adjectives*) About to happen, impending, coming, destined, imminent, inevitable, ineluctable, inexorable, fated, doomed, devoted

(*Phrases*) On the cards; on the knees of the gods.

(*Adverbs*) Necessarily, inevitably.

(*Phrases*) What must be, must; *che sarà sarà*; 'It is written'; the die is cast.

To pass off, wear off, blow over.

To experience, meet with, go through, pass through, endure (821), suffer, fare.

(*Adjectives*) Happening, occurring, etc., going on, current, incidental, eventful, stirring, bustling.

(*Phrase*) The plot thickening.

(*Adverbs*) Eventually, in the event of, on foot, on the *tapis*, as it may happen, happen what may, at all events, sink or swim, come what may.

(*Phrases*) In the course of things; in the long run; as the world wags.

Section VIII—Causation

1°. *Constancy of Sequence in Events*

153 Constant antecedent.

CAUSE (*Substantives*), origin, source, principle, element, occasioner, prime mover, *primum mobile*, spring, mainspring, agent, seed, leaven, groundwork, basis (215), fountain, well, fount, fountain-head, spring-head, author (164), parent (166), *fons et origo, raison d'être*.

Pivot, hinge, turning-point, key, lever.

Final cause, proximate cause, immediate cause, ground, reason, the reason why, the why and the wherefore, rationale, occasion, derivation, provenance.

Rudiment, germ, embryo, bud, root, *radix*, radical, etymon, nucleus, seed, ovum, stem, stock, trunk, taproot.

Nest, cradle, womb, *nidus*, birthplace, hot-bed, forcing-bed.

Causality, origination, causation, production (161), aetiology.

Theories of causation, creationism; evolution, Lamarckism, Darwinism, Spencerism, orthogenesis.

(*Verbs*) To be the cause of, to originate, germinate, give origin to, cause, occasion, give rise to, kindle, suscitate, bring on, bring to pass, give occasion to, produce, bring about, institute, found, lay the foundation of, lie at the root of, procure, draw down, induce, realize, evoke, provoke, elicit, entail, develop, evolve, operate (161).

154 Constant sequent.

EFFECT (*Substantives*), consequence, product, result, resultant, resultance, upshot, issue, end (67), fruit, crop, aftermath, harvest, development, outgrowth, derivative, derivation.

Production, produce, work, handiwork, performance, creature, creation, offshoot, fabric, offspring, first-fruits, firstlings, output, *dénouement*, derivation, heredity, evolution (161).

(*Verbs*) To be the effect, work, fruit, result, etc., of; to be owing to, originate in or from, rise from, take its rise from, arise, spring, proceed, evolve, come of, emanate, come, grow, germinate, bud, sprout, stem, issue, flow, result, follow, accrue, etc., from; come to; to come out of, be derived from, be caused by, depend upon, hinge upon, turn upon, result from, to be dependent upon, hang upon; to pan out.

(*Phrase*) To take the consequences.

(*Adjectives*) Owing to, due to, attributable to, ascribable to, resulting from, through, etc., all along of, hereditary, genetic, derivative.

(*Adverbs*) Of course, consequently, necessarily, eventually.

(*Phrases*) *Cela va sans dire*; thereby hangs a tale.

To conduce, contribute, tend to (176); to determine, decide.

(*Phrases*) To have a hand in; to have a finger in the pie; to open the door to; to be at the bottom of; to sow the seeds of; to turn the scale.

(*Adjectives*) Caused, occasioned, etc., causal, original, primary, primordial, having a common origin, connate, radical, embryonic, embryotic, in embryo.

Evolutionary, Darwinian; aetiological.

(*Phrase*) Behind the scenes.

155 Assignment of cause.

ATTRIBUTION (*Substantives*), theory, aetiology, ascription, reference to, rationale, accounting for, imputation to, derivation from, filiation, affiliation, genealogy, pedigree, paternity, maternity (166), explanation (522), cause (153).

(*Verbs*) To attribute, ascribe, impute, refer to, derive from, lay to, point to, charge on, ground on, invest with, assign as cause, trace to, father upon, account for, theorize, ground, etc.

(*Phrases*) To put the saddle on the right horse; to point out the reason of; to lay at the door of.

(*Adjectives*) Attributable, imputable, assignable, traceable, ascribable, referable, owing to, derivable from.

Putative, attributed, imputed, etc.

(*Adverbs*) Hence, thence, therefore, because, from that cause, for that reason, on that account, owing to, thanks to, forasmuch as, whence, *propter hoc*, wherefore, since, inasmuch as.

Why? wherefore? whence? how comes it? how is it? how happens it? how does it happen?

In some way, somehow, somehow or other, in some such way.

(*Phrase*) *Hinc illae lacrimae.*

156 Absence of assignable cause.

CHANCE (*Substantives*), indetermination, accident, fortune, hazard, hap, haphazard, chance-medley, luck, lot, fate (152), casualty, contingency, adventure, venture, pot-luck, lucky dip, treasure trove, hit.

A lottery, toss-up, game of chance, *sortes Virgiliance, rouge et noir*, heads or tails, gambling (621), sweepstake.

Possibility, probability, odds, long odds, a near shave, bare chance.

(*Phrases*) The turn of the cards; a cast or throw of the dice; a pig in a poke; a blind date.

(*Verbs*) To chance, hap, turn up; to fall to one's lot, to be one's fate (152); to light upon; stumble upon. .

To game, gamble, cast lots, raffle, play for.

(*Phrases*) To take one's chance; to toss up for; to chance one's arm; to take a flyer.

(*Adjectives*) Casual, fortuitous, random, accidental, adventitious, causeless, incidental, contingent, uncaused, undetermined, indeterminate, suppositional, possible (470); aleatory.

(*Adverbs*) By chance, by accident, perchance, peradventure, perhaps, maybe, mayhap, haply, possibly.

Casually, etc., at random, at a venture, as it may be, as it may chance, as it may turn up, as it may happen; as chance, luck, fortune, etc., would have it.

2°. *Connection between Cause and Effect*

157 POWER (*Substantives*), potentiality, potency, prepotence, prepotency, prepollence, puissance, strength, (159), might, force, energy, metal, dint, right hand, ascendancy, sway, control, almightiness, ability, ableness, competency, efficiency, effectiveness, efficacy, efficaciousness, validity, cogency, enablement; agency

158 IMPOTENCE (*Substantives*), inability, disability, disablement, impuissance, weakness (160), imbecility, paralysis, inaptitude, incapacity, incapability, invalidity, inefficacy inefficiency, inefficaciousness, ineffectualness, disqualification, helplessness, incompetence.

(*Phrases*) A dead letter; waste

(170), casualty (153), influence (175), authority (737).

Capability, capacity, faculty, quality, attribute, endowment, virtue, gift, property.

Pressure, high pressure, mechanical energy, applied force, motive power.

(*Verbs*) To be powerful, etc., to gain power; to exercise power, sway, etc., to constrain.

To be the property, virtue, attribute, etc., of; to belong to, pertain to, appertain to, to lie or be in one's power.

To give or confer power, to empower, enable, invest, endue, endow, arm, render strong (159).

(*Adjectives*) Powerful, high-powered, potent, puissant, potential, capable, able, equal to, cogent, valid, effective, effectual, efficient, efficacious, adequate, competent.

Forcible, energetic, vigorous, nervous, dynamic, vivid, sturdy, rousing, all-powerful, omnipotent, resistless, irresistible, inextinguishable, sovereign, invincible, unconquerable, indomitable.

(*Adverbs*) Powerfully, etc., by virtue of, in full force.

159 Degree of power.

STRENGTH (*Substantives*), energy (171), power (157), vigour, vitality, force, main force, physical force, brute force, spring, elasticity, tone, tension, tonicity.

Stoutness, sturdiness, lustiness, lustihood, stamina, physique, nerve, muscle, thews and sinews, backbone, pith, pithiness.

Feats of strength, athletics, gymnastics.

Strengthening, invigoration, bracing, recruital, recruitment, refreshment, refocillation (689).

Science of forces, dynamics, statics.

Adamant, steel, iron, oak, heart of oak.

An athlete, gymnast, acrobat; an Atlas, a Hercules, Sampson, Cyclops, Goliath.

(*Phrases*) A giant refreshed; a tower of strength.

paper; *brutum fulmen*; blank cartridge.

(*Verbs*) To be impotent, powerless, etc.; to collapse, fail, flunk, break down, fizzle out, fold up.

To render powerless, etc., to deprive of power, disable, disenable, incapacitate, disqualify, unfit, invalidate, nullify, deaden, cripple, cramp, paralyse, muzzle, hamstring, bowl over, render weak (160).

(*Phrases*) To go by the board; to end in smoke.

To clip the wings of; spike the guns; to tie a person's hands; to put a spoke in one's wheel; to take the wind out of one's sails.

(*Adjectives*) Powerless, impotent, unable, incapable, incompetent, inadequate, unequal to, inefficient, inefficacious, inept, ineffectual, ineffective, inoperative, nugatory, incapacitated, harmless, imbecile, disqualified, disabled, armless, disarmed, unarmed, weaponless, defenceless; unnerved, paralysed, palsied, disjointed, nerveless, adynamic, unendowed.

(*Phrases*) Laid on the shelf; *hors de combat*; not having a leg to stand on.

160 WEAKNESS (*Substantives*),

feebleness, impotence (158), debility, atony, relaxation, helplessness, languor, slackness, enervation, nervousness, faintness, languidness, infirmity, emasculation, effeminacy, feminality, femineity, flaccidity, softness, defencelessness.

Childhood, etc. (127, 129); orphan, chicken.

Declension, loss, failure, etc., of strength, invalidation, delicacy, delicateness, decrepitude, asthenia, neurasthenia, anaemia, bloodlessness, palsy, paralysis, exhaustion, collapse, prostration, faintness, cachexy (or cachexia).

A reed, thread, rope of sand, house of cards; a weakling, sissy, jellyfish.

(*Verbs*) To be weak, etc., to droop, fade, faint, swoon, languish, decline, flag, fail, totter, drop, crock; to go by the board.

(*Verbs*) To be strong, etc., to be stronger, to overmatch.

To render strong, etc., to give strength, tone, etc., to strengthen, invigorate, brace, buttress, sustain, fortify, harden, case-harden, steel, gird up, screw up, wind up, set up, tone up.

To reinforce, refit, recruit, vivify, restore (660), refect, refocillate (689).

(*Phrase*) To set on one's legs.

(*Adjectives*) Strong, mighty, vigorous, stout, robust, sturdy, powerful, puissant, hard, adamantine, invincible, able-bodied, athletic, Herculean, muscular, brawny, sinewy, made of iron, strapping, well-set, well-knit, stalwart, doughty, husky, lusty, hardy, irresistible; strengthening, etc., invigorative, tonic.

Manly, manlike, masculine, male, virile, manful, full-blooded.

Unweakened, unallayed, unwithered, unshaken, unworn, unexhausted, unrelaxed, undiluted, unwatered, neat.

(*Phrases*) Made of iron; as strong as a lion, as a horse; in great form; fit as a fiddle.

(*Adverbs*) Strongly, forcibly, etc., by main force, *vi et armis*, by might and main, tooth and nail, hammer and tongs, for all one is worth.

———

To render weak, etc., to weaken, enfeeble, debilitate, devitalize, deprive of strength, relax, enervate, unbrace, unman, emasculate, castrate, geld, hamstring, disable, unhinge, cripple, cramp, paralyse, maim, sprain, exhaust, prostrate, blunt the edge of, deaden, dilute, water, water down.

(*Adjectives*) Weak, feeble, debile, strengthless, nerveless, imbecile, unnerved, relaxed, unstrung, unbraced, enervated, nervous, sinewless, spineless, lustless, effeminate, feminine, womanly, unmanned, emasculated, castrated.

Crippled, maimed, lamed, shattered, broken, frail, fragile, flimsy, gimcrack, halting, shaken, crazy, shaky, paralysed, palsied, paralytic, decrepit, puny, shilpit, drooping, languid, faint, sickly, flagging, dull, slack, limp, spent, effete, weatherbeaten, worn, seedy, exhausted, deadbeat, all in, whacked, done up, languishing, wasted, washy, vincible, untenable, laid low, run down, asthenic, neurasthenic, neurotic, rickety, invertebrate, feckless.

Unstrengthened, unsustained, unsupported, unaided, unassisted, defenceless, indefensible, unfortified, unfriended, fatherless, etc.

(*Phrases*) On one's last legs; the worse for wear; weak as a child, as a baby, as a kitten, as water, good or fit for nothing.

3°. *Power in Operation*

161 PRODUCTION (*Substantives*), creation, formation, construction, fabrication, manufacture, building, architecture, erection, edification, coinage, organization, putting together, establishment, setting up, performance (729), workmanship, output.

Development, breeding, evolution, flowering, genesis, generation, *epigenesis*, procreation, propagation, fecundation, impregnation, gestation, birth, bringing forth, parturition, growth, proliferation.

162 Non-production.

DESTRUCTION (*Substantives*), waste, dissolution, breaking up, disruption, consumption, disorganization, falling to pieces, crumbling, etc.

Fall, downfall, ruin, perdition, crash, smash, havoc, desolation, *bouleversement, débacle*, upset, wreck, shipwreck, cataclysm, extinction, annihilation; doom, destruction of life (360), prang (716, 732),

Demolition, demolishment, overthrow, subversion, suppression, dismantling, cutting up, corrosion,

Theory of development, Mendelism, eugenics.

(*Verbs*) To produce, effect, perform, operate, do, make, form, construct, fabricate, frame, contrive, manufacture, weave, forge, coin, carve, sculp, chisel, build, raise, edify, rear, erect, run up, establish.

To constitute, compose, organize, institute, work out, realize, bring to bear, bring to pass, accomplish, bring off.

To create, generate, engender, beget, bring into being, breed, propagate, proliferate, conceive, bear, procreate, give birth to, bring forth, yield, flower, fructify, hatch, develop, bring up.

To induce, superinduce, suscitate (153).

(*Phrases*) To be brought to bed of; to usher into the world.

(*Adjectives*) Produced, etc., producing, productive of, etc., creative, formative, parturient, pregnant, *enceinte*, genetic; eugenic.

(*Phrase*) In the family way.

163 REPRODUCTION (*Substantives*), renovation, restoration (660), reconstruction, revival, regeneration, revivication, resuscitation, reanimation, resurrection, resurgence, reappearance, palingenesis, reincarnation, multiplication; phoenix.

(*Verbs*) To reproduce, revive, renew, renovate, rebuild, reconstruct, regenerate, revivify, resurrect, resuscitate, reanimate, reincarnate, quicken; come again into life, reappear.

(*Phrase*) To spring up like a mushroom.

(*Adjectives*) Reproduced, etc., renascent, reappearing; hydra-headed.

erosion, crushing, upsetting, abolition, abolishment, sacrifice, immolation, holocaust, dilapidation, devastation, *razzia*, ravaging, extermination, eradication, extirpation, rooting out, averruncation, sweeping, etc., death-blow, *coup de grâce*, the crack of doom.

(*Verbs*) To be destroyed, etc., to perish, waste, fall to pieces, break up, crumble, break down, crack.

To destroy, do or make away with, demolish, overturn, upset, throw down, overthrow, overwhelm, subvert, put an end to, uproot, eradicate, extirpate, root out, grub up, break up, pull down, do for, dish, ditch, crumble, smash, crash, crush, quell, quash, squash, squelch, cut up, shatter, shiver, batter, tear or shake to pieces, tear to tatters, pick to pieces, put down, suppress, strike out, throw or knock down, cut down, knock on the head, stifle, dispel, fell, sink, swamp, scuttle, engulf, submerge, wreck, corrode, erode, consume, sacrifice, immolate, burke, blow down, sweep away, erase, expunge, liquidate, wipe out, mow down, blast.

To waste, lay waste, ravage, dilapidate, dismantle, disorganize, devour, swallow up, desolate, devastate, sap, mine, blow up, stifle, dispatch, exterminate, extinguish, quench, annihilate, kill (361), unroot, root out, rout out, averruncate, deracinate.

(*Phrases*) To go to the dogs, or to pot; to go to the devil, or to rack and ruin; to be all over with one.

To lay the axe to the root of; to make short work of; make a clean sweep of; to make mincemeat of; to scatter to the winds; cut up root and branch; knock on the head; to wipe the floor with; to knock into a cocked hat; to sap the foundations of; to nip in the bud; to strike at the root of; to pluck up by the root; to ravage with fire and sword.

(*Adjectives*) Destroyed, done for, dished, etc.; destructive, subversive, pernicious, ruinous, deadly, incendiary, demolitionary.

164 PRODUCER (*Substantives*), originator, author, artist, creator, prime mover, founder, workman, doer, performer, manufacturer, forger, agent (690), builder, architect, factor.

166 PATERNITY (*Substantives*), fatherhood, maternity, motherhood, parentage, parent, father, sire, paterfamilias, pater, dad, daddy, papa, pa; mother, mamma, ma, mummy, mum, dam, materfamilias, mater, procreator, pregenitor, begetter, ancestor, ancestry, forefathers, forbears, grandsire; house, parent stem, trunk, stock, pedigree.

(*Adjectives*) Paternal, maternal, parental, fatherly, motherly, family, ancestral, patriarchal.

---

168 PRODUCTIVENESS (*Substantives*), fecundity, fruitfulness, fertility, prolificness; creativeness, inventiveness.

Pregnancy, gestation, pullulation, fructification, multiplication, propagation, procreation.

A milch cow, rabbit, warren, hydra.

(*Phrase*) A land flowing with milk and honey.

(*Verbs*) To procreate (161), multiply, teem, pullulate, fructify, proliferate, generate, fertilize, impregnate, conceive.

(*Adjectives*) Productive, prolific, teeming, fertile, fruitful, luxuriant, fecund, pregnant, great, gravid, *enceinte*, with child, with young.

Procreant, procreative, generative, propagable, life-giving.

165 DESTROYER (*Substantives*), extinguisher, exterminator, assassin (361), executioner (975), ravager, annihilator, subverter, demolisher; iconoclast, vandal.

167 POSTERITY (*Substantives*), progeny, breed, issue, offspring, brood, seed, litter, spawn, scion, offset, child, son, daughter, grandchild, grandson, granddaughter, etc., bantling, shoot, sprout, sprig, slip, branch, line, lineage, filiation, family, offshoot, ramification, descendant, heir, heiress, heir apparent, heir presumptive.

Straight descent, sonship, primogeniture, ultimogeniture.

(*Adjectives*) Filial, daughterly, dutiful, lineal, hereditary.

(*Phrase*) A chip of the old block; the rising generation.

169 UNPRODUCTIVENESS (*Substantives*), infertility, barrenness, sterility, unfruitfulness, unprofitableness, infecundity, fruitlessness (645), nonagency.

(*Verbs*) To be unproductive, etc., to come to nothing.

To render unproductive, sterilize, castrate, spay, pasteurize.

(*Adjectives*) Unproductive, inoperative, barren, addle, infertile, unprolific, sterile, unfruitful, fallow, fruitless, infecund, issueless, unprofitable (645).

---

170 AGENCY (*Substantives*), operation, force, working, strain, function, office, hand, intervention, intercession, interposition, exercise, work, swing, play, causation (153), impelling force, mediation (631), action (680).

Modus operandi, quickening power, maintaining power.

(*Verbs*) To be in action, to operate, function, work, act, perform, play, support, sustain, strain, maintain, take effect, quicken, strike, strike hard, strike home, bring to bear.

(*Phrases*) To come into play; to make an impression.

(*Adjectives*) Acting, operating, etc., operative, practical, efficient, efficacious, effectual, in force.

Acted upon, wrought upon.

171 Physical ENERGY (*Substantives*), force, power, activity, keenness, intensity, sharpness, pungency, vigour, strength, edge, point, raciness, metal, mettle, vim, dash, fire, punch, go, pep.

Seasoning, mordant, pepper, mustard, cayenne, caviare (392).

Mental energy (604), mental excitation (824), voluntary energy (682).

Exertion, activity, stir, bustle, hustle, agitation, effervescence, fermentation, ferment, ebullition, splutter, perturbation, briskness, voluntary activity (682), quicksilver.

(*Verbs*) To give energy, energize, stimulate, invigorate, kindle, galvanize, electrify, intensify, excite, exert (173).

(*Adjectives*) Strong, energetic, emphatic, forcible, forceful, active, keen, vivid, intense, severe, sharp, acute, pungent, poignant, racy, brisk, ebullient, mettlesome, enterprising, go-ahead, double-edged, double-barrelled, double-distilled, drastic, intensive, trenchant.

(*Phrases*) *Fortiter in re*; with telling effect; with full steam; at high pressure; flat out.

172 Physical INERTNESS (*Substantives*) inertia, *vis inertiae*, inertion, passiveness, passivity, inactivity, torpor, latency, torpidity, dullness, stagnation, deadness, heaviness, flatness, slackness, tameness, slowness, languor, lentor, quiescence (265), sleep (683), intermission (141).

Mental inertness, indecision (605), placidity (826).

(*Verbs*) To be alert, inactive, passive, etc.; to hang fire, smoulder.

(*Phrase*) To sit on the fence.

(*Adjectives*) Inert, inactive, passive, torpid, flaccid, limp, lymphatic, sluggish, dull, heavy, flat, slack, tame, slow, supine, slothful, stagnant, blunt, lifeless, dead.

Latent, dormant, smouldering, unexerted, unstrained, uninfluential.

(*Adverbs*) Inactively, in suspense, in abeyance.

---

173 VIOLENCE (*Substantives*), inclemency, vehemence, might, impetuosity, boisterousness, abruptness, ebullition, turbulence, horseplay, bluster, uproar, shindy, row, riot, rumpus, fierceness, rage, wildness, fury, heat, exacerbation, exasperation, malignity, fit, paroxysm, orgasm, force, brute force, *coup de main*, strain, shock, spasm, convulsion, throe.

Outbreak, burst, outburst, dissilience, discharge, volley, explosion, blow-up, blast, detonation, rush, eruption, displosion, torrent.

Turmoil, tumult, storm, tempest, squall, hurricane, tornado, typhoon, cyclone, earthquake, volcano, thunder-storm.

A rowdy (949), berserk (or berserker), spitfire, fireater, hellhound, fury, termagant, virago, vixen, hellcat, dragon, demon, tiger, beldam, Tisiphone, Megaera, Alecto, Maenad.

174 MODERATION (*Substantives*), gentleness, temperateness, calmness, mildness, composure, sobriety, slowness, tameness, quiet (740), restfulness, reason.

Relaxation, remission, measure, golden mean, mitigation, tranquillization, assuagement, soothing, allaying, etc., contemperation, pacification (723), restraint, check (751), lullaby, sedative, lenitive, demulcent, palliative, opiate, anodyne, balm, opium.

Mental calmness (826).

(*Verbs*) To be moderate, etc., to keep within bounds or within compass, to settle down, to keep the peace, to sober down, remit, relent.

To moderate, soften, soothe, mitigate, appease, temper, attemper, contemper, mollify, lenify, tame, dull, take off that edge, blunt, obtund, tone down, subdue.

To tranquillize, assuage, appease, lull, cool, compose, still, calm, quiet,

(*Verbs*) To be violent, etc., to run high, ferment, effervesce, run wild, run riot, run amuck, rush, tear, rush headlong, bluster, rage, rampage, riot, storm, boil, fume, let off steam, foam, wreak, bear down.

To break out, fly out, bounce, go off, explode, displode, fly, fulminate, detonate, blow up, flash, flare, burst, burst out, shock, strain.

To render violent, sharpen, stir up, quicken, excite, incite, stimulate, kindle, lash, suscitate, urge, accelerate, foment, aggravate, exasperate, exacerbate, convulse, infuriate, madden, lash into fury, inflame, let off, discharge.

(*Phrases*) To break the peace; to see red; to out-herod Herod; add fuel to the flame.

(*Adjectives*) Violent, vehement, warm, acute, rough, rude, wild, boisterous, impetuous, ungentle, tough, brusque, abrupt, rampant, knock-about, rampageous, bluff, turbulent, blustering, riotous, rowdy, noisy, thundering, obstreperous, uproarious, outrageous, frantic, phrenetic, headstrong, rumbustious, disorderly (59).

hush, quell, sober, pacify, damp, lay, allay, rebate, slacken, smooth, soften, alleviate, rock to sleep, deaden (376), check, restrain, slake, curb, bridle, rein in, hold in, repress, smother, counteract (179).

(*Phrases*) To pour oil on the waves; to pour balm into; to throw cold water on.

(*Adjectives*) Moderate, gentle, mild, sober, temperate, measured, reasonable, tempered, calm, unruffled, tranquil, smooth, untroubled; unexciting, unirritating, soft, bland, oily, demulcent, lenitive, cool, quiet, anodyne, hypnotic, sedative, peaceful, peaceable, pacific, lenient, tame, halcyon, restful.

(*Phrases*) Gentle as a lamb; mild as milk.

(*Adverbs*) Moderately, gently, temperately, softly, etc.

(*Phrases*) Softly, softly, catchee monkey; *suaviter in modo*; *est modus in rebus.*

Savage, fierce, ferocious, fiery, fuming, excited, unquelled, unquenched, unextinguished, unrepressed, unbridled, unruly, boiling, boiling over, furious, outrageous, raging, running riot, storming, hysteric, hysterical, wild, running wild, ungovernable, unappeasable, immitigable, uncontrollable, insuppressible, irrepressible, raging, desperate, mad, rabid, infuriate, exasperated.

Tempestuous, stormy, squally, spasmodic, spastic, paroxysmal, convulsive, galvanic, bursting, explosive, detonating, volcanic, meteoric, seismic.

(*Phrases*) Fierce as a tiger; all the fat in the fire.

(*Adverbs*) Violently, etc., by force, by main force, like mad.

(*Phrases*) By might and main; tooth and nail; *vi et armis*; at the point of the sword, or bayonet.

4°. Indirect Power

175 INFLUENCE (*Substantives*), weight, pressure, prevalence, sway, ascendancy (or ascendency), preponderance, predominance, predominancy, dominance, prepotency, importance (642), reign, ableness, capability (157).

Footing, hold, foothold, purchase,

175A Absence of INFLUENCE, impotence (158), weakness (160), inertness (172).

(*Verb*) To have no influence.

(*Phrase*) To cut no ice.

(*Adjective*) Uninfluential.

fulcrum, stance, *point d'appui*, *pou sto, locus standi*, leverage, vantage-ground; aegis, protection, patronage, auspices.

(*Phrases*) A tower of strength; a host in himself.

(*Verbs*) To have influence, etc., to have a hold upon, to have a pull, to gain a footing, work upon, take root, take hold, permeate, penetrate, infiltrate, prevail, dominate, predominate, outweigh, overweigh, carry weight, weigh, tell, to bear upon.

(*Phrases*) To be in the ascendant; to cut some ice; to pull wires; to pull the strings; to set the fashion; to have a voice.

(*Adjectives*) Influential, valid, weighty, prevailing, prevalent, dominant, regnant, predominating, predominant, prepotent, ascendant, rife.

(*Adverb*) With telling effect.

176 TENDENCY (*Substantives*), aptness, proneness, proclivity, conduciveness, bent, bias, quality, inclination, trend, propensity, predisposition, leaning, drift, conducement, temperament, idiosyncrasy, vein, humour, mood.

(*Verbs*) To tend, contribute, conduce, lead, dispose, incline, trend, verge, bend to, affect, carry, promote, redound to, subserve to (644), bid fair to, make for, gravitate towards.

(*Adjectives*) Tending, contributing, conducing, conducive, working towards, calculated to, disposing, inclining, bending, leading, carrying to, subservient, subsidiary (644, 707); apt, liable, prone, disposed, predisposed.

(*Adverbs*) For, whither, in a fair way to.

177 LIABILITY (*Substantives*), subjection to, dependence on, exposure to, contingency, possibility (156), susceptivity, susceptibility.

(*Verbs*) To be liable, etc., incur, to lay oneself open to, lie under, expose oneself to, stand a chance, to open a door to.

(*Phrase*) To stick one's neck out.

(*Adjectives*) Liable, apt, prone, subject, open to, incident to, exposed to, dependent on; answerable, accountable, responsible.

Contingent, incidental, possible, casual.

(*Phrases*) Within range of; at the mercy of.

5°. *Combinations of Causes*

178 CONCURRENCE (*Substantives*), co-operation, collaboration (709), union, agreement, consent (488), pulling together, alliance; complicity, connivance, collusion.

Voluntary concurrence (709).

(*Verbs*) To concur, co-operate, conspire, agree, conduce, contribute, unite, to pull together, hang together, join forces.

(*Phrases*) To have a hand in; to be in the same boat; to go hand in hand (709).

(*Adjectives*) Concurring, concurrent, conjoined, concomitant, associate, co-operating, conspiring, agreeing, correspondent, conformable, pulling

179 COUNTERACTION (*Substantives*), opposition, antagonism, polarity, clashing, etc., collision, contrariety (14), resistance, interference, friction.

Neutralization, nullification, compensation (30).

Reaction, retroaction (277), repercussion, rebound, recoil, ricochet, counterblast.

Check, obstacle, hindrance (706); antidote, counter-irritant, preventive, corrective, remedy (662).

Voluntary counteraction (708).

(*Verbs*) To counteract, oppose, cross, contravene, antagonize, interfere or conflict with, collide with,

together, etc., of one mind, in alliance with, with one consent, of one mind, with one accord.

———

clash, neutralize, undo, nullify, render null; to militate against, withstand, resist (719), hinder (706), repress, control, curb, check, rein in (174).

To react (277), countervail, counterpoise (30), overpoise.

(*Adjectives*) Counteracting, opposing, etc., counteractive, antagonistic, conflicting, reactionary, recalcitrant, opposite, retroactive, cohibitive, counter, contrary (14).

(*Adverbs*) Counter, notwithstanding, nevertheless, nathless, none the less, yet, still, although, though, albeit, howbeit, maugre, at all events.

But, even, however, in defiance of, in the teeth of, in the face of, in spite of, in despite of (708).

(*Phrases*) For all that; all the same; be that as it may; even so.

CLASS II

WORDS RELATING TO SPACE

1°. *Abstract Space*

180 Indefinite space.

SPACE (*Substantives*), extension, extent, expanse, room, scope, range, purview, way, expansion, compass, sweep, play, amplitude, latitude, field, swing, spread, stretch; spare room, headway, elbow-room, freedom, house-room, stowage, roomage, margin.

Open space, void space, vacuity (4), opening, waste, wilderness, moor, moorland, campagna, tundra.

Abyss (198); unlimited space, infinity (105).

(*Adjectives*) Spatial, two-dimensional, three-dimensional.

Spacious, roomy, commodious, extensive, expansive, capacious, ample.

Boundless, unlimited, unbounded, limitless, illimitable, infinite, uncircumscribed, shoreless, trackless, pathless.

(*Adverbs*) Extensively, etc., wherever, everywhere.

(*Phrases*) The length and the breadth of the land; far and near, far and wide; all over; all the world over; from. China to Peru; from Land's End to John o' Groat's; in every quarter; in all quarters; in all lands; every hole and corner; here, there, and everywhere; from pole to pole; throughout the world; to the four winds; under the sun.

181 Definite space.

REGION (*Substantives*), sphere, ground, area, realm, quarter, district, orb, circuit, circle, compartment, domain, tract, department, territory, country, canton, county, shire, township, riding, hundred, parish, bailiwick, province, satrapy, *arrondissement*, commune, enclave, principality, duchy, kingdom, empire, dominion, colony, protectorate, mandate.

Arena, precincts, *enceinte*, walk, patch, plot, paddock, enclosure, enclosure, field, compound.

Clime, climate, zone, meridian.

(*Adjectives*) Regional, territorial, provincial, parochial, local, etc.

Limited space, locality.

182 PLACE (*Substantives*), spot, point, nook, corner, recess, hole, niche, compartment, premises, precinct, station, pitch, venue, abode (189).

Indefinite place.

(*Adverbs*) Somewhere, in some place, wherever it may be.

2°. *Relative Space*

183 SITUATION (*Substantives*), position, locality, locale, status, latitude and longitude, footing, standing, post, stage, bearings, aspect, orientation, attitude, posture, lie, emplacement.

Place, site, station, pitch, seat, venue, whereabouts, direction, azimuth, etc. (278).

Topography, geography, chorography.

A map, chart, plan (554).

(*Verbs*) To be situated, to lie, to have its seat in.

(*Adjectives*) Local, topical; situate.

(*Adverbs*) *In situ*, here and there, *passim*, whereabouts.

184 LOCATION (*Substantives*), localization, lodgment, deposition, reposition, stowage, establishment, settlement, fixation, grafting, insertion (300), lading, encampment, billet, installation.

A colony, settlement, cantonment.

A habitation, residence, dwelling (189).

(*Phrases*) *Genius loci*; the spirit of the place.

(*Verbs*) To place, situate, locate, localize, put, lay, set, seat, station, lodge, park, post, install, house, settle, stow, dump, establish, fix, root, plant, graft, stick in, tuck in, insert, wedge in, shelve, pitch, camp, posit, deposit, reposit, cradle, encamp, moor, pack, embed (or imbed), vest, stock, populate, people, colonize, domicile.

To billet on, quarter upon.

To pocket, pouch, put up, bag, load.

To inhabit, reside (186), domesticate, put up at, colonize.

(*Phrase*) To pitch one's tent.

185 DISPLACEMENT (*Substantives*), dislodgment, eviction, ejectment (297), deportation, extradition, expatriation, banishment, exile.

Removal, remotion, transposition, relegation (270).

(*Verbs*) To displace, dislodge, unhouse, unkennel, break bulk, take off, eject, evict, chuck out, hoof out, expel, etc. (297), extradite, expatriate, banish, exile, relegate, oust, rusticate, ostracize, remove, transfer, transpose, transplant, transport (270), empty, clear, clear out, sweep off, sweep away, do away with, get rid of, root out, disestablish, unpeople, depopulate.

To vacate, leave (293), get out, heave out, bale out, lade out, pour out (297).

(*Phrase*) To make a clean sweep of.

(*Adjectives*) Displaced, etc., unhoused, houseless, homeless, stateless.

(*Phrase*) Like a fish out of water.

(*Adjectives*) Placed, located, etc., situate, situated, ensconced, nestled, embosomed, housed, moored, rooted, unremoved.

3°. *Existence in Space*

186 PRESENCE (*Substantives*), occupancy, occupation, attendance, whereness.

Diffusion, permeation, pervasion, interpenetration, dissemination (73).

Ubiquity, ubiety, ubiquitousness, omnipresence.

(*Verbs*) To exist in space, to be present, attend, remain.

To occur in a place, lie, stand, occupy, colonize.

To inhabit, dwell, reside, live, abide, sojourn, lodge, nestle, perch, roost, put up at, hang out at, stay at,

187 ABSENCE (*Substantives*), nonexistence (2), non-residence, nonattendance, alibi, absenteeism.

Emptiness, void, vacuum, voidness, vacuity, vacancy, vacuousness.

An absentee, truant, nobody, nobody on earth.

(*Verbs*) To be absent, not present, etc., vacate, to keep away, to keep out of the way.

(*Phrases*) Make oneself scarce; absent oneself; take oneself off; stay away; play truant; be conspicuous by one's absence.

stop at, squat, hive, burrow, camp, encamp, bivouac, anchor, settle, take up one's quarters, pitch one's tent, get a footing, frequent, haunt, tenant, take root, strike root, revisit.

To fill, pervade, permeate, penetrate, interpenetrate, infiltrate, be diffused through, be disseminated through, overspread, run through.

(*Adjectives*) Present, occupying, inhabiting, etc., moored, at anchor, resident, residentiary, domiciled.

Ubiquitous, omnipresent.

(*Adverbs*) Here, there, where? everywhere, in residence, aboard, on board, at home, afield, etc., on the spot.

(*Phrases*) Here, there, and everywhere; at every turn.

188 INHABITANT   (*Substantives*), resident, residentiary, dweller, indweller, occupier, occupant, lodger, boarder, paying guest, inmate, tenant, sojourner, settler, squatter, backwoodsman, national, colonist, denizen, citizen, cit, cockney, townsman, burgess, countryman, villager, cottar, compatriot, garrison, crew, population, people.

N a t i v e, indigene, a b o r i g i n e s, autochthones, son of the soil.

A colony, settlement, household.

Newcomer (57).

(*Adjectives*) Indigenous, native, aboriginal, autochthonous, domestic, domiciliated, domesticated, domiciliary.

(*Adjectives*) Absent, not present, away, gone, from home, missing, non-resident.

Empty, void, vacant, vacuous, blank, untenanted, tenantless, uninhabited, deserted, devoid, unoccupied, unpeopled.

(*Phrases*) Nowhere to be found; A.W.O.L. (absent without leave); *non est inventus*; not a soul; nobody present; the bird being flown.

(*Adverbs*) Without, minus, nowhere, elsewhere, sans.

(*Phrases*) One's back being turned; behind one's back.

189 Place of habitation.

ABODE (*Substantives*), dwelling, lodging, domicile, residence, address, habitation, berth, seat, lap, sojourn, housing, quarters, accommodation, headquarters, throne, ark, tabernacle.

Nest, nidus, lair, haunt, eyrie (or aerie), den, hole, earth, warren, rookery, hive, habitat, haunt, resort, retreat, nidification, perch, roost.

Bivouac, camp, encampment, cantonment, castrametation, tent, marquee, teepee, igloo.

Cave, cavern, cell, grove, grot, grotto, alcove, bower, arbour, cove, chamber (191).

Home, fatherland, motherland, native land, country, homestead, homestall, fireside, snuggery, hearth, Lares and Penates, household gods, roof, household, housing; 'dulce domum.'   Blighty.

Building, structure, edifice, fabric, erection, pile, tenement, messuage, farm, farmhouse, steading, grange.

Cot, cabin, hut, shack, chalet, croft, shed, hangar, penthouse, lean-to, booth, stall, hovel, outhouse, barn, kennel, sty, coop, hutch, cage, cote, stable, garage, offices.

House, mansion, villa, flat, flatlet, prefab, maisonnette, cottage, box, lodge, *pied-à-terre*, bungalow, hermitage, summer-house, gazebo, folly, rotunda, tower, temple (1000), château, castle, pavilion, court, hall, palace, kiosk, house-boat.

Inn, hostel, hotel, roadhouse, motel, tavern, caravansery, hospice, rest-house, dak-bungalow, barrack, lodging-house, guest-house, dosshouse, lodgings, apartments, diggings, digs.

Hamlet, village, clachan, thorp, dorp, kraal, borough, burgh, municipality, town, city, garden city, metropolis, suburb (227), conurbation, province, country.

Street, place, terrace, parade, road, avenue, row, lane, alley, court, wynd, close, yard, passage, rents, slum; square, polygon, quadrant, circus, crescent, mall, place, piazza, arcade, gardens.

Anchorage, roadstead, dock, basin, wharf, quay, port, harbour, haven.

(*Adjectives*) Urban, civic, metropolitan, municipal, provincial, rural, rustic, countrified; home-like, homy.

190 Things contained.
CONTENTS (*Substantives*), cargo, lading, filling, stuffing, freight, load, burden, ware (798).

191 RECEPTACLE (*Substantives*), recipient, receiver, reservatory, compartment (636).

Cell, cellule, loculus, follicle, hole, corner, niche, recess, nook, crypt, stall, pigeon-hole, lodging (189), bed, berth, bunk, doss, etc. (215), store-room, strong-room.

Capsule, vesicle, cyst, bladder, pod.

Stomach, belly, paunch, ventricle, crop, craw, maw, gizzard, bread-basket, kyte, ovary, womb (221).

Pocket, pouch, sporran, fob, sheath, scabbard, socket, bag, sac, sack, wallet, scrip, poke, kit, knapsack, rucksack, haversack, sabretache, satchel, cigar-case, cigarette-case, reticule, powder-box, flapjack, compact, vanity-case, vanity-bag, portfolio, budget.

Chest, box, hutch, coffer, case, casket, caddy, pyx (or pix), caisson, desk, davenport, escritoire, bureau, cabinet, reliquary; trunk, portmanteau, saratoga, grip-sack, grip, bandbox, valise, hold-all, attaché-case, dispatch-case, dispatch-box, writing-case, suit-case, dressing-case, kit-bag, brief-bag, brief-case, gladstone bag, boot, creel, crate, packing-case, snuff-box, mull.

Vessel, vase, bushel, barrel, canister, jar, can, pottle, basket, pannier, corbeille, punnet, hamper, tray, hod.

For liquids: cistern, reservoir, tank, vat, cauldron, barrel, cask, keg, runlet, firkin, kilderkin, demijohn, carboy, amphora, bottle, jar, decanter, carafe, tantalus, ewer, cruse, crock, kit, canteen, flagon, flask, flasket, thermos flask, vacuum flask, stoup, noggin, vial (or phial), cruet, caster, urn, samovar, billy.

Tub, bucket, pail, pot, tankard, beaker, jug, pitcher, mug, noggin, pipkin, gallipot, matrass, receiver, alembic, retort, test-tube, pipette, capsule, kettle, spittoon.

Bowl, basin, jorum, punch-bowl, cup, goblet, chalice, quaich, tumbler, glass, horn, can, pan, pannikin, plate, dish, trencher, tray, salver, patera, calabash, porringer, saucepan, skillet, casserole, tureen, saucer, platter, hod, scuttle, baikie, shovel, trowel, spoon, spatula, ladle.

Closet, cupboard, cellaret, chiffonier, wardrobe, bunker, locker, bin, buffet, press, safe, sideboard, whatnot, drawer, chest of drawers, tallboy, lowboy, till.

Chamber, flat, storey, apartment, room, cabin, bower, office, court, hall, saloon, *salon*, parlour, state-room, presence-chamber, reception-room, drawing-room, sitting-room, living-room, gallery, cabinet, nursery, boudoir, library, study, snuggery, adytum, sanctum, den, phrontistery, lumber-room (636), dormitory, bedroom, dressing-room, refectory, dining-room, breakfast-room, billiard-room, smoking-room, pew, harem, seraglio, zenana.

Attic, loft, garret, cockloft, belfry, cellar, vault, hold, cockpit, ground-floor, *rez-de-chaussée*, basement, kitchen, kitchenette, pantry, scullery, bath-room, lavatory, water-closet, w.c., urinal, latrine, rear, toilet, convenience, comfort station, heads, thunder-box, offices.

Portico, porch, veranda, piazza, stoop, lobby, court, hall, vestibule, foyer, lounge, corridor, loggia, passage, anteroom, antechamber.

(*Adjectives*) Capsular, saccular, sacculate, recipient, ventricular, cystic, vascular, celled, cellular, cellulous, cellulose, camerated, chambered, locular, multilocular, roomed, two-roomed, etc., polygastric, pouched, marsupial.

Section II—Dimensions

1°. *General Dimensions*

192 Size (*Substantives*), magnitude, dimension, bulk, volume, large-ness, bigness, greatness (31), expanse, amplitude, mass, massiveness.

Capacity, capaciousness, tonnage (or tunnage), calibre, scantling.

Average size, stock size.

Corpulence, adiposity, obesity, chubbiness, plumpness, *embonpoint*, stoutness, out-size; corporation, flesh and blood, brawn, brawniness.

Hugeness, vastness, enormousness, enormity, immensity, monstrousness, monstrosity; expansion (194), infinity (105).

A giant, Goliath, Brobdingnagian, Antaeus, Gargantua, monster, whale, leviathan, elephant, mammoth, colossus, tun, lump, chunk, bulk, block, boulder, mass, bushel, whacker, thumper, whopper, spanker, behemoth.

A mountain, mound, heap (72).

(*Phrases*) A Triton among the minnows; the lion's share.

(*Verbs*) To be large, etc., to become large (194).

(*Adjectives*) Large, big, great, considerable, bulky, voluminous, ample, massive, massy, capacious, comprehensive, mighty, king-sized.

Corpulent, obese, stout, fat, plump, rotund, buxom, sonsy, lusty, strapping, bouncing, portly, burly, brawny, fleshy, beefy, goodly, in good case, chopping, jolly, chubby, full-grown, chub-faced, lubberly, hulking, unwieldy, lumpish, husky, stalwart.

193 Littleness (*Substantives*), smallness (32), minuteness, diminutiveness, exiguity, inextension, puniness, dwarfishness, epitome, duodecimo, rudiment, microcosm.

Leanness, emaciation, thinness, macilency, flaccidity, meagreness.

A dwarf, runt, pygmy, midget, Lilliputian, chit, bantam, urchin, elf, doll, puppet, skeleton, ghost, spindle-shanks, shadow, Tom Thumb, manikin, *homunculus*.

Animalcule, mite, insect, emmet, fly, gnat, midge, shrimp, minnow, worm, grub, tit, tomtit, mouse, small fry, smout, mushroom, pollard, millet-seed, mustard-seed, grain of sand, molehill.

Atom, point, speck, dot, mote, ace, jot, iota, tittle, whit, particle, corpuscle, electron, molecule, monad, granule, grain, crumb, globule, nutshell, minim, drop, droplet, mouthful, thimbleful, sprinkling, dash, suspicion, *soupçon*, minimum, powder (330), driblet, patch, scrap, chip, inch, mathematical point; minutiae.

(*Phrases*) The shadow of a shade; a drop in the ocean; chicken feed; tip of the ice-berg.

(*Verbs*) To be small, etc., to become small, contract (195).

(*Adjectives*) Little, small, minute, diminutive, inconsiderable, exiguous, puny, tiny, wee, weeny, teeny-weeny, petty, mini, minikin, hop-o'-my-thumb, miniature, bijou, *petite*, pygmy, undersized, half-pint, dwarf,

Squab, dumpy (202), tubby, roly-poly, pursy, blowsy.

Huge, immense, enormous, mighty, unbounded, vast, vasty, amplitudinous, stupendous, inordinate, herculean, thumping, whacking, whopping, spanking, thundering, monstrous, monster; gigantic, giant-like, colossal, titanic, mountainous, elephantine, mammoth, cyclopean, Antaean, Gargantuan, Falstaffian, Brobdingnagian, infinite, unbounded.

(*Phrases*) Large as life; plump as a partridge; fat as a pig; fat as butter; fat as bacon.

---

194 EXPANSION (*Substantives*), enlargement, extension, augmentation, increase of size, amplification, ampliation, aggrandisement, spread, increment, growth, development, pullulation, swell, dilatation, rarefaction, turgescence, turgidity, thickening, tumefaction, intumescence, swelling, tumour, diastole, distension, puffing, inflation.

Overgrowth, hypertrophy, over-distension, tympany.

Bulb, knot, knob (249).

Superiority of size.

(*Verbs*) To become larger, to expand, widen, enlarge, extend, grow, increase, swell (202), gather, fill out, deploy, dilate, stretch, largen, spread, mantle, bud, burgeon, shoot, spring up, sprout, germinate, vegetate, pullulate, open, burst forth, put on flesh, outgrow.

To render larger, to expand, aggrandize, etc., distend, develop, open out, broaden, thicken, largen, amplify, tumefy, magnify, rarefy, inflate, puff, blow up, stuff, cram, pad, fill out.

To be larger than, to surpass, exceed, be beyond, cap, overtop (206, 33).

(*Adjectives*) Expanded, enlarged, increased, etc., swelled out, swollen, distended, bulbous; exaggerated,

stunted, dwarfed, dwarfish, pollard, Lilliputian; pocket, thumb-nail, portative, portable, duodecimo.

Microscopic, infra-microscopic, evanescent, impalpable, imperceptible, invisible, inappreciable, infinitesimal, homoeopathic, atomic, corpuscular, molecular, rudimentary, rudimental.

Lean, thin, gaunt, meagre, emaciated, lank, macilent, ghostly, starved, starveling, fallen away, scrubby, reduced, shrunk, shrunken, attenuated, extenuated, shrivelled, tabid, flaccid, starved, skinny, wizen, wizened, scraggy, lanky, raw-boned, scrawny, spindle-shanked, lantern-jawed (203).

(*Phrases*) In a small compass; in a nutshell; on a small scale.

Worn to a shadow; skin and bone.

---

195 CONTRACTION (*Substantives*), reduction, diminution, decrease of size, defalcation, lessening, decrement, shrinking, shrivelling, systole, collapse, emaciation, attenuation, tabefaction, tabes, consumption, marasmus, atrophy; hour-glass, neck (203).

Condensation, compression, squeezing.

Inferiority of size.

Corrugation, contractility, astringency.

(*Verbs*) To become smaller, to lessen, diminish, decrease, dwindle, shrink, contract, shrivel, collapse, wither, wilt, lose flesh, wizen, fall away, decay, purse up, waste, wane, ebb, to grow less.

To render smaller, to contract, lessen, etc., draw in, to condense, reduce, clip, compress, constrict, cramp, squeeze, attenuate, chip, dwarf, bedwarf, stunt, cut short (201), corrugate, crumple, crush, purse up, pinch (203), deflate.

To be smaller than, to fall short of, not to come up to.

(*Phrases*) To grow 'small by degrees, and beautifully less' (659); to be on the wane; to hide its diminished head.

(*Adjectives*) Contracting, etc., astringent, styptic, tabid, contracted, lessened, etc., shrivelled, wasted,

bloated, tumid, turgid, puffy, full-blown, full-grown, full-formed, over-grown, hypertrophied, pot-bellied, swag-bellied, dropsical, oedematous.

(*Phrase*) 'A-swellin' wisibly.'

196 DISTANCE (*Substantives*), remoteness, farness, longinquity, elongation, offing, removedness, parallax, reach, span.

Antipodes, outpost, outskirts, aphelion, apogee, horizon.

Separation (44), transference (270).

Diffusion, dispersion (73).

(*Phrases*) *Ultima Thule*; *ne plus ultra*; the uttermost parts of the earth; the back of beyond.

(*Verbs*) To be distant, etc.; to extend to, stretch to, reach to, spread to, go to, get to, stretch away to; outgo, outstep (303); to go great lengths.

To remain at a distance, keep away, stand off, keep off, keep clear, stand aloof, hold off.

(*Adjectives*) Distant, far, far off, remote, removed, distal, wide of, clear of, yon, yonder, at arm's length, apart, aloof, asunder, ulterior, trans-alpine, transatlantic, ultramundane, hyperborean, antipodean, hull down. Inaccessible, un-get-at-able, out of the way, unapproachable, unreachable; incontiguous.

(*Adverbs*) Far, away, far away, afar, off, a long way off, afar off, wide away, aloof, wide of, clear of, out of the way, a great way off, out of reach, abroad.

Apart, asunder, few and far between.

Yonder, farther, beyond, *longo intervallo*, wide apart, poles apart.

(*Phrases*) Far and near; far and wide; over the hills and far away; a far cry to; from end to end; from pole to pole; from Indus to the Pole; from China to Peru; from Dan to Beersheba; to the ends of the earth; out of the sphere of; wide of the mark.

wizened, stunted, waning, ebbing, etc., neap, condensed.

Unexpanded, contractile, compressible.

(*Phrase*) *Multum in parvo.*

197 NEARNESS (*Substantives*), nighness, proximity, propinquity, vicinity, vicinage, neighbourhood, adjacency, closeness; perihelion, perigee.

A short distance, a step, an ear-shot, close quarters, a stone's throw, a hair's breadth, a span, bowshot, gunshot, pistol-shot.

Purlieus, neighbourhood, environs (227), vicinity, *alentours*, suburbs, whereabouts, *banlieue*, borderland.

A bystander, neighbour.

Approach, approximation, appropinquation, appulse (286), junction (43), concentration, convergence (290).

Meeting, *rencontre* (292).

(*Verbs*) To be near, etc., to adjoin, hang about, trench on, border upon, stand by, approximate, tread on the heels of, cling to, clasp, hug, crowd, get near, etc., to approach (287), to meet (290).

To bring near, to crowd, pack, huddle together.

(*Adjectives*) Near, nigh, close, close at hand, neighbouring, proximate, approximate, adjacent, adjoining, intimate, bordering upon, close upon, hard upon, trenching on, treading on the heels of, verging on, at hand, handy, near the mark, home, at the point of, near run, in touch with, nearish.

(*Adverbs*) Near, nigh, hard by, fast by, close to, next door to, within reach, within call, within hearing, within an ace of, close upon, at hand, on the verge of, near the mark, in the environs, round the corner, at one's door, at one's feet, at one's elbow, at close quarters; within range, pistol-shot, a stone's throw, etc.; cheek by jowl, beside, alongside, at the heels of, at the threshold.

About, hereabouts, thereabouts, in the way, in presence of, in round numbers, approximately, roughly, as good as, *à peu près* (32).

198 INTERVAL (*Substantives*), interspace (70), break, gap, opening (260), chasm, hiatus, caesura, interstice, lacuna, cleft, fosse, mesh, crevice, chink, creek, cranny, crack, slit, fissure, scissure, chap, rift, flaw, gash, cut, leak, dike (350), ha-ha, fracture, breach, rent, oscitation, gaping, yawning, pandiculation, insertion (300), pass, gorge, defile, ravine, canyon (or cañon), crevasse, chimney, couloir, *bergschrund*, gulf, gully, gulch, nullah, strait, sound, kyle, frith, furrow (*see* 259).

Thing interposed, go-between, interjacence (228).

(*Verbs*) To separate (44), gape, yawn.

---

199 CONTIGUITY (*Substantives*), contact, proximity, apposition, juxtaposition, touching, tangency, tangent, osculation, meeting (292), syzygy, coincidence, register, co-existence, adhesion (46).

Confine, frontier, demarcation, border (233).

(*Verbs*) To be contiguous, etc., to touch, meet, adhere (46), osculate, coincide, register, coevist, join, adjoin, abut on, graze, border, march with.

(*Adjectives*) Contiguous, touching, bordering on, meeting, in contact, conterminous, osculating, osculatory, tangential, proximate.

(*Phrases*) Hand to hand; end to end; tête-à-tête; next door to; with no interval; in juxtaposition, apposition, etc.; in register.

2°. *Linear Dimensions*

200 LENGTH (*Substantives*), longitude, span, stretch.

A line, bar, rule, stripe, spoke, radius.

Lengthening, elongation, prolongation, production, producing, protraction, extension, tension, stretching.

(*Verbs*) To be long, etc., to extend to, reach, stretch to.

To render long, lengthen, extend, elongate, prolong, produce, stretch, draw out, protract, spin out, drawl.

(*Phrase*) To drag its slow length along.

(*Adjectives*) Long, longsome, lengthy, tedious, tiresome, wiredrawn, outstretched, lengthened, produced, etc., sesquipedalian, interminable, endless, unending, never-ending, there being no end of.

Linear, lineal, longitudinal, oblong.

(*Phrases*) As long as my arm; as long as to-day and to-morrow.

(*Adverbs*) Lengthwise, longitudinally, in a line, along, from end to end, endways, from stem to stern, fore and aft, from head to foot, from top to toe, cap-à-pie.

201 SHORTNESS (*Substantives*), brevity, briefness, a span, etc., *see* Smallness (193).

Shortening, abbreviation, abbreviature, abridgment, curtailment, reduction, contraction, compression (195), retrenchment, elision, ellipsis, compendium (596), conciseness (in style) (572).

(*Verbs*) To be short, brief, etc.

To render short, to shorten, curtail, abridge, abbreviate, epitomize, reduce, contract, compress, scrimp, skimp, boil down.

To retrench, cut short, cut down, pare down, whittle down, clip, dock, lop, poll, prune, pollard, crop, bob, shingle, bingle, snub, truncate, cut, hack, hew, foreshorten.

(*Adjectives*) Short, brief, curt, laconic, compendious, compact, stubby, squab, squabby, squat, chunky, stubby, stocky, dumpy, podgy, fubsy, skimpy, stumpy, pug, snub.

Oblate, elliptical.

Concise (572), summary.

202 BREADTH (*Substantives*), width, latitude, amplitude, diameter, bore, calibre, superficial extent, expanse.

THICKNESS, crassitude (192), thickening, expansion, dilatation, etc. (194).

(*Verbs*) To be broad, thick, etc.

To broaden, to swell, dilate, expand, outspread, etc. (194); to thicken, incrassate.

(*Adjectives*) Broad, wide, ample, extended, fan-like, outstretched, etc.

Thick, corpulent, fat (192), squab, squabby, squat, chunky, stubby, stocky, dumpy, podgy, fulsy, thickset.

(*Phrases*) Wide as a church door; thick as a rope.

———

203 NARROWNESS (*Substantives*), slenderness, closeness, scantiness, exility, lankness, lankiness, fibrousness.

A line (205), a hair's breadth, a finger's breadth, strip, streak, vein.

THINNESS, tenuity, leanness, meagreness.

A shaving, a slip (205), a mere skeleton, a shadow, an anatomy.

A middle constriction, stricture, neck, waist, isthmus, wasp, hourglass, bottle-neck, ridge, ravine, defile, gorge, pass (198).

Narrowing, coarctation, tapering, compression, squeezing, etc. (195).

(*Phrases*) A bag of bones; a living skeleton.

(*Verbs*) To be narrow, etc., to taper, contract, shrink.

To render narrow, etc., to narrow, contract, coarctate, attenuate, constrict, constringe, cramp, pinch, squeeze, compress, tweak, corrugate, warp.

To shave, pare, shear, etc.

(*Adjectives*) Narrow, strait, slender, thin, fine, tenuous, filiform, filamentary, filamentous, fibrous, funicular, capillary, stringy, wiredrawn, fine-spun, anguine, taper, dapper, slim, slight, gracile, scanty, scant, spare, delicate.

Meagre, lean, emaciated, lank, lanky, weedy, rangy, gangling, starveling, attenuated, pinched, skinny, scraggy, gaunt, cadaverous, skin and bone, raw-boned, scrawny, spindle-shanked (193), hatchet-faced, wasp-waisted, herring-gutted, spidery, spindly, reedy.

(*Phrases*) Thin as a lath; thin as a whipping-post; lean as a rake; thin as a thread-paper; thin as a wafer; thin as a shadow.

204 LAYER (*Substantives*), stratum, bed, zone, substratum, slab, escarpment, floor, flag, stage, course, storey, tier.

Plate, lamina, lamella, sheet, flake, scale, coat, pellicle, membrane, film, slice, shive, cut, shaving, rasher, board, plank, platter, trencher, spatula, leaf.

Stratification, scaliness, a nest of boxes, coats of an onion.

(*Verbs*) To slice, shave, etc.

(*Adjectives*) Lamellar, laminated, lamelliform, laminiferous, scaly, squamous, filmy, membranous, flaky, foliated, foliaceous, stratified, stratiform, tabular, nested.

205 FILAMENT (*Substantives*), line, fibre, fibril, tendril, hair, gossamer, wire, thread, cord, funicle, rope, yarn, string, twine (45), cilium, gimp.

Strip (51), shred, slip, spill, list, string, band, fillet, fascia, ribbon (or riband); roll, lath, slat, splinter, sliver, shiver, shaving; arborescence (256); strand.

A hair-stroke.

(*Adjectives*) Filamentary, fibrous, hairy, capillary, thread-like, wiry, funicular, stringy.

———

206 HEIGHT (*Substantives*), altitude, elevation, eminence, pitch, loftiness, sublimity.

Stature, tallness, procerity, culmination (210).

A giant, grenadier, guardsman, colossus, giraffe.

Alp, mountain, mount, hill, butte, ben, brae, hillock, kopje, monticule, fell, moorland, hummock, knap, knoll, cape, headland, foreland, promontory, ridge, *arête*, peak, pike, uplands, highlands, rising ground, downs, dune, mound, mole, steep, bluff, cliff, crag, vantage-ground, tor, eagle's nest, aerie.

Orography, Orology.

Tower, pillar, column, obelisk, monument, steeple, spire, *flèche*, campanile, belfry, minaret, turret, cupola, pilaster, skyscraper.

Pole, pikestaff, maypole, flagstaff, topmast, topgallant mast, crow's nest.

207 LOWNESS (*Substantives*), lowlands, depression, a molehill, recumbency, prostration.

Dwarf, pygmy bantam, Lilliputian. Lowlands; molehill.

A ground-floor, basement, cellar, *rez de chaussée* (191), hold.

(*Verbs*) To be low, etc., lie low, grovel, wallow, crouch, slouch, lie flat.

To lower, depress (306), take down a peg, prostrate, subvert.

(*Adjectives*) Low, low-lying, neap, nether, prostrate, flat, level with the ground, grovelling, crouched, crouching, subjacent, underground, underlying, squat.

(*Adverbs*) Under, beneath, underneath, below, down, adown, downstairs, below stairs, over head and ears, downwards, underfoot, at the foot of, underground, at a low ebb.

Ceiling, roof, awning, canopy (*see* 210), attic, loft, garret, housetop.

Growth, upgrowth (194).

(*Verbs*) To be high, etc., to tower, soar, ride, beetle, hover, cap, overtop, culminate, overharg, hang over, impend, overlie, bestride, mount, surmount, to cover (222), perch.

To render high, to heighten, exalt (307).

To become high, grow, upgrow, soar, tower, rise (305).

(*Adjectives*) High, elevated, eminent, exalted, lofty, supernal, tall, towering, beetling, soaring, colossal, gigantic (192), Patagonian, culminating, raised, elevated, etc., perched up, hanging (gardens), crowning, coronary.

Upland, moorland, hilly, mountainous, cloud-touching, heaven-kissing, cloud-topt, cloud-capt, Alpine, subalpine, aerial; orographical.

Upper, uppermost (210), topgallant.

Overhanging, impending, incumbent, overlying, superincumbent, supernatant, superimposed, hovering.

(*Phrases*) Tall as a maypole; tall as a steeple; tall as a poplar.

(*Adverbs*) On high, high up, aloft, above, upstairs, overhead, in the clouds, on tiptoe, on stilts, on the shoulders of, over head and ears.

Over, upwards, from top to bottom, from top to toe, from head to foot, cap-à-pie.

(*Interjection*) Excelsior!

208 DEPTH (*Substantives*), deepness, profundity, profoundness, depression, bathos, anti-climax, depth of water, draught.

A hollow, pit, shaft, well, crater, gulf, abyss, abysm, bottomless pit, hell.

209 SHALLOWNESS (*Substantives*), shoaliness, shoals.

(*Adjectives*) Shallow, skin-deep, superficial, shoaly.

Soundings, submersion, plunge, dive (310).
Plummet, lead, sounding-rod, probe; bathymetry.
Bathysphere, diving-bell, caisson, submarine; diver, frogman.
(*Verbs*) To be deep, etc.
To render deep, etc., to deepen, sink, submerge, plunge, dip, dive (310).
To dig, scoop out, hollow, sink, delve (252).
(*Adjectives*) Deep, deep-seated, profound, sunk, buried, submerged, etc., subaqueous, submarine, subterranean, underground, subterrene, abysmal; bathymetrical, bathymetric.
Bottomless, soundless, fathomless, unfathomed, unsounded, unplumbed, unfathomable.
(*Phrases*) Deep as a well; ankle-deep; knee-deep; breast-deep; chin-deep.
(*Adverbs*) Beyond one's depth, out of one's depth, underground.
(*Phrases*) Over head and ears; to Davy Jones's locker; in the bowels of the earth.

210 SUMMIT (*Substantives*), top, vertex, apex, zenith, pinnacle, acme, climax, culminating point, apogee, pitch, meridian, sky, pole, watershed.

Tip, tiptop, crest, crow's nest, mast-head, truck, peak, turning-point, pole.

Crown, brow, nib, head, nob, noddle, pate.

Capital, cornice, sconce, architrave, pediment, entablature, frieze.

Roof, ceiling, thatch, tiling, slating, awning, canopy (222).

(*Adjectives*) Top, topmost, uppermost, tiptop, culminating, meridian, capital, head, polar, supreme, crowning, coronary.

(*Phrase*) At the top of the tree.

211 BASE (*Substantives*), basement, plinth, foundation, substratum, ground, earth, pavement, floor, paving, flag, ground floor, deck, substructure, infrastructure, footing, groundwork.

The bottom, rock-bottom, nadir, foot, sole, toe, root, keel.

Dado, wainscot, skirting-board.

(*Adjectives*) Bottom, undermost, nethermost, fundamental, basic.

212 VERTICALITY (*Substantives*), erectness, uprightness, perpendicularity, aplomb, right angle, normal, plummet, plumb - line, azimuth, circle.

Wall, precipice, cliff.

Erection, raising, rearing.

(*Verbs*) To be vertical, etc., to stand up, to stand on end, to stand erect, to stand upright, to stick up.

To render vertical, to set up, stick up, erect, rear, raise up, cock up, prick up, raise on its legs.

(*Adjectives*) Vertical, upright, erect, perpendicular, sheer, normal, straight, standing up, etc., up on end, bolt upright, rampant.

213 HORIZONTALITY (*Substantives*), a level, plane, dead level, flatness (251).

Recumbency, lying, lying down, reclination, decumbence, decumbency, supination, resupination, prostration; spirit-level.

A plain, floor, level, flat, platform, bowling-green, billiard-table, plateau, terrace, estrade, esplanade, parterre, table-land (204, 215).

(*Verbs*) To be horizontal, recumbent, etc., to lie, recline, lie down, couch, sit down, squat, lie flat, lie prostrate, sprawl, loll.

To render horizontal, etc., to lay, lay down, lay out, level, flatten, prostrate, knock down, fell, floor.

(*Adverbs*) Up, vertically, etc., on end, up on end, endways, endwise.

(*Phrase*) Straight up and down.

(*Adverbs*) Horizontally, etc., hunkers.

(*Phrases*) Like a millpond.

(*Adjectives*) Horizontal, level, plane, flat, even, discoid.

Recumbent, decumbent, lying, prone, supine, couchant, couching, jacent, prostrate, squat, squatting, sitting, reclining.

on one's back, on all fours, on one's

214 PENDENCY (*Substantives*), dependency, suspension, hanging.

A pendant, pedicel, peduncle, tail, train, flap, skirt, plait, pigtail, queue, tassel, earring, pendulum.

A peg, knob, button, stud, hook, nail, ring, fastener, zipper, clip, staple, knot (45), tenterhook.

(*Verbs*) To be pendant, etc., to hang, swing, dangle, swag, daggle, flap, trail.

To suspend, append, hang, sling, hook up, hitch, fasten to.

(*Adjectives*) Pendent, pendulous, pensile, hanging, dependent, swinging, etc., suspended, etc., loose, flowing, caudal.

Having a peduncle, etc., pedunculate, tailed, caudate.

(*Adverbs*) Dingle-dangle.

(*Phrase*) In the air.

215 SUPPORT (*Substantives*), ground, foundation, base, basis, *terra firma*, fulcrum, foothold, toehold, *point d'appui, pou sto, locus standi*, landing, landing-place, resting-place, ground-work, substratum, floor, bed, stall, berth, lap, mount.

A supporter, prop, stand, strut, stray, shore, boom, yard, outrigger, truss, sleeper, staff, stick, walking-stick, crutch, stirrups, stilts, alpenstock, baton, anvil.

Post, pillar, shaft, column, buttress, pedicle, pedestal, plinth (211), baluster, banister.

A frame, framework, scaffold, scaffolding, skeleton, cadre, beam, rafter, lintel, joist, jamb, mullion, corner-stone, stanchion, summer, girder, cantilever, sponson, tie-beam, (45), columella, backbone, keystone, axle, axle-tree, axis, fuselage, chassis.

A board, form, ledge, platform, floor, stage, shelf, hob, bracket, arbor, rack, mantel, mantelpiece, mantel-shelf, counter, slab, console, dresser, flange, corbel, table, trestle, shoulder, perch, truss, horse, easel, desk.

A seat, throne, dais, divan, musnud, chair, arm-chair, easy-chair, *chaise longue*, hammock-chair, deck-chair, bench, sofa, davenport, lounge, settee, chesterfield, couch, *fauteuil*, stool, tripod, footstool, *tabouret*, trivet, woolsack, ottoman, settle, squab, bench, saddle, pillion, dicky, hassock, pouffe, cushion, howdah.

Bed, bedstead, chair-bedstead, bedding, pillow, bolster, mattress, shake-down, tester, pallet, hammock, bunk, stretcher, crib, cradle, cot, palliasse, donkey's breakfast, sleeping-bag, flea-bag.

Atlas, Persides, Atlantes, Caryatides, Hercules, Yggdrasil.

(*Verbs*) To be supported, etc., to lie, sit, recline, lean, loll, lounge, abut, bear, rest, stand, step, repose, etc., on, be based on, bestride, straddle, bestraddle.

To support, bear, carry, hold, sustain, shoulder, uphold, hold on, upbear, prop, underprop, shore up, underpin, bolster up, pillow.

To give, furnish, afford, supply, lend, etc., support or foundations; to bottom, found, ground, base, embed.

(*Adjectives*) Supported, etc., astride, astraddle; fundamental, basic.

216 PARALLELISM (*Substantives*), coextension.

(*Verbs*) To be parallel, etc.

(*Adjectives*) Parallel, coextensive.

(*Adverbs*) Alongside, abreast, beside.

(*Phrases*) Side by side; cheek by jowl.

——

217 OBLIQUITY (*Substantives*), inclination, slope, leaning, slant, crookedness, bias, bend, bevel, tilt, list, dip, swag, cant, lurch, skew, skewness, bevelling, squint.

Acclivity, uphill, rise, ascent, gradient, rising ground, bank, ramp.

Declivity, downhill, fall, devexity.

A gentle or rapid slope, easy ascent or descent, chute, helter-skelter, switchback, *montagnes russes*.

Steepness, precipitousness, cliff, precipice, talus, scarp, escarp, escarpment; measure of inclination, clinometer.

Diagonal, zigzag, distortion, hypotenuse, angle (244).

(*Phrase*) The leaning tower of Pisa.

(*Verbs*) To be or render oblique, etc., to slope, slant, tilt, lean, incline, shelve, stoop, descend, bend, heel, careen, sag, swag, slouch, cant, sidle, skew, scarp, escarp, bevel, distort.

(*Adjectives*) Oblique, inclined, leaning, recumbent, sloping, shelving, skew, askew, skew-whiff, slant, aslant, slanting, slantendicular, plagioclastic, indirect, distorted, wry, awry, ajee, drawn, crooked, canted, tilted, biased, saggy, bevel, slouched, slouching, etc., out of the perpendicular, backhanded.

Uphill, rising, ascending, acclivitous.

Downhill, falling, descending, declining, declivitous, anticlinal.

Steep, abrupt, precipitous, break-neck.

Diagonal, transverse, athwart, transversal, antiparallel.

(*Adverbs*) Obliquely, etc., on one side, askew, edgewise, askant, askance, sideways, aslope, slopewise, all on one side, crinkum-crankum, asquint, at an angle.

(*Phrase*) *Facilis descensus Averni.*

218 INVERSION (*Substantives*), contraposition, overturn, somersault (or somerset), *culbute*, subversion, retroversion, reversion, reversal, introversion, eversion, transposition, pronation and supination.

Anastrophe, metathesis, hysteron, proteron, spoonerism, palindrome.

(*Verbs*) To be inverted, etc., to turn turtle, loop the loop, bunt.

To render inverted, etc., to invert, reverse, upset, overset, overturn, turn over, upturn, subvert, retrovert, transpose, turn topsy-turvy, tilt over, *culbuter*, keel over, topple over, capsize.

(*Adjectives*) Inverted, inverse, upside down, topsy-turvy, top-heavy.

(*Adverbs*) Inversely, topsy-turvy, etc., inside out.

(*Phrases*) To turn the tables; to put the cart before the horse; to the

219 CROSSING (*Substantives*), intersection, decussation, transversion, convolution.

Reticulation, network, inosculation, anastomosis, interweaving, twining, intertwining, matting, plaiting, interdigitation, mortise (or mortice).

Net, knot, plexus, web, mesh, twill, skein, hank, felt, lace, tulle, wattle, wicker, basket-work, basketry, mat, matting, plait, trellis, lattice, grille, *cancelli*, grid, griddle, grating, gridiron, tracery, fretwork, filigree, reticle, diaper.

Cross, chain, wreath, braid, cat's-cradle, dovetail, Greek cross, Latin cross, Maltese cross, cross of St. Anthony, St. Andrew's cross, cross of Lorraine, swastika, fylfot.

(*Verbs*) To cross, lace, intersect, decussate, interlace, intertwine, inter-

right about; bottom upwards; head over heels; the wrong side up; base over apex.

———

twist, pleach, plash, entwine, enlace, enmesh, weave, interweave, inweave, twine, twist, wreathe, interdigitate, interlock, anastomose, inosculate, dovetail, splice (43).

To mat, plait, plat, braid, felt, twill, tangle, entangle, ravel, net, knot (43), dishevel, raddle.

(*Adjectives*) Crossing, intersecting, etc., crossed, intersected, matted, etc., crucial, cruciform.

Retiform, reticulate, areolar, areolate, cancellated, grated, barred, streaked, traceried.

(*Adverbs*) Across, thwart, athwart, transversely, crosswise.

3°. *Centrical Dimensions*

I. GENERAL

220 EXTERIORITY (*Substantives*), externality, outness, outside, exterior, surface, superficies, superstratum, eccentricity, extremity, frontage.

Disk, face, facet, front (234), skin (222).

(*Verbs*) To be exterior, etc.

To place exteriorly, or outwardly, to turn out.

(*Adjectives*) Exterior, external, outer, outward, outlying, outdoor, outside, extramural, superficial, skindeep, frontal, discoid, eccentric, extrinsic.

(*Adverbs*) Externally, etc., out, without, outwards, outdoors, abroad.

(*Phrases*) Out of doors; *extra muros*; *ab extra*; in the open air; *sub Jove*; *à la belle étoile*; al fresco.

———

221 INTERIORITY (*Substantives*), inside, interior, hinterland, backblocks, interspace, substratum, subsoil.

Vitals, viscera, pith, marrow, heart, bosom, breast, entrails, bowels, belly, intestines, guts, inwards, womb, lap, backbone, *penetralia*, inmost recesses, cave, cavern (191).

(*Verbs*) To be interior, internal, within, etc.

To place or keep within, to enclose, circumscribe (*see* 231, 232).

(*Adjectives*) Interior, internal, inner, inside, intramural, inward, inlying, inmost, innermost, deep-seated, intestine, intestinal, splanchnic, intercostal, inland, interstitial, subcutaneous, intrinsic.

Home, domestic, indoor.

(*Adverbs*) Internally, inwards, inwardly, within, inly, therein, *ab intra*, withinside, indoors, within doors, ben, at home, *chez soi*, up country.

222 COVERING (*Substantives*), cover, roof, ceiling, slates, tiles, thatch, cowling, canopy, baldachin, awning, tarpaulin, tilt, tent (189), lid, hatch, operculum (263), shed.

Integument, skin, tegument, pellicle, fleece, cuticle, scarf-skin, epidermis, hide, pelt, peel, crust, bark, rind, cortex, husk, scale, shell, carapace, capsule, coat, tunic, tunicle, sheath, case, casing, calyx, theca,

223 CENTRALITY (*Substantives*), centre (68), middle, focus, epicentre, hub, core, kernel, marrow, pith, nucleus, nucleolus, heart, pole, axis, bull's-eye, nave, navel, umbilicus, omphalos; concentration, centralization.

(*Verbs*) To be central, etc.

To render central, centralize, concentrate.

To bring to a focus.

(*Adjectives*) Central, centrical,

sheathing, scabbard, wrapping, wrapper, envelope, tarpaulin, cloth, table-cloth, blanket, rug, quilt, eiderdown, coverlet (or coverlid), counterpane, carpet, drugget, oilcloth, waxcloth, linoleum.

Superposition, coating, facing, veneer, paint, enamel, varnish, anointing, inunction, incrustation, plaster, stucco, wash, parget, patina.

(*Verbs*) To cover, superpose, superimpose, overspread, over-canopy, wrap, lap, overlap, face, case, encase, veneer, pave, upholster.

To coat, paint, enamel, varnish, pave, plaster, beplaster, daub, bedaub, encrust, stucco, dab, smear, besmear, anoint, spray, do over, gild, japan, lacquer (or lacker), plate, electroplate, parget.

(*Phrase*) To lay it on thick.

(*Adjectives*) Covering, etc., cutaneous, dermal, cortical, cuticular, tegumentary, skinny, scaly, squamous, imbricated, epidermal, loricated, armour-plated, iron-clad.

middle, middlemost, midmost, median, azygous, axial, focal, umbilical, concentric.

(*Adverbs*) Midway, centrally, etc.

224 LINING (*Substantives*), coating, facing, internal incrustation, puddle, stalactite, stalagmite, wainscot, dado, wall.

Filling, stuffing, wadding, padding.

(*Verbs*) To line, encrust, stuff, pad, wad, face, puddle, bush.

(*Adjectives*) Lined, encrusted, etc.

---

225 INVESTMENT (*Substantives*), dress, clothing, raiment, drapery, costume, attire, toilet, trim, rig, rig-out, fig, habiliment, vesture, apparel, underwear, full dress, evening dress, soup-and-fish, glad rags, dinner-jacket, tuxedo, fancy dress, accoutrement, outfit, wardrobe, trousseau, uniform, regimentals, battle-dress, kit, equipment, livery, gear, harness, turn-out, caparison, suit, dress suit, lounge suit, bathing suit, swim-suit, tweeds, flannels, rigging, trappings, slops, traps, duds, togs, clobber, frippery, bloomers, haberdashery, housing.

Dishabille, morning dress, dressing-gown, undress, mufti, civvies, rags, *négligé*, tea-gown.

Clothes, garment, garb, garniture, vestment, pontificals, robe, tunic, caftan, paletot, habit, gown, coat, dress-coat, claw-hammer, frock, stole, blouse, shirt-waist, toga, haik, smock-frock, kimono, bikini.

Cloak, opera-cloak, cape, mantle, mantlet, dolman, shawl, wrap, wrapper, veil, fichu, yashmak, tippet, kirtle, plaid, mantilla, tabard, burnous, overcoat, great-coat, British

226 DIVESTMENT (*Substantives*), nudity, bareness, nakedness, baldness, undress, dishabille, threadbareness.

Denuding, denudation, stripping, uncovering, decortication, peeling, flaying, excoriation, desquamation, moulting, exfoliation.

(*Verbs*) To divest, uncover, denude, bare, strip, unclothe, undress, unrobe, disrobe, disapparel, debag, disarray, take off, doff, cast off, peel, pare, decorticate, husk, uncoif, unbonnet, excoriate, skin, flay, expose, exfoliate, lay open, dismantle, unroof, uncase, unsheathe, moult, mew.

(*Adjectives*) Bare, naked, nude, stripped, denuded, undressed, unclothed, unclad, undraped, uncovered, unshod, barefoot, bareheaded, unbonneted, exposed, in dishabille, in buff, bald, threadbare, ragged, callow, roofless.

(*Phrases*) In a state of nature; stark-naked; *in puris naturalibus*; stripped to the buff; in one's birthday suit; bald as a coot; as bare as the back of one's hand; out at elbows.

---

warm, duffle coat, surtout, spencer, rain-coat, ulster, mackintosh, water-proof, oilskin, slicker, burberry, poncho, surplice, alb, cassock, pallium, etc., mask, domino, cardinal, pelerine.

Jacket, vest, under-vest, semmit, singlet, jerkin; lumberjacket, waist-coat, cardigan, sweater, jersey, pullover, slipover, jumper, windbreaker, windcheater, doublet, gaberdine, camisole, combinations, stays, corset, bodice, under-bodice, brassière, bra, corsage, cestus, petticoat, kilt, filibeg (or philibeg), stomacher, skirt, kirtle, crinoline, farthingale, underskirt, slip, apron, pinafore.

Trousers, trews, breeches, galligaskins, knickerbockers, plus-fours, knickers, drawers, scanties, pantaloons, pants, overalls, dungarees, boiler suit, rompers, unmentionables, inexpressibles, smalls, tights, bags, breeks, slacks, shorts, jeans, briefs.

Cap, hat, top-hat, silk hat, tile, bowler, panama, slouch-hat, trilby, Stetson, titfer, deerstalker, billycock, wide-awake, sou'wester, beaver, castor, bonnet, forage-cap, tam-o'-shanter, tammy, balmoral, glengarry, toque, sun-bonnet, hood, head-gear, head-dress, kerchief, scarf, muffler, comforter, boa, snood, coiffure, coif, skull-cap, calotte, biretta, cowl, chaplet, capote, calash, pelt, wig, peruke, periwig, toupee, transforma-tion, chignon, caftan, turban, puggaree, fez, helmet, topi, shako, busby, képi, casque, beret.

Shirt, smock, shift, chemise, chemisette, nightshirt, nightgown, nightdress, pyjamas, bed-jacket, bed-gown, collar, cravat, neck-cloth, neck-tie, stock, handkerchief.

Shoe, pump, high-low, Oxford shoe, sabot, brogue, sand-shoe, plim-soll, rubbers, sneakers, boot, jack-book, top-boot, Wellington, gum-boot, slipper, mule, galosh, overshoe, legging, puttee, buskin, greaves, galligaskins, mocassin, gaiter, spatterdash, spat, stocking, sock, nylons, hose, sandal, clog, babouche.

Glove, gauntlet, mitten, sleeve, cuff, muff.

Outfitter, tailor, clothier, milliner, sempstress, costumier, hatter, hosier, shoemaker, cobbler.

(*Verbs*) To invest, cover, envelop, lap, involve, drape, enwrap, wrap up, lap up, sheathe, vest, clothe, array, enrobe, dress, dight, attire, apparel, accoutre, trick out, rig, fit out, fig out, caparison, adonize, dandify, titivate, don, put on, wear, have on, huddle on, slip on, roll up in, muffle, perk up, mantle, swathe, swaddle, equip, harness.

(*Adjectives*) Invested, clothed, arrayed, dight, etc., clad, shod, etc.; sartorial.

227 Circumjacence (*Substantives*), circumambiency, encompassment, surroundings, environment, atmo-sphere, medium, setting, scene, out-post, skirt, outskirts, boulevards, suburbs, suburbia, rurbania, purlieus, precincts, faubourgs, environs, en-tourage, *banlieue*, green belt.

(*Verbs*) To lie around, surround, beset, set about, compass, encom-pass, environ, enclose, encircle, em-brace, lap, gird, begird, engirdle, orb, enlace, skirt, twine round, hem in (231).

228 Interjacence (*Substantives*), interlocation, intervention, insertion, interposition, interspersion, inter-penetration, interdigitation, inter-polation, interlineation, intercurrence, intrusion, obtrusion, insinuation, in-tercalation, insertion, intertwine-ment, interference, permeation, in-filtration.

An intermedium, intermediary, a go-between, bodkin, intruder, interloper; interlude, episode; parenthesis, gag, flyleaf, *entresol* (68).

(*Adjectives*) Circumjacent, ambient, circumambient, surrounding, etc., circumfluent, circumferential, suburban, extramural, embosomed.

(*Adverbs*) Around, about, without, on every side, on all sides, right and left, all around, round about.

229 OUTLINE (*Substantives*), circumference, perimeter, periphery, ambit, circuit, lines, tournure, contour, profile, silhouette, sky-line.

Zone, belt, girth, band, baldric, zodiac, cordon, girdle, cingulum, clasp (247).

230 EDGE (*Substantives*), verge, brink, brow, brim, margin, marge, border, skirt, rim, side, mouth, jaws, lip, muzzle, door, porch, portal (260), kerb; shore, coast.

Frame, flounce, frill, ruffle, jabot, list, fringe, valance, edging, trimming, hem, selvedge, welt, furbelow.

(*Verbs*) To border, edge, skirt, coast, verge on.

(*Adjectives*) Border, marginal, coastal, skirting.

A partition, septum, panel, diaphragm, midriff, party-wall.

A half-way house, no-man's-land.

(*Verbs*) To lie, come, or get between, intervene, intrude, butt in, slide in, permeate, put between, put in, interpose, interject, chip in, throw in, wedge in, thrust in, foist in, insert, intercalate, interpolate, parenthesize, interline, interleave, interlard, interdigitate, dovetail, sandwich, worm in, insinuate, obtrude (300), intersperse, infiltrate; to gag.

(*Phrases*) To put one's oar in; to stick one's nose into; to have a finger in the pie.

(*Adjectives*) Interjacent, intervening, etc., intermediary, intermediate, intercalary, interstitial, parenthetical, mediterranean.

(*Adverbs*) Between, betwixt, 'twixt, among, amongst, amid, amidst, midst, betwixt and between, sandwich-wise, parenthetically, between the lines, in the thick of.

---

231 CIRCUMSCRIPTION (*Substantives*), limitation, enclosure, confinement shutting up, circumvallation, entombment.

Imprisonment, incarceration (751).

(*Verbs*) To circumscribe, limit, delimit, localize, bound, confine, enclose, surround (227), compass about, impound, restrict, restrain (751), shut in, shut up, lock up, bottle up, dam, hem in, hedge in, wall in, rail in, fence, picket, pen, enfold, coop, corral, encage, cage, mew, entomb, bury, immure, encase, pack up, seal up, wrap up (225), etc.

(*Adjectives*) Circumscribed, etc., imprisoned, pent up (754), landlocked.

(*Phrase*) Not room to swing a cat.

232 ENCLOSURE (*Substantives*), envelope, case, box (191), pen, penfold, fold, sheep-fold, pound, paddock, enclave, *enceinte*, corral, ring fence, wall, hedge, hedgerow, espalier, exclosure, play-pen.

Barrier, bar, gate, gateway, door, barricade, cordon.

Dike (or dyke), ditch, fosse, moat.

Fence, pale, paling, balustrade, rail, railing, hurdle, palisade, battlement, rampart, embankment, breakwater, mole, groyne (717), circumvallation, contravallation.

233 LIMIT (*Substantives*), boundary, bounds, confine, term, bourne, line of demarcation, termination, stint, frontier, border, precinct, marches, line of circumvallation, pillars of Hercules, Rubicon, turning-point, last word, *ne plus ultra*.

(*Adjectives*) Definite, conterminal, terminal, frontier.

(*Phrases*) To cross the Rubicon; thus far and no farther.

2. SPECIAL

234 FRONT (*Substantives*), face, anteriority, fore-part, front rank, foreground, van, vanguard, advanced guard, outpost, proscenium, façade, frontage, foreword, preface, frontispiece (64).

Forehead, visage, physiognomy, phiz, countenance, mug, dial, puss, pan, beak, rostrum, bow, stem, prow.

Pioneer, avant-courier (64).

(In a medal) obverse; (in a coin) head.

(*Verbs*) To be in front, etc., to front, face, envisage, confront, bend forward, etc.

(*Adjectives*) Fore, anterior, front, frontal, facial.

(*Adverbs*) Before, in front, ahead, right ahead, in the van, foremost, vis-à-vis, in the foreground, face to face, before one's eyes.

---

236 LATERALITY (*Substantives*), side, flank, quarter, hand, cheek, jowl, wing, profile, temple, loin, haunch, hip, broadside, lee-side, lee.

East, orient; West, occident.

(*Verbs*) To be on one side, etc., to flank, outflank, to sidle, skirt.

(*Adjectives*) Lateral, sidelong, collateral, sideling, bilateral, trilateral, quadrilateral, multilateral, many-sided, eastern, oriental, western, occidental, eastward, westward.

(*Adverbs*) Sideways, side by side (216), sidelong, abreast, abeam, alongside, aside, by the side of, to windward, to leeward.

(*Phrases*) Cheek by jowl; broadside on.

238 DEXTRALITY (*Substantives*), right, right hand, dexter, offside, starboard, recto.

(*Adjectives*) Dextral, right-handed; ambidextrous, ambidexter.

235 REAR (*Substantives*), back, posteriority, the rear rank, rear-guard, the background, heels, tail, scut, rump, croup, crupper, breech, backside, posterior, fanny, catastrophe, buttocks, haunches, hunkers, hurdies, hind quarters, *dorsum*, dorsal region, stern, poop, after-part, tail-piece, wake.

(In a medal) reverse; (in a coin) tail.

(*Verbs*) To be in the rear, behind, etc., to fall astern, to bend backwards, to back on,

(*Phrases*) Turn the back upon; bring up the rear.

(*Adjectives*) Back, rear, postern, hind, hinder, hindmost, sternmost, posterior, dorsal, after.

(*Adverbs*) Behind, in the rear, aft, abaft, astern, aback, rearward.

(*Phrases*) In the background; behind one's back; at the heels of; at the tail of; at the back of; back to back.

237 ANTIPOSITION (*Substantives*), opposite side, contraposition, reverse, inverse, antipodes, opposition, inversion (218)

Polarity, opposite poles, North and South.

(*Verbs*) To be opposite, etc., subtend.

(*Adjectives*) Opposite, reverse, inverse, antipodal, subcontrary.

Fronting, facing, diametrically opposite, vis-à-vis.

Northern, boreal, septentrional, arctic; southern, austral, antarctic.

(*Adverbs*) Over, over the way, over against, facing, against, fronting (234), face to face, vis-à-vis.

239 SINISTRALITY (*Substantives*), left, left hand, sinister, near side, port, larboard, verso.

(*Adjectives*) Sinistral, left-handed.

Section III—Form

1°. *General Form*

240 Form (*Substantives*), figure, shape, configuration, make, formation, frame, construction, conformation, cut, set, trim, build, make, stamp, cast, mould, fashion, structure.

Feature, lineament, phase (448), turn, attitude, posture, pose.

Morphology, isomorphism.

Formation, figuration, efformation, sculpture.

(*Phrase*) The cut of one's jib.

(*Verbs*) To form, shape, figure, fashion, carve, cut, chisel, chase, emboss, hew, rough-hew, cast, rough-cast, hammer out, block out, trim, work, lick into shape, knock together, mould, sculpture, sculp, grave, stamp.

241 Absence of form.

Amorphism (*Substantives*), amorphousness, formlessness, shapelessness, disfigurement, defacement, mutilation (846).

Vandalism, vandal, Goth.

(*Verbs*) To destroy form, deform, deface, disfigure, disfeature (846), mutilate.

(*Adjectives*) Shapeless, amorphous, formless, unhewn, rough, rude, Gothic, unfashioned, unshapen, misshapen, inchoate.

(*Adjectives*) Formed, graven, etc., receiving form, plastic, fictile. Giving form, formative, plastic, plasmatic, plasmic.

242 Regularity of form.

Symmetry (*Substantives*), shapeliness, eurhythmy, uniformity, finish, beauty (845), proportion, balance.

(*Adjectives*) Symmetrical, regular, shapely, eurhythmic, well-set, uniform, finished, well-proportioned, balanced, chaste, classic.

(*Phrase*) *Teres atque rotundus.*

243 Irregularity of form.

Distortion (*Substantives*), twist, kink, wryness, asymmetry, gibbosity, contortion, malformation, ugliness, etc. (846), teratology.

(*Verbs*) To distort, twist, wrest, writhe, wring, contort, kink, buckle.

(*Adjectives*) Irregular, unsymmetrical, asymmetrical, distorted, twisted, wry, awry, askew, crooked, on one side, misshapen, deformed, ill-proportioned, ill-made, round-shouldered, pigeon-chested, humpbacked, hunchbacked, gibbous, gibbose; knock-kneed, bandy-legged, bow-legged, club-footed, splay-footed.

(*Phrases*) All manner of ways; all over the place.

2°. *Special Form*

244 Angularity (*Substantives*), angulation, angle, cusp, bend, elbow, knee, knuckle, groin, crinkle-crankle, kink, crotch, crutch, crane, fluke, scythe, sickle, zigzag, anfractuosity, refraction; fold (258), corner (182).

Fork, bifurcation, dichotomy.

Right angle (212), salient angle, re-entrant angle, acute angle, obtuse angle.

A polygon, square, rectangle, triangle, pentagon, hexagon, heptagon, octagon, nonagon, decagon, lozenge, diamond, rhomb, rhombus, rhomboid, parallelogram, gore, gusset, wedge.

Cube, parallelepiped, pyramid, prism, rhombohedron, tetrahedron, pentahedron, hexahedron, octahedron, dodecahedron, icosahedron.

T-square, set-square, protractor, goniometer, theodolite, sextant, quadrant, clinometer.

(*Verbs*) To bend, refract, diffract, fork, bifurcate, angulate, crinkle, crankle, splay.

(*Adjectives*) Angular, triangular, quadrangular, rectangular, bent, crooked, hooked, aduncous, aquiline, jagged, serrated, falciform, falcated, furcated, forked, bifurcate, zigzag; dovetailed, knock-kneed, crinkled, akimbo, geniculated, polygonal, trigonal, pentagonal, etc., fusiform, sagittate, arrow-headed, wedge-shaped, cuneate, cuneiform, splayed, angulate, cubical, pyramidal, rhombohedral, tetrahedral, etc.

---

245 CURVATURE (*Substantives*), curvation, incurvity, incurvation, bend, flexure, flexion, hook, crook, camber, bending, deflexion, inflexion, arcuation, diffraction, turn, deviation, detour, sweep, sinuosity, curl, curling, winding, recurvature, recurvation, refraction, flexibility (324).

A curve, arc, circle, ellipse (247), parabola, hyperbola, catenary, festoon, arch, arcade, vault, bow, crescent, half-moon, lunette, horseshoe, loop, bight, crane-neck, conchoid, ogee.

(*Verbs*) To be curved, etc., to bend, curve, etc., decline, turn, trend, deviate, re-enter, sweep.

To render curved; to bend, curve, incurvate, camber, deflect, inflect, crook, hook, turn, round, arch, arcuate, bow, curl, recurve, loop, frizzle.

(*Adjectives*) Curved, vent, etc., curvilinear, curviform, recurved, recurvous, circular, oval (247), parabolic, hyperbolic, bowed, crooked, bandy, arched, vaulted, arcuated, camerated, hooked, falcated, falciform, crescent-shaped, semilunar, semicircular, conchoidal, lunular, lunulate, cordiform, heart-shaped, reniform, pear-shaped; bow-legged, bandy-legged, knock-kneed, devious.

246 STRAIGHTNESS (*Substantives*), rectilinearity, directness.

A straight line, a right line, a direct line; inflexibility (323).

(*Verbs*) To be straight, etc.

To render straight, to straighten, rectify, set or put straight, take the curl out of, unbend, unfold, uncurl, uncoil, unroll, unwind, unravel, untwist, unwreathe, unwrap.

(*Adjectives*) Straight, rectilinear (or rectilineal), direct, even, right, in a line; unbent; not inclining, not bending, not turning, not deviating to either side, undeviating, unturned, undistorted, unswerving.

(*Phrases*) Straight as an arrow; as the crow flies; in a bee line.

---

247 Simple circularity.

CIRCULARITY (*Substantives*), roundness, rotundity (249).

A circle, circlet, ring, areola, hoop, roundlet, *annulus*, annulet, bracelet, bangle, armlet, anklet, ringlet, eye, loop, wheel, cycle, orb, orbit, rundle, zone, belt, cordon, band, sash, girdle, cestus, cincture, baldric, bandolier, fillet, cummerbund, fascia, wreath, garland, crown, corona, coronal, coronet, chaplet, necklace, rivière; noose, lasso.

An ellipse, oval, ovule, ellipsoid,

248 Complex circularity.

CONVOLUTION (*Substantives*), winding, wave, undulation, circuit, tortuosity, anfractuosity, sinuosity, involution, sinuation, circumvolution, meander, circumbendibus, twist, twirl, squiggle, curl, curlicue, curliewurlie, tirlie-whirlie, crimp, frizz, frizzle, permanent wave, perm, windings and turnings, *ambages*, inosculation, peristalsis.

A coil, reel, roll, spiral, helix, corkscrew, worm, volute, scroll, cartouche, rundle, scallop (or scollop), escallop.

cycloid, epicycloid, epicycle, semi-circle, quadrant, sextant, sector, segment.

(Verbs) To make round, round, circle, encircle, environ (227).

(Adjectives) Round, rounded, circular, annular, orbicular.

Oval, elliptical, elliptic, ovate, egg-shaped; cycloidal, etc., moniliform.

Serpent, eel, maze, labyrinth.

(Verbs) To be convoluted, etc.

To wind, twine, twist, coil, roll, turn and twist, weave, twirl, wave, undulate, meander, scallop, curl, crimp, frizz, frizzle, perm, inosculate, entwine (219), enlace, twist together, goffer.

(Adjectives) Convoluted, winding, twisting, contorted, waving, waved, wavy, curly, undulating, undulant, undulatory, undated, serpentine, anguilline, mazy, labyrinthine, Daedalian, tortuous, sinuous, flexuous, snaky, involved, sigmate, sigmoid, sigmoidal, vermiform, vermicular, peristaltic, meandrine; scalloped (or scolloped), wreathed, wreathy, crisped, crimped, frizzed, frizzy, frizzled, frizzly, ravelled, twisted, dishevelled (61).

Spiral, coiled, helical, turbinate.

(Adverb) In and out.

249 ROTUNDITY (Substantives), roundness, cylindricity; cylinder, barrel, drum, cylindroid, roll, roller, rouleau, column, rolling-pin, rundle.

Cone, conoid; pear-shape, bell-shape.

Sphericity, spheroidity, globosity; a sphere, globe, ball, spheroid, ellipsoid, drop, spherule, globule, vesicle, bulb, bullet, pellet, pill, clue, marble, pea, knob, pommel.

(Verbs) To form into a sphere, render spherical, to sphere, ensphere, to roll into a ball, round off, give rotundity, etc.

(Adjectives) Rotund, round, cylindric, cylindrical, cylindroid, columnar, lumbriciform; conic, conical, conoidal.

Spherical, spheral, spheroidal, globular, globated, globous, globose, ovoid, egg-shaped, gibbous, bulbiform, bulbous, bell-shaped, campaniliform, campaniform, campanulate, fungiform, bead-like, moniliform, pyriform, cigar-shaped.

(Phrases) Round as an apple; round as a ball; teres atque rotundus.

3°. Superficial Form

250 CONVEXITY (Substantives), prominence, projection, swelling, gibbosity, bulge, protuberance, intumescence, tumour, cancer, tuberosity, tubercle, tooth, knob, excrescence, elbow, process, condyle, bulb, nub, nubble, node, nodule, nodosity, tongue, dorsum, hump, hunch, hunk, bunch, boss, embossment, bump, lump, clump, sugarloaf, point (253), bow, bagginess.

Pimple, wen, papula, pustule, carbuncle, corn, wart, polyp, boil, furuncle, fungus, fungosity, bleb, blister, blain, chilblain, bunion.

Papilla, nipple, teat, pap, breast,

251 FLATNESS (Substantives), plane; horizontality (213), layer (204), smoothness (255); plate, platter, slab, table, tablet; level.

(Verbs) To render flat, flatten, smooth, level.

(Adjectives) Flat, plane, even, level, etc. (213), flush, scutiform, scutellate.

(Phrases) Flat as a pancake; flat as a flounder; flat as a board; flat as my hand; a dead flat; a dead level.

252 CONCAVITY (Substantives). depression, hollow, hollowness, indentation, intaglio, cavity, dent, dint, dimple, follicle, pit, sinus, alveolus,

dug, udder, mamilla, proboscis, nose, neb, beak, snout, nozzle, belly, paunch, corporation, kyte, back, shoulder, elbow, lip, flange.

Peg, button, stud, ridge, rib, jetty, snag, eaves, mole, cupola, dome, balcony.

Cameo, high and low relief, bas-relief, *basso rilievo*, *alto rilievo*; repoussé work.

Mount, hill (206); cape, promontory, foreland, headland, ness, mull, salient, point of land, hummock, spur, hog's back, offset.

(*Verbs*) To be prominent, etc., to project, bulge, belly, jut out, bristle up, to hang over, overhang, beetle, bend over, protrude, stand out, stick out, poke out, stick up, start up, cock up, shoot up, swell.

To render prominent; to raise (307), to emboss, chase, stud, bestud, ridge.

lacuna, honeycomb, excavation, trough (259).

Cup, basin, crater, etc. (191); socket, thimble.

Valley, vale, dale, dell, dingle, coombe, strath, bottom, corrie, glade, glen, cave, cell, cavern, cove, grotto, grot, alcove, gully (198), cul-de-sac.

(*Verbs*) To be depressed, etc., to cave in, subside, retire.

To depress, hollow, scoop, gouge, dig, delve, excavate, dent, dint, stave in, mine, undermine, burrow, tunnel.

(*Adjectives*) Depressed, concave, hollow, stove in, retiring, retreating, cavernous, honeycombed, alveolar, cellular, funnel-shaped, infundibular, bell-shaped, campaniliform, porous (260).

(*Adjectives*) Convex, prominent, projecting, bulging, etc., bold, bossed, bossy, knobby, nubbly, lumpy, bumpy, nodose, embossed, chased, gibbous, salient, mamilliform, in relief, bowed, arched, bellied, baggy, cornute, odontoid, tuberous, tuberculous, ridged, ridgy.

---

253   SHARPNESS (*Substantives*), keenness, pointedness, acuteness, acuity, acumination, spinosity, prickliness.

A point, spike, spine, spicule, needle, bodkin (262), aiguille, pin, prickle, prick, prong, tine, caltrop, *chevaux de frise*, arrow, spear, bayonet, pike, sword, dagger (727), spur, rowel, barb, spit, cusp, horn, antler,

254   BLUNTNESS (*Substantives*), obtuseness, dullness.

(*Verbs*) To be blunt, etc., to render blunt, etc., to obtund, dull, take off the point or edge, turn.

(*Adjectives*) Blunt, obtuse, dull, bluff.

---

snag, tag, jag, thorn, brier, bramble, thistle, nib, tooth, tusk, denticle, spoke, cog, ratchet, comb, bristle, beard, awn, *arête*, crest, cone, peak, spire, pyramid, steeple, porcupine, hedgehog.

Cutlery, blade, edge-tool, knife, jack-knife, penknife, clasp-knife, bowie, jocteleg, chisel, razor, scalpel, bistoury, lancet, axe, hatchet, pole-axe, pick-axe, pick, mattock, spade, adze, coulter, ploughshare, scythe, sickle, reaping-hook, bill, billhook, cleaver, scissors, shears, sécateurs.

Sharpener, knife-sharpener, strop, hone, grinder, grindstone, whetstone, steel, emery, carborundum.

(*Verbs*) To be sharp, etc., to taper to a point, to bristle with.

To render sharp, etc., to sharpen, point, aculeate, set, whet, strop, hone, grind, barb, bristle up.

(*Adjectives*) Sharp, keen, pointed, conical, acute, acicular, aculeated, arrowy, needle-shaped, spiked, spiky, spicular, spiculate, mucronate, mucronated, ensiform, peaked, acuminated, salient, cusped, cuspidate, cuspidated, cornute, prickly, spiny, spinous, thorny, jagged, bristling, muricate, pectinated, studded, thistly, briery, snaggy, digitated, barbed, spurred, two-edged, tapering, fusiform, dentiform, denticular, denticulated, toothed, odontoid, cutting, trenchant, sharp-edged.

Starlike, stellated, stelliform.

(*Phrases*) Sharp as a needle, as a razor.

255 SMOOTHNESS (*Substantives*), evenness, level (213), polish, gloss, glossiness, sleekness, slipperiness, lubricity, lubrication (332), down, velvet, velveteen, velour, silk, satin, plush, glass, ice, enamel, macadam.

Burnisher, calender, mangle, iron, file, plane, sandpaper, emery-paper, roller.

(*Verbs*) To smooth, smoothen, plane, polish, burnish, calender, mangle, enamel, glaze, iron, file, roll, lubricate, macadamize.

(*Adjectives*) Smooth, even, level, plane, sleek, slick, polished, glazed, glossy, sleeky, silken, silky, satiny, velvety, glabrous, slippery, oily, soft, unwrinkled.

(*Phrases*) Smooth as glass, as velvet, as satin, as soil; slippery as an eel.

256 ROUGHNESS (*Substantives*), unevenness, asperity, rugosity, ruggedness, scabrousness, salebrosity, cragginess, craggedness, corrugation, nodosity, crispness, plumosity, villosity; grain, texture, nap, pile.

Arborescence, branching, ramification.

Brush, bur, beard, shag, whisker, dundreary, mutton-chop, sideboards, side-burns, down, goatee, imperial, moustache, feather, plume, crest, tuft, *panache*, byssus, hair, chevelure, toupee, wool, fur, mane, cilia, fringe, *fimbriae*, tress, moss, plush, velvet, velveteen, velour, stubble.

(*Verbs*) To be rough, etc.

To render rough, to roughen, crisp, crumple, corrugate, rumple.

(*Adjectives*) Rough, uneven, scabrous, gnarled, rugged, rugose, rugous, salebrous, unpolished, matt, frosted, rough-hewn, craggy, cragged, prickly, scrubby.

Arborescent, dendriform, arboriform, branching, ramose, ramulose, dendroid.

Feathery, plumose, plumous, plumigerous, tufted, fimbriated, hairy, ciliated, hirsute, flocculent, bushy, hispid, tomentous, downy, woolly, velvety, villous (or villose), bearded, pilous, shaggy, shagged, stubbly, fringed, befringed, setaceous, filamentous.

(*Phrases*) Rough as a nutmeg-grater; like quills upon the fretful porcupine; against the grain.

257 NOTCH (*Substantives*), dent, dint, nick, cut, indent, indentation, dimple.

Embrasure, battlement, machicolation, machicoulis, saw, tooth, sprocket, crenelle, scallop (or scollop).

(*Verbs*) To notch, nick, cut, dent, indent, dint, jag, scotch, slash, scallop (or scollop), crenelate.

(*Adjectives*) Notched, etc., jagged, crenate, crenated, crenelated, dented, dentated, denticulated, toothed, palmated, indented, serrated.

258 FOLD (*Substantives*), plication, plait, ply, crease, pleat, tuck, hem, flexion, flexure, joint, elbow, doubling, duplicature, gather, wrinkle, crow's-foot, rimple, crinkle, crankle, crumple, rumple, rivel, ruck, ruffle, ruche, dog's-ear, corrugation, flounce, frounce, lapel, pucker, crimp.

(*Verbs*) To fold, double, plicate, plait, crease, wrinkle, crinkle, crankle, curl, cockle up, cocker, rimple, frizz, frizzle, rumple, flounce, frounce, rivel, twill, corrugate, ruffle, crimp, crumple, pucker, to turn down, turn under, tuck, ruck.

(*Adjectives*) Folded, dog's-eared (or dog-eared), etc.

259 FURROW (*Substantives*), groove, rut, slit, scratch, streak, stria, crack, score, rib.

Channel, gutter, trench, ditch, dike, moat, fosse, trough, kennel, chamfer, ravine (198), fluting.

(*Verbs*) To furrow, etc., flute, plough.

(*Adjectives*) Furrowed, etc., ribbed, striated, striate, sulcated, fluted, canaliculate, bisulcate, trisulcate, etc., corduroy, corded, corrugated.

260 OPENING (*Substantives*), hole, foramen, perforation, eye, eyelet, keyhole, loophole, porthole, scuttle, mouse-hole, pigeon-hole, eye of a needle, pinhole, peep-hole, puncture.

Aperture, hiatus, yawning, oscitancy, dehiscence, patefaction, slot, chink, crevice (198).

Window, light, fanlight, skylight, casement, lattice, embrasure.

Orifice, inlet, intake, outlet, mouth, throat, muzzle, gullet, weasand, nozzle, portal, porch, gate, lychgate, wicket, postern, gateway, door, embouchure, doorway, exit, vomitory, hatch, hatchway, gangway, arcade.

Channel (350), passage, pass, tube, pipe, vessel, tubule, canal, thoroughfare, gut, fistula, ajutage, tap, faucet, chimney, flue, vent, funnel, gully, tunnel, main, adit, pit, shaft, gallery, alley, aisle, glade, vista, bore, mine, calibre, pore, follicle, porosity, porousness, lacuna.

Sieve, cullender, colander, strainer, tamis, riddle, screen, honeycomb.

261 CLOSURE (*Substantives*), occlusion, blockade, shutting up, filling up, plugging, sealing, obstruction, impassableness, blocking up, obstipation, constipation, blind alley, blind corner, cul-de-sac, impasse, caecum.

Imperforation, imperviousness, impermeability, imporosity.

(*Verbs*) To close, occlude, steek, plug, block up, fill up, blockade, obstruct, bar, stop, bung up, seal, clinch, plumb, cork up, shut up, choke, throttle, ram down, dam up, cram, stuff up.

(*Adjectives*) Closed, shut, unopened, occluded, etc., impervious, imperforate, caecal, impassable, invious, pathless, untrodden, unpierced, unventilated, impermeable, imporous, operculated, tight, water-tight, airtight, hermetic.

(*Phrase*) Hermetically sealed.

Apertion, perforation, piercing, boring, mining, terebration, drilling, etc., impalement, pertusion, puncture, acupuncture, penetration (302).

Opener, tin-opener, key, master-key.

(*Verbs*) To open, ope, gape, yawn.

To perforate, lay open, pierce, empierce, tap, bore, mine, drill, scoop out, canalize, tunnel, transpierce, transfix, enfilade, rake, impale, spike, spear, gore, stab, pink, stick, prick, lance, puncture, riddle, honeycomb, punch, jab; uncover, unrip, stave in.

(*Phrase*) To cut a passage through.

(*Adjectives*) Open, pierced, perforated, etc., perforate, wide open, ajar, unclosed, unstopped, patulous, gaping, yawning, patent.

Tubular, tubulous, tubulate, tubuliform, cannular, fistulous, fistular, fistulate, pervious, permeable, foraminous, porous, follicular, cribriform, honeycombed, infundibular, windowed, fenestrated.

(*Phrase*) Open sesame!

262 PERFORATOR (*Substantives*), borer, auger, gimlet, stylet, drill, wimble, awl, bradawl, brog, scoop, corkscrew, dibble, trepan, probe, bodkin, needle, stiletto, lancet, punch, spike, bit, brace and bit, gouge, fleam.

(*Verbs*) To spike, gouge, scoop, punch, lance.

———

263 STOPPER (*Substantives*), stopple, plug, cork, bung, spigot, spike, spile, vent-peg, stopcock, tap, stopgap, rammer, ramrod, piston, wad, dossil, wadding, tompion, stuffing, tourniquet.

Cover, lid, operculum, covering, covercle, door, etc. (222), valve.

A janitor, door-keeper, commissionaire, chucker-out, ostiary, concierge, porter, warder, beadle, Cerberus.

SECTION IV—MOTION

1°. *Motion in General*

264 MOTION (*Substantives*), movement, transit, transition, move, going, etc., passage, course, stir.

Step, gait, stride, tread, port, footfall, carriage, transference (270), locomotion, travel (266), voyage (267).

Mobility, restlessness, unrest, movability, movableness, inquietude, flux; kinematics.

(*Verbs*) To be moving, etc., to move, go, stir, hie, gang, budge, pass, flit, shift, glide, roll, roll on, flow (347, 348), sweep along, wander (279), change or shift one's place or quarters, dodge, keep going.

To put in motion, impel, etc. (276); to propel, project (284); to mobilize, motorize.

(*Adjectives*) Moving, in motion, on the move, going, transitional; kinematic.

Shifting, movable (270), mobile, restless, nomadic, wandering, vagrant, discursive, erratic (279), mercurial, unquiet.

(*Adverbs*) *In transitu*, under way, on the move.

———

265 QUIESCENCE (*Substantives*), rest, stillness, stagnation, stagnancy, fixedness, immobility, catalepsy, paralysis.

Quiet, quietness, quietude, tranquillity, calm, calmness, sedentariness, peace; steadiness, balance, equilibrium.

Pause, suspension, suspense, lull, stop, stoppage, interruption, stopping, stand, standstill, standing still, lying to, repose (687), respite.

Lock, deadlock, dead stop, embargo.

Resting-place, anchorage, moorings, bivouac, port (189, 666), bed, pillow, etc. (215).

(*Verbs*) To be quiescent, etc., to remain, stand, stand still, lie to, pull up, hold, halt, stop, anchor, stop short, stop dead, freeze, heave to, rest, pause, repose, keep quiet, take breath, stagnate, vegetate, settle; to mark time.

To stay, tarry, sojourn, dwell (186), pitch one's tent, cast anchor, settle, encamp, bivouac, moor, tether, picket, plant oneself, alight, land, etc. (292) ride at anchor.

(*Phrases*) Not to stir a peg (or step or inch); '*j'y suis, j'y reste*'; to come to a standstill; to come to a deadlock; to rest on one's oars or laurels.

To stop, suspend, arrest, lay to, hold one's hand, interrupt, intermit, discontinue (142), put a stop to, quell, becalm.

(*Phrases*) To bring to a standstill; to lay an embargo on.

(*Adjectives*) Quiescent, still, motionless, moveless, at rest, stationary, untravelled, stay-at-home, at a stand, at a standstill, stock-still, standing still, sedentary, undisturbed, unruffled, fast, stuck fast, fixed, transfixed, rooted, moored, aground, at anchor, tethered, becalmed, stagnant, quiet, calm, breathless, peaceful, unmoved, unstirred, immovable, immobile, restful, cataleptic, paralysed, frozen, irremovable, stable, steady, steadfast.

(*Phrases*) Still as a statue; still as a post; quiet or still as a mouse.

(*Interjections*) Soho! stop! stay! avast! belay! halt! as you were! hold hard! hold your horses! hold on! whoa!

266 Locomotion by land.

JOURNEY (*Substantives*), travel, travelling, excursion, expedition, tour, trip, trek, circuit, peregrination, discursion, ramble, outing, pilgrimage, Odyssey, course, ambulation, march, route march, marching, walk, walking, promenade, stroll, saunter, dander, turn, trot, tramp, hike, stalk, noctambulation, perambulation, ride, equitation, drive, jogtrot, airing, constitutional, spin, jaunt, joy-ride, change of scene.

Roving, vagrancy, flit, flitting, migration, emigration, immigration, intermigration; *Wanderlust*.

Map, plan, itinerary, road-book, guide, Baedeker, Bradshaw, A B C.

Procession, caravan, cavalcade, column, cortège.

Organs and instruments of locomotion, legs, feet, pins, stilt, skate, ski, snow-shoe, locomotive, vehicle (272, 273), velocipede, penny-farthing, bone-shaker, bicycle, cycle, bike, push cycle, tandem, tricycle, fairycycle, scooter.

(*Phrase*) Shanks's mare.

(*Verbs*) To travel, journey, trek, walk, ramble, roam, rove, course, wander, itinerate, perambulate, stroll, straggle, expatiate, range, gad about, gallivant, knock about, to go or take a walk, journey, tour, turn, trip, etc.; to prowl, stray, saunter, tour, make a tour, knock about, emigrate, flit, migrate.

To walk, march, counter-march, step, tread, pace, wend, wend one's way, promenade, perambulate, circumambulate, take a walk, go for a walk, take the air, trudge, trapes, stalk, stride, straddle, strut, foot it, hoof it, stump, clump, plod, peg along, bundle, toddle, patter, shuffle on,

267 Locomotion by water, or air, or through space.

NAVIGATION (*Substantives*), voyage, sail, cruise, Odyssey, circumnavigation, periplus, seafaring, yachting, boating; drifting, headway, sternway, leeway.

Natation, swimming, surf-riding.

Flight, flying, flip, volitation, aerostation, aeronautics, aerostatics, ballooning, aviation, gliding.

Space travel, astronautics.

Wing, pinion, fin, flipper; oar, scull, canvas, sail, rotor, paddle, punt-pole, paddle-wheel, screw, turbine, jet.

(*Verbs*) To sail, make sail, warp, put to sea, navigate, take ship, get under way, spread sail, spread canvas, carry sail, plough the waves, plough the deep, scud, boom, drift, course, cruise, coast, circumnavigate, aviate.

To row, pull, paddle, scull, punt, steam.

To swim, float, buffet the waves, skim, *effleurer*, dive, wade.

To fly, aviate, hedge-hop, be wafted, hover, soar, glide, wing; to flush.

(*Phrases*) To take wing; to take flight.

(*Adjectives*) Sailing, etc., seafaring, under way, under sail, on the wing, volant, nautical; airborne, aeronautic, aeronautical, aerostatic; astronautical.

(*Phrases*) In sail; under canvas.

tramp, hike, footslog, traverse, bend one's steps, thread one's way, make one's way, find one's way, tread a path, take a course, take wing, take flight, defile, file off.

Ride, jog on, trot, amble, canter, gallop, take horse, prance, frisk, tittup, caracole, have a run, ride and tie, hitch-hike, lorry-hop.

To drive, slide, glide, skim, skate, tobaggon, ski.

To go to, repair to, resort to, hie to.

(*Phrase*) To pad the hoof; to hump bluey.

(*Adjectives*) Travelling, etc., ambulatory, itinerant, wayfaring, peripatetic, discursive, vagrant, migratory, nomadic, on the wing, etc., circumforanean, overland.

(*Adverbs*) By the way, *chemin faisant*, on the road, *en passant*, *en route*, on foot, afoot.

268 TRAVELLER (*Substantives*), wayfarer, voyager, itinerant, passenger, commuter, tourist, tripper, excursionist, wanderer, rover, straggler, rambler, hiker, bird of passage, gad-about, globe-trotter, vagrant, tramp, hobo, bum, swagman, sundowner, vagabond, rolling-stone, nomad, pilgrim, hadji, palmer, runner, courier, pedestrian, peripatetic, emigrant, fugitive.

Rider, horseman, equestrian, cavalier, jockey, postilion, rough-rider, scout, motorist.

Mercury, Iris, Ariel.

269 MARINER (*Substantives*), navigator, seaman, sailor, seafarer, shipman, tar, old salt, bluejacket, marine, jolly, boatman, *voyageur*, ferryman, waterman, lighterman, bargee, gondolier, longshoreman, crew, oarsman.

An aerial navigator, aeronaut, balloonist, aviator, airman, flying man, pilot.

Astronaut, cosmonaut, spaceman.

————

270 TRANSFERENCE (*Substantives*), transfer, displacement, metathesis, transposition (148), remotion, removal (185), relegation, deportation, extradition, conveyance, draft, carriage, carrying, convection, conduction, export, import.

Transmission, passage, transit, transition, ferry, transport, gestation, portage, porterage, cartage, carting, shovelling, shipment, transhipment, air lift, air drop, freight, wafture, transportation, transumption, transplantation, transfusion, translation, shifting, dodging, dispersion (73), traction (285).

(*Verbs*) To transfer, convey, transmit, transport, transplant, transfuse, carry, bear, carry over, hand over, pass forward, remove (185), transpose (148), shift, export, import, convey, conduct, convoy, send, relegate, extradite, turn over to, deliver, waft, ship, tranship, ferry over.

To bring, fetch, reach, draft.

To load, lade, charge, unload, shovel, ladle, decant, empty, break bulk.

(*Adjectives*) Transferred, etc., movable, portable, portative.

(*Adverbs*) From hand to hand, on the way, *en route*, *en passant*, *in transitu*, from pillar to post.

271 CARRIER (*Substantives*), porter, bearer, coolie, *hammal*, conveyer, transport-worker, stevedore (690), conductor, locomotive (285).

Beast of burden, cattle, horse, blood-horse, arab, steed, nag, palfrey, galloway, charger, destrier, war-horse, courser, racer, racehorse, hunter, pony, filly, colt, foal, barb, jade, hack, *bidet*, pad, cob, tit, punch, roadster, goer, pack-horse, draught-horse, cart-horse, post-horse, shelty, jennet, bayard, mare, stallion, gelding, gee-gee, gee, stud.

Ass, donkey, moke, cuddy, jackass, mule, hinny, sumpter-mule.

Camel, dromedary, llama, zebra, reindeer, yak, elephant, carrier-pigeon.

272 VEHICLE (*Substantives*), conveyance.

Carriage, caravan, van, furniture van, pantechnicon, wagon, stage-wagon, wain, dray, cart, float, trolley, sledge, sleigh, bob-sleigh, *luge*, toboggan, truck, tumbril, pontoon, barrow, wheelbarrow, hand-barrow, lorry.

Train, railway train, goods train, freight train, rolling stock, Pullman car, parlour car, restaurant-car, dining-car, diner, buffet-car, sleeping-car, sleeper, horse-box, cattle-truck, rail-car, tender.

Equipage, turn-out, carriage, coach, chariot, chaise, post-chaise, phaeton, curricle, tilbury, whisky, victoria, landau, brougham, clarence, gig, calash, dog-cart, governess-cart, trap, buggy, carriole, jingle, wagonette, jaunting-car, shandrydan, droshky, kibitka, berlin, stage, stage-coach, diligence, car, omnibus, bus, charabanc, brake, cabriolet, cab, hackney cab, four-wheeler, growler, fly, hansom.

Motor-car, motor, automobile, autocar, touring-car, tourer, sports car, torpedo, landaulette, limousine, saloon, sedan, two-seater, runabout, coupé, jalopy, tricar, motor-cycle, side-car, autocycle, moped, corgi, motor-bus, motor-coach, autobus, taxi-cab, taxi, motor-van, jeep; trolley-bus, tram-car, tram, street-car.

Tank, armoured car, half-track, amtrac, duck.

Bath-chair, wheel-chair, sedan chair, palanquin (or palankeen), litter, jinricksha (or rickshaw), brancard, stretcher, perambulator, pram, mail-cart, bassinette, baby carriage.

Shovel, spoon, spatula, ladle, hod.

273 SHIP (*Substantives*), vessel, bottom, craft, shipping, marine, fleet, flotilla, squadron, three-master, barque (or bark), barquentine, brig, brigantine, schooner, sloop, cutter, skiff, yawl, ketch, smack, dogger,

hoy, lugger, barge, wherry, lighter, hulk, buss, packet, clipper, rotor ship.

Navy, armada, warship, man-of-war, ironclad, capital ship, super-dreadnought, dreadnought, battle-ship, battle-cruiser, cruiser, frigate, corvette, gunboat, aircraft-carrier, monitor, torpedo boat destroyer, destroyer, torpedo boat, mine-sweeper, mine-layer, submarine, Q-boat, troop-ship, trooper, transport, hsopital ship, flagship; ship of the line, first-rate, seventy-four, fireship.

Liner, merchantman, tramp, slaver, steamer, steamboat, steam-packet, paddle-steamer, stern-wheeler, screw-steamer, turbine, tender, tug, collier, whaler, coaster, tanker.

Argosy, bireme, trireme, quadrireme, quinquereme, galley, galleon, carrack, caravel, galliot, polacca, tartan, junk, praam, saic, dhow, proa, sampan, xebec.

Boat, motor-boat, long-boat, pinnace, launch, cabin cruiser, yacht, shallop, jolly-boat, gig, funny, dinghy, bumboat, fly-boat, wherry, coble, cock-boat, punt, cog, kedge, out-rigger, catamaran, fishing-boat, coracle, hooker, life-boat, gondola, felucca, dahabeeyah, caique, canoe, dug-out, raft, float.

(*Adverbs*) Afloat, aboard.

273A AIRCRAFT (*Substantives*), flying machine, aeroplane, monoplane, biplane, seaplane, hydroplane, plane, flying boat, amphibian, air-liner, flying wing, stratocruiser, stratoliner, sky-master, jet aircraft, jet, turbo-jet, autogiro, helicopter, hoverplane, whirlybird, planicopter, glider; fighter, bomber, fighter-bomber, flying fortress, super-fortress.

Balloon, air-balloon, aerostat, Montgolfier, pilot balloon, blimp, kite, airship, dirigible, Zeppelin.

Space ship, rocket, sputnik, lunik, satellite.

(*Adjective*) Airborne; orbital.

2°. *Degrees of Motion*

274 VELOCITY (*Substantives*), speed, celerity, swiftness, rapidity, fleetness, expedition, speediness, quickness, nimbleness, briskness, agility, promptness, promptitude (682), dispatch, acceleration (684).

Gallop, full gallop, canter, trot, run, rush, scamper, scoot, scorch, handgallop, lope; flight, dart, bolt, dash, spurt, sprint.

Haste, hurry, scurry, bounce, bolt, precipitation, precipitancy (684), forced march, race, steeplechase, Marathon race.

Rate, pace, step, gait, course, progress.

Lightning, light, cannon-ball, bullet, wind, rocket, arrow, dart, quicksilver, telegraph, express train, clipper.

An eagle, antelope, doe, courser, racehorse, racer, gazelle, greyhound, hare, squirrel, bandersnatch.

Mercury, Ariel, Camilla.

Speed indicator, speedometer, tachometer, log, log-line.

(*Verbs*) To move quickly; to trip, speed, haste, hie, hasten, hurry, fly, press, press on, press forward, post, push on, whip, scamper, run, sprint, race, scud, scour, scurry, scuttle, spin, scoot, scorch, rip, clip, shoot, tear, whisk, sweep, skim, brush, glance, cut along, dash on, dash forward, trot, gallop, lope, rush, bound, bounce, flounce, frisk, tittup, bolt, flit, spring, boom, dart.

To hasten, accelerate, expedite, dispatch, urge, whip, forward, buck up, express, speed-up, hurry, precipitate, quicken pace, gather way, ride hard.

To keep up with, keep pace with, race, race with, outpace, outmarch, distance, outdistance, lap, leave behind, outrun, outstrip, gain ground.

(*Phrases*) To cover the ground; to clap on sail; take to one's heels; clap spurs to one's horse; to run like mad; ride hard; outstrip the wind; to make rapid strides; wing one's way; be off like a shot; run a race; stir one's stumps; do a scoot; get a move on; get cracking; step on it; give her the gun; let it rip.

275 SLOWNESS (*Substantives*), tardiness, dilatoriness, slackness, lentor, languor (683), drawl.

Hobbling, creeping, lounging, etc., shambling, claudication, halting, walk, amble, jog-trot, dog-trot, mincing steps, foot-pace, crawl.

A slow-goer, dawdle, dawdler, lingerer, slow-coach, lame duck, drone, tortoise, snail, slug, sluggard, slacker.

Retardation, slackening, slowing down, delay (133).

(*Verbs*) To move slowly, to creep, crawl, lag, slug, drawl, dawdle, linger, loiter (683), plod, trudge, flag, saunter, lounge, lumber, trail, drag, grovel, glide, laze, amble, steal along, inch along, jog on, rub on, bundle on, toddle, waddle, shuffle, halt, hobble, limp, claudicate, shamble, mince, falter, totter, stagger.

To retard, slacken, relax, check, rein in, curb, strike sail, reef, slow up, slow down.

(*Phrases*) To 'drag its slow length along'; to hang fire; to march in slow time, in funeral procession; to lose ground.

To put on the drag; apply the brake; clip the wings; take in sail; take one's time; ca' canny; *festina lente*.

(*Adjectives*) Slow, slack, tardy, dilatory, easy, gentle, leisurely, deliberate, lazy, languid, drowsy, sleepy, heavy, drawling, leaden, sluggish, snail-like, creeping, crawling, etc., dawdling, lumbering, hobbling, tardigrade.

(*Adverbs*) Slowly, etc., gingerly, softly, leisurely, deliberately, gradually, etc. (144), *piano, adagio, largo*.

(*Phrases*) In slow motion; just ticking over; under easy sail; at a snail's pace; with mincing steps; with clipped wings; by degrees; little by little; inch by inch.

(*Adjectives*) Fast, speedy, swift, rapid, full-drive, quick, double-quick, fleet, nimble, agile, expeditious, prompt, brisk, frisky, hasty, hurried, flying, etc., precipitate, furious, light-footed, nimble-footed, winged, eagle-winged, mercurial, electric, telegraphic, light-legged; accelerative.

(*Phrases*) Swift as an arrow, as a doe, as a lamplighter; off like a shot; quick as lightning; quick as thought.

(*Adverbs*) Swiftly, with speed, speedily, trippingly, etc., full-tilt, full speed, apace, post-haste, *presto*, tantivy, by express, by telegraph, slap, slap-dash, headlong, hurry-scurry, hand over hand, at a round trot.

(*Phrases*) Under press of sail, or canvas; *velis et remis*; on eagle's wings; at the double, in double-quick time; with giant, or gigantic steps; *à pas de géant*; in seven-league boots; whip and spur; *ventre à terre*; as fast as one's legs or heels will carry one; *sauve qui peut*; the devil take the hindmost; *vires acquirit eundo*; with rapid strides; at top speed; on top gear; flat out; all out; like greased lightning; like the wind.

3°. Motion conjoined with Force

276 IMPULSE (*Substantives*), momentum, impetus, push, impulsion, thrust, shove, fling, jog, jolt, brunt, throw, volley, explosion (173), propulsion (284).

Percussion, collision, concussion, impact, clash, encounter, cannon, carom, carambole, appulse, shock, crash, bump, charge, tackle (716), foul.

Blow, stroke, knock, tap, fillip, pat, rap, dab, dig, jab, smack, slap, hit, putt, cuff, bang, crack, whack, thwack, slog, belt, wipe, clout, swipe, clip, squash, dowse, punch, thump, pelt, kick, lunge, buffet, beating (972).

Hammer, mallet, mall, maul, beetle, flail, cudgel, bludgeon, life-preserver, cosh, baton, truncheon, knobkerrie, shillelagh, staff, lathi, cane, stick, club, racket, bat, driver, brassy, baffy, spoon, putter, cleek, iron, mashie, niblick, ram, battering-ram, monkey-engine, catapult, pile-driver, rammer, sledge-hammer, steam hammer.

Dynamics; seismometer.

(*Verbs*) To impel, push, give impetus, etc., drive, urge, hurtle, boom, thrust, elbow, shoulder, charge, tackle, jostle, justle, hustle, shove, jog, jolt, encounter, collide, clash, cannon, foul.

To strike, knock, tap, slap, dab, pat, slam, hit, bat, putt, rap, prod, jerk, dig, cuff, smite, butt, impinge, thump, bethump, beat, bang, whang, biff, punch, thwack, whack, spank, skelp, swat, lay into, shin, slog, clout, wipe, swipe, batter, dowse, baste, pummel, pelt, patter, drub, buffet, belabour, cane, whip (972), poke at, hoof, jab, pink, lunge, kick, recalcitrate.

To throw, etc. (284), to set going, mobilize.

(*Adjectives*) Impelling, etc., impulsive, impellent, impelled, etc., dynamic, dynamical.

(*Interjections*) Bang! boom! wham!

277 RECOIL (*Substantives*), retro-action, revulsion, reaction, rebound, bounce, stot, repercussion, ricochet, rebuff, reverberation, reflux, reflex, kick, springing back, ducks and drakes.

A boomerang, spring (325).

(*Verbs*) To recoil, react, spring back, fly back, bound back, rebound, stot, reverberate, repercuss.

(*Adjectives*) Recoiling, etc., on the recoil, etc., refluent, repercussive, reactionary, retroactive.

(*Phrase*) On the rebound.

4°. *Motion with reference to Direction*

278 DIRECTION (*Substantives*), bearing, course, route, bent, inclination, drift, tenor, tendency, incidence, set, leaning, bending, trend, dip, steerage, tack, steering, aim, alignment (or alinement), orientation, collimation.

A line, bee-line, path, road, aim, range, quarter, point of the compass, rhumb, great circle, azimuth, line of collimation.

(*Verbs*) To tend towards, go to, point to, or at; trend, verge, align (or aline), incline, conduct to, determine.

To make for, or towards, aim at, take aim, level at, steer for, keep or hold a course, be bound for, bend one's steps towards, direct or shape one's course.

To ascertain one's direction, orient (or orientate) oneself, to see which way the wind blows.

(*Adjectives*) Directed, etc., direct, straight, undeviating, unswerving, aligned (or alined) with, determinate, point-to-point.

(*Adverbs*) Towards, to, *versus*, thither, directly, straight, point-blank, full tilt at, whither, in a line with, as the crow flies.

By way of, via, in all directions, *quaquaversum*, in all manner of ways, to the four winds.

---

279 DEVIATION (*Substantives*), swerving, aberration, obliquation, *ambages*, warp, bending, flexion, deflection, refraction, sidling, side-slip, skid, half-roll, barrel-roll, loop, straying, straggling, warping, etc., digression, circuit, detour, departure from, divergence (291), desultory motion; slice, pull, hook, leg-break, off-break, googly.

Motion sideways, side-step.

(*Verbs*) To alter one's course, divert, deviate, depart from, turn, bend, swerve, break, switch, skid, side-slip, zoom, bank, loop, bunt, jib, shift, warp, stray, straggle, sidle, diverge (291), digress, wander, meander, veer, wear, tack, yaw, turn aside, turn a corner, turn away from, face about, wheel, wheel about, steer clear of, ramble, rove, go astray, step aside, shunt, side-track, jay walk.

(*Phrases*) To fly off at a tangent; to face to the right-about; to go out of one's way; to lose one's way.

(*Adjectives*) Deviating, etc., aberrant, discursive, devious, desultory, erratic, vagrant, stray, undirected, circuitous, roundabout, crab-like, zigzag.

(*Adverbs*) Astray from, round about.

(*Phrases*) To the right-about; all manner of ways; like the knight's move in chess.

---

280 Going before.
PRECESSION (*Substantives*), leading, heading.

Precedence in order (62), priority (116), precursor (64), front (234).

(*Verbs*) To precede, forerun, lead, head, herald, introduce, usher in (62), go ahead.

(*Phrases*) Go in the van; take the lead; lead the way; open the ball; have the start; to get before; steal a march.

(*Adjectives*) Preceding, leading, etc.

(*Adverbs*) In advance, before (62), in the van, ahead.

---

281 Going after.
SEQUENCE (*Substantives*), following, pursuit, chase, hunt (622).

A follower, pursuer, attendant, shadow, satellite, hanger-on, train.

Sequence in order (63), in time (117).

(*Verbs*) To follow, pursue, chase, hunt, hound, shadow, dog, tail, trail, lag.

(*Phrases*) Go in the rear, or in the wake of; tread in the steps of; tread on the heels of; go after; fly after; to follow as a shadow; to lag behind; to bring up the rear; to fall behind; to tail off.

(*Adjectives*) Following, etc.

(*Adverbs*) Behind, in the rear, etc.

282 Motion forwards.

PROGRESSION (*Substantives*), advance, advancement, progress (658), on-going, progressiveness, progressive motion, flood-tide, headway, advancing, etc., pursuit, steeplechase (622), journey, march (266).

(*Verbs*) To advance, proceed, progress, go, move, bend or pass forward, go on, move on, pass on, get on, get along, jog on, push on, go one's way, go ahead, forge ahead, make head, make way, make headway, work one's way, press forward, edge forward, get over the ground, gain ground, make progress, keep or hold on one's course, keep up with, get forward, distance.

(*Phrases*) To make up leeway; to go with the stream; to make rapid strides; to push or elbow or cleave one's way; to go full tilt at.

(*Adjectives*) Advancing, etc., progressive, go-ahead, avant-garde, profluent, undeviating.

(*Adverbs*) Forward, onward, forth, on, in advance, ahead, under way, straightforward.

(*Phrases*) *Vestigia nulla retrorsum; en avant.*

283 Motion backwards.

REGRESSION (*Substantives*), regress, recess, retrogression, retrogradation, retreat, withdrawal, retirement, recession (287), refluence, reflux, retroaction, return, reflexion, reflex (277), ebb, countermovement, countermarch, veering, regurgitation, backwash.

(*Verbs*) To recede, retrograde, return, rebound, back, fall back, fall or drop astern, lose ground, put about, go back, turn back, hark back, double, countermarch, turn tail, draw back, get back, retrace one's steps, wheel about, back water, regurgitate, yield, give.

(*Phrases*) Dance the back step; beat a retreat.

(*Adjectives*) Receding, etc., retrograde, retrogressive, regressive, refluent, reflex, recidivous, resilient.

(*Adverbs*) Backwards, reflexively, to the right-about, about turn, *à reculons, à rebours.*

(*Phrase*) *Revenons à nos moutons.*

---

284 Motion given to an object in front.

PROPULSION (*Substantives*), push, pushing (276), projection, jaculation, ejaculation, throw, fling, fillip, toss, shot, discharge, shy.

Ballistics, gunnery; *vis a tergo.*

Missile, projectile, shot, shell, ball, bolt, dart, arrow, bullet, stone, shaft, brickbat, discus, quoit, caber.

Bow, sling, pea-shooter, catapult, etc. (727).

(*Verbs*) To propel, project, throw, fling, cast, pitch, chuck, bung, toss, lob, loft, jerk, jaculate, ejaculate, hurl, boost, bolt, drive, sling, flirt, flip, flick, shy, dart, send, roll, send

285 Motion given to an object behind.

TRACTION (*Substantives*), drawing, draught, pull, pulling, towage, haulage.

Traction engine, locomotive; hauler, haulyer, tractor, tug; trailer.

(*Phrase*) A long pull, a strong pull, and a pull all together.

(*Verbs*) To draw, pull, haul, lug, drag, tug, tow, trail, train, wrench, jerk, twitch, yank.

(*Phrase*) To take in tow.

(*Adjectives*) Drawing, etc., tractile.

---

off, let off, discharge, fire off, shoot, launch, let fly, dash, punt, volley, heave, pitchfork.

To bowl, trundle, roll along (312).

To put in motion, start, give an impulse, impel (276), expel (297).

(*Phrases*) To carry off one's feet; to put to flight.

(*Adjectives*) Propelling, etc., propulsive, projectile, etc.

286 Motion towards.
APPROACH (*Substantives*), approximation, appropinquation, access, appulse, afflux, affluxion, pursuit (622), collision (276), arrival (292).

(*Verbs*) To approach, draw near, approximate, to near; to come, get, go, etc., near; to set in towards, make up to, snuggle up to, gain upon, gain ground upon.

(*Phrases*) To tread on the heels of; to hug the shore.

(*Adjectives*), Approaching, etc., approximative.

287 Motion from.
RECESSION (*Substantives*), retirement, withdrawal, retreat, retrocession (283), departure (293), recoil (277), decampment, flight, stampede, skedaddle.

A runaway, a fugitive.

(*Verbs*) To recede, go, move or fly from, retire, retreat, withdraw, come away, go or get away, draw back, shrink, move away.

To move off, stand off, draw off, buzz off, fall back, turn tail, march off, decamp, absquatulate, skedaddle, vamoose, sheer off, bolt, scram, hop it, beat it, slip away, run away, pack off, fly, remove, abscond, sneak off, slink away.

(*Phrases*) To take French leave; to cut and run; take to one's heels; to give leg-bail; take one's hook; *sauve qui peut*; the devil take the hindmost; beat a retreat; make oneself scarce; do a bolt; do a guy; make tracks; cut one's lucky.

(*Adjectives*) Receding, etc., fugitive, runaway (671).

288 Motion towards, actively.
ATTRACTION (*Substantives*), drawing to, pulling towards, adduction, attractiveness, magnetism, gravity, gravitation.

A loadstone, magnet.

(*Verbs*) To attract, draw, pull, drag, etc., towards, adduce.

(*Adjectives*) Attracting, etc., adducent, attrahent, adductive, attractive, magnetic, gravitational.

(*Interjections*) Come! come here! approach! come near!

289 Motion from, actively.
REPULSION (*Substantives*), push (276), driving from, repulse, expulsion (297).

(*Verbs*) To repel, repulse; push, drive, etc., from, drive away, cold-shoulder, send packing.

(*Phrases*) To give the frozen mitt to; send away with a flea in one's ear; send to the right-about (678).

(*Adjectives*) Repelling, etc., repellent, repulsive, forbidding.

(*Interjections*) Get out! be off! scram! avaunt! (293, 297).

290 Motion nearer to.
CONVERGENCE (*Substantives*), appulse, meeting, confluence, concourse, conflux, congress, concurrence, concentration.

Resort, assemblage, synod (72), focus (74), asymptote.

(*Verbs*) To converge, come together, unite, meet, fall in with, close in upon, centre in, enter in, meet, come across, come up against.

To gather together, unite, concentrate, etc.

291 Motion farther off.
DIVERGENCE (*Substantives*), aberration, peregrination, wandering, divarication, radiation, ramification, separation (44), dispersion, diffusion, dissemination (73); deviation (279).

(*Verbs*) To diverge, divaricate, deviate, wander, stray (279), radiate, branch off, ramify, file off, draw aside.

To spread, disperse, scatter, distribute, decentralize, diffuse, disseminate, shed, sow broadcast, broadcast, sprinkle.

(*Adjectives*) Converging, etc., convergent, confluent, concurring, concurrent, centripetal, asymptotical.

---

292 Terminal motion at.

ARRIVAL (*Substantives*), advent, reception, welcome, return, disembarkation, debarkation, remigration.

Home, goal, resting-place, destination, journey's end, harbour, haven, port, dock, pier, landing-place, landing-stage, landing-ground, airfield, airstrip, airstop, airport, aerodrome, helidrome, terminus, station.

Meeting, rencontre, rencounter, encounter.

Caller, visitor, visitant, guest.

(*Verbs*) To arrive, get to, come, come to, reach, attain, come up with, come up to, catch up, make, fetch, overtake, overhaul.

To light, alight, land, dismount, disembark, debark, detrain, outspan, debus, put in, put into, visit, cast, anchor.

To come upon, light upon, pitch upon, hit, drop in, pop upon, bounce upon, plump upon, bump against, run against, run across, close with.

To come back, return, get back, get home, sit down.

To meet, encounter, rencounter, contact, come in contact (199).

(*Phrase*) To be in at the death.

(*Adjectives*) Arriving, etc., homeward bound.

(*Adverbs*) Here, hither.

(*Interjections*) Welcome! hallo! hail! all hail! good day! good morrow! *ave!*

To part, part company, turn away from, wander from, separate (44).

(*Phrase*) To go or fly off at a tangent.

(*Adjectives*) Diverging, etc., divergent, radiant, wandering, aberring, aberrant, centrifugal.

(*Adverb*) Broadcast.

293 Initial motion from.

DEPARTURE (*Substantives*), outset, removal, exit, exodus, decampment, embarkation, flight, hegira.

Valediction, adieu, farewell, goodbye, leave-taking, send-off; stirrupcup, doch-an-doris, one for the road.

A starting point or post, place of departure or embarkation, airfield, terminus, etc. (292).

(*Phrase*) The foot being in the stirrup.

(*Verbs*) To depart, go, set out, set off, start, start off, issue, go forth, sally, debouch, sally forth, set forward, be off, move off, pack off, buzz off, scram, begone, get off, sheer off, clear out, vamoose, skedaddle, absquatulate.

To leave a place, quit, retire, withdraw, go one's way, take wing, flit, embus, inspan, entrain, embark, go on board, set sail, put to sea, weigh anchor, slip cable, decamp (671).

(*Phrases*) To take leave; bid or take adieu; bid farewell; to say goodbye; make one's exit; take a run-out powder.

(*Adjectives*) Departing, etc., valedictory, outward bound.

(*Adverbs*) Whence, hence, thence.

(*Interjections*) Be off! get out! clear out! scram! buzz off! hop it! beat it! begone! get you gone! go along! off with you! avaunt! away with you! go about your business!

Good-bye! bye-bye! 'bye! ta ta! farewell! fare you well! adieu! *au revoir! auf wiedersehen! a rivederci!* bon voyage! vale! hasta la vista! sayonara! so long! cheerio! chin-chin! tinkety-tonk! pip-pip! tootle-oo! bung-ho!

294 Motion into.

INGRESS (*Substantives*), ingoing, entrance, entry, introgression, admission, admittance, intromission,

295 Motion out of.

EGRESS (*Substantives*), exit, issue, emersion, emergence.

Exudation, extravasation, transu-

introduction, insinuation, insertion (300), intrusion, inroad, incursion, influx, irruption, invasion, penetration, interpenetration, infiltration, import, importation, illapse, immigration.

A mouth, door (260); an entrant.

(*Verbs*) To enter, go into, come into, set foot in, intrude, invade, flow into, pop into, insinuate itself, penetrate, interpenetrate, infiltrate, soak into; to put into, etc., bring in, insert, drive in, run in, wedge in, ram in (300), intromit, introduce, import, smuggle.

(*Phrases*) To find one's way into; creep into; worm oneself into; to darken one's door; have the *entrée*; to open the door to.

(*Adjectives*) Ingoing, incoming, penetrative, penetrant.

(*Adverb*) Inwards.

---

296 Motion into, actively.

RECEPTION (*Substantives*), admission, admittance, importation, immission, introduction, ingestion, imbibition, absorption, resorption, ingurgitation, inhalation (300).

Eating, swallowing, deglutition, devouring, gulp, gulping, gorge, gorging, carousal.

Drinking, potation, sipping, supping, suction, sucking, draught, libation; smoking, snuffing.

Mastication, manducation, rumination, chewing; hippophagy, ichthyophagy, anthropophagy.

(*Verbs*) To admit, receive, intromit, import, ingest, absorb, resorb, imbibe, inhale, let in, take in, readmit, resorb, reabsorb, snuff up, sop up, suck, suck in, swallow, take down, ingurgitate, engulf.

To eat, fare, feed, devour, tuck in, gulp, bolt, snap, get down, pick, peck, gorge, engorge, fall to, stuff, cram, gobble, guttle, guzzle, wolf, raven, eat heartily, do justice to, overeat, gormandize (957), dispatch, discuss.

To feed upon, live on, feast upon,

dation (348), leakage, seepage, percolation, distillation, oozing, effluence, efflux, effusion, drain, dropping, dripping, dribbling, drip, dribble, drainage, filtering, defluxion, trickling, eruption, outbreak, outburst, outpouring, gush (348), emanation, aura.

Export, expatriation, emigration, remigration, repatriation, exodus (293).

An outlet, vent, spout, tap, faucet, sluice, flue, chimney, pore, drain, sewer (350).

(*Verbs*) To emerge, emanate, issue, go, come, move, pass, pour, flow, etc., out of, find vent, pass off, evacuate.

To transude, exude, leak, seep, well out, percolate, transcolate, strain, distil, drain, ooze, filter, filtrate, dribble, trickle, drizzle, drip, gush, spout, run, flow out, effuse, extravasate, disembogue, debouch (348).

(*Adjectives*) Dripping, outgoing, etc., oozy, leaky, trickly, dribbly.

---

297 Motion out of, actively.

EJECTION (*Substantives*), emission, effusion, rejection, expulsion, detrusion, extrusion, eviction.

Discharge, egestion, evacuation, vomition, eructation, belch; bloodletting, venesection, phlebotomy, tapping.

Deportation, exile, rustication, banishment, relegation, extradition.

(*Phrases*) The rogue's march; the bum's rush.

(*Verbs*) To emit, eject, expel, export, reject, discharge, give out, let out, cast out, clear out, sweep out, clean out, gut, fillet, wipe off, turn out, chuck out, elbow out, kick out, hoof out, sack, dismiss, bounce, drive out, root out, pour out, ooze, shed, void, evacuate, disgorge, extrude, empty, detrude, throw off, spit, spit out, expectorate, spirt, spill, slop, drain.

To vomit, spue, cat, puke, cast up, keck, retch, spatter, splutter, slobber, slaver, slabber, squirt, eructate, belch, burp, give vent to, tap, broach, open the sluices, heave out, bale out, shake off.

regale, carouse, batten upon, fatten upon, dine, etc., browse, graze, crop, chew, champ, munch, gnaw, nibble, crunch, ruminate, masticate, manducate, mumble.

To drink, quaff, swill, swig, booze, drench, sip, sup, lap, drink up, drain up, toss off, drain the cup, tipple (959).

(*Phrases*) To give entrance or admittance to; open the door to; usher in.

To refresh the inner man; restore one's tissues; play a good knife and fork; get outside of; wrap oneself round.

To drink one's fill; wet one's whistle; empty one's glass; crook or lift one's elbow; crack a bottle.

(*Adjectives*) Admitting, etc., admitted, etc., admissible; absorbent, absorptive.

Hippophagous, ichthyophagous, anthropophagous, herbivorous, graminivorous, granivorous, omnivorous.

To throw, project (284); to push, thrust (276).

To unpack, unlade, unload (270).

To banish, exile, extradite, deport; ostracize, boycott, send to Coventry.

(*Phrases*) To send packing; to send to the right about; to send about one's business; to give the sack to; to show the door to; to turn out neck and crop; to make a clean sweep of; to send away with a flea in one's ear.

(*Adjectives*) Emitting, etc., emitted, etc.

(*Interjections*) Be off! get out! scram! (293), scat! fade! chase yourself! *allez-vous-en!*

298 FOOD (*Substantives*), pabulum, aliment, nourishment, nutriment, sustenance, sustentation, nurture, subsistence, provender, fodder, provision, prey, forage, pasture, pasturage, keep, fare, cheer, rations, diet, regimen.

Comestibles, eatables, victuals, prog, grub, chow, chuck, toke, eats, meat, bread, breadstuffs, cake, pastry, viands, cates, delicacy, delicatessen, dainty, creature comforts, bellytimber, staff of life, dish, flesh-pots, pottage, pudding, ragout, omelet, sundae, kickshaws.

299 EXCRETION (*Substantives*), discharge, emanation, exhalation, exudation, secretion, extrusion, effusion, extravasation, evacuation, faeces, excrement (653), perspiration, sweat, saliva, salivation, spittle, diaphoresis; bleeding, haemorrhage, flux.

(*Verbs*) To emanate, exhale, excern, excrete, exude, effuse, secrete, secern, extravasate, evacuate, urinate, discharge, etc. (297).

Table, board, commons, good cheer, bill of fare, menu, commissariat, table d'hôte, ordinary, cuisine.

Canteen, Naffy, restaurant, chop-house, café, cafeteria, eating-house, tea-room, tea-shop, coffee-house, coffee-stall, bar, milk bar, snack bar, public-house, pot-house, ale-house, wineshop, brasserie, bodega, tavern (189).

Meal, repast, feed, mess, spread, course, regale, regalement, entertainment, feast, banquet, junket, refreshment, refection; breakfast, *chota hazri*, elevenses, *déjeuner*, lunch, bever, luncheon, tiffin, tea, afternoon tea, five-o'clock tea, high tea, dinner, supper, whet, appetizer, aperitif, bait, dessert, *entremet*, *hors d'œuvre*, picnic, bottle-party, wayzgoose, beanfeast, blow-out, tuck-in, snack, pot-luck table d'hôte, *déjeuner à la fourchette*.

Mouthful, bolus, gobbet, sip, sup, sop, tot, snort, hoot, dram, peg, cocktail (615), nip, *chasse*, liqueur.

Drink, hard drink, soft drink, tipple, beverage, liquor, broth, soup, etc., symposium.

(*Phrases*) A good tuck-in; a modest quencher.

(*Adjectives*) Eatable, edible, esculent, comestible, alimentary, cereal, culinary, nutritious, nutritive, nutrient, nutrimental, succulent, potable, drinkable.

298A TOBACCO, the weed, bacca, baccy, honeydew, cavendish, bird's-eye, shag, virginia, latakia, perique, plug, twist.

Cigar, segar, cheroot, havana, manila, weed, whiff, cigarette, fag, gasper, stinker, coffin-nail.

Snuff, rappee.

A smoke, draw, puff, pinch, quid, chew, chaw.

Tobacco-pipe, pipe, briar, meerschaum, calabash, corncob, clay pipe, clay, churchwarden, dudeen (or dudheen), cutty, hookah, hubble-bubble, chibouque, narghile, calumet.

(*Verbs*) To smoke, chew, take snuff.

(*Adjective*) Nicotian.

300 Forcible ingress.

INSERTION (*Substantives*), putting in, implantation, introduction, interjection, insinuation, planting, intercalation, embolism, injection, inoculation, vaccination, importation, intervention (228), dovetailing, tenon, wedge.

Immersion, dip, plunge, bath (337), submergence, submersion, souse, duck, soak.

Interment, burying, etc. (363).

(*Verbs*) To insert, introduce, intromit, put into, import, throw in, interlard, inject, interject, intercalate, infuse, instil, inoculate, vaccinate, pasteurize, impregnate, imbue, imbrue, graft, engraft, bud, plant, implant, embed, obtrude, foist in, worm in, thrust in, stick in, ram in, stuff in, tuck in, plough in, let in, dovetail, mortise (or mortice), insinuate, wedge in, press in, impact, drive in, run in, empierce (260).

301 Forcible egress.

EXTRACTION (*Substantives*), taking out, removal, elimination, extrication, evulsion, avulsion, eradication, extirpation, wrench.

Expression, squeezing; ejection (297).

Extractor, corkscrew, pincers, pliers, forceps.

(*Verbs*) To extract, take out, draw, draw out, pull out, tear out, pluck out, extort, wring from, prise, wrench, sake out, rake up, grub up, root up, uproot, eradicate, extirpate, dredge, remove, get out (185), elicit, extricate, eliminate.

To express, squeeze out, wring out, pick out, disembowel, eviscerate, exenterate.

(*Adjectives*) Extracted, etc.

To immerse, dip, steep, immerge, merge, submerge, bathe, plunge, drop in, souse, douse, soak, duck, drown.

To inter, bury, etc. (363).

(*Adjectives*) Inserting, inserted, implanted, embedded, etc., ingrowing.

302 Motion through.

PASSAGE (*Substantives*), transmission, permeation, penetration, interpenetration (294), filtration, infiltration, percolation, transudation, osmosis (or osmose), capillary attraction, endosmosis (or endosmose), exosmosis (or exosmose), intercurrence; way, path (627); channel, pipe (350).

Terebration, impalement, etc. (260).

(*Verbs*) To pass, pass through, traverse, terebrate, stick, pierce, impale, spear, spike, spit (260), penetrate, percolate, permeate, thread, thrid, enfilade, go through, cross, go across, go over, pass over, get over, clear, negotiate, cut across, pass and repass; work, thread or worm one's way, force a passage; to transmit.

(*Adjectives*) Passing, intercurrent, penetrative, transudatory, etc.

303 Motion beyond.

TRANSCURSION (*Substantives*), transilience, transgression, trespass, encroachment, infringement, extravagation, transcendence, enjambement, overrunning.

(*Verbs*) To transgress, overstep, surpass, overpass, overrun, overgo, beat, outstrip, outgo, outstep, outrun, outdo, overreach, overleap, outleap, pass, go by, strain, overshoot the mark, overjump, overskip, overlap, go beyond, outpace, outmarch, transcend, distance, outdistance, lap, encroach, exceed, trespass, infringe, trench upon.

(*Phrases*) To stretch a point; to steal a march on; to pass the Rubicon; to shoot ahead of; to throw into the shade.

(*Adverbs*) Beyond the mark, out of bounds.

304 Motion short of.

SHORTCOMING (*Substantives*), failure, falling short (732), defalcation, default, backlog, leeway, incompleteness (53); imperfection (651); insufficiency (640).

(*Verbs*) To come or fall short of, not to reach, keep within bounds, keep within compass, to stop short, be wanting, lose ground, miss the mark.

(*Adjectives*) Unreached, deficient (53), short, minus.

(*Adverbs*) Within the mark, within compass, within bounds, etc., behindhand.

305 Motion upwards.

ASCENT (*Substantives*), rise, climb, ascension, upgrowth, leap (309).

A rocket, sky-rocket, lark, skylark; a climber, mountaineer, Alpinist, stegophilist.

(*Verbs*) To ascend, rise, mount, arise, uprise, go up, get up, climb, clamber, swarm, shin, scale, scramble, escalade, surmount, aspire.

To tower, soar, zoom, hover, spire, plane, swim, float, surge.

(*Phrase*) To make one's way up.

(*Adjectives*) Rising, etc., scandent, buoyant, floating, supernatant, superfluitant.

(*Adverbs*) Uphill, on the up grade.

(*Interjection*) Excelsior!

306 Motion downwards.

DESCENT (*Substantives*), fall, descension, declension, declination, drop, cadence, subsidence, lapse, downfall, tumble, tilt, toppling, trip, lurch, *culbute*, spill, cropper, purler, crash.

Titubation, shamble, shambling, stumble.

An avalanche, landslip, landslide, debacle, slump.

(*Phrase*) The fate of Icarus.

(*Verbs*) To descend, come or go down, fall, sink, gravitate, drop, drop down, droop, decline, come down, dismount, alight, light, settle, subside, slide, slip, slither, glissade, toboggan, coast, volplane, dive (310).

To tumble, slip, trip, stumble, pitch, lurch, swag, topple, topple over, swoop, tilt, sprawl, plump down, measure one's length, bite the dust, heel over, careen (217), slump, crash.

To alight, dismount, get down.

(*Adjectives*) Descending, etc., descendent, decurrent, decursive, deciduous.

(*Phrase*) Nodding to its fall.

(*Adverbs*) Downhill, on the down grade.

307 ELEVATION (*Substantives*), raising, lifting, erection, lift, uplift, upheaval, upcast.

Lift, elevator, hoist, escalator, crane, derrick, winch, windlass, jack, lever.

(*Verbs*) To elevate, raise, lift, uplift, upraise, set up, erect, stick up, rear, uprear, upbear, upcast, hoist, uphoist, heave, upheave, weigh, exalt, promote, give a lift, help up, prick up, perk up.

To drag up, fish up, dredge.

To stand up, rise up, ramp.

(*Phrases*) To set on a pedestal; to get up on one's hind legs.

(*Adjectives*) Elevated, etc., rampant.

(*Adverbs*) On stilts, on the shoulders of.

---

309 LEAP (*Substantives*), jump, hop, spring, bound, vault, saltation.

Dance, caper, curvet, caracole, *entrechat*, gambade, gambado, capriole, dido, demivolt.

Kangaroo, jerboa, chamois, goat, frog, grasshopper, flea, buck-jumper.

(*Phrases*) Hop, skip, and jump; on the light fantastic toe.

(*Verbs*) To leap, jump, bound, spring, take off, buck, buck-jump, hop, skip, vault, dance, bob, curvet, romp, caracole, caper, cut capers.

(*Adjectives*) Leaping, etc., saltatory, Terpsichorean, frisky.

308 DEPRESSION (*Substantives*), lowering, abasement, abasing, detrusion, reduction.

Overthrow, upset, prostration, subversion, overset, overturn, precipitation.

Bow, curtsy (or curtsey), genuflexion, obeisance, kowtow, salaam.

(*Verbs*) To depress, lower, let down, take down, sink, debase, abase, reduce, demote, detrude, let fall, cast down, to grass, send to grass.

To overthrow, overturn, upset, overset, subvert, prostrate, level, raze, fell; cast, take, throw, fling, dash, pull, cut, knock, hew, etc., down.

To stoop, bend, bow, curtsy (or curtsey), bob, duck, kneel, crouch, cower, lout, kowtow, salaam, bend the head or knee; to recline, sit, sit down, couch, squat.

(*Phrases*) To take down a peg; to pull about one's ears; to trample in the dust.

(*Adjectives*) Depressed, sunk, prostrate.

---

310 PLUNGE (*Substantives*), dip, dive, ducking, header.

Diver, frogman.

(*Verbs*) To plunge, dip, souse, duck, dive, plump, plop, submerge, submerse, bathe, douse, sink, engulf, founder.

---

311 Curvilinear motion.

CIRCUITION (*Substantives*), turn, wind, circuit, curvet, detour, excursion, circumbendibus, circumvention, circumnavigation, north-west passage, circulation.

Turning, winding, twist, twisting, wrench, evolution, twining, coil, circumambulation, meandering.

(*Verbs*) To turn, bend, wheel, put about, switch, circle, go round, or round about, circumnavigate, circumambulate, turn a corner, double a point, wind, meander, whisk, twirl, twist (248), twill; to turn on one's heel.

(*Phrases*) To lead a pretty dance; to go the round; to turn on one's heel.

(*Adjectives*) Turning, etc., circuitous, circumforaneous, circumfluent.

(*Adverb*) Round about.

312 Motion in a continued circle.

ROTATION (*Substantives*), revolution, gyration, roll, circumrotation, circumgyration, gurgitation, pirouette, circumvolution, convolution, turbination, whir, whirl, eddy, vortex, whirlpool, cyclone, anticyclone, tornado, typhoon, whirlwind, willy-willy, waterspout, surge, dizzy round, maelstrom, Charybdis.

A wheel, flywheel, screw, reel, whirligig, rolling stone, windmill, top, teetotum, merry-go-round, roundabout, gyroscope, gyrostat.

313 Motion in a reverse circle.

EVOLUTION (*Substantives*), unfolding, etc., development, introversion, reversion, eversion.

(*Verbs*) To evolve, unfold, unroll, unwind, uncoil, untwist, unfurl, untwine, unravel, disentangle (44), develop, introvert, reverse.

(*Adjectives*) Evolving, evolved, etc.

(*Adverbs*) Against.

———

Axis, axle, spindle, pivot, pin, hinge, pole, swivel, gimbals, mandrel.

(*Verbs*) To rotate, roll, revolve, spin, turn, turn round, circumvolve, circulate, gyre, gyrate, gimble, wheel, reel, whirl, twirl, birl, thrum, trundle, troll, twiddle, bowl, roll up, furl, wallow, welter.

(*Phrases*) To box the compass; to spin like a top.

(*Adjectives*) Rotating, etc., rotatory, rotary, circumrotatory, turbinate, trochoid, vortiginous, vortical, gyratory.

(*Phrase*) Like a squirrel in a cage.

(*Adverbs*) Clockwise, with the sun, deiseal (or deisil); counter-clockwise, against the sun, withershins (or widdershins).

314 Reciprocating motion, motion to and fro.

OSCILLATION (*Substantives*), vibration, undulation, pulsation, pulse, systole, diastole, libration, nutation, swing, beat, shake, seesaw, alternation, wag, evolution, vibratiuncle, coming and going, ebb and flow, flux and reflux; vibratility.

Fluctuation, vacillation, dance, lurch, dodge, rolling, pitching, tossing, etc. A pendulum, seesaw, rocker, rocking-chair, rocking-horse, etc.

(*Verbs*) To oscillate, vibrate, undulate, librate, wave, rock, swing, sway, pulsate, beat, wag, waggle, wiggle, wobble, shoogle, nod, bob, tick, play, wamble, wabble, waddle, dangle, swag, curtsy.

To fluctuate, vacillate, alternate, dance, curvet, reel, quake, quiver, quaver, roll, top, pitch, flounder, stagger, totter, brandish, shake, flicker, flourish, seesaw, teeter, move up and down, to and fro, backwards and forwards, to pass, and repass, to beat up and down.

(*Adjectives*) Oscillating, etc., oscillatory, vibratory, vibratile, vibrant, vibrational, undulatory, pulsatory, pendulous, libratory, systaltic.

(*Adverbs*) To and fro, up and down, backwards and forwards, seesaw, zigzag, wibble-wabble.

315 Irregular motion.

AGITATION (*Substantives*), stir, tremor, shake, ripple, jog, jolt, jar, succussion, trepidation, quiver, quaver, dance, jactitation, jactitancy, restlessness, shuffling, twitter, flicker, flutter, bobbing.

Disturbance, perturbation, commotion, turmoil, welter, bobbery; turbulence, tumult, tumultuation, bustle, fuss, flap, tirrivee, jerk, throw, convulsion, spasm (173), twitch, tic, staggers, St. Vitus's dance, epilepsy, writhing, ferment, fermentation, effervescence, ebullition, hurly-burly, hubbub, stramash, *tohu-bohu*; tempest, storm, whirlwind, cyclone (312), ground swell.

(*Verbs*) To be agitated, to shake, tremble, quiver, quaver, shiver, dither, twitter, twire, writhe, toss about, tumble, stagger, bob, reel, sway, wag, waggle, wiggle, wobble, shoogle, dance, wriggle, squirm, stumble, flounder, shuffle, totter, dodder, shamble, flounce, flop, curvet, prance, cavort, throb, pulsate, beat, palpitate, go pit-a-pat, fidget, flutter, flitter, flicker, bicker, twitch, jounce, ferment, effervesce, boil.

To agitate, shake, convulse, toss, tumble, bandy, wield, brandish, flap, flourish, whisk, switch, jerk, hitch, jolt, jog, hoggle, jostle, hustle, disturb, shake up, churn.

(*Phrases*) To jump like a parched pea; to be in a spin; to shake like an aspen leaf; to drive from pillar to post.

(*Adjectives*) Shaking, etc., agitated, tremulous, shivery, tottery, jerky, shaky, shoogly, quivery, quavery, trembly, choppy, rocky, wriggly, desultory, subsultory, shambling, giddy-paced, saltatory.

(*Phrases*) All of a tremble or twitter; like a pea on a drum; like a cat on hot bricks; like a hen on a hot griddle.

(*Adverbs*) By fits and starts; subsultorily, *per saltum* (139).

CLASS III

WORDS RELATING TO MATTER

Section I—Matter in General

316 MATERIALITY (*Substantives*), corporeity, corporality, materialness, substantiality, physical, condition.

Matter, body, substance, brute matter, stuff, element, principle, parenchyma, material, substratum, frame, *corpus pabulum*, flesh and blood.

Thing, object, article, still life, stocks and stones.

Physics, somatology, somatics, natural philosophy, physiography, physical science, experimental philosophy, positivism, materialism.

(*Verbs*), To materialize, embody, incarnate, objectify, externalize.

(*Adjectives*) Material, bodily, corporeal, corporal, carnal, temporal, physical, somatic, somatological, materialistic, sensible, palpable, tangible, ponderable, concrete, impersonal, objective, bodied.

317 IMMATERIALITY (*Substantives*), incorporeity, spirituality, spirit, etc. (450), inextension.

Personality, I, me, myself, ego.

Spiritualism, spiritism, idealism, immaterialism.

(*Verbs*) To disembody, spiritualize, immaterialize.

(*Adjectives*) Immaterial, incorporeal, ideal, unextended, intangible, impalpable, imponderable, bodiless, unbodied, disembodied, extra-sensory, astral, psychical, psychic, extramundane, unearthly, supernatural, supranatural, transcendent, transcendental, pneumatoscopic, spiritualistic, spiritual (450).

Personal, subjective.

---

318 WORLD (*Substantives*), nature, creation, universe; earth, globe, wide world, cosmos, sphere, macrocosm.

The heavens, sky, welkin, empyrean, starry heaven, firmament, ether; vault or canopy of heaven; celestial spaces, starry host, heavenly bodies, star, constellation, galaxy, Milky Way, *via lactea*, nebula, etc., sun, moon, planet, asteroid, planetoid, satellite, comet, meteor, meteorite, shooting star.

Zodiac, ecliptic, colure, orbit.

Astronomy, astrophysics, uranography, uranology, cosmology, cosmography, cosmogony; planetarium, orrery.

An astronomer, star-gazer, cosmographer; observatory.

(*Adjectives*) Cosmic, cosmical, mundane, terrestrial, terraqueous, terrene, telluric, sublunary, under the sun, subastral, worldwide, global.

Celestial, heavenly, spheral, starry, stellar, nebular, etc., sidereal, sideral, astral, solar, lunar.

---

319 HEAVINESS (*Substantives*), weight, gravity, gravitation, ponderosity, ponderousness, avoirdupois, pressure, load, burden, ballast; a

320 LIGHTNESS (*Substantives*), levity, imponderability, subtlety, buoyancy, airiness, portability, volatility.

99

lump, mass, weight, counterweight, counterpoise; ponderability.

Lead, millstone, mountain.

Balance, spring balance, scales, steelyard, weighbridge.

Statics.

(*Phrase*) Pelion on Ossa.

(*Verbs*) To be heavy, to gravitate, weigh, press, cumber, load.

(*Adjectives*) Weighty, heavy, ponderous, gravitating, weighing, etc., ponderable, lumpish, cumbersome, hefty, massive, unwieldy, cumbrous, incumbent, superincumbent; gravitational.

(*Phrase*) Heavy as lead.

A feather, dust, mote, down, thistledown, flue, ooss, fluff, cobweb, gossamer, straw, cork, bubble; float, buoy; featherweight.

(*Verbs*) To be light, float, swim, be buoyed up.

(*Adjectives*) Light, subtle, airy, vaporous, imponderous, astatic, weightless, imponderable, ethereal, sublimated, floating, swimming, buoyant, air-borne, portable, uncompressed, volatile.

(*Phrases*) Light as a feather; light as thistledown; 'trifles light as air.'

Section II—Inorganic Matter

1°. *Solid Matter*

321 DENSITY (*Substantives*), denseness, solidness, solidity, impenetrability, incompressibility, cohesion, coherence, cohesiveness (46), imporosity, impermeability, closeness, compactness, constipation, consistence, spissitude, thickness.

Specific gravity; hydrometer, araeometer.

Condensation, consolidation, solidification, concretion, coagulation, conglomeration, petrifaction, lapidification, vitrification, crystallization, precipitation, inspissation, thickening, grittiness, knottiness, induration (323).

Indivisibility, indiscerptibility, indissolubility.

322 RARITY (*Substantives*), tenuity, absence of solidity, subtility, sponginess, compressibility; hollowness (252).

Rarefaction, expansion, dilatation, inflation, dilution, attenuation, subtilization.

Ether, vapour, air, gas (334).

(*Verbs*) To rarefy, expand, dilate, dilute, attenuate, subtilize, thin out.

(*Adjectives*) Rare, subtle, sparse, slight, thin, fine, tenuous, compressible.

Porous, cavernous, spongy, bibulous, spongious, spongeous.

Rarefied, expanded, dilated, subtilized, unsubstantial, hollow (252).

A solid body, mass, block, knot, lump, concretion, concrete, cake, clot, stone, curd, coagulum, clinker, nugget; deposit, precipitate.

(*Verbs*) To be dense, etc.

To become or render solid; solidify, solidate, concrete, set, consolidate, congeal, jelly, jell, coagulate, curdle, curd, fix, clot, cake, cohere, crystallize, petrify, vitrify, condense, incrassate, thicken, inspissate, compact, concentrate, compress, squeeze, ram down, constipate.

(*Adjectives*) Dense, solid, solidified, consolidated, etc., coherent, cohesive, compact, close, thick-set, serried, substantial, massive, lumpish, impenetrable, incompressible, impermeable, imporous, constipated, concrete, knotted, gnarled, crystalline, crystallizable, vitreous, coagulated, thick, incrassated, inspissated, curdled, clotted, grumous.

Undissolved, unmelted, unliquefied, unthawed.

Indivisible, indiscerptible, infrangible, indissolvable, indissoluble, insoluble, infusible.

323 HARDNESS (*Substantives*), rigidity, rigescence, firmness, renitence, inflexibility, stiffness, starchiness, starchedness, temper, callosity, durity, induration, grittiness, petrifaction, etc. (321), ossification, sclerosis.

A stone, pebble, flint, marble, rock, granite, brick, iron, steel, corundum, diamond, adamant, bone, callus.

(*Verbs*) To render hard, harden, stiffen, indurate, petrify, vitrify, temper, ossify.

(*Adjectives*) Hard, horny, corneous, bony, osseous, rigid, rigescent, stiff, firm, starch, stark, unbending, unyielding, inflexible, tense, indurate, indurated, gritty, stony, proof, adamantean, adamantine.

(*Phrases*) Hard as iron, etc.; hard as a brick; hard as a nail; hard as a deal board; 'as hard as a piece of the nether millstone'; stiff as buckram; stiff as a poker.

324 SOFTNESS (*Substantives*) tenderness, flexibility, pliancy, pliableness, pliantness, litheness, pliability, suppleness, sequacity, ductility, malleability, tractility, extensibility, plasticity, inelasticity, laxity, flaccidity, flabbiness, limpness.

Clay, wax, butter, dough; a cushion, pillow, featherbed, down, padding, wadding, cotton-wool.

Mollification, softening, etc.

(*Verbs*) To render soft, soften, mollify, relax, temper, mash, pulp, knead, squash.

To bend, yield, give, relent, relax.

(*Adjectives*) Soft, tender, supple, pliable, limp, limber, flexible, flexile, lithe, lissom, *svelte*, willowy, pliant, plastic, waxen, ductile, tractile, tractable, malleable, extensile, sequacious.

Yielding, bending, flabby, flaccid, lymphatic, flocculent, downy, flimsy, spongy, oedematous, doughy, argillaceous, mellow; emollient, softening, etc.

(*Phrases*) Soft as butter; soft as down; soft as silk; yielding as wax; tender as a chicken.

325 ELASTICITY (*Substantives*), springiness, spring, resilience, buoyancy, renitency, contractility (195), compressibility.

Indiarubber, rubber, caoutchouc, whalebone, elastic.

(*Verbs*) To be elastic, etc., to spring back, fly back, rebound, recoil (277).

(*Adjectives*) Elastic, tensile, springy, resilient, buoyant.

326 INELASTICITY (*Substantives*), want or absence of elasticity, softness, etc. (324).

(*Adjectives*) Inelastic, ductile, limber, etc. (324).

327 TOUGHNESS (*Substantives*), tenacity, strength, cohesion (46), stubbornness (606).

Leather, gristle, cartilage.

(*Verbs*) To be tenacious, etc., to resist fracture.

(*Adjectives*) Tenacious, tough, wiry, sinewy, stringy, stubborn, cohesive, strong, resisting, resistant, leathery, coriaceous.

(*Phrase*) Tough as leather.

328 BRITTLENESS (*Substantives*), fragility, crispness, friability, frangibility, fissility.

(*Verbs*) To be brittle, break, crack, snap, split, shiver, splinter, fracture, crumble, break short, burst, fly.

(*Adjectives*) Brittle, frangible, fragile, frail, jerry-built, gimcrack, shivery, fissile, splitting, splintery, lacerable, crisp, friable, short, crumbling.

(*Phrases*) Brittle as glass; a house of cards.

329 Texture (*Substantives*), structure, construction, organization, set-up, organism, anatomy, frame, mould, fabric, framework, carcass, architecture, *compages*; substance, stuff, parenchyma, constitution, intertexture, contexture, tissue, grain, web, warp, woof, nap (256).

Fineness or coarseness of grain.

Histology.

(*Adjectives*) Textural, structural, organic, anatomic, anatomical; fine, delicate, subtle, fine-grained; coarse, homespun, rough-grained, coarse-grained; flimsy, unsubstantial, gossamery, filmy, gauzy.

330 Pulverulence (*Substantives*), state of powder, powderiness, efflorescence, sandiness, friability.

Dust, stour (or stoor), powder, sand, shingle, sawdust, grit, meal, bran, flour, limature, filings, debris, detritus, moraine, scobs, crumb, seed, grain, spore, atom, particle (32), flocculence.

Reduction to powder, pulverization, comminution, granulation, disintegration, weathering, subaction, contusion, trituration, levigation, abrasion, detrition, filing, etc. (331).

Mill, quern, grater, nutmeg grater, rasp, file, pestle and mortar.

(*Verbs*) To reduce to powder, to pulverize, comminute, granulate, triturate, levigate, scrape, file, abrade, rub down, grind, grate, rasp, mill, pound, bray, bruise, contuse, contund, beat, crush, crunch, scrunch, crumble, disintegrate, weather.

(*Adjectives*) Powdery, granular, mealy, floury, branny, farinaceous, furfuraceous, flocculent, dusty, sandy, sabulous, arenaceous, gritty, efflorescent, impalpable; pulverizable, pulverulent, friable, crumbly, shivery, pulverized, etc., attrite.

---

331 Friction (*Substantives*), attrition, rubbing, massage, abrasion, rub, scouring, limature, filing, rasping, frication, elbow-grease.

Grindstone, whetstone, buff, hone, strop (253).

(*Verbs*) To rub, abrade, scratch, scrape, scrub, grate, fray, rasp, pare, scour, polish, massage, curry, shampoo, rub out.

332 Absence of friction.

Lubrication (*Substantives*), prevention of friction, oiling, etc., anointment.

Lubricant, oil, lard, grease, etc. (356); synovia, saliva.

(*Verbs*) To lubricate, oil, grease, anoint, wax; smooth (255).

(*Adjectives*) Lubricated, etc.

2°. *Fluid Matter*

I. FLUIDS IN GENERAL

333 Fluidity (*Substantives*), fluid (including both inelastic and elastic fluids).

Inelastic fluid.

Liquidity, liquidness, aquosity, a liquid, liquor, lymph, humour, juice, sap, blood, serum, serosity, gravy, chyle, rheum, ichor, sanies; solubility.

Hydrology, hydrostatics, hydrodynamics.

334 Elastic fluid.

Gaseity, vaporousness, flatulence, flatulency; gas, air, vapour, ether, steam, fume, reek, effluvium.

Smoke, cloud (353).

Pneumatics, aerostatics, aerodynamics; gas-meter, gasometer.

(*Verbs*) To be fluid or liquid, to flow, run (348).

(*Adjectives*) Liquid, fluid, fluent, running, flowing, serous, juicy, succulent, sappy, lush.

Liquefied, uncongealed, melted, etc. (335).

335 LIQUEFACTION (*Substantives*), liquescence, fusion, melting, thaw, deliquation, deliquescence, lixiviation. Solution, dissolution, decoction, infusion, apozem, flux.

Solvent, menstruum, alkahest.

(*Verbs*) To render liquid, to liquefy, deliquesce, run, melt, thaw, fuse, solve, dissolve, resolve, to hold in solution.

(*Adjectives*) Liquefied, melted, unfrozen, molten, liquescent, liquefiable, deliquescent, diffluent, soluble, dissoluble.

(*Verbs*) To emit vapour, evaporate, to steam, fume, reek, smoke, puff, smoulder.

(*Adjectives*) Gaseous, aeriform, ethereal, aerial, airy, vaporous, vapoury, flatulent, volatile, evaporable.

336 VAPORIZATION (*Substantives*), gasification, volatilization, evaporation, distillation, sublimation, exhalation, volatility.

Vaporizer, retort, still.

(*Verbs*) To render gaseous, vaporize, volatilize, evaporate, exhale, distil, sublime, sublimate.

(*Adjectives*) Volatilized, etc., volatile, evaporable, vaporizable.

---

2. SPECIFIC FLUIDS

337 WATER (*Substantives*), heavy water, serum, lymph, rheum, whey.

Dilution, immersion, maceration, humectation, infiltration, sprinkling, washing, spraying, aspersion, affusion, irrigation, douche, balneation, bath, shower-bath, inundation, deluge (348), a diluent.

(*Verbs*) To be watery, etc., to reek.

To add water, to water, wet, moisten (339), dilute, dip, immerse, plunge, merge, immerge, steep, souse, duck, submerge, drown, soak, saturate, sop, macerate, pickle, blunge, wash, lave, springle, asperge, asperse, dabble, bedabble, affuse, splash, splatter, spray, swash, douse, drench, slop, slobber, irrigate, inundate, deluge, flood.

To take a bath, to tub, bathe, bath, paddle.

To syringe, inject, gargle.

(*Adjectives*) Watery (339), aqueous, aquatic, lymphatic, diluted, etc., reeking, dripping, sodden, drenched, soaking, sopping.

338 AIR (*Substantives*), common air, atmospheric air.

The atmosphere, troposphere, tropopause, stratosphere, ionosphere, Heaviside layer, Appleton layer; the sky, the ether, the open air, ozone, weather, climate.

Meteorology, climatology, isobar, barometer, aneroid barometer, weather-glass, weather-chart, weather station, weather ship.

Exposure to the air or weather, airing, weathering (330).

(*Verbs*) To aerate, oxygenate, arterialize, ventilate, air-condition.

(*Adjectives*) Containing air, windy, flatulent, aerated, effervescent.

Atmospheric, airy, open-air, *plein-air*, alfresco, aerial, aeriform; meteorological, barometric, weather-wise.

(*Adverbs*) In the open air, *à la belle étoile, sub Jove.*

Wet, washy, sloppy, squashy, splashy, soppy, soggy, slobbery, diluent, balneal.

(*Phrases*) Wet as a drowned rat; soaked to the skin; wet as a rag; wet through.

339 MOISTURE (*Substantives*), moistness, humidity, dampness, damp, wetness, wet, humectation, madefaction, dew, muddiness, marsh (345).

Hygrometer, hygrometry, hygrology.

(*Verbs*) To be moist, etc.

To moisten, wet, humectate, sponge, damp, dampen, bedew, imbue, infiltrate, imbrue; soak, saturate (337).

(*Adjectives*) Moist, damp, watery, humid, wet, dank, muggy, dewy, roral, rorid, roscid, juicy, swampy (345), humectant, sopping, dripping, sodden.

(*Phrase*) Wringing wet.

341 OCEAN (*Substantives*), sea, main, the deep, brine, salt water, blue water, high seas, offing, tide, wave, surge, ooze, etc. (348).

Hydrography, oceanography.

Neptune, Thetis, Triton, Oceanid, Nereid, sea-nymph, siren, mermaid, merman, dolphin; trident.

(*Phrases*) The vasty deep; the briny; the ditch; the drink.

(*Adjectives*) Oceanic, marine, maritime, thalassic, pelagic, pelagian, sea-going, hydrographic.

(*Adverbs*) At sea, on sea, afloat.

343 GULF (*Substantives*), bay, inlet, bight, estuary, roadstead, roads, arm of the sea, armlet, sound, frith, firth, fiord, lagoon, cove, creek, strait, belt, kyle, Euripus.

(*Adjective*) Estuarine.

LAKE (*Substantives*), loch, lough, mere, tarn, linn, plash, broad, pond, dew-pond, pool, puddle, well, reservoir, standing water, dead water, a sheet of water, fish-pond, ditch, dike, backwater.

(*Adjectives*) Lacustrine (or lacustrian), lacuscular.

340 DRYNESS (*Substantives*), siccity, aridity, drought.

Exsiccation, desiccation, arefaction, drainage.

(*Verbs*) To be dry, etc.

To render dry, to dry, dry up, sop up, swab, wipe, blot, exsiccate, desiccate, dehydrate, drain, parch.

(*Adjectives*) Dry, anhydrous, dehydrated, arid, dried, etc., unwatered, undamped, waterproof, husky, juiceless, sapless; siccative, desiccative.

(*Phrases*) Dry as a bone; dry as dust; dry as a stick; dry as a mummy; dry as a biscuit; dry as a limekiln.

342 LAND (*Substantives*), earth, ground, terra firma, continent, mainland, peninsula, delta, alluvium, polder, tongue of land, neck of land, isthmus, oasis.

Coast, shore, seaboard, seaside, sea-bank, strand, beach, bank, lea.

Cape, promontory, etc. (250), headland, point of land, highland (206).

Soil, glebe, clay, humus, loam, marl, clod, clot, rock, crag, chalk, gravel, mould, subsoil.

(*Adjectives*) Terrene, continental, earthy, terraqueous, terrestrial.

Littoral, riparian, alluvial, midland.

(*Adverbs*) Ashore, on shore, on land.

344 PLAIN (*Substantives*), tableland, open country, the face of the country, champaign country, basin, downs, waste, wild, weald, steppe, pampas, savanna, llano, prairie, tundra, heath, common, wold, moor, moorland, the bush; plateau, flat (213).

Meadow, mead, haugh, pasturage, park, field, lawn, green, plot, plat, terrace, esplanade, sward, turf, sod, heather, lea, grounds, pleasure-grounds, playing-fields, campus.

(*Phrase*) A weary waste.

(*Adjectives*) Campestrian, champaign, lawny.

345 MARSH (*Substantives*), marsh, swamp, morass, moss, fen, bog, quag, quagmire, slough, sump, wash.

(*Adjectives*) Marshy, marish, swampy, boggy, quaggy, fenny, soft, plashy, poachy, paludal.

346 ISLAND (*Substantives*), isle, islet, ait, eyot, inch, holm, reef, atoll; archipelago.

(*Adjectives*) Insular, sea-girt.

---

3. FLUIDS IN MOTION

347 Fluid in motion.

STREAM (*Substantives*), flow, current, jet, undercurrent, course (348).

(*Verbs*) To flow, stream, issue, run.

348 Water in motion.

RIVER (*Substantives*), running water, jet, spurt, squirt, spout, splash, rush, gush, water-spout, sluice, linn, waterfall, cascade, force, catadupe, cataract, debacle, cataclysm, inundation, deluge, avalanche, spate.

Rain, shower, scud, driving rain, downpour, drencher, soaker, cloudburst, mizzle, drizzle, Scotch mist, smirr, dripping, stillicidium; flux, flow, profluence, effluence, efflux, effluxion, defluxion.

Irrigation (337).

Spring, fountain, fount, rill, rivulet, gill, gullet, rillet, streamlet, runnel, sike, burn, beck, brooklet, brook, stream, reach, torrent, rapids, race, flush, flood, swash.

Tide, spring tide, high tide, tidal wave, bore, eagre, freshet, current, indraught, reflux, eddy, whirlpool, vortex, maelstrom, regurgitation.

Tributary, confluent, effluent, billabong; corrivation, confluence, effluence.

Wave, billow, surge, swell, chop, ripple, ground swell, surf, breaker, roller, comber, white caps, white horses.

Irrigation (337); sprinkler, sprayer, spray, atomizer, aspergillum, aspersorium, water-cart, watering-pot, watering-can, pump, syringe, hydrant.

Hydraulics, hydrodynamics, hydrography; rain-gauge.

(*Verbs*) To flow, run, meander, gush, spout, roll, billow, surge, jet, well, drop, drip, trickle, dribble, ooze (295), percolate, distil, transude,

349 Air in motion.

WIND (*Substantives*), draught, current, breath, air, breath of air, puff, whiff, zephyr, blow, drift, aura.

Gust, blast, breeze, squall, gale, storm, tempest, hurricane, whirlwind, tornado, cyclone, typhoon, blizzard, simoom, samiel, harmattan, monsoon, trade wind, sirocco, mistral, *bise, tramontana, föhn,* pampero; windiness, ventosity.

Aeolus, Boreas, Auster, Euroclydon, the cave of Aeolus.

Bellows, blowpipe, fan, ventilator, punkah.

Anemometer, anemograph, windgauge, weathercock, vane.

Insufflation, sufflation, perflation, blowing, fanning, ventilation, blowing up, inflation, afflation; respiration, inspiration, expiration, sneezing, sternutation, cough, hiccup.

(*Phrase*) A capful of wind.

(*Verbs*) To blow, waft, blow hard, blow a hurricane, breathe, respire, inspire, expire, insufflate, puff, whiff, sough, whiffle, wheeze, gasp, snuffle, sniffle, sneeze, cough.

To fan, ventilate, inflate, perflate, blow up.

(*Phrase*) To blow great guns.

(*Adjectives*) Blowing, etc., rough, blowy, windy, breezy, gusty, squally, puffy, stormy, tempestuous, blustering.

---

stream, sweat, perspire (299), overflow, flow over, splash, swash, guggle, murmur, babble, bubble, purl, gurgle, sputter, spurt, regurgitate, surge.

To rain, rain hard, pour with rain, drizzle, spit, mizzle, set in.

To flow into, fall into, open into, drain into, discharge itself, disembogue, disgorge, debouch.

(*Phrases*) To rain cats and dogs; to rain in torrents.

To cause a flow, to pour, drop, distil, splash, squirt, spill, drain, empty, discharge, pour out, open the sluices or flood-gates; shower down, irrigate (337).

To stop a flow, to stanch, dam, dam up (261), intercept.

(*Adjectives*) Fluent, profluent, affluent, confluent, diffluent, tidal, flowing, etc., babbling, bubbling, gurgling, meandering, meandrous.

Fluviatile, fluvial, riverine, streamy, showery, drizzly, rainy, pluvial, pouring.

350 Channel for the passage of water.

Conduit (*Substantives*), channel, duct, watercourse, watershed, race, adit, aqueduct, canal, sluice, dike main, gully, moat, ditch, lode, leat, rhine, trough, gutter, drain, sewer, culvert, cloaca, sough, kennel, siphon, pipe (260), emunctory, gully-hole, artery, aorta, pore, spout, funnel, tap, faucet, scupper, adjutage (or ajutage), waste-pipe, hose, rose, gargoyle, artesian well.

Floodgate, dam, weir, levee, water-gate, lock, valve.

351 Channel for the passage of air.

Air-pipe (*Substantives*), air-tube, shaft, flue, chimney, lum, funnel, smoke-stack, exhaust-pipe, exhaust, vent, blow-hole, nostril, nozzle, throat, weasand, trachea, larynx, windpipe, thrapple, spiracle, ventiduct.

Ventilator, louvre, register.

Tobacco-pipe, pipe, etc. (298A).

3°. *Imperfect Fluids*

352 Semiliquidity (*Substantives*), pulpiness, viscidity, viscosity, ropiness, sliminess, gumminess, glutinosity, gummosity, siziness, clamminess, mucosity, spissitude, lentor, thickness, crassitude.

Inspissation, thickening, incrassation.

Jelly, mucilage, gelatine, mucus, chyme, phlegm, gum, glue, gluten, goo, colloid, albumen, size, milk, cream, emulsion, soup, broth, starch, treacle, squash, mud, clart, glaur, slush, slime, ooze, dope, glycerine; lava.

Pitch, tar, bitumen, asphalt, resin, rosin, varnish, copal, mastic, wax, amber.

(*Verbs*) To inspissate, thicken, incrassate, jelly, jellify, mash, squash, churn, beat up, pulp.

(*Adjectives*) Semi-fluid, semi-liquid,

353 Mixture of air and water.

Bubble (*Substantives*), soda-water, aerated water, foam, froth, head, spume, lather, bleb, spray, spindrift, surf, yeast, barm, suds.

Cloud, vapour, fog, mist, smog, haze, steam, nebulosity (422); scud, rack, cumulus, cirrus, stratus, nimbus mare's tail, mackerel sky.

Nephelology; Fido.

Effervescence, foaming, mantling, fermentation, frothing, etc.

(*Verbs*) To bubble, boil, foam, froth, mantle, sparkle, guggle, gurgle, effervesce, fizz, ferment.

(*Adjectives*) Bubbling, etc., frothy, yeasty, barmy, nappy, effervescent, fizzy, up, boiling, fermenting, sparkling, mantling, *mousseux*.

Cloudy, foggy, misty, vaporous, nebulous.

---

milky, emulsive, creamy, lacteal, lacteous, curdy, curdled, soupy, muddy, slushy, clarty, thick, succulent, squashy.

Gelatinous, albuminous, gummy, colloid, amylaceous, mucilaginous, glairy, slimy, ropy, stringy, clammy, glutinous (46), viscid, viscous, sticky, gooey, slab, slabby, sizy, lentous, tacky.

Tarry, pitchy, resinous, bituminous.

354 PULPINESS (*Substantives*), pulp, paste, dough, curd, pap, pudding, poultice, soup, squash, mud, slush, grume, jam, preserve.

(*Adjectives*) Pulpy, pulpous, pultaceous, doughy, grumous.

———

355 UNCTUOUSNESS (*Substantives*), unctuosity, oiliness, greasiness, slipperiness, lubricity.

Lubrication (332), anointment, unction; ointment (356).

(*Verbs*) To oil, grease, anoint, wax, lubricate (332).

(*Adjectives*) Unctuous, oily, oleaginous, adipose, sebaceous, fat, fatty, greasy, waxy, butyraceous, soapy, saponaceous, pinguid, stearic, lardaceous.

356 OIL (*Substantives*), fat, butter, margarine, cream, grease, tallow, suet, lard, dripping, blubber, pomatum, pomade, stearin, lanoline, soap, soft soap, wax, beeswax, sealing-wax, ambergris, spermaceti, adipocere, ointment, unguent, liniment, paraffin, kerosene, gasolene, petroleum, petrol, mineral oil, vegetable oil, olive oil, castor oil, linseed oil, train oil.

SECTION III—ORGANIC MATTER

1°. *Vitality*

I. VITALITY IN GENERAL

357 ORGANIZATION (*Substantives*), the organized world, organized nature, living nature, animated nature, living beings; protoplasm, protein.

Biology, ecology (or oecology), natural history, organic chemistry, zoology (368), botany (369).

(*Adjectives*) Organic, animate.

358 INORGANIZATION (*Substantives*), the mineral world or kingdom; unorganized, inorganic, brute or inanimate matter.

Mineralogy, geognosy, petrology, lithology, geology, metallurgy, inorganic chemistry.

(*Adjectives*) Inorganic, azoic, mineral, inanimate.

359 LIFE (*Substantives*), vitality, animation, viability, the vital spark or flame or principle, the breath of life, life-blood; existence (1).

Vivification, revivification.

Physiology, biology; metabolism.

(*Phrase*) The breath of one's nostrils.

(*Verbs*) To be living, alive, etc., to live, subsist (1), breathe, fetch breath, respire, draw breath, to be born, be spared.

360 DEATH (*Substantives*), decease, dissolution, demise, departure, obit, expiration; termination, close or extinction of life, existence, etc.; mortality, fall, doom, fate, release, rest, end, quietus, loss, bereavement, euthanasia, katabolism.

Last breath, last gasp, last agonies, the death-rattle, dying breath, agonies of death, dying agonies.

Necrology, death-roll, obituary.

(*Phrases*) The ebb of life; the king

To come to life, to revive, come to.

To give birth to (161); to bring, restore, or recall to life, to vivify, revive, revivify, quicken, reanimate, vitalize.

(*Phrases*) To see the light; to come into the world; to walk the earth; to draw breath.

To keep body and soul together; to support life.

(*Adjectives*) Living, alive, in life, above ground, breathing, animated, quick, viable.

Vital, vivifying, vivified, Promethean, metabolic.

(*Phrases*) Alive and kicking; in the land of the living; on this side of the grave.

of terrors; the jaws of death; the swan-song; the Stygian shore; the sleep that knows no waking; a watery grave.

(*Verbs*) To die, perish, expire.

(*Phrases*) Breathe one's last; cease to live; depart this life; end one's days; be no more; go off; drop off; pop off; peg out; lose one's life; drop down dead; resign, relinquish, lay down, or surrender one's life; drop or sink into the grave; close one's eyes; break one's neck.

To give up the ghost; to be all over with one; to pay the debt to nature; to make the great change; to take one's last sleep; to shuffle off this mortal coil; to go to one's last home; to go the way of all flesh; to kick the bucket; to hop the twig; to turn up one's toes; to slip one's cable; to cross the Stygian ferry.

To snuff out; to go off the hooks; to go to one's account; to go aloft; to join the majority; to go west; to have had it; to be numbered with the dead; to die a natural death; to hand in one's checks; to pass away or over.

(*Adjectives*) Dead, lifeless, deceased, demised, gone, departed, defunct, exanimate, inanimate, *kaput*, out of the world, mortuary; still-born.

Dying, expiring, moribund, *in articulo mortis*, *in extremis*, in the agony of death, etc., going, life ebbing, going off, life failing, *aux abois*, booked, having received one's death warrant.

(*Phrases*) Dead and gone; dead as a door-nail, as mutton, as a doorpost, as a herring; stone-dead; launched into eternity; gone to one's last home; gathered to one's fathers; gone to Davy Jones's locker; gone west; gone for a Burton; pushing up the daisies.

At death's door; on one's death-bed; in the jaws of death; death staring one in the face; one's hour being come; one's days being numbered; one's race being run; one foot in the grave; on one's last legs; life hanging by a thread; at one's last gasp.

(*Adverbs*) Post-mortem, post-obit.

361 Destruction of life, violent death.

KILLING (*Substantives*), homicide, parricide, matricide, fratricide, sororicide, infanticide, regicide, tyrannicide, vaticide, genocide, manslaughter, murder, assassination, blood, gore, bloodshed, slaughter, carnage, butchery, massacre, immolation, holocaust, fusillade, *noyade*, thuggee, thuggery, thuggism; casualty, fatality.

Death-blow, *coup de grâce*, grace-stroke, mercy killing, euthanasia.

Suicide, felo-de-se, hara-kiri, happy dispatch, suttee, martyrdom, execution (972).

Destruction of animals, slaughtering, battue, hecatomb.

Slaughter-house, shambles, abattoir.

A butcher, slayer, murderer, homicide, parricide, matricide, etc., assassin, cut-throat, bravo, thug, executioner (975).

(*Verbs*) To kill, put to death, do to death, slay, murder, assassinate, slaughter, butcher, immolate, massacre, decimate, take away or deprive of life, make away with, dispatch, burke, lynch, settle, do for, do in, bump off, brain, spiflicate.

To strangle, throttle, bowstring, choke, garrotte, stifle, suffocate, smother, asphyxiate, drown, hang, turn off, string up.

To cut down, sabre, cut to pieces, cut off, cut the throat, stab, knife, bayonet, shoot, behead, decapitate, stone, lapidate, execute (972).

To commit suicide, to make away with oneself.

(*Phrases*) To put to the sword; put to the edge of the sword; give no quarter to; run through the body; knock on the head; give one the works; put one on the spot; blow the brains out; give the death blow, the *coup de grâce*; put out of one's misery; launch into eternity; give a quietus to.

(*Adjectives*) Killing, etc., murderous, slaughterous, sanguinary, ensanguined, gory, bloody, blood-stained, blood-guilty, red-handed.

Mortal, fatal, deadly, lethal, internecine, suicidal, homicidal, fratricidal, etc.

362 CORPSE (*Substantives*), corse, carcass, bones, skeleton, carrion, defunct, relic, remains, ashes, earth, dust, clay, mummy.

Shade, ghost, *manes*; the dead, the majority, the great majority.

(*Phrases*) All that was mortal; this tenement of clay; food for worms or fishes.

(*Adjectives*) Cadaverous, corpse-like.

363 INTERMENT (*Substantives*), burial, sepulture, inhumation, obsequies, exequies, funeral, wake, lyke-wake, pyre, funeral pile, cremation.

Funeral rite or solemnity, knell, passing-bell, tolling, dirge, lament, coronach, keening (839), requiem, epicedium, obit, elegy, funeral oration, epitaph, death march, dead march, lying in state.

Grave-clothes, shroud, winding-sheet, cerecloth, cerement.

Coffin, casket, shell, sarcophagus, urn, pall, bier, hearse, catafalque.

Grave, pit, sepulchre, tomb, vault, catacomb, mausoleum, house of death, burial-place, cemetery, necropolis, churchyard, graveyard, God's acre, burial-ground, cromlech, dolmen, barrow, tumulus, cairn, ossuary, charnel-house, morgue, mortuary, crematorium, cinerator; Valhalla.

Monument, tombstone, gravestone, shrine, cenotaph.

Exhumation, disinterment; autopsy, necropsy, post-mortem.

Undertaker, mortician, mute, sexton, grave-digger.

(*Verbs*) To inter, bury, lay in the grave, consign to the grave or tomb, entomb, inhume, cremate, lay out, embalm, mummify.

To exhume, disinter.

(*Adjectives*) Buried, etc., burial, funereal, funebrial, funerary, mortuary, sepulchral, cinerary; elegiac.

(*Phrases*) *Hic jacet*; R.I.P.

2. SPECIAL VITALITY

364 ANIMALITY (*Substantives*), animal life, animality, animation, breath, animalization.

Flesh, flesh and blood, physique.

(*Verb*) To animalize.

(*Adjectives*) Fleshly, corporal, carnal.

365 VEGETABILITY (*Substantives*), vegetable life, vegetation.

(*Adjectives*) Lush, rank, luxuriant.

366 ANIMAL (*Substantives*), the animal kingdom, brute creation, fauna, avifauna.

A beast, brute, creature, created being; creeping or living thing, dumb creature, flocks and herds, live-stock.

Cattle, kine, etc.

Game, *fera natura*, wild life.

Mammal, quadruped, bird, reptile, fish, mollusc, worm, insect, zoophyte, animalcule, etc.

(*Phrases*) The beasts of the field; fowls of the air: denizens of the deep.

(*Adjectives*) Animal, zoological, piscatory, fishy, molluscous, vermicular, etc., feral.

---

368 The science of animals.

ZOOLOGY (*Substantives*), zoography, anatomy, zootomy, comparative anatomy, physiology, morphology.

Ornithology, ichthyology, herpetology, ophiology, malacology, helminthology, entomology; palaeontology.

370 The economy or management of animals.

TAMING (*Substantives*), domestication, domesticity; training, breaking-in, manège, breeding, pisciculture; veterinary art.

Menagerie, zoological garden, game reserve, aviary, apiary, vivarium, aquarium, fishery, fish-pond, duck-pond.

(*Verbs*) To tame, domesticate, train, tend, break in.

(*Adjectives*) Pastoral, bucolic.

---

367 PLANT (*Substantives*), vegetable, the vegetable kingdom, flora.

Tree, fruit-tree, shrub, bush, creeper, herb, herbage, grass, fern, fungus, lichen, moss, weed, seaweed, alga; annual, biennial, perennial; exotic.

Forest, wood, hurst, holt, greenwood, woodland, brake, grove, copse, coppice, hedgerow, boscage, plantation, thicket, spinney, underwood, undergrowth, brushwood, clump of trees, park, chase, weald, scrub, jungle, prairie.

Foliage, florescence, flower, blossom, branch, bough, spray, twig, leaf.

(*Adjectives*) Vegetable, vegetal, arboreal, herbaceous, herbal, botanic, sylvan, woodland, woody, wooded, well-wooded, shrubby, grassy, verdurous, verdant, floral, mossy.

369 The science of plants.

BOTANY (*Substantives*), phytography, phytology, vegetable physiology, herborization, dendrology, mycology, Pomona, Flora, Ceres

Herbarium, herbal, *hortus siccus*, vasculum.

(*Verbs*) To botanize, herborize.

371 The economy or management of plants.

AGRICULTURE (*Substantives*), cultivation, culture, intensive cultivation, husbandry, agronomy, geoponics, hydroponics, georgics, tillage, gardening, horticulture, forestry, vintage, etc., arboriculture, floriculture, the topiary art.

Vineyard, vinery, garden, kitchen garden, market garden, nursery, bed, plot, herbaceous border, parterre, hothouse, greenhouse, conservatory, espalier, shrubbery, orchard, rock garden, rockery, winter garden, pinery, arboretum, allotment.

A husbandman, horticulturist, gardener, florist, agriculturist, agriculturalist, woodcutter, backwoodsman, forester, land girl, farmer, yeoman, cultivator.

(*Verbs*) To cultivate, till, garden, farm; delve, dibble, dig, sow, plant, graft; plough, harrow, rake, reap, mow, cut, weed.

(*Adjectives*) Agricultural, agrarian, arable, rural, country, rustic, agrestic.

372 MANKIND (*Substantives*), the human race or species; man, human nature, humanity, mortality, flesh, generation; Everyman.

Anthropology, anthropography, ethnology, ethnography, demography, sociology, social economics; civics.

Anthropomorphism.

Human being, person, individual, type, creature, fellow creature, mortal, body, somebody, one, someone, a soul, living soul, earthling, party personage, inhabitant; *dramatis personae*.

People, persons, folk, population, public, world, race, society, community, the million, commonalty (876), nation, state, realm, community, commonwealth, republic, commonweal, polity, nationality; civilized society, civilization.

Anthropologist, ethnologist, sociologist, etc.

(*Phrases*) The lords of creation; the body politic.

(*Adjectives*) National, civic, public, human, mortal, personal, individual, social, cosmopolitan, ethnic, racial; sociological, anthropological, ethnological, anthropomorphic, anthropomorphous, anthropoid, manlike.

373 MAN (*Substantives*), manhood, manliness, virility, he, menfolk.

A human being, man, male, mortal, person, body, soul, individual, fellow creature, one, someone, somebody, so-and-so.

Personage, a gentleman, sir, master, yeoman, citizen, denizen, burgess, burgher, cosmopolite, wight, swain, fellow, blade, bloke, beau, chap, guy, bod, type, cove, gossoon, buffer, gaffer, goodman; husband (903).

(*Adjectives*) Human, manly, male, masculine, manlike, mannish, virile, mannish, unwomanly, unfeminine.

(*Phrase*) The spear side.

────

374 WOMAN (*Substantives*), female, feminality, femininity, womanhood, muliebrity, girlhood, she, womenfolk.

Womankind, the sex, the fair, the fair sex, the softer sex, the weaker vessel, a petticoat, skirt.

Dame, madam, madame, ma'am, mistress, lady, gentlewoman, donna, belle, matron, dowager, goody, gammer, good woman, goodwife; wife (903).

Damsel, girl, lass, lassie, maid (209), maiden, *demoiselle*, flapper, miss, missie, nymph, wench, bint, floosy, popsy, pusher, jade, dona, grisette, colleen.

(*Adjectives*) Female, feminine, womanly, ladylike, matronly, maidenly, girlish; womanish, effeminate, unmanly, pansy.

(*Phrase*) The distaff side.

2°. *Sensation*

I. SENSATION IN GENERAL

375 PHYSICAL SENSIBILITY (*Substantives*), sensitiveness, sensitivity, feeling, perceptivity, acuteness; allergy, idiosyncrasy; moral sensibility (822).

Sensation, impression, consciousness (490).

The external senses.

(*Verbs*) To be sensible of, to feel, perceive, be conscious of, respond to, react to.

376 PHYSICAL INSENSIBILITY (*Substantives*), obtuseness, dullness, paralysis, anaesthesia, analgesia, sleep, trance, stupor, coma, catalepsy; moral insensibility (823).

Anaesthetic, opium, ether, chloroform, chloral, cocaine, morphia, laudanum, nitrous oxide, laughing gas.

Anaesthetics.

(*Verbs*) To be insensible, etc. To

To render sensible, to sharpen, cultivate, train, tutor, condition.

To cause sensation; to impress, excite, or produce an impression.

(*Adjectives*) Sensible, conscious, sensitive, sensuous, aesthetic, perceptive.

Hypersensitive, thin-skinned, neurotic, hyperaesthetic, allergic.

Acute, sharp, keen, vivid, lively, impressive.

(*Adverb*) To the quick.

377 PHYSICAL PLEASURE (*Substantives*), bodily enjoyment, gratification, titillation, comfort, luxury, voluptuousness, sensuousness, sensuality; mental pleasure (827).

(*Phrases*) The flesh-pots of Egypt; creature comforts; a bed of roses; a bed of down; on velvet; in clover.

(*Verbs*) To feel, experience, receive, etc., pleasure, to enjoy, relish, luxuriate, revel, riot, bask, wallow in, feast on, gloat over, have oneself a ball.

To cause or give physical pleasure, to gratify, tickle, regale, etc. (829).

(*Adjectives*) Enjoying, etc., luxurious, sensual, voluptuous, comfortable, cosy, snug.

Pleasant, pleasing, agreeable, grateful, refreshing, comforting.

———

render insensible, to blunt, dull, obtund, benumb, deaden, stupefy, stun, paralyse, anaesthetize, dope, hocus, gas.

(*Adjectives*) Insensible, unfeeling, senseless, impercipient, impassable, thick-skinned, pachydermatous, hardened, proof, apathetic, obtuse, dull, anaesthetic, paralytic, palsied, numb, dead, unaffected, untouched.

(*Phrase*) Having a rhinoceros hide.

378 PHYSICAL PAIN (*Substantives*), bodily pain, suffering, sufferance, dolour, ache, aching, smart, smarting, shoot, shooting, twinge, twitch, gripe, headache, toothache, earache, sore, hurt, discomfort, malaise; mental pain (828).

Spasm, cramp, nightmare, crick, stitch, convulsion, throe.

Pang, anguish, agony, torment, torture, rack, cruciation, crucifixion, martyrdom.

(*Verbs*) To feel, experience, suffer, etc., pain; to suffer, ache, smart, bleed, tingle, shoot, twinge, lancinate, wince, writhe, twitch.

(*Phrases*) To sit on thorns; to sit on pins and needles.

To give or inflict pain; to pain, hurt, chafe, sting, bite, gnaw, pinch, tweak, grate, gall, fret, prick, pierce, gripe, etc., wring, torment, torture, rack, agonize, break on the wheel, put on the rack, convulse.

(*Adjectives*) In pain, in a state of pain; uncomfortable, pained, etc.

Painful, aching, etc., sore, raw, agonizing, excruciating.

2. SPECIAL SENSATION

(1) *Touch*

379 Sensation of pressure.

TOUCH (*Substantives*), taction, tactility, feeling, palpation, manipulation, tangibility, palpability.

Organ of touch: hand, finger, forefinger, thumb, paw, feeler, antenna.

(*Verbs*) To touch, feel, handle, finger, thumb, paw, fumble, grope, grabble, scrabble; pass, or run the fingers over, manipulate.

(*Phrase*) To throw out a feeler.

(*Adjectives*) Tactual, tangible, palpable, tactile.

380 SENSATIONS OF TOUCH (*Substantives*), itching, titillation, formication, etc., creeping, aura, tingling, thrilling.

(*Verbs*) To itch, tingle, creep, thrill; sting, prick, prickle, tickle, kittle, titillate.

(*Adjectives*) Itching, etc., ticklish, kittly.

381 Insensibility to touch.

NUMBNESS (*Substantives*), deadness, anaesthesia (376); pins and needles.

(*Verbs*) To benumb, paralyse, anaesthetize; to chloroform, inject with cocaine, etc. (376).

(*Adjectives*) Numb, benumbed; intangible, impalpable.

(2) *Heat*

382 HEAT (*Substantives*), caloric, temperature, warmth, fervour, calidity, incalescence, candescence, incandescence, glow, flush, hectic, fever, pyrexia, hyperpyrexia.

Fire, spark, scintillation, flash, flame, blaze, bonfire, firework, wildfire, pyrotechny, ignition (384).

Insolation, summer, dog-days, tropical heat, heat-wave, summer heat, blood heat, sirocco, simoom; isotherm.

Hot spring, thermal spring, geyser.

Pyrology, thermology, thermotics, calorimetry, thermodynamics; thermometer (389).

(*Phrase*) The devouring element.

(*Verbs*) To be hot, to glow, flush, sweat, swelter, bask, smoke, reek, stew, simmer, seethe, boil, burn, broil, bake, parch, fume, blaze, smoulder.

(*Phrases*) To be in a heat, in a glow, in a fever, in a blaze, etc.

(*Adjectives*) Hot, warm, mild, unfrozen, genial, tepid, lukewarm, blood-hot, thermal, thermotic, calorific, sunny, close, sweltering, stuffy, sultry, baking, boiling, broiling, torrid, tropical, aestival, canicular, glowing, piping, scalding, reeking, etc., on fire, afire, ablaze, alight, aglow, fervid, fervent, ardent, unquenched; isothermal, sotheral; feverish, pyretic, pyrexial, pyrexical.

383 COLD (*Substantives*), coldness, frigidity, coolness, coolth, gelidity, chill, chilliness, freshness, inclemency; cold storage.

Frost, ice, snow, snowflake, sleet, hail, hailstone, rime, hoar-frost, icicle, iceberg, ice-floe, glacier, winter.

Sensation of cold: chilliness, shivering, shuddering, goose-skin, goose-pimples, goose-flesh, rigor, horripilation, chattering of teeth.

(*Verbs*) To be cold, etc., to shiver, quake, shake, tremble, shudder, dither, quiver, starve.

(*Adjectives*) Cold, cool, chill, chilly, gelid, frigid, algid, bleak, raw, inclement, bitter, biting, cutting, nipping, piercing, pinching, clay-cold, fresh, keen; pinched, starved, perished, shivering, etc., aguish, frozen, frost-bitten, frost-nipped, frost-bound, unthawed, unwarmed; isocheimal, isochimenal.

Icy, glacial, frosty, freezing, wintry, brumal, hibernal, boreal, arctic, hiemal, hyperborean, icebound.

(*Phrases*) Cold as a stone; cold as marble; cold as a frog; cold as charity; cold as Christmas; cool as a cucumber; cool as a custard.

Igneous, plutonic, fiery, candescent, incandescent, red-hot, white-hot, incalescent, smoking, blazing, unextinguished, smouldering.

(*Phrases*) Hot as fire; warm as toast; warm as wool; piping hot; like an oven; hot enough to roast an ox.

---

384 CALEFACTION (*Substantives*), increase of temperature, heating, tepefaction.

Melting, fusion, liquefaction, thaw,

385 REFRIGERATION (*Substantives*), infrigidation, reduction of temperature, cooling, freezing, congealing, congelation, glaciation.

liquescence (335), liquation, incandescence.

Burning, combustion, incension, accension, cremation, cautery, cauterization, roasting, broiling, frying, ustulation, torrefaction, scorification, branding, calcination, carbonization, incineration, cineration.

Boiling, coction, ebullition, simmering, scalding, decoction, smelting.

Ignition, inflammation, setting fire to, flagration, deflagration, conflagration, arson, incendiarism, fire-raising; *auto da fé*, suttee.

Inflammability, combustibility; incendiary, fire-bug, fire-ship, *pétroleur*.

Transmission of heat, diathermancy.

Fire-brigade, fire-extinguisher, fire-engine, fireman; incombustibility.

(*Verbs*) To cool, refrigerate, congeal, freeze, glaciate, ice, benumb, refresh, damp, slack, quench, put out, blow out, extinguish, starve, pinch, pierce, cut.

To go out.

(*Adjectives*) Cooled, frozen, benumbed, etc., shivery, frigorific, refrigerant.

Incombustible, non-inflammable, fire-proof.

———

(*Verbs*) To heat, warm, mull, chafe, fire, set fire to, set on fire, kindle, enkindle, light, ignite, relume, rekindle.

To melt, thaw, fuse, liquefy (335); defrost, de-ice.

To burn, inflame, roast, toast, broil, fry, grill, brander, singe, parch, sweal, scorch, brand, scorify, torrify, bake, cauterize, sear, char, carbonize, calcine, incinerate, smelt.

To boil, stew, cook, seethe, scald, parboil, simmer.

To take fire, catch fire, kindle, light, ignite.

(*Phrases*) To stir the fire; blow the fire; fan the flame; apply a match to; make a bonfire of; to take the chill off.

To consign to the flames; to reduce to ashes; to burn to a cinder.

(*Adjectives*) Combustible, inflammable, heating, etc., heated, warmed, melted, molten, unfrozen, boiled, stewed, sodden, adust.

---

386 FURNACE (*Substantives*), fire, gas fire, electric fire, stove, kiln, oven, bakehouse, hothouse, conservatory, fire-place, grate, hearth, radiator, register, reverberatory, range, hob, hypocaust, crematorium, incinerator, forge, blast-furnace, brasier, salamander, geyser, heater, hot-plate, hot-water bottle, electric blanket, warming-pan, stew-pan, boiler, cauldron, kettle, pot, urn, chafing-dish, gridiron, saucepan, frying-pan; sudatorium, sudatory, Turkish bath, *hammam*, vapour bath.

387 REFRIGERATORY (*Substantives*), refrigerator, frig, ice-pail, ice-bag, ice-house, freezing-mixture, cooler, freezer.

———

---

388 FUEL (*Substantives*), firing, coal, anthracite, coke, charcoal, briquette, peat, combustible, log, tinder, touchwood.

Lucifer, ingle, brand, match, vesuvian, vesta, safety-match, fusee, lighter, spill, embers, faggot, firebrand, incendiary, port-fire, fire-ball, fire-barrel.

---

389 THERMOMETER (*Substantives*), clinical thermometer, pyrometer, calorimeter, thermoscope, thermograph, thermostat, thermopile.

Fahrenheit, Centigrade, Celsius, Réaumur.

Thermometry, therm.

(3) *Taste*

390 TASTE (*Substantives*), flavour, gust, gusto, zest, savour, sapor, tang, twang, smack, relish, aftertaste, smatch, sapidity.

Tasting, gustation, degustation.

Palate, tongue, tooth, sweet tooth, stomach.

(*Verbs*) To taste, savour, smack, smatch, flavour, twang.

(*Phrases*) To tickle the palate; to smack the lips.

(*Adjectives*) Sapid, gustable, gustatory, saporific, strong, appetizing, palatable (394).

391 INSIPIDITY (*Substantives*), tastelessness, insipidness, vapidness, vapidity, mawkishness, wershness, mildness; wish-wash, milk and water, slops.

(*Verbs*) To be void of taste, tasteless, etc.

(*Adjectives*) Insipid, tasteless, savourless, mawkish, wersh, flat, vapid, *fade*, wishy-washy, watery, weak, mild; untasted.

---

392 PUNGENCY (*Substantives*), *haut-goût*, strong taste, twang, raciness, race, saltness, sharpness, roughness.

Ginger, caviare, cordial, condiment (393).

(*Verbs*) To be pungent, etc.

To render pungent, to season, spice, salt, pepper, pickle, brine, devil.

(*Adjectives*) Pungent, high-flavoured, high-tasted, high, sharp, strong, rough, stinging, piquant, racy, biting, mordant, spicy, seasoned, hot, peppery, gingery, high-seasoned, gamy, salt, saline, brackish.

(*Phrases*) Salt as brine; salt as a herring; salt as Lot's wife; hot as pepper.

393 CONDIMENT (*Substantives*), salt, mustard, pepper, cayenne, vinegar, curry, chutney, seasoning, spice, ginger, sauce, dressing, *sauce piquante*, caviare, pot-herbs, pickles, onion, garlic, sybo.

394 SAVOURINESS (*Substantives*), palatableness, toothsomeness, daintiness, delicacy, relish, zest.

A titbit, dainty, delicacy, ambrosia, nectar, *bonne-bouche*.

(*Verbs*) To be savoury, etc.

To render palatable, etc.

To relish, like, fancy, be partial to.

(*Adjectives*) Savoury, well-tasted, palatable, nice, good, dainty, delectable, toothsome, tasty, appetizing, delicate, delicious, exquisite, rich, luscious, ambrosial, meaty, fruity.

395 UNSAVOURINESS (*Substantives*), unpalatableness, bitterness, acridness, acridity, acrimony, roughness, acerbity, austerity; gall and wormwood, rue; sickener, scunner.

(*Verbs*) To be unpalatable, etc.

To sicken, disgust, nauseate, pall, turn the stomach.

(*Adjectives*) Unsavoury, unpalatable, ill-flavoured, bitter, acrid, acrimonious, unsweetened, rough, austere, uneatable, inedible.

Offensive, repulsive, nasty, fulsome, sickening, nauseous, nauseating, disgusting, loathsome, palling.

(*Phrases*) Bitter as gall; bitter as aloes.

---

396 SWEETNESS (*Substantives*), dulcitude, dulcification, sweetening.

Sugar, saccharine, glucose, syrup, treacle, molasses, honey, manna, confection, confectionery, candy,

397 SOURNESS (*Substantives*), acid, acidity, tartness, crabbedness, hardness, roughness, acetous fermentation.

Vinegar, verjuice, crab, alum.

(*Verbs*) To be sour, etc.

conserve, jam, jelly, marmalade, preserve, liquorice, julep, sugar-candy, toffee, caramel, butterscotch, plum, sugar-plum, lollipop, bonbon, jujube, lozenge, pastille, comfit, fudge, chocolate, sweet, sweetmeat, marzipan, marchpane, fondant, nougat; mead, nectar, hydromel, honeysuckle.

(*Verbs*) To be sweet, etc.

To render sweet, to sweeten, sugar, mull, edulcorate, candy, dulcify, saccharify.

To render or turn sour, to sour, acidify, acidulate.

(*Phrase*) To set the teeth on edge.

(*Adjectives*) Sour, acid, acidulous, acidulated, sourish, subacid, vinegary, tart, crabbed, acerb, acetic, acetous, acescent, acetose, styptic, hard, rough.

(*Phrases*) Sour as vinegar; sour as a crab.

(*Adjectives*) Sweet, saccharine, sacchariferous, sugary, dulcet, candied, honeyed, luscious, edulcorated, nectarous, nectareous, sweetish, sugary.

(*Phrases*) Sweet as a nut: sweet as honey.

(4) *Odour*

398 ODOUR (*Substantives*), smell, scent, effluvium, emanation, fume, exhalation, essence; trail, nidor, redolence.

The sense of smell, act of smelling.

(*Verbs*) To have an odour, to smell of, to exhale, to give out a smell, etc.

To smell, scent, snuff, sniff, inhale, nose, snowk.

399 INODOROUSNESS (*Substantives*), absence or want of smell; deodorization.

(*Verbs*) To be inodorous, etc., deodorize (652).

(*Adjectives*) Inodorous, odourless, scentless, smell-less, wanting smell.

(*Adjectives*) Odorous, odorant, odoriferous, smelling, strong-scented, graveolent, redolent, nidorous, pungent.

Relating to the sense of smell: olfactory, keen-scented.

400 FRAGRANCE (*Substantives*), aroma, redolence, perfume, savour, bouquet.

Incense, musk, myrrh, frankincense, ambrosia, attar (or otto), eau-de-Cologne, civet, castor, ambergris, bergamot, lavender, sandalwood, orris root, balm, pot-pourri, pulvil; scent-bag, scent-bottle, sachet, nosegay.

(*Phrase*) 'All the perfumes of Arabia.'

(*Verbs*) To perfume, scent, embalm.

(*Adjectives*) Fragrant, aromatic, redolent, balmy, scented, sweet-smelling, sweet-scented, ambrosial, perfumed, musky.

401 FETOR (*Substantives*), bad smell, empyreuma, stench, stink, mustiness, fustiness, frowziness, frowst, fug, rancidity, foulness, putrescence, putridity, mephitis.

A pole-cat, skunk, badger, teledu, asafoetida, cacodyl, stinkard, stink-bomb, stinkpot.

(*Verbs*) To smell, stink, hum, niff, pong.

(*Phrase*) To stink in the nostrils.

(*Adjectives*) Fetid, strong-smelling, smelly, whiffy, malodorous, noisome, offensive, rank, rancid, reasty, mouldy, fusty, musty, stuffy, frowsty, fuggy, foul, frowzy, olid, nidorous, stinking, rotten, putrescent, putrid, putrefying, tainted, high (653), mephitic, empyreumatic.

(5) *Sound*

(I) SOUND IN GENERAL

402 SOUND (*Substantives*), sonance, noise, strain, voice (580), accent, twang, intonation, tone, resonance (408); sonority, sonorousness, audibleness, audibility.

Acoustics, phonics, phonetics, phonology, diacoustics.

(*Verbs*) To produce sound; to sound, make a noise, give out or emit sound, to resound.

(*Adjectives*) Sonorous, sounding, soniferous, sonorific, sonoriferous, resonant, canorous, audible, distinct, phonic, phonetic.

403 SILENCE (*Substantives*), stillness, quiet, peace, calm, hush, lull; muteness (581).

A silencer, mute, damper, sordine.

(*Verbs*) To be silent, etc.

To render silent, to silence, still, hush, stifle, muffle, stop, muzzle, mute, damp, gag.

(*Phrases*) To keep silence; to hold one's tongue; to hold one's peace.

(*Adjectives*) Silent, still, stilly, noiseless, soundless, inaudible, hushed, etc., mute, mum, mumchance (581), solemn, awful, deathlike.

(*Phrases*) Still as a mouse; deathlike silence; silent as the grave; one might hear a pin drop.

(*Adverbs*) Silently, softly, etc., *sub silentio*.

(*Interjections*) Hush! silence! soft! mum! whist! chut! *tace!*

---

404 LOUDNESS (*Substantives*), clatter, din, clangour, clang, roar, uproar, racket, hubbub, flourish of trumpets, tucket, tantara, taratantara, fanfare, blare, alarum, peal, swell, blast, boom, echo, fracas, shindy, row, rumpus, bobbery, clamour, hullaballoo, chorus, hue and cry, shout, yell, whoop, charivari, shivaree, vociferation; Stentor, Boanerges.

Speaking-trumpet, megaphone, loud-speaker, microphone, mike, amplifier, resonator.

Artillery, cannon, thunder.

(*Verbs*) To be loud, etc., to resound, echo, re-echo, peal, swell, clang, boom, blare, thunder, fulminate, roar, whoop, shout (411).

(*Phrases*) To din in the ear; to pierce, split, or rend the ears, or head; to shout, or thunder at the pitch of one's breath, or at the top of one's voice; to make the welkin ring; to rend the air; *faire le diable à quatre*.

405 FAINTNESS (*Substantives*), lowness, faint sounds, whisper, undertone, breath, underbreath, murmur, mutter, hum, susurration, tinkle, rustle.

Hoarseness, huskiness, raucity.

(*Verbs*) To whisper, breathe, murmur, mutter, mumble, purl, hum, croon, gurgle, ripple, babble, tinkle.

(*Phrases*) Steal on the ear; melt, float on the air.

(*Adjectives*) Inaudible, scarcely audible, low, dull, stifled, muffled, hoarse, husky, gentle faint, breathed, etc., soft, floating, purling, etc., liquid, mellifluous, dulcet, flowing, soothing.

(*Adverbs*) In a whisper, with bated breath, under one's breath, *sotto voce*, between the teeth, from the side of one's mouth, aside, *piano, pianissimo, à la sourdine*.

(*Adjectives*) Loud, sonorous, resounding, etc., high-sounding, big-sounding, deep, full, swelling, clamorous, clangorous, multisonous, noisy, blatant, plangent, vocal, vociferous, stunning, piercing, splitting, rending, thundering, deafening, ear-deafening, ear-piercing, obstreperous, blaring, deep-mouthed, open-mouthed, trumpet-tongued, uproarious, rackety, stentorian.

(*Phrases*) Enough to split the head or ears; enough to wake the dead; enough to wake the Seven Sleepers.

(*Adverbs*) Loudly, aloud, etc., *forte, fortissimo.*

(*Phrases*) At the top of one's voice; in full cry.

(2) SPECIFIC SOUNDS

406 Sudden and violent sounds.

SNAP (*Substantives*), knock, rap, tap, click, clash, slam, clack, crack, crackle, crackling, crepitation, decrepitation, report, pop, plop, bang, thud, thump, ping, zip, clap, burst, explosion, discharge, crash, detonation, firing, salvo, atmospherics.

Squib, cracker, gun, pop-gun.

(*Verbs*) To snap, knock, etc.

(*Adjectives*) Snapping, etc.

407 Repeated and protracted sounds.

ROLL (*Substantives*), rumble, rumbling, hum, humming, shake, trill, whirr, chime, tick, beat, toll, ticking, tick-tack, patter, tattoo, ding-dong, drumming, quaver, tremolo, ratatat, tantara, rataplan, rat-tat, clatter, clutter, rattle, racket, rub-a-dub; reverberation (408).

(*Phrases*) The devil's tattoo; tuck of drum.

(*Verbs*) To roll, beat, tick, toll, drum, etc., rattle, clatter, patter, shake, trill, whirr, chime, beat; to drum or din in the ear.

(*Adjectives*) Rolling, rumbling, etc.

408 RESONANCE (*Substantives*), ring, ringing, jingle, chink, tinkle, ting, tink, tintinnabulation, gurgle, chime, toot, tootle, clang, etc. (404). Reflection, reverberation, echo.

(*Verbs*) To resound, reverberate, re-echo, ring, jingle, clink, chime, tinkle, etc.

(*Adjectives*) Resounding, resonant, tintinnabular, ringing, etc.

(*Phrase*) Clear as a bell.

BASS (*Substantives*), low, flat or grave note, chest-note, baritone, contralto.

409 Hissing sounds.

SIBILATION (*Substantives*), hiss, swish, buzz, whiz, rustle, fizz, fizzle, wheeze, whistle, snuffle, sneeze, sternutation.

(*Verbs*) To hiss, buzz, etc.

(*Adjectives*) Sibilant, hissing, buzzing, etc., wheezy.

SOPRANO (*Substantives*), high note (410).

(*Adjectives*) Deep-toned, deep-sounding, deep-mouthed, hollow, sepulchral, *basso profondo.*

410 Harsh sounds.

STRIDOR (*Substantives*), jar, grating, creak, clank, twang, jangle, jarring, creaking, rustling, roughness, gruffness, sharpness, cacophony.

High note, shrillness, acuteness, soprano, falsetto, treble, alto, counter-tenor, penny trumpet, head-note.

(*Verbs*) To creak, grate, jar, burr, pipe, twang, jangle, rustle, clank; to shrill, shriek, screech, squeal, skirl (411), stridulate.

(*Phrases*) To set the teeth on edge; to grate upon the ear.

(*Adjectives*) Strident, stridulous, jarring, etc., harsh, hoarse, horrisonous, discordant, scrannel (414), cacophonous, rough, gruff, sepulchral, grating.

Sharp, high, acute, shrill, piping, screaming.

411 Human sounds.

CRY (*Substantives*), voice (580), vociferation, outcry, roar, shout, bawl, bellow, brawl, halloo, hullaballoo, hoop, whoop, yell, cheer, hoot, howl, chorus, scream, screech, screak, shriek, squeak, squawk, squeal, skirl, yawp, squall, whine, pule, pipe, grumble, plaint, groan, moan, snore, snort.

(*Verbs*) To vociferate, roar, shout, bawl, etc., sing out, thunder, raise or lift up the voice.

(*Adjectives*) Vociferating, etc., clamant, clamorous, vociferous, stertorous.

412 Animal sounds.

ULULATION(*Substantives*),latration, cry, roar, bellow, reboation, bark, yelp, howl, bay, baying, yap, growl, grunt, gruntle, snort, neigh, nicker, whinny, bray, croak, snarl, howl, caterwauling, mew, mewl, miaow, miaul, purr, pule, bleat, baa, low, moo, boo, caw, coo, croodle, cackle, gobble, quack, gaggle, squeak, squawk, squeal, chuckle, chuck, cluck, clack, chirp, chirrup, crow, woodnote, twitter, peep.

Insect cry, drone, buzz, hum.

Cuckoo, screech-owl.

(*Verbs*) To cry, bellow, rebellow, etc., bell, boom, trumpet, give tongue.

(*Phrases*) To bay the moon; to roar like a bull or lion.

(*Adjectives*) Crying, etc., blatant, latrant, remugient.

(3) MUSICAL SOUND

413 MELODY (*Substantives*), melodiousness, *melos.*

Pitch, note, interval, tone, intonation, timbre; high or low, acute or grave notes, treble, alto, tenor, bass, soprano, mezzo-soprano, contralto, counter-tenor, baritone, *basso profondo.*

Scale, gamut, diapason; diatonic, chromatic, enharmonic, whole-tone, etc., scales; key, clef; major, minor, Dorian, Phrygian, Lydian, etc., modes; tetrachord, hexachord, pentatonic scale; tuning, modulation, temperament; solmization, solfeggio, sol-fa.

Staff (or stave), lines, spaces, brace; bar, double bar, rest.

414 DISCORD (*Substantives*), discordance, dissonance, jar, jarring, caterwauling, cocophony.

Hoarseness, croaking, etc. (410).

Confused sounds, babel, Dutch concert, cat's concert, marrow-bones and cleavers, charivari (404).

(*Verbs*) To be discordant, etc., to croak, jar (410).

(*Adjectives*) Discordant, dissonant, out of tune, sharp, flat, tuneless, absonant, unmusical, inharmonious, unmelodious, untuneful, untunable, singsong.

Cacophonous, harsh, hoarse, croaking, jarring, stridulous, etc. (410).

Notes of the scale: sharps, flats, naturals, accidentals; breve, semibreve, minim, crotchet, quaver, semiquaver, demisemiquaver, etc.

Tonic, keynote, supertonic, mediant, subdominant, dominant, submediant, leading note, octave; primes, seconds, triads, etc.

Harmonic, overtone, partial, fundamental, note, hum-note.

Harmony, harmoniousness, concord, concordance, unison, homophony, chord, chime, consonance, concent, euphony; counterpoint, polyphony; tonality, atonality; thorough-bass, figured bass.

Rhythm, time, tempo; common, duple, triple, six-eight, etc., time; *tempo rubato,* syncopation, ragtime, jazz, swing, jive, boogie-woogie, bebop, skiffle, rock-and-roll.

(*Verbs*) To harmonize, chime, be in unison; put in tune, tune, accord.

(*Adjectives*) Harmonious, harmonic, harmonical, in harmony, in tune, etc., unisonant, unisonal, univocal, symphonic, homophonous; contrapuntal, chordal; diatonic, chromatic, enharmonic, tonal, atonal.

Measured, rhythmical, in time, on the beat, hot.

Melodious, musical, tuneful, tunable, sweet, dulcet, canorous, mellow, mellifluous, silver-toned, silvery, euphonious, euphonic, euphonical; enchanting, ravishing, etc., Orphean.

415 MUSIC (*Substantives*), tune, air, lilt, melody, refrain, burden, cadence, theme, motive, motif, *leit-motiv*, subject, counter-subject, episode, modulation, introduction, finale, etc.

Composition, work, opus, score, full score, vocal score, etc.

Solo, duet, trio, quartet, etc., concerted music, chorus, chamber music.

Instrumental music: Symphony, *sinfonietta*, symphonic poem, tone-poem, concerto, sonata, sonatina; *allegro*, *andante*, *largo*, scherzo, rondo, etc.; overture, prelude, intermezzo, postlude, voluntary; ballade, nocturne, serenade, aubade, barcarolle, *berceuse*, etc.; fugue, fugato, canon; variations, humoresque, rhapsody, caprice, *capriccio*, fantasia, impromptu; arrangement, pot-pourri; march, pibroch, minuet, gavotte, waltz, mazurka, etc. (840); accompaniment, *obbligato*; programme music.

Vocal music: Chant, plain-song, Gregorian music, neume, psalmody, psalm, hymn, anthem, motet, antiphon, canticle, introit, etc., service, song, ballad, lied, *chanson*, cavatina, canzonet, serenade, lullaby, ditty, chanty, folk-song, dithyramb; part-song, glee, catch, round, canon, madrigal, chorus, cantata, oratorio, etc.; opera (599).

Dirge, requiem, *nenia*, knell, lament, coronach, dead march.

Musical ornament; grace-note, appoggiatura, trill, shake, turn, beat, mordent, etc.; cadenza, roulade, bravura, colorature, *coloratura*.

Scale, run, arpeggio, chord; five-finger exercise, study, *étude*, toccata.

Performance, execution, technique, touch, expression, tone-colour, rendering, interpretation; voice-production, *bel canto*; *embouchure*, lipping, bowing.

Concert, recital, performance, ballad concert, etc., musicale, sing-song.

Minstrelsy, musicianship, musicality, musicalness, an ear for music; composition, composing, orchestration, scoring, filling in the parts.

Composer, harmonist, contrapuntist.

Apollo, the Muses, Erato, Euterpe, Terpsichore.

(*Verbs*) To play, fiddle, bow, strike, strike up, thrum, strum, grind, touch, tweedle, scrape, blow, pipe, tootle, blare, etc.; to execute, perform, render, interpret, conduct, accompany, vamp, arrange, prelude, improvise (612).

To sing, chant, vocalize, warble, carol, troll, lilt, hum, croon, chirp, chirrup, twitter, quaver, trill, shake, whistle, yodel.

To compose, set to music, score, harmonize, orchestrate.

To put in tune, tune, attune, accord, string, pitch.

(*Adjectives*) Musical, harmonious, etc. (413), instrumental, orchestral, pianistic, vocal, choral, operatic, etc.; musicianly, having a good ear.

(*Phrase*) *Fanatico per la musica.*

(*Adverbs*) *Adagio, largo, larghetto, andante, andantino, maestoso, moderato, allegretto, con moto, vivace, veloce, allegro, presto, prestissimo, strepitoso,* etc.; *scherzando, legato, staccato, crescendo, diminuendo, morendo, sostenuto, sforzando, accelerando, stringendo, più mosso, meno mosso, allargando, rallentando, ritenuto, a piacere,* etc.; *arpeggiando, pizzicato, glissando, martellato, da capo.*

416 MUSICIAN (*Substantives*), minstrel, performer, player, soloist, virtuoso, maestro.

Organist, pianist, violinist, fiddler, cellist, harper, harpist, flautist, fifer, clarinettist, trombonist, etc., trumpeter, bugler, piper, bagpiper, drummer, timpanist; campanologist; band, orchestra, brass band, military band, string band, pipe band, waits; conductor, bandmaster, drum-major, leader, *chef d'orchestre*, etc., accompanist.

Vocalist, singer, songster, songstress, chanter, chantress, *cantatrice, lieder-singer*, ballad-singer, etc.; troubadour, minnesinger, gleeman; nightingale, Philomel, thrush, throstle, Orpheus.

Chorus, choir, chorister.

(*Phrase*) The tuneful Nine.

417 MUSICAL INSTRUMENTS.

1. Stringed instruments: Monochord, polychord, harp, lyre, lute, theorbo, mandolin, guitar, gittern, cithern, banjo, ukelele, balalaika.

Violin, fiddle, Cremona, Stradivarius (or Strad), kit, viola (or tenor), violoncello (or cello), double-bass (or bass-viol), viol, viola d'amore, viola da gamba, violone, rebeck, psaltery.

Pianoforte (or piano), harpsichord, clavier, clavichord, clavicembalo, spinet, cembalo, virginal, zither, dulcimer.

2. Wind instruments: Organ, siren, pipe, pitch-pipe, Pan-pipes; piccolo, flute, bass-flute, oboe (or hautboy), oboe d'amore, cor anglais, clarinet, basset-horn, bass-clarinet, bassoon, double-bassoon, saxophone, horn, French horn, tuba, trumpet, cornet, cornet-à-piston, trombone, euphonium; fife, flageolet, whistle, penny-whistle, ocarina, bugle, serpent, ophicleide, clarion, bagpipe, musette; harmonium, American organ, seraphina, concertina, accordion, melodeon, mouth-organ, etc.; great, swell, choir, solo and echo organs.

3. Vibrating surfaces: Cymbal, bell, carillon, gong, tabor, tambourine, timbrel, drum, side-drum, bass-drum, kettle-drum, timpano, military drum, tom-tom, castanet; musical glasses, harmonica, glockenspiel; sounding-board.

4. Vibrating bars: Tuning-fork, triangle, xylophone, Jew's harp.

5. Mechanical instruments: Musical box, hurdy-gurdy, barrel-organ, piano-organ, orchestrion, piano-player, pianola, etc.; gramophone, phonograph, tape recorder, juke box, nickelodeon.

Key, string, bow, drumstick, bellows, sound-box, pedal, stop; loud or sustaining pedal, soft pedal, mute, sordine, sourdine, damper, swell-box; keyboard, finger-board, console; organ-loft, concert platform, orchestra, choir, singing-gallery, belfry, campanile.

(4) PERCEPTION OF SOUND

418 Sense of sound.

HEARING (*Substantives*), audition, auscultation, listening, eavesdropping; audibility.

Acuteness, nicety, delicacy, of ear.

Ear, auricle, acoustic organs, auditory apparatus, lug, ear-drum, tympanum.

Telephone, speaking-tube, ear-trumpet, audiphone, audiometer, ear-phone, phone, gramophone, phonograph, dictaphone, intercom, receiver.

Wireless telephony, broadcasting, wireless, radio, transmitter, walkie-talkie, radiogram, microphone, mike.

419 DEAFNESS (*Substantives*), hardness of hearing, surdity; inaudibility.

(*Verbs*) To be deaf, to shut, stop, or close one's ears.

To render deaf, to stun, deafen.

(*Phrase*) To turn a deaf ear to.

(*Adjectives*) Deaf, stone deaf, tone deaf, hard of hearing, earless, surd, dull of hearing, deaf-mute, stunned, deafened, having no ear.

Inaudible, out of earshot.

(*Phrases*) Deaf as a post; deaf as a beetle; deaf as an adder.

A hearer, auditor, listener, eavesdropper, auditory, audience.
(*Verbs*) To hear, overhear, hark, listen, list, hearken, give or lend an ear, prick up one's ears, give a hearing or audience to, listen in.
To become audible, to catch the ear, to be heard.
(*Phrases*) To hang upon the lips of; to be all ears.
(*Adjectives*) Hearing, etc., auditory, auricular, acoustic.
(*Interjections*) Hark! list! hear! listen! oyez! (or oyes!)
(*Adverbs*) *Arrectis auribus*; with ears flapping.

(6) *Light*

(1) LIGHT IN GENERAL

420 LIGHT (*Substantives*), ray, beam, stream, gleam, streak, pencil, sunbeam, moonbeam, starbeam.

Day, daylight, sunshine, sunlight, moonlight, starlight, the light of day, the light of heaven, noontide, noonday, noontide light, broad daylight.

Glimmer, glimmering, glow, afterglow, phosphorescence, lambent flame, play of light.

Flush, halo, aureole, nimbus, glory, corona.

Spark, sparkle, scintilla, sparkling, scintillation, flame, flash, blaze, coruscation, fulguration, lightning, flood of light, glint.

Lustre, shine, sheen, gloss, tinsel, spangle, brightness, brilliancy, refulgence, dazzlement, splendour, resplendence, luminousness, luminosity, luminescence, lucidity, lucidness, incandescence, radiance, illumination, irradiation, glare, flare, flush, effulgence, fulgency, fluorescence, lucency, lambency.

Optics, photology, photometry, dioptrics, catoptrics.

Radioactivity, radiography, radiograph, radiometer, radioscopy, radiotherapy.

(*Verbs*) To shine, glow, glitter, glisten, glister, glint, twinkle, gleam, flicker, flare, glare, beam, radiate, shoot beams, shimmer, sparkle, scintillate, coruscate, flash, blaze, fizzle, daze, dazzle, bedazzle; to clear up, to brighten.

To illuminate, illume, illumine, lighten, enlighten, light, light up, irradiate, flush, shine upon, cast lustre upon; cast, throw, or shed a light upon, brighten, clear, relume.

421 DARKNESS (*Substantives*), night, midnight, obscurity, dusk (422), duskiness, gloom, gloominess, murk, mirk, murkiness, shadow, shade, umbrage, shadiness, umbra, penumbra, Erebus.

Obscuration, adumbration, obumbration, obtenebration, obfuscation, black-out, extinction, eclipse, gathering of the clouds, dimness (422).

(*Phrases*) Dead of night; darkness visible; darkness that can be felt; blind man's holiday.

(*Verbs*) To be dark, etc.; to lour (or lower).

To darken, obscure, shade, shadow, dim, bedarken, overcast, overshadow, obfuscate, obumbrate, adumbrate, cast in the shade, becloud, overcloud, bedim, put out, snuff out, blow out, extinguish, dout, douse.

To cast, throw, spread a shade or gloom.

(*Phrase*) To douse the glim.

(*Adjectives*) Dark, obscure, darksome, darkling, tenebrous, tenebrific, rayless, beamless, sunless, moonless, starless, pitch-dark, pitchy; Stygian, Cimmerian.

Sombre, dusky, unilluminated, unillumined, unlit, unsunned, nocturnal, dingy, lurid, overcast, louring (or lowering), cloudy, murky, murksome, shady, shadowy, umbrageous.

Benighted, noctivagant, noctivagous.

(*Phrases*) Dark as pitch; dark as a pit; dark as Erebus; dark as a wolf's mouth; the palpable obscure.

422 DIMNESS (*Substantives*), dimout, brown-out, paleness, glimmer, glimmering, owl-light, nebulousness,

(*Phrase*) To strike a light.

(*Adjectives*) Luminous, luminiferous, shining, glowing, etc., lambent, glossy, lucid, lucent, luculent, lustrous, lucific, glassy, clear, bright, scintillant, light, lightsome, unclouded, sunny, orient, noonday, noontide, beaming, beamy, vivid, alight, splendent, radiant, radiating, cloudless, unobscured; radioactive, fluorescent, phosphorescent.

Garish, resplendent, refulgent, fulgent, effulgent, in a blaze, ablaze, relucent, splendid, blazing, rutilant, meteoric, burnished.

(*Phrases*) Bright as silver, as day, as noonday.

nebulosity, nebula, cloud, film, mist, haze, fog, brume, smog, smoke, haziness, eclipse, dusk, cloudiness, dawn, aurora, twilight, crepuscule, cockshut time, gloaming, daybreak, dawn, half-light, moonlight; moonshine, moonbeam, starlight, starshine, starbeam, candle-light.

(*Verbs*) To be dim, etc., to glimmer, loom, lour, twinkle.

To grow dim, to fade, to render dim, to dim, obscure, pale.

(*Adjectives*) Dim, dull, lack-lustre, dingy, darkish, glassy, faint, confused.

Cloudy, misty, hazy, foggy, brumous, muggy, fuliginous, nebulous, lowering, overcast, crepuscular, muddy, lurid, looming.

(*Phrase*) Shorn of its beams.

---

423 Source of light, self-luminous body.

LUMINARY (*Substantives*), sun, Phoebus, star, orb, meteor, galaxy, constellation, blazing star, glow-worm, firefly.

Meteor, northern lights, aurora borealis, aurora australis, fire-drake, ignis fatuus, jack-o'-lantern, will-o'-the-wisp, friar's lantern.

Artificial light, flame, gas-light, incandescent gas-light, electric light, limelight, acetylene, torch, candle, flash-lamp, flashlight, flambeau, link, light, taper, lamp, arc-lamp, mercury vapour lamp, neon lighting, lantern (or lanthorn), rushlight, farthing rushlight, night-light, firework, rocket, Very light, blue lights, fizgig, flare.

Chandelier, gaselier, electrolier, candelabra, girandole, lustre, sconce, gas-bracket, gas-jet, gas-burner, batswing; gas-mantle, electric bulb, filament.

Lighthouse, lightship, pharos, beacon, watch-fire, cresset, brand.

(*Adjectives*) Self-luminous, phosphoric, phosphorescent, radiant (420).

424 SHADE (*Substantives*), awning, parasol, sunshade, screen, curtain, veil, mantle, mask, gauze, blind, shutter, cloud, mist.

A shadow, chiaroscuro, umbrage, penumbra (421).

(*Adjectives*) Shady, umbrageous.

---

425 TRANSPARENCY (*Substantives*), transparence, diaphaneity, translucence, translucency, lucidity, pellucidity, limpidity, clarity.

Glass, crystal, mica, lymph, water.

(*Verbs*) To be transparent, etc., to transmit light.

(*Adjectives*) Transparent, pellucid,

426 OPACITY (*Substantives*), thickness, opaqueness, turbidity, turbidness, muddiness.

Cloud, film, haze.

(*Verbs*) To be opaque, etc., to obfuscate, not to transmit, to obstruct the passage of light.

(*Adjectives*) Opaque, turbid, roily,

lucid, diaphanous, translucent, relucent, limpid, clear, crystalline, vitreous, transpicuous, glassy, hyaline.
(*Phrase*) Clear as crystal.

thick, muddy, opacous, obfuscated, fuliginous, cloudy, hazy, misty, foggy, impervious to light.

---

427 SEMITRANSPARENCY, opalescence, pearliness, milkiness.
Film, gauze, muslin.

(*Adjectives*) Semitransparent, semi-diaphanous, semi-opaque, opalescent, gauzy, pearly, milky.

(2) SPECIFIC LIGHT

428 COLOUR (*Substantives*), hue, tint, tinge, dye, complexion, shade, spectrum, tincture, blazonry, cast, livery, coloration, glow, flush, tone, key.
Pure or positive colour, primary colour.
Broken colour, secondary or tertiary colour.
Chromatics; prism, spectroscope.
A pigment, colouring matter, medium, paint, dye, wash, stain, distemper, mordant.
(*Verbs*) To colour, dye, tinge, stain, tinct, tincture, paint, wash, illuminate, blazon, emblazon, bedizen, imbue, distemper.
(*Adjectives*) Coloured, colorific, chromatic, prismatic, full-coloured, lush, dyed; tinctorial.
Bright, deep, vivid, florid, fresh, high-coloured, unfaded, gay, showy, gaudy, garish, flaunting, vivid, gorgeous, glaring, flaring, flashy, tawdry, meretricious, raw, intense, double-dyed, loud, noisy.
Mellow, harmonious, pearly, light, quiet, delicate, pastel.

429 Absence of colour.
ACHROMATISM (*Substantives*), decoloration, discoloration, paleness, pallidity, pallidness, pallor, etiolation, anaemia, chlorosis, albinism, neutral tint, colourlessness; monochrome, black and white.
(*Verbs*) To lose colour, to fade, pale, blanch, become colourless.
To deprive of colour, discolour, bleach, tarnish, decolour, decolorate, decolorize, achromatize, tone down.
(*Adjectives*) Colourless, uncoloured, untinged, untinctured, achromatic, aplanatic, hueless, undyed, pale, pallid, pale-faced, pasty, etiolated, anaemic, chlorotic, faint, faded, dull, cold, muddy, wan, sallow, dead, dingy, ashy, ashen, cadaverous, glassy, lack-lustre, tarnished, bleached, discoloured.
(*Phrases*) Pale as death, as ashes, as a witch, as a ghost, as a corpse.

---

430 WHITENESS (*Substantives*), milkiness, hoariness.
Albification, etiolation.
Snow, paper, chalk, milk, lily, sheet, ivory, silver, alabaster.
(*Verbs*) To be white, etc.
To render white, whiten, bleach, whitewash, blanch, etiolate.
(*Adjectives*) White, milk-white, snow-white, snowy, niveous, chalky, hoary, hoar, silvery, argent.

431 BLACKNESS (*Substantives*), darkness (421), swarthiness, dinginess, lividity, inkiness, pitchiness, nigritude.
Nigrification.
Jet, ink, ebony, coal, pitch, charcoal, soot, sloe, smut, raven, crow; negro, nigger, darkie, coon, blackamoor.
(*Verbs*) To be black, etc.
To render black, to blacken, nigrify,

Whitish, off-white, cream-coloured, creamy, pearly, fair, blonde, etiolated, albescent.

(*Phrases*) White as the driven snow; white as a sheet.

432 GREY (*Substantives*), neutral tint, dun.

(*Adjectives*) Grey, etc., drab, dingy, sombre, leaden, livid, ashen, mouse-coloured, slate-coloured, stone-coloured, cinereous, cineritious, grizzly, grizzled.

denigrate, blot, blotch, smirch, smutch.

(*Adjectives*) Black, sable, swarthy, swart, sombre, inky, ebon, livid, coal-black, jet-black, pitch-black, fuliginous, dingy, dusky, Ethiopic, nigrescent.

(*Phrases*) Black as my hat; black as ink; black as coal; black as a crow; black as thunder.

433 BROWN (*Substantives*), bistre, ochre, sepia.

(*Adjectives*) Brown, etc., bay, dapple, auburn, chestnut, nut-brown, umber, cinnamon, fawn, russet, olive, hazel, tawny, fuscous, chocolate, liver-coloured, tan, brunette, maroon, khaki, foxy, bronzed, sunburnt, tanned.

(*Phrases*) Brown as a berry, as mahogany, as a gipsy.

(*Verbs*) To render brown, embrown, to tan, bronze, etc.

Primitive Colours

434 REDNESS (*Substantives*), red, scarlet, vermilion, crimson, carmine, pink, lake, maroon, carnation, damask, ruby, rose, blush colour, peach colour, flesh colour, gules, solferino.

Rust, cinnabar, cochineal, madder, red lead, ruddle; blood, lobster, cherry, pillar-box.

Erubescence, rubescence, rubefaction, rosiness, rufescence, ruddiness, rubicundity.

(*Verbs*) To become red, to blush, flush, mantle, redden, colour.

435 GREENNESS (*Substantives*), verdure, viridescence, viridity.

Emerald, jasper, verd-antique, verdigris, beryl, aquamarine, malachite, grass.

(*Adjectives*) Green, verdant, pea-green, grass-green, apple-green, sea-green, turquoise-green, olive-green, bottle-green, glaucous, virescent, aeruginous, vert.

(*Phrase*) Green as grass.

To render red, redden, rouge, rubefy, rubricate, incarnadine.

(*Adjectives*) Red, scarlet, vermilion, carmine, rose, ruby, crimson, pink, etc., ruddy, rufous, florid, rosy, roseate, auroral, rose-coloured, blushing, mantling, etc., erubescent, blowzy, rubicund, stammel, blood-red, ensanguined, rubiform, cardinal, cerise, *sang-de-bœuf*, murrey, carroty, sorrel, brick-coloured, brick-red, lateritic, cherry-coloured, salmon-coloured.

(*Phrases*) Red as fire, as blood, as scarlet, as a turkey-cock, as a cherry.

436 YELLOWNESS (*Substantives*), buff colour, orpiment, yellow ochre, gamboge, crocus, saffron, xanthin, topaz.

437 PURPLE (*Substantives*), violet, plum, prune, lavender, lilac, peach colour, puce, gridelin, lividness, lividity, bishop's purple, magenta, mauve.

Lemon, mustard, jaundice, gold.

(*Adjectives*) Yellow, citron, gold, golden, aureate, citrine, fallow, tawny, flavous, fulvous, saffron, croceate, lemon, xanthic, xanthous, sulphur, amber, straw-coloured, sandy, lurid, Claude-tint, luteous, primrose-coloured, cream-coloured, buff, chrome.

(*Phrases*) Yellow as a quince, as a guinea, as a crow's foot.

Amethyst, murex.

(*Verb*) To empurple.

(*Adjectives*) Purple, violet, plum-coloured, lilac, mauve, livid, etc.

———

438 BLUENESS (*Substantives*), bluishness, azure, indigo, ultramarine, Prussian blue, mazarine, bloom, bice.

Sky, sea, lapis lazuli, cobalt, sapphire, turquoise.

(*Adjectives*) Blue, cerulean, sky-blue, sky-coloured, sky-dyed, watchet, azure, bluish, sapphire, Garter-blue.

439 ORANGE (*Substantives*), gold, flame, copper, brass, apricot colour; aureolin, nacarat.

Ochre, cadmium.

(*Adjectives*) Orange, golden, ochreous, etc., buff, flame-coloured.

———

440 VARIEGATION (*Substantives*), dichroism, trichroism, iridescence, play of colours, *reflet*, variegatedness, patchwork, check, plaid, chess-board, tartan, maculation, spottiness, pointillism, parquetry, marquetry, mosaic, inlay, buhl, striae, spectrum.

A rainbow, iris, tulip, peacock, chameleon, butterfly, tortoise-shell, leopard, zebra, harlequin, motley, mother-of-pearl, nacre, opal, marble.

(*Verbs*) To be variegated, etc.

To variegate, speckle, stripe, streak, chequer, bespeckle, fleck, freckle, inlay, stipple, spot, dot, damascene, embroider, tattoo.

(*Adjectives*) Variegated, varicoloured, many-coloured, versicolour, many-hued, divers-coloured, particoloured, polychromatic, bicolour, tricolour, dichromatic.

Iridescent, prismatic, opaline, nacreous, pearly, opalescent, shot, watered, *chatoyant, gorge de pigeon*, all manner of colours, pied, piebald, skewbald, daedal, motley, mottled, veined, marbled, paned, dappled, clouded, cymophanous.

Mosaic, inlaid, tessellated, chequered, tartan, tortoiseshell.

Dotted, spotted, bespotted, spotty, speckled, bespeckled, punctate, maculated, freckled, fleckered, flecked, flea-bitten, studded, tattooed.

Striped, striated, streaked, barred, veined, brinded, brindled, tabby, roan, grizzled, listed, stippled.

(*Phrase*) All the colours of the rainbow.

(3) PERCEPTIONS OF LIGHT

441 VISION (*Substantives*), sight, optics, eyesight.

View, espial, glance, glimpse, peep, peek, look, squint, dekko, gander, the once-over, gaze, stare, leer, perlustration, contemplation, sight-seeing, regard, survey, reconnaissance, introspection, inspection, speculation,

442 BLINDNESS (*Substantives*), night-blindness, snow-blindness, cecity, amaurosis, cataract, ablepsy, nictitation, wink, blink.

A blinkard.

(*Verbs*) To be blind, etc., not to see, to lose sight of.

Not to look, to close or shut the

watch, *coup d'œil*, œillade, glad eye, bo-peep, ocular demonstration, autopsy, visualization, envisagement.

A point of view, gazebo, vista, loop-hole, peep-hole, look-out, belvedere, field of view, watch-tower, observation post, crow's nest, theatre, amphitheatre, horizon, arena, commanding view, bird's-eye view, coign of vantage, observatory, periscope.

The organ of vision, eye, the naked or unassisted eye, retina, pupil, iris, cornea, white, optics, peepers.

Perspicacity, penetration, discernment.

Cat, hawk, lynx, eagle, Argus.

Evil eye; cockatrice, basilisk.

(*Verbs*) To see, behold, discern, have in sight, descry, sight, catch a sight, glance, or glimpse of, spy, espy, to get a sight of.

eyes, to look another way, to turn away or avert the eyes, to wink, blink, nictitate.

To render blind, etc., to put out the eyes, to blind, blindfold, hoodwink, daze, dazzle.

(*Phrase*) To throw dust in the eyes.

(*Adjectives*) Blind, eyeless, sightless, visionless, dark, stone-blind, sand-blind, stark-blind, mope-eyed, dazzled, hoodwinked, blindfolded, undiscerning.

(*Phrases*) Blind as a bat, as a buzzard, as a beetle, as a mole, as an owl.

(*Adverbs*) Blindly, etc., blindfold, darkly.

———

To look, view, eye, open one's eyes, glance on, cast or set one's eyes on, clap eyes on, look on or upon, turn or bend one's looks upon, turn the eyes to, envisage, visualize, peep, peer, peek, pry, scan, survey, reconnoitre, contemplate, regard, inspect, recognize, mark, discover, distinguish, see through, speculate; to see sights, lionize.

To look intently, strain one's eyes, be all eyes, look full in the face, look hard at, stare, gaze, pore over, gloat on, leer, to see with half an eye, to blink, goggle, ogle, make eyes at; to play at bo-peep.

(*Phrases*) To have an eye upon; keep in sight; look about one; glance round; run the eye over; lift up one's eyes; see at a glance, or with half an eye; keep a look-out for; to keep one's eyes skinned; to be a spectator of; to see with one's own eyes.

(*Adjectives*) Visual, ocular, optic, optical, ophthalmic.

Seeing, etc., the eyes being directed to, fixed, riveted upon.

Clear-sighted, sharp-sighted, quick-sighted, eagle-eyed, hawk-eyed, lynx-eyed, keen-eyed, Argus-eyed, piercing, penetrating.

(*Phrase*) The scales falling from one's eyes.

(*Adverbs*) Visibly, etc., at sight, in sight of, to one's face, before one's face, with one's eyes open, at a glance, at first sight, at sight.

(*Interjections*) Look! behold! see! lo! mark! observe! lo and behold!

443 Imperfect vision.

DIM-SIGHTEDNESS (*Substantives*), purblindness, lippitude, confusion of vision, scotomy, failing sight, short-sightedness, near-sightedness, myopia, nictitation, long-sightedness, amblyopia, presbyopia, hypermetropia, nyctalopia (or nyctalopy), nystagmus, astigmatism, squint, strabismus, wall-eye, swivel-eye, cast of the eye, double sight; an albino, blinkard.

Fallacies of vision: *deceptio visus*, refraction, false light, phantasm, anamorphosis, distortion, looming, mirage, *fata morgana*, the spectre of the Brocken, ignis fatuus, phantasmagoria, dissolving views.

Colour-blindness, Daltonism.

Limitation of vision, blinker, screen.

(*Verbs*) To be dim-sighted, etc., to see double, to have a mote in the eye, to squint, goggle, look askance (or askant), to see through a prism, wink, nictitate.

To glare, dazzle, loom.

(*Adjectives*) Dim-sighted, half-sighted, short-sighted, near-sighted, purblind, myopic, long-sighted, hypermetropic, presbyopic, moon-eyed, mope-eyed, blear-eyed, goggle-eyed, wall-eyed, one-eyed, nictitating, winking, monoculous, amblyopic, astigmatic.

444 SPECTATOR (*Substantives*), looker-on, onlooker, watcher, sightseer, bystander, *voyeur*, inspector, snooper, rubberneck (455), spy, beholder, witness, eye-witness, observer, star-gazer, etc., scout.

(*Verbs*) To witness, behold, look on at, spectate.

445 OPTICAL INSTRUMENTS (*Substantives*), lens, meniscus, magnifier, reading-glass, microscope, megascope, spectacles, specs, glasses, barnacles, goggles, pince-nez, lorgnette, folders, eye-glass, monocle, contact lens, periscope, telescope, spy-glass, monocular, binoculars, field-glass, night-glass, opera-glass, glass, view-finder, range-finder.

Mirror, reflector, speculum, looking-glass, pier-glass, cheval-glass, kaleidoscope.

Prism, camera, cine-camera, cinematograph (448), camera lucida, camera obscura, magic lantern, phantasmagoria, thaumatrope, chromatrope, stereoscope, pseudoscope, bioscope.

Photometer, polariscope, spectroscope, collimator, polemoscope, eriometer, actinometer, exposure meter, lucimeter.

446 VISIBILITY (*Substantives*), perceptibility, conspicuousness, distinctness, conspicuity, appearance, exposure.

(*Verbs*) To be visible, etc., to appear, come in sight, come into view, heave in sight, open to the view, catch the eye, show its face, present itself, show itself, manifest itself, produce itself, discover itself, expose itself, come out, come to light, come forth, come forward, stand forth, stand out, arise, peep out, peer out, show up, turn up, crop up, start up, loom, burst forth, break through the clouds, glare, reveal itself, betray itself.

(*Phrases*) To show its colours; to see the light of day; to show one's face; to tell its own tale; to leap to the eye; *cela saute aux yeux*; to stare one in the face.

(*Adjectives*) Visible, perceptible, perceivable, discernible, in sight, apparent, plain, manifest, patent, obvious (525), clear, distinct, definite, well-defined, well-marked, recognizable, evident, unmistakable, palpable, naked, bare, barefaced, ostensible,

447 INVISIBILITY (*Substantives*), indistinctness, inconspicuousness, imperceptibility, nonappearance, delitescence, latency (526), concealment (528).

(*Verbs*) To be invisible, escape notice, etc., to lie hidden, concealed, etc. (528), to be in or under a cloud, in a mist, in a haze, etc.; to lurk, lie in ambush, skulk.

Not to see, etc., to be blind to.

To render invisible, to hide, conceal (528).

(*Adjectives*) Invisible, imperceptible, unseen, unbeheld, undiscerned, viewless, undiscernible, indiscernible, sightless, undescried, unespied, unapparent, non-apparent, inconspicuous, unconspicuous, hidden, concealed, etc. (528), covert, eclipsed.

Confused, dim, obscure, dark, misty, hazy, foggy, indistinct, ill-defined, indefinite, ill-marked, blurred, shadowy, nebulous, shaded, screened, veiled, masked.

(*Phrases*) Out of sight; not in sight; out of focus.

conspicuous, prominent, staring, glaring, notable, notorious, overt; periscopic, panoramic, stereoscopic.

(*Phrases*) Open as day; clear as day; plain as a pikestaff; there is no mistaking; plain as the nose on one's face; before one's eyes; above-board; exposed to view; under one's nose; in bold relief; in the limelight.

448 APPEARANCE (*Substantives*), phenomenon, sight, spectacle, show, premonstration, scene, species, view, *coup d'œil*, look-out, prospect, outlook, vista, perspective, bird's-eye view, scenery, landscape, seascape, streetscape, picture, tableau, *mise en scène*, display, exposure, exhibition, manifestation.

Pageant, pageantry, peep-show, raree-show, panorama, diorama, cosmorama, georama, *coup de théâtre, jeu de théâtre*.

Bioscope, biograph, magic lantern, epidiascope, cinematograph (or kinematograph).

Phantasm, phasma, phantom, spectrum, apparition, spectre, mirage, etc. (4, 443).

Aspect, phase, *phasis*, seeming, guise, look, complexion, shape, mien, air, cast, carriage, manner, bearing, deportment, port, demeanour, presence, expression.

Lineament, feature, trait, lines, outline, contour, face, countenance, physiognomy, visage, phiz, mug, dial, puss, pan, profile, *tournure*.

(*Verbs*) To seem, look, appear; to present, wear, carry, have, bear, exhibit, take, take on, or assume the appearance of; to play, to look like, to be visible, to reappear; to materialize.

To show, to manifest.

(*Adjectives*) Apparent, seeming, etc., ostensible.

(*Adverbs*) Apparently, to all appearance, etc., ostensibly, seemingly on the face of it, *prima facie*, at the first blush, at first sight.

449 DISAPPEARANCE (*Substantives*), evanescence, eclipse, occultation.

Dissolving views, fade-out.

(*Verbs*) To disappear, vanish, dissolve, fade, melt away, pass, be gone, be lost, etc.

To efface, blot, blot out, erase, rub out, expunge (552).

(*Phrase*) To go off the stage.

(*Adjectives*) Disappearing, etc., lost, vanishing, evanescent, gone, missing.

Inconspicuous, unconspicuous (447).

(*Phrases*) Lost in the clouds; leaving no trace; out of sight.

(*Interjections*) Avaunt! vanish! disappear! (297).

CLASS IV

WORDS RELATING TO THE INTELLECTUAL FACULTIES

DIVISION I—FORMATION OF IDEAS

Section I—Operations of Intellect in General

450 Intellect (*Substantives*), mind, understanding, reason, thinking principle, nous, noesis, faculties, sense, common sense, consciousness, capacity, intelligence, percipience, intellection, intuition, instinct, conception, judgment, talent, genius, parts, wit, wits, shrewdness, intellectuality; the five senses; rationalism; ability, skill (698); wisdom (498).

Subconsciousness, subconscious mind, unconscious, id.

Soul, spirit, psyche, ghost, inner man, heart, breast, bosom.

Organ or seat of thought: *sensorium*, sensory, brain, head, headpiece, pate, noddle, nut, loaf, skull, brain-pan, grey matter, pericranium, cerebrum, cerebellum, cranium, upper storey, belfry.

Science of mind, phrenology, mental philosophy, metaphysics, psychology, psychics, psycho-analysis; ideology, idealism, ideality, pneumatology, immaterialism, intuitionism, realism; transcendentalism, spiritualism.

Metaphysician, psychologist, psychiatrist, psycho-analyst, psychotherapist.

(*Verbs*) Appreciate, realize, be aware of, be conscious of, take in, mark, note, notice.

(*Adjectives*) Intellectual, noetic, rational, reasoning, gnostic, mental, spiritual, subjective, metaphysical, psychical, psychological, noumenal, ghostly, immaterial (317), cerebral; subconscious, subliminal, Freudian.

450a Absence or want of intellect, imbecility (499), materialism.

(*Adjectives*) Material, objective, unreasoning.

————

451 Thought (*Substantives*), reflection, cogitation, cerebration, consideration, meditation, study, lucubration, speculation, deliberation, pondering, head-work, brain-work, application, attention (457).

Abstraction, contemplation, musing, brown study, reverie (458); depth of thought, workings of the mind, inmost thoughts, self-counsel, self-communing, self-examination, introspection; succession, flow, train,

452 Absence or want of thought.

Incogitancy (*Substantives*), vacancy, inanity, fatuity (499), thoughtlessness (458).

(*Verbs*) Not to think, to take no thought of, not to trouble oneself about, to put away thought; to inhibit, dismiss, discard, or discharge from one's thoughts, or from the mind; to drop the subject, set aside, turn aside, turn away from, turn

current, etc., of thought or of ideas,
brain-wave.

Afterthought, second thoughts,
hindsight, reconsideration, retrospection, retrospect (505), examination
(461), imagination (515).

Thoughtfulness, pensiveness, intentness.

Telepathy, thought-transference,
mind-reading, extra-sensory perception, retrocognition, telekinesis.

(*Verbs*) To think, reflect, cogitate,
excogitate, consider, deliberate, speculate, contemplate, mediate, intro-
spect, ponder, muse, ruminate, think
over, brood over, reconsider, animad-
vert, con, con over, mull over, study, bend or apply the mind, digest,
discuss, hammer at, puzzle out, weigh, perpend, fancy, trow, dream of.

To occur, present itself, pass in the mind, suggest itself, strike one.

To harbour, entertain, cherish, nurture, etc., an idea, a thought,
a notion, a view, etc.

(*Phrases*) Take into account; take into consideration; to take counsel;
to commune with oneself; to collect one's thoughts; to advise with
one's pillow; to sleep on or over it; to chew the cud upon; revolve in
the mind; turn over in the mind; to rack or cudgel one's brains; to put
on one's thinking-cap.

To flash on the mind; to flit across the view; to enter the mind; come
into the head; come uppermost; run in one's head.

To make an impression; to sink or penetrate into the mind; fasten
itself on the mind; to engross one's thoughts.

(*Adjectives*) Thinking, etc., thoughtful, pensive, meditative, reflective,
ruminant, introspective, wistful, contemplative, speculative, deliberative,
studious, abstracted, introspective, sedate, philosophical, conceptual.

Close, active, diligent, mature, deliberate, laboured, steadfast, deep,
profound, intense, etc., thought, study, reflection, etc.

Intent, engrossed, absorbed, deep-musing, rapt (or wrapt), abstracted;
sedate.

(*Phrases*) Having the mind on the stretch; lost in thought; the mind
or head running upon.

one's attention from, abstract oneself, dream.

To unbend, relax, divert the mind.

(*Adjectives*) Vacant, unintellectual
(499), unoccupied, unthinking, inconsiderate, thoughtless, idealess,
unidea'd, absent, *distrait*, abstracted,
inattentive (458), diverted, distracted,
distraught, unbent, relaxed.

Unthought-of, unconsidered, in-
cogitable, undreamed-of, off one's
mind.

(*Phrase*) *In nubibus.*

---

453 Object of thought.

IDEA (*Substantives*), notion, conception, apprehension, concept,
thought, fancy, conceit, impression,
perception, apperception, percept,
ideation, image, eidolon, sentiment,
(484), fantasy, flight of fancy.

Point of view, light, aspect (448),
field of view, standpoint; theory
(514); fixed idea (481).

---

454 Subject of thought.

TOPIC (*Substantives*), subject,
matter, theme, motif, thesis, text,
subject-matter, point, proposition,
theorem, business, affair, case, matter
in hand, question, argument, motion,
resolution, moot point (461), head,
chapter; nice or subtle point, quodlibet.

(*Phrases*) Food for thought; mental
pabulum.

(*Adverbs*) In question, under consideration, on the carpet, *sur le tapis*,
relative to, *re*, *in re* (9), concerning,
touching.

SECTION II—PRECURSORY CONDITIONS AND OPERATIONS

455 The desire of knowledge.
CURIOSITY (*Substantives*), curiousness, inquisitiveness, an inquiring mind.

A quidnunc, busybody, eavesdropper, snooper, rubberneck, Peeping Tom, Nosy Parker, Paul Pry, newsmonger, gossip.

(*Verbs*) To be curious, etc., to take an interest in, to stare, gape, pry, snoop, rubber, lionize.

(*Adjectives*) Curious, inquisitive, inquiring, inquisitorial, all agog, staring, prying, snoopy, gaping, agape, over-curious, nosy.

(*Adverbs*) With open mouth, on tiptoe, with ears flapping, *arrectis auribus*.

456 Absence of curiosity.
INCURIOSITY (*Substantives*), incuriousness, insouciance, nonchalance, want of interest, indifference (866).

(*Verbs*) To be incurious, etc., to have no curiosity, take no interest in, not to care, not to mind; to mind one's own business.

(*Phrases*) Not to trouble oneself about; one couldn't care less; the devil may care; san fairy ann.

(*Adjectives*) Incurious, uninquisitive, indifferent, *sans souci*, insouciant, nonchalant, aloof, detached, apathetic, uninterested.

---

457 ATTENTION (*Substantives*), advertence, advertency, observance, observation, interest, notice, heed, look, regard, view, remark, inspection, introspection, heedfulness, mindfulness, look-out, watch, vigilance, circumspection, surveillance, consideration, scrutiny, revision, revisal, recension, review, revise, particularity (459).

Close, intense, deep, profound, etc., attention, application, or study.

(*Verbs*) To be attentive, etc.; to attend, advert to, mind, observe, look, look at, see, view, look to, see to, remark, heed, notice, spot, twig, pipe, take heed, take notice, mark; give or pay attention to; give heed to, have an eye to; turn, apply, or direct the mind, the eye, or the attention to; look after, give a thought to, animadvert on, occupy oneself with, be interested in, devote oneself to, give oneself up to, see about.

To examine cursorily; to glance at, upon, or over; cast or pass the eyes over, run over, turn over the leaves, dip into, skim, perstringe.

To examine closely or intently, scrutinize, consider, give one's mind to, overhaul, pore over, perpend, note, mark, inspect, review, size up, take stock of, fix the eye, mind,

458 INATTENTION (*Substantives*), inconsideration, inconsiderateness, inadvertence, inadvertency, non-observance, inobservance, disregard, oversight, unmindfulness, giddiness, respectlessness, thoughtlessness (460), insouciance; wandering, distracted, etc., attention.

Absence of mind, abstraction, preoccupation, distraction, reverie, brown study, day-dream, day-dreaming, wool-gathering.

(*Phrases*) The wits going wool-gathering; the attention wandering; building castle in the air, or castles in Spain.

(*Verbs*) To be inattentive, etc., to overlook, disregard, pass by, slur over, pass over, gloss over, blink, miss, skim, skim the surface, *effleurer* (460).

To call off, draw off, call away, divert, etc., the attention; to distract; to disconcert, put out, rattle, discompose, confuse, perplex, bewilder, bemuse, moider, bemuddle, muddle, dazzle, obfuscate, faze, fluster, flurry, flummox, befog.

(*Phrases*) To take no account of; to drop the subject; to turn a deaf ear to; to come in at one ear and go out of the other; to reckon without one's host.

thoughts, or attention on, keep in view, contemplate, revert to, etc. (451).

To fall under one's notice, observation, etc., to catch the eye; to catch, awaken, wake, invite, solicit, attract, claim, excite, engage, occupy, strike, arrest, fix, engross, monopolize, preoccupy, obsess, absorb, rivet, etc., the attention, mind, or thoughts; to interest.

To call attention to, point out, indicate (550).

(*Phrases*) To trouble one's head about; lend or incline an ear to; to take cognizance of; to prick up one's ears; to have one's eyes open; to keep one's eyes skinned.

(*Adjectives*) Inattentive, mindless, unobservant, unmindful, uninterested, inadvertent, heedless, regardless, respectless, careless (460), insouciant, unwatchful, listless, cursory, blind, deaf, etc.

Absent, abstracted, *distrait*, absent-minded, lost, preoccupied, bemused, dreamy, moony, napping.

Disconcerted, put out, etc., dizzy, muzzy (460).

(*Phrase*) Caught napping.

(*Adverbs*) Inattentively, etc., cavalierly.

———

To have one's wits about one; to bear in mind; to come to the point; to take into account; to read, mark, learn.

(*Adjectives*) Attentive, mindful, heedful, regardful, alive to, awake to, bearing in mind, occupied with, engaged, taken up with, interested, engrossed, wrapped in, absorbed, rapt.

Awake, watchful, on the watch (459), broad awake, wide awake, agape, intent on, with eyes fixed on, open-eyed, unwinking, undistracted, with bated breath, breathless, upon the stretch.

(*Interjections*) See! look! say! attention! hey! oy! mark! lo! behold! *achtung! nota bene!* N.B.

459 CARE (*Substantives*), caution, heed, heedfulness, attention (457), wariness, prudence, discretion, watch, watchfulness, alertness, vigil, vigilance, circumspection, watch and ward, deliberation, forethought (510), predeliberation, solicitude, precaution (673), scruple, scrupulousness, scrupulosity, particularity, surveillance.

(*Phrases*) The eyes of Argus; *l'œil du maître*.

(*Verbs*) To be careful, etc., to take care, have a care, beware, look to it, reck, heed, take heed, provide for, see to, see after, keep watch, keep watch and ward, look sharp, look about one, set watch, take precautions, take tent, see about.

(*Phrases*) To have all one's wits about one; to mind one's P's and Q's; to speak by the card; to pick one's steps; keep a sharp look out; keep one's weather eye open; to keep an eye on.

(*Adjectives*) Careful, cautious,

460 NEGLECT (*Substantives*), negligence, omission, trifling, laches, heedlessness, carelessness, perfunctoriness, remissness, imprudence, secureness, indiscretion, *étourderie*, incautiousness, indiscrimination, rashness (863), recklessness, non-chalance, inattention (458); slovenliness, sluttishness.

Trifler, flibbertigibbet, Micawber; slattern, slut, sloven.

(*Verbs*) To be negligent, etc., to neglect, scamp, pass over, cut, omit, pretermit, set aside, cast or put aside.

To overlook, disregard, ignore, slight, pay no regard to, make light of, trifle with, blink, wink at, connive at; take or make no account of; gloss over, slur over, slip over, skip, skim, miss, shelve, sink, jump over, shirk (623), discount.

To waste time, trifle, frivol, fribble (683).

heedful, wary, canny, guarded, on one's guard, alert, on the alert, on the watch, watchful, on the look out, *aux aguets*, awake, vigilant, circumspect, broad awake, having the eyes open, Argus-eyed.

Discreet, prudent, sure-footed, provident, scrupulous, particular, meticulous.

(*Phrase*) On the *qui vive*.

(*Adverbs*) Carefully, etc., with care, etc., gingerly, considerately.

(*Phrases*) Let sleeping dogs lie; catching a weasel asleep.

(*Interjections*) Look out! mind your eye! watch! beware! cave! fore! heads!

To render neglectful, etc., to put or throw off one's guard.

(*Phrases*) To give to the winds; take no account of; turn a deaf ear to; shut one's eyes to; not to mind; think no more of; set at naught; give the go-by to.

(*Adjectives*) Neglecting, etc., unmindful, heedless, careless, *sans souci*, negligent, neglectful, slovenly, sluttish, remiss, perfunctory, thoughtless, unthoughtful, unheedful, off one's guard, unwary, incautious, unguarded, indiscreet, inconsiderate, imprudent, improvident, rash, headlong, reckless, heels over head, witless, hare-brained, giddy-brained, offhand, slapdash, happy-go-lucky, cursory, brain-sick, scatterbrained.

Neglected, missed, abandoned, shunted, shelved, unheeded, unperceived, unseen, unobserved, unnoticed, unnoted, unmarked, unattended to, untended, unwatched, unthought-of, overlooked, unmissed, unexamined, unsearched, unscanned, unweighed, unsifted, untested, unweeded, undetermined.

(*Phrases*) In an unguarded moment; buried in a napkin.

(*Adverbs*) Negligently, etc., anyhow, any old way.

(*Interjections*) Let it pass! never mind! no matter! I should worry! san fairy ann! *nichevo!*

---

461 INQUIRY (*Substantives*), search, research, quest, pursuit (622), examination, review, scrutiny, investigation, perquisition, perscrutation, referendum, straw vote, Gallup poll; discussion, symposium, inquest, inquisition, exploration, exploitation, sifting, screening, calculation, analysis, dissection, resolution, induction; the Baconian method.

Questioning, asking, interrogation, interpellation, interrogatory, the Socratic method, examination, cross-examination, cross-questioning, third degree, quiz, catechism.

Reconnoitring, reconnaissance, feeler, *ballon d'essai*, prying, spying, espionage, the lantern of Diogenes, searchlight.

QUESTION, query, difficulty, problem, proposition, desideratum, point to be solved; point or matter in dispute; moot point, question at issue,

462 ANSWER (*Substantives*), response, reply, replication, riposte, rejoinder, rebutter, surrejoinder, surrebutter, retort, come-back, repartee, rescript, antiphony, rescription, acknowledgment.

Explanation, solution, deduction, resolution, exposition, rationale, interpretation (522).

A key, master-key, open sesame, *passepartout*, clue.

Oedipus, oracle (513); solutionist.

(*Verbs*) To answer, respond, reply, rebut, retort, rejoin, return for answer, acknowledge, echo.

To explain, solve, resolve, expound, decipher, spell, interpret (522), to unriddle, unlock, cut the knot, unravel, fathom, pick or open the lock, discover, fish up, to find a clue to, get to the bottom of.

(*Phrases*) To turn the tables upon; Q.E.D.

bone of contention, plain question, fair question, open question, knotty point, vexed question, crux.

Enigma, riddle, conundrum, crossword, bone to pick, quodlibet, Gordian knot.

(*Adjectives*) Answering, responding, etc., responsive, respondent.

(*Adverb*) On the right scent.

(*Interjection*) Eureka!

An inquirer, querist, questioner, heckler, inquisitor, scrutator, scrutineer, examiner, inspector, analyst, quidnunc, newsmonger, gossip (527, 532); investigator, detective, bloodhound, sleuth-hound, sleuth, inquiry agent, private eye, Sherlock Holmes, busy, dick, rozzer, flattie, G-man; secret police, Cheka, Ogpu, Gestapo.

(*Verbs*) To inquire, seek, search, look for, look about for, look out for, cast about for, beat up for, grope for, feel for, reconnoitre, explore, sound, rummage, fossick, ransack, pry, snoop, look round, look over, look through, scan, peruse.

To pursue, hunt, track, trail, mouse, dodge, trace, shadow, tail, dog (622), nose out, ferret out, unearth, hunt up.

To investigate; to take up, follow up, institute, pursue, conduct, carry on, prosecute, etc., an inquiry, etc.; to overhaul, examine, study, consider, fathom, take into consideration, dip into, look into, calculate, pre-examine, dive into, to delve into, rake, rake over, discuss, canvass, thrash out, probe, fathom, sound, scrutinize, analyse, anatomize, dissect, sift, screen, winnow, resolve, traverse, see into.

To ask, speer, question, query, demand; to put, propose, propound, moot, raise, stir, suggest, put forth, start, pop, etc., a question; to interrogate, catechize, pump, cross-question, cross-examine, grill, badger, heckle, dodge, require an answer.

(*Phrases*) To look, peer, or pry into every hole and corner, to beat the bushes; to leave no stone unturned; to seek a needle in a bundle of hay; to scratch the head.

To subject to examination; to grapple with a question; to put to the proof; pass in review; take into consideration; to ventilate a question; seek a clue; throw out a feeler.

To undergo examination; to be in course of inquiry; to be under consideration.

(*Adjectives*) Inquiring, etc., inquisitive, requisitive, requisitory, catechetical, inquisitorial, heuristic, analytic, in search of, in quest of, on the look out for, interrogative, zetetic.

Undetermined, untried, undecided, to be resolved, etc., in question, in dispute, under discussion, under consideration, *sub judice*, moot, proposed, doubtful.

(*Adverbs*) Why? wherefore? whence? *quaere?* how comes it? how happens it? how is it? what is the reason? what's in the wind? what's cooking?

463 EXPERIMENT (*Substantives*), essay, trial, tryout, tentative method, *tâtonnement*, verification, probation, proof, criterion, test, acid test, reagent, check, control, touchstone, pyx, assay, ordeal; empiricism, rule of thumb method of trial and error.

A feeler, *ballon d'essai*, pilot-balloon, messenger-balloon; pilot-engine; straw to show the wind.

(*Verbs*) To experiment, essay, try, explore, grope, angle, cast about, beat the bushes; feel or grope one's way; to thread one's way; to make an experiment, make trial of.

To subject to trial, etc., to experiment upon, try over, rehearse, give a trial to, put, bring, or submit to the test or proof; to prove, verify, test, assay, touch, practise upon.

(*Phrases*) To see how the land lies; to see how the wind blows; to feel the pulse; to throw out a feeler; to have a try; to have a go.

(*Adjectives*) Experimental, crucial, tentative, probationary, empirical, *sub judice*, under probation, on trial, on approval.

(*Adverb*) A *tâtons*.

464 COMPARISON (*Substantives*), collation, contrast, antithesis, identification.

A comparison, simile, similitude, analogy, parallel, parable, metaphor, allegory (521).

(*Verbs*) To compare to or with; to collate, confront, place side by side or in juxtaposition, to draw a parallel, institute a comparison, contrast, balance, identify.

(*Adjectives*) Comparative, metaphorical, figurative, allegorical, comparable, compared with, pitted against, placed by the side of.

465 DISCRIMINATION (*Substantives*), distinction, differentiation, perception or appreciation of difference, nicety, refinement, taste (850), judgment, discernment, nice perception, tact, critique.

(*Verbs*) To discriminate, distinguish, differentiate, draw the line, sift, screen.

(*Phrases*) To split hairs; to cut blocks with a razor; to separate the chaff from the wheat or the sheep from the goats.

465A INDISCRIMINATION (*Substantives*), indistinctness, indistinction (460).

(*Verbs*) Not to distinguish or discriminate, to confound, confuse; to neglect, overlook, lose sight of a distinction.

(*Adjectives*) Indiscriminate, undistinguished, undistinguishable, unmeasured, sweeping, wholesale.

(*Adjectives*) Discriminating, etc., discriminative, distinctive, diagnostic, nice, judicial.

466 MEASUREMENT (*Substantives*), admeasurement, mensuration, triangulation, survey, valuation, appraisement, assessment, assize, estimation, reckoning, evaluation, gauging; mileage, voltage, horse power.

Geometry, geodetics, geodesy, orthometry, altimetry, sounding, surveying, weighing, ponderation, trutination, dead reckoning, metrology.

A measure, standard, rule, yardstick, compass, callipers, dividers, gauge, meter, line, rod, plumb-line, plummet, log, log-line, sound, sounding-rod, sounding-line, lead-line, index, flood-mark, Plimsoll line (or mark), check.

Scale, graduation, graduated scale, vernier, quadrant, theodolite, slide-rule, balance, spring balance, scales, steelyard, beam, weather-glass, barometer, aneroid, barograph, araeometer, altimeter, clinometer, graphometer, goniometer, thermometer, speedometer, tachometer, pedometer, ammeter, voltmeter, micrometer, etc.

A surveyor, geometer, leadsman, etc.

(*Verbs*) To measure, mete, value, assess, rate, appraise, estimate, form an estimate, set a value on, appreciate, span, pace, step; apply the compass, rule, scale, etc., gauge, plump, probe, sound, fathom, heave the log, survey, weigh, poise, balance, hold the scales, take an average, graduate, evaluate, size up, to place in the beam, to take into account, price.

(*Adjectives*) Measuring, etc., metrical, ponderable, measurable, mensurable.

Section III—Materials for Reasoning

467 Evidence, on one side, (*Substantives*), premises, data, grounds, *praecognita*, indication (550).

Oral, hearsay, internal, external, documentary, presumptive evidence.

Testimony, testimonial, deposition, declaration, attestation, testification, authority, warrant, warranty, guarantee, surety, handwriting, autograph, signature, endorsement, seal, sigil, signet (550), superscription, entry, finger-print.

Voucher, credential, certificate, deed, indenture, docket, dossier, probate, affidavit, diploma; admission, concession, allegation, deposition, citation, quotation, reference; admissibility.

Criterion, test, reagent, touchstone, check, control, prerogative, fact, argument, shibboleth.

A witness, eye-witness, indicator, ear-witness, deponent, telltale, informer, sponsor, special pleader.

Assumption, presumption, show of reason, postulation, postulate, lemma.

Reason, proof (478), circumstantial evidence.

Ex-parte evidence, one-sided view.

Secondary evidence, confirmation, corroboration, ratification, authentication, support, approval, compurgation.

(*Phrases*) A case in point; *ecce signum*; *ex pede Herculem.*

(*Verbs*) To be evidence, etc., to evidence, evince, show, indicate (550), imply, involve, entail, necessitate, argue, bespeak, admit, allow, concede, homologate, certify, testify, attest, bear testimony, depose, depone, witness, vouch for, sign, seal, set one's hand and seal to, endorse, confirm, ratify, corroborate, support, establish, uphold, bear upon, bear out, warrant, guarantee.

To adduce, cite, quote, refer to, appeal to, call, bring forward, produce, bring into court, confront witnesses, collect, bring together, rake up evidence, to make a case, make good, authenticate, substantiate, go bail for.

To allege, plead, assume, postulate, posit, presume; to beg the question.

468 Evidence on the other side, on the other hand.

Counter-evidence (*Substantives*), disproof, contradiction, rejoinder, rebutter, answer (462), weak point, conflicting evidence, refutation (479), negation (536).

(*Phrases*) A *tu quoque* argument; the other side of the shield.

(*Verbs*) To countervail, oppose, rebut, check, weaken, invalidate, contradict, contravene.

(*Phrases*) To tell another story; to cut both ways.

(*Adjectives*) Countervailing, etc., contradictory; unauthenticated, unattested, unvouched-for.

(*Adverbs*) Although, though, albeit, but, *per contra.*

(*Phrase*) *Audi alteram partem.*

469 Qualification (*Substantives*), limitation, modification, allowance, grains of allowance, consideration, extenuating circumstance, condition, proviso, saving clause, penalty clause, exception (83), assumption (514).

(*Verbs*) To qualify, limit, modify, tone down, colour, discount, allow for, make allowance for, take into account, introduce new conditions, admit exceptions, take exception.

(*Adjectives*) Qualifying, etc., conditional, exceptional (83), contingent, postulatory, hypothetical, supposititious (514).

(*Adverbs*) Provided, if, unless, but, yet, according as, conditionally, admitting, supposing, granted that; on the supposition, assumption, presumption, allegation, hypothesis, etc., of; with the understanding, even, although, for all that, at all events, after all.

(*Phrases*) With a grain of salt; *cum grano salis.*

(*Phrases*) To hold good, hold water; to speak volumes; to bring home to; to bring to book; to quote chapter and verse; to speak for itself; tell its own tale.

(*Adjectives*) Showing, etc., indicating, indicative, indicatory, evidential, evidentiary, following, deducible, consequential, collateral, corroborative, confirmatory, postulatory, presumptive.

Sound, logical, strong, valid, cogent, decisive, persuasive, persuasory, demonstrative, irrefragable, irresistible, etc. (578).

(*Adverbs*) According to, witness, admittedly, confessedly, *a fortiori*, still more, still less, all the more reason for.

Degrees of Evidence

470 POSSIBILITY (*Substantives*), potentiality, contingency (156), what may be, what is possible, etc.

Practicability, feasibility (705), compatibility (23).

(*Verbs*) To be possible, etc., to admit of, to bear.

To render possible, etc., to put into the way of.

(*Adjectives*) Possible, contingent (475), conceivable, credible.

Practicable, feasible, achievable, performable, viable, accessible, surmountable, attainable, obtainable, compatible.

(*Adverbs*) Possibly, by possibility, maybe, perhaps, mayhap, haply, perchance, peradventure, *in posse* (156).

(*Phrases*) Wind and weather permitting; within the bounds of possibility; on the cards; D.V.

471 IMPOSSIBILITY (*Substantives*), what cannot be, what can never be, imposs, no go, hopelessness (859).

Impracticability, incompatibility (704), incredibility.

(*Verbs*) To be impossible, etc., to have no chance whatever.

(*Phrases*) To make a silk purse out of a sow's ear; to wash a blackamoor white; to make bricks without straw; to get blood from a stone; to take the breeks off a highlandman; to square the circle; to eat one's cake and have it too.

(*Adjectives*) Impossible, contrary to reason, inconceivable, unreasonable, absurd, incredible, visionary, chimerical, prodigious (870), desperate, hopeless, unheard-of, unthinkable.

Impracticable, unattainable, unachievable, unfeasible, infeasible, beyond control, unobtainable, unprocurable, insuperable, unsurmountable, inaccessible, inextricable.

(*Phrases*) Out of the question; sour grapes; *non possumus*.

472 PROBABILITY (*Substantives*), likelihood, *vraisemblance*, verisimilitude, plausibility, show of, colour of, credibility, reasonable chance, favourable chance, fair chance, hope, prospect, presumption, presumptive evidence, circumstantial evidence, the main chance, a *prima facie* case.

Probabilism, probabiliorism.

(*Verbs*) To be probable, likely, etc.; to think likely, dare say, expect (507).

(*Phrases*) To bid fair; to stand fair for; to stand a good chance; to stand to reason.

473 IMPROBABILITY (*Substantives*), unlikelihood, unfavourable chances, small chance, off-chance, bare possibility, long odds, incredibility.

(*Verbs*) To be improbable, etc., to have or stand a small, little, poor, remote, etc., chance; to whistle for.

(*Adjectives*) Improbable, unheard-of, incredible, unbelievable, unlikely.

(*Phrases*) Contrary to all reasonable expectation; having scarcely a chance; a chance in a thousand.

(*Adjectives*) Probable, likely, hopeful, well-founded.

Plausible, specious, ostensible, colourable, standing to reason, reasonable, credible, tenable, easy of belief, presumable, presumptive, *ben trovato*.

(*Phrases*) Likely to happen; in a fair way; appearances favouring; according to every reasonable expectation; the odds being in favour.

(*Adverbs*) Probably, etc., belike, in all probability, or likelihood, apparently, to all appearance, on the face of it, in the long run, *prima facie*, very likely, like enough, ten to one.

(*Phrase*) All Lombard Street to a china orange.

474 CERTAINTY (*Substantives*), certitude, positiveness, a dead certainty, dead cert, infallibleness, infallibility, gospel, scripture, surety, assurance, indisputableness, moral certainty.

Fact, matter of fact, *fait accompli*.

Bigotry, dogmatism, *ipse dixit*.

Bigot, dogmatist, Sir Oracle.

(*Verbs*) To be certain, etc., to believe (484).

To render certain, etc., to ensure, to assure, clinch, determine, decide.

To dogmatize, lay down the law.

(*Phrases*) To stand to reason; to make assurance doubly sure.

(*Adjectives*) Certain, sure, assured, solid, absolute, positive, flat, determinate, categorical, unequivocal, inevitable, unavoidable, avoidless, unerring, infallible, indubitable, indubious, indisputable, undisputed, uncontested, undeniable, incontestable, irrefutable, unimpeachable, incontrovertible, undoubted, doubtless, without doubt, beyond a doubt, past dispute, unanswerable, decided, unquestionable, beyond all question, unquestioned, questionless, irrefragable, evident, self-evident, axiomatic, demonstrable (478), authoritative, authentic, official, unerring, infallible, trustworthy (939).

(*Phrases*) Sure as fate; and no mistake; sure as a gun; clear as the sun at noonday; sure as death (and taxes); bet your life; you bet; *cela va sans dire*; it's in the bag; that's flat.

(*Adverbs*) Certainly, assuredly, etc., for certain, *in esse*, sure, surely, sure enough, to be sure, of course, as a matter of course, yes (488), depend upon it, that's so, by all manner of means, beyond a peradventure.

475 UNCERTAINTY (*Substantives*), incertitude, doubt (485), doubtfulness, dubiety, dubiousness, suspense, precariousness, indefiniteness, indetermination, slipperiness, fallibility, perplexity, embarrassment, dilemma, ambiguity (520), hesitation, vacillation (605), equivoque, vagueness, peradventure, touch-and-go.

(*Phrases*) A blind bargain; a pig in a poke; a leap in the dark; a moot point; an open question.

(*Verbs*) To be uncertain, etc; to vacillate, hesitate, waver.

To render uncertain, etc., to perplex, embarrass, confuse, moider, confound, bewilder, disorientate.

(*Phrases*) To be in a state of uncertainty; not to know which way to turn; to be at a loss; to be at fault; to lose the scent.

To tremble in the balance; to hang by a thread.

(*Adjectives*) Uncertain, doubtful, dubious, precarious (665), chancy, casual, random, contingent, indecisive, dependent on circumstances, undecided, unsettled, undetermined, pending, pendent, vague, indeterminate, indefinite, ambiguous, undefined, equivocal, undefinable, puzzling, enigmatic, debatable, disputable, questionable, apocryphal, problematical, hypothetical, controvertible, fallible, fallacious, suspicious, fishy, slippery, ticklish.

Unauthentic, unconfirmed, undemonstrated, undemonstrable, unreliable, untrustworthy.

SECTION IV—REASONING PROCESSES

476 REASONING (*Substantives*), ratiocination, dialectics, induction, deduction, generalization; inquiry (461).

Argumentation, discussion, *pourparler*, controversy, polemics, debate, wrangling, logomachy, apology, apologetics, ergotism, disputation, disceptation.

The art of reasoning, logic, process, train or chain of reasoning, analysis, synthesis, argument, lemma, proposition, terms, premises, postulate, data, starting-point, principle, inference, result, conclusion.

Syllogism, prosyllogism, enthymeme, sorites, dilemma, *perilepsis*, pros and cons, a comprehensive argument.

Correctness, soundness, force, validity, cogency, conclusiveness.

A thinker, reasoner, disputant, controversialist, logician, dialectician, polemic, wrangler, arguer, debater.

(*Phrases*) A paper war; a war of words; a battle of the books; a full-dress debate.

The horns of a dilemma; *reductio ad absurdum*; *argumentum ad hominem*; *onus probandi*.

(*Verbs*) To reason, argue, discuss, debate, dispute, wrangle; bandy words or arguments; hold or carry on an argument, controvert, contravene (536), consider (461), comment upon, moralize upon, spiritualize.

(*Phrases*) To open a discussion or case; to moot; to join issue; to ventilate a question; to talk it over; to have it out; to take up a side or case.

To chop logic; to try conclusions; to impale on the horns of a dilemma; to cut the matter short; to hit the nail on the head; to take one's stand upon; to have the last word.

(*Adjectives*) Reasoning, etc., rational, rationalistic, ratiocinative, argumentative, controversial, dialectic, polemical, discursory, discursive, debatable, controvertible, disputatious; correct, just, fair, sound, valid,

477 The absence of reasoning.

INTUITION (*Substantives*), instinct, association, presentiment, insight, second sight, sixth sense.

False or vicious reasoning, show of reason.

Misjudgment, miscalculation (481).

SOPHISTRY (*Substantives*), paralogy, fallacy, perversion, casuistry, jesuitry, quibble, equivocation, evasion, chicanery, special pleading, quiddity, mystification; nonsense (497).

Sophism, solecism, paralogism, elenchus, fallacy, quodlibet, subterfuge, subtlety, quillet, inconsistency, antilogy.

Speciousness, plausibility, illusiveness, irrelevancy, invalidity; claptrap, hot air.

Quibbler, casuist, *advocatus diaboli*.

(*Phrases*) Begging the question; *petitio principii*; *ignoratio elenchi*; reasoning in a circle; *post hoc, ergo propter hoc*; *ignotum per ignotius*.

The meshes or cobwebs of sophistry; a flaw in an argument; an argument falling to the ground.

(*Verbs*) To envisage, to judge intuitively, etc.

To reason ill, falsely, etc.; to pervert, quibble, equivocate, mystify, evade, elude, gloss over, varnish, misjudge, miscalculate (481).

To refine, subtilize, cavil, sophisticate, mislead.

(*Phrases*) To split hairs; to cut blocks with a razor; throw off the scent; to beg the question; reason in a circle; beat about the bush; prove that black is white; not have a leg to stand on; lose one's reckoning.

(*Adjectives*) Intuitive, instinctive, impulsive, unreasoning, independent of or anterior to reason.

Sophistical, unreasonable, irrational, illogical, false, unsound, not following, not pertinent, inconsequent, inconsequential, unwarranted, untenable, inconclusive, incorrect, fallacious, inconsistent, groundless,

cogent, logical, demonstrative (478), relevant, pertinent (9, 23).

(*Phrases*) To the point; in point; to the purpose; *ad rem.*

(*Adverbs*) For, because, for that reason, forasmuch as, inasmuch as, since, hence, whence, whereas, considering, therefore, consequently, *ergo*, then, thus, accordingly, wherefore, *a fortiori, a priori, ex concesso.*

(*Phrases*) In consideration of; in conclusion; in fine; after all; *au bout du compte*; on the whole; taking one thing with another.

---

478 DEMONSTRATION (*Substantives*), proof, conclusiveness, probation, comprobation, clincher, *experimentum crucis*, test, etc. (463), argument (476).

(*Verbs*) To demonstrate, prove, establish, show, evince, verify, substantiate; to follow.

(*Phrases*) Make good; set at rest; settle the question; reduce to demonstration; to make out a case; to prove one's point; to clinch an argument; bring home to; bear out.

(*Adjectives*) Demonstrating, etc., demonstrative, probative, demonstrable, unanswerable, conclusive, final, apodictic (or apodeictic), irrefutable, irrefragable, unimpeachable, categorical, decisive, crucial.

Demonstrated, proved, proven, etc., unconfuted, unrefuted; evident, self-evident, axiomatic (474); deducible, consequential, inferential.

(*Phrases*) *Probatum est*; it stands to reason; it holds good; there being nothing more to be said; Q.E.D.

(*Adverbs*) Of course, in consequence, consequently, as a matter of course, no wonder.

fallible, unproved, indecisive, deceptive, illusive, illusory, specious, hollow, jesuitical, plausible, irrelevant.

Weak, feeble, poor, flimsy, trivial, trumpery, trashy, puerile, childish, irrational, silly, foolish, imbecile, absurd (499), extravagant, far-fetched, pettifogging, quibbling, fine-spun, hair-splitting.

(*Phrases*) *Non constat*; *non sequitur*; not holding water; away from the point; foreign to the purpose or subject; having nothing to do with the matter; not of the essence; *nihil ad rem*; not bearing upon the point in question; not the point; beside the mark.

---

479 CONFUTATION (*Substantives*), refutation, disproof, conviction, redargution, invalidation, exposure, exposition; demolition of an argument; answer, come-back, counter, retort.

(*Phrases*) *Reductio ad absurdum*; a knock-down argument; a *tu quoque* argument.

(*Verbs*) To confute, refute, disprove, redargue, expose, show the fallacy of, knock the bottom out of, rebut, parry, negative, defeat, overthrow, demolish, explode, riddle, overturn, invalidate, silence, reduce to silence, shut up, put down.

(*Phrases*) To cut the ground from one's feet; to give one a set-down.

(*Adjectives*) Confuting, etc., confuted, etc., capable of refutation, refutable, confutable, etc.; unproved, etc.

(*Phrases*) The argument falls to the ground; it won't hold water; that cock won't fight.

Section V—Results of Reasoning

480 Judgment (*Substantives*), conclusion, determination, deduction, inference, result, illation, corollary, rider, porism, consectary.

Estimation, valuation, appreciation, judication, adjudication, arbitrament, arbitration, assessment, award, ponderation.

Decision, sentence, verdict, moral, ruling, finding; detection, discovery, estimate; *chose jugée.*

Criticism, critique, review, report, notice; plebiscite, casting vote.

A judge, umpire, arbiter, arbitrator, assessor, censor, referee, critic, connoisseur, reviewer.

(*Verbs*) To judge, deduce, conclude, draw a conclusion, infer, make a deduction, draw an inference, put two and two together; come to, arrive or jump at a conclusion; to derive, gather, collect.

To estimate, appreciate, value, count, assess, rate, account, rank, regard, review, settle, decide, pronounce, arbitrate, perpend, size up.

(*Phrases*) To sit in judgment; to hold the scales; to pass an opinion; to pass judgment.

(*Adjectives*) Judging, etc., deducible (467); impartial, unbiased, unprejudiced, unwarped, unbigoted, equitable, fair, sound, rational, judicious, shrewd.

480A Detection (*Substantive*), discovery.

(*Verbs*) To ascertain, determine, find, find out, make out, detect, discover, elicit, recognize, trace, get at; get or arrive at the truth; meet with, fall upon, light upon, hit upon, fall in with, stumble upon, lay the finger on, spot, solve, resolve, unravel, fish out, worm out, ferret out, root out, nose out, disinter, unearth, grub up, fish up, investigate (461).

To be near the truth, to get warm, to burn.

(*Phrase*) To smell a rat.

(*Interjection*) Eureka!

481 Misjudgment (*Substantives*), obliquity of judgment, misconception, error (495), miscalculation, miscomputation, presumption.

Prejudgment, prejudication, prejudice, prenotion, *parti pris*, prevention, preconception, predilection, prepossession, preapprehension, presentiment, *esprit de corps*, clannishness, party spirit, partisanship, partiality.

Bias, warp, twist, fad, whim, crotchet, fike; narrow-mindedness, bigotry, dogmatism, intolerance, tenacity, obstinacy (606); blind side; one-sided, partial, narrow or confined views, ideas, conceptions, or notions; *idée fixe*, fixed idea, obsession, monomania, infatuation.

(*Phrases*) A bee in one's bonnet; a mote in the eye; a fool's paradise.

(*Verbs*) To misjudge, misestimate, misconceive, misreckon, etc. (495).

To prejudge, forejudge, prejudicate, dogmatize, have a bias, etc., presuppose, presume.

To produce a bias, twist, etc.; to bias, warp, twist, prejudice, obsess, infatuate, prepossess.

(*Phrases*) To have on the brain; to look only at one side of the shield; to view with jaundiced eye; to run away with the notion; to jump to a conclusion.

(*Adjectives*) Prejudging, misjudging, etc., prejudiced, jaundiced, narrow-minded, dogmatic, intolerant, illiberal, blimpish, besotted, infatuated, fanatical, *entêté*, positive, obstinate (606), tenacious, pig-headed, having a bias, twist, etc., warped, partial, one-sided, biased, bigoted, hide-bound, tendentious, opinionated, opinionative, opinioned, self-opinioned, self-opinionated, crotchety, pernickety, faddy, fussy, fiky.

(*Phrases*) Wedded to an opinion; the wish being father to the thought.

————

482 OVERESTIMATION (*Substantive*), exaggeration.

(*Phrases*) Much ado about nothing; much cry and little wool; a storm in a tea-cup.

(*Verbs*) To overestimate, estimate too highly, overrate, overvalue, overprize, overpraise, overweigh, outreckon; exaggerate, extol, puff, boost, make too much of, overstrain.

(*Phrases*) To set too high a value upon; to make a mountain out of a molehill; *parturiunt montes, nascetur ridiculus mus;* to make two bites of a cherry; all his geese are swans.

(*Adjectives*) Overestimated, etc.

483 UNDERESTIMATION (*Substantives*), depreciation, disparagement, detraction (934), underrating, undervaluing, etc.

(*Verbs*) To depreciate, disparage, detract, underrate, underestimate, undervalue, underreckon, underprize, misprize, disprize, not to do justice to, make light of, slight, belittle, knock, slam, make little of, think nothing of, hold cheap, cheapen, disregard, to care nothing for, despise, set at naught, minimize, discount, deride, derogate, decry, cry down, crab, denigrate, smear, vilipend, run down (934).

To scout, deride, pooh-pooh, mock, scoff at, laugh at, whistle at, play with, trifle with, fribble, niggle, ridicule (856).

(*Phrases*) To snap one's fingers at; throw into the shade; not to care a pin, rush, hoot, tinker's cuss, etc., for; to damn with faint praise.

(*Adjectives*) Depreciating, etc., derogatory, cynical.

Depreciated, etc., unvalued, unprized.

---

484 BELIEF (*Substantives*), credence, faith, trust, troth, confidence, credit, dependence on, reliance, assurance.

Opinion, notion, idea (453), conception, apprehension, impression, conceit, mind, view, persuasion, conviction, convincement, sentiment, voice, conclusion, judgment (480), estimation, self-conviction.

System of opinions, creed, credo, religion (983, 987), doctrine, tenet, dogma, principle, school, ideology, articles of belief, way of thinking, popular belief, *vox populi*, public opinion, *esprit de corps*, partisanship; ism, doxy.

Change of opinion (607), proselytism, propagandism (537).

A convert, pervert, vert, proselyte.

(*Verbs*) To believe, credit, receive, give faith to, give credit to, rely upon, make no doubt, reckon, doubt not, confide in, count upon, depend upon, build upon, calculate upon, take upon trust, swallow, gulp down, take one's word for, take upon credit, swear by.

To be of opinion, to opine, presume;

485 UNBELIEF (*Substantives*), disbelief, misbelief, discredit, agnosticism, atheism (988), heresy (984), dissent (489).

DOUBT, dubitation, scepticism, *diaporesis*, misgiving, demur, cliff-hanging, suspense; shade or shadow of doubt, distrust, mistrust, misdoubt, suspicion, shyness, embarrassment, hesitation, uncertainty (475), scruple, qualm, dilemma; casuistry, paradox; schism (489), incredulity (487).

Unbeliever, sceptic (487); Doubting Thomas.

(*Verbs*) To disbelieve, discredit, not to believe; refuse to admit or believe; misbelieve, controvert; put or set aside; join issue, dispute, etc.

To doubt, be doubtful, etc., diffide, distrust, mistrust, suspect, scent, jalouse; have, harbour, entertain, etc., doubts; demur, stick at, pause, hesitate, scruple, question, query, call in question, look askance (or askant).

To cause, raise, suggest, or start a doubt; to pose, stagger, floor, startle, embarrass, puzzle (704); shake or stagger one's faith or belief.

(*Phrases*) Not to know what to

to have, hold, possess, entertain, adopt, imbibe, embrace, foster, nurture, cherish, etc., a notion, idea, opinion, etc.; to think, look upon, view, consider, take, take it, hold, trow, ween, conceive, fancy, apprehend, regard, esteem, deem, account; meseems, methinks.

To cause to be believed, thought, or esteemed; to satisfy, persuade, assure, convince, convert, bring over, win over, indoctrinate, proselytize (537), evangelize; to vert.

(*Phrases*) To pin one's faith to; to take at one's word.

To take it into one's head; to run away with the notion; to come round to an opinion.

To cram down the throat; to bring home to; to find credence; to carry conviction; pass current; pass muster; to hold water; to go down.

make of; to smell a rat; to hang in doubt; to have one's doubts; to float in a sea of doubts.

(*Adjectives*) Unbelieving, doubting, etc., incredulous, scrupulous, suspicious, sceptical, shy of belief, at sea, at a loss (487).

Unworthy or undeserving of belief, hard to believe, doubtful (475), dubious, unreliable, fishy, questionable, suspect, staggering, puzzling, etc., paradoxical, incredible, inconceivable.

(*Phrases*) With a grain of salt; *cum grano salis*; *timeo Danaos et dona ferentes*; all is not gold that glitters; the cowl does not make the monk.

————

(*Adjectives*) Believing, etc., impressed with, imbued with, wedded to, unsuspecting, unsuspicious, void of suspicion, etc., credulous (486), convinced, positive, sure, assured, cocksure, certain, confident.

Believed, etc., credited, accredited, unsuspected, received, current, popular.

Worthy or deserving of belief, commanding belief, believable, persuasive, impressive, reliable, dependable, trustworthy (939), credible, probable (572), fiducial, fiduciary; relating to belief, doctrinal.

(*Adverbs*) In the opinion of, in the eyes of, on the strength of, to the best of one's belief, *me judice*.

486 CREDULITY (*Substantives*), credulousness, gullibility, infatuation, self-delusion, self-deception, superstition, gross credulity, bigotry, dogmatism.

A credulous person, gull, gobemouche; dupe (547).

(*Verbs*) To be credulous, etc., to follow implicitly, swallow, take on trust, take for gospel.

To impose upon, practise upon, palm off upon, cajole, etc., deceive (545).

(*Phrases*) *Credo quia absurdum*; the wish being father to the thought.

(*Adjectives*) Credulous, gullible, confiding, trusting; easily deceived, cajoled, etc.; green, verdant, superstitious, simple, unsuspicious, etc. (484), soft, childish, silly, stupid, over-credulous, over-confident.

487 INCREDULITY (*Substantives*), incredulousness, scepticism, pyrrhonism, nihilism, suspicion (485), suspiciousness, scrupulousness, scrupulosity.

An unbeliever, sceptic, misbeliever, pyrrhonist; nihilist.

(*Verbs*) To be incredulous, etc., to distrust (485).

(*Adjectives*) Incredulous, hard of belief, sceptical, unbelieving, inconvincible, shy of belief, doubting, distrustful, suspicious (485).

(*Phrases*) Oh yeah? says you! a likely story! rats! that be hanged for a tale; tell that to the marines; it won't wash; that cock won't fight; *credat Judaeus Apella*.

————

488 ASSENT (*Substantives*), acquiescence, admission, assentation, nod, consent, concession, accord, accordance, agreement (23), concord (714), concordance, concurrence, ratification, confirmation, corroboration, approval, recognition, acknowledgment, acceptance, granting, avowal, confession.

Unanimity, chorus; affirmation (535), common consent, acclamation, consensus.

Yes-man, sycophant, echo.

(*Verbs*) To assent, acquiesce, agree, yield assent, accord, concur, consent, nod assent, accept, coincide, go with, go along with, be at one with, chime in with, strike in with, close with, vote for, conform with, defer to; say yes, ay, ditto, amen, etc.

To acknowledge, own, avow, confess, concede, subscribe to, abide by, admit, allow, recognize, grant, endorse, ratify, countersign, O.K., okay, approve, carry.

(*Phrases*) To go or be solid for; to come to an understanding; to come to terms; one could not agree more.

(*Adjectives*) Assenting, etc., acquiescent, content, consentient, willing; approved, agreed, carried; uncontradicted, unchallenged, unquestioned, uncontroverted; unanimous.

(*Phrase*) Of one mind.

(*Adverbs*) Affirmatively, in the affirmative (535).

Yes, yea, yeah, yep, ay, aye, uh-huh, sure, very well, even so, just so, quite so, to be sure, all right, right oh! right you are, you said it, definitely, absolutely, exactly, precisely, truly, certainly, assuredly, no doubt, doubtless, verily, very true (494), *ex concesso.*

489 DISSENT (*Substantives*), dissidence, discordance, denial (536), dissonance, disagreement; difference or diversity of opinion, recusancy, contradiction, nonconformity, schism (984), secession; protest.

A dissentient, dissenter, protestant, nonconformist, recusant, heretic; deviationist, nonjuror, schismatic, seceder.

(*Verbs*) To dissent, demur, deny, disagree, refuse assent, say no, differ, cavil, ignore, protest, contradict, secede, repudiate, refuse to admit.

(*Phrases*) To shake the head; to shrug the shoulders; to join issue; to give the lie; to differ *toto caelo*.

(*Adjectives*) Dissenting, etc., dissentient, dissident, discordant, protestant, nonconforming, recusant, nonjuring, non-content, schismatic, deviationist; unconvinced, unconverted, unavowed, unacknowledged.

Unwilling, reluctant, extorted, etc.

(*Adverbs*) Negatively, in the negative (536), at variance with.

No, nay, nope, nit, na, not, not so, not at all, nohow, nowise, not in the least, not a bit, not a whit, not a jot, by no means, by no manner of means, not for the world, on no account, in no respect.

(*Phrases*) Many men, many minds; *quot homines, tot sententiae*; *tant s'en faut*; the answer is in the negative; *il s'en faut bien*.

(*Interjections*) No sir! God forbid! I'll be hanged first! I'll see you far enough! not bloody likely! not on your nelly! not if I know it! over my dead body! pardon me! I beg your pardon!

———

Be it so, so be it, by all means, granted, O.K., okay, oke, okeydoke, by all manner of means, *à la bonne heure*, amen, willingly, etc. (602).

With one voice, with one accord, *una voce*, unanimously, in chorus, as one man, to a man, *nem. con.* or *nemine contradicente, nemine dissentiente, en bloc*, without a dissentient voice, one and all, on all hands.

490 KNOWLEDGE (*Substantives*), cognizance, cognition, cognoscence, awareness, gnosis, acquaintance, experience, ken, privity, insight,

491 IGNORANCE (*Substantives*), nescience, nescientness, unacquaintance, unconsciousness, darkness, blindness, incomprehension,

familiarity, apprehension, comprehension, understanding, recognition; discovery (480), appreciation; knowability.

Intuition, clairvoyance, consciousness, conscience, perception, precognition, light, enlightenment, glimpse, inkling, glimmer, dawn, scent, suspicion; conception, notion, idea (453).

Self-consciousness, self-knowledge, apperception.

System or body of knowledge, science, philosophy, pansophy, pandect, doctrine, ideology, theory, aetiology, literature, *belles-lettres, literae humaniores,* the humanities, humanism; ology.

Erudition, learning, lore, scholarship, letters, book-learning, bookishness, bibliomania, bibliolatry, education, instruction, information, acquisitions, acquirements, accomplishments, attainments, proficiency, cultivation, culture; a liberal education, encyclopaedic knowledge, omniscience.

Elements, rudiments, abecedary (542), cyclopaedia, encyclopaedia, school, academy, etc.

Depth, extent, profoundness, profundity, stores, etc., solidity, accuracy, etc., of knowledge.

(*Phrases*) The march of intellect; the progress, advance, etc., of science; the schoolmaster being abroad.

(*Verbs*) To know, be aware of, savvy, ken, wot, ween, trow, have, possess, perceive, conceive, apprehend, ideate, understand, comprehend, make out, recognize, be master of, know full well, possess the knowledge of, experience, discern, perceive, see, see through, have in one's head.

(*Phrases*) To know what's what; to know how the wind blows; to know the ropes; to have at one's finger-tips or finger-ends.

(*Adjectives*) Knowing, aware of, etc., cognizant of, acquainted with, privy to, conscious of, no stranger to, *au fait, au courant,* versed in, hep,

incognizance, inexperience, emptiness.

Imperfect knowledge, smattering, sciolism, glimmering; bewilderment, perplexity (475); incapacity.

Affectation of knowledge, pedantry, charlatanry, quackery, dilettantism.

(*Phrases*) Crass ignorance; monumental ignorance.

A sealed book; unexplored ground; an unknown quantity; *terra incognita.*

(*Verbs*) To be ignorant, etc., not to know, to know nothing of, not to be aware of, to be at a loss, to be out of it, to be at fault, to ignore, to be blind to, etc., not to understand, etc.

(*Phrases*) To be caught tripping; not to know what to make of; to have no idea or notion; not to be able to make head or tail of; not to know one's hawk from a handsaw; to lose one's bearings.

(*Adjectives*) Ignorant, unknowing, unconscious, unaware, unwitting, witless, a stranger to, unacquainted, unconversant, unenlightened, unilluminated, incognizant, unversed, uncultivated, clueless.

Uninformed, uninstructed, untaught, unapprised, untutored, unschooled, unguided.

Shallow, superficial, green, verdant, rude, half-learned, illiterate, unread, uneducated, unlearned, uncultured, Philistine, unlettered, empty-headed, having a smattering, etc., pedantic.

Confused, puzzled, bewildered, bemused, muddled, bemuddled, lost, benighted, belated, at sea, at fault, posed, blinded, abroad, distracted, in a maze, misinformed, hoodwinked, in the dark, at a loss, *désorienté.*

Unknown, novel, unapprehended, unexplained, unascertained, uninvestigated, unexplored, untravelled, uncharted, chartless, unheard-of, unperceived, unknowable.

(*Phrases*) Having a film over the eyes; wide of the mark; at cross purposes.

(*Adverbs*) Ignorantly, unwittingly,

up in, up to, alive to, wise to, conversant with, proficient in, read in,
familiar with.

Apprised of, made acquainted with,
informed of; undeceived.

Erudite, instructed, learned, well-
read, lettered, literate, educated,
cultivated, cultured, knowledgeable, enlightened, well-informed, shrewd,
bookish, scholarly, scholastic, deep-read; self-taught, well-grounded,
well-conned.

Known, etc., well-known, recognized, received, notorious, noted, proverbial, familiar; hackneyed, trite, commonplace; cognoscible, know-
able; experiential.

(*Phrases*) Behind the scenes; in the know; at home in; the scales fallen
from one's eyes.

(*Adverbs*) To one's knowledge, to the best of one's knowledge.

(*Phrase*) *Experto crede.*

unawares; for anything one knows;
for aught one knows.

(*Phrase*) 'A little learning is a
dangerous thing.'

———

492 SCHOLAR (*Substantives*),
student (541), savant, scientist,
humanist, grammarian, intellectual,
pundit, schoolman, don, professor,
lecturer, reader, demonstrator, graduate, doctor, master of arts, licentiate,
wrangler, gownsman, philosopher,
philomath, clerk, encyclopaedist.

Linguist; *littérateur, literati, illumi-
nati,* intelligentsia.

Pedant, pedagogue, bookworm,
helluo librorum, bibliomaniac, bibliophile, blue-stocking, *bas-bleu,* high-
brow, bigwig, bookman; swot, grind.

493 IGNORAMUS (*Substantives*),
sciolist, smatterer, novice, greenhorn,
half-scholar, schoolboy, booby, dunce
(501); bigot (481); quack, mountebank, charlatan, dilettante, low-brow,
amateur, Philistine, obscurant, obscurantist.

(*Phrase*) The wooden spoon.

(*Adjectives*) Bookless, shallow (499),
ignorant, etc. (491), prejudiced (481),
obscurantist.

———

(*Phrases*) Man of letters; man of learning; at the feet of Gamaliel;
a walking dictionary.

(*Adjectives*) Erudite, learned, scholarly (490).

494 Object of knowledge.

TRUTH (*Substantives*), verity, actual
existence (1), reality, fact, matter of
fact, actuality, nature, principle,
orthodoxy, gospel, holy writ, substantiality, genuineness, authenticity,
realism.

Accuracy, exactness, exactitude,
precision, preciseness, nicety, delicacy, fineness, strictness, rigour,
punctuality.

(*Phrases*) The plain truth; the
honest truth; the naked truth; the
sober truth; the very thing; a stubborn fact; not a dream, fancy, illusion, etc.; the exact truth; 'the truth,
the whole truth, and nothing but the

495 Untruth (546).

ERROR (*Substantives*), mistake,
miss, fallacy, misconception, misapprehension, misunderstanding, in-
accuracy, incorrectness, inexactness,
misconstruction (523), miscomputation, miscalculation (481).

Fault, blunder, *faux pas,* bull, Irish
bull, Irishism, bloomer, howler,
floater, clanger, boner, lapse, slip of
the tongue, *lapsus linguae,* Spoonerism, slip of the pen, malapropism,
equivoque, cross purposes, oversight,
flaw, misprint, erratum; heresy, misstatement, misreport, bad shot.

Illusion, delusion, self-deceit, self-
deception, hallucination, monomania,

truth'; 'a round unvarnished tale'; *ipsissima verba*; the real Simon Pure.

(*Verbs*) To be true, real, etc., to hold good, to be the case.

To render true, legitimatize, legitimize, substantiate, realize, actualize, to make good, establish.

To get at the truth (480).

(*Phrases*) *Vitam impendere vero*; *magna est veritas et praevalebit.*

(*Adjectives*) True, real, veritable, veracious, actual, certain, positive, absolute, existing (1), substantial, categorical, realistic, factual; unrefuted, unconfuted, unideal, unimagined.

Exact, accurate, definite, precise, well-defined, just, correct, right, strict, hard-and-fast, literal, rigid, rigorous, scrupulous, conscientious, religious, punctilious, nice, mathematical, axiomatic, demonstrable, scientific, unerring, constant, faithful, *bona fide*, curious, delicate, meticulous.

Genuine, authentic, legitimate, pukka, orthodox, official, *ex officio*, pure, sound, sterling, hall-marked, unsophisticated, unadulterated, unvarnished; solid, substantial, undistorted, undisguised, unaffected, unflattering, unexaggerated, unromantic.

(*Phrases*) Just the thing; neither more nor less; to a hair.

(*Adverbs*) Truly, verily, veritable, troth, certainly, certes, assuredly, in truth, in good truth, of a truth, really, indubitably, in sooth, forsooth, in reality, in fact, in point of fact, as a matter of fact, strictly speaking, *de facto*, indeed, in effect, actually, *ipso facto*, definitely, literally, positively, virtually, at bottom, *au fond*.

Precisely, accurately, *ad amussim*, etc., mathematically, to a nicety, to a hair, to a T, to an inch; to the letter, *au pied de la lettre*.

aberration; fable, dream, shadow, fancy, bubble, false light (443), the mists of error, will-o'-the-wisp, jack-o'-lantern, ignis fatuus, chimera (515), *maya.*

(*Verbs*) To be erroneous, false, etc., to cause error, to mislead, lead astray, lead into error, delude, give a false impression or idea, to falsify, misstate, misrelate, misinform, misrepresent (544), deceive (545), beguile.

To err, be in error, to mistake, to receive a false impression; to lie or labour under an error, mistake, etc., to blunder, be in the wrong, be at fault, to misapprehend, misconceive, misunderstand, misremember, misreckon, miscalculate, miscount, misestimate, misjudge, misthink, flounder, trip.

(*Phrases*) To take the shadow for the substance; to go on a fool's errand; to have the wrong sow by the ear; to put one's foot in it; to pull a boner; to drop a brick.

(*Adjectives*) Erroneous, untrue, false, fallacious, duff, unreal, unsubstantial, baseless, groundless, less, ungrounded, unauthenticated, untrustworthy, heretical.

Inexact, incorrect, wrong, illogical, partial, one-sided, unreasonable, absonous, absonant, indefinite, unscientific, inaccurate, aberrant.

In error, mistaken, etc., tripping, floundering, etc.

Illusive, illusory, ideal, imaginary. fanciful, chimerical, visionary, shadowy, mock, futile.

Spurious, apocryphal, bogus, illegitimate, phoney, pseudo, bastard, meretricious, deceitful, sophisticated, adulterated.

(*Phrases*) Wide of the mark; on the wrong scent; barking up the wrong tree; out of it; without a leg to stand upon.

————

In every respect, in all respects, *sous tous les rapports*, at any rate, at all events, by all means.

(*Phrases*) Joking apart; in good earnest; in sober earnest; sooth to say.

496 MAXIM (*Substantives*), aphorism, apophthegm, dictum, saying, *mot*, adage, gnome, saw, proverb, wisecrack, sentence, precept, rule, formula, tag, code, motto, slogan, catchword, word, byword, moral, sentiment, phylactery, conclusion, reflection, thought, golden rule, axiom, theorem, scholium, lemma, triusm.

Catechism, creed (484), profession of faith.

(*Adjectives*) Aphoristic, gnomic, proverbial, phylacteric, axiomatic; hackneyed, trite.

(*Phrases*) 'Wise saws and modern instances'; as the saying is or goes.

---

497 ABSURDITY (*Substantives*), absurdness, nonsense, folly, paradox, inconsistency, quibble, sophism (477), stultiloquy, stultiloquence, Irish bull, Irishism, Hibernicism, sciamachy, imbecility (499).

Jargon, gibberish, rigmarole, double-Dutch, fustian, rant, bombast, bathos, amphigouri, rhapsody, extravagance, rodomontade, romance; nonsense verse, limerick, clerihew.

Twaddle, claptrap, flapdoodle, bunkum, blah, fudge, rubbish, piffle, verbiage, trash, truism, stuff, balderdash, slipslop, *bavardage*, palaver, *baragouin*, moonshine, fiddlestick, wish-wash, platitude, cliché, flummery, inanity, fiddle-faddle, rot, tommy-rot, bosh, tosh, hot air, havers, blethers, tripe, bilge, bull, hooey, hokum, boloney.

Vagary, foolery, tomfoolery, mummery, monkey-trick, monkey-shine, dido, *boutade*, lark, escapade, ploy, rag.

(*Phrases*) A cock-and-bull story; a mare's-nest; a wild-goose chase; talking through one's hat; 'a tale told by an idiot, full of sound and fury, signifying nothing'; clotted nonsense; arrant rot.

(*Adjectives*) Absurd, nonsensical, foolish, senseless, preposterous (499), sophistical, inconsistent, extravagant, ridiculous, cock-and-bull, quibbling, trashy, washy, wishy-washy, twaddling, etc.; topsy-turvy, Gilbertian.

---

498 INTELLIGENCE (*Substantives*), capacity, nous, parts, talent, sagacity, sagaciousness, wit, mother-wit, *esprit*, gumption, comprehension, understanding, quick parts, grasp of intellect.

Acuteness, acumen, shrewdness, astuteness, arguteness, sharpness, aptness, aptitude, quickness, receptiveness, subtlety, archness, penetration, perspicacity, perspicaciousness, clear-sightedness, discrimination, discernment, flair, refinement (850).

Head, brains, headpiece, a long head.

WISDOM, sapience, sense, good sense, common sense, plain sense, horse-sense, reason, reasonableness, rationality, judgment, judiciousness, solidity, depth, profoundness, catholicity, breadth of view, enlarged views, reach or compass of thoughts.

Genius, inspiration, the fire of genius.

---

499 IMBECILITY (*Substantives*), incapacity, vacancy of mind, poverty of intellect, shallowness, dullness, stupidity, asininity, obtuseness, stolidity, hebetude, doltishness, muddleheadedness, vacuity, short-sightedness, incompetence.

Silliness, simplicity, childishness, puerility, babyhood; dotage, second childhood, anility, fatuity, idiocy, idiotism (503).

FOLLY, unwisdom, absurdity, infatuation, irrationality, senselessness, foolishness, frivolity, inconsistency, lip-wisdom, conceit, vanity, irresponsibility, giddiness, extravagance, oddity, eccentricity (503), ridiculousness, desipience.

Act of folly (497), imprudence (699), rashness, fanaticism.

(*Phrases*) A fool's paradise; apartments to let; one's wits going woolgathering; the meanest capacity.

Wisdom in action, prudence, discretion, self-possession, aplomb (698), sobriety, tact, ballast.

(*Phrase*) Discretion being the better part of valour.

(*Verbs*) To be intelligent, wise, etc., to reason (476), to discern (441), discriminate (465), to penetrate, to see far into.

(*Phrases*) To have all one's wits about one; to see as far through a brick wall as anybody.

(*Adjectives*) Applied to persons: Intelligent, sagacious, receptive, quick, sharp, acute, fly, smart, shrewd, gumptious, canny, astute, sharp-sighted, quick-sighted, quick-eyed, keen, keen-eyed, keen-sighted, keen-witted, sharp-witted, quick-witted, needle-witted, penetrating, piercing, clear-sighted, perspicacious, discerning, discriminating, discriminative, clever (698), knowledgeable.

Wise, sage, sapient, sagacious, reasonable, rational, sound, common-sense, sane, sensible, judicious, judgmatic, enlightened, impartial, catholic, broad-minded, open-minded, unprejudiced, unbiased, unprepossessed, undazzled, unperplexed, judicial, impartial, fair, progressive.

Cool, cool-headed, long-headed, hard-headed, long-sighted, calculating, thoughtful, reflective, oracular, heaven-directed.

Prudent, discreet, sober, staid, deep, solid, considerate, provident, politic, diplomatic, tactful.

Applied to actions: Wise, sensible, reasonable, judicious, well-judged, well-advised, prudent, prudential, politic (646), expedient.

(*Phrases*) Wise as a serpent; wise in one's generation; not born yesterday; up to snuff; no flies on him; wise as Solomon.

(*Verbs*) To be imbecile, foolish, etc., to trifle, drivel, ramble, dote, *radoter*, blether, haver; to fool, to monkey, to footle.

(*Phrases*) To play the fool; to play the giddy goat; to make an ass of oneself; to go on a fool's errand; to pursue a wild-goose chase; *battre la campagne*; Homer nods.

(*Adjectives*) Applied to persons: Unintelligent, unintellectual, witless, reasonless, not bright, imbecile, shallow, *borné*, weak, soft, simple, sappy, spoony, weak-headed, weak-minded, feeble-minded, half-witted, short-witted, half-baked, not all there, deficient, wanting, shallow-pated, shallow-brained, dull, dumb, dense, crass, stupid, heavy, obtuse, stolid, doltish, asinine, addle-headed, dull-witted, blunt, dull-brained, dim-sighted, vacuous.

Childish, infantine, infantile, baby-ish, childlike, puerile, callow; anile.

Fatuous, idiotic, lack-brained, drivelling, blatant, brainless, blunt-witted, beef-witted, fat-witted, fat-headed, boneheaded, insulse, having no head or brains, thick-skulled, ivory-skulled, blockish, Boeotian.

Foolish, silly, senseless, irrational, insensate, nonsensical, blunder-headed, chuckle-headed, puzzle-headed, muddle-headed, muddy-headed, undiscerning, unenlightened, unphilosophical; prejudiced, bigoted, purblind, narrow-minded, wrong-headed, tactless, crotchety, conceited, self-opinionated, pig-headed, mulish, unprogressive, one-ideaed, stick-in-the-mud, reactionary, blimpish, besotted, infatuated, unreasoning.

Wild, giddy, dizzy, thoughtless, eccentric, odd, extravagant, quixotic, light-headed, rantipole, high-flying, crack - brained, cracked, cranky, hare-brained, scatter-brained, scatter - pated, unballasted, ridiculous, frivolous, balmy (or barmy), daft (503).

Applied to actions: Foolish, unwise, injudicious, improper, imprudent, unreasonable, nonsensical, absurd, ridiculous, silly, stupid, asinine, ill-imagined, ill-advised, ill-judged, ill-devised, tactless, inconsistent, irrational, unphilosophical, extravagant, preposterous, egregious, footling, imprudent, indiscreet, improvident, impolitic, improper (645, 647).

(*Phrases*) Dead from the neck up; concrete above the ears.
Without rhyme or reason; penny-wise and pound-foolish.

500 SAGE (*Substantives*), wise man, master-mind, thinker, *savant*, expert, luminary, adept, authority, egghead.

Oracle, a shining light, *esprit fort*, intellectual, high-brow, pundit, academist, academician, philomath, schoolman, magi, a Solomon, Nestor, Solon, Socrates, a second Daniel.

(*Adjectives*) Venerable, reverend, authoritative.

(*Phrases*) 'A Daniel come to judgment'; the wise men of the East.

(*Ironically*) Wiseacre, know-all, bigwig.

---

501 FOOL (*Substantives*), blockhead, bonehead, idiot, tom-fool, lowbrow, simpleton, simp, sap, softy, sawney, witling, ass, donkey, goat, goose, ninny, dolt, booby, boob, noodle, muff, mug, muggins, juggins, owl, cuckoo, gowk, numskull, noddy, dumb-bell, gomeril, half-wit, imbecile, ninnyhammer, mutt, driveller, cretin, moron, natural, lackbrain, child, infant, baby, innocent, greenhorn, zany, zombie, gaby.

Dunce, lout, loon, oaf, dullard, duffer, calf, colt, buzzard, block, stick, stock, clod-poll, clot-poll, clodhopper, clod, lubber, bull-calf, bullhead, fat-head, thick-skull, dunderhead, addle-head, dizzard, hoddy-doddy, looby, Joe Soap, nincompoop, poop, put, *un sot à triple étage*, loggerhead, sot, shallow-brain, jobbernowl, changeling, dotard, driveller, moon-calf, giddy-head, gobemouche, rantipole, muddler, stick-in-the-mud, old woman, April fool.

(*Phrases*) One who is not likely to set the Thames on fire; one who did not invent gunpowder; one who is no conjurer; *qui n'a pas inventé la poudre*; who could not say 'Bo' to a goose; one with his upper storey to let; no fool like an old fool.

Men of Gotham; men of Boeotia.

502 SANITY (*Substantives*), rationality; being in one's senses, in one's right mind, in one's sober senses; sobriety, lucidity, lucid interval, sound mind, *mens sana*.

(*Verbs*) To be sane, etc., to retain one's senses, reason, etc.

To become sane, come to one's senses, sober down.

To render sane, bring to one's senses, to sober.

(*Adjectives*) Sane, rational, reasonable, *compos*, in one's sober senses, in one's right mind, sober-minded.

(*Phrase*) In full possession of one's faculties.

(*Adverbs*) Sanely, soberly, etc.

---

503 INSANITY (*Substantives*), lunacy, madness, unsoundness, derangement, psychosis, neurosis, alienation, aberration, schizophrenia, split personality, dementia, paranoia, mania, melancholia, hypochondria, calenture, frenzy, phrenitis, raving, monomania, megalomania, kleptomania, dipsomania, etc., disordered intellect, incoherence, wandering, delirium, hallucination, lycanthropy, eccentricity (499), dementation; Bedlam.

(*Phrases*) The horrors; the jim-jams; pink spiders; snakes in the boots.

(*Verbs*) To be or become insane, etc., to lose one's senses, wits, reason, faculties, etc., to run mad, run amuck, go off one's head, rave, dote, ramble, wander, drivel.

To render or drive mad; to madden, dementate, turn the brain, addle the wits, turn one's head, befool, infatuate, craze.

(*Phrases*) *Battre la campagne; avoir le diable au corps.*

(*Adjectives*) Insane, mad, lunatic, crazy, crazed, *non compos*, cracked, cranky, loco, touched, deficient, wanting, out of one's mind, off one's head or nut or onion, bereft of reason, unsettled in one's mind, unhinged, insensate, reasonless, beside oneself.

Demented, daft, dotty, potty, dippy, scatty, loopy, batty, bats, wacky, crackers, cuckoo, haywire, bughouse, bugs, nuts, possessed, maddened, moon-struck, mad-brained, maniac, maniacal, delirious, incoherent, rambling, doting, doited, gaga.

Wandering, frantic, phrenetic, paranoiac, schizophrenic, megalo-maniacal, kleptomaniacal, etc., raving, corybantic, dithyrambic, rabid, pixillated, light-headed, giddy, vertiginous, wild, haggard, flighty, neurotic, distracted, distraught, hag-ridden, *écervelé, tête montée.*

(*Phrases*) The head being turned; having a screw (or a tile) loose; far gone; stark staring mad; mad as a March hare; mad as a hatter; of unsound mind; up the pole; bats in the belfry; the devil being in one; dizzy as a goose; candidate for Bedlam; like one possessed.

The wits going wool-gathering or bird's-nesting.

504 MADMAN (*Substantives*), lunatic, maniac, bedlamite, energumen, raver, monomaniac, paranoiac, schizophrenic, nut, screwball, crackpot, madcap, megalomaniac, dipsomaniac, kleptomaniac, psychopath, hypochondriac, *malade imaginaire,* crank, maenad.

SECTION VI—EXTENSION OF THOUGHT

1°. *To the Past*

505 MEMORY (*Substantives*), re-membrance, reminiscence, recognition, anamnesis, retention, retentiveness, readiness, tenacity.

Recurrence, recollection, retrospection, retrospect, flash-back, afterthought, hindsight.

Token of remembrance, reminder, memorial, memento, souvenir, keepsake, relic, reliquary, memorandum, aide-mémoire, remembrancer, prompter.

Things to be remembered, *memorabilia.*

Art of memory, artificial memory, *memoria technica,* mnemonics; Mnemosyne.

(*Phrases*) The tablets of the memory; *l'esprit de l'escalier.*

(*Verbs*) To remember, retain, mind, bear or keep in mind, have or carry in the memory, know by heart or by rote; recognize.

506 OBLIVION (*Substantives*), forgetfulness, amnesia, obliteration (552), a short memory; a lapse of memory; the memory failing, being in fault, or deserting one; the waters of Lethe, Nepenthe, *tabula rasa.*

(*Verbs*) To forget, lose, unlearn, efface, expunge, blot out, etc. (552); discharge from the memory.

To slip, escape, fade, die away from the memory, to sink into oblivion.

(*Phrases*) To cast behind one's back; to have a short memory; to put out of one's head: to apply the sponge; to think no more of; to consign to oblivion; to let bygones be bygones.

(*Adjectives*) Forgotten, etc., lost, effaced, blotted out, obliterated, discharged, sponged out, buried or sunk in oblivion, out of mind, clean out

To be deeply impressed, live, remain, or dwell in the memory; to be stored up, bottled up, to sink in the mind, to rankle, etc.

To recollect, call to mind, bethink oneself, recall, call up, retrace, carry one's thoughts back, review, look back, rake up, brush up, think upon, call to remembrance, tax the memory.

To suggest, prompt, hint, recall to mind, put in mind, remind, whisper, call up, summon up, renew, commend to.

To say by heart, repeat by rote, say one's lesson, repeat as a parrot.

To commit to memory, get or learn by heart or rote, memorize, con, con over, repeat; to fix, imprint, impress, stamp, grave, engrave, store, treasure up, bottle up, embalm, enshrine, etc., in the memory; to load, store, stuff, or burden the memory with; to commemorate (883).

(*Phrase*) To have at one's fingers' ends.

To jog or refresh the memory; to pull by the sleeve; to bring back to the memory; to keep the memory alive; to keep the wound green; to reopen old sores; to put in remembrance.

(*Adjectives*) Remembering, etc., mindful, remembered, etc., fresh, green, unforgotten, present to the mind; living in, being in, or within one's memory; indelible, ineffaceable, green in remembrance, reminiscential, commemorative.

(*Adverbs*) By heart, by rote, *memoriter*, without book; in memory of, in memoriam.

of one's head or recollection, past recollection, unremembered.

Forgetful, oblivious, unmindful, mindless; Lethean.

———

2°. To the Future

507 EXPECTATION (*Substantives*), expectance, expectancy, anticipation, forestalling, foreseeing (510); reckoning, calculation.

Contemplation, prospect, look-out, outlook (121), perspective, horizon, vista, hope, trust (858), abeyance, waiting, suspense.

(*Phrase*) The torments of Tantalus.

(*Verbs*) To expect, look for, look out for, look forward to, anticipate, contemplate, flatter oneself, to dare to say, foresee (510), forestall, reckon upon, count upon, lay one's account to, to calculate upon, rely upon, build upon, make sure of, prepare oneself for, keep in view, not to wonder at.

To wait, tarry, lie in wait, watch for, abide, to bide one's time.

To hold out, raise, or excite expectation, to bid fair, to promise, to augur, etc. (511).

(*Phrases*) To count one's chickens before they are hatched.

508 INEXPECTATION (*Substantives*), non-expectation; blow, shock, surprise (870).

False or vain expectation, miscalculation.

(*Phrase*) A bolt from the blue.

(*Verbs*) Not to expect, not to look for, etc., to be taken by surprise, to start, come upon, to fall upon, not to bargain for, to miscalculate.

To be unexpected, etc., to crop up, pop up, to come unawares, suddenly, abruptly, like a thunderbolt, creep upon, burst upon, bounce upon; surprise, take aback, stun, stagger, startle.

(*Phrases*) To reckon without one's host; to trust to a broken reed.

To drop from the clouds; you could have knocked me down with a feather.

(*Adjectives*) Non-expectant, surprised, taken by surprise, unwarned, unaware, startled, etc., taken aback.

Unexpected, unanticipated, unlooked-for, unhoped-for, unforeseen,

To have in store for; to have a rod in pickle.

(*Adjectives*) Expectant, expecting, etc., prepared for, gaping for, ready for, agog, anxious, ardent, eager, breathless, sanguine.

Expected, anticipated, foreseen, etc., long expected, impending, prospective, in prospect.

(*Adverbs*) With breathless expectation, on tenterhooks.

(*Phrases*) On the tiptoe of expectation; on edge; looming in the distance; the wish father to the thought; we shall see; *nous verrons.*

beyond expectation, abrupt, sudden, contrary to or against expectation, unannounced, unheralded; backhanded.

(*Adverbs*) Suddenly, abruptly, unexpectedly, plump, pop, *à l'improviste*, unawares, without notice or warning (113).

(*Phrases*) Like a thief in the night; who would have thought it?

509 Failure of expectation.

DISAPPOINTMENT (*Substantives*), vain expectation, blighted hope, surprise, astonishment (870); balk, afterclap, miscalculation.

(*Phrase*) 'There's many a slip 'twixt cup and lip.'

(*Verbs*) To be disappointed, etc., to miscalculate; to look blank, to look blue, to look or stand aghast.

To disappoint, balk, bilk, tantalize, let down, play false, stand up, dumbfound, dash one's hope (859), sell.

(*Adjectives*) Disappointed, disconcerted, aghast, blue, out of one's reckoning.

Happening, contrary to or against expectation.

(*Phrase*) *Parturiunt montes, nascetur ridiculus mus.*

510 FORESIGHT (*Substantives*), prospiscience, prescience, foreknowledge, forethought, forecast, prevision, prognosis, precognition, second sight, clairvoyance.

Anticipation, foretaste, prenotion, presentiment, foregone conclusion, providence, discretion, prudence, sagacity.

Announcement, prospectus, programme, policy (626).

(*Verbs*) To foresee, foreknow, forejudge, forecast, predict (511), anticipate, look forwards or beyond; look, peep, or pry into the future.

(*Phrases*) To keep a sharp look out for; to have an eye to the future; *respice finem.*

(*Adjectives*) Foreseeing, etc., prescient, weather-wise, far-sighted, far-seeing; provident, prudent, rational, sagacious, perspicacious.

511 PREDICTION (*Substantives*), announcement, prognosis, forecast, weird, prophecy, vaticination, mantology, prognostication, astrology, horoscopy, haruspicy, auguration, auspices, bodement, omination, augury, foreboding, abodement, aboding, horoscope, nativity, genethliacs, fortune-telling, crystal-gazing, palmistry, chiromancy, oneiromancy, sortilege, *sortes Virgilianae*, soothsaying, ominousness, divination (992).

Place of prediction, adytum, tripod.

(*Verbs*) To predict, prognosticate, prophesy, vaticinate, presage, augur, bode, forebode, divine, foretell, croak, soothsay, auspicate, to cast a horoscope or nativity, tell one's fortune, read one's hand.

To foretoken, betoken, prefigure, portend, foreshadow, foreshow, usher in, herald, signify, premise, announce, point to, admonish, warn, forewarn, advise.

(*Adjectives*) Predicting, etc., predictive, prophetic, fatidical, vaticinal, oracular, Sibylline.

Ominous, portentous, augural, auspicious, monitory, premonitory, significant of, pregnant with, weatherwise, bodeful, big with fate.

(*Phrase*) 'Coming events cast their shadows before.'

512 OMEN (*Substantives*), portent, presage, prognostic, augury, auspice, sign, forerunner, precursor (64), harbinger, herald, monition, warning, avant-courier, pilot-balloon, handwriting on the wall, rise and fall of the barometer, a bird of ill omen, a sign of the times, gathering clouds.

(*Phrases*) Touch wood! *absit omen.*

513 ORACLE (*Substantives*), prophet, seer, soothsayer, haruspex, fortune-teller, spaewife, palmist, gipsy, wizard, witch, geomancer, Sibyl, Python, Pythoness, *Pythia*, Pythian oracle, Delphic oracle, Old Moore, Zadkiel, Mother Shipton, Witch of Endor, Sphinx, Tiresias, Cassandra, Oedipus, Sibylline leaves.

SECTION VII—CREATIVE THOUGHT

514 SUPPOSITION (*Substantives*), conjecture, surmise, presurmise, speculation, inkling, guess, guess-work, shot, divination, conceit; assumption, postulation, hypothesis, presupposition, postulate, *postulatum*, presumption, theory, thesis; suggestion, proposition, motion, proposal, allusion, insinuation, innuendo.

(*Phrases*) A rough guess; a lucky shot.

(*Verbs*) To suppose, conjecture, surmise, guess, divine, theorize, give a guess, make a shot, hazard a conjecture, throw out a conjecture, etc., presuppose, fancy, wis, take it, dare to say, take it into one's head, assume, believe, postulate, posit, presume, presurmise.

To suggest, hint, insinuate, put forth, propound, propose, start, allude to, prompt, put a case, move, make a motion.

To suggest itself, occur to one, come into one's head; to run in the head; to haunt (505).

(*Phrases*) To put it into one's head; 'thereby hangs a tale.'

(*Adjectives*) Supposing, etc., supposed, supposititious, suppositious, suppositive, reputed, putative, suggestive, allusive, conjectural, presumptive, hypothetical, theoretical, warranted, authorized, mooted, conjecturable, supposable.

(*Adverbs*) If, if so be, an, gin, maybe, perhaps, on the supposition, in the event of, as if, *ex hypothesi, quasi.*

515 IMAGINATION (*Substantives*), fancy, conception, ideality, idealism, inspiration, afflatus, verve, dreaming, somnambulism, frenzy, ecstasy, excogitation, reverie, *Schwärmerei*, trance, imagery, vision; Pegasus.

Invention, inventiveness, originality, fertility, romanticism, utopianism, castle-building.

Conceit, maggot, figment, coinage, fiction, romance, novel (594), myth, Arabian Nights, fairyland, faerie, the man in the moon, dream, day-dream, pipe-dream, nightmare, vapour, chimera, phantom, phantasy, fantasia, whim, whimsy, vagary, rhapsody, extravaganza, air-drawn dagger, bugbear, men in buckram, castle in the air, air-built castle, castle in Spain, will-o'-the-wisp, ignis fatuus, jack-o'-lantern, Utopia, Atlantis, Shangri-la, land of Prester John, millennium, golden age, *fata morgana* (443).

A visionary, romancer, rhapsodist, high-flyer, enthusiast, idealist, energumen, dreamer, seer, fanatic, knight-errant, Don Quixote.

(*Phrases*) Flight of fancy; fumes of fancy; fine frenzy; thick-coming fancies; coinage of the brain; the mind's eye; a stretch of imagination; 'such stuff as dreams are made on.'

(*Verbs*) To imagine, fancy, conceive, ideate, idealize, realize, objectify; fancy or picture to oneself; create, originate, devise, invent, coin, fabricate, make up, mint, improvise, excogitate, conjure up.

(*Phrases*) To take into one's head; to figure to oneself; to strain or crack one's invention; to strike out something new; to give a loose to the fancy; to give the reins to the imagination; to set one's wits to work; to rack or cudgel one's brains.

(*Adjectives*) Imagining, imagined, etc.; ideal, unreal, unsubstantial, imaginary, *in nubibus*, fabulous, fictitious, legendary, mythological, chimerical, *ben trovato*, fanciful, faerie, fairylike, air-drawn, air-built, original, fantastic, fantastical, whimsical, high-flown.

Imaginative, inventive, creative, fertile, romantic, flighty, extravagant, high-flown, fanatic, enthusiastic, Utopian, Quixotic.

DIVISION II—COMMUNICATION OF IDEAS

SECTION I—NATURE OF IDEAS COMMUNICATED

516 Idea to be conveyed.

MEANING (*Substantives*), signification, sense, import, purport, significance, drift, gist, acceptation, acceptance, bearing, interpretation (522), reading, tenor, allusion, spirit, colouring, expression.

Literal meaning, literality, obvious meaning, grammatical sense, first blush, *prima facie* meaning; after-acceptation.

Equivalent meaning, synonym, synonymity.

Thing signified: Matter, subject, substance, pith, marrow, argument, text; sum and substance.

(*Verbs*) To mean, signify, express, import, purport, convey, breathe, imply, bespeak, speak of, tell of, touch on, bear a sense, involve, declare (527), insinuate, allude to, point to, indicate, drive at; to come to the point, give vent to; to stand for.

To take, understand, receive, or accept in a particular sense.

(*Adjectives*) Meaning, etc., significant, significative, significatory, literal, expressive, explicit, suggestive, allusive; pithy, pointed, epigrammatic, telling, striking, full of meaning, pregnant with meaning.

517 Absence of meaning.

UNMEANINGNESS (*Substantives*), empty sound, a dead letter, scrabble, scribble; inexpressiveness, vagueness (519).

Nonsense, stuff, balderdash (497), jabber, gibberish, palaver, rigmarole, twaddle, tosh, bosh, bull, rubbish, rot, empty babble, empty sound, verbiage, *nugae*, truism, moonshine, inanity.

(*Verbs*) To mean nothing, to be unmeaning, etc.; to scribble, jabber, gibber, babble.

(*Adjectives*) Unmeaning, meaningless, nonsensical, void of meaning, of sense, etc., senseless, not significant, undefined, tacit, not expressed.

Inexpressible, indefinable, undefinable, unmeant, unconceived.

Trashy, trumpery, twaddling, etc.

(*Phrases*) *Vox et praeterea nihil*; 'a tale told by an idiot, full of sound and fury, signifying nothing'; 'sounding brass and tinkling cymbal.'

(*Adverb*) Tacitly.

———

Synonymous, equivalent, tantamount; the same thing as.
Implied, tacit, understood, implicit, inferred, latent.
(*Adverbs*) Meaningly, literally, etc., *videlicet* (522), viz., i.e.
(*Phrases*) *Au pied de la lettre*; so to speak; to that effect; so to express oneself; as it were; that is to say; *façon de parler*.

518 INTELLIGIBILITY (*Substantives*), clearness, lucidity, perspicuity, explicitness, distinctness, plain speaking, expressiveness, legibility, visibility (446); precision (494).

Intelligence, comprehension, understanding, learning (539).

(*Phrases*) A word to the wise; *verbum sapienti*.

(*Verbs*) To be intelligible, etc.

To render intelligible, etc., to simplify, clear up, throw light upon.

To understand, comprehend, follow, take, take in, catch, catch on to, twig, dig, get the hang of, get wise to, grasp, sense, make out, get, collect; master, tumble to, rumble.

(*Phrases*) It tells its own tale; he who runs may read; to stand to reason; to speak for itself.

To come to an understanding; to see with half an eye.

(*Adjectives*) Intelligible, clear, lucid, understandable, explicit, expressive, significant, express, distinct, precise, definite, well-defined, perspicuous, transpicuous, striking, plain, obvious, manifest, palpable, glaring, transparent, above-board, unambiguous, unmistakable, legible, open, positive, expressive (516), unconfused, unequivocal, pronounced, graphic, readable.

(*Phrases*) Clear as day; clear as crystal; clear as noonday; not to be mistaken; plain to the meanest capacity; plain as a pikestaff; in plain English.

519 UNINTELLIGIBILITY (*Substantives*), incomprehensibility, inconceivability, darkness (421), imperspicuity, obscurity, confusion, perplexity, imbroglio, indistinctness, mistiness, indefiniteness, vagueness, ambiguity, looseness, uncertainty, mysteriousness (526), paradox, inexplicability, incommunicability, spinosity.

Jargon, gibberish, rigmarole, rodomontade, etc. (497); paradox, riddle, enigma, puzzle (533).

Double or High Dutch, Greek, Hebrew, etc.

(*Verbs*) To be unintelligible, etc., to pass comprehension.

To render unintelligible, etc., to perplex, confuse, confound, bewilder, darken, moither (475).

Not to understand, etc., to lose, miss, etc., to lose the clue.

(*Phrases*) Not to know what to make of; not to be able to make either head or tail of; to be all at sea; to play at cross purposes; to beat about the bush.

(*Adjectives*) Unintelligible, incognizable, inapprehensible, incomprehensible, inconceivable, unimaginable, unknowable, inexpressible, undefinable, incommunicable, above or past or beyond comprehension, inexplicable, illegible, undecipherable, inscrutable, unfathomable, beyond one's depth, paradoxical, insoluble, impenetrable.

Obscure, dark, confused, indistinct, indefinite, misty, nebulous, intricate, undefined, ill-defined, indeterminate, perplexed, loose, vague, ambiguous, disconnected, incoherent, unaccountable, puzzling, enigmatical, hieroglyphic, mysterious, mystic, mystical, at cross purposes.

Hidden, recondite, abstruse, crabbed, transcendental, far-fetched, *in nubibus*, searchless, unconceived, unimagined.

(*Phrases*) Greek to one; without rhyme or reason; *obscurum per obscurius; lucus a non lucendo.*

520 Having a double sense.

EQUIVOCALNESS (*Substantives*), double meaning, quibble, equivoque, equivocation, *double-entendre*, paragram, anagram, amphibology, amphiboly, ambiloquy, prevarication, white lie, mental reservation, tergiversation, slip of the tongue, *lapsus linguae*, a pun, play on words, homonym.

Having a doubtful meaning, ambiguity (475), homonymy.

Having a false meaning (544), *suggestio falsi*.

(*Verbs*) To be equivocal, etc., to have two senses, etc., to equivocate, prevaricate, tergiversate, palter to the understanding, to pun.

(*Adjectives*) Equivocal, ambiguous, amphibolous, amphibological, homonymous, double-tongued, double-edged, left-handed, equivocatory, paltering.

(*Adverb*) Over the left.

521 METAPHOR (*Substantives*), figure, metonymy, trope, catachresis, synecdoche, figure of speech, figurativeness, image, imagery, metalepsis, type (22), symbol, symbolism (550), tropology.

Personification, prosopopaeia, allegory, apologue, parable.

Implication, inference, allusion, application, adumbration, hidden meaning. Allegorist, tropist, symbolist.

(*Verbs*) To employ metaphor, etc., to personify, allegorize, adumbrate, shadow forth, imply, understand, apply, allude to.

(*Adjectives*) Metaphorical, figurative, catachrestical, typical, tropical, parabolic, allegorical, allusive, symbolic (550), symbolistic, implied, inferential, implicit, understood.

(*Adverbs*) So to speak, as it were.

(*Phrases*) Where more is meant than meets the ear; in a manner of speaking; *façon de parler*; in a Pickwickian sense.

522 INTERPRETATION (*Substantives*), exegesis, explanation, meaning (516), explication, expounding, exposition, rendition, reddition.

Translation, version, rendering, construction, reading, spelling, restoration, metaphrase, literal translation, free translation, paraphrase.

Comment, commentary, inference, illustration, exemplification, definition, *éclaircissement*, elucidation, crib, cab, gloss, glossary, annotation, *scholium*, marginalia, note, clue, key, sidelight, master-key (631), rationale, denouement, solution, answer (462), object lesson.

Palaeography, dictionary, glossology, etc. (562), semantics, semasiology, oneirocritics, oneirocriticism, hermeneutics.

(*Verbs*) To interpret, expound, explain, clear up, construe, translate, render, English, do into, turn into, transfuse the sense of.

To read, spell, make out, decipher, decode, unfold, disentangle, elicit the

523 MISINTERPRETATION (*Substantives*), misapprehension, misunderstanding, misacceptation, misconstruction, misspelling, misapplication, catachresis, mistake (495), cross-reading, cross-purpose.

Misrepresentation, perversion, falsification, misquotation, garbling, exaggeration (549), false colouring, abuse of terms, parody, travesty, misstatement, etc. (544).

(*Verbs*) To misinterpret, misapprehend, misunderstand, misconceive, misdeem, misspell, mistranslate, misconstrue, misapply, mistake (495).

To misstate, etc. (544); to pervert, falsify, distort, misrepresent, torture, travesty; to stretch, strain, wring, or wrest the sense or meaning; to put a bad or false construction on; to misquote, garble, belie, explain away.

(*Phrases*) To give a false colouring to; to be or play at cross-purposes; to put a false construction on.

meaning of, make sense of, find the key of, unriddle, unravel, solve, resolve (480), restore.

To elucidate, throw light upon, illustrate, exemplify, expound, annotate, comment upon, define, unfold.

(*Adjectives*) Explanatory, expository, explicatory, explicative, exegetical, hermeneutic, constructive, inferential.

Paraphrastic, metaphrastic; literal, plain, simple, strict, synonymous; polyglot.

(*Adverbs*) That is to say, *id est* (or i.e.), *videlicet* (or viz.), in other words, in plain words, simply, in plain English.

Literally, word for word, verbatim, *au pied de la lettre*, strictly speaking (494).

(*Adjectives*) Misinterpreted, etc., untranslated, untranslatable.

(*Phrase*) *Traduttori traditori.*

———

524 INTERPRETER (*Substantives*), expositor, expounder, exponent, demonstrator, scholiast, commentator, annotator, metaphrast, paraphrast, palaeographer, spokesman, speaker, mouthpiece, guide, dragoman, cicerone, conductor, courier, showman, barker, oneirocritic; Oedipus (513).

SECTION II—MODES OF COMMUNICATION

525 MANIFESTATION (*Substantives*), expression, showing, etc., disclosure (529), presentation, indication, exposition, demonstration, exhibition, production, display, showing off.

An exhibit, an exhibitor.

Openness, frankness, plain speaking (543), publication, publicity (531).

(*Verbs*) To manifest, make manifest, etc., show, express, indicate, point out, bring forth, bring forward, trot out, set forth, exhibit, expose, produce, present, bring into view, set before one, hold up to view, lay open, lay bare, expose to view, set before one's eyes, show up, shadow forth, bring to light, display, demonstrate, unroll, unveil, unmask, disclose (529).

To elicit, educe, draw out, bring out, unearth, disinter.

To be manifested, etc., to appear, transpire, come to light (446), to come out, to crop up, get wind.

(*Phrases*) Hold up the mirror; draw, lift up, raise, or remove the curtain; show one's true colours; throw off the mask.

To speak for itself; to stand to reason; to stare one in the face; to tell its own tale; to give vent to.

526 LATENCY (*Substantives*), secrecy, secretness, privacy, invisibility (447), mystery, occultness, darkness, reticence, silence (585), closeness, reserve, inexpression; a sealed book, a dark horse, an undercurrent.

Retirement, delitescence, seclusion (893).

(*Phrases*) More is meant than meets the ear (or eye).

(*Verbs*) To be latent, etc., to lurk, underlie, escape observation, smoulder; to keep back, reserve, suppress, keep close, etc. (528).

To render latent (528).

(*Phrases*) Hold one's tongue; hold one's peace; leave in the dark; to keep one's own counsel; to keep mum; to seal the lips; not to breathe a syllable about.

(*Adjectives*) Latent, lurking, secret, close, unapparent, unknown (491), dark, delitescent, in the background, occult, cryptic, snug, private, privy, *in petto*, anagogic, sequestered, dormant, smouldering.

Inconspicuous, unperceived, invisible, (447) unseen, unwitnessed, impenetrable, unespied, unsuspected.

(*Adjectives*) Manifest, clear, apparent, evident, visible (446), prominent, in the foreground, salient, signal, striking, notable, conspicuous, palpable, patent, overt, flagrant, stark, glaring, open.

Manifested, shown, expressed, etc., disclosed (529), frank, capable of being shown, producible.

(*Phrases*) As plain as a pikestaff; as plain as the nose on one's face.

(*Adverbs*) Openly, before one's eyes, face to face, above-board, in open court, in open daylight, in the light of day, in the open streets, on the stage, on show.

---

527 INFORMATION (*Substantives*), gen, pukka gen, low-down, enlightenment, communication, intimation, notice, notification, enunciation, announcement, annunciation, statement, specification, report, advice, monition, mention, acquaintance (490), acquainting, etc., outpouring, intercommunication, communicativeness.

An informant, teller, tipster, spy, nose, nark, stool-pigeon, intelligencer, correspondent, reporter, messenger, newsmonger, gossip (532).

Hint, suggestion (514), wrinkle, tip, pointer, insinuation, innuendo, wink, glance, leer, nod, shrug, gesture, whisper, implication, cue, office, byplay, eye-opener.

(*Phrases*) A word to the wise; *verbum sapienti*; a broad hint; a straight tip; a stage whisper.

(*Verbs*) To inform, acquaint, tell, mention, express, intimate, impart, communicate, apprise, post, make known, notify, signify to, let one know, advise, state, specify, give notice, announce, annunciate, publish, report, set forth, bring word, send word, leave word, write word, declare, certify, depose, pronounce, explain, undeceive, enlighten, put wise, set right, open the eyes of, convey the knowledge of, give an account of; instruct (537).

To hint, give an inkling of; give, throw out, or drop a hint, insinuate, allude to, glance at, touch on, make

Untold, unsaid, unwritten, unpublished, unmentioned, unbreathed, untalked-of, unsung, unpronounced, unpromulgated, unreported, unexposed, unproclaimed, unexpressed, not expressed, tacit, implicit, implied, undeveloped, embryonic, unsolved, unexplained, undiscovered, untraced, untracked, unexplored.

(*Phrase*) No news being good news.

(*Adverbs*) Secretly, etc., *sub silentio*.

(*Phrases*) In the background; behind one's back; under the table; behind the scenes; between the lines.

---

528 CONCEALMENT (*Substantives*), hiding, occultation, etc., secrecy, stealth, stealthiness, slyness (702), disguise, incognito, privacy, masquerade, camouflage, smoke screen, mystery, mystification, freemasonry, reservation, suppression, secretiveness, reticence, reserve, uncommunicativeness; secret path.

A mask, visor, ambush, etc. (530), enigma, etc. (533).

(*Phrases*) A needle in a bundle of hay; a nigger in the woodpile; a skeleton in the cupboard; a family skeleton.

(*Verbs*) To conceal, hide, put out of sight, secrete, cover, envelop, screen, cloak, veil, shroud, enshroud, shade, muffle, mask, disguise, camouflage, ensconce, eclipse.

To keep from, lock up, bury, cache, sink, suppress, stifle, withhold, reserve, burke, hush up, keep snug or close or dark.

To keep in ignorance, blind, hoodwink, mystify, pose, puzzle, perplex, embarrass, flummox, bewilder, bamboozle, etc. (545).

To be concealed, etc., to lurk, skulk, smoulder, lie hid, lie in ambush, lie perdu, lie low, lie doggo, sneak, slink, prowl, gumshoe, retire, steal into, steal along.

To conceal oneself, put on a veil, etc. (530), masquerade.

(*Phrases*) To draw or close the curtain; not breathe a word about;

allusion to, to wink, to tip the wink, glance, leer, nod, shrug, give the cue, give the office, give the tip, wave, whisper, suggest, prompt, whisper in the ear, give one to understand.

To be informed, etc., of, made acquainted with; to hear of, get a line on, understand.

To come to one's ears, to come to one's knowledge, to reach one's ears.

(*Adjectives*) Informed, etc., of, made acquainted with, in the know, hep; undeceived.

Reported, made known (531), bruited.

Expressive, significant, pregnant with meaning, etc. (516), declaratory, enunciative, nuncupatory, expository, communicatory, communicative, insinuative.

(*Adverbs*) Expressively, significantly, etc.

(*Phrases*) A little bird told me; *on dit*; from information received.

___

To play at bo-peep; to play at hide-and-seek; to hide under a bushel; to throw dust in the eyes.

(*Adjectives*) Concealed, hid, hidden, etc., secret, clandestine, perdu, close, private, privy, furtive, surreptitious, stealthy, feline, underhand, sly, sneaking, skulking, hole-and-corner, undivulged, unrevealed, undisclosed, incognito, incommunicado.

Mysterious, mystic, mystical, dark, enigmatical, problematical, anagogical, paradoxical, occult, cryptic, gnostic, cabbalistic, esoteric, recondite, abstruse, unexplained, impenetrable, undiscoverable, inexplicable, unknowable, bewildering, baffling.

Covered, closed, shrouded, veiled, masked, screened, shaded, disguised, under cover, under a cloud, veil, etc., in a fog, haze, mist, etc., under an eclipse; inviolate, inviolable, confidential, under wraps.

Reserved, uncommunicative, secretive, buttoned up, taciturn (585).

(*Phrase*) Close as wax.

let it go no farther; keep it under your hat.

(*Adverbs*) Secretly, clandestinely, incognito, privily, in secret, *in camera*, with closed doors, *à huis clos, à la dérobée*, under the rose, *sub rosa*, privately, in private, aside, on the sly, *sub silentio*, behind one's back, under the counter, behind the curtain, behind the scenes.

Confidentially, between ourselves, between you and me, *entre nous, inter nos*, in strict confidence, on the strict q.t., off the record, it must go no farther.

(*Phrases*) Like a thief in the night; under the seal of secrecy, of confession; between you and me and the gate-post; 'tell it not in Gath'; nobody any the wiser.

___

529 DISCLOSURE (*Substantives*), revealment, revelation, disinterment, exposition, show-down, exposure, effusion, outpouring.

Acknowledgment, avowal, confession; an *exposé*, denouement.

A telltale, talebearer, informer, stool-pigeon, nark, nose.

(*Verbs*) To disclose, open, lay open, divulge, reveal, bewray, discover, unfold, let drop, let fall, let out, let on, spill, lay open, acknowledge, allow, concede, grant, admit, own, own up, confess, avow, unseal, unveil, unmask, uncover, unkennel, unearth (525).

530 AMBUSH (*Substantives*), hiding-place, hide, retreat, cover, lurking-hole, secret place, cubby-hole, recess, closet, priest's hole, crypt, cache, ambuscade, *guet-apens, adytum*, dungeon, oubliette.

A mask, veil, visor (or vizor), eye-shade, blinkers, cloak, screen, hoarding, curtain, shade, cover, disguise, masquerade dress, domino.

(*Verbs*) To lie in ambush, lurk, couch, lie in wait for, lay or set a trap for (545).

___

To blab, peach, squeal, let out, let fall, let on, betray, give away, tell tales, speak out, blurt out, vent, give vent to, come out with, round on, split; publish (531).

To make no secret of, to disabuse, unbeguile, undeceive, set right, correct.

To be disclosed, revealed, etc., to come out, to transpire, to ooze out, to leak out, to creep out, to get wind, to come to light.

(*Phrases*) To let into the secret; to let the cat out of the bag; to spill the beans; to unburden or disburden one's mind or conscience; to open one's mind; to unbosom oneself; to make a clean breast of it; to come clean; to give the show away; to own the soft impeachment; to tell tales out of school; to show one's hand; to turn Queen's (or King's or State's) evidence.

Murder will out.

(*Adjectives*) Disclosed, revealed, divulged, laid open, etc., unriddled, etc.; outspoken, etc. (543).

Open, public, exoteric.

(*Interjection*) Out with it!

531 PUBLICATION (*Substantives*), announcement, notification, enunciation, annunciation, advertisement, promulgation, circulation, propagation, edition, redaction, proclamation, hue and cry, the Press, journalism, wireless, radio, broadcasting, television.

Publicity, notoriety, currency, cry, bruit, rumour, fame, report (532), *on dit*, flagrancy, limelight, town-talk, small talk, table-talk, puffery, bally-hoo, *réclame*, the light of day, daylight.

Notice, notification, manifesto, propaganda, advertisement, blurb, circular, placard, bill, *affiche*, poster, newspaper, journal, daily, periodical, weekly, gazette; personal column, agony column.

Publisher (593), publicity agent, advertising agent: tout, barker, town crier.

(*Phrases*) An open secret; *un secret de Polichinelle*.

(*Verbs*) To publish, make known, announce, notify, annunciate, gazette, set forth, give forth, give out, broach, voice, utter, advertise, circularize, placard, *afficher*, circulate, propagate, spread, spread abroad, broadcast, edit, redact, rumour, diffuse, disseminate, celebrate, blaze about; blaze or noise abroad; bruit, buzz, bandy, hawk about, trumpet, proclaim, herald, puff, boost, splash, plug, boom, give tongue, raise a cry, raise a hue and cry, tell the world, popularize; bring, lay or drag before the public, give currency to, ventilate, bring out.

(*Phrases*) To proclaim from the house-tops; to publish in the gazette; to send round the crier; with beat of drum.

To be published, etc., to become public, to go forth, get abroad, get about, get wind, take air, get afloat, acquire currency, get in the papers, spread, go the rounds, buzz about, blow about.

To pass from mouth to mouth; to spread like wildfire.

(*Adjectives*) Published, etc., made public, in circulation, exoteric, rumoured, rife, current, afloat, notorious, flagrant, whispered, buzzed about, in every one's mouth, reported, trumpet-tongued; encyclical.

(*Phrases*) As the story runs; to all whom it may concern.

(*Interjections*) Oyez! O yes! notice is hereby given!

532 NEWS (*Substantives*), piece of information, intelligence, tidings, budget of news, word, advice, message, communication, errand, embassy, dispatch, bulletin.

533 SECRET (*Substantives*), *arcanum*, *penetralia*, profound secret, mystery, crux, problem, enigma, teaser, poser, riddle, puzzle, conundrum, charade, rebus, logogriph,

Report, story, scoop, beat, rumour, canard, hearsay, *on dit*, fame, talk, gossip, tittle-tattle, *oui-dire*, scandal, buzz, bruit, *chronique scandaleuse*, town talk.

Letter, postcard, airgraph, telegram, wire, cable, wireless message, radiogram.

Newsmonger, scandalmonger, scaremonger, alarmist, talebearer, tattler, gossip (527), local correspondent, special correspondent, reporter (590).

anagram, acrostic, cross-word, cipher, code, cryptogram, monogram, paradox, maze, labyrinth, perplexity, chaos (528), the Hercynian wood; *terra incognita.*

Iron curtain, bamboo curtain, censorship, counter-intelligence.

(*Phrases*) The secrets of the prisonhouse; a sealed book.

(*Adjectives*) Secret, top secret, hush-hush, undercover, clandestine (528).

534 MESSENGER (*Substantives*), envoy, nuncio, internuncio, intermediary, go-between, herald, ambassador, legate, emissary, *corps diplomatique.*

Marshal, crier, trumpeter, pursuivant, *parlementaire*, courier, runner, postman, telegraph-boy, errand-boy, bell-boy, bell-hop, Mercury, Hermes, Iris, Ariel, carrier pigeon.

Narrator, etc., talebearer, spy, secret-service agent, scout.

Mail, post (592), post office, telegraph, telephone, wireless, radio; grapevine, bush telegraph.

535 AFFIRMATION (*Substantives*), statement, predication, assertion, declaration, word, averment, asseveration, protestation, swearing, adjuration, protest, profession, deposition, avouchment, affirmance, assurance, allegation, acknowledgment, avowal, confession, confession of faith, oath, affidavit; vote, voice.

Remark, observation, position, thesis, proposition, saying, dictum, theorem, sentence.

Positiveness (474), dogmatism, *ipse dixit.*

A dogmatist, doctrinaire.

(*Phrase*) The big bow-wow style.

(*Verbs*) To assert, make an assertion, etc., say, affirm, predicate, enunciate, state, declare, profess, aver, avouch, put forth, advance, express, allege, pose, propose, propound, broach, set forth, maintain, contend, pronounce, pretend, pass an opinion, etc.; to reassert, reaffirm, reiterate; quoth; *dixit, dixi.*

To vouch, assure, vow, swear, take oath, depose, depone, recognize, avow, acknowledge, own, confess, announce, hazard or venture an opinion.

536 NEGATION (*Substantives*), abnegation, denial, denegation, disavowal, disclaimer, abjuration, contradiction, *démenti*, contravention, recusation, retraction, retractation, recantation, renunciation, palinode, recusancy, protest.

Qualification, modification (469); rejection (610); refusal (764).

(*Verbs*) To deny, disown, contradict, negative, gainsay, contravene, disclaim, withdraw, recant, disavow, retract, revoke, abjure, negate.

(*Phrases*) To deny flatly; eat one's words; go back from, or upon one's word.

To dispute, impugn, controvert, confute (479), question, call in question, give the lie to, rebut, belie.

(*Adjectives*) Denying, etc., denied, etc., negative, contradictory, recusant.

(*Adverbs*) No, nay, not, nohow, not at all, by no means (489), far from it, anything but, on the contrary, quite the reverse.

To dogmatize, lay down, lay down the law; to call heaven to witness, protest, certify, warrant, posit, go bail for.

(*Phrases*) I doubt not; I warrant you; I 'll engage; take my word for it; depend upon it; I 'll be bound; I am sure; I have no doubt; sure enough; to be sure; what I have said, I have said; faith! that 's flat.

To swear till one is black in the face; to swear by all the saints in the calendar; to call heaven to witness.

(*Adjectives*) Asserting, etc., dogmatic, positive, emphatic, declaratory, affirmative, predicable, pronounced, unretracted.

Positive, broad, round, express, explicit, pointed, marked, definitive, distinct, decided, formal, solemn, categorical, peremptory, absolute, flat, pronounced.

(*Adverbs*) *Ex cathedra*, positively, avowedly, confessedly, broadly, roundly, etc.; ay, yes, indeed; by Jove, by George, by James, by jingo.

537 TEACHING (*Substantives*), instruction, direction, guidance, tuition, culture, inculcation, inoculation, indoctrination.

Education, co-education, initiation, preparation, practice, training, upbringing, schooling, discipline, exercise, drill, exercitation, breaking in, taming, drilling, etc., preachment, persuasion, edification, proselytism, propagandism.

A lesson, lecture, prolusion, prelection, exercise, task; curriculum, course.

Rudiments, ABC, elements, three Rs, grammar, text-book, vademecum, school-book (593).

Physical training, P.T., gymnastics, callisthenics.

(*Verbs*) To teach, instruct, enlighten, edify, inculcate, indoctrinate, instil, imbue, inoculate, infuse, impregnate, graft, infix, engraft, implant, sow the seeds of, infiltrate, give an idea of, cram, coach, put up to.

To explain, expound, lecture, hold forth, read a lecture or sermon, give a lesson, preach; sermonize, moralize, point a moral.

To educate, train, discipline, school, form, ground, tutor, prepare, qualify prime, drill, exercise, practise, bring up, rear, nurture, dry-nurse, breed, break in, tame, domesticate, condition.

To direct, guide, initiate, put in the way of, proselytize, bring round to an opinion, bring over, win over, brainwash, re-educate, persuade, convince, convict, set right, enlighten, give one new ideas, put one up to, bring home to.

538 MISTEACHING (*Substantives*), misdirection, misleading, misinformation, misguidance, perversion, false teaching, sophistry.

Indocility, incapacity, misintelligence, dullness, backwardness.

(*Verbs*) To misinform, misteach, mislead, misdirect, misguide, miscorrect, pervert, lead into error, bewilder, mystify (528), throw off the scent; to unteach.

(*Phrases*) To teach one's grandmother; *obscurum per obscurius*; the blind leading the blind.

(*Adjectives*) Misteaching, etc., unedifying.

539 LEARNING (*Substantives*), acquisition of knowledge, acquirement, attainment, scholarship, erudition, instruction, study, etc. (490).

Docility (602), aptitude (698), aptness to be taught, teachableness, persuasibility, capacity.

(*Verbs*) to learn; to acquire, gain, catch, receive, imbibe, pick up, gather, collect, glean, etc., knowledge or information.

To hear, overhear, catch hold of, take in, fish up, drink in, run away with an idea, to make oneself acquainted with, master, read, spell, turn over the leaves, pore over, run through, peruse, study, grind, cram, mug, swot, go to school; to get up a subject; to serve one's time or apprenticeship.

To be taught, etc.

(*Phrases*) To teach the young idea how to shoot; to sharpen the wits; to enlarge the mind.

(*Adjectives*) Teaching, etc., taught, etc., educational.

Didactic, academic, doctrinal, disciplinal, disciplinary, instructive, scholastic, persuasive.

540 TEACHER (*Substantives*), instructor, apostle, master, director, tutor, preceptor, institutor, mentor, adviser, monitor, counsellor, expositor, dry-nurse, trainer, coach, crammer, grinder, governor, bear-leader, disciplinarian, martinet, guide, cicerone, pioneer, governess, duenna.

Orator, speaker, mouthpiece (582).

Professor, lecturer, reader, demonstrator, praelector, prolocutor, schoolmaster, schoolmistress, schoolmarm, usher, pedagogue, monitor, pupil-teacher, dominie, dame, moonshee; missionary, propagandist.

(*Adjectives*) Tutorial, professorial.

(*Adjectives*) Docile, apt, teachable, persuasible, studious, industrious, scholastic, scholarly.

(*Phrase*) To burn the midnight oil.

———

541 LEARNER (*Substantives*), scholar, student, alumnus, disciple, pupil, *élève*, schoolboy, schoolgirl, beginner, tyro (or tiro), abecedarian, novice, neophyte, chela, inceptor, probationer, apprentice, tenderfoot, freshman, bejan (or bejant), undergraduate, undergraduette, sophomore.

Proselyte, convert, catechumen, sectator; class, form.

Pupilage, pupilarity, pupilship, tutelage, apprenticeship, novitiate, leading-strings, matriculation.

(*Phrases*) Freshwater sailor; *in statu pupillari*.

542 SCHOOL (*Substantives*), day school, boarding school, public school, council school, national school, board school, private school, preparatory school, elementary school, primary school, secondary school, senior school, grammar school, high school, academy, university, Alma Mater, university extension, correspondence school, college, seminary, lyceum, polytechnic, nursery, institute, institution, palaestra, gymnasium, class, form, standard; nursery school, infant school, kindergarten, crèche; reformatory, Borstal, approved school.

Horn-book, rudiments, vade-mecum, abecedary, manual, primer, school-book, text-book.

Professorship, lectureship, readership, chair; pulpit, ambo, theatre, amphitheatre, forum, stage, rostrum, platform.

(*Adjectives*) Scholastic, academic, collegiate.

543 VERACITY (*Substantives*), truthfulness, truth, sincerity, frankness, straightforwardness, ingenuousness, candour, honesty, fidelity, bona fides, openness, unreservedness, bluntness, plainness, plain speaking, plain dealing; simplicity, bonhomie, naïveté, artlessness (703), love of truth.

A plain-dealer, truth-teller, man of his word.

(*Verbs*) To speak the truth, speak one's mind, open out, think aloud.

(*Phrases*) Tell the truth and shame the devil; to deal faithfully with; to show oneself in one's true colours.

544 FALSENESS (*Substantives*), falsehood, untruthfulness, untruth (546), falsity, mendacity, falsification, perversion of truth, perjury, fabrication, romance, forgery, prevarication, equivocation, shuffling, evasion, fencing, duplicity, double-dealing, unfairness, dishonesty, fraud, misrepresentation, *suggestio falsi*, *suppressio veri*, Punic faith, giving the go-by, disguise, disguisement, irony, understatement.

Insincerity, dissimulation, dissembling, deceit (545), shiftiness, hypocrisy, cant, humbug, gammon,

(*Adjectives*) Truthful, true, veracious, uncompromising, veridical, veridicous, sincere, candid, frank, open, outspoken, unreserved, free-spoken, open-hearted, honest, simple, simple-hearted, ingenuous, blunt, plain-spoken, true-blue, straightforward, straight, fair, fair-minded, single-minded, artless, guileless, natural, unaffected, simple-minded, undisguised, unfeigned, unflattering, warts and all.

(*Adverbs*) Truly, etc. (494), aboveboard, broadly.

(*Phrases*) In plain English; without mincing the matter; honour bright; honest Injun; bona fide; *sans phrase.*

jesuitry, pharisaism, mental reservation, lip-service, simulation, acting, sham, malingering, pretending, pretence, crocodile tears, false colouring, art, artfulness (702).

Deceiver (548).

(*Verbs*) To be false, etc., to play false, speak falsely, lie, fib, tell a lie or untruth, etc. (546), to mistake, misreport, misrepresent, misquote, belie, falsify, prevaricate, equivocate, quibble, palter, shuffle, fence, hedge, understate, mince the truth.

To forswear, swear false, perjure oneself, bear false witness.

To garble, gloss over, disguise, pervert, distort, twist, colour, varnish, cook, doctor, embroider, fiddle, wangle, gerrymander, put a false colouring or construction upon (523).

To invent, make up, fabricate, concoct, trump up, forge, fake, romance.

To dissemble, dissimulate, feign, pretend, assume, act or play a part, simulate, pass off for, counterfeit, sham, malinger, make believe, cant, put on.

(*Phrases*) To play the hypocrite; to give the go-by; to play fast and loose; to play a double game; to blow hot and cold; to lie like a conjurer; sham Abraham; to look as if butter would not melt in one's mouth; to sail under false colours; to ring false.

(*Adjectives*) False, dishonest, faithless, deceitful, mendacious, unveracious, truthless, trothless, unfair, uncandid, disingenuous, shady, shifty, underhand, underhanded, hollow, insincere, canting, hypocritical, jesuitical, sanctimonious, pharisaical, tartuffian, double, double-tongued, double-faced, smooth-spoken, smooth-tongued, plausible, mealy-mouthed, snide.

Artful, insidious, sly, designing, diplomatic, Machiavellian.

Untrue, unfounded, fictitious, invented, made up, *ben trovato*, forged, falsified, counterfeit, spurious, factitious, self-styled, bastard, sham, bogus, phoney, mock, pseudo, disguised, simulated, artificial, colourable, catchpenny, meretricious, tinsel, Brummagem, postiche, pinchbeck, illusory, elusory, supposititious, surreptitious, ironical, apocryphal.

(*Phrase*) All is not gold that glitters.

(*Adverbs*) Falsely, etc., slyly, stealthily, underhand.

545 DECEPTION (*Substantives*), falseness (544), fraud, deceit, imposition, artifice, juggle, juggling, sleight of hand, legerdemain, conjuration, hocus-pocus, jockeyship, trickery, coggery, fraudulence, imposture, *supercherie*, chicane, chicanery, covin, cozenage, circumvention, ingannation, prestidigitation, subreption, collusion, complicity, guile, gullery, hanky-panky, jiggery-pokery, rannygazoo.

Quackery, charlatanism, charlatanry, empiricism, humbug, hokum, eye-wash, hypocrisy, gammon, flapdoodle, bunkum, *blague*, bluff, mummery, borrowed plumes.

Stratagem, trick, cheat, wile, artifice, cross, deception, take-in, camouflage, make-believe, ruse, manœuvre, finesse, hoax, canard, hum, kid, chouse, bubble, fetch, catch, spoof, swindle, plant, sell, hocus, dodge, bite, forgery, counterfeit, sham, fake, fakement, rig, delusion, stalking-horse.

Snare, trap, pitfall, decoy, gin, spring, noose, hook, bait, net, meshes, mouse-trap, trap-door, false bottom, ambush, ambuscade (530), masked battery, mine, mystery-ship, Q-boat.

(*Phrases*) A wolf in sheep's clothing; a whited (or painted) sepulchre; a pious fraud; a man of straw.

(*Verbs*) To deceive, mislead, cheat, impose upon, practise upon, circumvent, play upon, put upon, bluff, dupe, mystify, blind, hoodwink, best, outreach, trick, hoax, kid, gammon, spoof, hocus, bamboozle, hornswoggle, juggle, trepan, nick, entrap, beguile, lure, inveigle, decoy, lime, ensnare, entangle, lay a snare for, trip up, stuff the go-by.

To defraud, fiddle, take in, jockey, do, do brown, cozen, diddle, have, have on, chouse, welsh, bilk, bite, pluck, swindle, victimize, outwit, over-reach, nobble, palm upon, work off upon, foist upon, fob off, balk, trump up.

(*Phrases*) To throw dust in the eyes; to play a trick upon; to pull one's leg; to try it on; to cog the dice; to mark the cards; to live by one's wits; to play a part; to throw a tub to the whale.

(*Adjectives*) Deceiving, cheating, etc.; hypocritical, Pecksniffian; deceived, duped, done, had, etc., led astray.

Deceptive, deceitful, deceptious, illusive, illusory, delusory, prestigious, elusive, bogus, counterfeit, insidious, *ad captandum, ben trovato.*

(*Phrase*) *Fronti nulla fides; timeo Danaos et dona ferentes.*

546 UNTRUTH (*Substantives*), falsehood, lie, falsity, fiction, fabrication, fib, whopper, bouncer, cracker, crammer, tarradiddle, story, fable, novel, romance, flam, bull, gammon, flim-flam, *guet-apens*, white lie, pious, fraud, canard, nursery tale, fairy-tale, tall story.

Falsification, perjury, forgery, false swearing, misstatement, misrepresentation, inexactitude.

Pretence, pretext, subterfuge, irony, evasion, blind, disguise, plea, claptrap, shuffle, make-believe, shift, mask, cloak, visor, veil, masquerade, gloss, cobweb.

(*Phrases*) A pack of lies; a tissue of falsehoods; a cock-and-bull story; a trumped-up story; all my eye and Betty Martin; a mare's-nest.

547 DUPE (*Substantives*), gull (486), gudgeon, gobemouche, cully, victim, sucker, flat, greenhorn, puppet, cat's-paw, April fool, simple Simon, Joe Soap, pushover, soft mark.

(*Phrases*) To be the goat; to hold the baby; to carry the can; *qui vult decipi, decipiatur.*

548 DECEIVER (*Substantives*), liar, hypocrite, tale-teller, shuffler, shammer, dissembler, serpent, cockatrice; Janus, Tartuffe, Pecksniff, Joseph Surface, Cagliostro.

Pretender, impostor, knave, cheat, rogue, trickster, swindler, spiv, adventurer, humbug, sharper, jockey, welsher, leg, blackleg, rook, shark, confidence man, con man, confidence trickster, decoy, decoy-duck, stool-pigeon, gipsy.

Quack, charlatan, mountebank, empiric, quacksalver, *saltimbanco*, medicaster, *soi-disant*.

Actor, player, mummer, tumbler, posture-master, jack-pudding; illusionist, conjurer, (994).

(*Phrases*) A wolf in sheep's clothing; a snake in the grass; one who lives by his wits.

549 EXAGGERATION (*Substantives*), hyperbole, overstatement, stretch, strain, colouring, bounce, flourish, vagary, bombast (884), yarn, figure of speech, flight of fancy, *façon de parler*, extravagance, rhodomontade, heroics, sensationalism, highfalutin; tale of Baron Munchausen, traveller's tale.

(*Phrases*) A storm in a teacup; much ado about nothing.

(*Verbs*) To exaggerate, amplify, magnify, heighten, overcharge, overstate, overcolour, overlay, overdo, strain, stretch, bounce, flourish, embroider; to hyperbolize, aggravate, to make the most of.

(*Phrases*) To make a song about; spin a long yarn; draw the long bow; deal in the marvellous; out-herod Herod; lay it on thick; pile it on; make a mountain of a molehill.

(*Adjectives*) Exaggerated, etc., hyperbolical, turgid, tumid, fabulous, extravagant, magniloquent, bombastic, *outré*, highly coloured, high-flying, high-flown, high-falutin, sensational, blood-and-thunder, lurid.

(*Phrases*) All his geese are swans; much cry and little wool.

SECTION III—MEANS OF COMMUNICATING IDEAS

1°. *Natural Means*

550 INDICATION (*Substantives*), symbolization, symbolism, typification, notation, connotation, prefigurement, representation (554), exposition, notice (527), trace (551), name (564).

A sign, symbol, index, placard, exponent, indicator, pointer, mark, token, symptom, type, emblem, figure, cipher, code, device, epigraph, motto, posy. Science of signs, sematology, semeiology, semeiotics.

Lineament, feature, line, stroke, dash, trait, characteristic, idiosyncracy, score, stripe, streak, scratch, tick, dot, point, notch, nick, asterisk, red letter, rubric, italics, print, stamp, impress, imprint, sublineation, underlining, display, jotting.

For identification: Badge, criterion, check, countercheck, countersign, stub, counterfoil, duplicate, tally, label, book-plate, *ex-libris*, ticket, billet, card, visiting-card, *carte de visite*, identity-card, passport, bill, bill-head, facia, sign-board, witness, voucher, coupon, trade mark, hall-mark, signature, hand-writing, sign manual, monogram, seal, sigil, signet, chop, autograph, auto-graphy, superscription, endorsement, *visé*, title, heading, caption, docket, watchword, password, shibboleth, *mot du guet*, catchword; fingerprint.

Insignia: Banner, banneret, flag, colours, bunting, streamer, standard, eagle, ensign, pennon, pennant, pendant, burgee, jack, ancient, labarum, oriflamme; gonfalon, banderole, Union Jack, Royal Standard, Stars and Stripes, Tricolour, etc.; crest, arms, coat of arms, armorial bearings, shield, scutcheon, escutcheon, uniform, livery, cockade, epaulet, chevron, cordon, totem.

Indication of locality: Beacon, cairn, post, staff, flagstaff, hand, pointer, vane, guide-post, finger-post, signpost, landmark, sea-mark, lighthouse, light-ship, pole-star, lodestar, cynosure, guide, address, direction, rocket, blue-light, watch-fire, blaze.

Indication of an event: Signal, nod, wink, glance, leer, shrug, beck, cue, gesture, gesticulation, deaf-and-dumb alphabet, by-play, dumb-show, panto-mime, touch, nudge, freemasonry, telegraph, heliograph, semaphore.

Indication of time: Time-signal, clock (114), alarm-clock, hooter, blower, buzzer, siren; tattoo, reveille, last post, taps.

Indication of danger: Alarm, alarum, alarm-bell, alert, fog-signal, detonator, red light, tocsin, fire-hooter, maroon, S O S, beat of drum, fiery cross, sound of trumpet, war-cry, war-whoop, slogan.

Indication of safety: all-clear, green light.

(*Verbs*) To indicate, point out, be the sign, etc., of, denote, betoken, connote, connotate, represent, stand for, typify, symbolize, shadow forth, argue, bear the impress of, witness, attest, testify.

To put an indication, mark, etc.; to note, mark, stamp, impress, earmark, brand, label, ticket, docket, endorse, sign, countersign; put, append, or affix a seal or signature; dot, jot down, book, score, dash, trace, chalk, underline, italicize, print, imprint, engrave, stereotype, rubricate, star, obelize, initial.

To make a sign, signal, etc., signalize; give or hang out a signal; give notice, gesticulate, beckon, beck, nod, wink, nudge, tip the wink; give the cue, tip, or office; wave, unfurl, hoist, or hang out a banner, flag, etc., show one's colours, give or sound an alarm, beat the drum, sound the trumpets, raise a cry, etc.

(*Adjectives*) Indicating, etc., indicatory, indicative, sematic, semeiological, denotative, representative, typical, typic, symbolic, symbolical, diacritical, connotative, pathognomic, symptomatic, exponential, emblematic, pantomimic, attesting; armorial, totemistic.

Indicated, etc., typified, impressed, etc.

Capable of being denoted, denotable, indelible.

(*Phrases*) *Ecce signum*; in token of.

---

551 RECORD (*Substantives*), trace, mark, tradition, vestige, footstep, footmark, footprint, footfall, wake, track, trail, slot, spoor, pug, scent.

Monument, relic, remains, trophy, hatchment, achievement, obelisk, monolith, pillar, stele, column, slab, tablet, medal, testimonial, memorial.

Note, minute, register, registry, index, inventory, catalogue, list (86), memorandum, jotting, document, account, score, tally, invoice, docket, voucher, protocol, inscription.

Paper, parchment, scroll, instrument, deed, indenture, debenture, roll, archive, schedule, file, dossier, cartulary, table, *procès verbal*, affidavit, certificate, attestation, entry, diploma, protest, round-robin, roster, rota, muster-roll, muster-book, note-book, commonplace-book, *adversaria*, portfolio.

552 Suppression of sign.

OBLITERATION (*Substantives*), erasure, rasure, cancel, cancellation, circumduction, deletion.

(*Verbs*) To efface, obliterate, erase, raze, expunge, cancel, delete, blot out, take out, rub out, scratch out, strike out, elide, wipe out, wash out, black out, write off, render illegible.

To be effaced, etc., to leave no trace.

(*Phrases*) To draw the pen through; to apply the sponge.

(*Adjectives*) Obliterated, effaced, etc., printless, leaving no trace

Unrecorded, unattested, unregistered, intestate.

(*Interjections*) *Dele*; out with it!

Chronicle, annals, gazette, Hansard, history (594), newspaper, magazine, gazetteer, blue-book, almanac, calendar, ephemeris, diary, log, journal, day-book, ledger.

Registration, tabulation, enrolment, booking.

(*Verbs*) To record, note, register, chronicle, calendar, make an entry of, enter, book, take a note of, post, enrol, jot down, take down, mark, sign, etc. (550), tabulate, catalogue, file, index, commemorate (883).

(*Adjectives*) Registered, etc.

(*Adverbs*) Under one's hand and seal, on record.

553 RECORDER (*Substantives*), notary, clerk, registrar, registrary, register, prothonotary, secretary, stenographer, amanuensis, scribe, remembrancer, journalist, historian, historiographer, annalist, chronicler, biographer, book-keeper.

Recordership, secretaryship, secretariat, clerkship.

554 REPRESENTATION (*Substantives*), delineation, representment, reproduction, depictment, personification.

Art, the fine arts, the graphic arts, design, designing, illustration, imitation (19), copy (21), portraiture, iconography, photography.

A picture, drawing, tracing, photograph.

555 MISREPRESENTATION (*Substantives*), distortion (243), caricature, burlesque (856), a bad likeness, daub, scratch, sign-painting, anamorphosis; misprint, *erratum*.

(*Verbs*) To misrepresent, distort, falsify, caricature, wrest the sense (or meaning).

An image, likeness, icon, portrait, effigy, facsimile, autotype, imagery, figure, puppet, dummy, lay figure, figurehead, doll, manikin, *mannequin*, mammet, marionette, *fantoccini* (599), statue (557), waxwork.

Hieroglyphic, hieroglyph, inscription, diagram, monogram, draught (or draft), outline, scheme, *schema*, schedule.

Map, plan, chart, ground-plan, projection, elevation, ichnography, atlas; cartography, chorography.

(*Verbs*) To represent, present, depict, portray, photograph, delineate, design, figure, adumbrate, shadow forth, copy, draft, mould, diagrammatize, schematize, map.

To imitate, impersonate, personate, personify, act, take off, hit off, figure as; to paint (556); carve (557); engrave (558).

(*Adjectives*) Representing, etc.; artistic, imitative, representative, illustrative, figurative, hieroglyphic, hieroglyphical, diagrammatic, schematic.

556 PAINTING (*Substantives*), depicting, drawing; perspective, composition, treatment.

Drawing in pencil, crayon, pastel, chalk, water-colour, etc.

Painting in oils, in distemper, in gouache, in fresco; encaustic painting, enamel painting, scene-painting; wash (428), body-colour, impasto.

A picture, drawing, painting, sketch, illustration, scratch, *graffito*, outline, tableau, cartoon, fresco, illumination; pencil, pen-and-ink, etc., drawing; oil, etc., painting; photograph; silver print; P.O.P.; bromide, gaslight, bromoil, platinotype, carbon print; autochrome, Kodachrome; daguerreotype, calotype; mosaic, tapestry, etc., picture-gallery.

Portrait, portraiture, likeness, full-length, etc., miniature, kitcat, shade, profile, silhouette, still, snapshot.

Landscape, seascape, nocturne, view, still-life, *genre*, panorama, diorama.

Pre-Raphaelitism, impressionism, etc. (559).

(*Verbs*) To paint, depict, portray, limn, draw, sketch, pencil, scratch, scrawl, block in, rough in, dash off, chalk out, shadow forth, adumbrate, outline, illustrate, illuminate; to take a portrait, take a likeness, to photograph, snap, pan.

(*Phrases*) Fecit, *pinxit, delineavit.*

(*Adjectives*) Painted, etc.; pictorial, graphic, picturesque, Giottesque, Raphaelesque, Turneresque, etc.; like, similar (17).

557 SCULPTURE (*Substantives*), insculpture, carving, modelling.

A statue, statuary, statuette, figure, figurine, model, bust, image, high relief, low relief, alto-rilievo, mezzo-rilievo, basso-rilievo, bas-relief, cast, marble, bronze, intaglio, anaglyph; medallion, cameo.

(*Verbs*) To sculpture, sculp, carve, cut, chisel, model, mould, cast.

(*Adjectives*) Sculptured, etc., sculptural, sculpturesque, anaglyphic, ceroplastic, ceramic.

558 ENGRAVING (*Substantives*), etching, wood-engraving, process-engraving, xylography, chalcography, cerography, glyptography; poker-work.

A print, engraving, impression, plate, cut, wood-cut, steel-cut, linocut, vignette.

An etching, dry-point, stipple, roulette; copper-plate, mezzotint, aquatint, lithograph, chromolithograph, chromo, photo-lithograph, photogravure, anastatic-printing, collotype, electrotype, stereotype.

Matrix, flong.

(*Verbs*) To engrave, etch, lithograph, print, etc.

559 ARTIST (*Substantives*), painter, limner, draughtsman, black-and-white artist, cartoonist, caricaturist, drawer, sketcher, pavement artist, screever, designer, engraver, copyist, photographer.

Academician; historical, landscape, portrait, miniature, scene, sign, etc., painter; an Apelles.

Primitive, Pre-Raphaelite, old master, quattrocentist, cinquecentist, impressionist, post-impressionist, futurist, vorticist, cubist, surrealist, Dadaist, pointillist.

A sculptor, carver, modeller, goldsmith, silversmith, *figuriste*; a Phidias, Praxiteles, Royal Academician, R.A.

Implements of art: pen, pencil, brush, charcoal, chalk, pastel, crayon; paint (428); stump, graver, style, burin; canvas, easel, palette, maul-stick, palette-knife; studio, *atelier*.

2°. *Conventional Means*

I. LANGUAGE GENERALLY

560 LANGUAGE (*Substantives*), tongue, speech, lingo, vernacular, mothertongue, native tongue, standard English, King's (or Queen's) English, the genius of a language.

Dialect, local dialect, class dialect, provincialism, vulgarism, colloquialism, Americanism, Scotticism, Cockney speech, brogue, patois, patter, slang, cant, argot, Anglic, Basic English, broken English, pidgin English, lingua franca.

Universal languages: Esperanto, Volapük, Ido, Interglossa.

Philology, etymology (562), linguistics, glossology, dialectology, phonetics.

Literature, letters, polite literature, belles-lettres, the muses, humanities, the republic of letters, dead languages, classics, *literae humaniores*.

Scholarship (490), linguist, scholar (492), writer (593), glossographer.

(*Verbs*) To express by words, to couch in terms, to clothe in language.

(*Adjectives*) Literary, belletristic, linguistic, dialectal, vernacular, colloquial, slang, current, polyglot, pantomimic.

(*Adverbs*) In plain terms, in common parlance, in household words.

561 LETTER (*Substantives*), alphabet, A B C, abecedary, spelling-book, horn-book, criss-cross-row; character (591), writing (590), hieroglyph, hieroglyphic; consonant, vowel, diphthong, triphthong; mute, liquid, labial, palatal, dental, guttural; spelling, orthography, phonetic spelling, misspelling; spelling-bee.

Syllable, monosyllable, dissyllable, trisyllable, polysyllable; anagram.

(*Verbs*) To spell, spell out.

(*Adjectives*) Literal, alphabetical, abecedarian, orthographic; syllabic, disyllabic, etc.

562 WORD (*Substantives*), term, vocable, terminology, part of speech (567), root, etymon.

Word similarly pronounced, homonym, homophone, paronym.

A dictionary, vocabulary, lexicon, index, polyglot, glossary, thesaurus, concordance, onomasticon, gradus; lexicography, lexicographer.

Derivation, etymology, glossology.

(*Adjectives*) Verbal, literal, titular, nominal, etymological, terminological.

Similarly derived, conjugate, paronymous.

(*Adverbs*) Nominally, etc., *verbatim,* word for word, in so many words, literally, *sic, totidem verbis, ipsissimis verbis, literatim.*

564 NOMENCLATURE (*Substantives*), nomination, naming, nuncupation.

A name, appellation, designation, appellative, denomination, term, expression, noun, byword, moniker, epithet, style, title, prenomen, forename, Christian name, baptismal name, given name, cognomen, agnomen, patronymic, surname, family name.

Synonym, namesake; euphemism, antonomasia, onomatopoeia.

Quotation, citation, chapter and verse.

(*Verbs*) To name, call, term, denominate, designate, style, clepe, entitle, dub, christen, baptize, characterize, specify, label (550).

To be called, etc., to take the name of, pass under the name of; to quote, cite.

563 NEOLOGY (*Substantives*), neologism, slang, cant, byword, hard word, jaw-breaker, dog Latin, monkish Latin, loan word, vogue word, nonce word, Gallicism.

A pun, play upon words, paronomasia, *jeu de mots, calembour,* palindrome, conundrum, acrostic, anagram (533).

Dialect (560).

Neologian, neologist.

(*Verbs*) To neologize, archaize, pun.

(*Phrase*) To coin or mint words.

(*Adjectives*) Neological, neologistic, paronomastic.

———

565 MISNOMER (*Substantives*), missaying, malaprop, malapropism, antiphrasis, nickname, sobriquet, byname, assumed name or title, alias, *nom de guerre, nom de plume,* penname, pseudonym, pet name, euphemism.

So-and-so, what's-his-name, thingummy, thingumbob, thingumajig, dingus, *je ne sais quoi.*

A Mrs. Malaprop.

(*Phrase*) *Lucus a non lucendo.*

(*Verbs*) To misname, missay, miscall, misterm, nickname.

To assume a name.

(*Adjectives*) Misnamed, etc., malapropian, pseudonymous, *soi-disant,* self-called, self-styled, so-called.

Nameless, anonymous, without a name, having no name, innominate, unnamed.

———

(*Phrases*) To call a spade a spade; to rejoice in the name of.

(*Adjectives*) Named, called, etc., hight, yclept, known as; nuncupatory, nuncupative, cognominal, titular, nominal.

Literal, verbal, discriminative.

566 PHRASE (*Substantives*), expression, phraseology, paraphrase, periphrasis, circumlocution (573), set phrase, round terms; mode or turn of expression; idiom, wording, *façon de parler*, mannerism, plain terms, plain English.

Sentence, paragraph, motto.

Figure, trope, metaphor (521), wisecrack, proverb (496).

(*Verbs*) To express, phrase, put; couch, clothe in words, give words to; to word.

(*Adjectives*) Expressed, etc., couched in, phraseological, idiomatic, paraphrastic, periphrastic, circumlocutory (573), proverbial.

(*Phrase*) As the saying is; in good set terms; *sans phrase*.

567 GRAMMAR (*Substantives*), accidence, syntax, parsing, analysis, praxis, punctuation, conjugation, declension, inflexion, case, voice, person, number; philology (560), parts of speech.

(*Phrase*) *Jus et norma loquendi.*

(*Verbs*) To parse, analyse, conjugate, decline, inflect, punctuate.

(*Adjectives*) Grammatical, syntactic, inflexional.

568 SOLECISM (*Substantives*), bad or false grammar, slip of the pen or tongue, bull, howler, floater, clanger, *lapsus linguae*, barbarism, vulgarism; dog Latin.

(*Verbs*) To use bad or faulty grammar, to solecize, commit a solecism.

(*Phrases*) To murder the king's English; to break Priscian's head.

(*Adjectives*) Ungrammatical, barbarous, slipshod, incorrect, faulty, inaccurate.

569 STYLE (*Substantives*), diction, phraseology, wording, turn of expression, idiom, manner, strain, composition, authorship; stylist.

(*Adjectives*) Stylistic, idiomatic, mannered.

(*Phrases*) Command of language; a ready pen; *le style, c'est l'homme même*.

Various Qualities of Style

570 PERSPICUITY (*Substantives*), lucidity, lucidness, clearness, clarity, perspicacity, plain speaking, intelligibility (518).

(*Adjectives*), Perspicuous, clear (525), lucid, intelligible, plain, transparent, explicit.

571 OBSCURITY (*Substances*), ambiguity (520), unintelligibility (519), involution, involvedness, vagueness.

(*Adjectives*) Obscure, confused, crabbed, ambiguous, vague, unintelligible, etc., involved, wiredrawn, tortuous.

572 CONCISENESS (*Substantives*), brevity, terseness, compression (195), condensation, concision, closeness, laconism, portmanteau word, telegraphese, pithiness, succinctness, quaintness, stiffness, ellipsis, ellipse, syncope.

Abridgment, epitome (596).

(*Verbs*) To be concise, etc., to condense, compress, abridge, abbreviate, cut short, curtail, abstract.

(*Phrase*) To cut the cackle and come to the horses.

573 DIFFUSENESS (*Substantives*), prolixity, verbosity, macrology, pleonasm, tautology, copiousness, exuberance, laxity, looseness, verbiage, flow, flow of words, fluency, *copia verborum*, loquacity (584), redundancy, redundance, digression, amplification, *longueur*, padding, circumlocution, ambages, periphrasis, officialese, commercialese, gobbledygook, episode, expletive.

(*Verbs*) To be diffuse, etc., to expatiate, enlarge, launch out, dilate, expand, pad out, spin out, run on,

(*Adjectives*) Concise, brief, crisp, curt, short, terse, laconic, sententious, gnomic, snappy, pithy, nervous, pregnant, succinct, *guindé*, stiff, compact, summary, compendious (596), close, cramped, elliptical, telegraphic, epigrammatic, lapidary.

(*Adverbs*) Concisely, briefly, etc., in a word, to the point, in short.

(*Phrases*) The long and short of it; *multum in parvo*; it comes to this; for shortness' sake; to make a long story short; to put it in a nutshell.

amplify, swell out, inflate, dwell on, harp on, descant, digress, ramble, maunder, rant.

(*Phrases*) To beat about the bush; to spin a long yarn; to make a long story of.

(*Adjectives*) Diffuse, wordy, verbose, prolix, copious, exuberant, flowing, fluent, bombastic, lengthy, long-winded, talkative (584), prosy, spun out, long-spun, loose, lax, slovenly, washy, slipslop, sloppy, frothy, flatulent, windy, digressive, discursive, excursive, tripping, rambling, ambagious, pleonastic, redundant, periphrastic, episodic, circumlocutory, roundabout.

Minute, detailed, particular, circumstantial.

(*Adverbs*) In detail, at great length, *in extenso*, about it and about, *currente calamo, usque ad nauseam*.

574 VIGOUR (*Substantives*), energy, power, force, spirit, point, vim, snap, punch, ginger, *élan*, pep, go, raciness, liveliness, fire, glow, verve, piquancy, pungency, spice, boldness, gravity, warmth, sententiousness, elevation, loftiness, sublimity, eloquence, individuality, distinction, emphasis, virility.

(*Phrase*) 'Thoughts that glow and words that burn.'

(*Adjectives*) Vigorous, energetic, powerful, strong, forcible, nervous, spirited, vivid, virile, expressive, lively, glowing, sparkling, racy, bold, slashing, incisive, trenchant, snappy, mordant, poignant, piquant, pungent, spicy, meaty, pithy, juicy, pointed, antithetical, sententious, emphatic, athletic, distinguished, original, individual, lofty, elevated, sublime, Miltonic, eloquent.

575 FEEBLENESS (*Substantives*), baldness, tameness, meagreness, coldness, frigidity, poverty, puerility, childishness, dullness, dryness, jejuneness, monotony.

(*Adjectives*) Feeble, bald, dry, flat, insipid, tame, meagre, invertebrate, weak, mealy-mouthed, wishy-washy, wersh, banal, uninteresting, jejune, vapid, cold, frigid, poor, dull (843), languid, anaemic, prosy, prosaic, pedestrian, platitudinous, conventional, mechanical, decadent, trashy, namby-pamby (866), puerile, childish, emasculate.

576 PLAINNESS (*Substantives*), simplicity, homeliness, chasteness, chastity, neatness, monotony, severity.

(*Adjectives*) Simple, unornamented, unvarnished, straightforward, artless, unaffected, downright, plain, unadorned, unvaried, monotonous, severe, chaste, blunt, homespun.

577 ORNAMENT (*Substantives*), floridness, floridity, flamboyance, richness, opulence, turgidity, tumidity, pomposity, inflation, altiloquence, spreadeagleism, pretension, fustian, affectation, euphuism, gongorism, mannerism, metaphor, preciosity, inversion, figurativeness, sesquipedalianism, *sesquipedalia verba*, rant, bombast, frothiness; flowers of speech, high-sounding words, well-rounded periods, purple patches.

A phrase-monger, euphuist.

(*Verbs*) To ornament, overcharge, overlay with ornament, lard or garnish with metaphors, lay the colours on thick, round a period, mouth.

(*Adjectives*) Ornamented, etc., ornate, florid, flamboyant, rich, opulent, golden-mouthed, figurative, metaphorical, pedantic, affected, pretentious, falsetto, euphuistic, Della Cruscan, pompous, fustian, high-sounding, mouthy, inflated, high-falutin (or high-faluting), bombastic, stilted, mannered, high-flowing, frothy, flowery, luscious, turgid, tumid, swelling, declamatory, rhapsodic, rhetorical, orotund, sententious, grandiose, grandiloquent, magniloquent, altiloquent, sesquipedalian, Johnsonian, ponderous.

(*Adverb*) *Ore rotundo.*

578 ELEGANCE (*Substantives*), grace, ease, naturalness, purity, concinnity, readiness, euphony; a purist.

(*Phrases*) A ready pen; flowing periods; *curiosa felicitas.*

(*Adjectives*) Elegant, graceful, Attic, Ciceronian, classical, natural, easy, felicitous, unaffected, unlaboured, chaste, pure, correct, flowing, mellifluous, euphonious, rhythmical, puristic, well-expressed, neatly put.

(*Phrases*) To round a period; 'to point a moral and adorn a tale.'

579 INELEGANCE (*Substantives*), stiffness, uncouthness, barbarism, archaism, rudeness, crudeness, bluntness, brusquerie, ruggedness, abruptness, artificiality, cacophony.

(*Phrases*) Words that dislocate the jaw, that break the teeth.

(*Verbs*) To be inelegant, etc.

(*Phrase*) To smell of the lamp.

(*Adjectives*) Inelegant, ungraceful, stiff, forced, laboured, clumsy, contorted, tortuous, harsh, cramped, rude, rugged, dislocated, crude, crabbed, uncouth, barbarous, archaic, archaistic, affected (577), artificial, abrupt, blunt, brusque, incondite.

2. SPOKEN LANGUAGE

580 VOICE (*Substantives*), vocality, vocalization, utterance, cry, strain, articulate sound, prolation, articulation, enunciation, delivery, vocalism, pronunciation, orthoepy, euphony.

Cadence, accent, accentuation, emphasis, stress, tone, intonation, exclamation, ejaculation, vociferation, ventriloquism, polyphonism.

A ventriloquist, polyphonist.

Phonetics, phonology; voice-production.

(*Verbs*) To utter, breathe, cry, exclaim, shout, ejaculate, vociferate; raise, lift, or strain the voice or lungs; to vocalize, prolate, articulate, enunciate, pronounce, accentuate, aspirate, deliver, mouth, rap out, speak out, speak up.

(*Phrase*) To whisper in the ear.

(*Adjectives*) Vocal, oral, phonetic, articulate.

Silvery, mellow, soft (413).

581 APHONY (*Substantives*), obmutescence, absence or want of voice, dumbness, muteness, mutism, speechlessness, aphasia, hoarseness, raucity; silence (585).

A dummy, a mute, deaf-mute.

(*Verbs*) To render mute, to muzzle, muffle, suppress, smother, gag (585); to whisper (405).

(*Phrases*) To stick in the throat; to close one's lips; to shut up.

(*Adjectives*) Aphonous, dumb, speechless, mute, tongueless, muzzled, tongue-tied, inarticulate, inaudible, unspoken, unsaid, mum, mumchance, lips close or sealed, wordless; raucous, hoarse, husky, sepulchral.

(*Phrases*) Mute as a fish; hoarse as a raven; with bated breath; *sotto voce*; with the finger on the lips; mum's the word.

582 SPEECH (*Substantives*), locution, talk, parlance, verbal intercourse, oral communication, word of mouth, palaver, prattle, effusion, narrative (594), tale, story, yarn, oration, recitation, delivery, say, harangue, formal speech, speechifying, sermon, homily, discourse (998), lecture, curtain lecture, pi-jaw, address, tirade, pep-talk, screed; preamble, peroration; soliloquy (589).

Oratory, elocution, rhetoric, declamation, eloquence, gift of the gab, *copia verborum*, grandiloquence, magniloquence.

A speaker, spokesman, prolocutor, mouthpiece, lecturer, orator, stumporator, speechifier; a Cicero, a Demosthenes.

(*Verbs*) To speak, break silence, say, tell, utter, pronounce (580), open one's lips, give tongue, hold forth, make or deliver a speech, speechify, harangue, talk, discourse, declaim, stump, flourish, spout, rant, recite, rattle off, intone, breathe, let fall, whisper in the ear, expatiate, run on; to lecture, preach, address, sermonize, preachify; to soliloquize (589); quoth he.

(*Phrases*) To have a tongue in one's head; to have on the tip of one's tongue; to have on one's lips; to pass one's lips; to find one's tongue.

(*Adjectives*) Speaking, etc., oral, spoken, unwritten, elocutionary, oratorical, rhetorical, declamatory, outspoken.

(*Adverbs*) Viva voce; *ore rotundo*; by word of mouth.

583 Imperfect speech.

STAMMERING (*Substantives*), inarticulateness, stuttering, impediment in one's speech, titubancy, faltering, hesitation, drawl, jabber, gibber, sputter, splutter, mumbling, mincing, muttering, mouthing, twang, a broken or cracked voice, broken accents or sentences, tardiloquence, falsetto, a whisper (405), mispronunciation.

(*Verbs*) to stammer, stutter, hesitate, falter, hem, haw, hum and ha, mumble, lisp, jabber, gibber, mutter, sputter, splutter, drawl, mouth, mince, lisp, croak, speak through the nose, snuffle, clip one's words, mispronounce, missay.

(*Phrases*) To clip the King's (or Queen's) English; *parler à tort et à travers*; not to be able to put two words together.

(*Adjectives*) Stammering, etc., inarticulate, guttural, nasal, tremulous.

———

584 LOQUACITY (*Substantives*), loquaciousness, talkativeness, garrulity, flow of words, prate, gas, jaw, gab, gabble, jabber, chatter, prattle, cackle, clack, clash, blether (or blather), patter, rattle, twaddle, bibble-babble, gibble-gabble, talkeetalkee, gossip.

Fluency, flippancy, volubility, verbosity, *cacoethes loquendi*, anecdotage.

A chatterer, chatterbox, blatherskite, babbler, wind-bag, gas-bag, rattle, ranter, tub-thumper, sermonizer, proser, driveller, gossip.

Magpie, jay, parrot, poll; Babel.

(*Phrases*) A twice (or thrice) told tale; a long yarn; the gift of the gab.

(*Verbs*) To be loquacious, etc., to prate, palaver, chatter, prattle, jabber,

585 TACITURNITY (*Substantives*), closeness, reserve, reticence (528), muteness, silence, curtness; aposiopesis; a clam, oyster.

(*Phrases*) A Quaker meeting; a man of few words.

(*Verbs*) To be silent, etc. (403), to hold one's tongue, keep silence, hold one's peace, say nothing, hold one's jaw, close one's mouth or lips, fall silent, dry up, shut up, stow it.

To render silent, silence, put to silence, seal one's lips, smother, suppress, stop one's mouth, gag, muffle, muzzle (581).

(*Adjectives*) Taciturn, silent, close, reserved, mute, sparing of words, buttoned up, curt, short-spoken, close-tongued, tight-lipped, reticent,

jaw, rattle, twaddle, blether, babble, gabble, gas, out-talk, descant, dilate, dwell on, reel off, expatiate, prose, launch out, yarn, gossip, wag one's tongue, run on.

(*Phrases*) To din in the ears; to drum into the ear; to spin a long yarn; to talk at random; to bum one's chat; to talk oneself out of breath; to talk nineteen to the dozen.

secretive, uncommunicative, inconversable.

(*Phrases*) Not a word escaping one; not having a word to say.

(*Interjections*) Hush! silence! mum! *chut!* hist! whist! wheesht!

(*Adjectives*) Loquacious, talkative, garrulous, gassy, gabby, openmouthed, chatty, chattering, etc.

Fluent, voluble, glib, flippant, long-tongued, long-winded, verbose, the tongue running fast.

(*Adverb*) Trippingly on the tongue.

586 ALLOCUTION (*Substantives*), address, apostrophe, interpellation, appeal, invocation, alloquialism, salutation, accost, greeting (894).

Feigned dialogue, imaginary conversation; inquiry (461).

(*Phrase*) A word in the ear.

(*Verbs*) To speak to, address, accost, buttonhole, apostrophize, appeal to, invoke, hail, make up to, take aside, call to, halloo (or hallo), salute.

587 RESPONSE (*Substantives*), answer, reply (462).

(*Verbs*) To answer, respond, reply, etc.

(*Phrase*) To take up one's cue.

(*Adjectives*) Answering, responding, etc., responsive, respondent.

(*Phrases*) To talk with one in private; to break the ice.

(*Adjectives*) Accosting, etc., alloquial, invocatory, apostrophic.

(*Interjections*) Hallo! hello! hullo! I say! hoy! oi! hey! what ho! psst!

588 INTERLOCUTION (*Substantives*), collocution, colloquy, conversation, converse, confabulation, confab, talk, discourse, verbal intercourse, dialogue, duologue, logomachy, communication, intercommunication, commerce, debate.

Chat, chit-chat, crack, small talk, table-talk, tattle, gossip, tittle-tattle, babblement, clack, prittle-prattle, idle talk, town-talk, bazaar talk, *on dit*, causerie, *chronique scandaleuse*.

589 SOLILOQUY (*Substantives*), monologue, apostrophe, aside.

Soliloquist, monologist, monologuist.

(*Verbs*) To soliloquize, monologize; to say or talk to oneself, to say aside, to think aloud, to apostrophize.

(*Adjectives*) Soliloquizing, etc.

Conference, parley, interview, audience, tête-à-tête, reception, conversazione, palaver, pow-wow; council (686).

A talker, interlocutor, interviewer, gossip, tattler, chatterer, babbler (584), conversationalist, *causeur*; *dramatis personae*.

(*Phrases*) 'The feast of reason and the flow of soul'; a heart-to-heart talk.

(*Verbs*) To talk together, converse, collogue, commune, debate, discourse with, engage in conversation, interview; hold or carry on a conversation; chat, gossip, have a crack, put in a word, chip in, tattle, babble, prate, clack, prattle.

To confer with, hold conference, etc., to parley, palaver, commerce, hold intercourse with, be closeted with, commune with, have speech with, compare notes, intercommunicate.

(*Adjectives*) Conversing, etc., interlocutory, verbal, colloquial, discursive, chatty, gossiping, etc., conversable, conversational.

3. WRITTEN LANGUAGE

590 WRITING (*Substantives*), chirography, pencraft, penmanship, longhand, calligraphy, quill-driving, pen-pushing, typewriting, typing.

Scribble, scrawl, scratch, cacography, scribbling, etc., jotting, interlineation, palimpsest.

Uncial writing, court hand, cursive writing, picture writing, hieroglyphics, hieroglyph, cuneiform characters, demotic text, heiratic text, ogham, runes.

Pothooks and hangers.

Transcription, inscription, superscription, minute.

Shorthand, stenography, phonography, brachygraphy, tachygraphy, steganography.

Secret writing, writing in cipher, cryptography, polygraphy, stelography; cryptogram.

Automatic writing, planchette.

Composition, authorship, *cacoethes scribendi.*

591 PRINTING (*Substantives*), print, letterpress, text, context, note, page, proof, pull, revise; presswork.

Typography, stereotypography, type, character, black-letter, fount (or font), capitals, majuscules, lower-case letters, minuscules, etc.; roman, italic, type; braille.

Folio, quarto, octavo, etc. (593).

Printer, pressman, compositor, corrector of the press, proof-reader, copyholder; printer's devil.

Printing-press, linotype, monotype, etc.

(*Verbs*) To print, put to press, publish, edit, get out a work, etc.

(*Adjectives*) Printed, etc.

———

Manuscript, MS., copy, transcript, rough copy, fair copy, carbon, black, duplicate, flimsy, handwriting, hand, fist, script, autograph, signature, sign-manual, monograph, holograph, endorsement, paraph.

A scribe, amanuensis, scrivener, secretary, clerk, penman, calligraphist, copyist, transcriber, stenographer, typist.

Writer, author, scribbler, quill-driver, ink-slinger, pamphleteer, essayist, critic, reviewer, novelist (593), journalist, editor, subeditor, reporter, pressman, penny-a-liner, hack, free-lance; Grub Street, Fleet Street.

Pen, quill, fountain-pen, stylograph, stylo, ball-point, Biro, pencil, stationery, paper, parchment, vellum, tablet, slate, marble, pillar, table, etc.

(*Phrase*) A dash or stroke of the pen.

(*Verbs*) To write, pen, typewrite, type, write out, copy, engross, write out fair, transcribe, scribble, scrawl, scratch, interline; to sign, undersign, countersign, endorse (497), set one's hand to.

To compose, indite, draw up, draft, minute, jot down, dash off, make or take a minute of, put or set down in writing; to inscribe, to dictate.

(*Phrases*) To take up the pen; to spill ink; to sling ink; set or put pen to paper; put on paper; commit to paper.

(*Adjectives*) Writing, etc., written, in writing, penned, etc., scriptorial; uncial, cursive, cuneiform, runic, heiroglyphical; editorial, journalistic, reportorial.

(*Phrases*) Under one's hand; in black and white; pen in hand; *currente calamo.*

592 Correspondence (*Substantives*), letter, epistle, note, line, airgraph, postcard, chit, billet, missive, circular, favour, *billet-doux*, dispatch, bulletin, memorial, rescript, rescription.

Letter-bag, mail, post; postage.

(*Verbs*) To correspond, write to, send a letter to.

(*Phrase*) To keep up a correspondence.

(*Adjectives*) Epistolary, postal.

---

593 Book (*Substantives*), writing, work, volume, tome, codex, opuscule, tract, manual, pamphlet, chap-book, booklet, brochure, enchiridion, circular, publication, part, issue, number, journal, album, periodical, magazine, digest, serial, ephemeris, annual, year-book.

Writer, author, publicist, scribbler, pamphleteer, poet, essayist, novelist, fabulist, editor (590).

Book-lover, bibliophile, bibliomaniac, paperback.

Bibliography, *incunabula*, Aldine, Elzevir, etc.; library.

Publisher, bookseller, bibliopole, bibliopolist, librarian.

Folio, quarto, octavo, duodecimo, sextodecimo, octodecimo.

Paper, bill, sheet, leaf, fly-leaf, page, title-page.

Chapter, section, paragraph, passage, clause.

(*Adjectives*) Auctorial, bookish, bibliographical, etc.

594 Description (*Substantives*), account, statement, report, return, delineation, specification, particulars, sketch, representation (554), narration, narrative, yarn, relation, recital, rehearsal, annals, chronicle, saga, *adversaria*, journal (551), itinerary, log-book.

Historiography; historicity, historic muse, Clio.

Story, history, memoir, tale, tradition, legend, folk-tale, folk-lore, anecdote, ana, analects (596), fable, fiction, novel, novelette, thriller, whodunit, romance, short story, *conte*, *nouvelle*, apologue, parable; word-picture; local colour.

Biography, necrology, obituary, life, personal narrative, adventures, autobiography, confessions, reminiscences.

A historian, historiographer, narrator, *raconteur*, annalist, chronicler, biographer, fabulist, novelist, fictionist, story-teller.

(*Verbs*) To describe, state (535), set forth, sketch, delineate, represent (554), portray, depict, paint, shadow forth, adumbrate.

To relate, recite, recount, sum up, run over, recapitulate, narrate, chronicle, rehearse, tell, give or render an account of, report, draw up a statement, spin a yarn, unfold a tale, novelize, actualize.

To take up or handle a subject; to enter into particulars, detail, etc., to characterize, particularize, detail, retail, elaborate, write up; to descend to particulars; to Boswellize.

(*Phrases*) To plunge *in medias res*; to fight one's battles over again.

(*Adjectives*) Descriptive, narrative, graphic, realistic, naturalistic, novelistic, historic, traditional, traditionary, legendary, storied, romantic, anecdotic, Boswellian, described, etc.

595 Dissertation (*Substantives*), treatise, tract, tractate, thesis, theme, monograph, essay, discourse, article, leading article, leader, leaderette, editorial, feuilleton, criticism, critique, review, memoir, prolusion, disquisition, exposition, exercitation, compilation, sermon, lecture, teach-in, homily, pandect, *causerie*, pamphlet (593).

Commentator, lecturer, critic, leader-writer, pamphleteer.

(*Verbs*) To dissert, descant, treat of, discuss, write, compile, touch upon, ventilate, canvass; deal with, do justice to a subject.

(*Adjectives*) Discursive, disquisitional, expository, compiled.

596 COMPENDIUM (*Substantives*), compend, summary, abstract, précis, epitome, *aperçu*, analysis, digest, sum and substance, *compte rendu*, *procès verbal*, draft, *exposé*, brief, recapitulation, résumé, conspectus, abridgment, abbreviation, minute, note, synopsis, argument, plot, syllabus, contents, heads, prospectus.

Scrap-book, album, note-book, commonplace-book, compilation, extracts, cuttings, clippings, text-book, analects, *analecta*, excerpts, flowers, anthology, *collectanea*, memorabilia.

(*Verbs*) To abridge, abstract, excerpt, abbreviate, recapitulate, run over, make or prepare an abstract, etc. (201), epitomize, sum up, summarize, boil down, anthologize.

(*Adjectives*) Compendious, etc., synoptic, abridged, etc., analectic.

(*Phrase*) In a nutshell; in substance; in short.

597 POETRY (*Substantives*), poetics, poesy, the Muse, the Nine, Calliope, Parnassus, Helicon, the Pierian spring.

Verse, metre, measure, foot, numbers, strain, rhyme (or rime), head-rhyme, alliteration, rhythm, heroic verse, Alexandrine, octosyllables, *terza rima*, blank verse, free verse, *vers libre*, sprung rhythm, assonance, versification, macaronics, doggerel, jingle, prosody, orthometry, scansion.

598 PROSE (*Substantives*), prose-writer, proser, prosaist.

(*Verb*) To prose.

(*Adjectives*) Prosaic, prosaical, prosing, prosy, rhymeless, unrhymed, unpoetical, commonplace, humdrum.

———

Poem, epic, epopee, epic poem, ballad, ode, epode, idyll, lyric, eclogue, pastoral, bucolic, macaronic, dithyramb, anacreontic, sonnet, lay, roundelay, rondeau, rondel, ballade, villanelle, triolet, sestina, rhyme royal, madrigal, canzonet, libretto, posy, anthology; distich, stanza, stave, strophe, antistrophe, couplet, triplet, quatrain, cento, monody, elegy, *vers de société*.

Iambic (or iamb), trochee, spondee, dactyl, anapaest, amphibrach, amphimacer, tribrach, paeon, etc.

A poet, laureate, bard, scald, poetess, rhymer, rhymist, versifier, rhymester, sonneteer, poetaster, minor poet, minnesinger, meistersinger, troubadour, *trouvère*.

(*Phrase*) *Genus irritabile vatum.*

(*Verbs*) To rhyme, versify, sing, make verses, scan, poetize.

(*Adjectives*) Poetical, poetic, Castalian, Parnassian, Heliconian, lyric, lyrical, metrical, epic, heroic; catalectic, dithyrambic, doggerel, macaronic, leonine; Pindaric, Homeric, Virgilian, Shakespearian, Miltonic, Tennysonian; etc.

599 THE DRAMA (*Substantives*), stage, theatre, the histrionic art, dramatic art, histrionics, acting; stage effect, *mise en scène*, stage production, setting, scenery; buskin, sock, cothurnus; Melpomene, Thalia, Thespis; play-writing, dramaturgy.

Play, stage-play, piece, tragedy, comedy, tragi-comedy, morality, mystery, melodrama, farce, knock-about farce, comedietta, curtain-raiser, interlude, after-piece, vaudeville, extravaganza, *divertissement*, burletta, burlesque, variety show, revue; opera, grand opera, music-drama, comic opera, *opéra bouffe*, operetta, ballad opera, *singspiel*, musical comedy; ballet, pantomime, harlequinade, charade, wordless play, dumb-show, by-play; monodrama, monologue, duologue; masque, pageant, show; scenario, libretto, book of words, part, role; matinée, benefit; act, scene, prologue, epilogue.

Theatre, playhouse, music-hall, variety theatre; stage, the boards, the footlights, green-room, foyer, proscenium, flies, wings, stalls, box, pit, circle, dress-circle, balcony, amphitheatre, gallery.

An actor, player, stage-player, performer, artiste, comedian, comedienne, tragedian, tragedienne, Thespian, Roscius, clown, harlequin, pantaloon, *buffo*, buffoon, pierrot, pierrette, impersonator, entertainer, etc., strolling player; ballet dancer, *ballerina*, figurant, mime, star; prima donna, *primo tenore*, etc., leading lady, heavy lead, juvenile lead, *ingénue*, soubrette; supernumerary, super, walking, gentleman or lady, chorus girl; *dramatis personae*, cast, company, stock company, touring company, repertory company; a star turn.

Mummer, guiser, masquer; dancer, nautch-girl, bayadère, geisha.

Stage manager, impresario, producer, prompter, stage hands, call-boy, etc.

Dramatic writer, pantomimist, playwright, play-writer, dramatist, dramaturge, librettist.

(*Phrase*) The profession.

(*Verbs*) To act, enact, play, perform, personate (554), play or interpret a part, rehearse, spout, rant, gag, star, walk on.

To produce, present, stage, stage-manager.

(*Phrases*) To strut and fret one's hour on the stage; to tread the boards.

(*Adjectives*) Dramatic, theatre, theatrical, scenic, histrionic, comic, tragic, buskined, farcical, knock-about, slapstick, tragi-comic, melodramatic, transpontine, stagy, operatic.

599A CINEMA (*Substantives*), picture theatre, picturedrome, film, motion picture, pictures, movies, flicks, pix, silver screen; silent film, sound film, talkie, flattie; three-dimensional film, 3-D, wide-screen film, deepie; documentary, trailer.

Close-up, flash-back, fade-out.

Scenario, star, vamp; cinema-goer, cinemaddict, film fan.

(*Verbs*) To feature, screen; dub.

599B RADIO (*Substantives*), wireless, receiving set, transistor, walkie-talkie; broadcast, radio play; teleprompter.

Announcer, listener.

Television, TV., video, telly; telecast, telefilm, newscast, script.

Looker-in, televiewer, viewer.

(*Verbs*) To broadcast, televise, telecast.

To listen in, look in, view, teleview.

(*Phrase*) On the air.

(*Adjective*) Telegenic.

CLASS V

WORDS RELATING TO THE VOLUNTARY POWERS

DIVISION I—INDIVIDUAL VOLITION

SECTION I—VOLITION IN GENERAL

1°. *Acts of Volition*

600 WILL (*Substantives*), volition, voluntariness, velleity, conation, free-will, spontaneity, spontaneousness, freedom (748).

Pleasure, wish, mind, animus, breast, mood, bosom, *petto*, heart, discretion, accord.

Libertarianism.

Determination (604), predetermination (611), intention (620), choice (609).

(*Verbs*) To will, list, think fit, see fit, think proper, determine, etc. (604), settle, choose (609), to take upon oneself, to have one's will, to do as one likes, wishes, or chooses; to use or exercise one's own discretion, to volunteer, lend oneself to.

(*Phrases*) To have a will of one's own; *hoc volo, sic jubeo, stet pro ratione voluntas*; to take the will for the deed; to know one's own mind; to know what one is about; to see one's way; to have one's will; to take upon oneself; to take the law into one's own hands.

(*Adjectives*) Voluntary, volitional, willing, content, minded, spontaneous, free, left to oneself, unconstrained, unfettered, autocratic, bossy, unbidden, unasked, unurged, uncompelled, of one's own accord, gratuitous, of one's own head, prepense, advised, express, designed, intended, calculated, premeditated, preconcerted, predetermined, deliberate.

(*Adverbs*) At will, at pleasure, *à volonté, à discrétion, ad libitum, ad*

601 NECESSITY (*Substantives*), instinct, blind impulse, necessitation, ἀνάγκη, fate, fatality, destiny, doom, kismet, weird (152), foredoom, destination, election, predestination, preordination, fore-ordination, compulsion (744), subjection (749), inevitability, inevitableness.

Determinism, necessitarianism, fatalism, automatism.

A determinist, necessarian, necessitarian; robot, automaton.

The Fates, Parcae, the Three Sisters, fortune's wheel, the book of fate, the stars, astral influence, spell (152).

(*Phrases*) Hobson's choice; what must be; a blind bargain; a *pis aller*.

(*Verbs*) To lie under a necessity, to be fated, doomed, destined, etc. (152), to need be, have no alternative.

To necessitate, destine, doom, foredoom, predestine, preordain.

To compel, force, constrain, etc. (744), cast a spell, etc. (992).

(*Phrases*) To make a virtue of necessity; to be pushed to the wall; to dree one's weird.

(*Adjectives*) Necessitated, fated, destined, predestined, foreordained, doomed, elect, spellbound.

Compelled, forced, etc., unavoidable, inevitable, irresistible, irrevocable.

Compulsory, involuntary, unintentional, undesigned, unintended, instinctive, automatic, blind, mechanical, impulsive, unconscious, reflex, unwitting, unaware.

arbitrium, spontaneously, freely, of one's own accord, voluntarily, advisedly, designedly, intentionally, expressly, knowingly, determinately, deliberately, pointedly, in earnest, in good earnest, studiously, purposely, *proprio motu, suo motu, ex mero motu*; *quo animo*.

(*Phrases*) With one's eyes open; in cold blood.

---

602 WILLINGNESS (*Substantives*), voluntariness, disposition, inclination, leaning, *penchant*, humour, mood, vein, bent, bias, propensity, proclivity, aptitude, predisposition, predilection (865), proneness, docility, pliability (324), alacrity, earnestness, readiness, assent (448).

(*Phrases*) A labour of love; *labor ipse voluptas*.

(*Verbs*) To be willing, etc., to incline to, lean to, not mind (865), to propend; to volunteer.

(*Phrases*) To find in one's heart; to set one's heart upon; to make no bones of; have a mind to; have a great mind to; 'Barkis is willin'.'

(*Adjectives*) Willing, fain, disposed, inclined, minded, bent upon, set upon, forward, predisposed, content, favourable, hearty, ready, wholehearted, cordial, genial, keen, prepense, docile, persuadable, persuasible, facile, tractable, easy-going, easily led.

Free, spontaneous, voluntary, gratuitous, unforced, unasked, unsummoned, unbiased, unsolicited, unbesought, undriven.

(*Adverbs*) Willingly, freely, readily, lief, heartily, with a good grace, without reluctance, etc., as soon, of one's own accord (600), certainly, be it so (488).

(*Phrases*) With all one's heart, *con amore*; with heart and soul; with a right good will; with a good grace; *de bon cœur*; by all means; by all manner of means; nothing loth; *ex animo*; to one's heart's content.

Deterministic, necessitarian, fatalistic.

(*Phrase*) Unable to help it.

(*Adverbs*) Necessarily, needs, of necessity, perforce, forcibly, compulsorily; on or by compulsion or force, willy-nilly, *nolens volens*; involuntarily, etc., impulsively (612), unwittingly (491).

(*Phrases*) It must be; it needs must be; it is written; one's fate is sealed; *che sarà sarà*; there is no help for it; there is no alternative; nothing for it but; necessity knows no law; needs must when the devil drives.

603 UNWILLINGNESS (*Substantives*), indisposition, indisposedness, backwardness, disinclination, averseness, aversion, reluctance, repugnance, demur, renitence, remissness, slackness, lukewarmness, indifference, nonchalance.

Hesitation, shrinking, recoil, suspense, dislike (867), scrupulousness, scrupulosity, delicacy, demur, scruple, qualm.

A recusant, pococurante.

(*Verbs*) To be unwilling, etc., to demur, stick at, hesitate (605), waver, hang in suspense, scruple, stickle, boggle, falter, to hang back, hang fire, fight shy of, jib, grudge.

To decline, reject, refuse (764), refrain, keep from, abstain, recoil, shrink, reluct.

(*Phrases*) To stick in the throat; to set one's face against; to draw the line at; I'd rather not.

(*Adjectives*) Unwilling, unconsenting, disinclined, indisposed, averse, reluctant, not content, laggard, backward, shy, remiss, slack, indifferent, lukewarm, frigid, scrupulous, repugnant, disliking (867).

Demurring, wavering, etc., refusing (764), grudging.

(*Adverbs*) Unwillingly, etc., perforce.

(*Phrases*) Against the grain; *invita Minerva*; *malgré lui*; *bon gré, mal gré*; *nolens volens*; in spite of one's teeth; with a bad grace; not for the world; willy-nilly.

604 Resolution (*Substantives*), determination, decision, resolve, resolvedness, fixedness, steadiness, constancy, indefatigability, unchangeableness, inflexibility, decision, finality, firmness, doggedness, tenacity of purpose, pertinacity, perseverance, constancy, solidity, stability.

Energy, manliness, vigour, spirit, spiritedness, pluck, bottom, backbone, stamina, gameness, guts, grit, sand, will, iron will; self-reliance; self-mastery; self-control.

A devotee, zealot, extremist, ultra, enthusiast, fanatic, fan; bulldog, British lion.

(*Verbs*) To be resolved, etc., to have resolution, etc., to resolve, decide, will, persevere, determine, conclude, make up one's mind; to stand, keep, or remain firm, etc., to come to a determination, to form a resolution, to take one's stand, to stand by, hold by, hold fast, stick to, abide by, adhere to, keep one's ground, persevere, keep one's course, hold on, hang on, not to fail.

To insist upon, to make a point of.

(*Phrases*) To determine once for all; to form a resolution; to steel oneself; to pass the Rubicon; take a decisive step; to burn one's boats; to nail one's colours to the mast; to screw one's courage to the sticking-place; to take the bull by the horns; to mean business; to set one's teeth; to keep a stiff upper lip; to keep one's chin up.

(*Adjectives*) Resolved, resolute, game, firm, steady, steadfast, staunch, constant; solid, manly, stout.

Decided, strong-willed, determined, uncompromising, purposive, self-possessed, fixed, unmoved, unshaken, unbending, unyielding, unflagging, unflinching, inflexible, unwavering, unfaltering, unshrinking, undiverted, undeterred, immovable, not to be moved, unhesitating, unswerving.

605 Irresolution (*Substantives*), indecision, indetermination, demur, hesitation, suspense, uncertainty (475), hesitancy, vacillation, unsteadiness, inconstancy, wavering, fluctuation, flickering, changeableness, mutability, fickleness, caprice (608), levity, *légèreté*, trimming, softness, weakness, instability.

A weathercock, trimmer, time-server, turncoat, shuttlecock, butterfly, harlequin, chameleon.

(*Verbs*) To be irresolute, etc., to hesitate, hang in suspense, demur, waver, vacillate, quaver, fluctuate, shuffle, boggle, flicker, falter, palter, debate, dilly-dally, shilly-shally, dally with, coquette with, swerve, etc.

(*Phrases*) To hang fire; to hum and ha; to blow hot and cold; not to know one's own mind; to leave '*ad referendum*'; letting 'I dare not' wait upon 'I would.'

(*Adjectives*) Irresolute, undecided, unresolved, undetermined, vacillating, wavering, hesitating, faltering, shuffling, etc., half-hearted, double-minded, indicisive.

Unsteady, unsteadfast, fickle, flighty, changing, changeable, versatile, variable, inconstant, mutable, protean, fluctuating, unstable, unsettled, unhinged, unfixed, weak-kneed, spineless.

Weak, feeble-minded, frail, soft, pliant, giddy, capricious, coquettish, volatile, fitful, frothy, freakish, lightsome, light-minded, invertebrate.

Revocable, reversible.

(*Phrases*) Infirm of purpose; without ballast; waiting to see which way the cat jumps, or the wind blows.

(*Adverbs*) Irresolutely, etc.; off and on.

Peremptory, inexorable, indomitable, persevering, pertinacious, persistent, irrevocable, irreversible, reverseless, decisive, final.

Strenuous, bent upon, set upon, intent upon, proof against, master of oneself, steeled, staid, serious, stiff, stiff-necked, obstinate (606).

(*Phrases*) Firm as a rock; game to the last; true to oneself; master of oneself; *in utrumque paratus.*
(*Adverbs*) Resolutely, etc., without fail.
(*Phrases*) Through thick and thin; through fire and water; at all hazards; sink or swim; *coûte que coûte*; *fortiter in re*; like grim death.

606 OBSTINACY (*Substantives*), obstinateness, wilfulness, self-will, pertinacity, pertinaciousness, pervicacity, pervicaciousness, tenacity, tenaciousness, inflexibility, immovability, doggedness, stubbornness, steadiness (604), restiveness, contumacy, cussedness, obduracy, obduration, unruliness.

Intolerance, dogmatism, bigotry, opinionatedness, opiniativeness, fanaticism, zealotry, infatuation, monomania, indocility, intractability, intractableness (481), pig-headedness.

An opinionist, *opiniâtre*, crank, diehard, blimp, stickler, enthusiast, monomaniac, zealot, dogmatist, fanatic, mule.

A fixed idea, rooted prejudice, blind side, obsession (481), King Charles's head.

(*Phrase*) A bee in one's bonnet.

(*Verbs*) To be obstinate, etc., to persist, stickle, opiniate.

(*Phrases*) To stick at nothing; to dig in one's heels; not yield an inch.

(*Adjectives*) Obstinate, opinionative, opinative, opinionated, opinioned, wedded to an opinion, self-opinioned, prejudiced (481), cranky, wilful, self-willed, positive, tenacious.

Stiff, stubborn, stark, rigid, stiff-necked, dogged, pertinacious, restive, pervicacious, dogmatic, arbitrary, bigoted, unpersuadable, mulish, unmoved, uninfluenced, hard-mouthed, unyielding, inflexible, immovable, pig-headed, wayward, intractable, hide-bound, headstrong, restive, refractory, unruly, infatuated, *entêté*, wrong-headed, cross-grained, obdurate, contumacious, fanatical, rabid, inexorable, impracticable.

(*Phrases*) Obstinate as a mule; impervious to reason.

(*Adverbs*) Obstinately, etc.

(*Phrases*) *Non possumus*; *vestigia nulla retrorsum.*

607 Change of mind, intention, purpose, etc.

TERGIVERSATION (*Substantives*), retractation, recantation, revocation, revokement, reversal, palinode, volteface, renunciation, disavowal (536), abjuration, abjurement, apostasy, relinquishment (624), repentance (950), vacillation, etc. (605).

A turncoat, rat, Janus, renegade, apostate, pervert, backslider, recidivist, trimmer, time-server, opportunist, Vicar of Bray, deserter, weathercock, etc. (605), Proteus.

(*Verbs*) To change one's mind, etc., to retract, recant, revoke, forswear, unsay, take back, abjure, renounce, apostatize, relinquish, trim, straddle, veer round, change sides, rat, go over; pass, change, or skip from one side to another; back out, back down, swerve, flinch, balance.

(*Phrases*) To eat one's words; turn over a new leaf; think better of it; play fast and loose; blow hot and cold; box the compass; swallow the leek; eat dirt.

(*Adjectives*) Changeful, changeable, mobile, unsteady (605), trimming, double-faced, ambidexter, fast and loose, time-serving, facing both ways. Fugacious, fleeting (111), revocatory.

608 CAPRICE (*Substantives*), fancy, fantasy, humour, whim, crotchet, fad, fike, craze, *capriccio*, quirk, freak, maggot, vagary, whimsy, whimwham, kink, prank, shenanigans, fit, flim-flam, escapade, ploy, dido, monkey-tricks, rag, monkey-shines, *boutade*, wild-goose chase, freakishness, skittishness, volatility, fancifulness, whimsicality, giddiness, inconsistency, contrariety; a madcap.

(*Verb*) To be capricious, etc.

(*Phrases*) To strain at a gnat and swallow a camel; to take it into one's head.

(*Adjectives*) Capricious, inconsistent, fanciful, fantastic, whimsical, full of whims, etc., erratic, crotchety, faddy, maggoty, fiky, perverse, humoursome, wayward, captious, contrary, contrarious, skittish, fitful.
(*Phrases*) The head being turned; the deuce being in him; by fits and starts.

609 Choice (*Substantives*), option, election, arbitrament, adoption, selection, excerption, co-optation, gleaning, eclecticism, lief, preference, predilection, preoption, discretion (600), fancy.
Decision, determination, adjudication, award, vote, suffrage, ballot, poll, plebiscite, referendum, verdict, voice, plumper.
Alternative, dilemma (704).
Excerpt, extract, cuttings, clippings; pick, *élite*, cream (650).
Chooser, elector, voter, constituent; electorate, constituency.
(*Verbs*) To choose, decide, determine, elect, list, think fit, use one's discretion, fancy, shape one's course, prefer, have rather, have as lief, take one's choice, adopt, select, fix upon, pitch upon, pick out, single out, vote for, plump for, co-opt, pick up, take up, catch at, jump at, cull, glean, pick, winnow.
(*Phrases*) To winnow the chaff from the wheat; to indulge one's fancy; to pick and choose; to take a decided step; to pass the Rubicon (604);

610 Absence of Choice (*Substantives*), Hobson's choice, necessity (601). Indifference, indecision (605).
(*Phrase*) First come, first served.
(*Adjectives*) Neutral; indifferent, undecided.
(*Phrase*) To sit on the fence.
Rejection (*Substantives*), refusal (764); declining, repudiation, exclusion.
(*Verbs*) To reject, refuse, etc., decline, give up, repudiate, exclude, lay aside, pigeon-hole, refrain, spare (678), abandon, turn down, blackball; to fail, plough, pluck, spin, cast.
(*Phrases*) To lay on the shelf; to return to store; to throw overboard; to draw the line at.
(*Adjectives*) Rejecting, etc., rejected, etc., not chosen, etc.
(*Phrases*) Not to be thought of; out of the question.
(*Adverbs*) Neither; neither the one nor the other, nothing to choose between them.

to hold out; offer for choice; commend me to; to swallow the bait; to gorge the hook; to yield to temptation.
(*Adjectives*) Optional, discretional, eclectic, choosing, etc., chosen, etc., decided, etc., choice, preferential; left to oneself.
(*Adverbs*) Discretionally, at pleasure, *à plaisir, a piacere*, at discretion, at will, *ad libitum*.
Decidedly, etc., rather; once for all, either the one or the other, for one's money, for choice.

611 Predetermination (*Substantives*), premeditation, predeliberation, foregone conclusion, *parti pris*.
(*Verbs*) To predetermine, premeditate, preconcert, resolve beforehand.
(*Adjectives*) Prepense, premeditated, predetermined, advised, predesigned, aforethought, calculated, studied, designed (620).

612 Impulse (*Substantives*), sudden thought, improvisation, inspiration, flash, spurt.
Improvisator, improvisatore, improvisatrice, creature of impulse.
(*Verbs*) To flash on the mind; to improvise, improvisate, make up, extemporize, vamp, ad-lib.
(*Adjectives*) Extemporaneous, extemporary, impulsive, unrehearsed,

(*Adverbs*) Advisedly, deliberately, etc., with the eyes open, in cold blood.

———

unpremeditated (674), improvised, improvisatorial, improvisatory, unprompted, instinctive, spontaneous, natural, unguarded, unreflecting, precipitate.

(*Adverbs*) Extempore, offhand, impromptu, à l'improviste, out of hand.

(*Phrases*) On the spur of the moment, or of the occasion.

---

613 HABIT (*Substantives*), habitude, wont, rule, routine, jog-trot, groove, rut.

Custom, consuetude, use, usage, practice, trick, run, run of things, way, form, prevalence, observance, fashion (852), etiquette, prescription, convention, *convenances*, red tape, red-tapery, red-tapism, routinism, conventionalism, vogue.

Seasoning, training, hardening, etc. (673), acclimatization, acclimation, acclimatation.

Second nature, *cacoethes*, taking root, diathesis.

A victim of habit, etc., an addict, junkie, *habitué*.

(*Verbs*) To be habitual, etc., to be in the habit of, be wont, be accustomed to, etc.

To follow, observe, conform to, obey, bend to, comply with, accommodate oneself to, adapt oneself to; fall into a habit, convention, custom, or usage; to addict oneself to, take to, get the hang of.

To become a habit, to take root, to gain or grow upon one, to run in the blood.

To habituate, inure, harden, season, form, train, accustom, familiarize, naturalize, acclimatize, conventionalize, condition.

To acquire a habit, to get into the way of, to learn, etc.

(*Phrases*) To follow the multitude; go with the current, stream, etc.; run on in a groove; do in Rome as the Romans do.

(*Adjectives*) Habitual, accustomed, prescriptive, habituated, etc.; in the habit, etc., of; used to, addicted to, attuned to, wedded to, at home in; usual, wonted, customary, hackneyed, commonplace, trite, ordinary, set, stock, established, accepted, stereotyped, received, acknowledged, recognized; groovy, fixed, rooted, permanent, inveterate, ingrained, running in the blood, hereditary, congenital, innate, inborn, besetting, natural, instinctive, etc. (5).

Fashionable, in fashion, in vogue, according to use, routine, conventional, etc.

(*Phrases*) Bred in the bone; in the blood.

(*Adverbs*) Habitually; as usual, as the world goes, *more suo, pro more, pro forma*, according to custom, *de rigueur*.

---

614 DESUETUDE (*Substantives*), disuse, want of habit or of practice, inusitation, newness to.

Non-observance (773), infraction, violation, infringement.

(*Phrase*) 'A custom more honoured in the breach than the observance.'

(*Verbs*) To be unaccustomed, etc., to be new to; to leave off, wean oneself of, break off, break through, infringe, violate, etc., a habit, usage, etc.; to disuse, to wear off.

(*Adjectives*) Unaccustomed, unused, unusual, unwonted, unpractised, unprofessional, unfashionable, non-observant, lax, disused, weaned.

Unseasoned, uninured, untrained, green.

Unhackneyed, unconventional, Bohemian (83).

———

2°. *Causes of Volition*

615 MOTIVE (*Substantives*), reason, ground, principle, mainspring, *primum mobile*, account, score, sake, consideration, calculation, *raison d'être*.

Inducement, recommendation, encouragement, attraction, allectation, temptation, enticement, bait, allurement, charm, witchery, bewitchment.

Persuasibility, softness, susceptibility, attractability, impressibility.

Influence, prompting, dictate, instance, impulse, impulsion, incitement, incitation, press, instigation, excitement, provocation, invitation, solicitation, advocacy, call, suasion, persuasion, hortation, exhortation, seduction, cajolery, tantalization, *agacerie*, seducement, fascination, blandishment, inspiration, honeyed words.

Incentive, stimulus, spur, fillip, urge, goad, rowel, provocative, whet, dram, cocktail, pick-me-up, appetizer.

Bribe, graft, sop, lure, decoy, charm, spell, magnetism, magnet, loadstone.

Prompter, tempter, seducer, seductor, siren, Circe, instigator, *agent provocateur*.

(*Phrases*) The pros and cons; the why and wherefore.

The golden apple; a red herring; a sop for Cerberus; the voice of the tempter; the song of the sirens.

(*Verbs*) To induce, move, lead, draw, draw over, carry, bring, to influence, to weigh with, bias, to operate, work upon, engage, incline, dispose, predispose, put up to, prompt, whisper, call, call upon, recommend, encourage, entice, invite, solicit, press, enjoin, entreat (765), court, plead, advocate, exhort, enforce, dictate, tantalize, bait the hook, tempt, allure, lure, seduce, decoy, draw on, captivate, fascinate, charm, bewitch, conciliate, wheedle, coax, speak fair, carny (or carney), cajole, pat on the back or shoulder, talk over, inveigle, persuade, prevail upon, get to do, bring over, procure, lead by the nose, sway, over-persuade, come over, get round, turn the head, enlist, retain, kidnap, bribe, suborn, tamper with.

To act upon, to impel, excite, suscitate, stimulate, key up, motivate, incite, animate, instigate, provoke, set on, urge, pique, spirit, inspirit,

616 ABSENCE OF MOTIVE, caprice (608).

(*Adjectives*) Aimless, motiveless, pointless, purposeless (621); uninduced, unmoved, unactuated, uninfluenced, unbiased, unimpelled, unswayed, impulsive, wanton, unprovoked, uninspired, untempted, unattracted.

(*Phrase*) Without rhyme or reason.

DISSUASION (*Substantives*), dehortation, discouragement, remonstrance, expostulation, deprecation (766).

Inhibition, check, restraint, curb (752), bridle, rein, stay, damper, chill; deterrent, disincentive.

Scruple, qualm, demur (867), reluctance, delicacy (868); counter-attraction.

(*Phrase*) A wet blanket.

(*Verbs*) To dissuade, dehort, discourage, disincline, indispose, dispirit, damp, choke off, dishearten, disenchant, disillusion, deter, keep back, put off, render averse, etc.

To withhold, restrain, hold, hold back, check, bridle, curb, rein in, keep in, inhibit, censor, repel (751).

To cool, blunt, calm, quiet, quench, slake, stagger, remonstrate, expostulate, warn, deprecate (766).

To scruple, refrain, abstain, etc. (603).

(*Phrases*) To throw cold water on; to turn a deaf ear to.

(*Adjectives*) Dissuading, etc., dissuasive, dehortatory, expostulatory, deprecatory.

Dissuaded, discouraged, etc.

Repugnant, averse, scrupulous, etc. (867), unpersuadable (606).

inspire, awaken, buck up, give a fillip, light up, kindle, enkindle, rekindle, quicken, goad, spur, prick, edge, egg on, hurry on, stir up, work
up, fan, fire, inflame, set on fire, fan the flame, blow the coals, stir the
embers, put on one's mettle, set on, force, rouse, arouse, lash into fury,
get a rise out of.

(*Phrases*) To grease the palm; to gild the pill; to work the oracle.

To follow the bent of; to follow the dictates of; to yield to temptation;
to act on principle.

(*Adjectives*) Impulsive, motive, persuasive, hortative, hortatory,
seductive, carnying, suasory, suasive, honey-tongued, attractive, tempt-
ing, alluring, piquant, exciting, inviting, tantalizing, etc.

Persuadable, persuasible, suasible, soft, yielding, facile, easily
persuaded, etc.

Induced, moved, disposed, led, persuaded, etc., spellbound, instinct
with or by.

(*Adverbs*) Because, for, since, on account of, out of, from; by
reason of, for the sake of, on the score of.

As, forasmuch as, therefore, hence, why, wherefore; for all the
world.

(*Phrase*) *Hinc illae lacrimae.*

617 Ostensible motive, or reason assigned.

PLEA (*Substantives*), allegation, pretext, pretence, excuse, alibi, cue, colour,
gloss, salvo, loophole, handle, shift, quirk, guise, stalking-horse, makeshift,
white lie, evasion, get-out, special pleading (477), claptrap, advocation, soft
sawder, blarney (933), moonshine; a lame excuse or apology.

(*Verbs*) To make a pretext, etc., of; to use as a plea, etc.; to plead, allege,
pretend, excuse, make a handle, etc., of, make capital of.

(*Adjectives*) Ostensible, colourable, pretended, alleged, etc.

(*Phrases*) *Ad captandum*; *qui s'excuse s'accuse*; playing to the gallery.

3°. *Objects of Volition*

618 GOOD (*Substantives*), benefit,
advantage, service, interest, weal,
boot, gain, profit, velvet, good turn,
blessing, boon; behoof, behalf.

Luck, piece of luck, windfall, strike,
treasure trove, godsend, bonus, bunce,
bonanza, prize; serendipity.

Goodness (648), utility (644),
remedy (662).

(*Phrases*) The main chance; *summum bonum*; *cui bono ?*

(*Adjectives*) Good, etc. (648), gainful (644).

(*Adverbs*) Aright, well, favourably,
satisfactorily, for the best.

In behalf of, in favour of.

619 EVIL (*Substantives*), harm, ill,
injury, wrong, scathe, curse, detriment,
hurt, damage, disservice, ill-turn, bale,
grievance, prejudice, loss, mischief,
devilry (or deviltry), gravamen.

Disadvantage, drawback, trouble,
vexation (828), annoyance, nuisance,
molestation, oppression, persecution,
plague, corruption (659.

Blow, dunt, knock (276), bruise,
scratch, wound, mutilation, outrage,
spoliation, mayhem, plunder, pillage,
rapine, destruction (791), dilapidation, havoc, ravage, devastation,
inroad, sweep, sack, foray (716),
desolation, *razzia*, dragonnade.

Misfortune, mishap, woe, disaster,
calamity, affliction, catastrophe,
downfall, ruin (735), prostration,
curse, wrack, blight, blast; Pandora's
box; a plague-spot.

Cause of evil, bane (663).

(*Phrases*) Bad show; there's the devil to pay.

(*Adjectives*) Bad, hurtful, etc. (649).

(*Adverbs*) Amiss, wrong, evil, ill.

SECTION II—PROSPECTIVE VOLITION

1°. *Conceptional Volition*

620 INTENTION (*Substantives*), intent, purpose, design, purport, mind, meaning, drift (516), animus, view, set purpose, point, bent, turn, proposal, study, scope, purview.

Final cause, object, aim, end, motive (615), *raison d'être*; destination, mark, point, butt, goal, target, prey, quarry, game, objective; the philosophers' stone.

Decision, determination, resolve, resolution (604), predetermination (611); set purpose.

A hobby, ambition, wish (865).

Study of final causes, teleology; study of final issues, eschatology.

(*Verbs*) To intend, purpose, plan (626), design, destine, mean, aim at, propose to oneself.

To be at, drive at, be after, point at, level at, take aim, aspire at or after, endeavour after.

To meditate, think of, dream of, premeditate (611), contemplate, compass.

To propose, project, devise, take into one's head.

(*Phrases*) To have in view; to have an eye to; to take upon oneself; to have to do; to see one's way; to find in one's heart.

(*Adjectives*) Intended, etc., intentional, deliberate, advised, studied, minded, express, prepense (611), aforethought; set upon, bent upon, intent upon, in view, *in petto*, in prospect; teleological, eschatological.

(*Phrases*) In the wind; *sur le tapis*; on the stocks; in contemplation.

(*Adverbs*) Intentionally, etc., expressly, knowingly, wittingly, designedly, purposely, on purpose, with a view to, with an eye to, for the

621 Absence of purpose in the succession of events.

CHANCE (*Substantives*), fortune, accident, hazard, hap, haphazard (156), lot, fate (601), chance-medley, hit, fluke, casualty, contingency, exigency, fate, adventure, random shot, off chance, toss-up, gamble.

A godsend, luck, a run of luck, a turn of the dice or cards, a break, windfall, etc. (618).

Drawing lots, sortilege, *sortes Virgilianae*.

Wager, bet, flutter, betting, gambling; pitch-and-toss, *roulette*, *rouge-et-noir*.

(*Phrases*) A blind bargain; a pig in a poke.

(*Verbs*) To chance, hap, turn up; to stand a chance.

To risk, venture, hazard, speculate, stake; incur or run the risk; bet, wager, punt, gamble, plunge, raffle.

(*Phrases*) To take one's chance; to chance it; to chance one's arm; try one's luck; shuffle the cards; put into a lottery; lay a wager; toss up; spin a coin; cast lots; draw lots; stand the hazard.

To buy a pig in a poke; *alea jacta est*; the die being cast; to go nap on; to put one's shirt on.

(*Adjectives*) Casual, fortuitous, accidental, inadvertent, fluky, contingent, random, hit-or-miss, happy-go-lucky, adventitious, incidental.

Unintentional, involuntary, aimless, driftless, undesigned, undirected; purposeless, causeless, without purpose, etc., unmeditated, unpurposed, indiscriminate, promiscuous.

On the cards, possible (470), at stake.

(*Adverbs*) Casually, etc., by chance,

purpose of, with the view of, in order to, to the end that, on account of, in pursuance of, pursuant to, with the intent, etc.

(*Phrases*) In good earnest; with one's eyes open; to all intents and purposes.

622 Purpose in action.

PURSUIT (*Substantives*), pursuance, undertaking, enterprise (676), emprise, adventure, game, hobby, endeavour.

Prosecution, search, angling, chase, venery, quest, hunt, shikar, race, battue, drive, course, direction, wild-goose chase, steeplechase, point-to-point.

Pursuer, huntsman, hunter, Nimrod, shikari, hound, greyhound, foxhound, whippet, bloodhound, sleuth-hound, beagle, harrier.

(*Verbs*) To pursue, undertake, engage in, take in hand, carry on, prosecute (461), endeavour.

To court, seek, angle, chase, give chase, course, dog, stalk, trail, hunt, drive, follow, run after, hound, bid for, aim at, take aim, make a leap at, rush upon, jump at, quest, shadow, tail, chivy.

(*Phrases*) Take or hold a course; tread a path; shape one's course; direct or bend one's steps or course; run a race; rush headlong; rush head-foremost; make a plunge; snatch at, etc.; start game; follow the scent; to run or ride full tilt at.

(*Adjectives*) Pursuing, etc., in hot pursuit; in full cry.

(*Adverbs*) In order to, in order that, for the purpose of, with a view to, etc. (620); on the scent of.

(*Interjections*) Yoicks! tally-ho!

by accident, accidentally, etc., at haphazard, at a venture; heads or tails.

(*Phrase*) As luck would have it.

623 Absence of pursuit.

AVOIDANCE (*Substantives*), forbearance, abstention, abstinence, sparing, refraining.

Flight, escape (671), evasion, elusion.

Motive for avoidance, counter-attraction.

Shirker, slacker, quitter, truant, fugitive, runaway.

(*Verbs*) To avoid, refrain, abstain; to spare, hold, shun, fly, slope, flee, eschew, run away from, shrink, hold back, draw back (287), recoil from, flinch, blench, shy, elude, evade, shirk, blink, parry, dodge, let alone.

(*Phrases*) To give the slip or go-by; to part company; to beat a retreat; get out of the way; to give one a wide berth; steer clear of; fight shy of; to take to one's heels.

(*Adjectives*) Avoiding, etc., elusive, evasive, flying, fugitive, runaway, shy, retiring; unattempted, unsought.

(*Adverbs*) Lest, with a view to prevent.

(*Phrases*) *Sauve qui peut*; the devil take the hindmost.

624 RELINQUISHMENT (*Substantives*), dereliction, abandonment (782), renunciation, desertion (607), discontinuance (142).

Dispensation, riddance.

(*Verbs*) To relinquish, give up (782); lay, set, or put aside; drop, yield, resign, abandon, renounce, discard, shelve, pigeon-hole, waive, desist from, desert, leave, leave off, back out of, quit, throw up, chuck up, give over, forgo, give up, forsake, throw over, forswear, swerve from (279), put away, discontinue (681).

(*Phrases*) To drop all idea of; to think better of it; to wash one's hands of; to turn over a new leaf; to throw up the sponge; to have other fish to fry; to draw in one's horns; to lay on the shelf; to move the previous question.

To give warning; to give notice; to ask for one's books.
(*Adjectives*) Relinquishing, etc., relinquished, etc., unpursued.
(*Interjections*) Hands off! keep off! give over! chuck it!

625 BUSINESS (*Substantives*), affair, concern, matter, task, work, job, job of
work, assignment, darg, chore, stint, stunt, errand, agenda, commission, office,
charge, part, duty, role; a press of business.

Province, department, beat, round, routine, mission, function, vocation,
calling, avocation, profession, occupation, pursuit, cloth, faculty, trade, industry, commerce, art, craft, mystery, walk, race, career, walk of life, *métier*.

Place, post, orb, sphere, field, line, capacity, employment, engagement,
exercise, occupation; situation, undertaking (676).

(*Verbs*) To carry on or run a business, ply one's trade, keep a shop, etc.;
to officiate, serve, act, traffic.

(*Phrases*) To have to do with; have on one's hands; betake oneself to;
occupy or concern oneself with; go in for; have on one's shoulders; make it
one's business; go to do; act a part; perform the office of or functions of; to
enter or take up a profession; spend time upon; busy oneself with, about, etc.

(*Adjectives*) Business-like, official, functional, professional, workaday, commercial, in hand.

(*Adverbs*) On hand, on foot, afoot, afloat, going.

(*Phrase*) In the swim.

626 PLAN (*Substantives*), scheme, device, design, project, proposal, proposition, suggestion.

Line of conduct, game, card course, tactics, strategy, policy, polity (692),
craft, practice, campaign, platform, plank, ticket, agenda, orders of the day,
gambit.

Intrigue, cabal, plot, conspiracy, complot, racket, machination, *coup d'état*.

Measure, step, precaution, proceeding, procedure, process, system, economy,
set-up, organization, expedient, resource, contrivance, invention, artifice, shift,
makeshift, gadget, stopgap, manœuvre, stratagem, fetch, trick, dodge, machination, intrigue, stroke, stroke of policy, masterstroke, great gun, trump card.

Alternative, loophole, counterplot, counter-project, side-wind, last resort,
dernier ressort, *pis aller*.

Sketch, outline, blue-print, programme, draft (or draught), scenario, *ébauche*,
rough draft, skeleton, forecast, prospectus, *carte du pays*, bill of fare, menu.

After-course, after-game, after-thought, *arrière-pensée*, under-plot.

A projector, designer, schemer, contriver, strategist, promoter, organizer,
entrepreneur, artist, schematist, intriguant.

(*Verbs*) To plan, scheme, devise, imagine, design, frame, contrive, project,
plot, conspire, cabal, intrigue (702), think out, invent, forecast, strike out,
work out, chalk out, rough out, sketch, lay out, lay down, cut out, cast,
recast, map out, countermine, hit upon, fall upon, arrange, mature, organize,
systematize, concert, concoct, digest, pack, prepare, hatch, elaborate, make
shift, make do, wangle.

(*Phrases*) To have many irons in the fire; to dig a mine; to lay a train;
to spring a project; to take or adopt a course; to make the best of a bad
job; to work the oracle.

(*Adjectives*) Planned, etc., strategic; planning, scheming, etc.

Well-laid, deep-laid, cunning, well-devised, etc., maturely considered, well-
weighed, prepared, organized, etc.

(*Adverbs*) In course of preparation, under consideration, on the anvil, on the
stocks, in the rough, *sur le tapis*; *faute de mieux*.

627 WAY (*Substantives*), method, manner, wise, form, mode, guise, fashion. Path, road, gait, route, channel, walk, access, course, pass, ford, ferry, passage, line of way, trajectory, orbit, track, ride, avenue, approach, beaten track, pathway, highway, roadway, causeway, footway, pavement, sidewalk, *trottoir*, footpath, bridle path, corduroy road, cinder-path, turnpike road, high road, arterial road, *autobahn*, clearway, boulevard, the King's (or Queen's) highway, thoroughfare, street, lane, alley, gangway, hatchway, cross-road, crossway, flyover, cut, short cut, royal road, cross-cut, *carrefour*, promenade, subway.

Railway, railroad, tramway, tube, underground, elevated; canal.

Bridge, viaduct, stepping-stone, stair, corridor, aisle, lobby, staircase, moving staircase, escalator, companion-way, flight of stairs, ladder, step-ladder, stile, scaffold, scaffolding, lift, hoist, elevator; speedwalk, travolator.

Indirect way: By-path, by-way, by-walk, by-road, back door, backstairs.

Inlet, gate, door, gateway (260), portal, porch, doorway, adit, conduit, tunnel.

(*Phrase*) *Modus operandi.*

(*Adverbs*) How, in what way, in what manner, by what mode.

By the way, *en passant*, by the by, via, *in transitu, chemin faisant.*

One way or another, somehow, anyhow, by hook or by crook.

(*Phrases*) All roads lead to Rome; *hae tibi erunt artes*; where there's a will there's a way.

---

628 MID-COURSE (*Substantives*), middle course, middle (68), mean (29), golden mean, *juste milieu, mezzo termine.*

Direct, straight, straightforward, course or path; great-circle sailing.

Neutrality, compromise.

(*Verbs*) To keep in a middle course, etc.; to compromise, go half-way.

(*Adjectives*) Undeviating, direct, straight, straightforward.

(*Phrases*) *In medio tutissimus ibis;* to sit on the fence.

629 CIRCUIT (*Substantives*), roundabout way, zigzag, circuition, detour, circumbendibus (311), wandering, deviation (279), divergence (291).

(*Verbs*) To perform a circuit, etc., to deviate, wander, go round about, meander, etc. (279).

(*Phrases*) To beat about the bush; to make two bites of a cherry; to lead one a pretty dance.

(*Adjectives*) Circuitous, indirect, roundabout, tortuous, zigzag, etc.

(*Adverbs*) By a roundabout way, by an indirect course, etc.

---

630 REQUIREMENT (*Substantives*), requisition, need, occasion, lack, wants, requisites, necessities, desideratum, exigency, pinch, *sine qua non*, the very thing, essential, must.

Needfulness, essentiality, necessity, indispensability, urgency, call for.

(*Phrases*) Just what the doctor ordered; a crying need; a long-felt want.

(*Verbs*) To require, need, want, have occasion for, stand in need of, lack, desire, be at a loss for, desiderate; not to be able to do without or dispense with; to want but little.

To render necessary, to necessitate, to create a necessity for, demand, call for.

(*Adjectives*) Requisite, required, etc., needful, necessary, imperative, exigent, essential, indispensable, irreplaceable, prerequisite, that cannot be spared or dispensed with, urgent.

2°. *Subservience to Ends*

I. ACTUAL SUBSERVIENCE

631 INSTRUMENTALITY (*Substantives*), medium, intermedium, vehicle, channel, intervention, mediation, dint, aid (707), agency (170).

Minister, handmaid; obstetrician, midwife, *accoucheur*.

Key, master-key, passport, safe-conduct, passe-partout, 'open sesame'; a go-between, middleman (758), a cat's-paw, jackal, pander, tool, ghost, mainstay, trump card.

(*Phrase*) Two strings to one's bow.

(*Verbs*) To subserve, minister, intervene, mediate, devil, pander to.

(*Adjectives*) Instrumental, intervening, intermediate, intermediary, subservient, auxiliary, ancillary.

(*Adverbs*) Through, by, with, by means of, by dint of, *à force de*, along with, thereby, through the medium, etc., of, wherewith, wherewithal.

632 MEANS (*Substantives*), resources, wherewithal, appliances, ways and means, convenience, 'expedients, step, measure (626), aid (707), intermedium, medium.

Machinery, mechanism, mechanics, engineering, mechanical powers, automation, scaffolding, ladder, mainstay.

(*Phrases*) Wheels within wheels; a shot in the locker.

(*Adjectives*) Instrumental, accessory, subsidiary, mechanical.

(*Adverbs*) How, by what means, by all means, by all manner of means, by the aid of, by dint of.

(*Phrases*) By hook or by crook; somehow or other; for love or money; by fair means or foul; *quocumque modo*.

633 INSTRUMENT (*Substantives*), tool, implement, appliance, contraption, apparatus, utensil, device, gadget, craft, machine, engine, motor, dynamo, generator, mill, lathe.

Equipment, gear, tackle, tackling, rigging, harness, trappings, fittings, accoutrements, paraphernalia, equipage, outfit, appointments, furniture, material, plant, appurtenances.

A wheel, jack, clockwork, wheel-work, spring, screw, turbine, wedge, flywheel, lever, bascule, pinion, crank, winch, crane, capstan, windlass, pulley, hammer, mallet, mattock, mall, bat, racket, sledge-hammer, mace, club, truncheon, pole, staff, bill, crow, crowbar, poleaxe, handspike, crutch, boom, bar, pitchfork, etc.

Organ, limb, arm, hand, finger, claw, paw, talons, tentacle, wing, oar, paddle, pincer, plier, forceps, thimble.

Handle, hilt, haft, shaft, shank, heft, blade, trigger, tiller, helm, treadle, pummel, peg (214, 215), key.

Edge-tool, hatchet, axe, pickaxe, etc. (253), axis (312).

634 SUBSTITUTE (*Substantives*), shift, makeshift, succedaneum (147), stopgap, expedient, *pis aller*, surrogate, understudy, pinch-hitter, stand-in, locum tenens, proxy, deputy (759).

635 MATERIALS (*Substantives*), material, matter, stuff, constituent, ingredient (56), pabulum, fuel, grist, provender, provisions, food (298).

Supplies, munition, ammunition, reinforcement, relay, contingents.

Baggage, luggage, bag and baggage, effects, goods, chattels, household

stuff, equipage, paraphernalia, impedimenta, stock-in-trade, cargo, lading (780).
Metal, stone, ore, brick, clay, wood, timber, composition, compo, plastic.

636 STORE (*Substantives*), stock, fund, supply, reserve, relay, budget, quiver, *corps de réserve*, reserve fund, mine, quarry, vein, lode, fountain, well, spring, milch cow.
Collection, accumulation, heap (72), hoard, cache, stockpile, magazine, pile, rick, nest-egg, savings, bank (802), treasury, reservoir, repository, repertory, repertoire, depot, depository, treasure, thesaurus, museum, storehouse, promptuary, reservatory, conservatory, menagerie, aviary, aquarium, receptacle, warehouse, godown, *entrepôt*, dock, larder, cellar, garner, granary, store-room, box-room, lumber-room, silo, cistern, well, tank, gasometer, mill-pond, armoury, arsenal, coffer (191).
(*Verbs*) To store, stock, stockpile, treasure up, lay in, lay by, lay up, file, garner, save, husband, hoard, deposit, amass, accumulate (72).
To reserve, keep back, hold back.
(*Phrase*) To husband one's resources.
(*Adjectives*) Stored, etc., in store, in reserve, spare, surplus, extra.

637 PROVISION (*Substantives*), supply, providing, supplying, sustentation (707), purveyance, purveying, reinforcement, husbanding, commissariat, victualling.
Forage, pasture, food, provender (298).
A purveyor, caterer, contractor, commissary, quartermaster, sutler, victualler, *restaurateur*, feeder, batman; bum-boat.
(*Verbs*) To provide, supply, furnish, purvey, suppeditate, replenish, fill up, feed, stock with, recruit, victual, cater, find, fend, keep, lay in, lay in store, store, stockpile, forage, husband (636), upholster.
(*Phrase*) To bring grist to the mill.

639 SUFFICIENCY (*Substantives*), adequacy, competence; enough, satiety.
Fullness, fill, plenitude, plenty, abundance, copiousness, amplitude, affluence, richness, fertility, luxuriance, uberty, foison.
Heaps, lots, bags, piles, lashings, oceans, oodles, mobs.
Impletion, repletion, saturation.
Riches (803), mine, store, fund, (636); a bumper, a brimmer, a belly-ful, a cart-load, truck-load, ship-load; a plumper; a charge.

638 WASTE (*Substantives*), consumption, expenditure, exhaustion, drain, leakage, wear and tear, dispersion (73), ebb, loss, misuse, prodigality (818), seepage, squandermania.
(*Verbs*) To waste, spend, expend, use, consume, spill, leak, run out, run to waste, disperse (73), ebb, dry up, impoverish, drain, empty, exhaust; to fritter away, squander.
(*Phrases*) to cast pearls before swine; to burn the candle at both ends; to employ a steam-hammer to crack nuts; to break a butterfly on a wheel; to pour water into a sieve.
(*Adjectives*) Wasted, spent, profuse, lavish, etc., at a low ebb.
(*Phrase*) Penny wise and pound foolish.

640 INSUFFICIENCY (*Substantives*), inadequacy, inadequateness, incompetence.
Deficiency, stint, paucity, defect, defectiveness, default, defalcation, deficit, shortcoming, falling short (304), too little, what will not do, scantiness, slenderness, a mouthful, etc. (32).
Scarcity, dearth, shortage, want, need, lack, exigency, inanition, indigence, poverty, penury (804), destitution, dole, pittance, short allowance, short commons, a banian day,

A flood, draught, shower, rain (347), stream, tide, spring tide, flush.

(*Phrases*) The horn of plenty; the horn of Amalthea; cornucopia; the fat of the land.

(*Verbs*) To be sufficient, etc., to suffice, serve, pass muster, to do, satisfy, satiate, sate, saturate, make up.

To abound, teem, stream, flow, rain, shower down, pour, swarm, bristle with.

To render sufficient, etc., to make up, to fill, charge, replenish, pour in; swim in, wallow in, roll in.

(*Adjectives*) Sufficient, enough, adequate, commensurate, what will just do.

Moderate, measured.

Full, ample, plenty, copious, plentiful, plenteous, plenary, wantless, abundant, abounding, flush, replete, laden, charged, fraught; well stocked or provided, liberal, lavish, unstinted, to spare, unsparing, unmeasured; *ad libitum*, wholesale.

Brimful, to the brim, chock-full, saturated, crammed, up to the ears, fat, rich, affluent, full up, luxuriant, lush.

Unexhausted, unwasted, exhaustless, inexhaustible.

(*Phrases*) Enough and to spare; cut and come again; full as an egg; ready to burst; plentiful as blackberries; flowing with milk and honey; enough in all conscience; enough to go round; *quantum sufficit*.

(*Adverbs*) Amply, etc., galore.

fast (956), a mouthful, starvation, malnutrition, famine, drought, depletion, emptiness, vacancy, flaccidity, ebb-tide, low water.

(*Phrase*) 'A beggarly account of empty boxes.'

(*Verbs*) To be insufficient, etc., not to suffice, to come short of, to fall short of, fail, run out of, stop short, to want, lack, need, require (630); caret.

To render insufficient, etc., to stint, grudge, hold back, withhold, starve, pinch, skimp, scrimp, famish.

(*Phrase*) To live from hand to mouth.

(*Adjectives*) Insufficient, inadequate, incompetent, too little, not enough, etc., scant, scanty, skimpy, scrimpy, deficient, defective, in default, scarce, empty, empty-handed, devoid, short of, out of, wanting, etc., hard up for.

Destitute, dry, drained, unprovided, unsupplied, unfurnished, unreplenished, unfed, unstored, untreasured, bare, meagre, poor, thin, spare, skimpy, stinted, starved, famished, pinched, fasting, starveling, jejune, without resources (735), shorthanded, undermanned, understaffed, etc.

(*Phrases*) In short supply; not to be had for love or money; at the end of one's tether; at one's last gasp.

---

641 REDUNDANCE (*Substantives*), superabundance, superfluity, superfluence, glut, exuberance, profuseness, profusion, plethora, engorgement, congestion, surfeit, gorge, load, turgidity, turgescence, dropsy.

Excess, nimiety, overdose, oversupply, overplus, surplus, surplusage, overflow, inundation, deluge, extravagance, prodigality (818), exorbitance, lavishness, immoderation.

An expletive (908), pleonasm.

(*Phrases*) *Satis superque*; a drug in the market; the lion's share.

(*Verbs*) To superabound, overabound, run over, overflow, flow over, roll in, wallow in.

To overstock, overdose, overlay, gorge, engorge, glut, sate, satiate, surfeit, cloy, load, overlord, surcharge, overrun, choke, drown, drench, inundate, flood, whelm, deluge.

(*Phrases*) To go begging; it never rains but it pours; to paint the lily; to carry coals to Newcastle.

(*Adjectives*) Redundant, superfluous, exuberant, superabundant, immoderate, extravagant, excessive, in excess, *de trop*, needless, unnecessary, uncalledfor, over and above (40), more than enough, buckshee, running to waste, overflowing, running over.

Turgid, gorged, plethoric, dropsical, replete, profuse, lavish, prodigal, supervacaneous, extra, spare, duplicate, supernumerary, supererogatory, expletive, surcharged, overcharged, sodden, overloaded, overladen, overburdened, overrun, overfed, overfull.

(*Phrase*) Enough and to spare.

(*Adverbs*) Over, over and above, too much, overmuch, over and enough, too far, without measure, without stint.

(*Phrase*) Over head and ears.

2. DEGREE OF SUBSERVIENCE

642 IMPORTANCE (*Substantives*), consequence, moment, weight, gravity, seriousness, consideration, concern, significance, import, influence (175), pressure, urgency, instancy, stress, emphasis, interest, preponderance, prominence (250), greatness (31).

The substance, essence, quintessence, core, kernel, nub, gist, pith, marrow, soul, point, gravamen.

The principal, prominent, or essential part.

A notability, somebody, personage (875), V.I.P., bigwig, toff, big pot, big gun, his nibs; great doings, *notabilia*, a red-letter day.

(*Phrases*) *A sine qua non*; a matter of life and death; no laughing matter.

(*Verbs*) To be important, or of importance, etc., to signify, import, matter, boot, weigh, count, to be prominent, etc., to take the lead.

To attach, or ascribe importance to; to value, care for, etc. (897); overestimate, etc. (482), exaggerate (549).

To mark, underline, italicize, score, accentuate, emphasize, stress, rub in.

(*Phrases*) To be somebody; to fill the bill; to make much of; to make a stir, a fuss, a piece of work, a song and dance; set store upon; to lay stress upon; to take *au grand sérieux*.

(*Adjectives*) Important, of importance, etc., grave, serious, material, weighty, influential, significant, emphatic, momentous, earnest, pressing, critical, preponderating, pregnant, urgent, paramount, essential, vital.

643 UNIMPORTANCE (*Substantives*), indifference, insignificance, triflingness, triviality, triteness; paltriness, emptiness, nothingness, inanity, lightness, levity, frivolity, vanity, frivolousness, puerility, child's play.

Poverty, meagreness, meanness, shabbiness, etc. (804).

A trifle, small matter, minutiae, bagatelle, cipher, moonshine, molehill, joke, jest, snap of the fingers, flea-bite, pinch of snuff, old song, *nugae*, fiddlestick, fiddlestick end, bubble, bulrush, nonentity, lay figure, nobody.

A straw, pin, fig, button, rush, feather, farthing, brass farthing, red cent, dime, dam, doit, peppercorn, pebble, small fry.

Trumpery, trash, codswallop, stuff, *fatras*, frippery, chaff, drug, froth, smoke, cobweb.

Toy, plaything, knick-knack, gimcrack, gewgaw, thingumbob, bauble, kickshaw, bric-à-brac, fal-lal, whimwham, whigmaleerie, curio, bibelot.

Refuse, lumber, junk, litter, orts, tares, weeds, sweepings, scourings, off-scourings; rubble, debris, dross, scoriae, dregs, scum, flue, dust (653).

(*Phrases*) 'Leather and prunella'; *peu de chose*; much ado about nothing; much cry and little wool; flotsam and jetsam; a man of straw; a stuffed shirt; a toom tabard.

(*Verbs*) To be unimportant, to be of little or no importance, etc.; not to signify, not to deserve, merit, or be

Great, considerable, etc. (31), capital, leading, principal, superior, chief, main, prime, primary, cardinal, prominent, salient, egregious, outstanding.

Signal, notable, memorable, remarkable, etc., grand, solemn, eventful, stirring, impressive; not to be despised, or overlooked, etc., unforgettable, worth while.

(*Phrases*) Being no joke; not to be sneezed at; no small beer.

worthy of notice, regard, consideration, etc.

(*Phrases*) To catch at straws; to make much ado about nothing; to cut no ice; *le jeu ne vaut pas la chandelle.*

(*Adjectives*) Unimportant, secondary, inferior, immaterial, inconsiderable, inappreciable, insignificant, unessential, non-essential, beneath notice, indifferent; of little or no account, importance, consequence, moment, interest, etc.; unimpressive, subordinate.

Trifling, trivial, trite, banal, mere, common, so-so, slight, slender, flimsy, trumpery, foolish, idle, puerile, childish, infantile, frothy, trashy, catchpenny, fiddling, frivolous, commonplace, contemptible, cheap.

Vain, empty, inane, poor, sorry, mean, meagre, shabby, scrannel, vile, miserable, scrubby, weedy, niggling, beggarly, piddling, peddling, pitiful, pitiable, despicable, paltry, ridiculous, farcical, finical, finicking, finicky, finikin, fiddle-faddle, wishy-washy, namby-pamby, gimcrack, twopenny, twopenny-halfpenny, two-by-four, one-horse, piffling, jerry, jerry built.

(*Phrases*) Not worth a straw; as light as air; not worth mentioning; not worth boasting about; no great shakes; nothing to write home about; small potatoes; neither here nor there.

(*Interjections*) No matter! pshaw! pooh! pooh-pooh! shucks! I should worry! fudge! fiddle-de-dee! nonsense! boloney! hooey! nuts! rats! stuff! *n'importe!*

(*Adverbs*) Meagrely, pitifully, vainly, etc.

---

644 UTILITY (*Substantives*), service, use, function, office, sphere, capacity, part, role, task, work.

Usefulness, worth, stead, avail, advantageousness, profitableness, serviceableness, merit, *cui bono*, applicability, adequacy, subservience, subserviency, efficacy, efficiency, help, money's worth.

(*Verbs*) To be useful, etc., of use, of service.

To avail, serve, subserve, help (707), conduce, answer, profit, advantage, accrue, bedstead.

To render useful, to use (677), to turn to account, to utilize, to make the most of.

(*Phrases*) To stand in good stead; to do yeoman service; to perform a function; to serve a purpose; to serve a turn.

645 INUTILITY (*Substantives*), uselessness, inefficacy, inefficiency, ineptness, ineptitude, inadequacy, inaptitude, unskilfulness, fecklessness, fruitlessness, inanity, worthlessness, unproductiveness, barrenness, sterility, vanity, futility, triviality, paltriness, unprofitableness, unfruitfulness, rustiness, obsoleteness, discommodity, supererogation, obsolescence.

Litter, rubbish, lumber, trash, junk, punk, job lot, orts, weeds (643), bilge, hog-wash.

A waste, desert, Sahara, wild, wilderness.

(*Phrases*) The labour of Sisyphus; the work of Penelope; a slaying of the slain; a dead loss; a work of supererogation.

(*Verbs*) To be useless, etc., to be of no avail, use, etc. (644).

(*Adjectives*) Useful, beneficial, advantageous, serviceable, helpful, gainful, profitable, lucrative, worth while.

Subservient, conducive, applicable, adequate, efficient, efficacious, effective, effectual, seaworthy.

Applicable, available, handy, ready.

(*Adverbs*) Usefully, etc.; *pro bono publico*.

To render useless, etc.; to dismantle, disable, disqualify, cripple.

(*Phrases*) To use vain efforts; to beat the air; to fish in the air; to lash the waves; to plough the sands.

(*Adjectives*) Useless, inutile, inefficient, inefficacious, unavailing, inadequate, inoperative, bootless, supervacaneous, unprofitable, unremunerative, unproductive, sterile, barren, unsubservient, supererogatory.

Worthless, valueless, at a discount, gainless, fruitless, profitless, unserviceable, rusty, effete, vain, empty, inane, wasted, nugatory, futile, feckless, inept, withered, good for nothing, wasteful, ill-spent, obsolete, obsolescent, stale, dud, punk, dear-bought, rubbishy.

Unneeded, unnecessary, uncalled-for, unwanted, incommodious, discommodious.

(*Phrases*) Not worth having; leading to no end; no good; not worth while; of no earthly use; a dead letter.

(*Adverbs*) Uselessly, etc., to no purpose.

646 Specific subservience.

EXPEDIENCE (*Substantives*), expediency, fitness, suitableness, suitability, aptness, aptitude, appropriateness, propriety, pertinence, seasonableness (134), adaptation, congruity, consonance (23), convenience, eligibility, applicability, desirability, seemliness, rightness.

An opportunist, time-server.

(*Verbs*) To be expedient, etc.

To suit, fit, square with, adapt itself to, agree with, consort with, accord with, tally with, conform to, go with, do for.

(*Adjectives*) Expedient, fit, fitting, worth while, suitable, applicable, eligible, apt, appropriate, adapted, proper, advisable, politic, judicious, desirable, pertinent, congruous, seemly, consonant, becoming, meet, due, consentaneous, congenial, well-timed, pat, seasonable, opportune, apropos, befitting, happy, felicitous, auspicious, acceptable, etc., convenient, commodious, right.

(*Phrases*) Being just the thing; just as well.

648 Capability of producing good.

GOODNESS (*Substantives*), excellence, integrity (939), virtue (944),

647 INEXPEDIENCE (*Substantives*), inexpediency, disadvantageousness, unserviceableness, disservice, unfitness, inaptitude, ineptitude, ineligibility, inappropriateness, impropriety, undesirability, unseemliness, incongruity, impertinence, inopportuneness, unseasonableness.

Inconvenience, incommodiousness, incommodity, discommodity, disadvantage.

Inefficacy, inefficiency, inadequacy.

(*Verbs*) To be inexpedient, etc., to embarrass, cumber, lumber, handicap, be in the way, etc.

(*Adjectives*) Inexpedient, disadvantageous, unprofitable, unfit, unfitting, unsuitable, undesirable, amiss, improper, unapt, inept, impolitic, injudicious, ill-advised, unadvisable, ineligible, objectionable, inadmissible, unseemly, inopportune, unseasonable, inefficient, inefficacious, inadequate.

Inconvenient, incommodious, cumbrous, cumbersome, lumbering, unwieldy, unmanageable, awkward, clumsy.

649 Capability of producing evil.

BADNESS (*Substantives*), hurtfulness, disserviceableness, injurious-

merit, value, worth, price, preciousness, estimation, rareness, exquisiteness.

Superexcellence, superiority, supereminence, transcendence, perfection (650).

Mediocrity (651), innocuousness, harmlessness, inoffensiveness.

Masterpiece, *chef d'œuvre*, flower, pick, cream, *crême de la crême*, *élite*, gem, jewel, treasure; a good man (948).

(*Phrases*) One in a thousand (or in a million); the salt of the earth.

(*Verbs*) To be good, beneficial, etc.; to be superior, etc., to excel, transcend, top, vie, emulate (708).

To be middling, etc. (651); to pass, to do.

To produce good, benefit, etc., to benefit, to be beneficial, etc., to confer a benefit, etc., to improve (658).

(*Phrases*) To challenge comparison; to pass muster; to speak well for.

(*Adjectives*) Good, beneficial, valuable, estimable, serviceable, advantageous, precious, favourable, palmary, felicitous, propitious.

Sound, sterling, standard, true, genuine, household, fresh, in good condition, unfaded, unspoiled, unimpaired, uninjured, undemolished, undamaged, unravaged, undecayed, natural, unsophisticated, unadulterated unpolluted, unvitiated.

Choice, select, picked, nice, worthy, meritorious (944), fine, rare, unexceptionable, excellent, admirable, first-rate, splendid, swell, bully, wizard, priceless, smashing, super, topping, top-hole, clipping, ripping, nailing, prime, tiptop, crack, jake, cardinal, superlative, superfine, super-excellent, pukka, gradely, champion, exquisite, high-wrought, inestimable, invaluable, incomparable, transcendent, matchless, peerless, inimitable, unrivalled, *nulli secundus*, second to none, *facile princeps*, spotless, immaculate, perfect (650), *récherché*, first-class, first chop.

Moderately good (651).

Harmless, innocuous, innoxious,

ness, banefulness, mischievousness, noxiousness, malignancy, malignity, malevolence, tender mercies, venomousness, virulence, destructiveness, scathe, curse, pest, plague, bane (663), plague-spot, evil star, ill wind; evildoer (913).

Vileness, foulness, rankness, depravation, depravity; injury, outrage, ill treatment, annoyance, molestation, oppression; sabotage; deterioration (659).

(*Phrases*) A snake in the grass; a fly in the ointment; a nigger in the woodpile; a thorn in the side; a skeleton in the cupboard.

(*Verbs*) To be bad, etc.

To cause, produce, or inflict evil; to harm, hurt, injure, mar, damage, damnify, endamage, scathe, prejudice, stand in the light of, worsen.

To wrong, molest (830), annoy, harass, infest, grieve, aggrieve, trouble, oppress, persecute, weigh down, run down, overlay.

To maltreat, abuse, ill use, ill treat, bedevil, bruise, scratch, maul, mishandle, man-handle, strafe, knock about, strike, smite, scourge (972), wound, lame, maim, scotch, cripple, mutilate, hamstring, hough, stab, pierce, etc., crush, crumble, pulverize.

To corrupt, corrode, pollute, etc. (659).

To spoil, despoil, sweep, ravage, lay waste, devastate, dismantle, demolish, level, raze, consume, overrun, sack, plunder, destroy (162).

(*Phrases*) To play the deuce with; to break the back of; crush to pieces; crumble to dust; to grind to powder; to ravage with fire and sword; to knock the stuffing out of; to queer one's pitch; to let daylight into.

(*Adjectives*) Bad, evil, ill, wrong, prejudicial, disadvantageous, unprofitable, unlucky, sinister, lefthanded, obnoxious, untoward, unadvisable, inauspicious, ill-omened.

Hurtful, harmful, injurious, grievous, detrimental, noxious, pernicious, mischievous, baneful, baleful.

Morbific, rank, peccant, malignant,

unoffending, inoffensive, unobjectionable.

(*Phrases*) The goods; the stuff to give them; a bit of all right; of the first water; precious as the apple of the eye; *ne plus ultra*; sound as a roach; worth its weight in gold; right as a trivet; up to the mark; an easy winner.

———

tabid, corroding, corrosive, virulent, cankering, mephitic, narcotic.

Deleterious, poisonous, venomous, envenomed, pestilent, pestilential, pestiferous, destructive, deadly, fatal, mortal, lethal, lethiferous, miasmal.

Vile, sad, wretched, sorry, shabby, scurvy, base, low, low-down (940), scrubby, lousy, stinking, horrid.

Hateful, abominable, loathsome, detestable, execrable, iniquitous, cursed, accursed, confounded, damnable, diabolic, devilish, demoniacal, infernal, hellish, Satanic, villainous, depraved, shocking (898).

(*Adverbs*) Wrong, wrongly, badly, to one's cost.

(*Phrases*) *Corruptio optimi pessima*; if the worst comes to the worst.

---

650 PERFECTION (*Substantives*), perfectness, indefectibility, impeccability, infallibility, unimpeachability, *beau idéal*, summit (210).

Masterpiece, *chef d'œuvre*, *magnum opus*, classic, model, pattern, mirror, phoenix, *rara avis*, paragon, cream, nonsuch (or nonesuch), nonpareil, *élite*.

Gem, bijou, jewel, pearl, diamond, ruby, brilliant.

A Bayard, a Galahad, an Admirable Crichton.

(*Phrases*) The philosophers' stone; the flower of the flock; the cock of the roost; the pink or acme of perfection; the pick of the bunch; the *ne plus ultra*.

(*Verbs*) To be perfect, etc., to excel, transcend, overtop, etc. (33).

To bring to perfection, to perfect, to ripen, mature, etc. (52, 729).

(*Phrases*) To carry everything before it; to play first fiddle; bear away the bell; to sweep the board.

(*Adjectives*) Perfect, best, faultless, finished, indeficient, indefectible, immaculate, spotless, impeccable, transcendent, matchless, peerless, unparagoned, etc. (648), inimitable, unimpeachable, superlative, superhuman, divine, classical.

(*Phrases*) Right as a trivet; sound as a bell; *ad unguem factus*; *sans peur et sans reproche*.

---

651 IMPERFECTION (*Substantives*), imperfectness, unsoundness, faultiness, deficiency, disability, weak point, drawback, inadequacy, inadequateness (645), handicap.

Fault, defect, flaw, lacuna (198), crack, twist, taint, blemish, shortcoming (304), peccancy, vice.

Mediocrity, mean (29), indifference, inferiority.

(*Verbs*) To be imperfect, middling, etc., to fail, fall short, lie under a disadvantage, be handicapped.

(*Phrases*) To play second fiddle; barely to pass muster.

(*Adjectives*) Imperfect, deficient, defective, faulty, dud, inferior, inartistic, inadequate, wanting, unsound, vicious, cracked, warped, lame, feeble, frail, flimsy, sketchy, botched, gimcrack, gingerbread, tottering, wonky, decrepit, rickety, ramshackle, rattletrap, battered, worn out, threadbare, seedy, wormeaten, moth-eaten, played out, used up, decayed, mutilated, unrectified, uncorrected.

Indifferent, middling, mediocre, below par, so-so, *couci-couci*, secondary, second-rate, third-rate, etc., second-best, second-hand.

Tolerable, passable, bearable, pretty well, well enough, rather good, decent, fair, admissible, not bad, not amiss, not so dusty, unobjectionable, respectable, betwixt and between.

(*Phrases*) Having a screw loose; out of order; out of kilter; no great catch; milk and water; no great shakes; nothing to boast of; on its last legs; no class.

652 Cleanness (*Substantives*), cleanliness, asepsis, purity (960), neatness, tidiness, spotlessness, immaculateness.

Cleaning, purification, mundification, lustration, abstersion, depuration, expurgation, purgation, castration.

Washing, ablution, lavation, elutriation, lixiviation, clarification, defecation, edulcoration, filtration.

Fumigation, ventilation, antisepsis, decontamination, disinfection, soap; detergent, shampoo, antiseptic, disinfectant.

Washroom, wash-house, laundry; washerwoman, laundress, charwoman, cleaner, scavenger, dustman, sweep.

Brush, broom, besom, vacuum-cleaner, duster, handkerchief, napkin, face-cloth, towel, sponge, tooth-brush, nail-brush; mop, sieve, riddle, screen, filter.

(*Verbs*) To be clean, etc.

To render, clean, etc., to clean, to mundify, cleanse, wipe, mop, sponge, scour, swab, scrub, brush, sweep, vacuum, dust, brush up.

To wash, lave, sluice, buck, launder, steep, rinse, absterge, deterge, descale, clear, purify, depurate, defecate, elutriate, lixiviate, edulcorate, clarify, drain, strain, filter, filtrate, fine, fine down.

To disinfect, deodorize, fumigate, delouse, ventilate, purge, expurgate, bowdlerize.

To sift, winnow, pick, screen, weed.

(*Phrase*) To make a clean sweep of.

(*Adjectives*) Clean, cleanly, pure, spotless, unspotted, immaculate, unstained, stainless, unsoiled, unsullied, taintless, untainted, sterile, aseptic, uninfected.

Cleansing, etc., detergent, detersive, abstersive, abstergent, purgatory, purificatory, etc., abluent, antiseptic.

Spruce, tidy, washed, swept, etc., cleaned, disinfected, purified, etc.

(*Phrases*) Clean as a whistle; clean as a new penny; neat as ninepence.

653 Uncleanness (*Substantives*), immundicity, uncleanliness, soilure, sordidness, foulness, impurity (961), pollution, nastiness, offensiveness, beastliness, muckiness, defilement, contamination, abomination, taint, tainture, corruption, decomposition (49).

Slovenliness, slovenly, untidiness, sluttishness, coarseness, grossness, dregginess, squalor.

Dirt, filth, soil, slop, dust, flue, ooss, cobweb, smoke, soot, smudge, smut, stour, clart, glaur, grime, *sordes*, mess, muck.

Slut, slattern, sloven, frump, mud-lark, riff-raff.

Dregs, grounds, sediment, lees, settlement, dross, drossiness, precipitate, scoriae, slag, clinker, scum, sweepings, off-scourings, garbage, *caput mortuum*, residuum, draff, fur, scurf, scurfiness, furfur, dandruff, vermin.

Mud, mire, slush, quagmire, slough, sludge, alluvium, silt, slime, spawn, offal, faeces, excrement, ordure, dung, droppings, guano, manure, compost, dunghill, midden, bog, laystall, sink, cesspool, sump, sough, *cloaca*, latrine, lavatory, water-closet, w.c., toilet, urinal, rear, convenience, privy, jakes, comfort station, heads, thunder-box, drain, sewer; hog-wash, bilge-water.

Sty, pigsty, dusthole, lair, den, slum.

Rottenness, corruption, decomposition, decay, drossiness, putrefaction, putrescence, putridity, purulence, pus, matter, suppuration, feculence, rankness, rancidity, mouldiness, mustiness, mucidness, mould, mother, must, mildew, dry-rot, fetor, (401).

Scatology, coprology.

(*Phrases*) A sink of corruption; an Augean stable.

(*Verbs*) To be unclean, dirty, etc., to rot, putrefy, corrupt, decompose, go bad, mould, moulder, fester, etc.

To render unclean, etc., to dirt, dirty, soil, tarnish, begrime, smear, besmear, mess, smirch, besmirch, smudge, besmudge, bemire, spatter, bespatter, splash, bedaggle, bedraggle, daub, bedaub, slobber, beslobber, beslime, to cover with dust.

To foul, befoul, sully, pollute, defile, debase, contaminate, taint, corrupt, deflower, rot.

(*Adjectives*) Unclean, dirty, soiled, filthy, grimy, clarty, dusty, dirtied, etc., smutty, sooty, smoky, reechy, thick, turbid, dreggy, slimy, filthy, mucky.

Slovenly, untidy, sluttish, blowzy, draggle-tailed, dowdy, frumpish, slipshod, unkempt, unscoured, unswept, unwiped, unwashed, unstrained, unpurified, squalid.

Nasty, foul, impure, offensive, abominable, beastly, lousy.

Mouldy, musty, mildewed, fusty, rusty, mouldering, moth-eaten, reasty, rotten, rotting, tainted, rancid, high, fly-blown, maggoty, putrescent, putrid, putrefied, bad, festering, purulent, feculent, fecal, stercoraceous, excrementitious.

(*Phrases*) Wallowing in the mire; rotten to the core.

---

654 HEALTH (*Substantives*), sanity, soundness, heartiness, haleness, vigour, freshness, bloom, healthfulness, euphoria, incorruption, incorruptibility.

(*Phrases*) *Mens sana in corpore sano*; a clean bill.

(*Verbs*) To be in health, etc., to flourish, thrive, bloom.

To return to health, to recover, convalesce, recruit, pull through, to get the better of.

To restore to health, to cure, recall to life, bring to.

(*Phrases*) To keep on one's legs; to take a new or fresh lease of life; to turn the corner.

(*Adjectives*) Healthy, in health, well, sound, healthful, hearty, hale, fresh, whole, florid, staunch, flush, hardy, vigorous, chipper, spry, bobbish, blooming, weather-proof, fit.

Unscathed, uninjured, unmaimed, unmarred, untainted.

(*Phrases*) Sitting up and taking nourishment; being on one's legs; sound as a bell, or roach; fresh as a daisy or rose; in fine or high feather; in good case; fit as a fiddle; in the pink of condition; in the pink; in good form.

---

655 DISEASE (*Substantives*), illness, sickness, ailment, ailing, indisposition, complaint, disorder, malady, distemper.

Attack, visitation, seizure, stroke, fit.

Sickliness, sickishness, infirmity, diseasedness, tabescence, invalidation, delicacy, weakness, cachexy, witheredness, atrophy, marasmus, incurableness, incurability, palsy, paralysis, decline, consumption, prostration.

Taint, pollution, infection, septicity, epidemic, endemic, murrain, plague, pestilence, virus, pox.

A sore, ulcer, abscess, fester, boil, gathering, issue, rot, canker, cancer, carcinoma, sarcoma, caries, gangrene, mortification, eruption, rash, congestion, inflammation, fever.

A valetudinarian, invalid, patient, case, cripple.

Pathology, aetiology, nosology.

(*Verbs*) To be ill, etc., to ail, suffer, be affected with, etc., to complain of, to droop, flag, languish, halt, sicken, gasp; to malinger.

(*Phrases*) To be laid up; to keep one's bed.

(*Adjectives*) Diseased, ill, taken ill, seized, indisposed, unwell, sick, sickish, seedy, queer, crook, toutie, ailing, suffering, confined, bedridden, invalided.

Unsound, sickly, poorly, delicate, weakly, cranky, healthless, infirm, groggy, unbraced, drooping, flagging, withered, palsied, paralytic, paraplectic, decayed, decrepit, lame, crippled, battered, halting, worn out, used up, run down, off colour, moth-eaten, worm-eaten.

Morbid, tainted, vitiated, peccant, contaminated, tabid, tabescent, mangy, poisoned, immedicable, gasping, moribund (360).

(*Phrases*) Out of sorts; good for nothing; on the sick-list; on the danger list; in a bad way; *hors de combat*; on one's last legs; at one's last gasp.

656 SALUBRITY (*Substantives*), healthiness, wholesomeness, innoxiousness.

Preservation of health, prophylaxis, hygiene, sanitation.

A health resort, spa, hydropathic, sanatorium (662).

(*Verbs*) To be salubrious, etc., to agree with.

(*Adjectives*) Salubrious, wholesome, healthy, sanitary, hygienic, salutary, salutiferous, healthful, tonic, prophylactic, bracing, benign.

Innoxious, innocuous, harmless, uninjurious, innocent.

Remedial, restorative, sanatory (662), nutritious, alterative (660).

658 IMPROVEMENT (*Substantives*), melioration, amelioration, betterment, mend, amendment, emendation, advance, advancement, progress, elevation, promotion, preferment, convalescence, recovery, recuperation, curability.

Repair, reparation, cicatrization, correction, reform, reformation, rectification, epuration, purification, etc. (652), refinement, relief, redress, second thoughts.

New edition; *réchauffé, rifacimento*, revision, revise, recension, rehash, redaction.

(*Verbs*) To be, become, or get better, etc., to improve, mend, advance, progress (282), to get on, make progress, gain ground, make way, go ahead, pick up, rally, recover, get the better of, get well, get over it, pull through, convalesce, recuperate.

To render better, improve, amend, better, meliorate, ameliorate, advance, push on, promote, prefer, forward, enhance.

To relieve, refresh, restore, renew, redintegrate, heal (660); to palliate, mitigate.

To repair, refit, cannibalize,

657 INSALUBRITY (*Substantives*), unhealthiness, unwholesomeness, deadliness, fatality.

Microbe, germ, virus, etc. (663).

(*Adjectives*) Insalubrious, insanitary, unsanitary, unhealthy, ungenial, uncongenial, unwholesome, morbific, mephitic, septic, deleterious, pestilent, pestiferous, pestilential, virulent, poisonous, toxic, contagious, infectious, catching, epidemic, epizootic, endemic, pandemic, zymotic, deadly, pathogenic, pathogenetic, lowering, relaxing; innutritious (645).

(*Phrase*) 'There is death in the pot.'

659 DETERIORATION (*Substantives*), wane, ebb, debasement, degeneracy, degeneration, degradation, degenerateness, demotion, relegation.

Impairment, injury, outrage, havoc, devastation, inroad, vitiation, adulteration, sophistication, debasement, perversion, degradation, demoralization, corruption, prostitution, pollution, contamination, alloy, venenation.

Decline, declension, declination, going downhill, recession, retrogression, retrogradation (283), caducity, decrepitude, decadence, falling off, pejoration.

Decay, disorganization, damage, scathe, wear and tear, mouldiness, rottenness, corrosion, moth and rust, dry-rot, blight, marasmus, atrophy, emaciation, falling to pieces, *délâbrement*.

(*Verbs*) To be, or become worse, to deteriorate, worsen, disimprove, wane, ebb, degenerate, fall off, decline, go downhill, sink, go down, lapse, droop, be the worse for, recede, retrograde, revert (283), fall into decay, fade, break, break up, break down, fall to pieces, wither, moulder,

retouch, revise, botch, vamp, tinker, cobble, clout, patch up, touch up, cicatrize, darn, fine-draw, rub up, do up, furbish, refurbish, polish, bolster up, caulk, careen; to stop a gap, to staunch.

To purify, depurate (652), defecate, strain, filter, rack, refine, disinfect, chasten.

To correct, rectify, redress, reform, review, remodel, prune, restore (660), mellow, set to rights, sort, fix, put straight, straighten out, revise.

(*Phrases*) To turn over a new leaf; to take a new lease of life; to make the most of; to infuse new blood into.

(*Adjectives*) Improving, etc., improved, etc., progressive, corrective, reparatory, emendatory, revisory, sanatory, advanced.

Curable, corrigible, capable of improvement.

———

rot, rust, crumble, totter, shake, tumble, fall, topple, perish, die (360).

To render less good; to weaken, vitiate, debase, alloy, pervert.

To spoil, embase, defile, taint, infect, contaminate, sophisticate, poison, canker, corrupt, tamper with, pollute, deprave, demoralize, envenom, debauch, prostitute, defile, degrade, downgrade, demote, adulterate, stain, spatter, bespatter, soil, tarnish (653), addle.

To corrode, erode, blight, rot, wear away, wear out, gnaw, gnaw at the root of, sap, mine, undermine, shake, break up, disorganize, dismantle, dismast, lay waste, do for, ruin, confound.

To embitter, acerbate, aggravate.

To wound, stab, maim, lame, cripple, mutilate, disfigure, deface.

To injure, harm, hurt, impair, dilapidate, damage, endamage, damnify, etc. (649).

(*Phrases*) To go to rack and ruin; to have seen better days; to go to the dogs; to go to pot; to go on from bad to worse; to go farther and fare worse; to run to seed; to play the deuce with; to sap the foundations of.

(*Adjectives*) Deteriorated, worse, impaired, etc., degenerate, *passé*, on the decline, on the down-grade, deciduous, unimproved, unrecovered, unrestored.

Decayed, etc., moth-eaten, worm-eaten, mildewed, rusty, time-worn, moss-grown, effete, wasted, worn, crumbling, tumbledown, dilapidated, overblown.

(*Phrases*) Out of the frying-pan into the fire; the worse for wear; worn to a thread; worn to a shadow; reduced to a skeleton; the ghost of oneself; a hopeless case.

660 RESTORATION (*Substantives*), restoral, reinstatement, replacement, rehabilitation, instauration, re-establishment, rectification, revendication, redintegration, refection, reconstitution, cure, sanation, refitting, reorganization, recruiting, redress, retrieval, refreshment.

Renovation, renewal, reanimation, recovery, resumption, reclamation, reconversion, recure, resuscitation, revivification, reviviscence, revival, renascence, renaissance, rejuvenation, rejuvenescence, regeneration, regeneracy, regenerateness, palingenesis, redemption; a Phoenix.

661 RELAPSE (*Substantives*), lapse, falling back, backsliding, retrogression, reaction, set-back, recidivism, retrogradation, etc. (659).

Return to or recurrence of a bad state.

A recidivist, backslider, throwback.

(*Verbs*) To relapse, lapse, backslide, fall back, slide back, sink back, go back, return, retrograde.

———

Réchauffé, *rifacimento* (658), recast.

(*Phrases*) A new lease of life; second youth; new birth; 'Richard's himself again.'

(*Verbs*) To return to the original state, to right itself, come to, come round, rally, revive, recover.

To restore, replace, re-establish, reinstate, reseat, replant, reconstitute, redintegrate, set right, set to rights, sort, fix, rectify, redress, reclaim, redeem, recover, recoup, recure, retrieve, cicatrize.

To refit, recruit, refresh, refocillate, rehabilitate, reconvert, renew, renovate, revitalize, revivify, reinvigorate, regenerate, rejuvenesce, rejuvenate, resuscitate, reanimate, recast, reconstruct, rebuild, reorganize.

To repair, retouch, revise (658).

To cure, heal, cicatrize, remedy, doctor, physic, medicate.

(*Phrases*) Recall to life; set on one's legs.

(*Adjectives*) Restoring, etc., restored, etc., restorative, recuperative, reparative, sanative, remedial, curative (662).

Restorable, sanable, remediable, retrievable, recoverable.

(*Adverbs*) *In statu quo*; as you were; Phoenix-like.

662 REMEDY (*Substantives*), help, redress, cure, antidote, counterpoison, vaccine, antitoxin, antibiotic, antiseptic, specific, prophylactic, corrective, restorative, pick-me-up, bracer, sedative, anodyne, opiate, hypnotic, nepenthe, tranquillizer.

Febrifuge, diaphoretic, diuretic, carminative, purgative, laxative, emetic, palliative.

Physic, medicine, drug, tonic, medicament, nostrum, placebo, recipe, prescription, catholicon.

Panacea, elixir, *elixir vitae*, balm, balsam, cordial, cardiac, theriac, ptisan.

Pill, pilule, pellet, tablet, tabloid, pastille, lozenge, powder, draught, tincture, suppository.

Salve, ointment, plaster, epithem, embrocation, liniment, lotion, cataplasm, styptic, poultice, compress, pledget.

Treatment, diet, dieting, regimen.

663 BANE (*Substantives*), scourge, curse, scathe, sting, fang, gall and wormwood.

Poison, virus, venom, toxin, microbe, germ, bacillus, miasma, mephitis, malaria, pest, rust, canker, cancer, canker-worm.

Hemlock, hellebore, nightshade, henbane, aconite, upas-tree.

Sirocco.

A viper, adder, serpent, cobra, rattlesnake, cockatrice, scorpion, wireworm, torpedo, hornet, vulture, vampire.

Science of poisons, toxicology.

(*Adjectives*) Poisonous, venomous, virulent, toxic, mephitic, pestilent, pestilential, miasmatic, baneful (649).

————

Pharmacy, pharmacology, materia medica, therapeutics, homoeopathy, allopathy, radiotherapy, actinotherapy, heliotherapy, thalassotherapy, hydrotherapy, hydropathy, osteopathy, dietetics, dietary, chirurgery, surgery, gynaecology, midwifery, obstetrics, paediatrics, geriatrics; psycho-analysis, psychiatry, psychotherapy; faith-healing.

A hospital, infirmary, pest-house, lazaretto, madhouse, asylum, lunatic asylum, mental hospital, *maison de santé*, ambulance, clinic, dispensary, sanatorium, spa, hydropathic, nursing home.

A doctor, physician, general practitioner, G.P., surgeon, anaesthetist, dentist, aurist, oculist, specialist, alienist, psycho-analyst, psychiatrist, psycho-therapist; apothecary, druggist; midwife, nurse.

(Verbs) To dose, physic, attend, doctor, nurse.

(Adjectives) Remedial, medical, medicinal, therapeutic, surgical, chirurgical, sanatory, sanative, curative, salutary, salutiferous, healing, paregoric, restorative, tonic, corroborant, analeptic, balsamic, anodyne, sedative, lenitive, demulcent, emollient, depuratory, detersive, detergent, abstersive, disinfectant, antiseptic, corrective, prophylactic, antitoxic, febrifuge, alterative, expectorant; veterinary.

Dietetic, alexipharmic, nutritious, nutritive, peptic, alimentary.

3. CONTINGENT SUBSERVIENCE

664 SAFETY (Substantives), security, surety, impregnability, invulnerability, invulnerableness, escape (671).

Safeguard, guard, guardianship, chaperonage, protection, tutelage, wardship, wardenship, safe-conduct, escort, convoy, garrison.

Watch, watch and ward, sentinel, sentry, scout, watchman, patrol, vedette, picket, bivouac.

Policeman, policewoman, police officer, constable, cop, copper, bobby, peeler, slop, bull, dick, rozzer.

Watch-dog, bandog, Cerberus.

Protector, guardian, guard (717), defender, warden, warder, preserver, chaperon, tutelary saint, guardian angel, palladium.

Custody, safe-keeping (751).

Isolation, segregation, quarantine; insurance, assurance; cover.

(Verbs) To be safe, etc.

To render safe, etc., to protect, guard, ward, shield, shelter, flank, cover, screen, shroud, ensconce, secure, fence, hedge in, entrench, house, nestle.

To defend, forfend, escort, convoy, garrison, mount guard, patrol, chaperon, picket.

(Phrases) To save one's bacon; to light upon one's feet; to weather the storm; to bear a charmed life; to make assurance doubly sure; to take no chances.

To play gooseberry.

(Adjectives) Safe, in safety, in security, secure, sure, protected, guarded, etc., snug, fireproof, waterproof, seaworthy, airworthy.

Defensible, tenable; insurable.

665 DANGER (Substantives), peril, insecurity, jeopardy, risk, hazard, venture, precariousness, slipperiness.

Liability, exposure (177), vulnerability, vulnerable point, Achilles heel.

Hopelessness (859), forlorn hope, alarm (860), defencelessness.

(Phrases) The ground sliding from under one: breakers ahead; a storm brewing; the sword of Damocles.

(Verbs) To be in danger, etc., to be exposed to, to incur or encounter danger, run the danger of, run a risk.

To place or put in danger, etc., to endanger, expose to danger, imperil, jeopardize, compromise, adventure, risk, hazard, venture, stake.

(Phrases) To sit on a barrel of gunpowder; stand on a volcano; to engage in a forlorn hope.

(Adjectives) In danger, peril, jeopardy, etc., unsafe, insecure, unguarded, unscreened, unsheltered, unprotected, guardless, helpless, guideless, exposed, defenceless, vulnerable, at bay.

Unwarned, unadmonished, unadvised.

Dangerous, perilous, hazardous, parlous, risky, chancy, untrustworthy, fraught with danger, adventurous, precarious, critical, touch-and-go, breakneck, slippery, unsteady, shaky, tottering, top-heavy, harbourless, ticklish, dicky.

Threatening, ominous, alarming, minacious (909).

(Phrases) Not out of the wood; hanging by a thread; neck or nothing; in a tight place; between two fires; out of the frying-pan into the fire;

Invulnerable, unassailable, unattackable, impregnable, inexpugnable.

Protecting, etc., guardian, tutelary.

Unthreatened, unmolested, unharmed, scatheless, unhazarded.

(*Phrases*) Out of harm's way; safe and sound; under lock and key; on sure ground; under cover; under the shadow of one's wing; the coast being clear; the danger being past; out of the wood; proof against.

(*Interjections*) All's well! *salva est res !* safety first!

between the devil and the deep sea; between Scylla and Charybdis; on the rocks; hard bested.

———

666 Means of safety.

REFUGE (*Substantives*), asylum, sanctuary, fastness, retreat, ark, hiding-place, dug-out, funk-hole, fox-hole, loophole, shelter, lee, cover.

Roadstead, anchorage, breakwater, mole, groyne, port, haven, harbour, harbour of refuge, pier.

Fort, citadel, fortification, stronghold, strong point, keep, shield, etc. (717).

Screen, covert, wing, fence, rail, railing, wall, dike, ditch, etc. (232).

Anchor, kedge, grapnel, grappling-iron, sheet-anchor, prop, stay, mainstay, jury-mast, lifeboat, lifebuoy, lifebelt, plank, stepping-stone, umbrella, parachute, lightning-conductor, safety-valve, safety curtain, safety-lamp.

667 Source of danger.

PITFALL (*Substantives*), rocks, reefs, sunken rocks, snags, sands, quicksands, breakers, shoals, shallows, bank, shelf, flat, whirlpool, rapids, current, undertow, precipice, lee shore, air-pocket.

Trap, snare, gin, springe, deadfall, toils, noose, net, spring-net, spring-gun, masked battery, mine.

(*Phrases*) The sword of Damocles; a snake in the grass; trusting to a broken reed; a lion's den; a hornet's nest; an ugly customer.

———

668

WARNING (*Substantives*), caution, *caveat*, notice, premonition, premonishment, lesson, dehortation, monition, admonition (864); alarm (669).

Beacon, lighthouse, lightship, pharos, watch-tower, signal-post, guide-post (550).

Sentinel, sentry, watch, watchman, patrol, vedette (664); monitor, Cassandra.

(*Phrases*) The writing on the wall; the yellow flag; a red light; a stormy petrel; gathering clouds.

(*Verbs*) To warn, caution, forewarn, premonish, give notice, give warning, admonish, dehort, threaten, menace (909).

To take warning; to beware; to be on one's guard (864).

(*Phrases*) To put on one's guard; to sound the alarm.

(*Adjectives*) Warning, etc., monitory, premonitory, dehortatory, cautionary, admonitory.

Warned, etc., careful, on one's guard (459).

(*Interjections*) Beware! look out! mind what you are about! watch your step! let sleeping dogs lie! *foenum habet in cornu!* fore! heads! mind your back! cave!

669 Indication of danger.

ALARM (*Substantives*), alert, alarum, alarm-bell, horn, siren, maroon, fog-signal, tocsin, tattoo, signal of distress, S O S, hue and cry.

False alarm, cry of wolf, bugbear, bugaboo, bogy.

(*Verbs*) To give, raise, or sound an alarm, to alarm, warn, ring the tocsin, dial 999; to cry wolf.

(*Adjectives*) Alarming, etc., threatening.

(*Phrases*) Each for himself; *sauve qui peut.*

670 PRESERVATION (*Substantives*), conservation, maintenance (141), support, upkeep, sustentation, deliverance, salvation, rescue, redemption, self-preservation, continuance (143).

Means of preservation, prophylaxis, preservative, preserver.

(*Verbs*) To preserve, maintain, support, keep, sustain, nurse, save, rescue, file (papers).

To embalm, mummify, dry, dehydrate, cure, kipper, smoke, salt, pickle, marinade, season, kyanize, bottle, pot, can, tin.

(*Adjectives*) Preserving, conservative, prophylactic, preservatory, hygienic. Preserved, intact, unimpaired, uninjured, unhurt, unsinged, unmarred.

671 ESCAPE (*Substantives*), getaway, flight, elopement, evasion, retreat, reprieve, reprieval, deliverance, redemption, rescue.

Narrow escape, hair's-breadth, escape, close shave, close call, narrow squeak.

Means of escape: Bridge, drawbridge, loophole, ladder, plank, stepping-stone, trap-door, fire-escape, emergency exit.

A fugitive, runaway, refugee, evacuee.

(*Verbs*) To escape, elude, evade, wriggle out of, make or effect one's escape, make off, march off, pack off, skip, skip off, slip away, steal away, slink away, flit, decamp, run away, abscond, levant, skedaddle, scoot, fly, flee, bolt, bunk, scarper, scram, hop it, beat it, vamoose, elope, whip off, break loose, break away, get clear.

(*Phrases*) To take oneself off; play truant; to beat a retreat; to give one the slip; to slip the collar; to slip through the fingers; to make oneself scarce; to fly the coop; to take to one's heels; to show a clean pair of heels; to take French leave; to do a bunk; to do a guy; to cut one's lucky; to cut and run; to live to fight another day; to run for one's life; to make tracks.

(*Interjections*) *Sauve qui peut!* the devil take the hindmost!

(*Adjectives*) Escaping, etc., escaped, etc., runaway.

(*Phrase*) The bird having flown.

672 DELIVERANCE (*Substantives*), extrication, rescue, reprieve, respite, redemption, salvation, riddance, release, liberation (750); redeemableness, redeemability.

(*Verbs*) To deliver, extricate, rescue, save, salvage, redeem, ransom, help out, bring off, *tirer d'affaire*, to get rid, to work off, to rid.

(*Phrases*) To save one's bacon; to find a hole to creep out of.

(*Adjectives*) Delivered, saved, etc., scot-free, scatheless.

Extricable, redeemable, rescuable.

3°. *Precursory Measures*

673 PREPARATION (*Substantives*), making ready, providing, provision, providence, anticipation, preconcertation, rehearsal, precaution; laying foundations, ploughing, sowing, semination, cooking, brewing, digestion,	**674 NON-PREPARATION** (*Substantives*), want or absence of preparation, inculture, inconcoction, improvidence. Immaturity, crudeness, crudity, greenness, rawness, disqualification.

gestation, hatching, incubation, concoction, maturation, elaboration, predisposition, premeditation (611), acclimatization (613).

Physical preparation, training, drill, drilling, discipline, exercise, exercitation, gymnastics, callisthenics, eurhythmics, athletics, gymnasium, *palaestra*, prenticeship, apprenticeship, qualification, inurement, education, novitiate (537).

Putting or setting in order, putting to rights, clearance, arrangement, disposal, organization, adjustment, adaptation, disposition, accommodation, putting in tune, tuning, putting in trim, dressing, putting in harness, outfit, equipment, accoutrement, armament.

Groundwork, basis, foundation, pedestal, etc. (215), stepping-stone, first stone, scaffold, scaffolding, cradle, sketch (626).

State of being prepared, preparedness, ripeness, maturity, readiness, mellowness.

Preparer, pioneer, avant-courier, sappers and miners.

(*Phrases*) A stitch in time; clearing decks; a note of preparation; a breather; a trial bout; a practice swing.

(*Verbs*) To prepare, get ready, make ready, get up, anticipate, forecast, pre-establish, preconcert, settle preliminaries, to found.

To arrange, set or put in order, set or put to rights, organize, dispose, cast the parts, mount, adjust, adapt, accommodate, trim, tidy, fit, predispose, inure, elaborate, mature, mellow, season, ripen, nurture, hatch, cook, concoct, brew, tune, put in tune, attune, set, temper, anneal, smelt, undermine, brush up, get up.

To provide, provide against, discount, make provision, keep on foot, take precautions, make sure, lie in wait for (507).

Absence of art, state of nature, virgin soil.

An embryo, skeleton, rough copy, draft (626); germ, rudiment (153), raw material, rough diamond.

Tyro, beginner, novice, neophyte, greenhorn, new chum, pommy, recruit, sprog.

(*Verbs*) To be unprepared, etc., to want or lack preparation.

To improvise, extemporize (612).

To render unprepared, etc., to dismantle, dismount, dismast, disqualify, disable (645), unrig, undress (226).

(*Phrases*) To put *hors de combat*; to put out of gear; to spike the guns; to remove the sparking-plug.

(*Adjectives*) Unprepared, rudimentary, immature, embryonic, unripe, raw, green, crude, rough, roughcast, rough-hewn, unhewn, unformed, unhatched, unfledged, unnurtured, uneducated, unlicked, unpolished, natural, in a state of nature, *au naturel*, unwrought, unconcocted, undigested, indigested, unrevised, unblown, unfashioned, unlaboured, unleavened, fallow, uncultivated, unsown, untilled, untrained, undrilled, unexercised, unseasoned, disqualified, unqualified, out of order, unseaworthy.

Unbegun, unready, unarranged, unorganized, unfurnished, unprovided, unequipped, undressed, in dishabille, dismantled, untrimmed.

Shiftless, improvident, unguarded, happy-go-lucky, feckless, thoughtless, unthrifty.

Unpremeditated, unseen, off-hand (612), from hand to mouth, extempore (111).

(*Phrases*) Caught on the hop; with their trousers down.

———

To equip, arm, man, fit out, fit up, furnish, rig, dress, dress up, furbish up, accoutre, array, fettle, vamp up, wind up.

To train, drill, discipline, break in, cradle, inure, habituate, harden, case-harden, season, acclimatize, qualify, educate, teach.

(*Phrases*) To take steps; prepare the ground; lay or fix the foundations, the basis, groundwork, etc.; to clear the ground or way or course; clear decks; clear for action; close one's ranks; plough the ground; dress the ground; till the soil; sow the seed; open the way; pave the way; lay a train; dig a mine; prepare a charge; erect the scaffolding; *reculer pour mieux sauter.*

Put in harness; sharpen one's tools; whet the knife; shoulder arms; put the horses to; oil up; crank up; warm up.

To prepare oneself; lay oneself out for; get into harvest; gird up one's loins; buckle on one's armour; serve one's time or apprenticeship; be at one's post; gather oneself together.

To set on foot; to lay the first stone; to break ground.

To erect the scaffold; to cut one's coat according to one's cloth; to keep one's powder dry; to beat up for recruits; to sound the note of preparation.

(*Adjectives*) Preparing, etc., in preparation, in course of preparation, in hand, in train, brewing, hatching, forthcoming, in embryo, afoot, afloat, on the anvil, on the carpet, on the stocks, *sur le tapis.*

Preparative, preparatory, provisional, in the rough, rough and ready (111).

Prepared, trained, drilled, etc., forearmed, ready, in readiness, ripe, mature, mellow, fledged, ready to one's hand, on tap, cut and dried, annealed, concocted, laboured, elaborated, planned (626).

(*Phrases*) Armed to the teeth; armed cap-à-pie; booted and spurred; in full feather; *in utrumque paratus*; in working order.

(*Adverbs*) In preparation, in anticipation of, etc., against.

675 ESSAY (*Substantives*), endeavour, try, trial, experiment (463), probation, attempt (676), venture, adventure, tentative, *ballon d'essai, coup d'essai*, go, crack, whack, slap, shot, speculation.

(*Verbs*) To try, essay, make trial of, try on, experiment, make an experiment, endeavour, strive, attempt, grope, feel one's way; to venture, adventure, speculate, take upon oneself.

(*Phrases*) To put out or throw out a feeler; to tempt fortune; to fly a kite; to send up a pilot balloon; to fish for information, compliments, etc.; to have a crack at; to try one's luck; to chance it; to risk it.

(*Adjectives*) Essaying, etc., experimental, tentative, empirical, on trial, probative, probatory, probationary.

(*Adverbs*) Experimentally, etc., at a venture.

676 UNDERTAKING (*Substantives*), enterprise, emprise, quest, mission, endeavour, attempt, move, first move, the initiative, first step.

(*Verbs*) To undertake, take in hand, set about, go about, set to, fall to, set to work, engage in, launch into, embark in, plunge into, take on, set one's hand to, tackle, grapple with, volunteer, take steps, launch out.

To endeavour, strive, use one's endeavours; to attempt, make an attempt, tempt.

To begin, set on foot, set agoing, take the first step.

(*Phrases*) To break the neck of the business; take the initiative; to get cracking; to break ground; break the ice; break cover; to pass the Rubicon; to take upon oneself; to take on one's shoulders; to put one's shoulder to the wheel; *ce n'est que le premier pas qui coûte*; well begun is half done.

To take the bull by the horns; to rush *in medias res*; to have too many irons in the fire; to attempt impossibilities.

(*Adverbs*) Undertaking, attempting, etc.

677 USE (*Substantives*), employment, employ, application, appliance, adhibition, disposal, exercise, exercitation.

Recourse, resort, avail, service, wear, usage, conversion to use, usufruct, utilization.

Agency (170); usefulness (644).

(*Verbs*) To use, make use of, utilize, exploit, employ (134), apply, adhibit, dispose of, work, wield, manipulate, handle, put to use; turn or convert to use; avail oneself of, resort to, have recourse to, take up with, betake oneself to.

To render useful, serviceable, available, etc.; to utilize, draw, call forth, tax, task, try, exert, exercise, practise, ply, work up, consume, absorb, expend.

To be useful, to serve one's turn (644).

(*Phrases*) To take advantage of; to turn to account; to make the most of; to make the best of; to bring to bear upon; to fall back upon; to press or enlist into the service; to make shift with; make a cat's-paw of.

To pull the strings or wires; put in action; set to work; set in motion; put in practice.

(*Adjectives*) Used, employed, etc., applied, exercised, tried, etc.

678 DISUSE (*Substantives*), forbearance, abstinence, dispensation, desuetude (614), relinquishment, abandonment (624, 782).

(*Verbs*) To disuse, not to use, to do without, to dispense with, neglect, to let alone, to spare, waive.

To lay by; set, put, or lay aside, to discard, dismiss (756); cast off, throw off, turn off, turn out, turn away, throw away, scrap, dismantle, shelve (133), shunt, side-track, get rid of, do away with; to keep back (636).

(*Phrases*) To lay on the shelf; to lay up in a napkin; to consign to the scrap-heap; to cast, heave, or throw overboard; to cast to the winds; to turn out neck and crop; to send to the right-about; to send packing.

(*Adjectives*) Disused, etc., not used, unused, unutilized, done with, unemployed, unapplied, unspent, unexercised, kept or held back.

Unessayed, untouched, uncalled-for, ungathered, unculled, untrodden.

679 MISUSE (*Substantives*), misusage, misemployment, misapplication, misappropriation, abuse, profanation, prostitution, desecration.

Waste (818), wasting, spilling, exhaustion (638).

(*Verbs*) To misuse, misemploy, misapply, misappropriate, desecrate, abuse, profane, prostitute.

To waste, spill, fritter away, exhaust, throw or fling away, squander (818).

(*Phrases*) To waste powder and shot; cut blocks with a razor; cast pearls before swine.

(*Adjectives*) Misused, etc.

SECTION III.—VOLUNTARY ACTION

1°. *Simple Voluntary Action*

680 ACTION (*Substantives*), performance, work, operation, execution, perpetration, proceeding, procedure, *démarche*, process, handiwork, handicraft, workmanship, manœuvre, evolution, transaction, bout, turn,

681 INACTION (*Substantives*), abstinence from action, inactivity (683), non-intervention, non-interference, neutrality, strike, Fabian tactics.

(*Verbs*) Not to do, to let be, abstain from doing; let or leave alone, refrain,

job, doings, dealings, business, affair.

Deed, act, overt act, touch, move, strike, blow, *coup*, feat, stunt, exploit, passage, measure, step, stroke of policy, *tour de force*, *coup de main*, *coup d'état*.

(*Verbs*) To act, do, work, operate, do or transact business, practise, prosecute, perpetrate, perform, execute (729), officiate, exercise, commit, inflict, strike a blow, handle, take in hand, put in hand, run.

To labour, drudge, toil, ply, set to work, pull the oar, serve, officiate, go about, turn one's hand to, dabble; to have in hand.

(*Phrases*) To have a finger in the pie; to take or play a part; to set to work; to put into execution (729); to lay one's hand to the plough; to ply one's task; to get on with the job; to discharge an office.

(*Adjectives*) Acting, etc., in action, in operation, etc., operative, in harness, in play, on duty, on foot, at work, red-handed.

(*Interjection*) Here goes!

desist, keep oneself from doing; let pass, lie by, let be, wait.

To undo, take down, take or pull to pieces, do away with.

(*Phrases*) To bide one's time; to let well alone; to cool one's heels; to stay one's hand; to wash one's hands of; to strike work; nothing doing; *nihil fit*; *dolce far niente*.

(*Adjectives*) Not doing, not done, let alone, undone, etc.; passive, neutral.

682 ACTIVITY (*Substantives*), briskness, quickness, promptness, promptitude, expedition, dispatch, readiness, alertness, smartness, sharpness, nimbleness, agility (274).

Spirit, ardour, animation, life, liveliness, vivacity, eagerness, *empressement*, *brio*, dash, *élan*, abandon, pep, go, alacrity, zeal, push, vim, energy (171), hustle, vigour, intentness.

Wakefulness, *pervigilium*, insomnia, sleeplessness.

Industry, assiduity, assiduousness, sedulity, sedulousness, diligence; perseverance, persistence, plodding, painstaking, drudgery, busyness, indefatigability, indefatigableness, patience, business habits.

Movement, bustle, commotion, stir, fuss, fluster, bother, pother, ado, fidget, restlessness, fidgetiness.

Officiousness, meddling, interference, interposition, intermeddling, tampering with, intrigue, *tripotage*, supererogation.

A man of action, busy bee, busybody, go-getter, zealot, devotee, meddler, hustler, whizz-kid.

(*Phrases*) The thick of the action; *in medias res*; too many cooks; new

683 INACTIVITY (*Substantives*), inaction (681), idleness, sloth, laziness, indolence, inertness, inertia (172), lumpishness, supineness, sluggishness, segnitude, languor, torpor, quiescence, stagnation, lentor, limpness, listlessness, remissness, slackness.

Dilatoriness, cunctation, procrastination (133), relaxation, truancy, lagging, dawdling, rust, rustiness, want of occupation, resourcelessness.

Somnolence, drowsiness, doziness, nodding, oscitation, sleepiness, hypnosis.

Hypnology.

Sleep, nap, doze, slumber, shuteye, bye-bye, snooze, dog-sleep, catnap, siesta, dream, faint, swoon, coma, trance, hypnotic state, snore, a wink of sleep, lethargy, hibernation, aestivation.

An idler, laggard, truant, donothing, lubber, sluggard, sleepyhead, slumberer, faineant, *flâneur*, loafer, drone, dormouse, slow-coach, stick-in-the-mud, lounger, slug, sundowner, bum, Weary Willie, lazybones, lotus-eater, slacker, trifler, dilettante.

brooms sweep clean; too many irons in the fire.

(*Verbs*) To be active, busy, stirring, etc., to busy oneself in, stir, bestir oneself, bustle, fuss, make a fuss, speed, hasten, push, make a push, go ahead, hustle; to industrialize.

To plod, drudge, keep on, hold on, persist, persevere, fag at, hammer at, peg away, stick to, buckle to, stick to work, take pains; to take or spend time in; to make progress.

To meddle, moil, intermeddle, interfere, interpose, kibitz, tamper with, fool with, get at, nobble, agitate, intrigue.

To overact, overdo, overlay, outdo, ride to death.

(*Phrases*) To look sharp; to lay about one; to have one's hands full; to kick up a dust; to stir one's stumps; to exert one's energies; to put one's best foot foremost; to do one's best; to do all one can; to leave no stone unturned; to have all one's eyes about one; make the best of one's time; not to let the grass grow under one's feet; to make short work of; to seize the opportunity; to come up to the scratch.

To take time by the forelock; to improve the shining hour; to make hay while the sun shines; to keep the pot boiling; to strike while the iron is hot; to kill two birds with one stone; to move heaven and earth; to go through fire and water; to do wonders; to go all lengths; to stick at nothing; to go the whole hog; to keep the ball rolling; to put one's back into it; to make things hum.

To have a hand in; to poke one's nose in; to put in one's oar; to have a finger in the pie; to mix oneself up with; steal a march upon.

(*Adjectives*) Active, brisk, quick, prompt, alert, on the alert, stirring, spry, sharp, smart, quick, nimble, agile, light-footed, tripping, ready, awake, broad awake, wide awake, alive, lively, live, animated, vivacious, frisky, forward, eager, strenuous, zealous, expeditious, enterprising, pushing, pushful, spirited, in earnest, up in arms, go-ahead.

Cause of inactivity (174), sedative, hypnotic, knock-out drops, hypnotism; lullaby.

(*Phrases*) The Castle of Indolence; *dolce far niente;* the Land of Nod; the Fabian policy; *laissez aller*; *laissez faire*; masterly inactivity; the thief of time.

Sleeping partner; waiter on Providence.

(*Verbs*) To be inactive, etc., to do nothing, let alone, lie by, lie idle, stagnate, lay to, keep quiet, hang fire, relax, slouch, loll, drawl, slug, dally, lag, dawdle, potter, lounge, loiter, laze, moon, moon about, loaf, hang about, stooge, mouch; to waste, lose, idle away, kill, trifle away, fritter away or fool away time; trifle, footle, dabble, fribble, peddle, fiddle-faddle.

To sleep, slumber, nod, close the eyes, close the eyelids, doze, drowse, fall asleep, take a nap, go off to sleep, hibernate, aestivate, vegetate.

To languish, expend itself, flag, hang fire.

To render idle, etc.; to sluggardize.

(*Phrases*) To fold one's arms; to let well alone; play truant; while away the time; to rest upon one's oars; to burn daylight; to take it easy; slack off.

To get one's head down; to hit the hay; to have forty winks; to sleep like a top or like a log; to sleep like a dormouse; to swing the lead; to eat the bread of idleness; to twiddle one's thumbs.

(*Adjectives*) Inactive, unoccupied, unemployed, unbusied, doing nothing (685), resourceless.

Indolent, easy-going, lazy, slothful, idle, thowless, fushionless, slack, inert, torpid, sluggish, languid, supine, heavy, dull, stagnant, lumpish, soulless, listless, moony, limp, languorous, exanimate.

Dilatory, laggard, lagging, tardigrade, drawling, creeping, dawdling, faddling, rusty, lackadaisical, fiddle-faddle, shilly-shally, unpractical, unbusiness-like.

Sleepy, dozy, dopy, dreamy,

Working, on duty, at work, hard at work, intent, industrious, up and coming, assiduous, diligent, sedulous, painstaking, business-like, practical, in harness, operose, plodding, toiling, hard-working, fagging, busy, bustling, restless, fussy, fidgety.

Persevering, indefatigable, untiring, unflagging, unremitting, unwearied, never-tiring, undrooping, unintermitting, unintermittent, unflinching, unsleeping, unslumbering, sleepless, persistent.

drowsy, somnolent, dormant, asleep, lethargic, comatose, napping, somniferous, soporific, soporous, soporose, somnific, hypnotic, narcotic, unawakened.

(*Phrases*) With folded arms; *les bras croisés*; with the hands in the pockets; at a loose end.

In the arms or lap of Morpheus.

Meddling, meddlesome, pushing, intermeddling, tampering, etc., officious, over-officious, intriguing, managing.

(*Phrases*) Up and doing; up and stirring; busy as a bee; on the *qui vive*; nimble as a squirrel; the fingers itching; no sooner said than done; *nulla dies sine linea*; a rolling stone gathers no moss; the used key is always bright.

(*Adverbs*) Actively, etc. (684).

(*Interjections*) Look alive! look sharp! get a move on! get cracking! get busy! hump yourself! get weaving!

684 HASTE (*Substantives*), dispatch, precipitancy, precipitation, precipitousness, impetuosity, posthaste, acceleration, spurt, quickness (274).

Hurry, flurry, drive, bustle, fuss, splutter, scramble, brusquerie, fidget, fidgetiness (682).

(*Verbs*) To haste, hasten, urge, press on, push on, bustle, hurry, hustle, buck up, precipitate, accelerate; to bustle, scramble, scuttle, scurry, scoot, plunge, rush, dash on, press on, scorch, speed.

(*Phrases*) To make the most of one's time; to lose not a moment; *festina lente*.

685 LEISURE (*Substantives*), leisureliness, spare time, breathing-space, off-time, slack time, holiday, bank holiday, Sunday, sabbath, vacation, recess, red-letter day, relaxation, rest, repose, halt, pause (142), respite.

(*Phrases*) *Otium cum dignitate*; time to spare; time on one's hands.

(*Verbs*) To have leisure, take one's ease, repose (687), pause.

(*Phrase*) To shut up shop.

(*Adjectives*) Leisurely, undisturbed, quiet, deliberate, calm, slow (683).

(*Adverbs*) Leisurely, etc., at leisure.

(*Adjectives*) Hasty, hurried, precipitate, scrambling, etc., headlong, boisterous, impetuous, brusque, abrupt, slapdash, cursory.

(*Adverbs*) Hastily, etc., headlong, in haste, slapdash, slap-bang, amain, hurry-scurry, helter-skelter, head and shoulders, head over heels, by fits and starts, by spurts.

(*Phrases*) No sooner said than done; a word and a blow.

686 EXERTION (*Substantives*), labour, work, toil, fag, exercise, travail, swink, sweat, exercitation, duty, trouble, pains, ado, drudgery, fagging, slavery, operoseness.

Effort, strain, grind, tug, stress,

687 REPOSE (*Substantives*), rest, halt, pause, relaxation, breathing-space, respite (685).

Day of rest, *dies non*, sabbath, holiday.

(*Verbs*) To repose, rest, relax, take

tension, throw, stretch, struggle, spell, heft.

Gymnastics, gym, physical jerks, P.T.

(*Phrases*) A stroke of work; the sweat of one's brow.

(*Verbs*) To labour, work, exert oneself, toil, strive, use exertion, fag, strain, drudge, moil, take pains, take trouble, trouble oneself, slave, pull, tug, ply the oar, rough it, sweat, bestir oneself, get up steam, get a move on, fall to work, buckle to, stick to.

rest, breathe, take breath, take one's ease, gather breath, recover one's breath, respire, pause, halt, stay one's hand, lay to, lie by, lie fallow, recline, lie down, go to rest, go to bed, go to sleep, etc., unbend, slacken.

(*Phrases*) To rest upon one's oars, to take a holiday; to shut up shop.

(*Adjectives*) Reposing, resting, etc., restful, unstrained; sabbatical.

———

(*Phrases*) To set one's shoulder to the wheel; to strain every nerve; to spare no pains; to do one's utmost or damnedest; to work day and night; to work one's fingers to the bone; to do double duty; to work double tides; to put forth one's strength; to work like a nigger or a horse; to go through fire and water; to put one's best foot forward (682); to do one's level best; to grub along; to lay oneself out.

(*Adjectives*) Labouring, etc., laborious, toilsome, troublesome, operose, herculean, gymnastic, palaestric.

Hard-working, painstaking, energetic, strenuous (682).

(*Adverbs*) Laboriously, lustily, roundly.

(*Phrases*) By the sweat of the brow; with all one's might; *totis viribus*; with might and main; *vi et armis*; tooth and nail; hammer and tongs; through thick and thin; heart and soul.

688 FATIGUE (*Substantives*), lassitude, weariness (841), tiredness, exhaustion, sweat, collapse, prostration, swoon, faintness, faint, *deliquium*, syncope, yawning, anhelation; overstrain.

(*Verbs*) To be fatigued, etc., to droop, sink, flag, wilt, lose breath, lose wind, gasp, pant, pech, puff, yawn, drop, swoon, faint, succumb.

To fatigue, tire, weary, fag, irk, jade, harass, exhaust, knock up, prostrate, wear out, strain, overtask, overwork, overburden, overtax, overstrain, drive, sweat.

(*Adjectives*) Fatigued, tired, unrefreshed, weary, wearied, jaded;

689 REFRESHMENT (*Substantives*), recovery of strength, recruiting, repair, refection, refocillation, relief, bracing, regalement, bait, restoration, revival; pick-up.

(*Phrase*) A giant refreshed.

(*Verbs*) To refresh, recruit, repair, refocillate, give tone, reinvigorate, reanimate, restore, recover.

To recover, regain, renew, etc., one's strength; perk up.

(*Adjectives*) Refreshing, etc., recuperative, tonic; refreshed, etc., untired, unwearied, etc. (682).

———

wayworn; overworked, hard-driven, toilworn, done up.

Breathless, out of breath, windless, out of wind, blown, winded, broken-winded.

Drooping, flagging, faint, fainting, done up, knocked up, exhausted, sinking, prostrate, spent, overspent, dead-beat, dog-tired, fagged out.

Worn out, played out, battered, shattered, weather-beaten, footsore, *hors de combat*, done for.

Fatiguing, etc., tiresome, irksome, wearisome, trying.

(*Phrases*) Ready to drop; tired to death; on one's last legs; run off one's legs; all in.

690 AGENT (*Substantives*), doer, performer, actor, perpetrator, practitioner, operator, hand, employee, commissionaire, executor, executrix, maker, effector, consignee, steward, broker, factor, middleman, jobber.

Artist, workman, workwoman, charwoman, worker, artisan, artificer, architect, craftsman, handicraftsman, mechanic, machinist, machineman, manufacturer, operative, journeyman, labourer, navvy, stevedore, docker, smith, wright, day-labourer, co-worker; *dramatis personae.*

Drudge, hack, fag, man or maid of all work, hired man, hired girl, factotum, handy-man.

(*Phrase*) Hewers of wood and drawers of water.

691 WORKSHOP (*Substantives*), laboratory, manufactory, mill, shop, works, factory, mint, forge, smithy, loom, cabinet, office, bureau, studio, atelier, hive, hive of industry, workhouse, nursery, hothouse, hotbed, kitchen, dock, slip, yard, foundry.

Crucible, alembic, cauldron, matrix.

2°. Complex Voluntary Action

692 CONDUCT (*Substantives*), course of action, practice, drill, procedure, business (625), transaction, dealing, ways, tactics, policy, polity, generalship, statesmanship, economy, strategy, husbandry, seamanship, stewardship, housekeeping, housewifery, *ménage*, regime, *modus operandi*, economy.

Execution, manipulation, handling, treatment, process, working-out, course, campaign, career, walk.

Behaviour, deportment, comportment, carriage, mien, air, demeanour, bearing, manner, observance.

(*Verbs*) To conduct, carry on, run, transact, execute, carry out, work out, get through, carry through, go through, dispatch, treat, deal with, proceed with, officiate, discharge, do duty, play a part or game, run a race.

To behave; to comport, acquit, demean, carry, hold, oneself.

(*Phrases*) To shape one's course; to paddle one's own canoe.

(*Adjectives*) Conducting, etc., strategical, business-like, practical, executive.

693 DIRECTION (*Substantives*), management, government, bureaucracy, statesmanship, conduct (692), regulation, charge, agency, senatorship, ministry, ministration, managery, directorate, directorship, chairmanship, guidance, steerage, pilotage, superintendence, stewardship, supervision, surveillance, proctorship, chair, portfolio, statecraft, politics, *haute politique*, kingcraft, cybernetics; council (696).

Helm, rudder, compass, needle, radar.

(*Phrase*) The reins of government.

(*Verbs*) To direct, manage, govern, guide, conduct, regulate, order, prescribe, brief, steer, con, pilot, have or take the direction, take the helm, have the charge of, administer, superintend, overlook, supervise, look after, see to, control, boss, run, preside, hold office, hold the portfolio.

To head, lead, show the way, etc.

(*Phrase*) To pull the wires.

(*Adjectives*) Directing, etc., managerial, gubernatorial, executive; dirigible.

694 DIRECTOR (*Substantives*), manager, executive, master (745), prime minister, premier, governor, statesman, legislator, controller, comptroller, intendant, superintendent, rector, matron, supervisor, president, preses, chairman, headman, supercargo, inspector, moderator, monitor, overseer, overlooker, shopwalker, taskmaster, leader, ringleader, demagogue, conductor, precentor, fugleman; official, jack-in-office, bureaucrat, minister, office-bearer, red-tapist, officer (726).

Conductor, steersman, helmsman, pilot, coxswain, guide, cicerone, guard, driver, engine-driver, motorman, whip, charioteer, coachman, Jehu, muleteer, teamster, chauffeur, postilion, *vetturino*.

Steward, factor, factotum, bailiff, landreeve, foreman, forewoman, gaffer, charge-hand, whipper-in, shepherd, proctor, procurator, housekeeper, major-domo, chef, master of ceremonies, M.C.

695 ADVICE (*Substantives*), counsel, suggestion, recommendation, advocacy, hortation, exhortation, dehortation, instruction, charge, monition, admonition (668), admonishment, caution, warning, expostulation (616), obtestation, injunction, persuasion.

Guidance, guide, handbook, chart, compass, manual, itinerary, road-book, reference.

An adviser, senator, counsellor, counsel, consultant, specialist, monitor, mentor, Nestor, guide, teacher (540), physician, leech, doctor.

Referee, arbiter, arbitrator, referendary, assessor.

(*Verbs*) To advise, counsel, give advice, recommend, advocate, admonish, submonish, suggest, prompt, caution, warn, forewarn.

To persuade, dehort, exhort, enjoin, expostulate, charge, instruct.

To deliberate, consult together, hold a council, etc., confer, call in, refer to take advice, be closeted with.

(*Phrases*) To lay their heads together; to compare notes; to go into a huddle; to take counsel of one's pillow; to take one's cue from.

(*Adjectives*) Monitory, monitive, admonitory, recommendatory, hortatory, dehortatory, exhortatory, exhortative, warning, etc.

(*Phrases*) A word to the wise; *verb sap*.

(*Interjection*) Go to!

696 COUNCIL (*Substantives*), conclave, court, chamber, cabinet, cabinet council, house, committee, subcommittee, board, bench, brains trust, *comitia*, staff.

Senate, *senatus*, parliament, synod, soviet, convocation, convention, congress, consistory, conventicle, chapter, chapel, witenagemot, junta, states-general, diet, Cortes, Riksdag, Thing, Storthing, Reichsrat, Reichstag, Duma, Politburo, Presidium, Comintern, Sobranje, Skupshtina, Tynewald, divan, durbar, kgotla, indala, Areopagus, sanhedrim, directory.

A meeting, assembly, sitting, session, séance, sederunt.

(*Adjectives*) Senatorial, curule.

697 PRECEPT (*Substantives*), direction, instruction, charge, prescript, prescription, recipe, receipt, order (741).

Rule, canon, code, formula, formulary, law, statute, act, rubric, maxim, apophthegm, etc. (496).

698 SKILL (*Substantives*), skilfulness, cleverness, ability, talent, genius, ingenuity, calibre, capacity, competence, shrewdness, sagacity, parts, endowment, faculty, gift, forte, strong point, turn, invention, headpiece.	**699 UNSKILFULNESS** (*Substantives*), inability, incompetence, incompetency, improficience, improficiency, infelicity, inexpertness, indexterity, unaptness, ineptitude, lefthandedness, awkwardness, maladroitness, clumsiness, gaucherie, rawness,

Address, dexterity, adroitness, aptness, aptitude, facility, felicity, knack,
expertness, quickness, sharpness, re-
sourcefulness, smartness, readiness,
excellence, habilitation, technique,
virtuosity, artistry, ambidexterity,
ambidextrousness, sleight of hand
(545), know-how, knowingness.

Qualification, proficiency, panurgy,
accomplishment, attainment, acquirement, craft, mastery, mastership.

Tact, knowledge of the world,
savoir faire, discretion, finesse,
worldly wisdom.

Prudence, discretion (864).

Art, science, management, tactics,
manœuvring, sleight, trick, policy,
strategy, jobbery, temporization,
technology.

A masterstroke, *chef-d'œuvre*, a
masterpiece, *tour de force*, a bold
stroke, *coup de maître*, a good hit
(650).

(*Verbs*) To be skilful, skilled, etc.,
to excel in, to specialize in, have the
trick of, be master of; to temporize,
manœuvre.

(*Phrases*) To play one's cards well;
to stoop to conquer; to have all one's
wits about one; to keep one's hand
in; to know your stuff; to cut one's
coat according to one's cloth; to
know what one is about; to know
what's what; to know the ropes.

(*Adjectives*) Skilled, skilful, etc.,
clever, able, accomplished, talented,
versatile, many-sided, resourceful,
ingenious, inventive, shrewd, gifted,
hard-headed, sagacious, sharp-
witted.

Expert, crack, dexterous, scientific,
adroit, apt, sharp, handy, deft, fluent,
facile, ready, quick, smart, slick,
spry, yare, nimble, ambidextrous,
neat-handed, fine-fingered.

Conversant, versed, proficient,
efficient, capable, competent, qualified, good at, up to, master of, cut
out for, at home in, knowing.

Experienced, practised, hackneyed,
trained, initiated, prepared, primed,
finished, schooled, thoroughbred,
masterly, consummate.

slovenliness, greenness, inexperience,
disability, disqualification.

Bungling, blundering, etc., blunder (495), *bêtise*; unteachable-
ness, dumbness, dullness, stupidity
(499).

Indiscretion, imprudence (863),
thoughtlessness, giddiness, wildness,
mismanagement, misconduct, mal-
administration, misrule, misgovern-
ment, misapplication, misdirection.

(*Phrases*) Rule of thumb; a bad
show.

(*Verbs*) To be unskilled, unskilful,
etc.

To mismanage, bungle, blunder,
botch, boggle, fumble, flounder,
stumble, muff, foozle, miscue, muddle,
murder, mistake, misapply, misdirect,
misconduct; stultify.

(*Phrases*) To make a mess or hash
of; to begin at the wrong end; to
make sad work or a bad job of; to
put one's foot in it; to lose or miss
one's way; to lose one's balance; to
stand in one's own light; to quarrel
with one's bread and butter; to pay
dear for one's whistle; to cut one's
own throat; to kill the goose which
lays the golden eggs; to reckon without one's host.

(*Adjectives*) Unskilled, etc., unskilful, bungling, etc., awkward,
clumsy, unhandy, unworkmanlike,
unscientific, shiftless, lubberly, *gauche*,
maladroit, left-handed, hobbling,
slovenly, sloppy, slatternly, giddy,
gawky, dumb, dull, unteachable, at
fault.

Unapt, unqualified, inhabile, incompetent, disqualified, untalented,
ill-qualified, inapt, inept, inexpert,
inartistic, raw, green, rusty.

Unaccustomed, unused, unhackneyed, unexercised, untrained, unpractised, undisciplined, uneducated,
undrilled, uninitiated, unschooled,
unconversant, unversed, inexperi-
enced, unstatesmanlike, non-profes-
sional.

Unadvised, misadvised, ill-judged,
ill-advised, unguided, misguided,
foolish, wild, ill-devised, miscon-
ducted.

Technical, artistic, workmanlike, business-like, daedalian.

Discreet, politic, tactful, diplomatic, sure-footed, felicitous, strategic.

(*Phrases*) Up to snuff; sharp as a needle; no flies on him.

(*Adverbs*) Skilfully, etc., aright.

(*Phrases*) His fingers are all thumbs; penny wise and pound foolish.

———

700 PROFICIENT (*Substantives*), adept, expert, specialist, genius, dab, crack, whiz, master, *maître*, masterhand, virtuoso, champion, first string, first fiddle, protagonist, ace, artist, tactician, marksman, old stager, veteran, top-sawyer, picked man, cunning man, conjurer, wizard, etc. (994); connoisseur (850); prodigy (872), an Admirable Crichton.

(*Phrases*) A man of the world; a practised hand; no slouch; a smart customer; an old file; an all-round man.

701 BUNGLER (*Substantives*), blunderer, marplot, greenhorn, lubber, landlubber, fumbler, muddler, duffer, butter-fingers, novice, no conjurer, flat, muff, babe.

(*Phrases*) A poor hand at; no good at; a fish out of the water; a freshwater sailor; the awkward squad; not likely to set the Thames on fire.

———

702 CUNNING (*Substantives*), craft, craftiness, wiliness, artfulness, subtlety, shrewdness, smartness, archness, insidiousness, slyness, opportunism, artificialness, artificiality.

Artifice, stratagem, wile, dodge, subterfuge, evasion, finesse, ruse, diplomacy, jobbery, backstairs influence.

Duplicity, guile, circumvention, chicane, chicanery, sharp practice, Machiavellism, legerdemain, trickery, etc. (545).

Net, toils, trap, etc. (667).

A slyboots, Ulysses, Machiavel, trickster, serpent, fox, intriguer, opportunist, time-server.

(*Verbs*) To be cunning, etc., to contrive, design, manœuvre, gerrymander, finesse, shuffle, wriggle, wangle, intrigue, temporize, overreach (545), circumvent, get round, nobble, undermine.

(*Phrases*) To play a deep game; to steal a march on; to know on which side one's bread is buttered.

703 ARTLESSNESS (*Substantives*), nature, naturalness, simplicity, ingenuousness, *bonhomie*, frankness, naïveté, openness, *abandon*, candour, outspokenness, sincerity, straightforwardness, honesty (939), innocence (946).

(*Phrases*) *Enfant terrible*; a rough diamond; a mere babe.

(*Verbs*) To be artless, etc.

(*Phrases*) To call a spade a spade; not to mince one's words; to speak one's mind; to wear one's heart upon one's sleeve.

(*Adjectives*) Artless, natural, native, plain, simple-minded, ingenuous, candid, untutored, unsophisticated, simple, naïve, sincere, frank (543), open, frank-hearted, open-hearted, above-board, downright, unreserved, guileless, inartificial, undesigning, single-minded, honest, straightforward, outspoken, blunt, matter-of-fact.

———

(*Adjectives*) Cunning, crafty, artful, knowing, wily, sly, fly, pawky, smooth, sharp, smart, slim, feline, subtle, arch, designing, intriguing, contriving, insidious, canny, downy, leery, tricky, deceitful (545), artificial, deep, profound, diplomatic, vulpine, Machiavellian, time-serving.

(*Phrases*) Cunning as a fox; too clever by half; not born yesterday; not to be caught with chaff.

SECTION IV—ANTAGONISM

1°. *Conditional Antagonism*

704 DIFFICULTY (*Substantives*), hardness, toughness, hard work, uphill work, hard task, troublesomeness, laboriousness.

Impracticability, infeasibility, intractability, toughness, perverseness (471).

Embarrassment, awkwardness, perplexity, intricacy, intricateness, entanglement, knot, Gordian knot, labyrinth, net, meshes, maze, etc. (248).

Dilemma, nice point, delicate point, knotty point, stumbling-block, snag, vexed question, crux; *pons asinorum*, poser, puzzle, floorer, teaser, nonplus, quandary, strait, pass, critical situation, crisis, trial, pinch, emergency, exigency, scramble.

Scrape, hobble, fix, hole, lurch, contretemps, hitch, how-d'ye-do, slough, quagmire, hot water, pickle, stew, imbroglio, mess, ado, false position, stand, deadlock, encumbrance, cul-de-sac, impasse.

(*Phrases*) A Herculean task; a labour of Sisyphus; a difficult role to play; a sea of troubles; horns of a dilemma; a peck of troubles; a kettle of fish; a pretty state of things; a handful; 'Ay, there's the rub.'

(*Verbs*) To be difficult, etc.

To meet with, experience, labour under, get into, plunge into, be surrounded by, be encompassed with, be entangled by, struggle, contend against or grapple with difficulties.

To come to a stand, to stick fast, to be set fast, to boggle, flounder, get left.

To render difficult, etc., to embarrass, perplex, put one out, bother, pose, puzzle, floor, nonplus, ravel, entangle, gravel, faze, flummox, run hard.

(*Phrases*) To come to a deadlock; to be at a loss; to get into hot water; to get into a mess; to be bunkered; to weave a tangled web; to fish in troubled waters; to buffet the waves;

705 FACILITY (*Substantives*), practicability, feasibility, practicableness (470).

Ease, easiness, smoothness, tractability, tractableness, ductility, flexibility, malleability, capability, disentanglement, freedom, advantage, vantage-ground.

A cinch, snap, cakewalk, walkover.

(*Phrases*) Plain sailing; smooth water; fair wind; a clear coast; a holiday task; a royal road; child's play; a soft job; a piece of cake.

(*Verbs*) To be easy, etc., to go, flow, swim, or drift with the tide or stream; to do with ease, to throw off.

To render easy, etc., to facilitate, popularize, smooth, ease, lighten, free, clear, disencumber, deobstruct, disembarrass, clear the way, smooth the way, disentangle, unclog, disengage, extricate, unravel, disburden, exonerate, emancipate, free from; to lubricate, etc. (332), relieve (834).

(*Phrases*) To have it all one's own way; to have a walk-over; to win in a canter; to make light (or nothing) of.

To leave a loophole; to open the door to; to pave the way to; to bridge over; to grease the wheels.

(*Adjectives*) Easy, facile, cushy, attainable, handy, practicable, feasible, achievable, performable, possible (470), superable, surmountable, accessible, come-at-able, get-at-able.

Easily managed or accomplished, etc., tractable, manageable, smooth, glib, pliant, yielding, malleable, ductile, flexible, plastic, submissive, docile.

At ease, free, light, unburdened, unencumbered, unloaded, disburdened, disencumbered, disembarrassed, exonerated, unrestrained, unobstructed, unimpeded, untrammelled, at home.

(*Phrases*) The coast being clear; as easy as falling off a log; like taking candy from a child.

to be put to one's shifts; not to know which way to turn; to skate over thin ice.

To lead one a pretty dance; to put a spoke in one's wheel; to leave in the lurch.

Quite at home; in one's element; in smooth water; on velvet.

(*Adverbs*) Easily, etc., swimmingly.

———

(*Adjectives*) Difficult, not easy, hard, stiff, troublesome, toilsome, formidable, laborious, onerous, operose, awkward, unwieldy, beset with or full of difficulties, Herculean, Sisyphean.

Unmanageable, tough, stubborn, hard to deal with, *difficile*, trying, provoking, ill-conditioned, refractory, perverse, crabbed, intractable, against the grain.

Embarrassing, perplexing, delicate, ticklish, pernickety, complicated, intricate, thorny, spiny, knotty, tricky, critical, pathless, trackless, labyrinthine.

Impracticable, not possible, impossible (471), not practicable, not feasible, unachievable, un-come-at-able, inextricable, impassable, innavigable, desperate, insuperable, insurmountable, unplayable.

In difficulty, perplexed, etc., beset, water-logged, put to it, hard put to it, run hard, hard pressed, thrown out, adrift, at fault, abroad, pushed.

Stranded, aground, stuck fast, at bay.

(*Phrases*) At a standstill; at a stand; up against it; up a gum-tree; out of one's depth; at the end of one's tether; in a cleft stick; on a wrong scent; driven from pillar to post; things being come to a pretty pass; at a pinch; between two stools; in the wrong box; in a fix; in a hole; in a tight place; in the cart; in the soup.

(*Adverbs*) With difficulty, hardly, etc., against the stream, against the grain, uphill.

2°. Active Antagonism

706 HINDRANCE (*Substantives*), prevention, preclusion, impedance, retardment, retardation.

Obstruction, stoppage, interruption, interclusion, oppilation, interception, restriction, restraint, inhibition, embargo, blockade, embarrassment.

Interference, interposition, obtrusion, discouragement, chill.

An impediment, hindrance, obstacle, obstruction, bunker, hazard, let, stumbling-block, snag, check, impasse, countercheck, *contretemps*, set-back, hitch, bar, barrier, barrage, barricade, turnpike, wall, dead wall, bulkhead, portcullis, etc. (717), dam, weir, broom, turnstile, tourniquet.

Drawback, objection.

An encumbrance, impedimenta, onus, clog, skid, drag, weight, dead weight, lumber, top-hamper, pack, millstone, incubus, nightmare; trammel, etc. (752).

707 AID (*Substantives*), assistance, help, succour, support, advocacy, relief, advance, furtherance, promotion.

Coadjuvancy, patronage, interest, championship, countenance, favour, helpfulness.

Sustentation, subvention, subsidy, alimentation, nutrition, nourishment, ministration, ministry, accommodation.

Supplies, reinforcements, succours, contingents, recruits; physical support (215); relief, rescue.

(*Phrases*) Corn in Egypt; a *deus ex machina*.

(*Verbs*) To aid, assist, help, succour, support, sustain, uphold, subscribe to, finance, promote, further, abet, advance, foster, cherish, foment; to give, bring, furnish, afford or supply support, etc., to reinforce, recruit, nourish, nurture.

A hinderer, marplot; killjoy, interloper, passenger; opponent (710).

(*Phrases*) A lion in the path; a millstone round one's neck; a wet blanket;
the old man of the sea; *damnosa
hereditas*; back to square one.

(*Verbs*) To hinder, impede, prevent,
preclude, retard, slacken, obviate, fore-
fend, avert, turn aside, ward off, draw
off, cut off, counteract, undermine.

To obstruct, stop, stay, let, make
against, bar, debar, inhibit, scotch,
squash, cramp, restrain, check, stone-
wall, set back, discourage, discountenance, foreclose.

To thwart, traverse, contravene,
interrupt, intercept, interclude, frustrate, defeat, disconcert, embarrass,
baffle, undo, intercept; to balk, un-
sight, cushion, stymie, spoil, mar.

To interpose, interfere, intermeddle,
obtrude (682).

To hamper, clog, cumber, encum-
ber, saddle with, load with, overload,
overlay, lumber, block up, incommode, hustle; to curb, shackle, fetter;
to embog.

(*Phrases*) To lay under restraint; to
tie the hands; to keep in swaddling-
bands.

To stand in the way of; to take the
wind out of one's sails; to break in
upon; to run or fall foul of; to put a
spoke in the wheel; to throw cold
water on; to nip in the bud; to apply
the closure.

(*Adjectives*) Hindering, etc., in the
way of, impedimental, inimical, unfavourable, onerous, burdensome,
cumbrous, intercipient, obstructive.

Hindered, etc., wind-bound, storm-stayed, water-logged, heavy-laden.
Unassisted, unaided, unhelped, unsupported, single-handed, un-
befriended.

(*Phrase*) Prevention is better than cure.

To favour, countenance, befriend,
smile upon, encourage, patronize,
make interest for.

To second, stand by, relieve,
rescue, back, back up, take part
with, side with, to come or pass
over to, to join, to rally round, play
up to.

To serve, do service, minister to,
oblige, humour, cheer, accommodate,
work for, administer to, pander to;
to tend, attend, take care of, wait on,
nurse, dry-nurse, entertain.

To speed, expedite, forward,
quicken, hasten, set forward.

(*Phrases*) To take the part of; consult the wishes of; to take up the
cudgels for; to espouse the cause of;
to enlist under the banners of; to
lend or bear a hand; to hold out a
helping hand; to give one a lift; to do
one a good turn; to see one through;
to take in tow; to pay the piper; to
help a lame dog over the stile; to
give a leg-up.

(*Adjectives*) Aiding, helping, assisting, etc., auxiliary, adjuvant, ancillary, accessory, ministrant, subservient, subsidiary, helpful.

Friendly, amicable, favourable,
propitious, well-disposed, neighbourly.

(*Adverbs*) On or in behalf of; in
the service of; under the auspices of;
hand in hand.

(*Interjections*) Help! save us! à
moi!

708 OPPOSITION (*Substantives*),
antagonism, oppugnancy, oppugnation, counteraction (179), contravention, impugnment, control, clashing, collision, competition, conflict,
rivalry, emulation.

Absence of aid, etc., counterplot
(718).

(*Phrase*) A head wind.

709 CO-OPERATION (*Substantives*),
coadjuvancy, collaboration, concert,
collusion, participation, complicity,
co-efficiency, concurrence (178).

Alliance, colleagueship, freemasonry, joint-stock, co-partnership,
coalition, combine, syndicate (778),
amalgamation, federation, confederation (712).

(*Verbs*) To oppose, antagonize, cross, counteract, control, contravene, countervail, counterwork, contradict, belie, controvert, oppugn, stultify, thwart, counter, countermine, run counter, go against, collide with, clash, rival, emulate, put against, militate against, beat against, stem, breast, encounter, compete with, withstand, to face, face down.

(*Phrases*) To set one's face against; to make a dead set against; to match (or pit) oneself against; to stand out against; to fly in the face of; to fall foul of; to come into collision with; to be or to play at cross-purposes; to kick against the pricks; to buffet the waves; to cut one another's throats; to join issue.

(*Adjectives*) Opposing, etc., adverse, antagonistic, opposed, conflicting, contrary, unfavourable, unfriendly, hostile, inimical; competitive, emulous.

(*Phrases*) Up in arms; at daggers drawn.

(*Phrases*) A helping hand; a long pull.

(*Verbs*) To co-operate, combine, concur, conspire, concert, collaborate, draw or pull together, to join with, collude, unite one's efforts, club together, fraternize, be in league, etc., with, be a party to, to side with.

(*Phrases*) To make common cause; to be in the same boat; to stand shoulder to shoulder; to play into the hands of; to hunt in couples; to hit it off together; to lay their heads together; to play ball.

(*Adjectives*) Co-operating, etc., co-operative, co-operant, in co-operation, etc., in concert, allied, clannish; favourable (707).

Unopposed, unobstructed, unimpeded.

(*Phrase*) Wind and weather permitting.

(*Adverbs*) As one man (488).

———

(*Adverbs*) Against, versus, counter to, against the grain; against the stream, tide, wind, etc., in the way of, in spite of, in despite of, in the teeth of, in the face of, *per contra*; single-handed.

Across, athwart, overthwart.

Though, although (179), even, *quand même*, all the same.

(*Phrases*) In spite of one's teeth; with the wind in one's teeth.

———

710 OPPONENT (*Substantives*), antagonist, adversary, adverse party, opposition, rival, competitor, pacemaker, enemy, foe (891), assailant; malcontent.

711 AUXILIARY (*Substantives*), assistant, adjuvant, adjunct, adjutant, help, helper, helpmate, helpmeet, colleague, partner, side-kick, *confrère*, coadjutor, co-operator, collaborator, co-belligerent, ally, aide-de-camp, accomplice, accessory, stand-in, stooge.

Friend (890), confidant, champion, partisan, right hand, stand-by; adherent, *particeps criminis*, confederate, bottle-holder, second, candle-holder, servant (746); *fidus Achates*.

(*Phrase*) *Deus ex machina*.

———

712 PARTY (*Substantives*), side, partnership, fraternity, sodality, company, society, firm, house, establishment, body, corporation, corporate body, union, association, syndicate, guild, tong, joint concern, combine, trust, cartel.

Fellowship, brotherhood, sisterhood, denomination, communion, community, clan, clanship, club, friendly society, clique, junto, coterie, faction, gang, ring, circle, *camarilla*, cabal, league, confederacy, confederation, federation; *esprit de corps*; alliance, partisanship.

Band, staff, crew, team, set, posse, phalanx, *dramatis personae*.

(*Verbs*) To unite, join, club together, join forces, federate, co-operate, befriend, aid, etc. (707), cement, form a party, league, etc., to be in the same boat.

(*Adjectives*) In partnership, alliance, etc., federal, federated, bounded, banded, linked, cemented, etc., together, embattled.

713 DISCORD (*Substantives*), disagreement (24), variance, difference, divergence, dissent, dissension, misunderstanding, jar, jarring, clashing, friction, odds, dissonance, disaccord.

Disunion, schism, breach, falling out, division, split, rupture, disruption, open rupture, *brouillerie*, feud, vendetta, contentiousness, litigiousness, strife, contention (720); enmity (889).

Dispute, controversy, polemics, quarrel, tiff, spat, *tracasserie*, altercation, imbroglio, bickering, snip-snap, chicanery, squabble, row, she-mozzle, rumpus, racket, fracas, brawl, bear garden, Donnybrook, debate (476).

Litigation, words, war of words, battle of the books, logomachy, wrangling, wrangle, jangle, breach of the peace, declaration of war (722).

Subject of dispute, ground of quarrel, disputed point, vexed question, bone of contention, apple of discord, *casus belli*.

(*Verbs*) To be discordant, etc., to differ, dissent, disagree, clash, jar, to misunderstand one another.

714 CONCORD (*Substantives*), accord, agreement (23), unison, unity, union, good understanding, quiet, peace, conciliation, unanimity (488), harmony, amity, sympathy (897), *entente cordiale*, *rapprochement*, alliance.

(*Phrases*) The bonds of harmony; a happy family; kittens in a basket; a happy band of brothers.

(*Verbs*) To agree, accord, be in unison, etc., to harmonize with, fraternize, stand in with.

(*Phrases*) To understand one another; to see eye to eye with; to hit it off; to keep the peace; to pull together.

(*Adjectives*) Concordant, congenial, agreeing, etc., united, in unison, etc., harmonious, allied, cemented, friendly (888), amicable, fraternal, at peace, peaceful, pacific, tranquil.

(*Phrases*) At one with; with one voice.

———

To fall out, dispute, controvert, litigate, to quarrel, argue, wrangle, squabble, bicker, spar, jangle, nag, brawl; to break with; to declare war.

To embroil, entangle, disunite, set against, pit against; to sow dissension, disunion, discord, etc. among.

(*Phrases*) To be at odds with; to fall foul of; to have words with; to have a bone to pick with; to have a crow to pluck with; to have a chip on one's shoulder; to be at variance with; to be at cross purposes; to join issue; to pick a quarrel with; to part brass rags; to chew the fat or rag; to go to the mat with; to live like cat and dog.

To set by the ears; to put the cat among the pigeons; to sow or stir up contention.

(*Adjectives*) Discordant, disagreeing, differing, disunited, clashing, jarring, discrepant, divergent, dissentient, sectarian, at variance, controversial.

Quarrelsome, disputatious, litigious, litigant, factious, pettifogging, polemic, schismatic; unpacified, unreconciled.

(*Phrases*) At odds; on bad terms; in hot water; at daggers drawn; up in arms; out of tune; at sixes and sevens; at loggerheads; a house divided against itself; no love lost between them.

715 Defiance (*Substantives*), challenge, dare, cartel, daring, war-cry, slogan, college yell, war-whoop.

(*Verbs*) To defy, challenge, dare, brave, beard, bluster, look big.

(*Phrases*) To set at naught; snap the fingers at; to cock a snook at; to bid defiance to; to set at defiance; to hurl defiance at; to double the fist; to show a bold front; to brave it out; to show fight; to throw down the gauntlet or glove; to call out.

(*Adjectives*) Defying, etc., defiant.

(*Adverbs*) In defiance of; with arms akimbo.

(*Interjections*) Come on! let 'em all come! do your worst!

(*Phrase*) *Nemo me impune lacessit.*

716 Attack (*Substantives*), aggression, offence, assault, charge, onset, onslaught, battue, brunt, thrust, pass, passado, cut, sally, inroad, invasion, irruption, incursion, excursion, sortie, *camisade*, storm, storming, boarding, escalade, foray, raid, air raid, *razzia*, dragonnade (619); siege, investment.

Fire, volley, cannonade, barrage, blitz, broadside, bombardment, stonk, hate, raking fire, platoon-fire, fusillade.

Kick, punch (276), lunge, a run at, a dead set at, carte and tierce, a backhander.

An assailant, aggressor, invader.

(*Verbs*) To attack, assault, assail, go for, fall upon, close with, charge, bear down upon, set on, have at, strike at, run at, make a run at, butt, tilt at, poke at, make a pass at, thrust at, stab, bayonet, cut and thrust, pitch into, kick, buffet, bonnet, beat (972), lay about one, lift a hand against, come on, have a fling at, slap on the face, pelt, throw stones, etc., to round on.

To shoot, shoot at, fire at, fire upon, let fly at, brown, pepper, bombard, shell, bomb, dive-bomb, blitz, strafe, prang.

To beset, besiege, lay siege to, invest, beleaguer, open the trenches, invade, raid, storm, board, scale the walls.

To press one hard, be hard upon, drive one hard.

(*Phrases*) To draw the sword against; to launch an offensive; take the offensive; assume the aggressive; make a dead set at.

To give the cold steel to; to lay down a barrage; to pour in a broadside; to fire a volley.

717 Defence (*Substantives*), self-defence, self-preservation, protection, ward, guard, guardianship, shielding, etc., resistance (719), safety (664).

Fence, wall, parapet, dike, ditch, fosse, moat (232), boom, mound, mole, outwork, trench, foxhole, dugout, shelter, Anderson shelter, Morrison shelter, entrenchment, fortification, embankment, bulwark, barbican, battlement, stockade, laager, zareba, abattis, turret, barbette, casemate, muniment, vallum, circumvallation, contravallation, barbedwire entanglement, sunk fence, ha-ha, buttress, abutment, breastwork, portcullis, glacis, bastion, redoubt, rampart.

Hold, stronghold, keep, donjon, palladium, fort, fortress, blockhouse, pillbox, hedgehog, sconce, citadel, tower, castle, capitol, fastness, asylum (666).

Anchor, sheet-anchor.

Shield, armour, buckler, aegis, breastplate, coat of mail, cuirass, hauberk, habergeon, *chevaux de frise*, screen, etc. (666), helmet, tin hat, battle bowler, casque, shako, bearskin, gas-mask, panoply; fender, torpedo-net, paravane, cow-catcher, buffer.

Defender, protector, guardian (664), champion, protagonist, knight errant; garrison, picket.

(*Verbs*) To defend, shield, fend, fence, entrench, guard (664), keep off, keep at bay, ward off, beat off, parry, repel, bear the brunt of, put to flight.

(*Phrases*) To act on the defensive; to maintain one's ground; to stand

(*Adjectives*) Attacking, etc., aggressive, offensive, up in arms.

———

loopholed, sandbagged, castellated, panoplied, proof, bullet-proof, bomb-proof.

at bay; to give a warm reception to.

(*Adjectives*) Defending, etc., defensive, defended, etc., armed, armoured, armour-plated, iron-clad,

(*Phrases*) Armed cap-à-pie; armed to the teeth.
(*Adverbs*) Defensively, on the defence, on the defensive, at bay.

---

718 RETALIATION (*Substantives*), reprisal, retort, come-back, counterstroke, reciprocation, *tu quoque*, recrimination, retribution, counterplot, counterproject, counterblast, *lex talionis*, revenge (919), compensation (30).

(*Phrases*) Tit for tat; a *quid pro quo*; a Roland for an Oliver; diamond cut diamond; the biter bit; catching a Tartar; a game two can play at; hoist with his own petard.

(*Verbs*) To retaliate, retort, cap, reciprocate, recriminate, counter, get even with one, pay off.

(*Phrases*) To turn the tables; to return the compliment; to pay off old scores; to pay in one's own coin; to give as good as one got.

(*Adjectives*) Retaliating, retaliatory, retaliative, recriminatory, recriminative.

(*Interjection*) You're another!

———

719 RESISTANCE (*Substantives*), stand, oppugnation, reluctation, front, repulse, rebuff, opposition (708), disobedience (742), recalcitration.

Strike, industrial action, lockout, tumult, riot, pronunciamento, *émeute*, mutiny.

Revolt, rising, insurrection, rebellion, *coup d'état*, *putsch*.

(*Verbs*) To resist, not to submit, etc., to withstand, stand against, stand firm, make a stand, repugn, reluct, reluctate, confront, grapple with, face down.

To kick, kick against, recalcitrate, lift the hand against (716), repel, repulse, rise, revolt, mutiny.

(*Phrases*) To show a bold front; to make head against; to stand one's ground; to stand the brunt of; to hold one's own; to keep at bay; to stem the torrent; to champ the bit; to sell one's life dearly.

To fly in the face of; to kick against the pricks; to take the bit between one's teeth.

(*Adjectives*) Resisting, etc., resistive, resistant, refractory, mutinous, recalcitrant, rebellious, up in arms, out.

Unyielding, unconquered, indomitable.
(*Interjections*) Hands off! keep off!

---

720 CONTENTION (*Substantives*), contest, struggle, contestation, debate (476), logomachy, paper war, litigation, high words, rivalry, corrivalry, corrivalship, competition, *concours*, gymkhana, race, heat, match, tie, bickering, strife (713).

Wrestling, jiu-jitsu, pugilism, boxing, fisticuffs, spar, prize-fighting, athletics, sports, gymnastics, set-to, round, fracas, row, shindy, scrap, dust, rumpus, shemozzle, stramash,

721 PEACE (*Substantives*), amity, truce, armistice, harmony (714), tranquillity.

(*Phrases*) Piping time of peace; a quiet life.

(*Verbs*) To be at peace, etc., to keep the peace, etc. (714), pacify (723).

(*Adjectives*) Pacific, peaceable, peaceful, tranquil, untroubled, bloodless, halcyon.

———

outbreak, clash, collision, shock, breach of the peace, brawl, Donny-brook (713).

Conflict, skirmish, rencounter, scuffle, encounter, velitation, tussle, scrimmage, scrummage, broil, fray, affray, *mêlée*, affair, brush, bout, fight, battle, combat, action, engagement, battle royal, running fight, free fight, joust, tournament, tourney, pitched battle, death struggle, Armageddon.

Naval engagement, naumachy, sea-fight; air duel, dogfight.

Duel, satisfaction, monomachy, single combat, passage of arms, affair of honour, a triangular duel.

(*Verbs*) To contend, contest, struggle, vie with, emulate, rival, race, race with, outvie, battle with, cope with, compete, join issue, bandy words with, try conclusions with, close with, square, buckle with, spar, box, tussle, fence, wrestle, joust, enter the lists, take up arms, take the field, encounter, struggle with, grapple with, tackle, engage with, pitch into, strive with, fall to, encounter, collide with.

(*Phrases*) Join battle; fall foul of; have a brush with; break the peace; take up the cudgels; unsheath the sword; break a lance; to run a tilt at; give satisfaction; measure swords; exchange shots; lay about one; cut and thrust; fight without the gloves; go on the warpath.

(*Adjectives*) Contending, etc., contentious, combative, bellicose (722); pugilistic, agonistic, competitive, rival, polemical (476), rough-and-tumble.

(*Phrases*) A word and a blow; pull devil, pull baker.

722 WARFARE (*Substantives*), war, hostilities, fighting, etc., arms, the sword, open war, *ultima ratio*, war to the knife.

Battle array, campaign, crusade, expedition, operation, mission, war-path.

Warlike spirit, military spirit, militarism, bellicosity.

The art of war, tactics, strategy, military evolutions, arms, service, campaigning, tented field; Mars, Bellona.

War-cry, slogan, fiery cross, trumpet, clarion, bugle, pibroch, war-whoop, beat of drum, tom-tom; mobilization.

(*Phrases*) The mailed fist; wager of battle.

(*Verbs*) To arm, fight, set to, spar, scrap, tussle, joust, tilt, box, skirmish, fight hand to hand, fence, measure swords, engage, combat, give battle, go to battle, join battle, engage in battle, raise or mobilize troops, declare war, wage war, go to war, come to blows, break a lance with, appeal to arms, appeal to the sword, give satisfaction, take the

723 PACIFICATION (*Substantives*), re-conciliation, accommodation, arrangement, *modus vivendi*, adjustment, terms, amnesty.

Peace-offering, olive-branch, calumet or pipe of peace, preliminaries of peace.

Pacifism, pacificism, appeasement.

Truce, armistice, suspension of arms, of hostilities, etc., convention, *détente*.

Flag of truce, white flag, cartel.

(*Phrases*) Hollow truce; cold war; *pax in bello*.

(*Verbs*) To make peace, pacify, make it up, reconcile, conciliate, pro-pitiate, appease, tranquillize, compose, allay, settle differences, restore harmony, heal the breach.

(*Phrases*) To put up the sword; to sheathe the sword; to beat swords into ploughshares; to bury the hatchet; to smoke the pipe of peace; to close the temple of Janus; to cry quits.

(*Adjectives*) Pacified, etc., pacific, conciliatory.

field, keep the field, fight it out, fight to a finish, spill blood, carry on
war, carry on hostilities, to fight one's way, to serve, to fight like
devils, to sell one's life dearly.
(*Phrases*) To see service; to smell powder; to go over the top.
(*Adjectives*) Contending, etc., unpeaceful, unpacific, contentious,
belligerent, bellicose, jingo, chauvinistic, martial, warlike, military,
militant, soldierly, soldierlike, gladiatorial, chivalrous, in arms, embattled.
(*Phrases*) Together by the ears; sword in hand.
(*Adverbs*) *Pendente lite*, the battle raging, in the cannon's mouth; in the
thick of the fray.
(*Interjections*) To arms! the Philistines be upon thee!

724 MEDIATION (*Substantives*), intervention, interposition, interference,
intermeddling, intercession, parley, negotiation, arbitration, conciliation,
mediatorship, good offices, diplomacy, peace-offering, eirenicon.
A mediator, intermediary, go-between, intercessor, peacemaker, diplomat,
diplomatist, negotiator, troubleshooter, ombudsman.
(*Verbs*) To mediate, intermediate, intercede, interpose, interfere, intervene, negotiate, arbitrate, compromise, meet half-way.
(*Phrase*) To split the difference.

725 SUBMISSION (*Substantives*), surrender, non-resistance, appeasement,
deference, yielding, capitulation, cession.
Homage, obeisance, bow, curtsy, kneeling, genuflexion, prostration, kowtow.
(*Verbs*) To surrender, succumb, submit, yield, give in, bend, cringe, crawl,
truckle to, knuckle down or under, knock under, capitulate, lay down or
deliver up one's arms, retreat, give way, cave in.
(*Phrases*) Beat a retreat; strike one's flag or colours; surrender at discretion; make a virtue of necessity; to come to terms.
To eat humble pie; to eat dirt; to swallow the pill; to kiss the rod; to turn
the other cheek; to lick a person's boots.
(*Adjectives*) Surrendering, etc., non-resisting, unresisting, submissive, downtrodden.
Undefended, untenable, indefensible.

726 COMBATANT (*Substantives*),
belligerent, champion, disputant,
controversialist, litigant, competitor,
rival, corrival, assailant, bully,
bruiser, fighter, duellist, fighting-
man, pugilist, pug, boxer, the fancy,
prize-fighter, fighting-cock, gladiator,
swashbuckler, fire-eater, berserker;
swordsman, wrestler, Amazon, Paladin, son of Mars; staff, *état-major*,
brass hats; militarist.

726A NON-COMBATANT (*Substantives*), civilian; passive resister, conscientious objector, conchy, Cuthbert,
pacifist, pacificist; non-effective.
Quaker, Quirites.
(*Adjectives*) Non-effective.

Warrior, soldier, campaigner, veteran, man-at-arms, redcoat, man in
khaki, Tommy Atkins, tommy, doughboy, G.I., *poilu*, trooper, dragoon,
hussar, grenadier, fusilier, guardsman, lifeguard, lancer, cuirassier, spear-
man, musketeer, carabineer, rifleman, sniper, sharpshooter, *bersagliere*;

ensign, standard-bearer, halberdier; private, subaltern, conscript, recruit, cadet; effectives, line, rank and file, cannon fodder, P.B.I.

Engineer, artilleryman, gunner, cannoneer, bombardier, sapper, miner; archer, bowman.

Paratrooper, aircraftman, erk, pilot, observer, aircrew.

Marine, jolly, leatherneck; seaman, bluejacket, tar, A.B.

Guerrilla, Maquis, partisan, cossack, sepoy, gurkha, spahi, janizary, zouave, bashi-bazouk.

Armed force, the army, the military, regulars, soldiery, infantry, mounted infantry, fencibles, volunteers, territorials, yeomanry, cavalry, artillery, guns, tanks, armour, commando.

Militia, irregulars, *francs-tireurs*, Home Guard, train-band.

Legion, phalanx, myrmidons, squadron, wing, group, troop, cohort, regiment, corps, platoon, battalion, unit, mob, company (72), column, detachment, brigade, division, garrison, battle array, order of battle.

727 ARMS (*Substantives*), weapons, armament, armour, armoury, quiver, arsenal, magazine, armature.

Mail, chain-mail, lorication; ammunition, powder, gunpowder, gun-cotton, dynamite, gelignite, T.N.T., cordite, lyddite, cartridge, cartouche (635).

Artillery, park, ordnance piece, gun, cannon, swivel, howitzer, carronade, culverin, field-piece, machine-gun, Gatling, Maxim, submachine-gun, tommygun, mitrailleuse, pom-pom, mortar, grenade, petronel, petard, falconet.

Fire-arms, side-arms, stand of arms, musketry, musket, smooth-bore, muzzle-loader, firelock, match-lock, flint-lock, fowling-piece, rifle, revolver, six-shooter, carbine, blunderbuss, pistol, gat, rod, betsy, automatic pistol, derringer, Winchester, Lee-Metford, Mauser, Bren gun, Bofors, Sten gun, Lewis gun, bazooka.

Bow, arquebus (or harquebus), cross-bow, sling, catapult.

Missile, projectile, shot, round-shot, ball, shrapnel; grape, grape-shot, chain-shot, bullet, stone, shell, gas-shell, bomb, land-mine, block-buster, flying bomb, buzz-bomb, doodlebug, guided missile, V1, V2, atomic bomb, hydrogen bomb, torpedo, rocket, ballistics.

Pike, lance, spear, javelin, assagai, dart, arrow, reed, shaft, bolt, boomerang, harpoon.

Bayonet, sword, sabre, broadsword, cutlass, falchion, scimitar, rapier, skean, toledo, tuck, claymore, kris (or creese), dagger, dirk, hanger, poniard, stiletto, stylet, dudgeon, axe, bill, pole-axe, battle axe, halberd, tomahawk, bowie-knife, snickersnee, yataghan, kukri.

Club, mace, truncheon, staff, bludgeon, cudgel, knobkerrie, life-preserver, knuckle-duster, shillelagh, bat, cosh, sandbag, lathi.

Catapult, battering-ram; tank.

728 ARENA (*Substantives*), field, walk, battle-field, field of battle, lists, palaestra, campus, playing field, recreation ground, playground, course, cinder-track, dirt-track, gridiron, diamond, pitch, links, rink, court, platform, stage, boards, racecourse, *corso*, circus, ring, cockpit, bear garden, scene of action, theatre of war, the enemy's camp, amphitheatre, hippodrome, coliseum (or colosseum), proscenium.

Section V—Results of Voluntary Action

729 COMPLETION (*Substantives*), accomplishment, performance, fulfilment, fruition, execution, achievement, dispatch, work done, superstructure, finish, termination, denouement, catastrophe, conclusion, culmination, climax, consummation, *fait accompli*, winding up, the last stroke, finishing stroke, *coup de grâce*, last finish, final touch, crowning touch, coping-stone, end (67), arrival (292), completeness (52).

(*Verbs*) To complete, effect, perform, do, execute, go through, accomplish, fulfil, discharge, achieve, compass, effectuate, dispatch, knock off, close, terminate, conclude, finish, end (67), consummate, elaborate, bring about, bring to bear, bring to pass, get through, carry through, bring through, bring off, pull off, work out, make good, carry out, wind up, dispose of, bring to a close, termination, conclusion, etc.

730 NON-COMPLETION (*Substantives*), inexecution, shortcoming (304), non-fulfilment, non-performance, neglect; incompleteness (53); a drawn battle or game, a draw, a stalemate.

(*Phrase*) The web of Penelope; one swallow does not make a summer.

(*Verbs*) Not to complete, perform, etc., to fall short of, leave unfinished, let slip, lose sight of, neglect, leave undone, etc., draw.

(*Phrases*) To scotch the snake, not kill it; hang fire; do by halves.

(*Adjectives*) Not completed, etc., uncompleted, incomplete, unfinished, left undone (53), short, unaccomplished, unperformed, unexecuted.

In progress, in hand, proceeding, going on, on the stocks.

(*Adverbs*) *Re infecta*; *nihil fit.*

To perfect, bring to perfection, stamp, put the seal to, polish off, crown.

To reach, arrive (292), touch, reach, attain the goal; to run one's race.

(*Phrases*) To give the last finish or finishing touch; to be through with; to get it over; to deliver the goods; to shut up shop.

(*Adjectives*) Completing, final, terminal, concluding, conclusive, exhaustive, crowning, etc., done, completed, wrought.

(*Phrases*) It is all over; *finis coronat opus; actum est.*

(*Adverbs*) Completely, etc. (52), out of hand, effectually, with a vengeance, with a witness.

---

731 SUCCESS (*Substantives*), successfulness, speed, thrift, advance, luck, good fortune (734), godsend, prize, windfall, trump card, hit, stroke, lucky strike, break; lucky or fortunate hit; bold stroke, masterstroke, *coup de maître*, knock-out blow (698), checkmate.

Continued success, run of luck, time well spent, tide, flood, high tide, heyday.

Advantage over, ascendancy, mastery, conquest, subdual, victory, subjugation, triumph, exultation (884).

732 FAILURE (*Substantives*), unsuccess, non-success, disappointment, blow, frustration, inefficacy, discomfiture, abortion, miscarriage, lost trouble; vain, ineffectual, or abortive attempt or effort.

A mistake, error, blunder, fault, miss, oversight, blot, slip, trip, stumble, claudication, breakdown, false step, wrong step, howler, floater, clanger, boner, *faux pas, bêtise*, titubation, scrape, botch, bungle, foozle, mess, washout, stalemate, botchery, fiasco, flop, frost, sad work, bad job, bad show, want of skill.

A conqueror, victor, winner.

(*Phrase*) A feather in one's cap.

(*Verbs*) To succeed, to be successful, to come off successful, to be crowned with success, to come or go off well, catch on, to thrive, speed, prosper, bloom, blossom, flourish, go on well, be well off.

To gain, attain, carry, secure, or win a point or object; to triumph, be triumphant, etc.; to surmount, overcome, conquer, master, or get over a difficulty or obstacle; to score, make a hit.

To advance (282), come on, get on, gain ground, make one's way, make progress, progress, worry along, get by.

To bring to bear, to bring about, to effect, accomplish, complete (729), manage, contrive to, make sure; to reap, gather, etc., the benefit of.

To master, get the better of, conquer, subdue, subjugate, quell, reduce, overthrow, overpower, vanquish, get under; get or gain the ascendancy, obtain a victory; to worst, defeat, beat, lick, drub, trim, settle, floor, knock out, put down, trip up, beat hollow, checkmate, nonsuit, trip up the heels of, capsize, shipwreck, ruin, kibosh, do for, victimize, put to flight, drown, etc.; to roll in the dust, to trample under foot, to wipe the floor with.

To baffle, disconcert, frustrate, confound, discomfit, dish, foil, outgeneral, outmanœuvre, outflank, outwit, overreach, balk, outvote, circumvent, score off, catch napping.

To answer, succeed, work well, turn out well.

(*Phrases*) To sail before the wind; to swim with the tide; to stem the torrent; to turn a corner; to weather a point; to fall on one's legs or feet; *se tirer d'affaire*; to take a favourable turn; to turn up trumps; to have the ball at one's feet; to come off with flying colours; to win or gain the day; to win the palm; to win one's spurs; to breast the tape; to bear away the bell.

To get the upper hand; to gain an

Mischance, mishap, misfortune, misadventure, disaster, bad or hard luck (735).

Repulse, rebuff, set-down, defeat, fall, downfall, rout, discomfiture, collapse, smash, crash, wreck, perdition, shipwreck, ruin, subjugation, overthrow, death-blow, quietus, knock-out, destruction.

A victim, loser, bankrupt, insolvent (808).

(*Phrases*) A losing game; a flash in the pan; a wild-goose chase; a mare's-nest; a fool's errand.

(*Verbs*) To fail, to be unsuccessful, etc., to come off badly, go badly, go amiss, abort, go wrong, fall flat, flop, fall through, fizzle out, turn out ill, work ill, lose ground, recede (283), fall short of (304), prang (162, 176).

To miss, miss one's aim; to labour, toil, etc., in vain; to lose one's labour, flounder, limp, miss one's footing, miscarry, abort; to make vain, ineffectual, or abortive efforts; to make a slip; to make or commit a mistake, commit a fault, make a mess of; to botch, make a botch of, bungle, foozle.

To be defeated, overthrown, foiled, worsted, let down, etc.; to break down, sink, drown, founder, go to ruin, etc., fall, slip, tumble, stumble, falter, be capsized, run aground, pack up, crock up, collapse.

(*Phrases*) To come to nothing; to end in smoke; to slip through one's fingers; to hang fire; to miss fire; to miss stays; to flash in the pan; to split upon a rock; to go to the wall; to have had it; to take a back seat; to get the worst of it; to go to the dogs; to go to pot; to be all up with; to be in the wrong box; to stand in one's own light; to catch a Tartar; to get hold of the wrong sow by the ear; to burn one's fingers; to shoot at a pigeon and kill a crow; to beat the air; to tilt against windmills; to roll the stone of Sisyphus; to fall between two stools; to pull a boner; to come a cropper or mucker.

(*Adjectives*) Unsuccessful, failing, etc., unfortunate, in a bad way,

advantage; to get the whip-hand of; to have on the hip; to get the start of; to have a run of luck; to make a hit; to make a killing; to score a success; to reap or gather the harvest; to strike oil; to give a good account of oneself; to carry all before one; to put to rout; to cook one's goose; to settle one's hash.

(*Adjectives*) Succeeding, etc., successful, home and dry, prosperous, felicitous, blooming, etc., set up, triumphant, victorious, cock-a-hoop.

Unfoiled, unbeaten, unsubdued, etc. Effective, well-spent.

(*Phrases*) Flushed with success; one's star being in the ascendant; the spoilt child of fortune.

(*Adverbs*) Successfully, etc., triumphantly, with flying colours, in truimph, *à merveille*, to good purpose.

(*Phrase*) *Veni, vidi, vici.*

unlucky, luckless, out of luck, ill-fated, ill-starred, disastrous.

Unavailing, abortive, addle, still-born, fruitless, bootless, ineffectual, stickit, unattained, lame, hobbling, impotent, futile.

Aground, grounded, swamped, stranded, cast away, wrecked, on the rocks, foundered, capsized, torpedoed, shipwrecked.

Defeated, overcome, overthrown, overpowered, mastered, worsted, vanquished, conquered, subjugated, routed, silenced, distanced, foiled, unhorsed, baffled, befooled, dished, tossed about, stultified, undone, done for, down and out, ruined, circumvented, planet-struck, nonplussed.

(*Phrases*) At a loss; wide of the mark; not having a leg to stand upon; ruined root and branch; the sport of fortune; bitched, bothered, and bewildered; hoist by one's own petard; left in the lurch; out of the running.

(*Adverbs*) Unsuccessfully, etc., in vain, to no purpose, all up with. (*Phrases*) The game is up; all is lost.

733 TROPHY (*Substantives*), laurel, palm, crown, bays, wreath, garland, chaplet, civic crown, medal, ribbon, cup, scalp, prize, award, oscar, triumphal arch, ovation, triumph (883), flourish of trumpets, flying colours.

(*Phrase*) A feather in one's cap.

734 PROSPERITY (*Substantives*), affluence (803), success (731), thrift, good fortune, welfare, well-being, felicity, luck, good luck, a run of luck, fair weather, sunshine, fair wind, a bed of roses, palmy days, the smiles of fortune, halcyon days, *Saturnia regna*, golden age.

An upstart, parvenu, *nouveau riche*, profiteer, skipjack, mushroom, self-made man.

A made man, a lucky dog.

(*Phrase*) A roaring trade.

(*Verbs*) To prosper, thrive, flourish, be well off; to flower, blow, blossom, bloom, fructify.

(*Phrases*) To feather one's nest; to line one's pockets; to make one's pile; to bask in the sunshine; to rise in the world; to make one's way; to better oneself; to light on one's feet.

735 ADVERSITY (*Substantives*), bad, ill, evil, adverse, etc., fortune, hap, or luck, tough luck, hard lines, reverse, set-back, come-down, broken fortunes, falling or going down in the world, hard times, iron age, evil day, rainy day.

Fall, ruin, ruination, ruinousness, undoing, mishap, mischance, misadventure, misfortune, disaster, calamity, catastrophe (619), failure (732); a hard life; trouble, hardship, blight, curse, evil star, evil genius, evil dispensation.

(*Phrases*) The frowns of fortune; the ups and downs of life; a black look-out; the time being out of joint.

(*Verbs*) To be ill off; to decay, sink, go under, fall, decline, come down in the world, lose caste; to have had it.

(*Adjectives*) Prosperous, fortunate, lucky, well-off, well-to-do, bein, affluent, solvent (803), thriving, set up, prospering, etc., blooming, palmy, halcyon.

Auspicious, propitious, in a fair way.

(*Phrases*) Born with a silver spoon in one's mouth; the spoilt child of fortune; in clover; on velvet; in luck's way.

(*Adverbs*) Prosperously, etc., swimmingly.

(*Adjectives*) Unfortunate, unlucky, luckless, untoward, ill-off, badly off, decayed, ill-fated, ill-starred, impecunious, necessitous (804), bankrupt (808), unprosperous, adverse, untoward.

Disastrous, calamitous, ruinous, dire, deplorable, etc.

(*Phrases*) Down on one's luck; in a bad way; in poor shape; having seen better days; born with a wooden ladle in one's mouth; one's star on the wane; from bad to worse; down and out.

736 MEDIOCRITY (*Substantives*), the golden mean, *aurea mediocritas*, moderation (174), moderate circumstances; the middle classes, bourgeoisie.

(*Adjectives*) Tolerable, fair, middling, passable, average, so-so, ordinary, mediocre; middle-class, bourgeois.

(*Verbs*) To keep a middle course, jog on, get along, get by.

(*Phrase*) *Medio tutissimus ibis.*

DIVISION II—INTERSOCIAL VOLITION

SECTION I—GENERAL INTERSOCIAL VOLITION

737 AUTHORITY (*Substantives*), influence, patronage, credit, power, prerogative, control, jurisdiction, censorship, authoritativeness, absoluteness, despotism, absolutism, tyranny.

Command, empire, sway, rule, dominion, domination, supremacy, sovereignty, suzerainty, lordship, headship, seigniory, seigniorship, mastery, mastership, office, government, administration, gubernation, empire, body politic, accession.

Hold, grasp, gripe, grip, reach, fang, clutches, talons, helm, reins.

Reign, dynasty, regime, directorship, proconsulship, prefecture, caliphate, seneschalship, magistrature, magistracy, presidency, presidentship, premiership.

Empire, autocracy, monarchy, kinghood, kingship, royalty, regality, kingcraft, aristocracy, oligarchy, feudalism, republic, republicanism, democracy, socialism, demagogy, ochlocracy, mobocracy, mob-rule, dictatorship of proletariat, ergatocracy, collectivism, communism, Bolshevism,

738 Absence of authority.

LAXITY (*Substantives*), laxness, licence, licentiousness, relaxation, looseness, loosening, slackness, toleration, *laissez-faire*, remission, liberty (748).

Misrule, anarchy, interregnum.

Deprivation of power, dethronement, deposition, usurpation.

Denial of authority: anarchism, nihilism; insubordination, mutiny (742).

Anarchist, nihilist, usurper, mutineer.

(*Phrases*) A dead letter; *brutum fulmen.*

(*Verbs*) To be lax, etc., to hold a loose rein, tolerate, to relax, to misrule.

To dethrone.

(*Phrases*) To give a loose rein to; to give rope enough.

(*Adjectives*) Lax, permissive, loose, slack, remiss, relaxed, licensed, reinless, unbridled, anarchic, anarchical, nihilistic.

Unauthorized (925).

bureaucracy, bumbledom, syndicalism, militarism, stratocracy, *imperium in imperio*, dictatorship, protectorate, protectorship, directorate, directory, executive, raj.

Limited monarchy, constitutional government, representative government, home rule, diarchy (or dyarchy), duumvirate, triumvirate.

Vicarious authority (755, 759).

Gynarchy, gynaecocracy, petticoat government, matriarchy; patriarchy, patriarchism.

(*Verbs*) To have, hold, possess, or exercise authority, etc.

To be master, etc.; to have the control, etc.; to overrule, override, overawe, dominate.

To rule, govern, sway, command, control, direct, administer, lead, preside over, boss; to dictate, reign, hold the reins; to possess or be seated on the throne; to ascend or mount the throne; to sway or wield the sceptre.

(*Phrases*) To have the upper hand; to have the whip-hand; to bend to one's will; to have one's own way; to rule the roast; to lay down the law; to be cock of the roost; to have under the thumb; to keep under; to lead by the nose; to wear the breeches; to have the ball at one's feet; to play first fiddle.

(*Adjectives*) Ruling, etc., regnant, dominant, paramount, supreme, authoritative, executive, gubernatorial, administrative, official.

Imperial, regal, sovereign, royal, royalist, kingly, monarchical, imperatorial, princely, baronial, feudal, seigneurial, seigniorial, aristocratic, democratic, etc.; totalitarian, ultramontane, absolutist.

Imperative, peremptory, arbitrary, absolute, overruling.

(*Adverbs*) In the name of, by the authority of, in virtue of, at one's command, under the auspices of, under the aegis of, *ex officio*, *ex cathedra*.

---

739 SEVERITY (*Substantives*), strictness, rigour, rigidity, rigidness, sternness, stringency, austerity, inclemency, harshness, acerbity, stiffness, rigorousness, inexorability.

Arbitrary power, absolutism, despotism, dictatorship, autocracy, domineering, tyranny; Moloch.

Assumption, usurpation.

A tyrant, disciplinarian, martinet, stickler, despot, oppressor, hard master; King Stork.

(*Phrases*) Iron rule; reign of terror; mailed fist; martial law; blood and iron; tender mercies; red tape.

740 LENITY (*Substantives*), mildness, lenience, leniency, gentleness, indulgence, clemency, tolerance, forbearance.

(*Verbs*) To be lenient, etc., to tolerate, indulge, spoil, bear with, to allow to have one's own way, to let down gently.

(*Adjectives*) Lenient, mild, gentle, soft, indulgent, tolerant, easy-going, clement.

(*Phrase*) Live and let live.

(*Verbs*) To be severe, etc.; to assume, usurp, arrogate, take liberties; to hold or keep a tight hand; to bear or lay a heavy hand on; to be down on; to dictate; to domineer, bully, oppress, override, tyrannize.

(*Phrases*) To lord it over; to carry matters with a high hand; to ride roughshod over; to rule with a rod of iron; to put on the screw; to deal faithfully with; to keep a person's nose to the grindstone.

(*Adjectives*) Severe, strict, rigid, stern, stiff, dour, strait-laced, rigorous, exacting, stringent, hard and fast, peremptory, absolute, positive, uncompromising, harsh, austere, arbitrary, haughty, overbearing.

arrogant, autocratic, bossy, dictatorial, imperious, domineering, tyranni-
cal, masterful, obdurate, unyielding, inflexible, inexorable, exigent,
inclement, Spartan, Rhadamanthine, Draconian.
(*Adverbs*) Severely, etc., with a heavy hand.

741 COMMAND (*Substantives*), order, fiat, bidding, dictum, hest, behest, call,
beck, nod, message, direction, injunction, charge, instructions, appointment,
demand, exaction, imposition, requisition, requirement, claim, reclamation,
revendication.

Dictation, dictate, mandate, caveat, edict, decree, decretal, enactment,
precept, prescript, writ, rescript, law, ordinance, ordination, bull, regulation,
prescription, brevet, placet, ukase, firman, warrant, passport, mittimus,
mandamus, summons, subpoena, interpellation, citation, word of command.

(*Verbs*) To command, to issue a command, order, give order, bid, require,
enjoin, charge, claim, call for, demand, exact, insist on, make a point of,
impose, entail, set, tax, prescribe, direct, brief, appoint, dictate, ordain,
decree, enact; to issue or promulgate a decree, etc.

To cite, summon, call for, call up, send for, requisition, subpoena; to set
or prescribe a task, to set to work, to give the word of command, to call
to order.

(*Phrase*) The decree is gone forth.
(*Adjectives*) Commanding, etc., authoritative, peremptory, decretive, de-
cretory (737).
(*Adverbs*) By order, with a dash of the pen.
(*Phrase*) Le roy le veult.

742 DISOBEDIENCE (*Substantives*),
non-compliance, insubordination,
contumacy, defection, infringement,
infraction, violation; defiance (715),
resistance (719), non-observance
(773).

Rising, insurrection, revolt, *coup
d'état*, *putsch*, rebellion, turn-out,
strike, riot, riotousness, mutinous-
ness, mutiny, tumult, sedition,
treason, lese-majesty.

An insurgent, mutineer, rebel,
rioter, traitor, apostate, renegade,
seceder, quisling, fifth columnist;
carbonaro, sansculotte, *frondeur*; agi-
tator, demagogue, Jack Cade, Wat
Tyler; ringleader.

(*Verbs*) To disobey, violate, infringe, resist (719), defy (715), turn
restive, shirk, kick, strike, mutiny,
rise, rebel, secede, lift the hand
against, turn out, come out, go on
strike.

(*Phrases*) To champ the bit; to
kick over the traces; to unfurl the
red flag.

(*Adjectives*) Disobedient, resisting,
rebellious, unruly, unsubmissive, un-

743 OBEDIENCE (*Substantives*),
submission, non-resistance, passiveness, resignation, cession, compliance,
surrender (725), subordination, deference, loyalty, devotion, allegiance,
obeisance, homage, fealty, prostration, kneeling, genuflexion, curtsy,
kotow, salaam, submissiveness, obsequiousness (886), servitorship, subjection (749).

(*Verbs*) To be obedient, etc.; to
obey, submit, succumb, give in, knock
under, cringe, yield (725), comply,
surrender, follow, give up, give way,
resign, bend to, bear obedience to.

To kneel, fall on one's knees, bend
the knee, curtsy, kowtow, salaam,
bow, pay homage to.

To attend upon, tend; to be under
the orders of, to serve.

(*Phrases*) To kiss the rod; to do
one's bidding; to play second fiddle;
to take it lying down; to dance
attendance on.

(*Adjectives*) Obedient, submissive,
resigned, passive, complying, compliant, loyal, faithful, devoted, yielding, docile, tractable, amenable,

governable, uncomplying, uncompliant, restive, insubordinate, contumacious, mutinous, riotous, seditious, disaffected, recusant, recalcitrant, refractory, naughty.

Unbidden, unobeyed, a dead letter.

(*Phrase*) The grey mare being the better horse.

biddable, unresisting, henpecked; restrainable, unresisted.

———

744 Compulsion (*Substantives*), coercion, coaction, force, constraint, enforcement, press, *corvée*, conscription, levy, duress, brute force, main force, *force majeure*, the sword, club law, *ultima ratio*, *argumentum baculinum*.

(*Verbs*) To compel, force, make, drive, coerce, constrain, steam-roller, enforce, put in force, oblige, force upon, press, conscribe, extort, put down, bind, pin down, bind over, impress, commandeer, requisition.

(*Phrases*) To cram down the throat; to take no denial; to insist upon; to make a point of.

(*Adjectives*) Compelling, etc., compulsory, compulsatory, obligatory, forcible, coercive, coactive, peremptory, rigorous, stringent, inexorable (739); being fain to do, having to do.

(*Adverbs*) By force, perforce, under compulsion, *vi et armis*, in spite of one's teeth; *bon gré, mal gré*; willy-nilly, *nolens volens*; *de rigueur*.

745 Master (*Substantives*), lord, laird, chief, leader, captain, skipper, mate, protagonist, coryphaeus, head, chieftain, commander, commandant, director (694), captain of industry, ruler, potentate, dictator, liege, sovereign, monarch, autocrat, despot, tyrant, *führer, duce*, demagogue, ringleader, boss, big shot, fugleman.

Crowned head, emperor, king, majesty, tetrarch, *imperator*, protector, president, stadtholder, governor.

Caesar, czar, sultan, soldan, caliph, sophy, khan, cacique, inca, lama, mogul, imam, shah, khedive, pasha (or bashaw), dey, cham, judge, aga, hospodar, mikado, shogun, tycoon, exarch.

Prince, seignior, highness, archduke, duke, marquis, earl, viscount, baron (875), margrave, landgrave, palatine, elector, doge, satrap, rajah, maharajah, emir, bey, effendi, nizam, nawab, mandarin, sirdar, ameer, sachem, sagamore.

Empress, queen, czarina, sultana, princess, duchess, marchioness, countess, viscountess, baroness, infanta, ranee, maharanee, margravine, etc.

Military authorities, marshal, field-marshal, *maréchal*, generalissimo,

746 Servant (*Substantives*), servitor, employee, attaché, secretary, subordinate, clerk, retainer, vassal, protégé, dependant, hanger-on, pensioner, client, emissary, *âme damnée*.

Retinue, cortège, staff, court, train, entourage, clientele, suite.

An attendant, squire, henchman, led captain, chamberlain, follower, usher, page, train-bearer, domestic, help, butler, footman, lackey, flunkey, parlour-man, valet, waiter, *garçon*, equerry, groom, jockey, ostler (or hostler), stable-boy, tiger, buttons, boot-boy, boots, livery servant, hireling, mercenary, underling, menial, gillie, under-strapper, journeyman, whipper-in, bailiff, castellan, seneschal, majordomo, cup-bearer, bottle-washer, scout, gyp.

Serf, villein, slave, galley-slave, thrall, peon, helot, bondsman, *adscriptus glebae*, wage-slave.

A maid, handmaid, abigail, chamber-maid, lady's maid, housekeeper, lady help, soubrette, *fille de chambre*, parlour-maid, housemaid, between-maid, kitchen-maid, nurse, *bonne*, scullion, laundress, bed-maker, skivvy, slavey, daily.

(*Verbs*) To serve, attend upon, dance attendance, wait upon, squire, valet.

commander-in-chief, admiral, commodore, general, lieutenant-general, major-general, brigadier, colonel, lieutenant-colonel, officer, captain, major, lieutenant, adjutant, midshipman, quartermaster, aide-de-camp, ensign, cornet, cadet, subaltern, non-commissioned officer, drum-major, sergeant-major, sergeant, corporal, air-marshal, group-captain, wing-commander, squadron-leader, flight-lieutenant, centurion, *seraskier*, hetman, subahdar, *condottiere*.

(*Adverbs*) In one's pay or employ, in the train of.

———

Civil authorities, mayor, prefect, chancellor, provost, magistrate, syndic, alcade (or alcayde), burgomaster, *corregidor*, sheik, seneschal, burgrave, alderman, warden, constable (965), beadle, alguazil, kavass, tribune, consul, proconsul, quaestor, praetor, aedile, archon, polemarch.

Statesman, politician, statist, legislator, lawgiver.

President, chairman, speaker, moderator, vice-president, comptroller, director (694), monitor, monitress.

747 Ensign, or badge of authority.

SCEPTRE (*Substantives*), regalia, insignia (550), crown, coronet, rod of empire, orb, mace, *fasces*, wand, baton, truncheon, staff, insignia (550), portfolio.

A throne, chair, divan, dais, woolsack.

Diadem, tiara, ermine, purple, signet, seals, keys, talisman, cap of maintenance, toga, robes of state, decoration.

748 FREEDOM (*Substantives*), independence, liberty, licence (760), self-government, autonomy, scope, range, latitude, play, swing, free play, elbow-room, *lebensraum*, margin.

Franchise, immunity, exemption, emancipation (750), naturalization, denizenship.

Freeland, freehold, allodium (780).

A freeman, freedman, denizen.

(*Phrases*) The four freedoms; *liberté, egalité, fraternité*; a place in the sun; Liberty Hall.

(*Verbs*) To be free, to have scope, etc.

To render free, etc., to free, to emancipate, enfranchise (750), naturalize.

(*Phrases*) To have the run of; to have one's own way; to have one's fling; to stand on one's own feet; to stand on one's rights; to have a will of one's own; to paddle one's own canoe; to play a lone hand.

To take a liberty; to make free with; to take the bit between one's teeth.

749 SUBJECTION (*Substantives*), dependence, thrall, thraldom, subjugation, subordination, bondage, serfdom, servitude, slavery, vassalage, villeinage, service, clientship, liability (177), enslavement, tutelage, constraint (751).

Yoke, harness, collar.

(*Verbs*) To be subject, dependent, etc., to fall under, obey, serve (743).

To subject, subjugate, enthral, enslave, keep under, control, etc. (751), to reduce to slavery, mediatize, break in.

(*Phrases*) To drag a chain; not dare to call one's soul one's own; to be led by the nose; to be or lie at the mercy of.

To keep in leading strings.

(*Adjectives*) Subject, subordinate, dependent, subjected, in subjection to, in thrall to, feudatory, feudal, enslaved, a slave to, at the mercy of, downtrodden, overborne, henpecked, enthralled, controlled, constrained (751).

(*Phrases*) Under the thumb of; at the feet of; tied to the apron-

(*Adjectives*) Free, independent, loose, at large, unconstrained, unrestrained, unchecked, unobstructed, unconfined, unsubdued, unsubjugated, self-governed, autonomous, self-supporting, untrammelled, unbound, uncontrolled, unchained, unshackled, unfettered, uncurbed, unbridled, unrestricted, unmuzzled, unbuttoned, unforced, uncompelled, unbiased, spontaneous, unhindered, unthwarted, heart-whole, uncaught, unenslaved, unclaimed, ungoverned, resting.

Free and easy, at ease, *dégagé*, wanton, rampant, irrepressible, unprevented, unvanquished, exempt, freehold, allodial, enfranchised, emancipated, released, disengaged (750), out of hand.

(*Phrases*) Free as air; one's own master; *sui juris*; a law to oneself; on one's own; a cat may look at a king.

strings of; the puppet, sport, plaything of.

---

750 LIBERATION (*Substantives*), disengagement, release, enlargement, emancipation, affranchisement, enfranchisement, manumission, discharge, dismissal.

Escape (671), deliverance (672), redemption, extrication, absolution, acquittance, acquittal (970).

Licence, toleration; parole, ticket of leave.

(*Verbs*) To gain, obtain, acquire, etc., one's liberty, freedom, etc., to get off, get clear, to deliver oneself from.

To break loose, escape, slip away, make one's escape, cut and run, slip the collar, bolt (671).

To liberate, free, set free, set at liberty, release, loose, let loose, loosen, relax, unloose, untie, unbind, unhand, unchain, unshackle, unfetter, unclog, disengage, unharness (44).

To enlarge, set clear, let go, let out, disenchain, disimprison, unbar, unbolt, uncage, unclose, uncork, discharge, disenthral, dismiss, deliver, extricate, let slip, enfranchise, affranchise, manumit, denizen, emancipate, assoil (748).

To clear, acquit, redeem, ransom, get off.

(*Phrases*) To throw off the yoke; to burst one's bonds; to break prison.

To give one one's head.

(*Adjectives*) Liberated, freed, etc.

---

751 RESTRAINT (*Substantives*), constraint, coercion, cohibition, repression, clamp down, control, discipline.

Confinement, durance, duress, detention, imprisonment, incarceration, prisonment, internment, blockade, quarantine, coarctation, mancipation, entombment, 'durance vile,' limbo, captivity, penal servitude.

Arrest, arrestation, custody, keep, care, charge, ward.

Prison, fetter (752); *lettre de cachet*.

(*Verbs*) To be under restraint or arrest, to be coerced, etc.

To restrain, constrain, coerce, check, trammel, curb, cramp, keep under, enthral, put under restraint, restrict, repress, cohibit, detain, debar; to chain, enchain, fasten, tie up (43), picket, fetter, shackle, manacle, handcuff, bridle, muzzle, gag, suppress, pinion, pin down, tether, hobble.

To confine, shut up, shut in, clap up, lock up, cage, encage, impound, pen, coop, hem in, jam in, enclose, bottle up, cork up, seal up, mew, wall in, rail in, cloister, bolt in, close the door upon, imprison, incarcerate, immure, entomb, seclude, corral.

To take prisoner, lead captive, send or commit to prison, give in charge or in custody, arrest, commit, run in, lag; re-commit, remand.

(*Phrases*) To put in irons; to clap under hatches; to put in a strait-waistcoat.

(*Adjectives*) Restrained, coerced, etc., sewn up, pent up.

Held up, wind-bound, weather-bound, storm-stayed.
Coactive, stiff, restringent, strait-laced, hide-bound.
(*Phrases*) In limbo; under lock and key; laid by the heels; 'cabined,
cribbed, confined'; in quod; in durance vile; doing time; bound
hand and foot.

752 Means of restraint.

PRISON (*Substantives*), jail (or gaol), prison-house, house of detention, lock-up,
the cells, clink, glasshouse, brig, jug, quod, cooler, choky, stir, calaboose,
cage, coop, den, cell, stronghold, fortress, keep, dungeon, bastille, oubliette,
bridewell, tollbooth, panopticon, hulks, galleys, penitentiary, guard-room,
hold, round-house, blackhole, station, enclosure, concentration camp, pen,
fold, pound, paddock, stocks, bilboes, nick.

Newgate, King's Bench, Fleet, Marshalsea, Pentonville, Holloway, Dart-
moor, Portland, Peterhead, Broadmoor, Sing Sing, the Bastille.

Fetter, shackle, trammel, bond, chain, irons, collar, cangue, pinion, gyve,
fetterlock, manacle, handcuff, darbies, strait waistcoat; yoke, halter, harness,
muzzle, gag, bridle, curb, bit, snaffle, rein, martingale, leading-strings,
swaddling-bands, tether, hobble, picket, band, brake.

Bolt, bar, lock, padlock, rail, wall, paling, palisade (232), fence, corral,
barrier, barricade.

753 KEEPER (*Substantives*), custodian, *custos*, warder, jailer (or
gaoler), turnkey, castellan, guard,
ranger, gamekeeper, watch, watchman, watch and ward, sentry, sentinel, coastguard, convoy, escort,
concierge, caretaker, watch-dog.

Guardian, duenna, nurse, ayah,
chaperon.

755 Vicarious authority.

COMMISSION (*Substantives*), delega-
tion, consignment, assignment, de-
volution, procuration, deputation,
legation, mission, agency, clerkship,
agentship; power of attorney; errand,
embassy, charge, brevet, diploma,
exequatur, committal, commitment.

Appointment, nomination, ordination, installation, inauguration, return, accession, investiture, coronation.

Vicegerency, regency, regentship.

Deputy (759).

(*Verbs*) To commission, delegate,
depute, devolve, send out, assign,
consign, charge, encharge, entrust
with, commit to, enlist.

To appoint, name, nominate,
accredit, engage, bespeak, ordain,
install, induct, inaugurate, invest,
crown, return, enrol.

754 PRISONER (*Substantives*),
prisoner-of-war, P.O.W., kriegie, captive, *détenu*, convict, jail-bird, lag;
ticket-of-leave man.

(*Adjectives*) In custody, in charge,
imprisoned, locked up, incarcerated,
pent.

756 ABROGATION (*Substantives*),
annulment, cancel, cancellation, revocation, repeal, rescission, rescinding,
deposal, deposition, dethronement,
defeasance, dismissal, sack, *congé*,
demission, disestablishment, disendowment.

Abolition, abolishment, counter-
order, countermand, repudiation,
nullification, recantation, palinode,
retractation (607).

(*Verbs*) To abrogate, annul, cancel,
revoke, repeal, rescind, reverse, override, overrule, abolish, disannul,
dissolve, quash, repudiate, nullify,
retract, recant, recall, countermand,
counter-order, break off, disclaim,
declare null and void, disestablish,
disendow, deconsecrate, set aside, do
away with.

To dismiss, send off, send away,
discard, turn off, turn away, cashier,

Employ, empower, set over.
To be commissioned, to represent.
(*Adverbs*) *Per procurationem per pro.*, p.p.

——————

sack, fire, bounce, oust, unseat, unthrone, dethrone, depose, uncrown, unfrock, disbar, disbench.
(*Phrases*) Send about one's business; put one's nose out of joint; give one the mitten, the chuck, the sack, the boot, the push.

To get one's books or cards; to get the key of the street.
(*Adjectives*) Abrogated, etc.; *functus officio.*
(*Interjections*) Get along with you! clear out! be off! beat it!

757 RESIGNATION (*Substantives*), retirement, abdication, renunciation, abjuration.
(*Verbs*) To resign, give up, throw up, retire, abdicate, lay down, abjure, renounce, forgo, disclaim, retract (756); to tender one's resignation, send in one's papers.
(*Phrases*) To swallow the anchor; to be given one's bowler.
(*Adjective*) Emeritus.
(*Phrase*) 'Othello's occupation's gone.'

758 CONSIGNEE (*Substantives*), delegate, commissary, commissioner, vice-regent, legate, representative, secondary, nominee, surrogate, functionary, trustee, assignee.
Corps diplomatique, plenipotentiary, emissary, embassy, ambassador, diplomatist, diplomat, consul, resident, nuncio, internuncio.
Agent, factor, attorney, broker, factotum, bailiff, man of business, go-between, intermediary, middleman, salesman, commission agent, commercial traveller, bagman, drummer, colporteur, commissionaire, employee, attaché, curator, clerk, placeman.

759 DEPUTY (*Substantives*), substitute, vice, proxy, locum tenens, baby-sitter, *chargé d'affaires*,, delegate, representative, *alter ego*, surrogate, understudy, stooge, stand-in, stopgap, pinch-hitter.
Regent, viceroy, vicegerent, vicar, satrap, exarch, vizier, minister, premier, commissioner, chancellor, prefect, warden, lieutenant, proconsul, legate.
(*Verbs*) To deputize; to be deputy, etc., for; to appear for; to understudy; to take duty for.
(*Phrase*) To hold a watching brief for.
(*Adjectives*) Acting, deputizing, etc.
(*Adverbs*) In place of, vice.

SECTION II—SPECIAL INTERSOCIAL VOLITION

760 PERMISSION (*Substantives*), leave, allowance, sufferance, tolerance, toleration, liberty, law, licence, concession, grant, vouchsafement, authorization, sanction, accordance, admission, favour, dispensation, exemption, connivance.
A permit, warrant, brevet, precept, authority, firman, pass, passport,

761 PROHIBITION (*Substantives*), inhibition, veto, disallowance, interdiction, estoppage, hindrance (706), restriction, restraints (751), embargo, an interdict, ban, injunction, taboo, proscription; *index librorum prohibitorum.*
(*Verbs*) To prohibit, forbid, inhibit, disallow, bar, debar, interdict, ban,

furlough, ticket, licence, charter, patent, *carte blanche*, exeat.

(*Verbs*) To permit; to give leave or permission; to let, allow, admit, suffer, tolerate, concede, accord, vouchsafe, humour, indulge, to leave it to one; to leave alone; to grant, empower, charter, sanction, authorize, warrant, license; to give licence; to give a loose to.

To let off, absolve, exonerate, dispense with, favour, wink, connive at.

(*Phrases*) To give *carte blanche*; to give rein to; to stretch a point; leave the door open; to let one have a chance; to give one a fair show.

To take a liberty; to use a freedom; to make so bold; to beg leave.

estop, veto, keep in, hinder, restrain (751), restrict, withhold, limit, circumscribe, keep within bounds.

To exclude, shut out, proscribe.

(*Phrase*) To clip the wings of; to forbid the banns.

(*Adjectives*) Prohibitive, restrictive, exclusive, prohibitory, forbidding, etc.

Not permitted, prohibited, etc., unlicensed, contraband, unauthorized.

(*Phrases*) Under the ban of; on the Index.

(*Interjections*) Hands off! keep off! God forbid!

(*Adjectives*) Permitting, etc., permissive, conceding, indulgent. Allowable, permissible, lawful, legitimate, legal. Unforbid, unforbidden, unconditional.

---

762 CONSENT (*Substantives*), compliance, acquiescence, assent (488), agreement, concession, yieldingness, acknowledgment, acceptance.

Settlement, ratification, confirmation.

(*Verbs*) To consent, give consent, assent, comply with, acquiesce, agree to, subscribe to, accede, accept.

To concede, yield, satisfy, grant, settle, acknowledge, confirm, homologate, ratify, deign, vouchsafe.

(*Phrase*) To take at one's word.

(*Adjectives*) Consenting, etc., having no objection, unconditional.

(*Adverbs*) Yes (488); if you please, as you please, by all means, by all manner of means, so be it, of course, certainly, sure, O.K.

(*Phrases*) Suits me; all right by me.

---

763 OFFER (*Substantives*), proffer, tender, present, overture, proposition, motion, proposal, invitation, candidature, presentation, offering, oblation, bid, bribe.

Sacrifice, immolation.

(*Verbs*) To offer, proffer, tender, present, invite, volunteer, propose, move, make a motion, start, press, bid, hold out, hawk about.

To sacrifice, immolate.

(*Phrases*) To be a candidate; to go a-begging.

(*Adjectives*) Offering, etc., in the market, for sale, on hire.

---

764 REFUSAL (*Substantives*), rejection, declining, non-compliance, declension, dissent (489), denial, repulse, rebuff, discountenance.

Disclaimer, recusancy, abnegation, protest.

Revocation, violation, abrogation (756), flat refusal, peremptory denial.

(*Verbs*) To refuse, reject, deny, decline, disclaim, repudiate, protest, resist, repel, veto, refuse or withhold one's assent; to excuse oneself, to negative, turn down, rebuff, snub, spurn, resist, cross, grudge, begrudge.

To discard, set aside, rescind, revoke, discountenance, forswear.

(*Phrases*) To turn a deaf ear to; to shake the head; not to hear of;

to send to the right-about; to hang fire; to wash one's hands of; to declare off.

(*Adjectives*) Refusing, etc., recusant, restive, uncomplying, unconsenting.

Refused, etc., out of the question, not to be thought of.

(*Adverbs*) No, by no means, etc. (489).

(*Phrases*) Excuse me; nix on that; not on your life; nothing doing.

765 REQUEST (*Substantives*), requisition, asking, petition, demand, suit, solicitation, craving, entreaty, begging, postulation, adjuration, canvass, candidature, prayer, supplication, impetration, imploration, instance, obsecration, obtestation, importunity, application, address, appeal, motion, invitation, overture, invocation, interpellation, apostrophe, orison, incantation, imprecation, conjuration.

Mendicancy, begging letter, round robin.

Claim, reclamation, revendication.

766 Negative request.

DEPRECATION (*Substantives*), expostulation, intercession, mediation.

(*Verbs*) To deprecate, protest, expostulate; to enter a protest; to intercede for.

(*Adjectives*) Deprecating, etc., deprecatory, expostulatory, intercessory; deprecated, protested.

Unsought, unbesought.

(*Interjections*) God forbid! forbid it heaven! *absit omen!*

————

(*Verbs*) To request, ask, sue, beg, cadge, crave, pray, petition, solicit, beg a boon, demand, prefer a request or petition, ply, apply to, make application, put to, make bold to ask, invite, beg leave, put up a prayer.

To beg hard, entreat, beseech, supplicate, implore, plead, conjure, adjure, invoke, evoke, kneel to, fall on one's knees, impetrate, imprecate, appeal to, apply to, put to, address, call for, press, urge, beset, importune, dun, tax, besiege, cry to, call on.

To bespeak, canvass, tout, make interest, court; to claim, reclaim.

(*Phrases*) To send the hat round; to beg from door to door.

(*Adjectives*) Requesting, asking, beseeching, etc., precatory, suppliant, supplicatory, postulant, importunate.

(*Phrases*) Cap in hand; on one's knees.

(*Adverbs*) Do, please, kindly, be good enough, pray, prithee, be so good as, have the goodness, vouchsafe.

For heaven's sake, for goodness' sake, for God's sake, for the love of Mike.

767 PETITIONER (*Substantives*), solicitor, applicant, suppliant, supplicant, mendicant, beggar, mumper, suitor, candidate, aspirant, claimant, postulant, canvasser, tout, cadger, sponger.

SECTION III—CONDITIONAL INTERSOCIAL VOLITION

768 PROMISE (*Substantives*), word, troth, plight, profession, pledge, parole, word of honour, assurance, vow, oath.

Engagement, guarantee, undertaking, insurance, contract (769), obligation; affiance, betrothal, betrothment.

768A Release from engagement, disengagement, liberation (750).

(*Adjectives*) Absolute, unconditional, uncovenanted, unsecured.

————

(*Verbs*) To promise, give a promise, undertake, engage, assure; to give, pass, pledge or plight one's word, honour credit, faith, etc.; to covenant, warrant, guarantee (467); to swear, vow, be sworn; take oath, make oath, kiss the book; to attest, adjure; to betroth, plight troth, affiance.

To answer for, be answerable for, secure, give security (771).

(*Phrases*) To enter on, make or form an engagement, take upon oneself; to bind, tie, commit, or pledge oneself; to be in for it; to contract an obligation; to be bound; to hold out an expectation.

To call heaven to witness; to swear by bell, book, and candle; to put on one's oath; to swear a witness.

(*Adjectives*) Promising, etc., promised, pledged, sworn, etc.; votive, promissory.

(*Phrases*) Under one's hand and seal; as one's head shall answer for.

(*Interjection*) So help me God!

769 COMPACT (*Substantives*), contract, agreement, understanding, bargain, bond, deal, pact, paction, stipulation, covenant, settlement, convention, cartel, protocol, charter, treaty, indenture, concordat, *zollverein*.

Negotiation, transaction, bargaining, haggling, chaffering; diplomacy.

Ratification, settlement, signature, endorsement, seal, signet.

A negotiator, diplomatist, diplomat, agent, contractor, underwriter, attorney, broker (758).

(*Verbs*) To contract, covenant, agree for, strike a bargain, engage (768); to underwrite.

To treat, negotiate, bargain, stipulate, haggle (or higgle), chaffer, stick out for, insist upon, make a point of, compound for.

To conclude, close, confirm, ratify, endorse, clench, come to an understanding, take one at one's word, come to terms.

To subscribe, sign, seal, indent, put the seal to, sign and seal.

(*Phrase*) Caveat emptor.

770 CONDITIONS (*Substantives*), terms, articles, articles of agreement, clauses, proviso, provisions, salvo, covenant, stipulation, obligation, ultimatum, *sine qua non*.

(*Verbs*) To make it a condition, make terms; to stipulate, insist upon; to tie up.

(*Adjectives*) Conditional, provisional, guarded, fenced, hedged in.

(*Adverbs*) Conditionally, on the understanding; provided (469).

(*Phrases*) With a string tied to it; wind and weather permitting; God willing; D.V.; *Deo volente*.

771 SECURITY (*Substantives*), surety, guaranty, guarantee, mortgage, warranty, bond, debenture, pledge, tie, plight, pawn, lien, caution, sponsion, hostage, sponsor, bail, parole.

Deed, instrument, deed-poll, indenture, warrant, charter, cartel, protocol, recognizance; verification, acceptance, endorsement, signature, execution, seal, stamp, I O U.

Promissory note, bill of exchange, bill.

Stake, deposit, pool, kitty, jack-pot, earnest, handsel.

Docket, certificate, voucher, verification, authentication.

(*Verbs*) To give security, go bail, pawn (787); guarantee, warrant, accept, endorse, underwrite, insure; execute, stamp.

To hold in pledge.

772 OBSERVANCE. *(Substantives),* performance, fulfilment, satisfaction, discharge, compliance, acquittance, quittance, acquittal, adhesion, acknowledgment, fidelity (939).

(Verbs) To observe, perform, keep, fulfil, discharge, comply with, make good, meet, satisfy, respect, abide by, adhere to, be faithful to, act up to, acquit oneself.

(Phrase) To redeem one's pledge.

(Adjectives) Observant, faithful, true, honourable (939), strict, rigid, punctilious.

(Adverb) Faithfully, etc., to the letter.

(Phrase) As good as one's word.

773 NON-OBSERVANCE *(Substantives),* inobservance, evasion, omission, failure, neglect, laches, laxity, infringement, infraction, violation, forfeiture, transgression.

Retractation, repudiation, nullification, protest.

Informality, lawlessness, disobedience, bad faith (742).

(Verbs) To break, violate, fail, neglect, omit, skip, cut, forfeit, infringe, transgress.

To retract, discard, protest, go back upon or from one's word, repudiate, nullify, ignore, set at naught, wipe off, cancel, etc. (552), to fob off, palter, elude, evade.

(Phrases) To wash out; to shut one's eyes to; to drive a coach and six through.

(Adjectives) Violating, etc., elusive, evasive, transgressive, unfulfilled; compensatory (30).

774 COMPROMISE *(Substantives),* composition, middle term, *mezzo termine, modus vivendi;* bribe, hush-money.

(Verbs) To compromise, compound, commute, adjust, take the mean, split the difference, come to terms, come to an understanding, meet one half-way, give and take, submit to arbitration.

SECTION IV—POSSESSIVE RELATIONS

1°. *Property in general*

775 ACQUISITION *(Substantives),* obtainment, gaining, earning, procuration, procuring, procurement, gathering, gleaning, picking, collecting, recovery, retrieval, totting, salvage, find.

Book-collecting, book-hunting, etc., philately, cartophily, phillumeny.

Gain, profit, benefit, emolument, the main chance, pelf, lucre, loaves and fishes, produce, product, proceeds, return, fruit, crop, harvest, scoop, takings, winnings.

Inheritance, bequest, legacy.

Fraudulent acquisition, subreption, stealing (791).

Profiteering, pot-hunting.

A collector, book-collector, etc., bird-fancier, etc., philatelist,

776 LOSS *(Substantives),* perdition, forfeiture, lapse.

Privation, bereavement, deprivation (789), dispossession, riddance.

(Verbs) To lose; incur, experience, or meet with a loss; to miss, mislay, throw away, forfeit, drop, let slip, allow to slip through the fingers; to get rid of (782), to waste (638, 679).

To be lost, lapse.

(Phrase) To throw good money after bad.

(Adjectives) Losing, etc., lost, etc. Devoid of, not having, unobtained, unpossessed, unblest with.

Shorn of, deprived of, bereaved of, bereft of, rid of, quit of, dispossessed, denuded, out of pocket, minus, cut off.

cartophilist, phillumenist; a profit-eer, money-grubber, pot-hunter.

(*Verbs*) To acquire, get, gain, win, earn, realize, regain, receive (785), take (789), obtain, procure, derive, secure, collect, reap, gather, glean, come in for, step into, inherit, come by, rake in, scrape together, get hold of, scoop, pouch.

To profit, make profit, turn to profit, make money by, obtain a return, make a fortune, coin money, profiteer.

To be profitable, to pay, to answer.

To fall to, come to, accrue.

(*Phrases*) To turn an honest penny; to earn an honest crust; to bring grist to the mill; to raise the wind; to line one's pockets; to feather one's nest; to reap or gain an advantage; to keep the wolf from the door; to keep the pot boiling.

(*Adjectives*) Acquisitive, acquiring, acquired, etc., profitable, lucrative, remunerative, paying.

(*Phrase*) On the make.

Irrecoverable, irretrievable, irremediable, irreparable.

(*Interjections*) Farewell to! adieu to!

_____

777 POSSESSION (*Substantives*), ownership, proprietorship, tenure, tenancy, seisin, occupancy, hold, holding, preoccupancy.

Exclusive possession, impropriation, monopoly, inalienability.

Future possession, heritage, heirship, inheritance, reversion.

(*Phrases*) A bird in the hand; nine points of the law; the haves and the have-nots.

(*Verbs*) To possess, have, hold, own, be master of, be in possession of, enjoy, occupy, be seised of, be worth, to have in hand or on hand; to inherit (775).

To engross, monopolize, corner, forestall, absorb, preoccupy.

To be the property of, belong to, appertain to, pertain to, be in the hands of, be in the possession of.

(*Adjectives*) Possessing, etc., possessed of, seised of, worth, endowed with, instinct with, fraught, laden with, charged with.

Possessed, etc., proprietary, proprietorial; on hand, in hand, in store, in stock, unsold, unshared; inalienable.

778 Joint possession.

PARTICIPATION (*Substantives*), joint stock, common stock, partnership, copartnership, possession in common, communion, community of possessions or goods, socialism, collectivism, communism, syndicalism.

Bottle party, share-out, picnic.

A syndicate, ring, corner, combine, cartel, trust, monopoly, pool.

A partner, co-partner, shareholder; co-tenant, co-heir; a communist, socialist.

(*Verbs*) To participate, partake, share, communicate, go snacks, go halves, share and share alike; to have or possess, etc., in common; to come in for a share, to stand in with, to socialize, to pool.

(*Adjectives*) Partaking, etc.; socialist, socialistic, communist.

(*Adverbs*) Share and share alike, fifty-fifty, even Stephen.

_____

779 POSSESSOR (*Substantives*), owner, holder, proprietor, proprietress, proprietary, master, mistress, heritor, occupier, occupant, landlord, landlady, landowner, lord of the manor, squire, laird, landed gentry; tenant, renter, lessee, lodger.

Future possessor, heir, heiress, inheritor.

780 PROPERTY (*Substantives*), possession, ownership, proprietorship, seisin, tenancy, tenure, lordship, title, claim, stake, legal estate, equitable estate, fee simple, fee tail, *meum et tuum*, occupancy.

Estate, effects, assets, resources, means, belongings, stock, goods, chattels, fixtures, plant, movables, furniture, things, traps, trappings, paraphernalia, luggage, baggage, bag and baggage, cargo, lading.

Lease, term, settlement, remainder, reversion, dower, jointure, apanage, heritage, inheritance, patrimony, heirloom.

Real property, land, landed estate, manor, demesne, domain, tenement, holding, hereditament, household, freehold, farm, ranch, *hacienda, estancia,* fief, feoff, seigniority, allodium.

Ground, acres, field, close.

State, realm, empire, kingdom, principality, territory, sphere of influence.

(*Adjectives*) Predial, manorial, freehold, etc., copyhold, leasehold.

781 RETENTION (*Substantives*), keep, holding, keeping, retaining, detention, custody, grasp, gripe, grip, tenacity.

Fangs, teeth, clutches, hooks, tentacles, claws, talons, nails.

Forceps, pincers, pliers, tongs, vice.

Incommunicableness, incommunicability.

(*Phrase*) A bird in the hand.

(*Verbs*) To retain, keep, keep in hand, secure, detain, hold fast, grasp, clutch, clench, cinch, gripe, grip, hug, withhold, keep back.

(*Adjectives*) Retaining, etc., retentive, tenacious.

Unforfeited, undeprived, undisposed, uncommunicated, incommunicable, inalienable, not transferable.

782 RELINQUISHMENT (*Substantives*), cession, abandonment (624), renunciation, surrender, dereliction, rendition, riddance (776), resignation (758).

(*Verbs*) To relinquish, give up, let go, lay aside, resign, forgo, drop, discard, dismiss, waive, renounce, surrender, part with, get rid of, lay down, abandon, cede, yield, dispose of, divest oneself of, spare, give away, throw away, cast away, fling away, maroon, jettison, chuck up, let slip, make away with, make way for.

(*Phrases*) To lay on the shelf; to throw overboard.

(*Adjectives*) Relinquished, etc., derelict, left, residuary (40), unculled.

2°. *Transfer of Property*

783 TRANSFER (*Substantives*), interchange, exchange, transmission, barter (794), conveyance, assignment, alienation, abalienation, demise, succession, reversion; metastasis.

(*Verbs*) To transfer, convey, assign, consign, make over, pass, transmit, interchange, exchange (148).

To change hands, change from one to another, alienate, devolve.

To dispossess, abalienate, disinherit.

(*Adjectives*) Alienable, negotiable, transferable.

784 GIVING (*Substantives*), bestowal, donation, accordance, presentation, oblation, presentment, delivery, award, investment, granting.

Cession, concession, consignment, dispensation, benefaction, charity, liberality, generosity, munificence, almsgiving.

Gift, donation, bonus, boon, present, testimonial, presentation, fairing, benefaction, grant, subsidy, subvention, offering, contribution, subscription, whip-round, donative, meed, tribute, gratuity, tip, Christmas box, handsel, trinkgeld, *douceur*, *pourboire*, baksheesh, cumshaw, dash, bribe, free gift, favour, bounty, largess, allowance, endowment, charity, alms, dole, peace-offering, payment (807).

Bequest, legacy, demise, dotation.

Giver, grantor, donor, benefactor.

(*Phrase*) *Panem et circenses.*

(*Verbs*) To give, bestow, accord, confer, grant, concede, present, give away, deliver, deliver over, make over, consign, entrust, hand, tip, render, impart, hand over, part with, fork out, yield, dispose of, put into the hands of, vest in, assign, put in possession, settle upon, endow, subsidize.

To bequeath, leave, demise, devise.

To give out, dispense, deal, deal out, dole out, mete out.

To contribute, subscribe, put up a purse, send round the hat, pay (807), spend (809).

To furnish, supply, administer, afford, spare, accommodate with, indulge with, shower upon, lavish.

To bribe, suborn, grease the palm, square.

(*Adjectives*) Giving, etc., given, etc., charitable, eleemosynary, tributary.

(*Phrase*) *Bis dat qui cito dat.*

785 RECEIVING (*Substantives*), acquisition (775), reception, acceptance, admission.

A recipient, donee, assignee, legatee, grantee, stipendiary, beneficiary, pensioner, almsman.

(*Verbs*) To receive, take (789), accept, pocket, pouch, admit, catch, catch at, jump at, take in.

To be received, etc.; to accrue, come to hand.

(*Adjectives*) Receiving, etc., recipient; pensionary, stipendiary.

---

786 APPORTIONMENT (*Substantives*), distribution, dispensation, allotment, assignment, consignment, partition, division, deal, share-out.

Dividend, portion, contingent, share, whack, meed, allotment, lot, measure, dole, pittance, quantum, ration, quota, modicum, allowance, appropriation.

(*Phrase*) Cutting up the melon.

(*Verbs*) To apportion, divide, distribute, administer, dispense, billet, allot, cast, share, mete, parcel out, serve out, deal, partition, appropriate, assign.

(*Adjectives*) Apportioning, etc., respective.

(*Adverbs*) Respectively, severally.

787 LENDING (*Substantives*), loan, advance, mortgage, accommodation, lease-lend, subsistence money, sub, pawn, pignoration, hypothecation, investment; pawnshop, *mont de piété*.

Lender, pawnbroker, uncle.

788 BORROWING (*Substantives*), pledging, replevin, borrowed plumes, plagiarism, plagiary; a touch.

(*Verbs*) To borrow, hire, rent, farm, raise money, raise the wind; to plagiarize.

(*Verbs*) To lend, loan, advance, mortgage, invest, pawn, impawn, pop, hock, hypothecate, impignorate, place or put out to interest, entrust, accommodate with.

(*Adjectives*) Lending, etc., lent, etc., unborrowed.

(*Adverb*) In advance; up the spout.

(*Adjectives*) Borrowing, etc., borrowed, second-hand.

(*Phrases*) To borrow of Peter to pay Paul; to run into debt.

---

789 TAKING (*Substantives*), appropriation, prehension, capture, seizure, abduction, ablation, catching, seizing, apprehension, arrest, kidnapping, round-up.

Abstraction, subtraction, deduction, subduction.

Dispossession, deprivation, deprival, bereavement, divestment, sequestration, confiscation, disendowment.

Resumption, reprise, reprisal, recovery (775).

Clutch, swoop, wrench, catch, take, haul.

(*Verbs*) To take, capture, lay one's hands on; lay, take, or get hold of; to help oneself to; to possess oneself of, take possession of, make sure of, make free with.

790 RESTITUTION (*Substantives*), return, reddition, rendition, restoration, rehabilitation, remission, reinvestment, reparation, atonement.

Redemption, recovery, recuperation, release, replevin.

(*Verbs*) To return, restore, give back, bring back, derequisition, denationalize, render, refund, reimburse, recoup, remit, rehabilitate, repair, reinvest.

To let go, disgorge, regorge, regurgitate.

(*Adjectives*) Restoring, etc., recuperative.

(*Phrase*) *Suum cuique.*

To appropriate, impropriate, pocket, put into one's pocket, pouch, bag; to ease one of.

To pick up, gather, collect, round up, net, absorb (296), reap, glean, crop, get in the harvest, cull, pluck; intercept, tap.

To take away, carry away, carry off, bear off, hurry off with, abduct, kidnap, crimp, shanghai.

To lay violent hands on, fasten upon, pounce upon, catch, seize, snatch, nip up, whip up, jump at, snap at, hook, claw, clinch, grasp, gripe, grip, grab, clutch, wring, wrest, wrench, pluck, tear away, catch, nab, capture, collar, throttle.

To take from, deduct, subduct (38), subtract, curtail, retrench, abridge of, dispossess, expropriate, take away from, abstract, deprive of, bereave, divest, disendow, despoil, strip, fleece, shear, impoverish, levy, distrain, confiscate, sequester, sequestrate, commandeer, requisition, oust, extort, usurp, suck, squeeze, drain, bleed, milk, gut, dry, exhaust.

(*Phrases*) To suck like a leech; to be given an inch and take an ell; to sweep the board; to scoop the pool.

(*Adjectives*) Taking, etc., privative, prehensile, predatory, rapacious, raptorial, predial, ravenous.

---

791 STEALING (*Substantives*), theft, thieving, thievery, abstraction, appropriation, plagiarism, depredation, pilfering, rape, larceny, robbery, shoplifting, burglary, house-breaking, abaction (of cattle), cattle-lifting, kidnapping.

Spoliation, plunder, pillage, sack, rapine, brigandage, foray, raid, hold-up, dragonnade, marauding.

Peculation, embezzlement, swindling (545), blackmail, *chantage*, smuggling, black market; thievishness, rapacity, kleptomania; den of thieves, Alsatia.

Licence to plunder, letter of marque.

(*Verbs*) To steal, thieve, rob, abstract, appropriate, filch, pilfer, purloin, nab, nim, prig, grab, bag, lift, pick, pinch, knock off.

To convey away, carry off, make off with, run or walk off with, abduct, spirit away, kidnap, crimp, seize, lay violent hands on, etc. (789), abact, rustle (of cattle), shanghai.

To scrounge, wangle, win, crib, sponge, rook, bilk, diddle, swindle (545), peculate, embezzle, fiddle, flog, poach, run, smuggle, hijack.

To plunder, pillage, rifle, sack, ransack, burgle, spoil, spoliate, despoil, hold up, stick up, bail up, strip, fleece, gut, loot, forage, levy blackmail, pirate, plagiarize.

(*Phrases*) To live by one's wits; to rob Peter to pay Paul; to obtain under false pretences; to set a thief to catch a thief.

(*Adjectives*) Stealing, etc., thievish, light-fingered, larcenous, stolen, furtive, piractical, predaceous.

792 THIEF (*Substantives*), robber, spoiler, pickpocket, cutpurse, dip, depredator, yegg, yeggman, footpad, highwayman, burglar, house-breaker, larcener, larcenist, pilferer, filcher, sneak-thief, shop-lifter, poacher, rustler; swell mob; the light-fingered gentry; kleptomaniac.

Swindler, crook, spiv, welsher, smuggler, bootlegger, hijacker, gangster, cracksman, magsman, mobsman, sharper, blackleg, shark, trickster, harpy, *chevalier d'industrie*, peculator, plagiarist, blackmailer; receiver, fence.

Brigand, freebooter, bandit, pirate, viking, corsair, buccaneer, thug, dacoit, picaroon, moss-trooper, rapparee, maurauder, filibuster, wrecker, bushranger; Autolycus, Turpin, Macheath, Bill Sikes, Jonathan Wild.

(*Phrases*) A snapper-up of unconsidered trifles; *homo triarum literarum*.

793 BOOTY (*Substantives*), spoil, plunder, swag, loot, boodle, prey, pickings, grab, forage, blackmail, graft, prize.

3°. Interchange of Property

794 BARTER (*Substantives*), exchange, truck, swop (or swap), chop, interchange, commutation.

Traffic, trade, commerce, dealing, business, custom, negotiation, transaction, jobbing, agiotage, bargain, deal, commercial, enterprise, speculation, brokery.

(*Phrases*) A Roland for an Oliver; a *quid pro quo*; payment in kind.

(*Verbs*) To barter, exchange, truck, interchange, commute, swap (or swop), traffic, trade, speculate, transact, or do business with, deal with, have dealings with; open or keep an account with; to carry on a trade; to rig the market.

To bargain; drive, make, or strike a bargain; negotiate, bid for, haggle (or higgle), chaffer, dicker, stickle, cheapen, compound for, beat down, outbid, underbid, outbargain, come to terms, do a deal, quote, underquote.

(*Phrase*) To throw a sprat to catch a whale.

(*Adjectives*) Commercial, mercantile, trading, interchangeable, marketable, negotiable; wholesale, retail.

795 PURCHASE (*Substantives*), emption, buying, purchasing, shopping, hire-purchase, never-never; pre-emption, bribery, co-emption.

A buyer, purchaser, customer, emptor, shopper, patron, client, clientele.

(*Verbs*) To buy, purchase, procure, hire, rent, farm, pay, fee, repurchase, buy in, keep in one's pay; pre-empt; bribe, suborn, square, buy over; shop, market.

(*Adjectives*) Purchased, etc.

(*Phrase*) *Caveat emptor.*

796 SALE (*Substantives*), disposal, custom.

Auction, Dutch auction, roup.

Lease, mortgage.

Vendibility, salability.

A vendor, seller (797).

To sell, vend, dispose of, retail, dispense, auction, auctioneer, hawk, peddle, undersell.

To let, sublet, lease, mortgage.

(*Phrases*) Put up to sale or auction; bring under the hammer.

(*Adjectives*) Vendible, marketable, salable; unpurchased, unbought, on one's hands, unsalable.

797 MERCHANT (*Substantives*), trader, dealer, tradesman, buyer and seller, vendor, monger, chandler, shopkeeper, shopman, salesman, saleswoman, changer.

Retailer, chapman, hawker, huckster, regrater, higgler, pedlar, cadger, sutler, bumboatman, middleman, coster, costermonger; auctioneer, broker, money-broker, bill-broker, money-changer, jobber, factor, go-between, cambist, usurer, money-lender.

House, firm, concern, partnership, company, guild, syndicate.

798 MERCHANDISE (*Substantives*), ware, mercery, commodity, effects, goods, article, stock, stock-in-trade, cargo (190), produce, freight, lading, ship-load, staple commodity.

799 MART (*Substantives*), market, change (or 'change), exchange, bourse, market-place, fair, hall, staple, bazaar, guildhall, tollbooth (or tolbooth), custom-house.

Office, shop, counting-house, bureau, counter, stall, booth, chambers.

Warehouse, depot, store (636), *entrepôt*, emporium, godown.

4°. *Monetary Relations*

800 MONEY (*Substantives*), funds, treasure, capital, stock, proceeds, assets, cash, bullion, ingot, nugget; sum, amount, balance.

Currency, soft currency, hard currency, circulating medium, legal tender, specie, coin, hard cash, sterling, pounds shillings and pence, L.S.D.

Ready, rhino, blunt, oof, lolly, splosh, chink, dibs, plunks, bucks, bones, siller, dust, tin, dough, jack, spondulicks, simoleons, mazuma, ducats, the needful, the wherewithal.

Gold, silver, copper, nickel, rouleau, dollar, etc.

Finance, gold standard, monometallism, bimetallism.

Pocket-money, pin money, chicken feed, petty cash, change, small coin; doit, farthing, bawbee, penny, shilling, stiver, mite, sou; plum, grand, monkey, pony, tenner, fiver, quid, wheel, bob, tanner, two bits.

Sum, amount, balance.

Paper money, note, bank-note, treasury note, greenback, note of hand, promissory note, I O U.

Cheque (or check), bill, draft (or draught), order, remittance, postal order, money order, warrant, coupon, debenture, bill of exchange, exchequer bill, treasury bill, assignat.

A drawer, a drawee.

False money, base coin, flash note, kite, stumer.

Science of coins, numismatics.

(*Phrases*) The sinews of war; the almighty dollar.

(*Verbs*) To draw, draw upon, endorse, issue, utter; to amount to, come to.

(*Adjectives*) Monetary, pecuniary, fiscal, financial, sumptuary; monometallic, bimetallic; numismatical.

(*Phrases*) To touch the pocket; *argumentum ad crumenam.*

801 TREASURER (*Substantives*), purse-bearer, purser, bursar, banker, moneyer, paymaster, cashier, teller, accountant, steward, trustee, almoner.

Chancellor of the Exchequer, minister of finance, Queen's Remembrancer.

802 TREASURY (*Substantives*), bank, savings-bank, exchequer, coffer, chest, money-box, money-bag, strong-box, strong-room, safe, bursary, till, note-case, wallet, purse, *porte-monnaie*, purse-strings, pocket, fisc.

Consolidated fund, sinking fund, the funds, consols, government securities, war loan, savings certificates.

803 WEALTH (*Substantives*), fortune, riches, opulence, affluence, independence, solvency, competence, easy circumstances, command of money; El Dorado, Golconda, plutocracy.

Means, provision, substance, resources, capital, revenue, income, alimony, livelihood, subsistence, loaves and fishes, pelf, mammon, lucre, dower (810), pension, superannuation, annuity, unearned increment, pin-money.

A rich man, capitalist, plutocrat, financier, money-bags, millionaire, a Nabob, Dives, Croesus, Midas; *rentier*.

(*Phrases*) The golden calf; a well-lined purse; the purse of Fortunatus; a mint or pot of money.

(*Verbs*) To be rich, etc., to afford. To enrich, fill one's coffers, etc.; to capitalize.

(*Phrases*) To roll in riches; to wallow in wealth; to make one's pile; to feather one's nest; to line one's pockets; to keep one's head above water.

(*Adjectives*) Wealthy, rich, well-off, affluent, opulent, flush, oofy, solvent (734), moneyed, plutocratic.

(*Phrases*) Made of money; in

804 POVERTY (*Substantives*), indigence, penury, pauperism, destitution, want, need, lack, necessity, privation, distress, an empty purse; bad, reduced, or straitened circumstances; narrow means, straits, insolvency, impecuniosity, beggary, mendicancy, mendicity.

A poor man, pauper, mendicant, beggar, tramp, bum, vagabond, gangrel, starveling; the proletariat; *un pauvre diable.*

Poorhouse, workhouse, the institution.

(*Phrases*) *Res angusta domi*; the wolf at the door.

(*Verbs*) To be poor, etc., to want, lack, starve.

To render poor, etc., to reduce, to impoverish, reduce to poverty, depauperate, ruin; to pauperize.

(*Phrases*) To live from hand to mouth; come upon the parish; not to have a penny; to have seen better days; to beg one's bread.

(*Adjectives*) Poor, indigent, penniless, moneyless, impecunious, short of money, out of money, out of cash, out of pocket, needy, destitute, necessitous, distressed, hard up, in need, in want, poverty-stricken,

funds; rich as Croesus; rolling in riches; one's ship come home.

———

badly off, in distress, pinched, straitened, dowerless, fortuneless, reduced, insolvent (806), bereft, bereaved, fleeced, stripped, stony broke, stony, stumped.

(*Phrases*) Unable to make both ends meet; out at elbows; in reduced circumstances; not worth a sou; poor as Job; poor as a church mouse; down at heels; on one's uppers; on the rocks.

805 CREDIT (*Substantives*), trust, tick, score, account.

Letter of credit, duplicate, traveller's cheque (or check); mortgage, lien, debenture.

A creditor, lender, lessor, mortgagee, debenture-holder; a dun, usurer, gombeen-man, Shylock.

(*Verbs*) To keep an account with, to credit, accredit.

To place to one's credit or account, give credit.

(*Adjective*) Crediting.

(*Adverbs*) On credit, on tick, on account, to pay, unpaid-for.

———

806 DEBT (*Substantives*), obligation, liability, debit, indebtment, arrears, deficit, default, insolvency.

Interest, usance, usury.

Floating debt, bad debt, floating capital, debentures; deferred payment, hire system, never-never system.

A debtor, debitor, borrower, lessee, mortgagor; a defaulter (808).

(*Verbs*) To be in debt, to owe, to answer for, to incur a debt, borrow (788).

(*Phrases*) To run up a hill; to go on tick; to outrun the constable.

(*Adjectives*) In debt, indebted, owing, due, unpaid, outstanding, in arrear, being minus, out of pocket, encumbered, involved, in difficulties, liable, chargeable, answerable for, insolvent, in the red.

Unrequited, unrewarded.

807 PAYMENT (*Substantives*), defrayment, discharge, quittance, acquittance, settlement, clearance, liquidation, satisfaction, remittance, instalment, stake, reckoning, arrangement, composition, acknowledgment, release.

Repayment, reimbursement, retribution, reward (973).

Bill, cheque, cash, ready money (800).

(*Phrase*) A *quid pro quo*.

(*Verbs*) To pay, defray, discharge, settle, quit, acquit oneself of, reckon with, remit, clear, liquidate, release; repay, refund, reimburse.

(*Phrases*) To honour a bill; to strike a balance; to settle, balance, or square accounts with; to be even with; to wipe off old scores; to satisfy all demands; to pay one's way or shot; to pay in full.

808 NON-PAYMENT (*Substantives*), default, defalcation, repudiation, protest.

Insolvency, bankruptcy, failure, whitewashing, application of the sponge.

Waste paper, dishonoured bills.

A defaulter, bankrupt, welsher, levanter, insolvent debtor, man of straw, lame duck.

(*Verbs*) Not to pay, to fail, break, become insolvent or bankrupt, default, defalcate.

To protest, dishonour, repudiate, nullify; hammer.

(*Phrases*) To run up bills; to tighten the purse-strings.

(*Adjectives*) Not paying, in debt, behindhand, in arrear, insolvent, bankrupt, gazetted.

(*Phrases*) Being minus or worse than nothing; plunged or over head

(*Adjectives*) Paying, etc., paid, owing nothing, out of debt.
(*Adverbs*) On the nail, money down, C.O.D.

809 EXPENDITURE (*Substantives*), money going out; outgoings, expenses, disbursement, outlay.

Pay, payment, fee, hire, wages, perquisites, vails, allowance, stipend, salary, screw, divided, tribute, subsidy, batta, bat-money, shot, scot.

Remuneration, recompense, reward (973), tips, *pourboire*, largess, honorarium, refresher, bribe, *douceur*, hush-money, extras, commission, rake-off.

Advance, subsistence money, sub, earnest, handsel, deposit, prepayment, entrance fee, entrance.

Contribution, donation, subscription, deposit, contingent, dole, quota.

Investment, purchase (795), alms (748).

(Verbs) To expend, spend, pay, disburse, lay out, lay or pay down, to cash, to come down with, brass up, shell out, fork out, bleed, make up a sum, to invest, sink money, prepay, tip.

(*Phrases*) To unloose the purse-strings; to pay the piper; to pay through the nose.

(*Adjectives*) Expending, etc., expended, etc., sumptuary.

and ears in debt; in the gazette; in Queer Street.

810 RECEIPT (*Substantives*), money coming in, incomings.

Income, revenue, earnings (775), rent, rental, rent-roll, rentage, return, proceeds, premium, bonus, gate-money, royalty.

Pension, annuity, tontine, jointure, dower, dowry, dot, alimony, compensation.

Emoluments, perquisites, recompense (809), sinecure.

(*Verbs*) To receive, pocket (789), to draw from, derive from.

To bring in, yield, return, afford, pay, accrue.

(*Phrases*) To get what will make the pot boil; keep the wolf from the door; bring grist to the mill.

(*Adjectives*) Receiving, etc., received, etc.

Gainful, profitable, remunerative, lucrative, advantageous (775).

811 ACCOUNTS (*Substantives*), money matters, finance, budget, bill, score, reckoning, balance-sheet, books, account-books, ledger, day-book, cash-book, cash account, current acount, deposit account, pass-book.

Book-keeping, audit, double entry.

An accountant, C.A., auditory, actuary, book-keeper.

(*Verbs*) To keep accounts, to enter, post, credit, debit, tot up, carry over; balance, make up accounts, take stock, audit.

To falsify, garble, cook, or doctor accounts.

812 PRICE (*Substantives*), cost, expense, amount, figure, charge, demand, damage, fare, hire.

Dues, duty, toll, tax, supertax, pay-as-you-earn, P.A.Y.E., rate, impost, cess, levy, gabelle, octroi, assessment, benevolence, custom, tithe, exactment, ransom, salvage, excise, tariff, brokerage, demurrage.

Bill, account, score, reckoning.

Worth, rate, value, valuation,

813 DISCOUNT (*Substantives*), abatement, reduction, deduction, depreciation, allowance, drawback, poundage, *agio*, percentage, rebate, set-off, backwardation, contango, tare and tret, salvage.

(*Verbs*) To discount, bate, abate, rebate, reduce, take off, allow, give, discount, tax.

(*Adjectives*) Discounting, etc.

(*Adverb*) At a discount.

evaluation, appraisement, market price, quotation; money's worth, pennyworth; price-current, price list.

(*Verbs*) To set or fix a price, appraise, assess, value, evaluate, price, charge, demand, ask, require, exact.

To fetch, sell for, cost, bring in, yield, make, change hands for, go for, realize, run into, stand one in; afford.

(*Phrases*) To run up a bill; to amount to; to set one back.

(*Adjectives*) Priced, charged, etc., to the tune of, *ad valorem*; mercenary, venal.

(*Phrases*) No penny, no paternoster; *point d'argent, point de Suisse.*

814 DEARNESS (*Substantives*), costliness, high price, expensiveness, rise in price, overcharge, surcharge, extravagance, exorbitance, extortion.

(*Phrase*) A pretty penny.

(*Verbs*) To be dear, etc., to cost much, to come expensive; to overcharge, surcharge, bleed, fleece (791).

To pay too much, to pay through the nose.

(*Adjectives*) Dear, high, high-priced, expensive, costly, dear-bought, precious, unreasonable, extortionate, extravagant, exorbitant, steep, stiff.

(*Adverbs*) Dear, at great cost, at a premium.

815 CHEAPNESS (*Substantives*), low price, inexpensiveness, drop in price, undercharge, bargain; absence of charge, gratuity, free admission.

(*Phrases*) A labour of love; the run of one's teeth; a drug in the market.

(*Verbs*) To be cheap, etc., to cost little, to come down or fall in price, to cut prices.

(*Phrase*) To have one's money's worth.

(*Adjectives*) Cheap, low, moderate, reasonable, inexpensive, unexpensive, low-priced, dirt-cheap, worth the money, half-price; catchpenny.

Gratuitous, gratis, free, for nothing, given away, free of cost, without charge, not charged, untaxed, scot-free, shot-free, expenseless, free of expense, free of all demands, honorary, unpaid.

(*Phrases*) Cheap as dirt; for a mere song; given away with a pound of tea; at cost price; at a reduction; at a sacrifice.

816 LIBERALITY (*Substantives*), generosity (942), bounty, munificence, bounteousness, bountifulness, charity (906), hospitality.

(*Verbs*) To be liberal, etc., spend freely, lavish, shower upon.

(*Phrases*) To loosen one's purse-strings; to give *carte blanche*; to spare no expense.

(*Adjectives*) Liberal, free, generous, charitable, hospitable, bountiful, bounteous, handsome, lavish, ungrudging, free-handed, open-handed, open-hearted, free-hearted, munificent, princely.

Overpaid.

817 ECONOMY (*Substantives*), frugality, thrift, thriftiness, care, husbandry, good housewifery, austerity, retrenchment; parsimony (819).

(*Verbs*) To be economical, etc., to save, economize, skimp, scrimp, scrape, meet one's expenses, retrench; to lay by, put by, save up, invest, bank, hoard, accumulate.

(*Phrases*) To cut one's coat according to one's cloth; to make ends meet; to pay one's way; to look at both sides of a shilling; to provide for a rainy day.

(*Adjectives*) Economical, frugal, thrifty, canny, careful, saving, chary, spare, sparing, cheese-paring.

(*Phrase*) Take care of the pence and the pounds will take care of themselves.

818 PRODIGALITY (*Substantives*), unthriftiness, thriftlessness, unthrift, waste, profusion, profuseness, extravagance, dissipation, squandering, squandermania, malversation.

A prodigal, spendthrift, squanderer, waster, wastrel.

(*Verbs*) To be prodigal, etc., to squander, lavish, waste, dissipate, exhaust, run through, spill, misspend, throw away money, drain.

(*Phrases*) To burn the candle at both ends; to make ducks and drakes of one's money; to spend money like water; to outrun the constable; to fool away, potter, muddle away, fritter away, etc., one's money; to pour water into a sieve; to go the pace.

(*Adjectives*) Prodigal, profuse, improvident, thriftless, unthrifty, wasteful, extravagant, lavish, dissipated.

(*Phrases*) Penny wise and pound foolish; money burning a hole in one's pocket.

819 PARSIMONY (*Substantives*), parsimoniousness, stint, stinginess, niggardliness, cheese-paring, extortion, illiberality, closeness, penuriousness, avarice, tenacity, covetousness, greediness, avidity, rapacity, venality, mercenariness, cupidity.

A miser, niggard, churl, screw, skinflint, money-grubber, codger, muckworm, hunks, curmudgeon, harpy.

(*Phrase*) *Auri sacra fames.*

(*Verbs*) To be parsimonious, etc., to grudge, begrudge, stint, pinch, screw, dole out.

(*Phrases*) To skin a flint; to drive a hard bargain; to tighten one's purse-strings.

(*Adjectives*) Parsimonious, stingy, miserly, mean, mingy, penurious, shabby, near, niggardly, cheese-paring, close, close-fisted, close-handed, chary, illiberal, ungenerous, churlish, sordid, mercenary, venal, covetous, avaricious, greedy, grasping, griping, pinching, extortionate, rapacious.

(*Phrases*) Having an itching palm; with a sparing hand.

CLASS VI

WORDS RELATING TO THE SENTIENT AND MORAL POWERS

SECTION I—AFFECTIONS IN GENERAL

820 AFFECTIONS (*Substantives*), character, qualities, disposition, nature, spirit, mood, tone, temper, temperament; cast or frame of mind or soul; turn, bent, idiosyncrasy, bias, turn of mind, predisposition, diathesis, predilection, propensity, proneness, proclivity, vein, humour, grain, mettle.

Soul, heart, breast, bosom, the inner man, inmost heart, heart's core, heart-strings, heart's-blood, heart of hearts, *penetralia mentis*.

Passion, pervading spirit, ruling passion, master-passion.

(*Phrases*) Flow of soul; fullness of the heart; the cockles of one's heart; flesh and blood.

(*Verbs*) To have or possess affections, etc.; be of a character, etc.; to breathe.

(*Adjectives*) Affected, characterized, formed, moulded, cast, tempered, attempered, framed, disposed, predisposed, prone, inclined, having a bias, etc., imbued or penetrated with; inbred, inborn, engrained (or ingrained).

821 FEELING (*Substantives*), endurance, experience, suffering, tolerance, sufferance, experience, sensibility (822), passion (825).

Impression, sensation, affection, response, emotion, pathos, warmth, glow, fervour, fervency, heartiness, effusiveness, effusion, gush, cordiality, ardour, exuberance, zeal, eagerness, *empressement*, *élan*, enthusiasm, verve, inspiration.

Blush, suffusion, flush, tingling, thrill, kick, excitement (824), turn, shock, agitation (315), heaving, flutter, flurry, fluster, twitter, stew, tremor, throb, throbbing, panting, palpitation, trepidation, perturbation, hurry of spirits, the heart swelling, throbbing, thumping, pulsating, melting, bursting; transport, rapture, ecstasy, ravishment (827).

(*Verbs*) To feel, receive an impression, etc.; to be impressed with, affected with, moved with, touched with, keen on.

To bear, bear with, suffer, endure, brook, tolerate, stomach, stand, thole, experience, taste, meet with, go through, put up with, prove; to harbour, cherish, support, abide, undergo.

To blush, change colour, mantle, tingle, twitter, throb, heave, pant, palpitate, go pit-a-pat, agitate, thrill, tremble, shake, quiver, wince, simmer, burble.

To swell, glow, warm, flush, redden, look blue, look black, catch the flame, catch the infection, respond, enthuse.

To possess, pervade, penetrate, imbue, absorb, etc., the soul.

(*Phrases*) To bear the brunt of; to come home to one's feelings or bosom; to strike a chord.

(*Adjectives*) Feeling, suffering, enduring; sentient, emotive, emotional. Impressed, moved, touched, affected with, etc., penetrated, imbued.

Warm, quick, lively, smart, strong, sharp, keen, acute, cutting, incisive, piercing, pungent, racy, piquant, poignant, caustic.

257

Deep, profound, indelible, ineffaceable, impressive, effective, deep-felt, home-felt, heart-felt, warm-hearted, hearty, cordial, swelling, thrilling, rapturous, ecstatic, soul-stirring, deep-mouthed, heart-expanding, electric.

Earnest, hearty, eager, exuberant, gushing, effusive, breathless, glowing, fervent, fervid, ardent, soulful, burning, red-hot, fiery, flaming, boiling, boiling over, zealous, pervading, penetrating, absorbing, hectic, rabid, fanatical; the heart being big, full, swelling, overflowing, bursting.

Wrought up, excited, passionate, enthusiastic (825).

(*Phrase*) Struck all of a heap.

(*Adverbs*) Heartily, cordially, earnestly, etc.

(*Phrases*) From the bottom of one's heart; *de profundis*; heart and soul; over head and ears.

---

822 SENSIBILITY (*Substantives*), impressibility, sensibleness, sensitiveness, hyperaesthesia (825), responsiveness, affectibility, susceptibleness, susceptibility, susceptivity, excitability, mobility, vivacity, vivaciousness, tenderness, softness, sentimentality, sentimentalism.

Physical sensibility (375).

(*Verbs*) To be sensible, etc., to shrink, have a tender heart.

(*Phrases*) To be touched to the quick; to feel where the shoe pinches; to take it hard; to take to heart.

(*Adjectives*) Sensible, sensitive, impressible, impressionable, susceptive, susceptible, responsive, excitable, mobile, thin-skinned, touchy, alive, vivacious, lively, mettlesome, high-strung, intense, emotional, tender, soft, sentimental, maudlin, sloppy, romantic, enthusiastic, neurotic.

(*Adverbs*) Sensibly, etc., to the quick.

823 INSENSIBILITY (*Substantives*), insensibleness, inertness, insensitivity, impassibility, impassibleness, impassivity, apathy, phlegm, dullness, hebetude, coolness, coldness, supineness, stoicism, insouciance, nonchalance, indifference, lukewarmness, frigidity, cold blood, sang-froid, dry eyes, cold heart, deadness, torpor, torpidity, ataraxia, pococurantism.

Lethargy, coma, trance, stupor, stupefaction, amnesia, paralysis, palsy, catalepsy, suspended animation, hebetation, anaesthesia (381), stock and stone, neutrality.

Physical insensibility (376).

(*Verbs*) To disregard, be insensible, not to be affected by, not to mind, to vegetate, *laisser aller*, not to care; to take it easy.

To render insensible (376), numb, benumb, paralyse, deaden, render callous, sear, inure, harden, steel, case-harden, stun, daze, stupefy, brutalize, hebetate.

(*Phrases*) To turn a deaf ear to; not care a straw (or a fig).

(*Adjectives*) Insensible, unconscious, impassive, unsusceptible, insusceptible, impassible, unimpressionable, unresponsive, unfeeling, blind to, deaf to, dead to, passionless, spiritless, soulless, apathetic, listless, phlegmatic, callous, hard-boiled, thick-skinned, pachydermatous, obtuse, dull, proof against, case-hardened, inured, steeled against, stoical, dull, frigid, cold, cold-blooded, cold-hearted, flat, inert, bovine, supine, sluggish, torpid, languid, tame, tepid, numb, numbed, sleepy, yawning, comatose, anaesthetic.

Indifferent, insouciant, lukewarm, careless, mindless, regardless, disregarding, nonchalant, unconcerned, uninterested, pococurante; taking no interest in.

Unfelt, unaffected, unruffled, unimpressed, unmoved, unperturbed, uninspired, untouched, etc.; platonic, imperturbable, vegetative, automatic.

(*Adverbs*) Insensibly, etc., *aequo animo*, with dry eyes, with withers unwrung.

(*Phrases*) No matter; never mind; *n'importe*; it matters not; it does not signify; it is of no consequence or importance (643); it cannot be helped; nothing coming amiss; it is all the same or all one to; what's the odds? *nichevo.*

824 EXCITATION (*Substantives*), of feeling, excitement, galvanism, stimulation, provocation, calling forth, infection, animation, inspiration, agitation, perturbation, subjugation, fascination, intoxication, enravishment, unction; a scene, sensation, tableau, shocker, thriller.

(*Verbs*) To excite, affect, touch, move, stir, wake, awaken, raise, raise up, evoke, call up, summon up, rake up.

To impress, strike, hit, quicken, swell, work upon.

To warm, kindle, stimulate, pique, whet, animate, hearten, inspire, impassion, inspirit, spirit, provoke, irritate, infuriate, sting, rouse, work up, hurry on, ginger up, commove.

To agitate, ruffle, flutter, fluster, flush, shake, thrill, penetrate, pierce, cut; to work oneself up, to simmer, bubble, burble.

To soften, subdue, overcome, master, overpower, overwhelm, bring under.

To shock, stagger, jar, jolt, stun, astound, electrify, galvanize, give one a shock, petrify.

To madden, intoxicate, fascinate, transport, ravish, enrapture, enravish, entrance, send.

(*Phrases*) To come home to one's feelings; to make a sensation; to prey on the mind; to give one a turn; to cut to the quick; to go through one; to strike one all of a heap; to make one's blood boil; to lash to a fury; to make one sit up.

(*Adjectives*) Excited, affected (825), wrought up, worked up, strung up, lost, *éperdu*, wild, haggard, feverish, febrile.

Exciting, etc., impressive, pathetic, sensational, provocative, piquant, aphrodisiac, dramatic, warm, glowing, fervid, swelling.

(*Phrases*) Being all of a twitter; all of a flutter; the head being turned.

825 Excess of sensitiveness.

EXCITABILITY (*Substantives*), intolerance, impatience, wincing, perturbation, trepidation, disquiet, disquietude, restlessness, fidgets, fidgetiness, fuss, hurry, agitation, flurry, fluster, flutter, irritability (901), hypersensitiveness, hyperaesthesia.

Passion, excitement, vehemence, impetuosity, flush, heat, fever, fire, flame, fume, wildness, turbulence, boisterousness, tumult, effervescence, ebullition, boiling, boiling over, whiff, gust, storm, tempest, outbreak, outburst, burst, explosion, fit, paroxysm, brain-storm, the blood boiling.

Fierceness, rage, fury, furore, tantrum, hysteria, hysterics, raving, delirium, frenzy, intoxication, fascination, infection, infatuation, fanaticism, Quixotism, *la tête montée.*

826 Absence of excitability.

INEXCITABILITY (*Substantives*), hebetude, tolerance, patience.

Coolness, composure, calmness, imperturbability, sang-froid, collectedness, tranquillity, quiet, quietude, quietness, sedateness, soberness, poise, staidness, gravity, placidity, sobriety, philosophy, stoicism, demureness, meekness, gentleness, mildness.

Submission, resignation, sufferance, endurance, longanimity, longsufferance, forbearance, fortitude, equanimity.

Repression, restraint (174), hebetation, tranquillization.

(*Phrases*) Patience of Job; even temper; cool head; Spartan endurance; a sober-sides.

(*Verbs*) To be composed, etc., to

(*Verbs*) To be intolerant, etc., not to bear, to bear ill, wince, chafe, fidget, fuss, not to be able to bear, stand, tolerate, etc.

To break out, fly out, burst out, explode, run riot, boil, boil over, fly off, flare up, fire, take fire, fume, rage, rampage, rave, run mad, run amuck, raise Cain.

(*Phrases*) To fly off at a tangent; to be out of all patience; to go off the deep end; to get the wind up; to make a scene; to go up in a blue flame.

(*Adjectives*) Excitable, etc., excited, etc.

Intolerant, impatient, unquiet, restless, restive, fidgety, irritable, mettlesome, chafing, wincing, etc.

Vehement, boisterous, impetuous, demonstrative, fierce, fiery, flaming, boiling, ebullient, over-zealous, passionate, impassioned, enthusiastic, rampant, mercurial, high-strung, skittish, overwrought, overstrung, hysterical, hot-headed, hurried, turbulent, furious, fuming, boiling, raging, raving, frantic, phrenetic, rampageous, wild, heady, delirious, intoxicated, demoniacal; hypersensitive.

Overpowering, overwhelming, uncontrolled, madcap, reckless, stanchless, irrepressible, ungovernable, uncontrollable, inextinguishable, volcanic.

(*Phrases*) More than flesh and blood can stand; stung to the quick; all hot and bothered.

(*Interjections*) Pish! pshaw! botheration!

bear, to bear well, tolerate, put up with, bear with, stand, bide, abide, aby, take easily, rub on, rub along, make the best of, acquiesce, submit, yield, bow to, resign oneself, suffer, endure, support, go through, reconcile oneself to, bend under; subside, calm down, pipe down.

To brook, digest, eat, swallow, pocket, stomach, brave, make light of.

To be borne, endured, etc., to go down.

To allay, compose, calm, still, lull, pacify, placate, quiet, tranquillize, hush, smooth, appease, assuage, mitigate, soothe, soften, temper, chasten, alleviate, moderate, sober down, mollify, lenify, tame, blunt, obtund, dull, deaden (823), slacken, damp, repress, restrain, check, curb, bridle, rein in, smother (174).

(*Phrases*) To take things as they come; to submit with a good grace; to shrug the shoulders.

To set one's heart at rest or at ease.

(*Adjectives*) Inexcitable, unexcited, calm, cool, temperate, composed, collected, placid, quiet, tranquil, unstirred, undisturbed, unruffled, serene, demure, sedate, staid, sober, dispassionate, unimpassioned, passionless, good-natured, easy-going, platonic, philosophic, stoical, imperturbable, cold-blooded, insensible (823).

Meek, tolerant, patient, submissive, unoffended, unresenting, content, resigned, subdued, bearing with, long-suffering, gentle, mild, sober-minded, cool-headed.

(*Phrases*) Gentle or meek as a lamb; mild as milk; patient as Job; armed with patience; cool as a cucumber.

SECTION II—PERSONAL AFFECTIONS

1°. *Passive Affections*

827 PLEASURE (*Substantives*), gratification, delectation, enjoyment, fruition, relish, zest, gusto, kick.

Well-being, satisfaction, complacency, content (831), ease, comfort, bed of roses, bed of down, velvet.

828 PAIN (*Substantives*), suffering; physical pain (378).

Displeasure, dissatisfaction, discontent, discomfort, discomposure, malaise.

Uneasiness, disquiet, inquietude,

Joy, gladness, delight, glee, cheer, sunshine.

Physical pleasure (377).

Treat, refreshment, feast, luxury, voluptuousness, clover.

Happiness, felicity, bliss, beatitude, beatification, enchantment, transport, rapture, ravishment, ecstasy, heaven, *summum bonum*, paradise, Eden, Arcadia, nirvana, elysium, empyrean (981).

Honeymoon, palmy days, halcyon days, golden age, *Saturnia regna*.

(*Verbs*) To be pleased, etc., to feel, receive, or derive pleasure, etc.; to take pleasure or delight in; to delight in, joy in, rejoice in, relish, like, enjoy, take to, take in good part.

To indulge in, treat oneself, solace oneself, revel, riot, luxuriate in, gloat over; to be on velvet, in clover, in heaven, etc.; to enjoy oneself; to congratulate oneself, hug oneself.

(*Phrases*) To slake the appetite; to bask in the sunshine; to tread on enchanted ground; to have a good time; to make whoopee.

(*Adjectives*) Pleased, enjoying, relishing, liking, gratified, glad, gladdened, rejoiced, delighted, overjoyed, charmed.

Cheered, enlivened, flattered, tickled, indulged, regaled, treated.

Comfortable, at ease, easy, cosy, satisfied, content (831), luxurious, on velvet, in clover, on a bed of roses, *sans souci*.

Happy, blest, blessed, blissful, overjoyed, enchanted, captivated, fascinated, transported, raptured, rapt, enraptured, in raptures, in ecstasies, in a transport, beatified, in heaven, in the seventh heaven, in paradise.

(*Phrases*) With a joyful face; with sparkling eyes; happy as a king; pleased as Punch; in the lap of luxury; happy as the day is long; *ter quaterque beatus*.

(*Adverbs*) Happily, etc.

---

weariness (841), dejection (837).

Annoyance, irritation, plague, bore, bother, botheration, worry, infliction, stew.

Care, anxiety, concern, mortification, vexation, chagrin, trouble, trial, solicitude, cark, dole, dule, load, burden, fret.

Grief, sorrow, distress, affliction, woe, bitterness, heartache, a heavy heart, a bleeding heart, a broken heart, heavy affliction.

Unhappiness, infelicity, misery, wretchedness, desolation, tribulation.

Dolour, sufferance, ache, aching, hurt, smart, cut, twitch, twinge, stitch, cramp, spasm, nightmare, convulsion, throe, angina.

Pang, anguish, agony, torture, torment, rack, crucifixion, martyrdom, purgatory, hell (982).

A sufferer, victim, prey, martyr.

(*Phrases*) Vexation of spirit; a peck of troubles; a sea of troubles; the ills that flesh is heir to; *mauvais quart d'heure*; the iron entering the soul.

(*Verbs*) To feel, suffer, or experience pain, etc.; to suffer, ache, smart, ail, bleed, twinge, tingle, gripe, wince, writhe.

To grieve, fret, pine, mourn, bleed, worry oneself, chafe, yearn, droop, sink, give way, despair (859).

(*Phrases*) To sit on thorns; to be on pins and needles; to labour under afflictions; to have a bad or thin time; to drain the cup of misery to the dregs; to fall on evil days.

(*Adjectives*) In pain; feeling, suffering, enduring, etc., pain; in a state of pain, of suffering, etc., sore, aching, suffering, ailing, etc., pained, hurt, stung (830).

Displeased, annoyed, dissatisfied, discontented, weary (832), uneasy, ungratified, uncomfortable, ill at ease.

Crushed, stricken, victimized, illused.

Concerned, afflicted, in affliction, sorry, sorrowful, in sorrow, cut up, bathed in tears (839).

Unhappy, unfortunate, hapless, unblest, luckless, unlucky, ill-fated, ill-starred, fretting, wretched, miserable, careworn, disconsolate, inconsolable, woebegone, poor, forlorn, comfortless, a prey to grief, etc., despairing, in despair (859), heart-broken, broken-hearted, the heart bleeding, doomed, devoted, accursed, undone.

829 Capability of giving pleasure.

PLEASURABLENESS (*Substantives*), pleasantness, gratefulness, welcomeness, acceptableness, acceptability, agreeableness, delectability, deliciousness, daintiness, sweetness, luxuriousness, lusciousness, voluptuousness, eroticism.

Charm, attraction, attractiveness, sex-appeal, S.A., It, oomph, fascination, witchery, prestige, loveliness, takingness, winsomeness, likableness, invitingness, glamour.

A treat, dainty, titbit, bonbon, *bonne bouche*, sweet, sweetmeat, sugarplum, nuts, *sauce piquante*.

(*Verbs*) To cause, produce, create, give, afford, procure, offer, present, yield, etc., pleasure, gratification, etc.

To please, take, gratify, satisfy, indulge, flatter, tickle, humour, regale, refresh, interest.

To charm, rejoice, cheer, gladden, delight, enliven (836), to transport, captivate, fascinate, enchant, entrance, bewitch, ravish, enrapture, enravish, beatify, enthral, imparadise.

(*Phrases*) To do one's heart good; to tickle one to death; to take one's fancy.

(*Adjectives*) Causing or giving pleasure, etc., pleasing, agreeable, grateful, gratifying, pleasant, pleasurable, acceptable, welcome, glad, gladsome, comfortable.

Sweet, delectable, nice, jolly, palatable, dainty, delicate, delicious, dulcet, savoury, toothsome, tasty, luscious, luxurious, voluptuous, genial, cordial, refreshing, comfortable, scrumptious.

Fair, lovely, favourite, attractive, engaging, winsome, winning, taking, prepossessing, inviting, captivating, bewitching, fascinating, magnetic, seductive, killing, stunning, ripping, smashing, likable.

Charming, delightful, exquisite, enchanting, enthralling, ravishing,

830 Capability of giving pain.

PAINFULNESS (*Substantives*), disagreeableness, unpleasantness, irksomeness, displeasingness, unacceptableness, bitterness, vexatiousness, troublesomeness.

Trouble, care, cross, annoyance, burden, load, nuisance, pest, plague, bore, bother, botheration, vexation, sickener, pin-prick.

Scourge, bitter pill, worm, canker, cancer, ulcer, curse, gall and wormwood, sting, pricks, scorpion, thorn, brier, bramble, hornet, whip, lash, rack, wheel.

A mishap, misadventure, mischance, pressure, infestation, grievance, trial, crosses, hardship, blow, stroke, affliction, misfortune, reverse, infliction, dispensation, visitation, disaster, undoing, tragedy, calamity, catastrophe, adversity (735).

Provocation, infestation, affront, aggravation, indignity, outrage (900, 929).

(*Phrases*) A thorn in one's side; a fly in the ointment; a sorry sight; a bitter pill; a crumpled rose-leaf.

(*Verbs*) To cause, produce, give, etc., pain, uneasiness, suffering, etc.

To pain, hurt, wound, sting, pinch, grate upon, irk, gall, jar, chafe, gnaw, prick, lacerate, pierce, cut, cut up, stick, gravel, hurt one's feelings, mortify, horrify, shock, twinge, gripe.

To wring, harrow, torment, torture, rack, scarify, cruciate, crucify, convulse, agonize.

To displease, annoy, incommode, discompose, trouble, disquiet, grieve, cross, tease, rag, josh, bait, tire, vex, worry, try, plague, fash, faze, fret, haunt, obsess, bother, pester, bore, gravel, flummox, harass, importune, tantalize, aggravate.

To irritate, provoke, nettle, pique, rile, ruffle, aggrieve, enchafe, enrage.

rapturous, heart-felt, thrilling, beatific, heavenly, celestial, elysian, empyrean, seraphic, ideal.

Palmy, halcyon, Saturnian, Arcadian.

(*Phrases*) To one's heart's content; to one's taste.

———

To maltreat, bite, assail, badger, infest, harry, persecute, haze, roast.

To sicken, disgust, revolt, turn the stomach, nauseate, disenchant, repel, offend, shock.

To horrify, prostrate.

(*Phrases*) To barb the dart; to set the teeth on edge; to stink in the nostrils; to stick in one's throat; to add a nail to one's coffin; to plant a dagger in the breast; to freeze the blood; to make one's flesh creep; to make one's hair stand on end; to break or wring the heart.

(*Adjectives*) Causing, occasioning, giving, producing, creating, inflicting, etc., pain, etc., hurting, etc.

Painful, dolorific, dolorous, unpleasant, unpleasing, displeasing, unprepossessing, disagreeable, distasteful, uncomfortable, unwelcome, unsatisfactory, unpalatable, unacceptable, thankless, undesirable, untoward, unlucky, undesired, obnoxious.

Distressing, bitter, afflicting, afflictive, cheerless, joyless, comfortless, depressing, depressive, mournful, dreary, dismal, bleak, melancholy, grievous, pathetic, woeful, disastrous, calamitous, ruinous, sad, tragic, tragical, deplorable, dreadful, frightful, lamentable, ill-omened.

Irritating, provoking, provocative, stinging, biting, vexatious, annoying, unaccommodating, troublesome, fashious, wearisome, tiresome, irksome, plaguing, plaguy, teasing, pestering, bothering, bothersome, carking, mortifying, galling, harassing, worrying, tormenting, aggravating, racking, importunate, insistent.

Intolerable, insufferable, insupportable, unbearable, unendurable, shocking, frightful, terrific, grim, appalling, dire, heart-breaking, heart-rending, heart-wounding, heart-corroding, dreadful, horrid, harrowing, horrifying, horrific, execrable, accursed, damnable.

Odious, hateful, unpopular, repulsive, repellent, uninviting, offensive, nauseous, disgusting, sickening, nasty, execrable, revolting, shocking, vile, foul, abominable, loathsome, rotten.

Sharp, acute, sore, severe, grave, hard, harsh, bitter, cruel, biting, caustic, corroding, consuming, racking, excruciating, grinding, agonizing.

(*Phrase*) More than flesh and blood can bear.

(*Adverbs*) Painfully, etc.

831 CONTENT (*Substantives*), contentment, contentedness, satisfaction, peace of mind, complacency, serenity, sereneness, ease.

Comfort, snugness, well-being.

Moderation, patience (826), endurance, resignation, reconciliation.

(*Verbs*) To be content, etc.; to rest satisfied, to put up with; to take up with; to be reconciled to.

To render content, etc., to set at ease, to conciliate, reconcile, disarm, propitiate, win over, satisfy, indulge, slake, gratify.

832 DISCONTENT (*Substantives*), discontentment, dissatisfaction, disappointment, mortification.

Repining, taking on, inquietude, heart-burning, regret (833).

Nostalgia, home-sickness, *maladie du pays*.

Grumbler, grouser, croaker.

(*Verbs*) To be discontented, dissatisfied, etc.; to repine, regret (833), grumble (839).

To cause discontent, etc., to disappoint, dissatisfy, mortify.

(*Phrases*) To take in bad part; to

(*Phrases*) To make the best of; to let well alone; to take in good part; to set one's heart at ease or at rest.

(*Adjectives*) Content, contented, satisfied, at ease, easy, snug, comfortable, cosy.

Patient, resigned to, reconciled to, unrepining; disarming, conciliatory.

Unafflicted, unvexed, unmolested, unplagued, etc., serene, at rest, *sine cura, sans souci.*

(*Phrases*) To one's heart's content; like patience on a monument.

(*Interjections*) Very well, all right, suits me.

833 REGRET (*Substantives*), bitterness, repining; lamentation (839); self-reproach, penitence (950).

(*Verbs*) To regret, deplore, repine, lament, rue, repent (950).

(*Phrase*) To rue the day.

(*Adjectives*) Regretting, etc., regretful, regretted, regrettable, lamentable.

(*Phrase*) What a pity!

835 AGGRAVATION (*Substantives*), heightening, exacerbation, exasperation.

(*Verbs*) To aggravate, render worse, heighten, intensify, embitter, sour, acerbate, envenom, exacerbate, exasperate.

(*Phrase*) To add fuel to the flame.

(*Adjectives*) Aggravating, etc., aggravated, etc., unrelieved; aggravable.

(*Phrases*) Out of the frying-pan into the fire; from bad to worse.

836 CHEERFULNESS (*Substantives*), gaiety, cheer, spirits, high spirits, high glee, light-heartedness, joyfulness, joyousness, good humour, geniality, hilarity, exhilaration, liveliness, sprightliness, briskness, vivacity, buoyancy, sunniness, jocundity, joviality, levity, sportiveness, playfulness, jocularity.

Mirth, merriment, merrymaking, laughter (838), amusement (840); nepenthe, Euphrosyne.

Gratulation, rejoicing, exultation,

have the hump; to quarrel with one's bread and butter.

(*Adjectives*) Discontented, dissatisfied, unsatisfied, malcontent, mortified, disappointed, cut up.

Repining, glum, grumbling, grousing, grouchy, exigent, *exigeant*, exacting; nostalgic, home-sick; disgruntled.

Disappointing, unsatisfactory.

(*Phrases*) Out of humour; in the dumps; in high dudgeon; down in the mouth.

___

834 RELIEF (*Substantives*), easement, alleviation, mitigation, palliation, solace, consolation, comfort, encouragement, refreshment (689), lullaby; deliverance, delivery.

Lenitive, balm, oil, restorative, cataplasm (662); cushion, pillow, bolster (215).

(*Phrases*) A crumb of comfort; balm in Gilead.

(*Verbs*) To relieve, ease, alleviate, mitigate, palliate, soften, soothe, assuage, allay, cheer, comfort, console, encourage, bear up, refresh, restore, remedy, cure.

(*Phrases*) To dry the tears; to pour balm into; to lay the flattering unction to one's soul; to temper the wind to the shorn lamb; to breathe again; to breathe freely.

(*Adjectives*) Relieving, etc., consolatory; balmy, balsamic, soothing, lenitive, anodyne. (662), remedial, curative; easeful.

837 DEJECTION (*Substantives*), depression, low spirits, lowness or depression of spirits, dejectedness, sadness.

Heaviness, dullness, infestivity, joylessness, gloom, dolefulness, dolesomeness, weariness (841), heaviness of heart, heart-sickness.

Melancholy, melancholia, dismals, mumps, dumps, doldrums, blues, mulligrubs, blue devils, megrims, vapours, accidie, spleen, hypochondria; *taedium vitae; maladie du pays.*

jubilation, jubilee, triumph, paean, Te Deum, heyday; joy-bells.

(*Verbs*) To be cheerful, etc.; to be of good cheer, to cheer up, perk up, brighten up, light up; take heart, bear up.

To rejoice, make merry, exult, congratulate oneself, triumph, clap the hands, crow, sing, carol, lilt, frisk, prance, galumph, rollick, maffick, frivol.

To cheer, enliven, elate, exhilarate, entrance, inspirit, animate, gladden, buck up, liven up.

(*Phrases*) To drive dull care away; to make whoopee; to keep up one's spirits; care killed the cat; *ride si sapis*; laugh and grow fat.

(*Adjectives*) Cheerful, gay, blithe, cheery, jovial, genial, gleeful, of good cheer, in spirits, in good or high spirits, *allegro*, light, lightsome, buoyant, debonair, bright, glad, light-hearted, hearty, free and easy, airy, jaunty, canty, perky, spry, chipper, saucy, sprightly, lively, vivacious, sunny, breezy, chirpy, hopeful (858).

Merry, joyous, joyful, jocund, playful, waggish, frisky, frolicsome, sportive, gamesome, jokesome, joky, jocose, jocular, jolly, frivolous.

Rejoicing, elated, exulting, jubilant, hilarious, flushed, rollicking, cock-a-hoop.

(*Phrases*) In high feather; walking on air; with one's head in the clouds; gay as a lark; happy as a king or as the day is long; playful as a kitten; jolly as a sandboy; merry as a grig; full of beans.

(*Adverbs*) Cheerfully, cheerily, cheerly, etc.

(*Interjections*) Cheer up! never say die! hurrah! huzza!

Despondency, despair, pessimism, disconsolateness, prostration; the Slough of Despond (859).

Demureness, seriousness, gravity, solemnity, solemnness, sullenness.

A hypochondriac, self-tormentor, *malade imaginaire*, kill-joy, Job's comforter, wet blanket, pessimist, futilitarian.

(*Verbs*) To be dejected, sad, etc.; to grieve, take on, take to heart, give way, droop, sink, lour, look downcast, mope, mump, pout, brood over, fret, pine, yearn, frown, despond (859).

To depress, discourage, dishearten, dispirit, dull, deject, lower, sink, dash, unman, prostrate, over-cloud.

(*Phrases*) To look blue; to hang down the head; to wear the willow; to laugh on the wrong side of the mouth; to get the hump.

To prey on the mind or spirits; to dash one's hopes.

(*Adjectives*) Cheerless, unmirthful, mirthless, joyless, dull, glum, flat, dispirited, out of spirits, out of sorts, out of heart, in low spirits, spiritless, lowering, frowning, sulky.

Discouraged, disheartened, downhearted, downcast, cast down, depressed, chap-fallen, crest-fallen, dashed, drooping, sunk, heart-sick, dumpish, mumpish, desponding, pessimistic.

Dismal, melancholy, sombre, tristful, *triste*, pensive, *penseroso*, mournful, doleful, moping, splenetic, gloomy, lugubrious, funereal, woebegone, comfortless, forlorn, overcome, prostrate, cut up, care-worn, care-laden.

Melancholic, hipped, hypochondriacal, bilious, jaundiced, atrabilious, atrabiliar, saturnine, adust.

Disconsolate, inconsolable, despairing; in despair (859).

Grave, serious, sedate, staid, sober, solemn, grim, grim-faced, grim-visaged (846), rueful, sullen.

Depressing, preying upon the mind (830).

(*Phrases*) Down in the mouth; down on one's luck; sick at heart; with a long face; a prey to melancholy; dull as a beetle; dull as ditchwater; as melancholy as a gib-cat; grave as a judge.

838 Expression of pleasure.

REJOICING (*Substantives*), exultation, heyday, triumph, jubilation, jubilee (840), paean (990).

Smile, simper, smirk, grin, broad grin.

Laughter, giggle, titter, snigger, crow, cheer, chuckle, guffaw, shout; hearty laugh, horse-laugh, cachinnation; a shout, burst, or peal of laughter.

Derision, risibility (856).

Momus, Democritus the Abderite.

(*Verbs*) To rejoice, exult, triumph (884), hug oneself, sing, carol, dance with joy.

To smile, simper, smirk, grin, mock; to laugh, giggle, titter, snigger, chuckle, chortle, burble, crow, cackle; to burst out, shout, guffaw.

To cause, create, occasion, raise, excite, or produce laughter, etc.; to tickle, titillate.

(*Phrases*) To clap one's hands; to fling up one's cap; to laugh in one's sleeve; to shake one's sides; to hold both one's sides; to split one's sides; to die with laughter.

To tickle one's fancy; to set the table in a roar; to convulse with laughter; to be the death of one.

(*Adjectives*) Laughing, rejoicing, etc.; jubilant (836), triumphant.

Laughable, risible, ludicrous (853), side-splitting.

(*Phrases*) Ready to burst or split oneself; 'Laughter holding both his sides.'

(*Interjections*) Hurrah! three cheers!

---

839 Expression of pain.

LAMENTATION (*Substantives*), complaint, murmur, mutter, plaint, lament, wail, sigh, suspiration, heaving.

Cry, whine, whimper, sob, tear, moan, snivel, grumble, groan.

Outcry, scream, screech, howl, whoop, yell, roar, (414).

Weeping, crying, etc.; lachrymation, complaining, frown, scowl, sardonic grin or laugh.

Dirge (363), elegy, requiem, monody, threnody, jeremiad; coronach, wake, keen, keening.

Plaintiveness, querimoniousness, languishment, querulousness.

Mourning, weeds, willow, cypress, crape, sackcloth and ashes.

A grumbler, grouser, croaker, drip; Heraclitus, Niobe.

(*Phrases*) The melting mood; wringing of hands; weeping and gnashing of teeth.

(*Verbs*) To lament, mourn, grieve, keen, complain, murmur, mutter, grumble, grouse, belly-ache, beef, squawk, sigh; give, fetch, or heave a sigh.

To cry, weep, sob, greet, blubber, blub; snivel, whimper; to shed tears; pule, take on, pine.

To grumble, groan, grunt, croak, whine, moan, bemoan, wail, bewail, frown, scowl.

To cry out, growl, mew, mewl, squeak, squeal, sing out, scream, cry out lustily, screech, skirl, bawl, howl, holloa, bellow, yell, roar, yammer.

(*Phrases*) To melt or burst into tears; to cry oneself blind; to cry one's eyes out; to beat one's breast; to wring one's hands; to gnash one's teeth; to tear one's hair; to cry before one is hurt; to laugh on the wrong side of one's mouth.

(*Adjectives*) Lamenting, complaining, etc.; mournful, doleful, sad, tearful, lachrymose, plaintive, plaintful, querulous, querimonious, elegiac.

(*Phrases*) With tears in one's eyes; bathed or dissolved in tears; the tears starting from the eyes.

(*Interjections*) O dear! ah me! alas! alack! heigh-ho! ochone! well-a-day! well-a-way! alas the day! woe worth the day! *O tempora, O mores!*

---

840 AMUSEMENT (*Substantives*), diversion, entertainment, sport, divertissement, recreation, relaxation, distraction, avocation, pastime.

841 WEARINESS (*Substantives*), tedium, ennui, boredom, lassitude, fatigue (688), dejection (837).

Disgust, nausea, loathing, sickness,

Fun, frolic, pleasantry, drollery, jollity, joviality, jovialness, jocoseness, laughter (838).

Play, game, gambol, romp, prank, quip, quirk, rig, lark, fling, bat, spree, burst, binge, razzle-dazzle, escapade, dido, monkey-shines, ploy, jamboree.

Dance (309), ball, ballet (599), hop, shindig, jig, fling, reel, strathspey, cotillion, quadrille, lancers, rigadoon, saraband, lavolta, pavane, galliard, hornpipe, can-can, tarantella, cachucha, fandango, bolero, minuet, gavotte, polka, mazurka, schottische, waltz (or valse), fox-trot, tango, maxixe, rumba, samba, blues, two-step, one-step; folk-dance, morris-dance, square dance, round dance, country dance, step-dance, clog-dance, sword-dance, egg-dance, cake-walk, break-down.

Festivity, festival, jubilee, party (892), merrymaking, rejoicing, fête, gala, ridotto, revelry, revels, carnival, corroboree, saturnalia, high jinks, night out.

Feast, banquet, entertainment, carousal, bean-feast, beano, wayz-goose, jollification, junketing, junket, wake, field-day, regatta, fair, kermess, fête champêtre, symposium, wassail.

Buffoonery, mummery, tomfoolery, raree-show, puppet-show, masquerade.

Bonfire, fireworks, feu de joie.

A holiday, gala day, red-letter day.

A place of amusement, theatre, music-hall, concert-hall, cinema, circus, hippodrome, ballroom, dance hall, arena, auditorium, recreation ground, playground, playing field, park.

Toy, plaything, bauble, doll, puppet, teddy-bear.

A master of ceremonies or revels; a sportsman, sportswoman, gamester, reveller; devotee, votary, enthusiast, fan.

(Phrases) A round of pleasure; a short life and a merry one; high days and holidays.

(Verbs) To amuse, divert, entertain, rejoice, cheer, recreate, enliven, solace; to beguile or while away the time; to drown care.

To play, sport, disport, make merry, take one's pleasure, make holiday, keep holiday; to game, gambol, revel, frisk, frolic, romp, jollify, skylark, dally; to dance, hop, foot it, jump, caper, cut capers, skip.

To treat, feast, regale, carouse, banquet.

(Phrases) To play the fool; to jump over the moon; to make a night of it; to make whoopee; to go on the bust; to have one's fling; desipere in loco.

disgust of life, taedium vitae, Weltschmerz.

Wearisomeness, irksomeness, tiresomeness, montony, sameness, treadmill, grind.

A bore, a buttonholer, proser, fossil, wet blanket.

(Phrases) A twice-told tale; time hanging heavily on one's hands; a thin time.

(Verbs) To tire, weary, fatigue, fag, jade, bore; set to sleep, send to sleep.

To sicken, disgust, nauseate.

(Phrases) To harp on the same string; to bore to tears; never hear the last of.

(Adjectives) Wearying, etc., wearisome, tiresome, irksome, uninteresting, devoid of interest, monotonous, humdrum, pedestrian, mortal, flat, tedious, prosy, prosing, slow, soporific, somniferous.

Disgusting, sickening, nauseating.

Weary, tired, etc.; aweary, uninterested, sick of, flagging, used up, blasé, bored, stale, fed up, browned off, brassed off, cheesed off, chokka, weary of life; drowsy, somnolent, sleepy (683).

(Adverbs) Wearily, etc.

(Phrase) Ad nauseam.

(*Adjectives*) Amusing, amusive, diverting, entertaining, etc., amused, etc.

Sportive, jovial, festive, jocose, tricksy, rompish.

(*Phrases*) On with the dance! *vogue la galère! vive la bagatelle!*

842 WIT (*Substantives*), humour, comicality, imagination (515), fancy, fun, drollery, whim, jocularity, jocosity, facetiousness, waggery, waggishness, wittiness, salt, Atticism, Attic wit, Attic salt, *esprit*, smartness, banter, chaff, persiflage, badinage, farce, *espièglerie.*

Jest, joke, jape, conceit, quip, quirk, quiddity, crank, wheeze, side-splitter, *concetto*, witticism, gag, wisecrack, repartee, retort, come-back, *mot, bon mot*, pleasantry, funniment, flash of wit, happy thought, sally, point, dry joke, idle conceit, epigram, quibble, play upon words, pun (563), conundrum, anagram (533), quodlibet, *jeu d'esprit, facetiae*; a chestnut, a Joe Miller; an absurdity (497).

A practical joke, a rag.

(*Phrases*) The cream of the jest; the joke of it; *le mot pour rire.*

843 DULLNESS (*Substantives*), heaviness, stolidness, stolidity, dumbness, stupidity (499), flatness, prosiness, gravity (837), solemnity; prose, matter of fact, platitude, commonplace, bromide.

(*Verbs*) To be dull, prose, fall flat. To render dull, etc., damp, depress.

(*Phrase*) To throw cold water on.

(*Adjectives*) Dull, prosaic, prosing, prosy, unentertaining, dismal (837), uninteresting, boring, flat, pointless, stolid, humdrum (841), pedestrian, literal, unimaginative, matter-of-fact, commonplace.

Slow, stupid, dumb, plodding, Boeotian.

(*Phrases*) Dull as ditch-water; *Davus sum, non Oedipus; aliquando bonus dormitat Homerus.*

———

(*Verbs*) To joke, jest, jape, retort; to cut jokes, crack a joke, perpetrate a joke or pun.

To laugh at, banter, rally, chaff, josh, jolly, jeer (856), rag, guy, kid; to make fun of, make merry with.

(*Phrase*) To set the table in a roar.

(*Adjectives*) Witty, facetious, humorous, fanciful, quick-witted, ready-witted, nimble-witted, imaginative (515), sprightly, *spirituel*, smart, jocose, jocular, waggish, comic, comical, laughable, droll, ludicrous, side-splitting, killing, funny, risible, farcical, roguish, sportive, pleasant, playful, sparkling, entertaining, arch.

(*Adverbs*) In joke, in jest, in sport, for fun.

844 A HUMORIST (*Substantives*), wag, wit, funny man, caricaturist, cartoonist, epigrammatist, *bel esprit*, jester, joker, punster, wise-cracker.

A buffoon (599), comedian, *farceur*, merry-andrew, jack-pudding, tumbler, mountebank, harlequin, punch, punchinello, scaramouch, clown, pantaloon.

(*Phrase*) The life and soul of the party.

2°. *Discriminative Affections*

845 BEAUTY (*Substantives*), handsomeness, beauteousness, beautifulness, pulchritude, aesthetics.

Form, elegance, grace, symmetry, *belle tournure*; good looks.

846 UGLINESS (*Substantives*), deformity, inelegance, plainness, homeliness, uncomeliness, ungainliness, uncouthness, clumsiness, stiffness, disfigurement, distortion, contortion,

Comeliness, seemliness, shapeliness, fairness, prettiness, neatness, spruceness, attractiveness, loveliness, quaintness, speciousness, polish, gloss, nattiness; a good effect.

Bloom, brilliancy, radiance, splendour, magnificence, sublimity.

Concinnity, delicacy, refinement, charm, style.

A beautiful woman, belle, charmer, enchantress, goddess; Helen of Troy, Venus, Hebe, the Graces, Peri, Houri; Cupid, Apollo, Hyperion, Adonis, Antinous, Narcissus.

Peacock, butterfly, flower, rose, lily; the flower of, the pink of, etc.; a garden, a picture.

(*Phrases*) *Je ne sais quoi; le beau idéal*; a sight for sore eyes.

(*Verbs*) To be beautiful; to shine, beam, bloom.

To render beautiful, etc., to beautify, embellish, adorn, deck, bedeck, decorate, set out, set off, ornament (847), dight, bedight, array, garnish, furbish, smarten, trick out, rig out, fig out, dandify, dress up, prank, prink, perk, preen, trim, embroider, emblazon, adonize.

To polish, burnish, gild, varnish, japan, enamel, lacquer.

To powder, rouge, make up, doll up, titivate.

(*Adjectives*) Beautiful, handsome, good-looking, fine, pretty, lovely, graceful, elegant, delicate, refined, fair, personable, comely, seemly, bonny, braw, well-favoured, proper, shapely, well-made, well-formed, well-proportioned, symmetrical, sightly, becoming, goodly, neat, dapper, tight, trig, spruce, smart, stylish, chic, dashing, swagger, dandified, natty, sleek, quaint, jaunty, bright-eyed, attractive, seductive, stunning.

Blooming, rosy, brilliant, shining, beaming, splendid, resplendent, dazzling, gorgeous, superb, magnificent, sublime, grand.

Picturesque, statuesque, artistic, aesthetic, decorative, photogenic, well-composed, well-grouped.

malformation, monstrosity, misproportion, inconcinnity, want of symmetry, roughness, repulsiveness, squalor, hideousness, unsightliness, odiousness.

An eyesore, object, figure, sight, fright, guy, spectre, scarecrow, hag, harridan, satyr, sibyl, toad, baboon, monster, gorgon, Caliban, Hecate.

(*Phrases*) A forbidding countenance; a wry face; a blot on the landscape; no oil-painting; '*monstrum horrendum, informe, ingens, cui lumen ademptum.*'

(*Verbs*) To be ugly, etc.

To render ugly, etc., to deform, deface, distort, disfigure (241), disfeature, misshape, blemish, spot, stain, distain, soil, tarnish, discolour, sully, blot, daub, bedaub, begrime, blur, smear, besmear (653), bespatter, maculate, denigrate, uglify.

(*Phrase*) To make faces.

(*Adjectives*) Ugly, plain, homely, unsightly, unornamental, unshapely, unlovely, ill-looking, ordinary, unseemly, ill-favoured, hard-favoured, evil-favoured, hard-featured, hard-visaged, ungainly, uncouth, gawky, hulking, lumbering, slouching, ungraceful, clumsy, graceless, rude, rough, rugged, homespun, gaunt, raw-boned, haggard, scraggy.

Misshapen, shapeless, misproportioned, ill-proportioned, deformed, ill-made, ill-shaped, inelegant, disfigured, distorted, unshapen, unshapely, humpbacked, crooked, bandy, stumpy, dumpy, squat, stubby, bald, rickety.

Squalid, grim, grisly, gruesome, grooly, macabre, grim-faced, grim-visaged, ghastly, ghost-like, death-like, cadaverous, repellent, repulsive, forbidding, grotesque.

Frightful, odious, hideous, horrid, shocking, monstrous, unprepossessing.

Foul, soiled, tarnished, stained, distained, sullied, blurred, blotted, spotted, maculated, spotty, splashed, smeared, begrimed,

Passable, presentable, not amiss, undefaced, spotless, unspotted.
(*Phrases*) Easy to look at; dressed up to kill.

847 ORNAMENT (*Substantives*), ornamentation, adornment, decoration, embellishment, enrichment, illustration, illumination, ornature, ornateness, flamboyancy.

Garnish, polish, varnish, gilding, japanning, enamel, lacquer, ormolu.

Cosmetic, rouge, powder, lipstick, mascara, hair-oil, brilliantine.

Jewel, jewellery, bijouterie, spangle, trinket, locket, bracelet, bangle, anklet, necklace, earring, brooch, chain, chatelaine, carcanet, tiara, coronet, diadem.

Gem, precious stone, diamond, brilliant, emerald, sapphire, ruby, agate, garnet, beryl, onyx, topaz, amethyst, opal; pearl, coral.

Embroidery, broidery, brocade, galloon, lace, fringe, trapping, trimming, edging, border, chiffon, hanging, tapestry, arras.

Wreath, festoon, garland, lei, chaplet, tassel, knot, epaulette, frog, star, rosette, bow.

Feather, plume, *panache*, aigrette.

Nosegay, bouquet, posy, buttonhole.

Tracery, moulding, arabesque.

Frippery, finery, bravery, gewgaw, gaud, fal-lal, tinsel, spangle, clinquant, bric-à-brac, knick-knack.

Trope, flourish, flowers of rhetoric, purple patches (577).

Excess of ornament, tawdriness (851).

(*Verbs*) To ornament, embellish, illustrate, illuminate, enrich, decorate, adorn, beautify, garnish, polish, gild, varnish, enamel, paint, whitewash, stain, japan, lacquer, fume, grain; bespangle, bedeck, bedizen (845), embroider, work, chase, emboss, fret, tool; emblazon, illuminate.

(*Adjectives*) Ornamented, etc., beautified, rigged out, figged out, well-groomed, dolled up, ornate, showy, dressy, gaudy (851), garish, gorgeous, fine, gay, rich.

(*Phrases*) Fine as fivepence; in full fig; in one's Sunday best; dressed up to the nines.

850 Good taste.

TASTE (*Substantives*), delicacy, refinement, gust, gusto, *goût*, virtuosity, virtuosoship, nicety, finesse, grace, culture, virtu, τὸ πρέπον, polish, elegance.

spattered, bedaubed, besmeared; ungarnished.
(*Phrases*) Ugly as sin; not fit to be seen.

848 BLEMISH (*Substantives*), disfigurement, defacement, deformity, eyesore, defect, fault, deficiency, flaw, fleck.

Stain, blot, spot, speck, mote, blur; macula, blotch, speckle, spottiness; soil, tarnish, smudge, smut, dirt, soot (653); freckle, birthmark.

Excrescence, pimple, pustule (250).

(*Verbs*) To blemish, disfigure, deface (846).

(*Adjectives*) Blemished, disfigured, etc.; spotted, speckled, freckled, pitted.

849 SIMPLICITY (*Substantives*), plainness, undress, chastity, chasteness; freedom from ornament or affectation, homeliness.

(*Phrase*) Simplex munditiis.

(*Verbs*) To be simple, etc., to render simple, etc., to simplify.

(*Adjectives*) Simple, plain, ordinary, household, homely, homespun, chaste, unaffected, severe, primitive.

Unadorned, unornamented, undecked, ungarnished, unarrayed, untrimmed, unsophisticated, in dishabille.

851 Bad taste.

VULGARITY (*Substantives*), vulgarism, barbarism, Vandalism, Gothicism, *mauvais goût*, sensationalism, flamboyance.

Coarseness, grossness, indecorum,

Science of taste, aesthetics.

A man of taste, connoisseur, judge, critic, *cognoscente*, virtuoso, dilettante, amateur, aesthete, purist, precision; an Aristarchus, Corinthian, *arbiter elegantiarum*.

(*Phrase*) Caviare to the general.

(*Verbs*) To appreciate, judge, discriminate, criticize (465).

(*Adjectives*) In good taste, tasteful, unaffected, pure, chaste, classical, attic, refined, aesthetic, cultivated, cultured, artistic, elegant.

(*Adverb*) Elegantly, etc.

(*Phrases*) To one's taste or mind; after one's fancy; *comme il faut*.

852 FASHION (*Substantives*), style, tonishness, *ton*, *bon ton*, mode, vogue, craze, rage, fad.

Manners, breeding, politeness, gentlemanliness, courtesy (894), decorum, *bienséance*, *savoir faire*, *savoir vivre*, punctilio, convention, conventionality, propriety, the proprieties, Mrs. Grundy, form, formality, etiquette, custom, demeanour, air, port, carriage, presence.

Show, equipage, turn-out (882).

The world, the fashionable world, the smart set, the *beau monde*, high life, society, town, court, gentility (875), civilization, civilized life, the *élite*.

(*Phrases*) The height of fashion; *dernier cri*; the latest thing.

(*Verbs*) To be fashionable, etc.

(*Phrases*) To cut a dash; to be in the swim.

(*Adjectives*) Fashionable, in fashion, in vogue, *à la mode*, modish, tony, tonish, stylish, smart, courtly, *recherché*, genteel, aristocratic, conventional, punctilious, *comme il faut*, well-bred, well-mannered, polished, gentlemanlike, ladylike, well-spoken, civil, presentable, *distingué*, refined, thorough-bred, county, *dégagé*, jaunty, swell, swagger, posh, dashing, unembarrassed; trendy.

(*Phrases*) Having a run; all the go.

(*Adverbs*) Fashionably, in fashion.

lowness, low life, *mauvais ton*, bad form, ribaldry, clownishness, rusticity, boorishness, brutishness, brutality, rowdyism, ruffianism, awkwardness, *gaucherie*, want of tact, tactlessness.

Excess of ornament, false ornament, tawdriness, loudness, gaudiness, flashiness, ostentation.

A rough diamond, a hoyden, tomboy, slattern, sloven, dowdy, frump, cub, unlicked cub, clown, cad, guttersnipe, ragamuffin (876); a Goth, Vandal.

(*Verbs*) To be vulgar, etc., to misbehave.

(*Adjectives*) In bad taste, vulgar, coarse, unrefined, gross, ribald, heavy, rude, unpolished, indecorous, home-spun, clownish, uncouth, awkward, *gauche*, ungraceful, slovenly, slatternly, dowdy, frumpish.

Ill-bred, ungenteel, impolite, ill-mannered, uncivil, tactless, underbred, caddish, ungentlemanly, unladylike, unfeminine, unmaidenly, unseemly, unpresentable, unkempt, uncombed.

Rustic, countrified, boorish, provincial, barbarous, barbaric, brutish, blackguardly, rowdy, raffish, Gothic, unclassical, heathenish, outlandish, untamed (876).

Obsolete, out of fashion, *démodé*, out of date, unfashionable, antiquated, fossil, old-fashioned, old-world, gone by.

New-fangled, odd, fantastic, grotesque, ridiculous (853), affected, meretricious, extravagant, sensational, monstrous, shocking, horrid, revolting.

Gaudy, tawdry, tinsel, bedizened, flamboyant, baroque, tricked out, gingerbread, loud, flashy, showy.

(*Phrase*) A back number.

853 RIDICULOUSNESS (*Substantives*), ludicrousness, risibility.

Oddness, oddity, whimsicality, comicality, drollery, grotesqueness, fancifulness, quaintness, frippery, gawkiness, preposterousness, extravagance, monstrosity, absurdity (497).

Bombast, bathos, fustian, doggerel, nonsense verse, amphigouri, extravaganza, clerihew, bull, Irish bull, spoonerism.

(*Adjectives*) Ridiculous, absurd, extravagant, *outré*, monstrous, preposterous, irrational, nonsensical.

Odd, whimsical, quaint, queer, rum, droll, grotesque, fanciful, eccentric, bizarre, strange, out-of-the-way, outlandish, fantastic, baroque, rococo.

Laughable, risible, ludicrous, comic, serio-comic, mock-heroic, comical, funny, derisive, farcical, burlesque, *pour rire*, quizzical, bombastic, inflated, stilted.

Awkward, gawky, lumbering, lumpish, hulking, uncouth.

854 FOP (*Substantives*), dandy, exquisite, swell, toff, dude, nut, masher, lady-killer, coxcomb, beau, macaroni, blade, blood, buck, spark, dog, popinjay, puppy, *petit-maître*, jackanapes, jack-a-dandy, tailor's dummy, man-milliner, man about town.

855 AFFECTATION (*Substantives*), mannerism, pretension, airs, dandyism, coxcombry, frills, side, swank, dog, conceit, foppery, affectedness, preciosity, euphuism, charlatanism, quackery, foppishness, pedantry, acting a part, pose, gush.

Prudery, Grundyism, demureness, coquetry, *minauderie*, sentimentality, lackadaisicalness, stiffness, formality, buckram, mock modesty, *mauvaise honte*.

Pedant, precisian, prig, square, bluestocking, *bas bleu*, formalist, *poseur*, mannerist, *précieuse ridicule*; prude, Mrs. Grundy.

(*Phrases*) A lump of affectation; prunes and prisms.

(*Verbs*) To affect, to give oneself airs, put on side or frills, to swank, simper, mince, to act a part, overact, attitudinize, gush, pose.

(*Adjectives*) Affected, conceited, precious, pretentious, stilted, pedantic, pragmatical, priggish, smug, puritanical, prim, prudish, starchy, up-stage, high-hat, stiff, formal, demure, goody-goody.

Foppish, namby-pamby, slip-slop, coxcombical, slipshod, simpering, mincing, niminy-piminy, la-di-da, sentimental, lackadaisical.

Exaggerated (549), overacted, overdone, high-falutin, gushing, stagy, theatrical.

856 RIDICULE (*Substantives*), derision, mockery, quiz, banter, chaff, badinage, irony, persiflage, raillery, send-up.

Jeer, gibe, quip, taunt, satire, scurrility, scoffing.

A parody, burlesque, travesty, skit, farce, comedy, tragi-comedy, doggerel, blunder, bull, *lapsus linguae*, slip of the tongue, malapropism, spoonerism, anticlimax.

Buffoonery, vagary, antic, mummery, tomfoolery, grimace, monkey-trick, escapade, prank, gambade, extravaganza, practical joke, booby-trap.

(*Verbs*) To ridicule, deride, laugh at (929), laugh down, scoff, mock, jeer, banter, quiz, rally, fleer, flout, rag, rot, chaff, josh, guy, rib, razz, roast, twit, taunt, point at, grin at.

To parody, caricature, burlesque, travesty, pillory, take off.

(*Phrases*) To raise a smile; to set the table in a roar; to make fun of; to poke fun at; to make merry with; to make a fool of; to make an ass of; to make game of; to make faces at; to make mouths at; to lead one a dance;

to run a rig upon; to make an April fool of; to laugh out of court; to laugh in one's sleeve; to take the micky out of.

(*Adjectives*) Derisory, derisive, sarcastic, ironical, quizzical, mock, scurrilous, burlesque, Hudibrastic.

857 Object and cause of ridicule.

LAUGHING-STOCK (*Substantives*), gazing-stock, butt, stooge, target, quiz; an original, guy, oddity, card, crank, eccentric, monkey, buffoon, jester (844), mime, mimer (599), scaramouch, punch, punchinello, mountebank, golliwog.

(*Phrases*) A figure of fun; a queer fish; fair game.

3°. Prospective Affections

858 HOPE (*Substantives*), trust, confidence, reliance, faith, assurance, credit, security, expectation, affiance, promise, assumption, presumption.

Hopefulness, buoyancy, reassurance, optimism, enthusiasm, aspiration.

A reverie, day-dream, pipe-dream, Utopia, millennium.

Anchor, mainstay, sheet-anchor, staff (215).

(*Phrases*) Castles in the air; castles in Spain; a ray, gleam, or flash of hope; the silver lining of the cloud.

(*Verbs*) To hope; to feel, entertain, harbour, cherish, feed, nourish, encourage, foster, etc., hope or confidence; to promise oneself.

To trust, confide, rely on, build upon, feel or rest assured, confident, secure, etc.; to flatter oneself, expect, aspire, presume, be reassured.

To give or inspire hope; to augur well, shape well, bid fair, be in a fair way; to encourage, assure, promise, flatter, buoy up, reassure, embolden, raise expectations.

(*Phrases*) To see daylight; to live in hopes; to look on the bright side; to pin one's hope or faith upon; to catch at a straw; to hope against hope.

(*Adjectives*) Hoping, etc., in hopes, hopeful, confident, secure, buoyant, buoyed up, in good heart, sanguine, optimistic, enthusiastic, utopian.

Fearless, unsuspecting, unsuspicious; free or exempt from fear, suspicion, distrust, etc., undespairing.

Auspicious, promising, propitious, bright, rose-coloured, rosy, of good omen, reassuring.

859 Absence, want, or loss of hope.

HOPELESSNESS (*Substantives*), despair, desperation, despondency, pessimism (837); forlornness, a forlorn hope, the Slough of Despond.

(*Phrases*) A black look-out; a bad business.

(*Verbs*) To despair, despond, give up, be hopeless; to lose, give up, abandon, relinquish, etc., all hope; to yield to despair.

To inspire or drive to despair; to dash, crush, or destroy one's hopes.

(*Phrases*) To trust to a broken reed; '*lasciate ogni speranza voi ch' entrate.*'

(*Adjectives*) Hopeless, having lost or given up hope, losing, etc., hope, past hope, despondent, pessimistic, forlorn, desperate, despairing.

Incurable, irremediable, irreparable, irrevocable, incorrigible, beyond remedy.

Inauspicious, unpropitious, unpromising, threatening, ill-omened.

860 FEAR (*Substantives*), cowardice (862), timidity, diffidence, nervousness, restlessness, inquietude, disquietude, solicitude, anxiety, care, distrust, mistrust, hesitation, misgiving, suspicion, qualm, want of confidence, nerves.

Apprehension, flutter, trepidation, tremor, shaking, trembling, palpitation, jitters, the jumps, the creeps, the needle, ague-fit, fearfulness, despondency; stage fright, cold feet, wind up.

Fright, affright, alarm, dread, awe, terror, horror, dismay, obsession,

(*Phrases*) *Nil desperandum*; while there's life there's hope; *dum spiro spero*; never say die; all for the best.

——

panic, funk, flap, stampede, scare, consternation, despair (859).

Intimidation, terrorism, reign of terror; an alarmist, scaremonger.

Object of fear, bugbear, bugaboo, bogy, scarecrow, goblin (980), *bête noire*, nightmare, Gorgon, ogre.

(*Phrases*) Raw head and bloody bones; fee-faw-fum; butterflies in the stomach.

(*Verbs*) To fear, be afraid, etc., to distrust, hesitate, have qualms, misgiving, suspicions.

To apprehend, take alarm, start, wince, boggle, skulk, cower, crouch, tremble, shake, quake, quaver, quiver, shudder, quail, cringe, turn pale, blench, flutter, flinch, funk.

To excite fear, raise apprehensions, to give, raise, or sound an alarm, to intimidate, put in fear, frighten, fright, affright, alarm, startle, scare, haunt, obsess, strike terror, daunt, terrify, unman, awe, horrify, dismay, petrify, appal.

To overawe, abash, cow, browbeat, bully, deter, discourage.

(*Phrases*) To shake in one's shoes; to shake like an aspen leaf; to stand aghast; to eye askance.

To fright from one's propriety; to strike all of a heap; to make the flesh creep; to give one the creeps; to cause alarm and despondency.

(*Adjectives*) Fearing, timid, timorous, faint-hearted, tremulous, fearful, nervous, nervy, jumpy, funky, diffident, apprehensive, restless, haunted with the fear, apprehension, dread, etc., of.

Frightened, afraid, cowed, pale, alarmed, scared, terrified, petrified, aghast, awestruck, dismayed, horror-struck, horrified, appalled, panic-stricken.

Inspiring fear, fearsome, alarming, formidable, redoubtable, portentous, perilous (665), ugly, fearful, dreadful, dire, shocking, terrible, tremendous, horrid, horrible, horrific, ghastly, awful, awesome, horripilant, hair-raising, creepy, crawly.

(*Phrases*) White as a sheet; afraid of one's shadow; the hair standing on end; letting 'I dare not' wait upon 'I would'; more frightened than hurt; frightened out of one's senses or wits; in a blue funk.

861 Absence of fear.

COURAGE (*Substantives*), bravery, value, boldness, spirit, moral fibre, spiritedness, daring, gallantry, intrepidity, contempt of danger, self-reliance, confidence, fearlessness, audacity.

Manhood, manliness, nerve, pluck, grit, guts, sand, mettle, gameness, heart, spunk, smeddum, virtue, hardihood, fortitude, firmness, resolution, sportsmanship.

Prowess, derring-do, heroism, chivalry.

A hero, heroine, ace, paladin, *preux chevalier*, Hector, Hotspur, Amazon, Joan of Arc, *beau sabreur*, fire-eater (863).

862 Excess of fear.

COWARDICE (*Substantives*), fear (860), pusillanimity, cowardliness, timidity, fearfulness, spiritlessness, faint-heartedness, softness, effeminacy, funk.

Poltroonery, baseness, dastardliness, yellow streak, a faint heart.

A coward, poltroon, dastard, recreant, funk, mollycoddle, milksop, cry-baby, 'fraid-cat, chicken, cowardy custard.

A runaway, fugitive, deserter, quitter.

(*Verbs*) To be cowardly, etc.; to quail (860), to flinch, fight shy, shy, turn tail, run away, cut and run, fly for one's life, stampede.

A lion, tiger, bulldog, gamecock, fighting-cock, sportsman.

(*Verbs*) To be courageous, etc., to face, front, affront, confront, despise, brave, defy, etc., danger; to take courage; to summon up, muster up, or pluck up courage; to rally.

To venture, make bold, face, dare, defy, brave (715), beard, hold out, bear up against, stand up to.

To give, infuse, or inspire courage; to encourage, embolden, inspirit, cheer, nerve.

(*Phrases*) To take the bull by the horns; to come up to the scratch; to face the music; to 'screw one's courage to the sticking-place'; to die game.

To pat on the back; to make a man of.

(*Adjectives*) Courageous, brave, valiant, valorous, gallant, intrepid.

Spirited, high-spirited, high-mettled, mettlesome, plucky, manly, manful, resolute, stout, stout-hearted, lion-hearted, heart of oak, firm, indomitable, game, sportsmanlike.

Bold, daring, audacious, fearless, unfearing, dauntless, undaunted, indomitable, unappalled, undismayed, unawed, unabashed, unalarmed, unflinching, unshrinking, unblenching, unblenched, unapprehensive, confident, self-reliant.

Enterprising, venturous, adventurous, venturesome, dashing, chivalrous, heroic, fierce, warlike (722).

Unfeared, undreaded, etc.

(*Phrases*) One's blood is up; brave as a lion; bold as brass; full of beans.

(*Phrases*) To show the white feather; to be in a sweat.

(*Adjectives*) Coward, cowardly, yellow, pusillanimous, shy, fearful, timid, skittish, timorous, poor-spirited, spiritless, weak-hearted, faint-hearted, chicken-hearted, white-livered.

Dastard, dastardly, base, craven, recreant, unwarlike, unheroic, unsoldierly, unmanly, womanish.

(*Phrase*) 'In face a lion, but in heart a deer.'

(*Interjections*) *Sauve qui peut !* the devil take the hindmost !

---

863 RASHNESS (*Substantives*), temerity, audacity, presumption, precipitancy, precipitation, impetuosity, recklessness, overboldness, foolhardiness, desperation, knight-errantry, Quixotism; carelessness (460), want of caution, overconfidence.

Imprudence, indiscretion.

A desperado, madcap, bravo, daredevil, *enfant perdu*, gambler, adventurer, knight errant; Hotspur, Don Quixote, Icarus.

(*Phrases*) A leap in the dark; a blind bargain; a wild-cat scheme.

(*Verbs*) To be rash, incautious, etc.

(*Phrases*) To buy a pig in a poke; to go on a forlorn hope; to go at it bald-headed; to play with fire; to tempt providence.

(*Adjectives*) Rash, temerarious,

864 CAUTION (*Substantives*), cautiousness, discretion, prudence, reserve, wariness, heed, circumspection, calculation, deliberation (459).

Coolness, self-possession, aplomb, presence of mind, sang-froid, self-command, steadiness, the Fabian policy.

(*Phrases*) The better part of valour; masterly inactivity.

(*Verbs*) To be cautious, etc., to beware, take care, have a care, take heed, ca' canny, be on one's guard, look about one, take no chances.

(*Phrases*) To look before one leaps; to think twice; to let sleeping dogs lie; to see which way the wind blows; to see how the land lies; to feel one's way; to count the cost; to be on the safe side; steady as she goes.

headstrong, insane, foolhardy, slap-dash, dare-devil, devil-may-care, overbold, wild, reckless, desperate, hot-headed, hare-brained, headlong, hot-blooded, over-confident, precipitate, impetuous, venturesome, impulsive, Quixotic.

Imprudent, indiscreet, uncalculating, incautious, improvident.

(*Phrases*) Without ballast; neck or nothing.

(*Interjections*) *Vogue la galère!* come what may!

865 Desire (*Substantives*), wish, mind, inclination, leaning, bent, fancy, partiality, penchant, predilection, liking, love, fondness, relish.

Want, need, exigency.

Longing, hankering, solicitude, anxiety, yearning, yen, coveting, eagerness, zeal, ardour, aspiration, ambition, over-anxiety.

Appetite, appetence, appetency, the edge of appetite, keenness, hunger, stomach, thirst, thirstiness, drouth, mouth-watering, dipsomania, itch, itching, prurience, lickerishness, *cacoethes*, cupidity, lust, libido, concupiscence, greed.

Avidity, greediness, covetousness, craving, voracity, bulimia, rapacity.

Passion, rage, furore, mania, kleptomania, inextinguishable desire, vaulting ambition, impetuosity.

A gourmand, gourmet, glutton, cormorant (957).

An amateur, votary, devotee, fan, aspirant, solicitant, candidate.

Object of desire, desideratum, attraction, lure, allurement, fancy, temptation, magnet, loadstone, whim, whimsy (608), maggot, hobby, hobby-horse, pursuit.

(*Phrases*) The height of one's ambition; *hoc erat in votis*; the wish being father to the thought; the torments of Tantalus.

(*Verbs*) To desire, wish, long for, fancy, affect, like, have a mind to, be glad of, want, miss, need, feel the want of, would fain have, to care for.

To hunger, thirst, crave, lust after; to hanker after, itch for.

(*Adjectives*) Cautious, wary, careful, heedful, cautelous, chary, canny, cagey, circumspect, prudent, prudential, reserved, discreet, politic, non-committal.

Unenterprising, unadventurous, cool, steady, self-possessed.

(*Phrases*) Safety first; better be sure than sorry.

———

866 Indifference (*Substantives*), coldness, coolness, unconcern, nonchalance, insouciance, inappetency, listlessness, lukewarmness, neutrality, impartiality; apathy (823), supineness (683), disdain (930).

(*Verbs*) To be indifferent, etc.; to have no desire, wish, taste, or relish for; to care nothing about, take no interest in, not mind, make light of; to disdain, spurn (930).

(*Phrase*) Couldn't care less.

(*Adjectives*) Indifferent, undesirous, cool, cold, frigid, unconcerned, insouciant, unsolicitous, unattracted, lukewarm, half-hearted, listless, lackadaisical, unambitious, unaspiring, phlegmatic.

Unattractive, unalluring, uninviting, undesired, undesirable, uncared-for, unwished, uncoveted, unvalued.

Vapid, tasteless, insipid (391), wersh, unappetizing, mawkish, namby-pamby, flat, stale, vain.

(*Phrases*) Never mind; all one to Hippocleides.

867 Dislike (*Substantives*), distaste, disrelish, disinclination, reluctance, backwardness, demur (603).

Repugnance, disgust, queasiness, turn, nausea, loathing, averseness, aversion, abomination, antipathy, abhorrence, horror, hatred, detestation (898), resentment (900); claustrophobia, agoraphobia, Anglophobia, Gallophobia.

(*Verbs*) To dislike, mislike, disrelish, mind, object to.

To desiderate, covet; to sigh, cry, gasp, pine, pant, languish, yearn for; to aspire after, catch at, jump at.

To woo, court, solicit, ogle, fish for.

To cause, create, raise, excite, or provoke, desire; to allure, attract, solicit, tempt, hold out temptation or allurement, to tantalize, appetize.

To gratify desire, slake, satiate (827).

(*Phrases*) To have at heart; to take a fancy to; to set one's heart upon; to make eyes at; to set one's cap at; to run mad after.

To whet the appetite; to make one's mouth water.

(*Adjectives*) Desirous, inclined, fain, keen, wishful, wishing, optative, desiring, wanting, needing, hankering after, dying for, partial to.

Craving, hungry, esurient, sharp-set, keen-set, peckish, thirsty, athirst, dry, drouthy.

Greedy, voracious, lickerish, open-mouthed, agog, covetous, ravenous, rapacious, extortionate; unsated, un-slaked, insatiable, insatiate, omni-vorous.

Eager, ardent, avid, fervent, bent on, intent on, aspiring, ambitious.

Desirable, desired, desiderated (829).

(*Phrases*) Pinched or perished with hunger; hungry as a hunter; parched with thirst; having a sweet tooth; nothing loth.

(*Interjections*) O for! would that!

To shun, avoid, eschew, withdraw from, shrink from, shrug the shoulders at, recoil from, shudder at.

To loathe, nauseate, abominate, detest, abhor, hate (898).

To cause or excite dislike; to dis-incline, repel, sicken, render sick, nauseate, disgust, shock, pall.

(*Adjectives*) Not to be able to bear or endure or stand; to have no taste for; to turn up one's nose at; to look askance at.

To go against the grain; to turn one's stomach; to stink in the nostrils; to stick in one's throat; to make one's blood run cold.

(*Adjectives*) Disliking, disrelishing, etc., averse to, adverse, shy of, sick of, fed up with, queasy, disinclined.

Disliked, disagreeable, unpalatable, unpopular, offensive, loathsome, loathly, sickening, nauseous, nau-seating, repulsive, disgusting, detest-able, execrable, abhorrent, abhorred (830), disgustful.

(*Adverbs*) Disagreeably, etc.

(*Phrase*) *Usque ad nauseam.*

(*Interjections*) Faugh! Ugh!

868 FASTIDIOUSNESS (*Substantives*), nicety, daintiness, squeamishness, niceness, particularity, finicality, me-ticulosity, difficulty in being pleased, epicurism.

Excess of delicacy, prudery.

Epicure, gourmet, gourmand, *bon vivant*, gastronomer.

(*Verbs*) To be fastidious, etc., to discriminate, differentiate, disdain.

(*Phrases*) To split hairs; to mince one's words; to see spots in the sun.

(*Adjectives*) Fastidious, nice, difficult, dainty, delicate, finicky, licker-ish, pernickety, squeamish, queasy, difficult to please, particular, choosy, punctilious, fussy, hypercritical; prudish, strait-laced.

869 SATIETY (*Substantives*), fullness, repletion, glut, saturation, surfeit.

A spoilt child; too much of a good thing.

(*Verbs*) To sate, satiate, satisfy, saturate, quench, slake, pall, glut, overfeed, gorge, surfeit, cloy, tire, spoil, sicken.

(*Adjectives*) Satiated, sated, blasé, used up, fed up, browned off, brassed off, cheesed off, chokka, sick of.

(*Phrases*) Enough is enough; *Toujours perdrix.*

(*Interjections*) Enough! that'll do!

4°. *Contemplative Affections*

870 WONDER (*Substantives*), surprise, marvel, astonishment, amazement, amazedness, wonderment, admiration, awe, bewilderment, stupefaction, fascination, thaumaturgy (992).

(*Verbs*) To wonder, marvel, be surprised, admire; to stare, gape, start.

To surprise, astonish, amaze, astound, dumbfound, dumbfounder, strike, dazzle, startle, take by surprise, take aback, strike with wonder, electrify, stun, petrify, flabbergast, confound, stagger, stupefy, bewilder, fascinate, boggle.

To be wonderful, etc.

871 Absence of wonder.

EXPECTANCE (*Substantives*), expectancy, expectation (507).

(*Verbs*) To expect, not to be surprised, not to wonder, etc., *nil admirari.*

(*Phrase*) To think nothing of.

(*Adjectives*) Expecting, etc., unamazed, astonished at nothing, blasé (841).

Common, ordinary (82); foreseen.

———

(*Phrases*) To open one's mouth or eyes; to look blank; to stand aghast; not to believe one's eyes; not to account for; not to know whether one stands on one's head or one's heels.

To make one sit up; to take one's breath away.

To beggar description; to stagger belief; imagination boggles at it.

(*Adjectives*) Surprised, astonished, amazed, astounded, struck, startled, taken by surprise, taken aback, struck dumb, awestruck, aghast, agape, dumbfounded, flabbergasted, thunder-struck, planet-struck, stupefied, open-mouthed, petrified.

Wonderful, wondrous, surprising, astonishing, amazing, astounding, startling, stunning, unexpected, unforeseen, strange, uncommon, unheard-of, unaccountable, incredible, inexplicable, indescribable, inexpressible, ineffable, unutterable, unspeakable, monstrous, prodigious, stupendous, marvellous, miraculous, passing strange, uncanny, weird, phenomenal.

(*Phrases*) Struck all of a heap; lost in wonder; like a dying duck in a thunder-storm; you could have knocked me down with a feather.

(*Adverbs*) Wonderingly, wonderfully, etc., with gaping mouth, all agog; *mirabile dictu.*

(*Interjections*) What! indeed! really! hallo! humph! you don't say so! my stars! good heavens! my goodness! good gracious! bless my soul! bless my heart! my word! O gemini! great Scott! gee! *wunderbar!* dear me! well, I'm damned! well, I never! lo! heyday! who'd have thought it!

872 PRODIGY (*Substantives*), phenomenon, wonder, cynosure, marvel, miracle, monster (83), unicorn, phoenix, gazing-stock, curiosity, *rara avis*, lion, sight, spectacle, wonderment, sign, portent (512), eye-opener; wonderland, fairyland.

Thunderclap, thunderbolt, bursting of a shell or bomb, volcanic eruption.

(*Phrases*) A nine days' wonder; *annus mirabilis.*

5°. *Extrinsic Affections*

873 REPUTE (*Substantives*), distinction, note, notability, name, mark, reputation, figure, *réclame*, *éclat*, celebrity, vogue, fame, famous-

874 DISREPUTE (*Substantives*), discredit, ingloriousness, derogation, abasement, degradation, odium, notoriety.

ness, popularity, renown, memory, immortality.

Glory, honour, credit, prestige, kudos, account, regard, respect, reputableness, respectability, respectableness, good name, illustriousness, gloriousness.

Dignity, stateliness, solemnity, grandeur, splendour, nobility, nobleness, lordliness, majesty, sublimity.

Greatness, highness, eminence, supereminence, pre-eminence, primacy, importance (642).

Elevation, ascent (305), exaltation, superexaltation, aggrandisement.

Rank, standing, condition, precedence, *pas*, station, place, status, order, degree, *locus standi*.

Dedication, consecration, enshrinement, glorification, beatification, canonization, deification, posthumous fame.

Chief, leader (745), hero, celebrity, notability, somebody, lion, cock of the roost, cock of the walk, man of mark, pillar of the state, prima donna.

A star, sun, constellation, galaxy, flower, pearl, paragon (650); honour, ornament, aureole.

(*Phrases*) A halo of glory; a name to conjure with; blushing honours; a feather in one's cap; the top of the tree; a niche in the temple of fame.

(*Verbs*) To glory in, to be proud of (878), to exult (884), to be vain of (880).

To be glorious, distinguished, etc., to shine, to figure, to make or cut a figure, dash, or splash; to rival, outrival, surpass, emulate, outvie, eclipse, outshine, overshadow, throw into the shade.

To live, flourish, glitter, flaunt.

To honour, lionize, dignify, glorify, ennoble, nobilitate, exalt, enthrone, signalize, immortalize, deify.

To consecrate, dedicate to, devote to, to enshrine.

To confer or reflect honour, etc., on; to do, pay, or render honour to; to redound to one's honour.

(*Phrases*) To acquire or gain honour, etc.; to bear the palm; to bear the bell; to take the cake; to win laurels;

Dishonour, shame, disgrace, disfavour, disapprobation (932), slur, scandal, obloquy, opprobrium, ignominy, baseness, turpitude, vileness, infamy.

Tarnish, taint, defilement, pollution.

Stain, blot, spot, blur, stigma, brand, reproach, imputation, slur, black mark.

(*Phrases*) A burning shame; *scandalum magnatum*; a badge of infamy; the bar sinister; a blot on the scutcheon; a byword of reproach; a bad reputation.

(*Verbs*) To be conscious of shame, to feel shame, to blush, to be ashamed, humiliated, humbled (879, 881).

To cause shame, etc.; to shame, disgrace, put to shame, dishonour; to throw, cast, fling, or reflect shame, etc., upon; to be a reproach to, to derogate from.

To tarnish, stain, blot, sully, taint, discredit, degrade, debase, defile.

To impute shame to, to brand, stigmatize, vilify, defame, slur, run down, knock.

To abash, humiliate, humble, dishonour, discompose, disconcert, shame, show up, put out, put down, snub, confuse, mortify; to obscure, eclipse, outshine.

(*Phrases*) To feel disgrace; to cut a poor figure; to hide one's face; to look foolish; to hang one's head; to laugh on the wrong side of the mouth; not to dare to show one's face; to hide one's diminished head; to lose caste; to be in one's black books.

To put to the blush; to put out of countenance; to put one's nose out of joint; to cast into the shade; to take one down a peg; to take the shine out of; to tread or trample under foot; to drag through the mud.

(*Adjectives*) Feeling shame, disgrace, etc.; ashamed, abashed, disgraced, blown upon, branded, tarnished.

Inglorious, mean, base (940), shabby, nameless, unnoticed, unnoted, unhonoured.

Shameful, disgraceful, despicable, discreditable, unbecoming, degrading,

to make a noise in the world; to go far; to make a sensation; to be all the rage; to have a run; to catch on. To exalt one's horn; to leave one's mark; to exalt to the skies.

(*Adjectives*) Distinguished, *distingué*, noted, notable, respectable, reputable, celebrated, famous, famed, far-famed, honoured, renowned, popular, deathless, imperishable, immortal (112) Illustrious, glorious, splendid, bright, brilliant, radiant, full-blown, heroic.

Eminent, prominent, conspicuous, kenspeckle, high, pre-eminent, peerless, signalized, exalted, dedicated, consecrated, enshrined.

humiliating, unworthy, disreputable, derogatory, vile, ribald, dishonourable, abject, scandalous, infamous, notorious.

(*Phrases*) Unwept, unhonoured, and unsung; shorn of its beams; unknown to fame; in bad odour; under a cloud; down in the world.

(*Interjections*) Fie! shame! for shame! *O tempora! O mores!*

——

Great, dignified, proud, noble, worshipful, lordly, grand, stately, august, imposing, transcendent, majestic, kingly, queenly, princely, sacred, sublime, commanding.

(*Phrases*) Redounding to one's honour; one's name living for ever; *sic itur ad astra*.

(*Interjections*) Hail! all hail! *vive! viva!* glory be to! honour be to!

875 NOBILITY (*Substantives*) noblesse, aristocracy, peerage, gentry, gentility, quality, rank, blood, birth, donship, fashionable world (852), the *haute monde*, high life, the upper classes, the upper ten, the four hundred.

A personage, notability, celebrity, man of distinction, rank, etc.; a nobleman, noble, lord, peer, grandee, magnate, magnifico, hidalgo, don, gentleman, squire, patrician, lordling, nob, swell, dignitary, bigwig, big gun.

House of Lords, Lords Spiritual and Temporal.

Gentlefolk, landed proprietors, squirearchy, *optimates*.

Prince, duke, marquis, earl, viscount, baron, thane, banneret, baronet, knight, count, armiger, laird, esquire; nizam, maharajah, rajah, nawab, sultan, emir (or ameer), effendi, sheik, pasha.

Princess, duchess, marchioness, marquise, countess, viscountess, baroness, lady, dame, maharanee, ranee, sultana, begum.

(*Verbs*) To be noble, etc.

(*Adjectives*) Noble, exalted, titled,

876 COMMONALTY (*Substantives*) the lower classes or orders, the vulgar herd, the crowd, the people, the commons, the proletariat, the multitude, Demos, οἱ πολλοί, the populace, the million, the masses, the mobility, the peasantry.

The middle classes, bourgeoisie.

The mob, rabble, rabble-rout, ruck, *canaille*, the underworld, riff-raff, *profanum vulgus*.

A commoner, one of the people, a proletarian, *roturier*, plebeian; peasant, yeoman, crofter, boor, carle, churl, serf, kern, tyke, (or tike), chuff, ryot, fellah, cottar.

A swain, clown, hind, clodhopper, bog-trotter, chaw-bacon, hodge, joskin, yokel, bumpkin, hayseed, rube, hick, ploughman, plough-boy, gaffer, loon, looby, lout, *gamin*, street arab, guttersnipe, mudlark, slubberdegullion.

A beggar, tramp, vagrant, gangrel, gaberlunzie, bum, hobo, sundowner, panhandler, pariah, muckworm, sansculotte, raff, tatterdemalion, ragamuffin.

A Goth, Vandal, Hottentot, savage,

patrician, aristocratic, high-born, well-born, genteel, *comme il faut*, gentlemanlike, ladylike, princely, courtly, fashionable (852).

(*Phrases*) *Noblesse oblige*; born in the purple.

877 TITLE (*Substantives*), honour, princedom, principality, dukedom, marquisate, earldom, viscounty, baronetcy, lordship, knighthood.

Highness, excellency, grace, worship, reverence, esquire, sir, master, sahib, Mr., monsieur, signor, señor, Herr.

Decoration, laurel, palm, wreath, medal, gong, ribbon, cross, star, garter, feather, crest, epaulette, colours, cockade, livery; order, arms, shield, scutcheon.

(*Phrase*) A handle to one's name.

---

878 PRIDE (*Substantives*), haughtiness, loftiness, hauteur, stateliness, pomposity, vainglory, superciliousness, assumption, lordliness, stiffness, primness, arrogance, *morgue*, starch, starchiness, side, swank, uppishness; self-respect, dignity.

A proud man, etc., a highflier.

(*Verbs*) To be proud, etc., to presume, assume, swagger, strut, prance, peacock, bridle.

To pride oneself on, glory in, pique oneself, plume oneself, preen oneself.

(*Phrases*) To look big; give oneself airs; to ride the high horse; to put on side; to put on dog; to hold up one's head; to get one's tail up.

To put a good face upon.

(*Adjectives*) Proud, haughty, lofty, high, mighty, high-flown, high-minded, high-mettled, puffed up, flushed, supercilious, patronizing, condescending, disdainful, overweening, consequential, on stilts, swollen, arrogant, pompous.

Stately, dignified, stiff, starchy, prim, perked up, buckram, strait-laced, vainglorious, lordly,

barbarian, yahoo, rough diamond, unlicked cub.

An upstart, parvenu, skipjack, *novus homo*, *nouveau riche*, outsider, vulgarian, snob, mushroom.

Barbarousness, barbarism.

(*Phrases*) The man in the street; the submerged tenth; ragtag and bobtail; the swinish multitude; hewers of wood and drawers of water; the great unwashed.

(*Verbs*) To be ignoble, etc.

(*Adjectives*) Ignoble, common, mean, low, plebeian, proletarian, vulgar, bourgeois, untitled, homespun, homely, Gorblimey.

Base, base-born, low-bred, beggarly, earth-born, rustic, agrestic, countrified, provincial, parochial; banausic, menial, sorry, scrubby, mushroom, dunghill, sordid, vile, uncivilized, loutish, boorish, churlish, rude, brutish, raffish, unlicked, barbarous, barbarian, barbaric.

879 HUMILITY (*Substantives*), humbleness, meekness, lowness, lowliness, abasement, self-abasement, self-contempt, humiliation, submission, resignation, verecundity, modesty (881).

(*Verbs*) To be humble, etc.; to deign; vouchsafe, condescend; to humble or demean oneself; stoop, submit, knuckle under, look foolish, feel small.

To render humble; to humble, humiliate, set down, abash, abase, shame, mortify, crush, take down, snub.

(*Phrases*) To sing small; to pipe down; to draw in one's horns; to hide one's diminished head; to eat humble-pie; to eat dirt; to kiss the rod; to pocket an affront; to stoop to conquer.

To throw into the shade; to put out of countenance; to put a person in his place; to put to the blush; to take down a peg, cut down to size; to send away with a flea in one's ear.

(*Adjectives*) Humble, lowly, meek, sober-minded, submissive (725), resigned, self-contemptuous, under correction.

magisterial, purse-proud, stand-offish, up-stage, toffee-nose.
Unabashed (880).
(*Phrases*) High and mighty; proud as a peacock; proud as Lucifer.
(*Adverbs*) Proudly, haughtily, arrogantly, etc.

880 VANITY (*Substantives*), conceit, conceitedness, self-conceit, self-confidence, self-sufficiency, self-esteem, self-approbation, self-importance, self-praise, self-laudation, self-admiration, complacency, self-complacency, swelled head, megalomania, *amour-propre*.
Pretensions, airs, mannerism, egotism, egoism, egomania, priggishness, coxcombry, gaudery, vainglory (943), elation, ostentation (882).
A coxcomb (854).
(*Verbs*) To be vain, etc., to egotize.
To render vain, etc., to puff up, to inspire with vanity, turn one's head.
(*Phrases*) To have a high or overweening opinion of oneself; to think no small beer of oneself; to thrust oneself forward; to give oneself airs; to show off; to fish for compliments.
(*Adjectives*) Vain, conceited, overweening, forward, vainglorious, puffed up, high-flown, inflated, flushed, stuck-up.
Self-satisfied, self-confident, self-sufficient, self-flattering, self-admiring, self-applauding, self-opinionated, self-centred, egocentric, egoistic, egoistical, egotistic, egotistical, complacent, self-complacent, pretentious, priggish.
Unabashed, unblushing, unconstrained, unceremonious, free and easy.
(*Phrases*) Vain as a peacock; wise in one's own conceit.
(*Adverbs*) Vainly, etc., ostentatiously (882).

Humbled, humiliated, abashed, ashamed, chapfallen, crestfallen.
(*Phrases*) Out of countenance; on one's bended knees; humbled in the dust; not having a word to say for oneself.
(*Adverbs*) Humbly, meekly, etc.

881 MODESTY (*Substantives*), humility (879), diffidence, timidity, bashfulness, shyness, coyness, sheepishness, *mauvaise honte*, shamefacedness, verecundity, self-consciousness.
Reserve, constraint, demureness.
(*Verbs*) To be modest, humble, etc.; to retire, keep in the background, keep private, reserve oneself.
(*Phrases*) To hide one's light under a bushel; to take a back seat.
(*Adjectives*) Modest, diffident, humble (879), timid, bashful, timorous, shy, skittish, coy, sheepish, shamefaced, blushing, self-conscious.
Unpretending, unpretentious, unassuming, unostentatious, unboastful, unaspiring.
Abashed, ashamed, dashed, out of countenance, crestfallen (879).
Reserved, constrained, demure, undemonstrative.
(*Adverbs*) Modestly, diffidently, quietly, privately, unostentatiously.

———

882 OSTENTATION (*Substantives*), display, show, flourish, parade, pomp, state, solemnity, pageantry, dash, splash, splurge, glitter, veneer, tinsel, magnificence, pomposity, showing off, swank, swagger, strut, *panache, coup de théâtre*, stage effect.
Flourish of trumpets, fanfare, salvo of artillery, salute, fireworks, *feu de joie*.
Pageant, spectacle, procession, march-past, review, promenade, turn-out, set-out, build-up, fête, gala, regatta, field-day.
Ceremony, ceremonial, mummery; formality, form, etiquette, ritual, protocol, punctilio, punctiliousness.
(*Verbs*) To be ostentatious, etc.; to display, exhibit, posture, attitudinize,

show off, swank, come forward, put oneself forward, flaunt, emblazon, prink, glitter; make or cut a figure, dash, or splash.

To observe or stand on ceremony, etiquette, etc.

(*Adjectives*) Ostentatious, showy, gaudy, garish, flashy, dashing, pretentious, flaunting, jaunty, glittering, sumptuous, spectacular, ceremonial, stagy, theatrical, histrionic.

Pompous, solemn, stately, high-sounding, formal, stiff, ritualistic, ceremonious, punctilious.

(*Phrases*) With flourish of trumpets; with beat of drum; with flying colours; in one's Sunday best; in one's best bib and tucker.

883 CELEBRATION (*Substantives*), jubilee, jubilation, commemoration, festival, feast, solemnization, ovation, paean, triumph.

Triumphal arch, bonfire, illuminations, fireworks, salute, salvo, *feu de joie*, flourish of trumpets, fanfare.

Inauguration, installation, presentation, coronation, fête (882).

Anniversary, silver wedding, golden wedding, diamond wedding, diamond jubilee, centenary, bicentenary, tercentenary, quatercentenary, quingentenary (or quincentenary), sexcentenary, etc., millenary.

(*Verbs*) To celebrate, keep, signalize, do honour to, pledge, drink to, toast, commemorate, solemnize.

To inagurate, install.

(*Phrase*) To paint the town red.

(*Adjectives*) Celebrating, etc., in honour of, in commemoration of, in memoriam.

(*Interjections*) Hail! all hail! 'See the conquering hero comes.' 'For he's a jolly good fellow.'

884 BOASTING (*Substantives*), boast, vaunt, vaunting, brag, bounce, *blague*, swank, bluff, puff, puffing, puffery, flourish, fanfaronade, gasconade, braggadocio, bravado, tall talk, heroics, vapouring, rodomontade, bombast, exaggeration (549), self-advertisement, *réclame*; jingoism, Chauvinism, spread-eagleism.

Exultation, triumph, flourish of trumpets (883).

A boaster, braggart, braggadocio, Gascon, peacock; a pretender, charlatan.

(*Verbs*) To boast, make a boast of, brag, vaunt, puff, flourish, vapour, blow, strut, swagger, swank, skite, gas.

To exult, crow, chuckle, triumph, gloat, glory.

(*Phrases*) To talk big; to shoot a line; to blow one's own trumpet.

(*Adjectives*) Boasting, vaunting, etc., thrasonical, vainglorious, braggart, jingo, jingoistic, chauvinistic.

Elate, elated, flushed, jubilant.

(*Phrases*) On stilts; cock-a-hoop; in high feather.

885 Undue assumption of superiority.

INSOLENCE (*Substantives*), haughtiness, arrogance, imperiousness, contumeliousness, superciliousness, bumptiousness, bounce, swagger, swank.

Impertinence, sauciness, pertness, flippancy, petulance, malapertness.

Assumption, presumption, presumptuousness, forwardness, impudence, assurance, front, face, neck, cheek, lip, side, brass, shamelessness,

886 SERVILITY (*Substantives*), obsequiousness, suppleness, fawning, slavishness, abjectness, prostration, prosternation, genuflexion (900), abasement, subjection (749).

Fawning, mealy-mouthedness, sycophancy, flattery (833), humility (879).

A sycophant, parasite, gate-crasher, toad-eater, toady, spaniel, bootlicker, lickspittle, flunkey, sponger, snob, hanger-on, tuft-hunter, time-server, reptile, cur (941); Uriah Heep.

hardihood, a hardened front, effrontery, audacity, procacity, self-assertion, nerve, gall, crust.

(*Verbs*) To be insolent, etc.; to bluster, vapour, swagger, swank, swell, roister, arrogate, assume, bluff. To domineer, bully, beard, snub, huff, outface, outlook, outstare, outbrazen, bear down, beat down, trample on, tread under foot, outbrave, hector.

To presume, take liberties or freedoms.

(*Phrases*) To give oneself airs; to lay down the law; to put on side; to ride the high horse; to lord it over; *traiter, ou regarder de haut en bas*; to ride roughshod over; to carry with a high hand; to throw one's weight about; to carry it off; to brave it out.

(*Verbs*) To cringe, bow, stoop, kneel, fall on one's knees, etc.

To sneak, crawl, crouch, cower, truckle to, grovel, fawn.

(*Phrases*) To pay court to; to dance attendance on; to do the dirty work of; to lick the boots of.

To go with the stream; to worship the rising sun; to run with the hare and hunt with the hounds.

(*Adjectives*) Servile, subservient, obsequious, sequacious, soapy, oily, unctuous, supple, mean, crouching, cringing, fawning, slavish, grovelling, snivelling, beggarly, sycophantic, parasitical, abject, prostrate.

(*Adverb*) Cap in hand.

———

(*Adjectives*) Insolent, etc.; haughty, arrogant, imperious, dictatorial, high-handed, contumelious, supercilious, snooty, uppish, self-assertive, bumptious, overbearing, intolerant, assumptive.

Flippant, pert, perky, cavalier, saucy, cheeky, fresh, forward, impertinent, malapert.

Blustering, swaggering, swanky, vapouring, bluff, roistering, rollicking, high-flown, assuming, presuming, presumptuous, self-assertive, impudent, free, brazen, brazen-faced, barefaced, shameless, unblushing, unabashed.

---

887 BLUSTERER (*Substantives*), bully, swaggerer, braggart (884), fire-eater, daredevil, roisterer, puppy, sauce-box, hussy, minx, malapert, jackanapes, jack-in-office, jingo, Drawcansir, Captain Bobadil, Sir Lucius O'Trigger, Bombastes Furioso, Hector, Thraso, Bumble.

(*Phrases*) The great Panjandrum himself; a cool hand.

SECTION III—SYMPATHETIC AFFECTIONS

1°. *Social Affections*

888 FRIENDSHIP (*Substantives*), amity, amicableness, amicability, friendliness, friendly regard, affection (897), goodwill, favour, brotherhood, fraternity, sodality, comradeship, *camaraderie*, confraternity, fraternization, cordiality, harmony, good understanding, concord (714), *entente cordiale*.

Acquaintance, introduction, intimacy, familiarity, fellowship, fellow-feeling, sympathy, welcomeness, partiality, favouritism.

889 ENMITY (*Substantives*), hostility, unfriendliness, antagonism, animosity, hate (898), dislike (867), malevolence (907), ill will, ill feeling, spite, bad blood, aversion, antipathy, alienation, estrangement; umbrage, pique.

(*Verbs*) To be inimical, etc.; to estrange, to fall out, alienate.

(*Phrases*) To keep at arm's length; to bear malice; to set by the ears.

(*Adjectives*) Inimical, unfriendly, hostile, antagonistic, adverse, at

(*Verbs*) To be friends, to be friendly, etc., to fraternize, sympathize with (897), to be well with, to be thick with, to befriend (707), to be in with, to keep in with.

To become friendly, to make friends with, to chum up with.

(*Phrases*) To take in good part; to hold out the right hand of fellowship; to break the ice; to scrape acquaintance with.

(*Adjectives*) Friendly, amical, amicable, brotherly, fraternal, harmonious, cordial, social, chummy, pally, neighbourly, on good terms, on a friendly footing, on friendly terms, well-affected, well-disposed, favourable.

Acquainted, familiar, intimate, thick, hand and glove, welcome.

Firm, staunch, intimate, familiar, bosom, cordial, devoted.

(*Phrases*) In one's good books; hail fellow well met.

(*Adverbs*) Friendly, amicably, etc., *sans cérémonie*.

variance, at loggerheads, at daggers drawn, on bad terms.

Estranged, alienated, irreconcilable.

———

890 FRIEND (*Substantives*), well-wisher, *amicus curiae*, *alter ego*, bosom friend, *fidus Achates*, partner (711); *persona grata*.

Partisan, sympathizer, ally, backer, patron, good genius, fairy godmother.

Neighbour, acquaintance, associate, compeer, comrade, companion, *confrère*, *camarade*, mate, messmate, shopmate, shipmate, crony, cummer, confidant, chum, pal, buddy, side-kick, boon companion, pot-companion, schoolfellow, playfellow, playmate, bed-fellow, bed-mate. bunkie, room-mate.

Arcades ambo, Pylades and Orestes, Castor and Pollux, Nisus and Euryalus, Damon and Pythias, David and Jonathan, *par nobile fratrum*.

Host, guest, visitor, *habitué*, protégé.

891 ENEMY (*Substantives*), foe, opponent (710), antagonist.

Public enemy, enemy to society, anarchist, terrorist, Ishmael.

———

892 SOCIALITY (*Substantives*), sociability, sociableness, social intercourse, companionship, companionableness, consortship, intercommunication, intercommunion, consociation.

Conviviality, good fellowship, hospitality, heartiness, welcome, the glad hand, joviality, jollity, *savoir vivre*, festivity, merrymaking.

Society, association, union, co-partnership, fraternity, sodality, coterie, clan, club (72), circle, clique, knot.

Assembly-room, casino, clubhouse, common-room.

Esprit de corps, nepotism (11).

An entertainment, party, social gathering, reunion, gaudy, levee, soirée, conversazione, rout, *ridotto*,

893 SECLUSION (*Substantives*), privacy, retirement, withdrawal, reclusion, recess, retiredness, rustication.

Solitude, singleness, estrangement from the world, loneliness, lonesomeness, retiredness, isolation; hermitage, cloister, nunnery (1000); study, den; ivory tower, Shangri-la.

Wilderness, depopulation, desolation.

Agoraphobia, claustrophobia.

EXCLUSION (*Substantives*), excommunication, banishment, expatriation, exile, ostracism, cut, cut direct, dead cut, inhospitality, inhospitableness, unsociability.

A recluse, hermit, cenobite, anchoret (or anchorite), stylite, santon,

at-home, house-warming, bee, tea-party, bun-fight, picnic, garden-party, festival (840), interview, assignation, appointment, date, tryst, call, visit, visiting, reception (588).

A good fellow, good scout, boon companion, good mixer, *bon vivant.*

(*Verbs*) To be sociable, etc., to associate with, keep company with, to club together, sort with, hobnob with, consort, make advances, fraternize, make the acquaintance of.

To visit, pay a visit, interchange visits or cards, call upon, leave a card.

To entertain, give a party, dance, etc.; to keep open house; to receive, to welcome.

(*Phrases*) To make oneself at home; to crack a bottle with.

To be at home to; to do the honours; to receive with open arms; to give a warm reception to; to kill the fatted calf.

(*Adjectives*) Sociable, social, companionable, neighbourly, gregarious, clannish, clubbable, conversable, affable, accessible, familiar, on visiting terms, welcome, hospitable, convivial, jovial, festive.

(*Phrases*) Free and easy; hail fellow well met.

(*Adverbs*) *En famille*; in the family circle; in the social whirl; *sans façon; sans cérémonie; sans gêne.*

---

894 COURTESY (*Substantives*), good manners, good breeding, good form, mannerliness, manners, *bienséance,* urbanity, civilization, polish, politeness, gentility, comity, civility, amenity, suavity, discretion, diplomacy, good temper, easy temper, gentleness, mansuetude, graciousness, gallantry, affability, obligingness, *prévenance,* amiability, good humour.

Compliment, fair words, soft words, sweet words, honeyed phrases, attentions, *petits soins,* salutation, reception, presentation, introduction, *accueil,* greeting, regards, remembrances, welcome, *abord,* respect, devoir.

troglodyte, solitary, ruralist; displaced person, outcast, pariah; foundling, waif, wastrel, castaway; Timon of Athens, Simon Stylites.

(*Phrase*) 'A lone lorn creetur.'

(*Verbs*) To be secluded, etc., to retire, to live retired, secluded, etc.; to keep aloof, keep snug, shut oneself up, deny oneself.

To cut, refuse to associate with or acknowledge; repel, cold-shoulder, blackball, outlaw, proscribe, excommunicate, boycott, exclude, banish, exile, ostracize, rusticate, send down, abandon, maroon.

To depopulate, dispeople, unpeople.

(*Phrases*) To retire from the world; to take the veil; to sport one's oak.

To send to Coventry; to turn one's back upon; to give one the cold shoulder.

(*Adjectives*) Secluded, sequestered, retired, private, snug, domestic, claustral.

Unsociable, unsocial, aloof, eremitical, offish, stand-offish, unclubbable, inhospitable, cynical, inconversible, retiring, unneighbourly, exclusive, unforthcoming.

Solitary, lonely, lonesome, isolated, single, estranged, unfrequented, uninhabited, unoccupied, tenantless.

Unvisited, cut, blackballed, uninvited, unwelcome, friendless, deserted, abandoned, derelict, lorn, forlorn, homeless, out of it.

(*Phrase*) Left to shift for oneself.

---

895 DISCOURTESY (*Substantives*), ill-breeding; ill, bad, or ungainly manners; rusticity, inurbanity, impoliteness, ungraciousness, uncourtliness, insuavity, rudeness, incivility, tactlessness, disrespect, impertinence, impudence, cheek, barbarism, misbehaviour, *grossièreté,* brutality, blackguardism, roughness, ruggedness, brusqueness, brusquerie, bad form.

Bad or ill temper, churlishness, crabbedness, tartness, crossness, peevishness, moroseness, sullenness, sulkiness, grumpiness, grouchiness, acrimony, sternness, austerity, moodi-

Obeisance, reverence, bow, curtsy, scrape, salaam, kowtow, capping, shaking hands, embrace, hug, squeeze, accolade, salute, kiss, buss, kissing hands, genuflexion, prostration, obsequiousness.

Mark of recognition, nod, wave, valediction (293).

(*Verbs*) To be courteous, civil, etc., to show courtesy, civility, etc., to speak one fair; to make oneself agreeable; to unbend, thaw.

To visit, wait upon, present oneself, pay one's respects, kiss hands. .

To receive, do the honours, greet, welcome, bid welcome, usher in, bid God speed; hold or stretch out the hand; shake, press, or squeeze the hand.

To salute, kiss, embrace, hug, drink to, pledge, hobnob; to wave to, nod to, smile upon, bow, curtsy, scrape, uncover, cap, present arms, take off the hat.

To pay homage or obeisance, kneel, bend the knee, prostrate oneself, etc.

To render polite, etc., to polish, civilize, humanize.

(*Phrases*) To mind one's p's and q's; to do the polite; to greet with open arms; to speed the parting guest.

(*Adjectives*) Courteous, courtly, civil, civilized, polite, Chesterfieldian, genteel, well-bred, well-mannered, mannerly, urbane, gentlemanly, ladylike, refined (850), polished, genial.

Gracious, affable, familiar, well-spoken, fair-spoken, soft-spoken, fine-spoken, suave, bland, mild, conciliatory, winning, obsequious, obliging, open-armed.

(*Phrases*) With a good grace; *suaviter in modo; à bras ouverts.*

(*Interjections*) Hail! welcome! good morning! good day! good afternoon! good evening! good night! well met! *pax vobiscum!*

ness, asperity, captiousness, sharpness, snappishness, perversity, cussedness, irascibility (901).

Sulks, dudgeon, mumps, scowl, frown, hard words, black looks.

A bear, brute, boor, blackguard, beast, cross-patch, grouch, sorehead.

(*Verbs*) To be rude, etc., frown, scowl, glower, lour, pout, snap, snarl, growl, nag; to cut, insult, etc.

To render rude, etc., to brutalize, decivilize, dehumanize.

(*Phrases*) To turn one's back upon; to turn on one's heel; to look black upon; to give one the cold shoulder, or the frozen face, or the frozen mitt; to take liberties with.

(*Adjectives*) Discourteous, uncourteous, uncourtly, ill-bred, ill-mannered, ill-behaved, unmannerly, mannerless, impolite, unpolished, ungenteel, ungentlemanly, unladylike, uncivilized.

Uncivil, rude, ungracious, cool, chilly, distant, stand-offish, offish, icy, repulsive, uncomplaisant, unaccommodating, ungainly, unceremonious, ungentle, rough, rugged, bluff, blunt, gruff, churlish, boorish, bearish, brutal, brusque, blackguardly, vulgar, stern, harsh, austere, cavalier.

Ill-tempered, out of temper or humour, cross, crusty, tart, sour, crabbed, sharp, short, snappish, testy, peevish, waspish, captious, grumpy, snarling, caustic, acrimonious, ungenial, petulant, pettish, pert.

Perverse, cross-grained, ill-conditioned, wayward, humoursome, naughty, cantankerous, intractable, curst, nagging, froward, sulky, glum, grim, morose, scowling, grouchy, glowering, surly, sullen, growling, splenetic, spleenful, spleeny, spleenish, moody, dogged, ugly.

(*Phrases*) Cross as two sticks; sour as a crab; surly as a bear.

(*Adverbs*) With a bad grace, grudgingly.

---

896 CONGRATULATION (*Substantives*), felicitation, wishing joy, the compliments of the season, good wishes.

(*Verbs*) To congratulate, felicitate, give or wish joy, tender or offer one's congratulations.

(*Adjectives*) Congratulatory, etc.
(*Phrases*) Many happy returns of the day! merry Christmas! happy New Year!

897 LOVE (*Substantives*), fondness, liking, inclination (865), regard, good graces, partiality, benevolence (906), admiration, fancy, tenderness, leaning, penchant, predilection; amativeness, amorousness.

Affection, sympathy, fellow-feeling, heart, affectionateness.

Attachment, yearning, amour, romance, gallantry, love-affair, *affaire de cœur*, passion, tender passion, *grande passion*, flame, pash, crush, rave, devotion, enthusiasm, fervour, enchantment, infatuation, adoration, idolatry, idolization.

Eros, Cupid, Aphrodite, Venus, Freya, the myrtle.

Maternal love, στοργή.

Attractiveness, etc., popularity.

Abode of love, love-nest, agapemone.

A lover, suitor, follower, admirer, adorer, wooer, beau, fiancé, gallant, young man, boy friend, sweetheart, flame, love, true-love, leman, paramour, amorist, *amoroso*, *cavaliere servente, cicisbeo*; turtle-doves.

Girl friend, lady-love, fiancée, sweetie, cutie, mistress, *inamorata*, idol, doxy, dona, Dulcinea, goddess.

Betrothed, affianced.

(*Verbs*) To love, like, affect, fancy, care for, regard, revere, cherish, admire, dote on, adore, idolize, fall for, hold dear, prize.

To bear love to; to take to; to be in love with; to be taken, smitten, etc., with; to have, entertain, harbour, cherish, etc., a liking, love, etc., for; to be fond of, be gone on.

To excite love; to win, gain, secure, etc., the love, affections, heart, etc.; to take the fancy of, to attract, attach, seduce, charm, fascinate, captivate, enamour, enrapture.

To get into favour; to ingratiate oneself, insinuate oneself, curry favour with, pay one's court to, *faire l'aimable.*

(*Phrases*) To take a fancy to; to

898 HATE (*Substantives*), hatred, disaffection, disfavour, alienation, estrangement, odium, dislike (867), enmity (899), animus, animosity (900).

Umbrage, pique, grudge, dudgeon, spleen, bitterness, ill feeling, acrimony, acerbity, malice (907), implacability.

Disgust, repugnance, aversion, averseness, loathing, abomination, horror, detestation, antipathy, abhorrence.

Object of hatred, abomination, *bête noir.*

(*Verbs*) To hate, dislike, disrelish (867), loathe, nauseate, execrate, detest, abominate, shudder at, recoil at, abhor, shrink from.

To excite hatred, estrange, incense, envenom, antagonize, rile, alienate, disaffect, set against; to be hateful, etc.

(*Phrases*) To make one's blood run cold; to have a down on; to hate one's guts.

To sow dissension among; to set by the ears.

(*Adjectives*) Hating, etc., averse to, set against.

Unloved, disliked, unwept, unlamented, undeplored, unmourned, unbeloved, uncared-for, unvalued.

Crossed in love, forsaken, jilted, rejected, lovelorn.

Obnoxious, hateful, abhorrent, odious, repulsive, offensive, shocking, loathsome, sickening, nauseous, disgusting, abominable, horrid (830).

Invidious, spiteful, malicious (907), spleenful, disgustful.

Insulting, irritating, provoking.

(*Phrases*) Not on speaking terms; there being no love lost between them; at daggers drawn.

make a fuss of; to look sweet upon; to cast sheep's eyes at; to fall in love with; to set one's affections on; to lose one's heart to.

To set one's cap at; to turn one's head.

(*Adjectives*) Loving, liking, etc., attached to, fond of, taken with, struck with, gone on, sympathetic, sympathizing with, charmed, captivated, fascinated, smitten, bitten, *épris*, enamoured, lovesick, love-lorn.

Affectionate, tender, sweet upon, loving, lover-like, loverly, amorous, amatory, amative, spoony, erotic, uxorious, motherly, ardent, passionate, devoted, amatorial.

Loved, beloved, etc., dear, precious, darling, favourite (899), pet, popular.

Lovely, sweet, dear, charming, engaging, amiable, winning, winsome, lovesome, attractive, adorable, enchanting, captivating, fascinating, bewitching, taking, seductive (829).

(*Phrases*) Head over ears in love; to one's mind, taste, or fancy; in one's good graces; nearest to one's heart.

899 FAVOURITE (*Substantives*), pet, cosset, dear, darling, honey, duck, moppet, jewel, idol, minion, spoilt child, blue-eyed boy, *persona grata*.

(*Phrases*) The apple of one's eye; a man after one's own heart; the idol of the people; the answer to the maiden's prayer.

900 RESENTMENT (*Substantives*), displeasure, animus, animosity, anger, wrath, indignation.

Pique, umbrage, huff, miff, soreness, dudgeon, moodiness, acerbity, bitterness, asperity, spleen, gall, heart-burning, heart-swelling, rankling; temper (901), bad blood, ill blood, ill humour.

Excitement, irritation, exasperation, warmth, bile, choler, ire, fume, dander, passion, fit, tantrum, burst, explosion, paroxysm, storm, rage, wax, fury, desperation.

Temper, petulance, procacity, angry mood, taking, snappishness.

Cause of umbrage, affront, provocation, offence, indignity, insult (929).

The Furies; the Eumenides.

(*Phrases*) The blood being up or boiling; a towering passion; the vials of wrath; fire and fury.

A sore subject; a rap on the knuckles; *casus belli.*

(*Verbs*) To resent, take amiss, take offence, take umbrage, take huff, bridle up, bristle up, frown, scowl, lour, snarl, growl, gnash, snap.

To chafe, mantle, redden, colour, fume, froth up, kindle; get, fall, or fly into a passion, rage, etc.; fly out, take fire, fire up, flare up, boil, boil over, rage, storm, foam.

To cause or raise anger; to affront, offend, give offence or umbrage; hurt the feelings; discompose, fret, ruffle, nettle, excite, irritate, provoke, rile, chafe, wound, sting, incense, inflame, enrage, aggravate, embitter, exasperate, rankle, infuriate, peeve.

(*Phrases*) To take in bad part; to take it ill; to take exception to; to stick in one's gizzard; to take in dudgeon; to have a bone (or crow) to pick with one; to get up on one's hind legs; to show one's teeth; to lose one's temper; to stamp, quiver, swell, or foam with rage; to see red; to look as black as thunder; to breathe revenge; to cut up rough; to pour out the vials of one's wrath; to blaze up; to blow one's top; to go up in a blue flame; to go on the war-path; to raise Cain.

To put out of humour; to stir up one's bile; to raise one's dander or choler; to work up into a passion; to make one's blood boil; to lash into a fury; to drive one mad; to put one's monkey up; to get one's goat.

(*Adjectives*) Angry, wroth, irate, ireful, warm, boiling, fuming, raging, etc., nettled, sore, bitter, riled, ruffled, chafed, exasperated, wrought up, worked up, snappish.

Fierce, wild, rageful, furious, infuriate, mad, fiery, savage, rabid, waxy, shirty, boiling over, rankling, bitter, virulent, set against.

Relentless, ruthless, implacable, unpitying, pitiless (919), inexorable, remorseless, stony-hearted, immitigable.

(*Phrases*) One's back being up; up in arms; in a stew; the gorge rising; in the height of passion.

(*Interjections*) Hell's bells! zounds! damme!

901 IRASCIBILITY (*Substantives*), susceptibility, excitability, temper, bad temper, procacity, petulance, irritability, fretfulness, testiness, grouchiness, tetchiness, touchiness, frowardness, peevishness, snappishness, hastiness, tartness, huffiness, resentfulness, vindictiveness, acerbity, protervity, aggressiveness, pugnacity (895).

A shrew, vixen, termagant, virago, scold, spitfire, Xanthippe; a tartar, fire-eater, fury; *genus irritabile*.

(*Verbs*) To be irascible, etc.; to take fire, fire up, flare up (900).

(*Adjectives*) Irascible, susceptible, excitable, irritable, fretful, fretty, on the fret, fidgety, peevish, hasty, over-hasty, quick, warm, hot, huffish, huffy, touchy, testy, tetchy (or techy), grouchy, restive, pettish, waspish, snappish, petulant, peppery, fiery, passionate, choleric, short-tempered.

Ill-tempered, bad-tempered, cross, churlish, sour, crabbed, cross-grained, sullen, sulky, grumpy, fractious, splenetic, spleenful, froward, shrewish.

Quarrelsome, querulous, disputatious, contentious, cranky, cantankerous, sarcastic (932), resentful, vindictive, pugnacious, aggressive.

(*Phrases*) Like touchwood or tinder; a word and a blow; as cross as two sticks.

902 Expression of affection or love.

ENDEARMENT (*Substantives*), caress, blandishment, fondling, billing and cooing, petting, necking, embrace, salute, kiss, buss, smack, osculation, deosculation.

Courtship, wooing, suit, addresses, attentions, *petits soins*, flirtation, coquetry, philandering, gallivanting, serenading, œillade, ogle, the glad eye, sheep's eyes, goo-goo eyes.

Love-tale, love-token, love-letter, *billet-doux*, valentine.

Flirt, coquette, gold digger, vamp; male flirt, masher, philanderer, lady killer, wolf, lounge lizard, cake eater, sheik.

(*Verbs*) To caress, fondle, wheedle, dandle, dally, cuddle, cockle, cosset, nestle, nuzzle, snuggle, clasp, hug, embrace, kiss, salute, bill and coo.

To court, woo, flirt, coquette; philander, spoon, canoodle, mash, spark, serenade.

(*Phrases*) To make much of; to smile upon; to make eyes at; to chuck under the chin; to pat on the cheek; to make love; to pay one's court or one's addresses to; to set one's cap at; to pop the question.

To win the heart, affections, love, etc., of.

(*Adjectives*) Caressing, etc., caressed, etc., flirtatious, spoony.

903 MARRIAGE (*Substantives*), matrimony, wedlock, union, bridal, match, intermarriage, coverture, cohabitation, bed, the marriage bond, the nuptial tie.

Wedding, nuptials, Hymen, spousals, espousals; leading to the altar;

904 CELIBACY (*Substantives*), singleness, misogamy; bachelorhood, bachelorship; virginity, maidenhood, maidenhead.

An unmarried man, bachelor, celibate, misogamist, misogynist.

An unmarried woman, spinster,

the torch of Hymen; nuptial benediction, marriage song, epithalamium.

Bride, bridegroom, groom, bridesmaid, maid of honour, matron of honour, bridesman, groomsman, best man.

Honeymoon, honeymooner.

A married man, a husband, spouse, benedick (or benedict), consort, goodman, lord and master, hubby.

A married woman, a wife, lady, matron, mate, helpmate, helpmeet, rib, better half, *femme couverte* (or *feme coverte*), squaw.

A married couple, wedded pair, Darby and Joan, man and wife.

A monogamist, bigamist, polygamist, a much-married man, a Turk, a Bluebeard, a Mormon.

maid, maiden, old maid, virgin, *feme sole*, bachelor girl.

(*Phrase*) Single blessedness.

(*Verb*) To live single.

(*Adjectives*) Unwedded, unmarried, single, celibate, wifeless, spouseless, lone.

905 DIVORCE (*Substantives*), dissolution of marriage, separation, divorcement.

A divorcee, co-respondent, cuckold.

(*Verbs*) To live separate, divorce, put away.

WIDOWHOOD, viduity, weeds.

Widow, relict, dowager, jointress, grass widow; widower, grass widower.

Monogamy, bigamy, digamy, deuterogamy, trigamy, polygamy, polygyny, polyandry, endogamy, exogamy.

A morgantic marriage, left-handed marriage, marriage of convenience, *mariage de convenance*, companionate marriage, trial marriage, misalliance, *mésalliance*.

(*Verbs*) To marry, wed, espouse, wive.

To join, give away, handfast, splice.

(*Phrases*) To lead to the altar; to take to oneself a wife; to take for better for worse; to give one's hand to; to get spliced.

To tie the nuptial knot; to give in marriage.

(*Adjectives*) Matrimonial, conjugal, connubial, nuptial, wedded, hymeneal, spousal, bridal, marital, epithalamic.

Monogamous, bigamous, polygamous, etc.

2°. *Diffusive Sympathetic Affections*

906 BENEVOLENCE (*Substantives*), goodwill, good nature, kindness, kindliness, benignity, brotherly love, beneficence, charity, humanity, fellow-feeling, sympathy, good feeling, kind-heartedness, amiability, complaisance, loving-kindness; toleration, consideration, generosity.

Charitableness, bounty, bounteousness, bountifulness, almsgiving, philanthropy (910), unselfishness (942).

Acts of kindness, a good turn, good works, kind offices, attentions, good treatment.

(*Phrases*) The milk of human kindness; the good Samaritan.

(*Verbs*) To be benevolent, etc., to do good to, to benefit, confer a benefit, be of use, aid, assist (707),

907 MALEVOLENCE (*Substantives*), ill will, unkindness, ill nature, malignity, malice, maliciousness, spite, spitefulness, despite, despitefulness.

Uncharitableness, venom, gall, rancour, rankling, bitterness, acerbity, harshness, mordacity, acridity, virulence, *acharnement*, misanthropy(911).

Cruelty, hardness of heart, obduracy, cruelness, brutality, brutishness, hooliganism, savageness, savagery, ferocity, barbarity, bloodthirstiness, immanity, pitilessness, truculence, devilry (or deviltry), devilment.

An ill turn, a bad turn, outrage, atrocity, affront (929).

(*Phrases*) A heart of stone; the evil eye; the cloven hoof.

render a service, treat well, to sympathize with.

(*Phrases*) To have one's heart in the right place; to enter into the feelings of others; to do a good turn to; to do as one would be done by.

(*Adjectives*) Benevolent, well-meaning, kind, obliging, accommodating, kind-hearted, tender-hearted, charitable, generous, beneficent, bounteous, bountiful, humane, clement, benignant, benign, considerate.

Good-natured, *bon enfant, bon diable,* a good sort, sympathizing, sympathetic, responsive, complaisant, accommodating, amiable, gracious.

Kindly, well-meant, well-intentioned, brotherly, fraternal, friendly (888).

(*Adverbs*) With a good intention, with the best intentions.

(*Interjections*) Good luck! God speed!

(*Verbs*) To be malevolent, etc.; to injure, hurt, harm, molest, disoblige, do harm to, ill treat, maltreat (649), do an ill office or turn to, (830) to wrong.

To worry, harass, bait, oppress, grind, haze, persecute, hunt down, dragoon, hound.

(*Phrases*) To wreak one's malice on; to bear or harbour malice against; to do one's worst.

(*Adjectives*) Malevolent, malicious, ill-disposed, evil-minded, ill-intentioned, maleficent, malign, malignant.

Ill-natured, disobliging, inofficious, unfriendly, unsympathetic, unkind, uncandid, unaccommodating, uncharitable, ungracious, unamiable.

Surly, churlish (895), grim, spitefull, despiteful, ill-conditioned, foulmouthed, acrid, rancorous, caustic, bitter, acrimonious, mordacious, vitriolic, venomous.

Cold, cold-blooded, cold-hearted, hard-hearted, iron-hearted, flint-hearted, marble-hearted, stony-hearted.

Pitiless, unpitying, uncompassionate, without bowels, ruthless, merciless, unmerciful, inexorable, relentless, unrelenting, virulent, dispiteous.

Cruel, brutal, savage, ferocious, atrocious, untamed, ferine, inhuman, barbarous, fell, Hunnish, bloody, blood-stained, bloodthirsty, bloody-minded, sanguinary, truculent (919), butcherly.

Fiendish, fiendlike, infernal, demoniacal, diabolical, devilish, hellish.

(*Adverbs*) Malevolently, etc., with bad intent or intention, despitefully.

908. MALEDICTION (*Substantives*), curse, malison, imprecation, denunciation, execration, anathema, ban, proscription, excommunication, commination, fulmination, *maranatha.*

Cursing, scolding, revilement, vilification, vituperation, invective, flyting, railing, Billingsgate, expletive, oath, bad language, unparliamentary language, ribaldry, scurrility.

(*Verbs*) To censure, curse, imprecate, damn, scold, swear at, flyte on, rail at or against, execrate.

To denounce, proscribe, excommunicate, fulminate against, anathematize, blaspheme.

(*Phrases*) To devote to destruction; to invoke or call down curses on one's head; to swear like a trooper; to rap out an oath; to curse with bell, book, and candle.

(*Adjectives*) Cursing, etc., accursed, cursed, etc., blue-pencil, asterisk; maledictory, imprecatory, blasphemous.

(*Interjections*) Curse! damn! blast! devil take it! dash! hang! blow! confound! plague on it! woe to! beshrew! *ruat coelum!* ill betide!

909 THREAT (*Substantives*), menace, defiance (715) abuse, minacity, intimidation, commination.

(*Verbs*) To threaten, threat, menace, fulminate, thunder, bluster, defy, snarl; growl, gnarl, mutter; to intimidate (860).

(*Phrases*) To hurl defiance; to throw down the gauntlet; to look daggers; to show one's teeth; to shake the fist at.

(*Adjectives*) Threatening, menacing, minatory, comminatory, minacious, abusive, sinister, ominous, louring, defiant (715).

(*Interjections*) Let them beware! You have been warned!

910 PHILANTHROPY (*Substantives*), humanity, humanitarianism, altruism, public spirit.

Patriotism, civicism, nationality, nationalism, love of country, *amor patriae*, sociology, socialism, utilitarianism.

A philanthropist, humanitarian, utilitarian, Benthamite, socialist, cosmopolitan, cosmopolite, citizen of the world, patriot, nationalist, lover of mankind.

(*Adjectives*) Philanthropic, philanthropical, humanitarian, humane, utilitarian, patriotic, altruistic, public-spirited.

(*Phrases*) '*Humani nihil a me alienum puto*'; *pro bono publico*; the greatest happiness of the greatest number.

911 MISANTHROPY (*Substantives*), egotism, egoism, incivism, want of patriotism, moroseness, selfishness (943); misogynism.

A misanthrope, egotist, cynic, man-hater, Timon, Diogenes.

Woman-hater, misogynist.

(*Adjectives*) Misanthropic, misanthropical, antisocial, unpatriotic, fish, egotistical, morose, sullen, maladjusted.

912 BENEFACTOR (*Substantives*), saviour, good genius, tutelary saint, guardian angel, fairy godmother, good Samaritan.

(*Phrase*) *Deus ex machina.*

913 Maleficent being.

EVILDOER (*Substantives*), wrongdoer, mischief-maker, marplot, anarchist, nihilist, terrorist, firebrand, incendiary, evil genius (980).

Frankenstein's monster.

Savage, brute, ruffian, blackguard, villain, scoundrel, cutthroat, barbarian, caitiff, desperado, jail-bird, hooligan, tough, rough, teddy boy, larrikin, hoodlum, gangster, crook, yegg, apache (949).

Fiend, tiger, hyena, bloodhound, butcher, blood-sucker, vampire, ogre, ghoul, serpent, snake, adder, viper, rattlesnake, scorpion, hellhound, hag, hellbag, beldam, harpy, siren, fury, Jezebel.

Monster, demon, imp, devil (980), anthropophagi, Attila, vandal, Hun, Goth.

(*Phrases*) A snake in the grass; a scourge of the human race; a fiend in human shape; worker of iniquity.

3°. Special Sympathetic Affections

914 PITY (*Substantives*), compassion, commiseration, sympathy, fellow-feeling, tenderness, yearning.

Forbearance, mercy, humanity, clemency, leniency, ruth, long-suffering, quarter.

(*Phrases*) The melting mood; *coup de grâce*; bowels of compassion; *argumentum ad misericordiam.*

(*Verbs*) To pity, commiserate, compassionate, sympathize, feel for, yearn for, console, enter into the feelings of, have or take pity; show or have mercy; to forbear, relent, thaw, spare, relax, give quarter.

To excite pity, touch, soften, melt, propitiate, disarm.

To ask for pity, mercy, etc.; to supplicate, implore, deprecate, appeal to, cry for quarter, etc.; beg one's life, kneel, fall on one's knees, etc.

(*Phrase*) To put one out of one's misery.

(*Adjectives*) Pitying, commiserating, etc.

Pitiful, compassionate, tender, clement, merciful, lenient, relenting, etc.; soft-hearted, sympathetic, touched, weak, soft, melting, unhardened (740). Piteous, pitiable, sorry, miserable.

(*Phrases*) Tender as a woman; one's heart bleeding for.

(*Interjections*) For pity's sake! mercy! God help you! poor thing! poor fellow!

915 CONDOLENCE (*Substantives*), lamentation, lament (839), sympathy, consolation.

(*Verbs*) To condole with, console, solace, sympathize; express, testify, etc., pity; to afford or supply consolation, grieve for, lament with, weep with (839).

4°. *Retrospective Sympathetic Affections*

916 GRATITUDE (*Substantives*), gratefulness, thankfulness, feeling of obligation.

Acknowledgment, recognition, thanksgiving, giving thanks.

Thanks, praise, benediction, grace, paean, Te Deum (990).

Requital, thank-offering.

(*Verbs*) To be grateful, etc.; to thank, to give, render, return, offer, tender thanks, acknowledgments, etc.; to acknowledge, appreciate, requite.

To lie under an obligation, to be obliged, beholden, etc.

(*Phrases*) To overflow with gratitude; to thank one's stars; never to forget.

(*Adjectives*) Grateful, thankful, obliged, beholden, indebted to, under obligation.

(*Interjections*) Thanks! many thanks! ta! *merci*! gramercy! much obliged! thank heaven! heaven be praised!

917 INGRATITUDE (*Substantives*), ungratefulness, thanklessness, oblivion of benefits.

(*Phrases*) 'Benefits forgot'; a thankless task.

(*Verbs*) To be ungrateful, etc.; to forget benefits.

(*Phrases*) To look a gift-horse in the mouth; to bite the hand that fed one.

(*Adjectives*) Ungrateful, unmindful, unthankful, thankless, ingrate, inappreciative.

Forgotten, unacknowledged, unthanked, unrequited, unrewarded, ill-requited.

(*Phrase*) Thank you for nothing.

---

918 FORGIVENESS (*Substantives*), pardon, condonation, grace, remission, absolution, amnesty, indemnity, oblivion, indulgence, reprieve.

Reconcilement, reconciliation, appeasement, mollification, shaking of hands, pacification (723).

919 REVENGE (*Substantives*), vengeance, revengement, avengement, vendetta, feud, retaliation.

Rancour, vindictiveness, implacability.

Revenger, avenger, vindicator, Nemesis, Furies.

Excuse, exoneration, quittance, acquittal, propitiation, exculpation. Longanimity, forbearance, placability.

(*Verbs*) To forgive, pardon, excuse, pass over, overlook, bear with, condone, absolve, pass, let off, remit, reprieve, exculpate, exonerate.

To allow for; to make allowance for.

To conciliate, propitiate, pacify, appease, placate, reconcile.

(*Phrases*) To make it up; to forgive and forget; to shake hands; to heal the breach; to kiss and be friends; to bury the hatchet; to wipe the slate clean; to let bygones be bygones.

(*Adjectives*) Forgiving, etc., unreproachful, placable, conciliatory. Forgiven, etc., unresented.

(*Verbs*) To revenge, take revenge, avenge.

(*Phrases*) To wreak one's vengeance; to visit the sins on; to breathe vengeance; to have a bone to pick with; to have accounts to settle; to have a rod in pickle; to get one's knife into; to take one's change out of.

To harbour vindictive feelings; to rankle in the breast.

(*Adjectives*) Revengeful, revanchist, vindictive, vengeful, rancorous, unforgiving, pitiless, ruthless, remorseless, unrelenting, relenting, implacable, rigorous.

---

920 JEALOUSY (*Substantives*), jealousy, heartburning.
(*Phrases*) A jaundiced eye; the green-eyed monster.
(*Verbs*) To be jealous, etc.; to view with jealousy.
(*Adjectives*) Jealous, jaundiced, yellow-eyed.
(*Phrase*) Eaten up with jealousy.

921 ENVY (*Substantives*), rivalry, emulation, covetousness; a Thersites, Zoilus.
(*Verbs*) To envy, rival, emulate, covet.
(*Adjectives*) Envious, invidious, covetous.
(*Phrase*) Bursting with envy.

SECTION IV—MORAL AFFECTIONS

1°. Moral Obligation

922 RIGHT (*Substantives*), what ought to be, what should be; goodness, virtue (944), rectitude, probity (939).

Justice, equity, equitableness, fitness, fairness, fair play, impartiality, reasonableness, propriety.

Astraea, Themis.

(*Phrases*) The scales of justice; even-handed justice; *suum cuique*; a fair field and no favour; *lex talionis*; '*Fiat justitia, ruat coelum.*'

Morality, morals, ethics, duty (926).

(*Verbs*) To stand to reason; to be right, just, etc.

To deserve, merit; to be worthy of, to be entitled to (924).

923 WRONG (*Substantives*), what ought not to be, badness, evil (945), turpitude, improbity (940).

Injustice, unfairness, inequity, foul play, partiality, favour, favouritism, leaning, bias, party spirit, undueness (925), unreasonableness, tort, unlawfulness (964), encroachment, imposition.

(*Verbs*) To be wrong, unjust, etc.; to favour, lean towards, show partiality, to encroach, impose upon.

(*Phrase*) To rob Peter to pay Paul.

(*Adjectives*) Wrong, wrongful, bad, unjust, unfair, undue, inequitable, unequal, partial, invidious, one-sided, improper, unreasonable, iniquitous, unfit, immoral (945).

(*Phrases*) To do justice to; to see justice done; to hold the scales even; to see fair play; to see one righted; to serve one right; to give the devil his due; to give and take; *audire alteram partem.*

(*Adjectives*) Right, just, equitable, fair, equal, even-handed, impartial, judicial, legitimate, justifiable, rightful, reasonable, fit, proper, becoming, decorous, decent (926).

Deserved, merited, condign (924).

(*Adverbs*) Rightly, in justice, in equity, fairly, etc., in reason, without distinction, without respect of persons.

(*Phrases*) *En règle*; *de jure.*

924 Dueness (*Substantives*), due.

Right, privilege, prerogative, title, claim, qualification, pretension, birthright, prescription, immunity, exemption, licence, liberty, franchise, enfranchisement, vested interest.

Sanction, authority, warranty, tenure, bond, security, lien, constitution, charter, warrant (760), patent, letters patent, copyright, *imprimatur.*

A claimant, pretender, appellant, plaintiff (938).

Women's rights, feminism; feminist, suffragist, suffragette.

(*Verbs*) To be due, etc., to.

To have a right to, to be entitled to, to be qualified for, to have a claim upon, a title to, etc.; to deserve, merit, be worthy of.

To demand, claim, call upon, exact, insist on, challenge, to come upon one for, to revendicate, make a point of, enforce, put in force, use a right.

To appertain to, belong to, etc. (777).

To lay claim to, assert, assume, arrogate, make good, substantiate; to vindicate a claim, etc., to make out a case.

To give or confer a right; to entitle, authorize, warrant, sanction, sanctify, privilege, enfranchise, license, legalize, ordain, prescribe, allot.

(*Adjectives*) Having a right to, a claim to, etc.; due to, entitled to, deserving, meriting, worthy of, claiming, qualified.

Unjustified, unjustifiable, unwarranted, unauthorized, unallowable, unwarrantable.

(*Phrases*) In the wrong; in the wrong box.

(*Adverbs*) Wrongly, unjustly, etc., amiss.

(*Phrase*) It won't do.

———

925 Absence of right.

Undueness (*Substantives*), unlawfulness, impropriety, unfitness, illegality (964).

Falseness, spuriousness, emptiness or invalidity of title, illegitimacy.

Loss of right, forfeiture, disfranchisement.

Usurpation, violation, breach, encroachment, stretch, imposition, relaxation.

(*Verbs*) Not to be due, etc., to; to be undue, etc.

Too infringe, encroach, violate, do violence to; to stretch or strain a point; to trench on, usurp.

To disfranchise, disentitle, disfrock, unfrock; to disqualify, invalidate, relax.

To misbecome, misbehave (945).

(*Adjectives*) Undue, unlawful, illicit, unconstitutional.

Unauthorized, unwarranted, unsanctioned, unjustified, unprivileged, illegitimate, bastard, spurious, supposititious, false, usurped, unchartered, unfulfilled, unofficial, unauthorized.

Unentitled, disentitled, unqualified, underprivileged; disfranchised, forfeit.

Undeserved, unmerited, unearned. Improper, unmeet, unbecoming, unfit, misbecoming, unseemly, preposterous.

(*Phrases*) Not the thing; out of the question; not to be thought of; out of court.

———

Privileged, allowed, sanctioned, warranted, authorized, permitted, licit, ordained, prescribed, chartered, enfranchised, constitutional, official.

Prescriptive, presumptive, absolute, indefeasible, unalienable, inalienable, imprescriptible, inviolable, unimpeachable, unchallenged, sacred, sacrosanct.

Condign, merited, deserved.

Allowable, permissible, lawful, legitimate, legal, legalized (963), proper, square, equitable, unexceptionable, reasonable (922), right, correct, meet, fitting (926).

(*Adverbs*) Duly, by right, by divine right, *ex officio, Dei gratia, de jure.*

926 DUTY (*Substantives*), what ought to be done; moral obligation, accountableness, accountability, liability, onus, responsibility, bounden duty; dueness (924).

Allegiance, fealty, tie, office, function, province, post, engagement (768).

Morality, morals, conscience, accountableness, conscientiousness; the Decalogue, the Ten Commandments.

Dueness, propriety, fitness, decency, seemliness, decorum.

Observance, fulfilment, discharge, performance, acquittal, satisfaction, redemption, good behaviour.

Science of morals, ethics, deontology; moral or ethical philosophy, casuistry.

(*Phrases*) The thing; the proper thing; a case of conscience; the still small voice.

(*Verbs*) To be the duty of, to be due to, to be up to; ought to be; to be incumbent on, to behove, befit, become, beseem, belong to, pertain to, devolve on, to be on one's head; to be, or stand, or lie under an obligation; to have to answer for, to be accountable for, to owe it to oneself, to be in duty bound, to be committed to, to be on one's good behaviour.

To impose a duty or obligation; to enjoin, require, exact, bind, pin down, saddle with, prescribe, assign, call upon, look to, oblige.

927 DERELICTION OF DUTY (*Substantives*), guilt (947), sin (945), neglect, negligence, non-observance, failure, evasion, dead letter.

(*Verbs*) To violate, break, break through, infringe, set at naught, slight, neglect, trample on, evade, contravene, disregard, renounce, repudiate, quit, forswear, fail, transgress.

(*Phrase*) To wash one's hands of.

927A EXEMPTION (*Substantives*), freedom, irresponsibility, immunity, liberty, licence, release, exoneration, excuse, dispensation, absolution, franchise, renunciation, discharge.

(*Verbs*) To be exempt, free, at liberty, released, excused, exonerated, absolved, etc.

To exempt, release, excuse, exonerate, absolve, acquit, free, set at liberty, discharge, set aside, let off, remit, passover, spare, excuse, license, dispense with; to give dispensation.

(*Phrase*) To stretch a point.

(*Adjectives*) Exempt, free, released, at liberty, absolved, exonerated, excused, let off, discharged, licensed, acquitted, unencumbered, dispensed, scot-free, immune.

Irresponsible, unaccountable, unanswerable, unbound.

To do one's duty, to enter upon a duty; to perform, observe, fulfil, discharge, adhere to; acquit oneself of an obligation.

(*Phrases*) To be at one's post; to redeem one's pledge; to toe the mark or line.

(*Adjectives*) Dutiful, duteous, docile, obedient, compliant, tractable.

Obligatory, binding, imperative, peremptory, mandatory, behoving, incumbent on, chargeable on, meet, due to.

Being under obligation, under obedience, obliged by, beholden to, bound by, tied by, saddled with, indebted to.

Amenable, liable, accountable, responsible, answerable.

Right, proper, fit, due, correct, seemly, fitting, befitting, decent, meet.

Moral, ethical, casuistical, conscientious.

(*Adverbs*) Conscientiously, with a safe conscience; as in duty bound; on one's own responsibility.

2°. *Moral Sentiments*

928 RESPECT (*Substantives*), deference, reverence, regard, consideration, attention, honour, esteem, estimation, distance, decorum, veneration, admiration.

Homage, fealty, obeisance, genuflexion, kneeling, salaam, kowtow, presenting arms (896), prostration, obsequiousness, devotion, worship (990).

(*Verbs*) To respect, honour, reverence, regard, defer to, pay respect or deference to, render honour to, look up to, esteem, revere, think much of, think highly of, venerate, hallow.

To pay homage to, bow to, take off one's hat to, kneel to, bend the knee to, present arms, fall down before, prostrate oneself.

To command or inspire respect; to awe, overawe, dazzle.

(*Phrases*) To keep one's distance; to make way for; to observe due decorum.

(*Adjectives*) Respecting, etc., respectful, considerate, polite, attentive, reverential, obsequious, ceremonious, bare-headed, cap in hand, on one's knees, prostrate.

Respected, esteemed, honoured, hallowed, venerable, emeritus.

(*Phrases*) Saving your presence; begging your honour's pardon.

929 DISRESPECT (*Substantives*), irreverence, dishonour, disparagement, slight, neglect, disesteem, disestimation, superciliousness, contumely, indignity, insult, rudeness.

Ridicule (856), sarcasm, derision, scurrility, mockery, scoffing, sibilation.

A jeer, gibe, taunt, scoff, sneer (930), hiss, hoot, fling, flout.

(*Verbs*) To treat with disrespect, etc., to disparage, dishonour, misprise, vilipend, slight, insult, affront, disregard, make light of, hold in, no esteem, esteem of no account, set at naught, speak slightingly of, set down, pass by, overlook, look down upon, despise (930).

To deride, scoff, sneer at, laugh at, ridicule (856), roast, guy, rag, mock, jeer, taunt, twit, flout, gibe, hiss, hoot, boo.

(*Phrases*) To make game of; to point the finger at; to make a fool of; to turn into ridicule; to laugh to scorn; to turn one's back upon.

(*Adjectives*) Disrespectful, slighting, disparaging (934), dishonouring, scornful (940), irreverent, supercilious, contumelious, scurrilous, deriding, derisive, derisory.

Unrespected, unworshipped, unregarded, disregarded, ignored.

(*Adverbs*) Disrespectfully, cavalierly, etc.

930 CONTEMPT (*Substantives*), disdain, scorn, contumely, despisal, slight, sneer, spurn, sniff; a byword.

Scornfulness, disdainfulness, haughtiness, contemptuousness, superciliousness, derision (929).

The state of being despised, despisedness.

(*Verbs*) To despise, contemn, scorn, disdain, scout, spurn, look down upon, disregard, slight, make light of, not mind, hold cheap, hold in contempt, pooh-pooh, sneeze at, sniff at, whistle at, hoot, flout, trample upon.

(*Phrases*) Not to care a straw, fig, button, etc., for (643); to turn up one's nose at; to shrug one's shoulders; to snap one's fingers at; to take no account of; to laugh to scorn; to make light of; to tread or trample under foot; to set at naught; to point the finger of scorn at.

(*Adjectives*) Contemptuous, disdainful, scornful, contumelious, cavalier, derisive, supercilious, toplofty, upstage, sniffy, sardonic.

Contemptible, despicable, poor, paltry (643), downtrodden, unenvied.

(*Interjections*) A fig for! hoots! bah! pshaw! pish! shucks! pooh-pooh! fiddlestick! fiddle-de-dee! tush! tut!

931 APPROBATION (*Substantives*), approval, approvement, endorsement, sanction, esteem, admiration, estimation, good opinion, appreciation, regard, account, popularity, kudos.

Commendation, praise, laud, laudation, advocacy, good word; meed or tribute of praise, encomium, eulogium, eulogy, *éloge*, panegyric, puff, blurb, homage.

Applause, plaudit, cheer, clap, clapping, clapping of hands, acclamation; paean, benediction, blessing, benison, hosanna; claque.

(*Phrases*) A peal, shout, or chorus of applause; golden opinions; *succès d'estime.*

(*Verbs*) To approve, think well or highly of, esteem, appreciate, value, prize, admire, countenance, endorse.

To commend, speak well of, recommend, advocate, praise, laud, belaud, compliment, bepraise, clap, clap hands, applaud, cheer, panegyrize, celebrate, eulogize, cry up, root for, crack up, write up, extol, glorify, magnify, puff, boom, boost, exalt, swell, bless, give a blessing to.

To deserve praise, etc., to be praised, etc.

(*Phrases*) To set great store by; to sing the praises of; to extol to the skies; to applaud to the echo; to stick up for; to say a good word for; to pat on the back.

To redound to the honour or praise of; to do credit to.

To win golden opinions; to be in high favour; to bring down the house.

(*Adjectives*) Approving, etc., commendatory, complimentary, bene-

932 DISAPPROBATION (*Substantives*), disapproval, dislike (867), blame, censure, reprobation, obloquy, dispraise, contumely, odium, disesteem, depreciation, detraction (934), condemnation, ostracism.

Reprobation, exprobration, insinuation, innuendo, animadversion, reflection, stricture, objection, exception, criticism, critique, correction, discommendation.

Satire, sneer, fling, gibe, skit, squib, quip, taunt, sarcasm, lampoon, cavil, pasquinade, recrimination, castigation.

Remonstrance, reprehension, reproof, admonition, expostulation, reproach, rebuke, reprimand, talking-to, telling-off.

Evil speaking, hard words, foul language, personalities, ribaldry, Billingsgate, unparliamentary language.

Upbraiding, abuse, invective, vituperation, scolding, wigging, dressing-down, objurgation, jaw, railing, jobation, nagging, reviling, contumely, execration (908).

A set-down, trimming, rating, slap, snub, frown, scowl, black look.

A lecture, curtain lecture, diatribe, jeremiad, tirade, philippic; clamour, outcry, hue and cry, hiss, hissing, sibilation, cat-call.

(*Phrases*) A rap on the knuckles; a slap in the face; a left-handed compliment.

(*Verbs*) To disapprove, dislike (867), dispraise, find fault with, criticize, glance at, insinuate, cut up, carp at, cavil, point at, peck at, nibble at, object to, take exception

dictory, laudatory, panegyrical, eulogistic, encomiastic.

Approved, praised, uncensured, unimpeached, admired, popular, deserving or worthy of praise, praiseworthy, commendable, estimable, plausible, meritorious.

(*Phrases*) Lavish of praise; lost in admiration.

(*Interjections*) Well done! good man! stout fellow! good show! attaboy! bravo! bravissimo! *euge!* that's the stuff! hear, hear!

to, animadvert upon, protest against, frown upon, bar.

To disparage, depreciate, deprecate, crab, knock, traduce, smear, speak ill of, decry, vilify, vilipend, defame, detract (934), revile, satirize, sneer, gibe, lampoon, inveigh against, write down, scalp.

To blame; to lay or cast blame upon, reflect upon, cast a slur upon, censure, pass censure on, impugn, show up, denounce, censure, brand, stigmatize, reprobate, improbate.

To reprehend, reprimand, admonish, remonstrate, expostulate, reprove, pull up, take up, set down, snub, twit, taunt, reproach, load with reproaches, rebuke, come down upon, sit on, pitch into, get on to, tell off, tick off.

To chide, scold, wig, rate, objurgate, upbraid, vituperate, recriminate, anathematize, abuse, call names, exclaim against, jaw, mob, trounce, trim, rail at, nag, nag at, bark at, blackguard, revile, ballyrag, rag, natter, blow up, roast, lecture; castigate, chastise, correct, lash, flay; to fulminate against, fall foul of.

To cry out against, cry down, run down, clamour, hiss, hoot; to accuse (938), to find guilty, ostracize, blacklist, blackball.

To scandalize, shock, revolt, incur blame, excite disapprobation.

(*Phrases*) To set one's face against; to shake the head at; to take a poor or dim view of; to view with dark or jaundiced eyes; to pick holes in; to give a thing the bird; to damn with faint praise; to pluck a crow with; to have a fling at; to read a lecture; to put on the carpet (or mat); to take to task; to bring to book; to haul over the coals; to tear one off a strip; to shoot down in flames; to pull to pieces; to cut up; to cast in one's teeth; to abuse like a pickpocket; to speak or look daggers; to rail in good set terms; to give it one hot; to throw mud; to give a person the rough side of one's tongue.

To forfeit the good opinion of; to catch it; to be under a cloud; to carry the can; to stand corrected.

(*Adjectives*) Disapproving, disparaging, etc., condemnatory, damnatory, denunciatory, reproachful, abusive, objurgatory, clamorous, vituperative, dyslogistic.

Censorious, critical, carping, satirical, sarcastic, sardonic, cynical, dry, hypercritical, captious; sharp, cutting, mordant, biting, withering, trenchant, caustic, severe, scathing; squeamish, fastidious, strait-laced (868).

Disapproved, chid, unapproved, blown upon, unblest, unlamented, unbewailed.

Blameworthy, uncommendable, exceptionable (649, 945).

(*Phrases*) Hard upon one; weighed in the balance and found wanting; not to be thought of.

(*Interjections*) Bad show! shame!

---

933 FLATTERY (*Substantives*), adulation, sycophancy, blandishment, cajolery, fawning, wheedling, coaxing.

934 DETRACTION (*Substantives*), obloquy, scurrility, scandal, vilification, smear, defamation, aspersion,

flunkeyism, toad-eating, toady-ism, tuft-hunting, back-scratching, blandiloquence.

Incense, honeyed words, flummery, soft sawder, soft soap, butter, apple-sauce, blarney, malarkey; mouth-honour, lip-service.

(*Verbs*) To flatter, wheedle, cajole, fawn upon, coax (615), humour, gloze, butter, toady, sugar, bespatter, beslaver, earwig, jolly, flannel, truckle to, pander to, court, pay court to.

(*Phrases*) To curry favour with; to lay it on thick; to lay it on with a trowel; to ingratiate oneself with; to fool to the top of one's bent.

(*Adjectives*) Flattering, adulatory, mealy-mouthed, smooth, honeyed, candied, soapy, oily, unctuous, fair-spoken, plausible, servile, sycophantic, fulsome; courtier-like.

935 FLATTERER (*Substantives*), adulator, eulogist, encomiast, white-washer, toady, sycophant, toad-eater, *prôneur*, touter, booster, *claqueur*, spaniel, back-scratcher, flunkey, lick-spittle, pick-thank, earwig, tuft-hunter, hanger-on, courtier, parasite, doer of dirty work, *âme damnée*, *Graeculus esuriens*.

937 VINDICATION (*Substantives*), justification, exoneration, exculpa-tion, acquittal, whitewashing.

Extenuation, palliation, mitiga-tion, softening; extenuating circum-stances.

Plea, excuse, apology, defence, gloss, varnish, salvo (617).

Vindicator, apologist, justifier, de-fender.

(*Verbs*) To vindicate, justify, warrant, exculpate, acquit, clear, set right, exonerate, disculpate, white-wash.

To extenuate, palliate, excuse, soften, apologize, varnish, slur, gloze, gloss over, bolster up.

To plead, advocate, defend, stand up for, stick up for, speak for, make good, bear out, say in defence, con-tend for.

traducement, slander, calumny, back-biting, criticism, slating, personality, evil-speaking, disparagement, de-preciation (932).

Libel, lampoon, skit, squib, sar-casm.

(*Verbs*) To detract, criticize, as-perse, depreciate, derogate, disparage, cheapen, blow upon, bespatter, blacken, denigrate, defame, brand, malign, decry, vilify, vilipend, back-bite, libel, slate, lampoon, traduce, slander, calumniate, run down, write down.

(*Phrases*) To speak ill of one behind one's back; to damn with faint praise; to sell oneself short.

(*Adjectives*) Detracting, disparag-ing, libellous, scurrilous, abusive, cynical (932), foul-tongued, foul-mouthed, slanderous, defamatory, calumnious, calumniatory.

936 DETRACTOR (*Substantives*), dis-approver, critic, censor, caviller, carper, knocker, *frondeur*, defamer, backbiter, slanderer, traducer, libeller, calumniator, lampooner, satirist, can-did friend, Thersites.

938 ACCUSATION (*Substantives*), charge, imputation, inculpation, ex-probration, delation, crimination, recrimination, invective, jeremiad (932).

Denunciation, denouncement, challenge, indictment, libel, delation, citation, arraignment, impeachment, appeachment, bill of indictment, true bill, condemnation (971), scandal (934), *scandalum magnatum*.

Accuser, prosecutor, plaintiff, pursuer, informer, appellant, com-plainant.

Accused, defendant, prisoner, panel, respondent.

(*Phrases*) The gravamen of a charge; *argumentum ad hominem*.

(*Verbs*) To accuse, charge, tax, im-pute, twit, taunt with, slur, reproach, brand with, stigmatize, criminate,

(*Phrases*) To put in a good word for; to plead the cause of; to put a good face upon; to keep in countenance; to make allowance for.

(*Adjectives*) Vindicatory, vindicative, palliative, exculpatory; vindicating, etc.

Excusable, defensible, pardonable, venial, specious, plausible, justifiable, warrantable.

(*Phrases*) '*Honi soit qui mal y pense*'; *qui s'excuse s'accuse.*

incriminate, inculpate (932), implicate, saddle with.

To inform against; to indict, denounce, arraign, impeach, challenge, show up, pull up, cite, prosecute, summon.

(*Phrases*) To lay to one's door; to lay to one's charge; bring home to; to call to account; to bring to book; to take to task; to trump up a charge; to brand with reproach.

(*Adjectives*) Accusing, etc., accusatory, accusative, imputative, denunciatory, criminative, criminatory, incriminatory, accusable, imputable.

Indefensible, inexcusable, unpardonable, unjustifiable (945).

3°. Moral Conditions

939 PROBITY (*Substantives*), integrity, uprightness, honesty, virtue (944), rectitude, faith, good faith, bona fides, fairness, honour, fair play, justice, principle, constancy, fidelity, incorruptibility.

Trustworthiness, trustiness, reliability, dependableness, grace, uncorruptedness, impartiality, equity, candour, veracity (545), straightforwardness, truth, equitableness, singleness of heart.

Conscientiousness, punctiliousness, nicety, scrupulosity, delicacy, sense of decency, strictness, punctuality.

Dignity, respectability, reputableness (873).

A man of honour, a gentleman, a man of his word, a sportsman, white man, trump, brick, *preux chevalier.*

(*Phrases*) The court of honour; a fair field and no favour; 'a verray parfit gentil knight.'

(*Verbs*) To be honourable, etc.; to keep one's word, to give and take, to deal honourably, squarely, impartially, fairly.

(*Phrases*) To hit straight from the shoulder; to play the game.

(*Adjectives*) Upright, honest, virtuous (944), honourable, fair, right, just, equitable, impartial, evenhanded, square, constant, faithful, loyal, staunch, straight.

940 IMPROBITY (*Substantives*), wickedness (945), bad faith, unfairness, infidelity, faithlessness, want of faith, dishonesty, disloyalty, falseness, falsity, one-sidedness, disingenuousness, shabbiness, littleness, meanness, caddishness, baseness, villainy, roguery, rascality, vileness, abjectness, turpitude, unreliability, untrustworthiness, insidiousness, knavery, knavishness, fraud (545), falsehood (544), shenanigans.

Disgrace, ignominy, infamy, tarnish, blot, stain, spot, slur, pollution, derogation, degradation (874).

Perfidy, perfidiousness, treason, high treason, perjury, apostasy (607), backsliding, breach of faith, defection, disloyalty, disaffection, foul play, sharp practice, graft, doubledealing, betrayal, treacherousness, treachery.

(*Phrases*) The kiss of Judas; divided allegiance; Punic faith.

(*Verbs*) To be of bad faith, dishonest, etc.; to play false, break one's word or faith, betray, forswear, shuffle (545).

To disgrace oneself, derogate, stoop, demean oneself, lose caste, dishonour oneself, sneak, crawl, grovel.

(*Phrases*) To seal one's infamy; to sell oneself; to go over to the enemy.

Trustworthy, trusty, reliable, dependable, tried, incorruptible, straightforward, ingenuous (703), frank, open-hearted, candid.

Conscientious, tender-conscienced, high-principled, high-minded, high-toned, scrupulous, strict, nice, punctilious, correct, punctual, inviolable, inviolate, unviolated, unbroken, unbetrayed.

Chivalrous, gentlemanlike, respectable, unbought, unbribed, unstained, stainless, untarnished, unsullied, untainted, unperjured, innocent (946).

(*Phrases*) Jealous of honour; as good as one's word; true to one's colours; *sans peur et sans reproche*; *integer vitao scelorisque purus.*

(*Adverbs*) Honourably, etc., bona fide; on the square; on the up and up.

(*Adjectives*) Dishonest, unfair, one-sided, fraudulent (545), knavish, wicked (945), false, faithless, unfaithful, foul, disingenuous, trothless, trustless, untrustworthy, unreliable, slippery, double-faced, double-tongued, crooked, tortuous, unscrupulous, insidious, treacherous, perfidious, false-hearted, perjured, rascally.

Base, vile, grovelling, dirty, scurvy, scabby, low, low-down, abject, shabby, caddish, mean, paltry, pitiful, inglorious, scrubby, beggarly, putid, unworthy, disgraceful, dishonourable, derogatory, low-thoughted, disreputable, unhandsome, unbecoming (925), unbefitting, ungentlemanly, unmanly, unwomanly, undignified, base-minded, recreant, low-minded, blackguard, pettifogging, underhand, underhanded, unsportsmanlike.

(*Phrases*) Lost to shame; dead to honour.

(*Adverbs*) Dishonestly, etc., *mala fide*, on the crook.

941 KNAVE (*Substantives*), bad man (949), rogue, rascal, scoundrel, villain, spiv, sharper, shyster, blackleg, scab, trimmer, time-server, timist, turncoat, badmash, Vicar of Bray, Judas (607).

Apostate, renegade, pervert, black sheep, traitor, arch-traitor, quisling, fifth columnist, deviationist, betrayer, recreant, miscreant, cullion, outcast, mean wretch, slubberdegullion, snake in the grass, wolf in sheep's clothing.

942 UNSELFISHNESS (*Substantives*), selflessness, disinterestedness, generosity, high-mindedness, nobleness, elevation, liberality, greatness, loftiness, exaltation, magnanimity, chivalry, chivalrous spirit, heroism, sublimity, altruism, self-forgetfulness, unworldliness.

Self-denial, self-abnegation, self-sacrifice, self-restraint, self-control, devotion, stoicism.

(*Phrases*) To put oneself in the background, in the place of others; to do as one would be done by.

(*Adjectives*) Unselfish, selfless, self-forgetful, handsome, generous, liberal, noble, princely, great, high, high-minded, elevated, lofty, exalted, spirited, stoical, self-denying, self-sacrificing, self-devoted, magnanimous, chivalrous, heroic, sublime, unworldly.

943 SELFISHNESS (*Substantives*), egotism, egoism, self-regard, self-love, self-indulgence, worldliness, worldly-mindedness, earthly-mindedness, self-interest, opportunism.

Illiberality, meanness, baseness.

A time-server, tuft-hunter, fortune-hunter, gold-digger, jobber, worldling, self-seeker, opportunist, hog, road-hog.

(*Phrase*) A dog in the manger.

(*Verbs*) To be selfish, etc., to indulge oneself, coddle oneself.

(*Phrases*) To look after one's own interest; to take care of number one; to have an eye for the main chance.

(*Adjectives*) Selfish, egotistical, egoistical, self-indulgent, apolaustic, self-regarding, self-centred, illiberal, self-seeking, mercenary, venal, mean, ungenerous, interested.

Unbought, unbribed, pure, un-corrupted, incorruptible.
(*Adverb*) En prince.

————

944 VIRTUE (*Substantives*), virtu-ousness, goodness, righteousness, morals, morality (926), rectitude, correctness, dutifulness, conscientiousness, integrity, probity (939), uprightness, nobleness, nobility; innocence (946).

Merit, worth, worthiness, desert, excellence, credit, self-control, self-conquest, self-government, self-respect.

Well-doing, good actions, good behaviour, a well-spent life.

(*Verbs*) To be virtuous, etc.; to act well; to do, fulfil, perform, or discharge one's duty, to acquit oneself well, to practise virtue; to command or master one's passions (926).

(*Phrases*) To have one's heart in the right place; to keep in the right path; to fight the good fight; to set an example; to be on one's good behaviour.

(*Adjectives*) Virtuous, good, innocent (946), meritorious, deserving, worthy, correct, dutiful, duteous (926), moral, ethical, righteous, right-minded (939), laudable, well-intentioned, creditable, commendable, praiseworthy, excellent, admirable, sterling, pure, noble, well-conducted, well-behaved.

Exemplary, matchless, peerless, saintly, saint-like, heaven-born, angelic, seraphic, godlike.

(*Phrase*) Mens sibi conscia recti.
(*Adverb*) Virtuously, etc.

————

Worldly, earthly, mundane, time-serving, worldly-minded.

(*Phrases*) To serve one's private ends; from interested motives; charity begins at home; I'm all right, Jack.

945 VICE (*Substantives*), evildoing, wrongdoing, wickedness, sin, iniquity, unrighteousness, demerit, unworthiness, worthlessness, badness.

Immorality, impropriety, indecorum, laxity, looseness of morals, want of principle, obliquity, backsliding, recidivism, gracelessness, infamy, demoralization, pravity, depravity, depravation, obduracy, hardness of heart, brutality (907), corruption, pollution, dissoluteness, debauchery, grossness, baseness, knavery, roguery, rascality, villainy (940), profligacy, abandonment, flagrancy, atrocity, devilry (or deviltry), criminality, guilt (947).

Infirmity, weakness, feebleness, frailty, imperfection, error, weak side or point, blind side, foible, failing, failure, defect, deficiency, indiscretion, peccability.

(*Phrases*) The cloven hoof; the old Adam; the lowest dregs of vice; a sink of iniquity; the primrose path.

(*Verbs*) To be vicious, etc.; to sin, commit sin, do amiss, misdo, err, transgress, go astray, misdemean or misconduct oneself, misbehave; to fall, lapse, slip, trip, offend, trespass.

To render vicious, etc., to demoralize, corrupt, seduce, debauch, debase, vitiate.

(*Phrases*) To deviate from the line of duty or from the paths of virtue, rectitude, etc.; to blot one's copybook; to hug a sin or fault; to sow one's wild oats.

(*Adjectives*) Vicious, bad, sinful, wicked, evil, evil-minded, immoral, iniquitous, unprincipled, demoralized, unconscionable, worthless, unworthy, good for nothing, graceless, heartless, virtueless, undutiful, unrighteous, unmoral, amoral, guilty (947).

Wrong, culpable, naughty, incorrect, indictable, criminal, dissolute, debauched, disorderly, raffish, corrupt, profligate, depraved, degenerate, abandoned, graceless, shameless, recreant, villainous, sunk, lost, obdurate, reprobate, incorrigible, irreclaimable, ill-conditioned.

Weak, frail, lax, infirm, spineless, invertebrate, imperfect, indiscreet, erring, transgressing, sinning, etc., peccable, peccant.

Blamable, reprehensible, blameworthy, uncommendable, discreditable, disreputable, shady, exceptionable.

Indecorous, unseemly, improper, sinister, base, ignoble, scurvy, foul, gross, vile, black, felonious, nefarious, scandalous, infamous, villainous, heinous, grave, flagrant, flagitious, atrocious, satanic, satanical, diabolic, diabolical, hellish, infernal, stygian, fiendlike, fiendish, devilish, miscreated, misbegotten, hell-born, demoniacal.

Unpardonable, unforgivable, indefensible, inexcusable, irremissible, inexpiable.

(*Phrases*) Past praying for; of the deepest dye; not having a word to say for oneself; weighed in the balance and found wanting; *in flagrante delicto*.

(*Adverbs*) Wrongly, etc.; without excuse, too bad.

---

946 INNOCENCE (*Substantives*), guiltlessness, harmlessness, innocuousness, incorruption, impeccability, inerrability, blamelessness, sinlessness.

A newborn babe, lamb, dove.

(*Phrases*) Clean hands; a clear conscience.

(*Verbs*) To be innocent, etc.

(*Adjectives*) Innocent, guiltless, not guilty, faultless, sinless, clear, spotless, stainless, immaculate, unspotted, innocuous, unblemished, untarnished, unsullied, undefiled.

Inculpable, unblamed, blameless, unblamable, clean-handed, irreproachable, unreproached, unimpeachable, unimpeached, unexceptionable, inerrable, unerring.

947 GUILT (*Substantives*), sin, guiltiness, culpability, criminality, criminousness, sinfulness.

Misconduct, misbehaviour, misdoing, malpractice, malefaction, malfeasance, misprision, dereliction, *corpus delicti*.

Indiscretion, peccadillo, lapse, slip, trip, *faux pas*, fault, error, flaw, blot, omission, failure.

Misdeed, offence, trespass, transgression, misdemeanour, delinquency, felony, sin, crime, enormity, atrocity.

Science of crime, criminology.

(*Phrases*) Besetting sin; deviation from rectitude; a deed without a name.

Harmless, inoffensive, unoffending, dovelike, lamblike, pure, uncorrupted, undefiled, undepraved, undebauched, chaste, unhardened, unsophisticated, unreproved.

(*Phrases*) Innocent as an unborn babe; in the clear; above suspicion; more sinned against than sinning.

(*Adverbs*) Innocently, etc.

---

948 GOOD MAN (*Substantives*), trump, brick, worthy, example, pattern, mirror, model, paragon, phoenix (650), superman, hero, demigod, seraph, angel, saint (987).

A good fellow, good sort, sportsman, white man.

(*Phrases*) One of the best; one in a million; the salt of the earth.

949 BAD MAN (*Substantives*), wrongdoer, evildoer, culprit, delinquent, criminal, recidivist, malefactor, outlaw, felon, convict, lag, outcast, sinner (988).

Knave, rogue, rascal, scoundrel, spiv, scamp, scapegrace, black sheep, scallywag, spalpeen, varlet, *vaurien*, blighter, rotter, good-for-nothing, twerp, heel, jerk, creep, goon, son of a gun, dastard, blackguard, sweep, loose fish, bad egg, bad lot, hard case, lost soul, vagabond, bum, *mauvais sujet,* cur, sad dog, rip, rascallion, rapscallion, slubberdegullion, cullion, roisterer.

Mohock, rowdy, hooligan, larrikin, teddy boy, apache, thug, reprobate, *roué,* recreant, jail-bird, crook, tough, rough, roughneck, gangster, gunman, hoodlum, yegg, villain, ruffian, miscreant, caitiff, wretch, *âme damnée,* castaway, monster, Jonathan Wilde, Jack Sheppard, Lazarillo de Tormes, Scapin (941).

Cur, dog, hound, skunk, swine, rat, viper, serpent, cockatrice, basilisk, reptile, urchin, tiger, imp, demon, devil, devil incarnate, Mephistopheles (978), hellhound, son of Belial, cut-throat, *particeps criminis,* incendiary.

Bad woman, hellcat, hellhag, bitch, witch, hag, harridan, trollop, jade, drab, hussy, minx, Jezebel.

Riff-raff, rabble, ragtag and bobtail, *canaille.*

(*Phrases*) A fiend in human shape; scum of the earth; poor white trash.

(*Interjection*) Sirrah!

950 PENITENCE (*Substantives*), contrition, compunction, regret (833), repentance, remorse.

Self-reproach, self-reproof, self-accusation, self-condemnation.

Confession, acknowledgment, shrift, apology, recantation (607).

A penitent, prodigal, Magdalen.

(*Phrases*) The stool of repentance; the cutty-stool; sackcloth and ashes; qualms or prickings of conscience; a sadder and a wiser man.

(*Verbs*) To repent, regret, rue, repine, deplore, be sorry for.

To confess (529), acknowledge, apologize, shrive oneself, humble oneself, reclaim, turn from sin.

(*Phrases*) To have a weight on one's mind; to plead guilty; to sing small; to cry *peccavi*; to eat humble pie; to turn over a new leaf; to stand in a white sheet.

(*Adjectives*) Penitent, repentant, contrite, repenting, remorseful, regretful, sorry, compunctious, self-reproachful, self-accusing, self-convicted, conscience-stricken, conscience-smitten.

Not hardened, unhardened, reclaimed.

(*Adverb*) *Meâ culpâ.*

951 IMPENITENCE (*Substantives*), obduracy, recusance, irrepentance, hardness of heart, a seared conscience, induration.

(*Verbs*) To be impenitent, etc.; to steel or harden the heart.

(*Phrases*) To make no sign; to die game.

(*Adjectives*) Impenitent, uncontrite, obdurate, hard, callous, unfeeling, hardened, seared, recusant, relentless, unrepentant, graceless, shiftless, lost, incorrigible, irreclaimable, irredeemable, unatoned, unreclaimed, unreformed, unrepented.

———

952 ATONEMENT (*Substantives*), reparation, compromise, composition, compensation (30), quittance, quits; propitiation, expiation, redemption, conciliation.

Amends, *amende honorable,* apology, satisfaction, peace-offering, olive branch, sin-offering, scapegoat, sacrifice, burnt-offering.

Penance, fasting, maceration, flagellation, sackcloth and ashes, white sheet, lustration, purgation, purgatory.

(*Verbs*) To atone, expiate, propitiate, make amends, redeem, make good, repair, ransom, absolve, do penance, apologize, purge, shrive, give satisfaction.

(*Phrases*) To purge one's offence; to pay the forfeit or penalty.

(*Adjectives*) Propitiatory, piacular, expiatory, expiational.

4°. *Moral Practice*

953 TEMPERANCE (*Substantives*), moderation, forbearance, abnegation, self-denial, self-conquest, self-control, self-command, self-discipline, sobriety, frugality, vegetarianism.

Abstinence, abstemiousness, teetotalism, prohibition, asceticism (955), gymnosophy, system of Pythagoras.

An abstainer, ascetic, gymnosophist, vegetarian, teetotaller, Pythagorean.

(*Phrases*) The simple life; the blue ribbon.

(*Verbs*) To be temperate, etc.; to abstain, forbear, refrain, deny oneself, spare.

(*Phrases*) To sign the pledge; to go on the water wagon.

(*Adjectives*) Temperate, moderate, sober, frugal, sparing, abstemious, abstinent, Pythagorean, vegetarian, teetotal, dry.

954 INTEMPERANCE (*Substantives*), excess, immoderation, unrestraint; epicurism, epicureanism, hedonism, sensuality, luxury, luxuriousness, animalism, carnality, effeminacy; the lap of pleasure or luxury; indulgence, self-indulgence, voluptuousness; drunkenness (959).

Dissipation, licentiousness, debauchery, dissoluteness, crapulence, brutishness.

Revels, revelry, carousal, orgy, spree, jag, toot, drinking bout, debauch, jollification, saturnalia.

A sensualist, epicure, epicurean, voluptuary, rake, rip, *roué*, sybarite, drug addict, dope fiend, hophead.

(*Phrases*) The Circean cup; a fast life; wine, women, and song.

(*Verbs*) To be intemperate, sensual, etc.

To indulge, exceed, revel, dissipate; give a loose to indulgence, live hard.

To debauch, pander to, sensualize, animalize, brutalize.

(*Phrases*) To wallow in voluptuousness, luxury, etc.; to plunge into dissipation; to paint the town red; to live on the fat of the land; to sow one's wild oats.

(*Adjectives*) Intemperate, sensual, pampered, self-indulgent, fleshly, inabstinent, licentious, wild, dissolute, dissipated, fast, rakish, debauched, brutish, crapulous, hedonistic, epicurean, sybaritical, Sardanapalian, voluptuous, apolaustic, orgiastic, swinish, piggish, hoggish; indulged, pampered.

955 ASCETICISM (*Substantives*), austerity, puritanism, mortification, maceration, sackcloth and ashes, flagellation, martyrdom, yoga.

An ascetic, anchoret, yogi, martyr; a recluse, hermit (893); puritan, Cynic.

(*Adjectives*) Ascetic, ascetical, austere, puritanical.

956 FASTING (*Substantives*), fast, spare diet, meagre diet, Lent, Quadragesima, a lenten entertainment, famishment, starvation, banian day, Ramadan.

(*Phrases*) A Barmecide feast; a hunger strike; short commons.

(*Verbs*) To fast, starve, clem, famish.

(*Phrases*) To dine with Duke Humphrey; to perish with hunger.

957 GLUTTONY (*Substantives*), epicurism, greediness, good cheer, high living, edacity, voracity, gulosity, crapulence, hoggishness, piggishness.

Gastronomy; feast, banquet, good cheer, blow-out.

A glutton, epicure, *bon vivant*, cormorant, gourmand, gourmet, belly-god, pig, hog, Apicius, gastronome, gastronomer, gastronomist.

(*Adjectives*) Fasting, etc., unfed, famished, starved; lenten, Quadragesimal.

(*Verbs*) To gormandize, gorge, cram, stuff, guzzle, bolt, devour, gobble up, pamper.

(*Phrases*) To eat out of house and home; to have the stomach of an ostrich; to play a good knife and fork.

(*Adjectives*) Gluttonous, greedy, gormandizing, edacious, voracious, crapulent, swinish, piggish, hoggish, pampered, overfed; gastronomical.

958 SOBRIETY (*Substantives*), teetotalism, total abstinence, temperance (953).

Compulsory sobriety, prohibition.

A water-drinker, teetotaller, abstainer, total abstainer, blue-ribbonite, Rechabite, Band of Hope; prohibitionist.

(*Verbs*) To abstain, to take the pledge.

(*Adjectives*) Sober, abstemious, teetotal.

(*Phrases*) Sober as a judge; on the water wagon.

959 DRUNKENNESS (*Substantives*), insobriety, ebriety, inebriety, inebriation, intoxication, ebriosity, bibacity, drinking, toping, tippling, sottishness, tipsiness, bacchanals, compotation, intemperance (954); dipsomania, alcoholism, delirium tremens, D.T.

A drunkard, sot, toper, tippler, hard drinker, winebag, winebibber, dram-drinker, soak, soaker, sponge, tun, tosspot, pub-crawler, reveller, carouser, Bacchanal, Bacchanalian, Bacchant, a devotee to Bacchus; a dipsomaniac.

Drink, hard drinks, intoxicant, alcohol, liquor, spirits, booze, blue ruin, grog, cocktail, highball, dram, peg, stirrup-cup, doch-an-doris.

(*Phrases*) The flowing bowl; one for the road.

(*Verbs*) To drink, tipple, tope, booze; to guzzle, swill, soak, swig, get or be drunk, etc.; to take to drinking, drink hard, drink deep. To inebriate, intoxicate, fuddle.

(*Phrases*) To liquor up; to wet one's whistle; to crack a bottle; to have a bucket; to look on the wine when it is red; to take a drop too much; to drink like a fish; to splice the main-brace; to crook or lift the elbow.

(*Adjectives*) Drunk, drunken, tipsy, intoxicated, in liquor, inebriated, fuddled, mellow, boozy, high, fou, boiled, tiddly, stinko, blotto, lit up, groggy, top-heavy, pot-valiant, glorious, overcome, overtaken, elevated, whiffled, sozzled, screwed, corned, raddled, sewed up, lushy, squiffy, muddled, oiled, canned, muzzy, maudlin, dead-drunk, disguised, tight, beery.

Bibacious, bibulous, sottish, Bacchanal, Bacchanalian.

(*Phrases*) In one's cups; *inter pocula;* the worse for liquor; half-seasover; three sheets in the wind; under the table; drunk as a piper, as a fiddle, as a lord, as an owl, as David's sow; stewed to the eyebrows; pickled to the gills; one over the eight.

(*Interjections*) Cheers! here's to you! down the hatch! mud in your eye! skin off your nose! *prosit! slainte! skoal!*

960 PURITY (*Substantives*), modesty, decency, decorum, delicacy, continence, chastity, honesty, pudency, virtue, virginity.

961 IMPURITY (*Substantives*), immodesty, grossness, coarseness, indelicacy, impropriety, impudicity, indecency, obscenity, obsceneness,

A virgin, maiden, maid, vestal; Joseph, Hippolytus, Lucrece.

(*Phrase*) The white flower of a blameless life.

(*Adjectives*) Pure, immaculate, undefiled, modest, delicate, decent, decorous.

Chaste, continent, honest, virtuous; Platonic.

———

ribaldry, smut, smuttiness, bawdiness. bawdry, *double entendre*, equivoque, pornography.

Concupiscence, lust, carnality, flesh, salacity, lewdness, prurience, lechery, lasciviousness, voluptuousness, lubricity.

Incontinence, intrigue, gallantry, debauchery, libertinism, libertinage, fornication, liaison, wenching, whoring, whoredom, concubinage, hetaerism.

Seduction, defloration, violation, rape, adultery, defilement, *crim. con.*, incest, harlotry, stupration, procuration, white slave traffic.

A scraglio, harem, brothel, bagnio, stew, bawdy-house, disorderly house, house of ill fame, red lamp district, Yoshiwara.

(*Phrase*) The morals of the farmyard; the oldest profession.

(*Verbs*) To intrigue, debauch, defile, seduce, abuse, violate, force, rape, ravish, deflower, ruin, prostitute, procure.

(*Adjectives*) Impure, immodest, indecorous, indelicate, unclean, unmentionable, unseemly, improper, suggestive, indecent, loose, coarse, gross, broad, equivocal, risky, *risqué*, high-seasoned, nasty, smutty, scabrous, ribald, obscene, bawdy, lewd, pornographic, Rabelaisian, Aristophanic.

Concupiscent, prurient, lickerish, rampant, carnal, fleshy, sensual, lustful, lascivious, lecherous, libidinous, goatish, erotic, ruttish, salacious.

Unchaste, light, wanton, debauched, dissolute, carnal-minded, licentious, frail, riggish, incontinent, meretricious, rakish, gallant, dissipated, adulterous, incestuous, bestial.

(*Phrases*) On the streets; of easy virtue; no better than she should be. Near the knuckle; not for ears polite; four-letter words.

962 A LIBERTINE (*Substantives*), voluptuary, man of pleasure, sensualist (954), rip, rake, *roué*, debauchee, loose fish, intriguant, gallant, seducer, fornicator, lecher, satyr, whoremonger, *paillard*, adulterer, a gay deceiver, Lothario, Don Juan, Bluebeard.

A prostitute, courtesan, tart, call-girl, strumpet, harlot, whore, punk, *fille de joie*, cocotte, *lorette*, woman of the town, streetwalker, pick-up, piece, the frail sisterhood, the *demi-monde*, soiled dove, demirep, wench, trollop, trull, baggage, hussy, drab, jade, quean, slut, harridan, an unfortunate, Jezebel, Messalina, Delilah, Thais, Aspasia, Phryne, Lais.

Concubine, odalisque, mistress, doxy, kept woman, *petite amie*, hetaera. Pimp, pander, ponce, *souteneur*, bawd, procuress.

5°. Institutions

963 LEGALITY (*Substantives*), legitimateness, legitimacy, justice (922).

Law, legislature, code, constitution, pandect, enactment, edict, statute, charter, rule, order, ordinance, injunction, institution, precept, regulation, by-law, decree, firman, bull, ukase, decretal.

964 Absence or violation of law.

ILLEGALITY (*Substantives*), lawlessness, arbitrariness, antinomy, violence, brute force, despotism, outlawry.

Mob law, lynch law, club law, martial law.

Legal process, form, formula, formality, rite.

Science of law, jurisprudence, legislation, codification.

Equity, common law, *lex non scripta*, unwritten law, law of nations, international law, *jus gentium*, civil law, canon law, statute law, *lex mercatoria*, ecclesiastical law.

(*Phrase*) The arm of the law.

(*Verbs*) To legalize, enact, ordain, enjoin, prescribe, order, decree (741); to pass a law, issue an edict or decree; to legislate, codify.

(*Adjectives*) Legal, lawful, according to law, legitimate, constitutional, chartered, vested.

Legislative, statutable, statutory.

(*Adverbs*) Legally, etc.

(*Phrases*) In the eye of the law; *de jure*.

Camorra, Ku Klux Klan. Judge Lynch.

Informality, unlawfulness, illegitimacy, bastardy, the baton or bar sinister.

Smuggling, poaching, bootlegging; black market, grey market.

(*Verbs*) To smuggle, run, poach.

To invalidate, annual, illegalize, abrogate, void, nullify, quash.

(*Phrases*) To take the law into one's own hands; to set the law at defiance; to drive a coach and six through the law.

(*Adjectives*) Illegal, unlawful, illicit, illegitimate, injudicial, unofficial, lawless, unauthorized, unchartered, unconstitutional, informal, contraband, hot.

Arbitrary, extrajudicial, despotic, autocratic, irresponsible, unanswerable, unaccountable.

(*Adverbs*) Illegally, with a high hand.

---

965 JURISDICTION (*Substantives*), judicature, soc (or soke), administration of justice.

Inquisition, inquest, coroner's inquest.

The executive, municipality, corporation, magistracy, police, police force, constabulary, posse, *gendarmerie*.

Lord lieutenant, sheriff, sheriff-substitute, deputy, officer, constable, policeman, traffic warden, bailiff, tipstaff, bum-bailiff, catchpoll, beadle; *gendarme*, lictor, mace-bearer.

(*Adjectives*) Juridical, judicial, forensic, municipal, executive, administrative, inquisitorial, causidical.

(*Phrases*) *Coram judice; ex cathedra.*

966 TRIBUNAL (*Substantives*), court, guild, board, bench, judicatory, senate-house, court of law, court of justice, criminal court, police-court, Court of Chancery, of King's Bench; Probate, Divorce, Admiralty Court, court of appeal, justice-seat, judgment-seat, mercy-seat, Star Chamber, Judicial Committee of the Privy Council, U.S. Supreme Court, durbar.

City hall, town hall, theatre, bar, dock, forum, hustings, drum-head, woolsack, jury-box, witness-box.

Assize, sessions, quarter sessions, petty sessions, eyre, court-martial, wardmote.

967 JUDGE (*Substantives*), justice, justiciar, justiciary, chancellor, magistrate, beak, recorder, common serjeant, stipendiary, coroner, arbiter, arbitrator, umpire, referee, jury, Justice of the Peace, J.P., Lord Chancellor, Lord Chief Justice, Master of the Rolls.

Mullah, ulema, mufti, cadi (or kadi), kavass.

Prosecutor, plaintiff, accuser, appellant, pursuer.

Defendant, panel, prisoner, the accused.

(*Verbs*) Judge, try, pass judgment, give verdict.

968 LAWYER (*Substantives*), the bar, advocate, counsellor, counsel, queen's or king's counsel, Q.C., K.C., pleader, special pleader, conveyancer, bencher, proctor, civilian, barrister, barrister-at-law, jurist, jurisconsult, publicist, draughtsman, notary, notary public, scrivener, attorney, solicitor, legal adviser, writer to the signet, writer, marshal, pundit; pettifogger.

(*Phrases*) The gentlemen of the long robe; the learned in the law; a limb of the law.

(*Verbs*) To practise law, plead.

(*Phrases*) To be called to the bar; to take silk.

969 LAWSUIT (*Substantives*), suit, action, case, cause, trial, litigation.

Denunciation, citation, arraignment, prosecution, indictment, impeachment, apprehension, arrest, committal, imprisonment (751).

Pleadings, writ, summons, subpoena, plea, bill, affidavit, libel; answer, counterclaim, demurrer, rebutter, rejoinder, surrebutter, surrejoinder.

Verdict, sentence, judgment, finding, decree, arbitrament, adjudication, award, decision, precedent.

(*Verbs*) To denounce, cite, apprehend, sue, writ, arraign, summons, prosecute, indict, contest, impeach, attach, distrain; to commit.

To try, hear a cause, sit in judgment.

To pronounce, find, judge, adjudge, sentence, give judgment; bring in a verdict; to doom, arbitrate, adjudicate, award, report.

(*Phrases*) To go to law; to appeal to the law; to file a claim; to inform against; to lodge an information; to serve with a writ; to bring an action against; to bring to trial or the bar; to give in charge or custody; to throw into prison; to clap in jail.

(*Adjectives*) Litigious, litigant, litigatory.

(*Adverbial phrases*) Sub judice; pendente lite.

970 ACQUITTAL (*Substantives*), acquitment, absolution, exculpation, quietus, clearance, discharge, release, reprieve (918), respite, compurgation.

Exemption from punishment, impunity.

(*Verbs*) To acquit, absolve, whitewash, extenuate, exculpate, exonerate, clear, assoil, discharge, release, reprieve, respite.

(*Adjectives*) Acquitted, etc.

Uncondemned, unpunished, unchastised.

971 CONDEMNATION (*Substantives*), conviction, proscription, damnation, death-warrant.

Attainder, attainture, attaintment.

(*Verbs*) To condemn, convict, cast, find guilty, proscribe, ban, outlaw, attaint, damn, doom, sentence, confiscate, sequestrate, non-suit.

(*Adjectives*) Condemnatory, damnatory, condemned; self-convicted.

972 PUNISHMENT (*Substantives*), punition, chastisement, castigation, correction, chastening, discipline, infliction.

Retribution, requital (973), penalty (974), reckoning, Nemesis.

Imprisonment (751), transportation, exile (297), cucking-stool, ducking-stool, treadmill, crank, hulks, galleys, penal servitude, preventive detention.

A blow, slap, spank, skelp, swish, hit, knock, rap, thump, bang, buffet stripe, stroke, cuff, clout, kick, whack, thwack, box, punch, pummel.

Beating, lash, flagellation, flogging, etc., dressing, lacing, tanning, knock-out, fustigation, leathering, lathering, jacketing, strap-oil, gruelling, spiflication, bastinado, strappado, pillory (975), running the gauntlet, coup de grâce, peine forte et dure.

Execution, capital punishment, hanging, beheading, decollation, decapitation, electrocution, guillotine, garrotte, *auto de fé, noyade,* crucifixion, impalement, *hara-kiri,* martyrdom.

(*Verbs*) To punish, chastise, castigate, chasten, correct, inflict punishment, pay, do for, serve out, pay out, visit upon, give it to, strafe, spiflicate.

To strike, hit, smite, knock, slap, flap, rap, bang, thwack, whack, thump, kick, punch, pelt, beat, buffet, thrash, swinge, pummel, clapper-claw, drub, trounce, baste, belabour, lace, strap, comb, lash, lick, whip, flog, scourge, knout, swish, spank, skelp, birch, tan, larrup, lay into, knock out, wallop, leather, flagellate, horsewhip, bastinado, lapidate, stone.

To execute, hang, behead, decapitate, decollate, electrocute, guillotine, garrotte, shoot, gibbet; to hang, draw, and quarter; break on the wheel; crucify, impale, torture, flay, keelhaul; lynch.

To banish, exile, transport, deport, expel, drum out, disbar, disbench, unfrock.

To be hanged, etc., to be spread-eagled.

(*Phrases*) To make an example of; to serve one out; to give it one; to dust one's jacket; to tweak or pull the nose; to box the ears; to beat to a jelly; to tar and feather; to give a black eye; to lay it on.

To come to the gallows; to swing for it; to go to the chair; to die in one's shoes.

(*Adjectives*) Punishing, etc., punitory, punitive, inflictive, penal, disciplinary, castigatory, borstal.

(*Interjection*) *A la lanterne!*

---

973 REWARD (*Substantives*), recompense, remuneration, meed, guerdon, premium, indemnity, indemnification, compensation, reparation, requital, retribution, quittance, hush-money, acknowledgment, amends, solatium, sop, atonement, redress, consideration, return, tribute, honorarium, perquisite, tip, vail; salvage.

Prize, purse, crown, laurel, bays, cross, medal, ribbon, decoration (877).

(*Verbs*) To reward, recompense, repay, requite, recoup, remunerate, compensate, make amends, indemnify, atone, satisfy, acknowledge, acquit oneself.

(*Phrase*) To get for one's pains.

(*Adjectives*) Remunerative, munerary, compensatory, retributive, reparatory.

---

974 PENALTY (*Substantives*), punishment (972), pain, penance.

Fine, mulct, amercement, forfeit, forfeiture, escheat, damages, deodand, sequestration, confiscation.

(*Phrases*) Pains and penalties; the devil to pay.

(*Verbs*) To fine, mulct, amerce, sconce, confiscate, sequester, sequestrate, escheat, estreat.

975 Instrument of punishment.

SCOURGE (*Substantives*), rod, cane, stick, rattan, switch, ferule, birch, cudgel.

Whip, lash, strap, thong, knout, cowhide, cat, cat-o'-nine-tails, sjambok, rope's end.

Pillory, stocks, cangue, whipping-post, ducking-stool, triangle, wooden horse, boot, thumbscrew, rack, wheel, treadmill.

Stake, tree, block, scaffold, gallows, halter, bowstring, gibbet, axe, maiden, guillotine, garrotte, electric chair, hot squat, lethal chamber.

Executioner, hangman, electrocutioner, firing squad, headsman, Jack Ketch.

Section V—Religious Affections

1°. *Superhuman Beings and Objects*

976 Deity (*Substantives*), Divinity, Godhead, Omnipotence, Omniscience, Providence.

Quality of being divine, divineness, divinity.

God, Lord, Jehovah, The Almighty; The Supreme Being; The First Cause, *Ens Entium*; The Author of all things, The Infinite, The Eternal, The All-powerful, The All-wise, The All-merciful, The All-holy.

Attributes and perfections, infinite power, wisdom, goodness, justice, mercy, omnipotence, omniscience, omnipresence, unity, immutability, holiness, glory, majesty, sovereignty, infinity, eternity.

The Trinity, The Holy Trinity, The Trinity in Unity, The Triune God.

God the Father, The Maker, The Creator.

Functions: creation, preservation, divine government, theocracy, thearchy, providence; the ways, dispensations, visitations of Providence.

God the Son, Christ, Jesus, The Messiah, The Anointed, The Saviour, The Redeemer, The Mediator, The Intercessor, The Advocate, The Judge, The Son of Man, The Lamb of God, The Word, The Logos, Emmanuel, The King of Kings and Lord of Lords, The King of Glory, The Prince of Peace, The Good Shepherd, The Way of Truth and Life, The Bread of Life, The Light of the World, The Sun of Righteousness, the Incarnation, the Word made Flesh.

Functions: salvation, redemption, atonement, propitiation, mediation, intercession, judgment.

God the Holy Ghost, The Holy Spirit, Paraclete, The Comforter, The Spirit of Truth, The Dove.

Functions: inspiration, unction, regeneration, sanctification, consolation.

(*Verbs*) To create, uphold, preserve, govern.

To atone, redeem, save, propitiate, mediate.

To predestinate, elect, call, ordain, bless, justify, sanctify, glorify.

(*Adjectives*) Almighty, all-powerful, omnipotent, omnipresent, omniscient, all-wise, holy, hallowed, sacred, divine, heavenly, celestial.

Superhuman, ghostly, spiritual, supernatural, theocratic.

---

977 Beneficent spirits.

Angel (*Substantives*), archangel.

The heavenly host; ministering spirits; the choir invisible.

Madonna, saint.

Seraphim, cherubim, thrones, principalities, powers, dominions.

(*Adjectives*) Angelic, angelical, seraphic, cherubic, celestial, heavenly, saintly.

---

978 Maleficent spirits.

Satan (*Substantives*), the Devil, Lucifer, Beelzebub, Belial, Mephistopheles, Mephisto, Abaddon, Apollyon, the Prince of the Devils.

His Satanic Majesty, the tempter, the evil one, the wicked one, the old Serpent, the Prince of darkness, the father of lies, the foul fiend, the arch-fiend, the common enemy, Old Harry, Old Nick, the Old Scratch, the Old Gentleman, Old Horny.

Diabolism, devilism, devilship; Satanism, the cloven hoof, the black mass.

Fallen angels, unclean spirits, devils, the powers of darkness, inhabitants of Pandemonium.

(*Adjectives*) Satanic, diabolic, devilish.

Gods of other Religions and Mythological Beings

979 GREAT SPIRIT (*Substantives*), deity, numen, god, goddess; Allah, Brahma, Vishnu, Siva, Krishna, Buddha, Mithra, Ormuzd, Isis, Osiris, Moloch, Baal, Asteroth.

Jupiter, Jove, Juno, Minerva, Apollo, Diana, Venus, Vulcan, Mars, Mercury, Neptune, Pluto; Zeus, Hera, Athena, Artemis, Aphrodite, Hephaestus, Ares, Hermes, Poseidon. Odin or Woden, Frigga, Thor.

Good genius, demiurge, familiar; fairy, fay, sylph, peri, kelpie, nymph, nereid, dryad, hamadryad, naiad, merman, mermaid (341), undine; Oberon, Mab, Titania, Puck, Robin Goodfellow; the good folk, the little people.

(*Adjectives*) Fairy, faery, fairy-like, sylph-like, sylphine.

Mythical, mythological, fabulous, legendary.

980 DEMON (*Substantives*), evil genius, fiend, unclean spirit, cacodemon, incubus, succubus, succuba, flibbertigibbet; fury, harpy, siren, faun, satur, Eblis, Demogorgon.

Vampire, werewolf, ghoul, afreet (or afrite), ogre, ogress, gnome, djinn, imp, genie (or jinnee), lamia, bogy, bogle, nix, nixie, kobold, brownie, leprechaun, elf, pixy, troll, sprite, gremlin, spandule.

Supernatural appearance, ghost, spectre, apparition, shade, vision, goblin, hobgoblin, banshee, spook, wraith, *revenant*, *doppelgänger*, poltergeist.

(*Phrases*) The powers of darkness.

(*Adjectives*) Supernatural, ghostly, apparitional, elfin, elfish, unearthly, uncanny, eerie, weird, spectral, spookish, spooky, ghostlike, fiendish, fiendlike, impish, demoniacal, haunted.

981 HEAVEN (*Substantives*), the kingdom of heaven; the kingdom of God, the heavenly kingdom; the throne of God, the presence of God.

Paradise, Eden, Zion, the Celestial City, the New Jerusalem, the abode of the blessed; celestial bliss or glory.

Mythological heaven, Olympus; mythological paradise, Elysium, the Elysian Fields, the garden of the Hesperides; Valhalla, Nirvana, happy hunting grounds.

Translation, apotheosis, deification, resurrection.

(*Adjectives*) Heavenly, celestial, supernal, unearthly, from on high, paradisaical, paradisical, paradisial, Elysian, beatific.

982 HELL (*Substantives*), bottomless pit, place of torment; the habitation of fallen angels, Pandemonium, Domdaniel.

Hell-fire, everlasting fire, the lake of fire and brimstone.

Purgatory, limbo, abyss.

Mythological hell, Tartarus, Hades, Pluto, Avernus, Styx, the Stygian creek, Acheron, Cocytus, Phlegethon, Lethe, Erebus, Tophet, Gehenna.

(*Phrases*) The fire that is never quenched; the worm that never dies.

The infernal or nether regions; the shades below; the realms of Pluto.

(*Adjectives*) Hellish, infernal, stygian, Tartarean, Plutonian.

2°. Religious Doctrines

983 Religious knowledge.

THEOLOGY (natural and revealed) (*Substantives*), divinity, religion, monotheism, hagiology, hagiography, hierography, theosophy; comparative religion, comparative mythology.

Creed, belief, faith, persuasion, tenet, dogma, articles of faith, declaration, profession or confession of faith.

Theologian, divine, schoolman, the Fathers.

(*Adjectives*) Theological, religious, patristic, ecumenical, denominational, sectarian.

983A CHRISTIAN RELIGION (*Substantives*), true faith, Christianity, Christianism, Christendom, Catholicism, orthodoxy.

A Christian, a true believer.

The Church, the Catholic or Universal Church, the Church of Christ, the body of Christ, the Church Militant.

The members of Christ, the disciples or followers of Christ, the Christian community.

Protestant, Church of England, Anglican, Church of Scotland; Church of Rome, Roman Catholic; Greek Church, Orthodox Church.

(*Adjectives*) Christian, Catholic, orthodox, sound, faithful, true, scriptural, canonical, schismless.

---

984 OTHER RELIGIONS (*Substantives*), paganism, heathenism, ethnicism, polytheism, ditheism, tritheism, pantheism, hylotheism.

Judaism, Gentilism, Mohammedanism (or Mahometanism), Islam, Buddhism, Hinduism, Taoism, Confucianism, Shintoism, Sufism.

A pagan, heathen, paynim, infidel, unbeliever, pantheist, etc.

A Jew, Mohammedan (or Mahometan), Mussulman, Moslem, Brahmin (or Brahman), Parsee, Sufi, Magus, Gymnosophist, Fire-worshipper, Buddhist, Rosicrucian.

(*Adjectives*) Pagan, heathen, ethnic, gentile, pantheistic, etc.

Judaical, Mohammedan, Brahminical, Buddhistic.

984A HERESY (*Substantives*), heterodoxy, false doctrine, schism, schismaticalness, latitudinarianism, recusancy, apostasy, backsliding, quietism, adiaphorism.

Bigotry, fanaticism, iconoclasm, bibliolatry, fundamentalism, puritanism, sabbatarianism.

Dissent, sectarianism, nonconformity, secularism, syncretism.

A heretic, deist, unitarian.

(*Adjectives*) Heretical, heterodox, unorthodox, unscriptural, uncanonical, schismatic, sectarian, nonconformist, recusant, latitudinarian.

Credulous, bigoted, fanatical, idolatrous, superstitious, visionary.

985 CHRISTIAN REVELATION (*Substantives*), Word, Word of God, Scripture, the Scriptures, Holy Writ, the Bible, the Holy Book.

Old Testament: Septuagint, Vulgate, Pentateuch, Hagiographa, the Law, the Prophets, the Apocrypha.

New Testament: the Gospel, the Evangelists, the Epistles, the Apocalypse, Revelations.

Talmud, Mishna, Masorah, Torah.

A prophet, seer, evangelist, apostle, disciple, saint, the Fathers.

(*Adjectives*) Scriptural, biblical, sacred, prophetic, evangelical, apostolic, apostolical, inspired, theopneustic, apocalyptic.

986 OTHER SACRED BOOKS (*Substantives*), the Koran (or Alcoran), Vedas, Upanishads, Puranas, Zend-Avesta.

Religious founders: Buddha (or Gautama), Zoroaster (or Zarathustra), Confucius, Lao-Tsze, Mohammed (or Mahomet).

Idols: Golden calf, Baal, Moloch, Dagon.

(*Adjectives*) Anti-scriptural, antichristian, profane, idolatrous, pagan, heathen, heathenish.

3°. *Religious Sentiments*

987 PIETY (*Substantives*), religion, theism, faith, religiousness, godliness, reverence, humility, veneration, devoutness, devotion, spirituality, grace, unction, edification, unworldliness, other-worldliness; holiness, sanctity, sanctitude, sacredness, consecration; virtue (944).

Theopathy, beatification, adoption, regeneration, conversion, justification, salvation, inspiration.

A believer, convert, theist, Christian, saint, one of the elect, a devotee.

The good, righteous, faithful, godly, elect, just.

(*Phrases*) The odour of sanctity; the beauty of holiness; spiritual existence.

The children of God, of light.

(*Verbs*) To be pious, etc., to believe, have faith; to convert, edify, sanctify, hallow, beatify, regenerate, inspire; to consecrate, enshrine.

(*Phrases*) To work out one's salvation; to stand up for Jesus; to fight the good fight.

(*Adjectives*) Pious, religious, devout, reverent, reverential, godly, humble, heavenly-minded, pure, holy, spiritual, saintly, saint-like, unworldly, other-worldly.

Believing, faithful, Christian.

Sanctified, regenerated, born again, justified, adopted, elected, inspired, consecrated, converted, unearthly, sacred, solemn, not of the earth.

988 IMPIETY (*Substantives*), irreverence, profaneness, profanity, blasphemy, desecration, sacrilege, sacrilegiousness, sin (945); scoffing, ribaldry, reviling.

Assumed piety, hypocrisy, cant, pietism, lip-devotion, lip-service, lip-reverence, formalism, sanctimony, sanctimoniousness, pharisaism, precisianism, sabbatism, sabbatarianism, sacerdotalism, religiosity, religionism, *odium theologicum.*

Hardening, backsliding, declension, reprobation, perversion.

Sinner, outcast, castaway, lost sheep, reprobate.

A scoffer, hypocrite, pietist, pervert, religionist, precisian, formalist; son of darkness, son of Belial, blasphemer, Pharisee; bigot, devotee, fanatic, sabbatarian.

The wicked, unjust, ungodly, unrighteous.

(*Phrase*) The unco guid.

(*Verbs*) To be impious, etc., to profane, desecrate, blaspheme, revile, scoff, commit sacrilege.

To play the hypocrite, cant.

(*Adjectives*) Impious, profane, irreverent, sacrilegious, desecrating, blasphemous; unhallowed, unsanctified, hardened, perverted, reprobate.

Bigoted, priest-ridden, fanatical, churchy.

Hypocritical, canting, pietistical, sanctimonious, unctuous, pharisaical, over-righteous, righteous overmuch.

(*Phrases*) Under the mask, cloak, or pretence of religion.

---

989 IRRELIGION (*Substantives*), ungodliness, unholiness, gracelessness, impiety (989).

Scepticism, doubt, unbelief, disbelief, incredulity, incredulousness, faithlessness, want of faith or belief (485, 487).

Atheism, hylotheism, materialism, positivism.

Deism, infidelity, freethinking, rationalism, agnosticism, unchristianness, antichristianity, antichristianism.

An atheist, sceptic, unbeliever, deist, freethinker, rationalist, agnostic, nullifidian, infidel, alien, giaour, heathen.

(*Verbs*) To be irreligious, disbelieve, lack faith, doubt.

To dechristianize, rationalize.

(*Adjectives*) Irreligious, undevout, godless, atheistic, atheistical, ungodly, unholy, unhallowed, unsanctified, graceless, without God, carnal-minded.

Sceptical, unbelieving, freethinking, agnostic, rationalistic, incredulous, unconverted, faithless, lacking faith.

Deistical, antichristian, unchristian, worldly-minded, mundane, carnal, earthly-minded.

(*Adverbs*) Irreligiously, etc.

4°. Acts of Religion

990 WORSHIP (*Substantives*), adoration, devotion, cult, homage, service, humiliation, kneeling, genuflexion, prostration.

Prayer, invocation, supplication, rogation, petition, orison, litany, the Lord's prayer, paternoster, collect.

Thanksgiving, giving or returning thanks, praise, glorification, benediction, doxology, hosanna, hallelujah, paean, Te Deum, Magnificat, Ave Maria, De Profundis, Nunc dimittis, Non nobis, Domine.

Psalmody, psalm, hymn, plainsong, chant, antiphon, response, anthem, motet.

Oblation, sacrifice, incense, libation, burnt-offering, votive offering; offertory, collection.

Discipline, self-discipline, self-examination, self-denial, fasting.

Divine service, religious service, office, duty, prime, terce, sext, matins, mass (998), angelus, nones, evensong, vespers, vigils, lauds, compline; prayer meeting, revival.

Worshipper, congregation, communicant, celebrant.

(*Verbs*) To worship, adore, reverence, venerate, do service, pay homage, humble oneself, bow down, kneel, bend the knee, prostrate oneself.

To pray, invoke, supplicate, petition, put up prayers or petitions; to ask, implore (765).

To return or give thanks; to say grace; to bless, praise, laud, glorify, magnify, sing praises, lead the choir, pronounce benediction.

To propitiate, offer sacrifice, fast, deny oneself; vow, offer vows, give alms.

(*Phrases*) To lift up the heart; to say one's prayers; to tell one's beads; to go to church; to attend divine service.

(*Adjectives*) Worshipping, etc., devout, solemn, devotional, reverent, pure, fervent, prayerful.

(*Interjections*) Hallelujah! alleluia! hosanna! glory be to God! *sursum corda!*

991 IDOLATRY (*Substantives*), idol-worship, idolism, demonism, demonolatry, fire-worship, devil-worship, fetishism.

Sacrifices, hecatomb, holocaust; human sacrifices, immolation, mactation, infanticide, self-immolation, suttee.

Idol, image, fetish, ju-ju, Mumbo-Jumbo, Juggernaut, joss.

(*Verbs*) To worship idols, pictures, relics, etc.; to idolize, idolatrize.

(*Adjectives*) Idolatrous, fetishistic.

992 OCCULT ARTS (*Substantives*), occultism, sorcery, magic, the black art, black magic, necromancy, theurgy, thaumaturgy, psychomancy, *diablerie,* bedevilment, witchcraft, witchery, bewitchment, wizardry, glamour, fetishism, vampirism, shamanism, voodooism, obeah (or obi), sortilege, conjuration, exorcism, fascination, mesmerism, hypnotism, animal magnetism, clairvoyance, telegnosis, telekinesis, psychokinesis, mediumship, spiritualism, extra-sensory perception, telepathy, parapsychology, second sight, spirit-rapping, table-turning, psychometry, crystal-gazing, divination, enchantment, hocus-pocus (545).

(*Verbs*) To practise sorcery, etc.; to conjure, exorcise, charm, enchant, bewitch, bedevil, hoodoo, entrance, mesmerize, hypnotize, fascinate; to taboo, wave a wand, cast a spell, call up spirits.

(*Adjectives*) Magic, magical, cabbalistic, talismanic, phylacteric, necromantic, incantatory, occult, mediumistic, charmed, exorcised, etc.

993 SPELL (*Substantives*), charm, fascination, incantation, exorcism, weird, cabbala, exsufflation, cantrip, runes, abracadabra, open sesame, taboo, countercharm, evil eye, jinx, hoodoo, Indian sign.

Talisman, amulet, mascot, periapt, phylactery, philtre, fetish, wishbone, merrythought.

Wand, caduceus, rod, divining-rod, the lamp of Aladdin, magic ring, wishing-cap, seven-league boots.

994 SORCERER (*Substantives*), sorceress, magician, conjurer, necromancer, enchanter, enchantress, thaumaturgist, occultist, adept, Mahatma, seer, wizard, witch, warlock, charmer, exorcist, mage, archimage, soothsayer (513), shaman, medicine-man, witch-doctor, mesmerist, hypnotist, medium, spiritualist, clairvoyant; control.

(*Phrase*) *Deus ex machina.*

5°. *Religious Institutions*

995 CHURCHDOM (*Substantives*), ministry, apostleship, priesthood, prelacy, hierarchy, church government, Christendom, church; clericalism, sacerdotalism, priestcraft, theocracy, popery, papistry.

Monachism, monasticism, monkdom, monkhood, monkery.

Ecclesiastical offices and dignities: Pontificate, papacy, primacy, archbishopric, archiepiscopacy, bishopric, bishopdom, episcopate, episcopacy, see, diocese, prelacy, deanery, stall, canonry, canonicate, prebend, prebendaryship; benefice, incumbency, advowson, living, cure, rectorship, vicarship, vicariate, deaconry, deaconship, curacy, chaplaincy, chaplainship; cardinalate, abbacy.

Holy orders, ordination, institution, consecration, induction, preferment, translation.

Council, conclave, sanhedrim, synod, presbytery, consistory, chapter, vestry (696).

(*Verbs*) To call, ordain, induct, install, prefer, translate, consecrate, canonize, beatify; to take the veil, to take vows.

(*Adjectives*) Ecclesiastical, clerical, sacerdotal, priestly, prelatical, hierarchical, pastoral, ministerial, capitular, theocratic.

Pontifical, papal, episcopal, archidiaconal, diaconal, canonical; monastic, monachal, monkish; levitical, rabbinical.

996 CLERGY (*Substantives*), ministry, priesthood, presbytery.

A clergyman, cleric, parson, divine, ecclesiastic, churchman, priest, presbyter, hierophant, pastor, father, shepherd, minister, father in Christ, patriarch, padre, abbé, curé; sky-pilot, holy Joe, devil-dodger.

Dignitaries of the church: Primate, archbishop, bishop, prelate,

997 LAITY (*Substantives*), flock, fold, congregation, assembly, brethren, people.

Temporality, secularization.

A layman, parishioner.

(*Verb*) To secularize.

(*Adjectives*) Secular, lay, laical, civil, temporal, profane.

diocesan, suffragan; dean, subdean, archdeacon, prebendary, canon, capitular, residentiary, beneficiary; rector, vicar, incumbent, chaplain, curate, deacon, sub-deacon, preacher, reader, evangelist, revivalist, missionary, missioner.

Churchwarden, sidesman; clerk, precentor, choir, chorister, almoner, verger, beadle, sexton, sacrist, sacristan, acolyte.

Roman Catholic priesthood: Pope, pontiff, cardinal, confessor, spiritual director.

Cenobite, conventual, abbot, prior, father superior, monk, oblate, friar, lay brother, mendicant, Franciscan (or Grey Friars, Friars minor, Minorites), Observant, Capuchin, Dominican (or Black Friars), Carmelite (or White Friars), Augustin (or Austin Friars), Crossed or Crutched Friars, Benedictine, Jesuit (or Society of Jesus).

Abbess, prioress, canoness, mother, mother superior, *religieuse*, nun, novice, postulant.

Greek Church: Patriarch, metropolitan, archimandrite, pope.

Under the Jewish dispensation: Prophet, priest, high-priest, Levite, rabbi (or rabbin), scribe.

Moslem: Imam, mullah, mufti, dervish, fakir, santon, hadji; muezzin.

Hindu: Brahmin, pundit, guru, yogi.

Buddhist: Lama, bonze.

(*Phrase*) The cloth.

(*Adjectives*) Reverend, ordained, in orders.

998 RITE (*Substantives*), ceremony, ordinance, observance, cult, duty, form, formulary, ceremonial, solemnity, sacrament.

Baptism, immersion, christening, chrism, baptismal regeneration.

Confirmation, imposition or laying on of hands, ordination (995), consecration.

The Eucharist, the Lord's Supper, the communion, the sacrament, consubstantiation, celebration, consecrated elements, bread and wine.

Matrimony (903), burial (363), visitation of the sick, offertory.

Roman Catholic rites and ceremonies: Mass, high mass, low mass, dry mass; the seven sacraments, transubstantiation, impanation, extreme unction, viaticum, invocation of saints, canonization, transfiguration, auricular confession, maceration, flagellation, penance (952), telling of beads.

Relics, rosary, beads, reliquary, pyx (or pix), host, crucifix, *Agnus Dei*, thurible, censer, patera.

Liturgy, ritual, euchology, book of common prayer, litany, etc.; rubric, breviary, missal, ordinal; psalter, psalm book, hymn book, hymnal.

Service, worship (990), ministration, psalmody; preaching, predication; sermon, homily, lecture, discourse, exhortation, address.

Ritualism, ceremonialism, liturgics, liturgiology.

(*Verbs*) To perform service, do duty, minister, officiate; to baptize, dip, sprinkle; to confirm, lay hands on; to give or administer the sacrament; to take or receive the sacrament, communicate.

To preach, sermonize, predicate, lecture, harangue, hold forth, address the congregation.

(*Adjectives*) Ritual, ceremonial, baptismal, eucharistical, pastoral, liturgical.

999 VESTMENTS (*Substantives*), canonicals, robe, gown, pallium, surplice, cassock, alb, scapular (or scapulary), dalmatic, cope, soutane, chasuble, tonsure, cowl, hood, amice, calotte, bands, apron, biretta.

Mitre, tiara, triple crown, crosier.

1000 Place of worship, house of God.

TEMPLE (*Substantives*), cathedral, pro-cathedral, minster, church, kirk, chapel, meeting-house, tabernacle, conventicle, bethesda, little Bethel, basilica, fane, holy place, chantry, oratory.

Synagogue, mosque, pantheon, pagoda, joss-house, dagobah, tope.

Parsonage, rectory, vicarage, manse, presbytery, deanery, bishop's palace, the Vatican.

Altar, shrine, sanctuary, *sanctum sanctorum*, the Holy of Holies, sacristy, communion table, holy table, table of the Lord; piscina, baptistery, font, aumbry.

Chancel, choir, nave, aisle, transept, vestry, crypt, apse, belfry, stall, pew, pulpit, ambo, lectern, reading-desk, confessional, prothesis, credence.

Monastery, priory, abbey, convent, nunnery, cloister.

(*Adjectives*) Claustral, monastic, monasterial, conventual.

INDEX

N.B.—The numbers refer to the headings under which the words occur. The headings or related words are given in italics, not to explain the meaning of the words, but to assist in the required reference. Words borrowed from another language have an asterisk prefixed to them.

Argent, *whiteness*, 430
Argillaceous, *softness*, 324
Argosy, *ship*, 273
Argot, *language*, 560
Arguably, *probably*, 471
Argue, *reason*, 476
  evidence, 467
  indicate, 550
  discord, 713
Argument, *evidence*, 467
  topic, 454; *meaning*, 516
  compendium, 596
* Argumentum ad crumenam, *money*, 800
* Argumentum ad hominem, *speciality*, 79
  accusation, 938
* Argumentum ad misericordiam, *pity*, 914
* Argumentum ad verecundiam, *probity*, 939
* Argumentum baculinum, *compulsion*, 744
Argus-eyed, *sight*, 441
  vigilant, 459
Argute, *wisdom*, 498
Aria, *music*, 415
Arid, *dryness*, 340
Ariel, *messenger*, 534
  swift, 274
  courier, 268
  spirit, 979
Arietta, *music*, 415
Aright, *goodness*, 618, 648
Arise, *begin*, 66
  mount, 305
  appear, 446
  happen, 151,
  proceed from, 154
  exist, 1
Aristarchus, *taste*, 850
Aristocracy, *power*, 737
  nobility, 875
Aristocratic, *fashionable*, 852
Arithmetic, *numeration*, 85
Ark, *asylum*, 666
Arm, *instrument*, 266, 633
  part, 51
  power, 157
  to provide, 637
  to prepare, 673
  war, 722
Armada, *ship*, 273
Armageddon, *contention*,
Armament, *arms*, 727 [720
Armature, *arms*, 727
Armiger, *nobility*, 875
Armistice, *pacification*, 721, 723
Armless, *impotence*, 158

Armlet, *roundness*, 247
  inlet, 343
Armorial, *indication*, 550
Armour, *arms*, 727
  defence, 717
  soldier, 726
Armour-plated, *covered*, 222
Armoured car, *vehicle*, 272
Armoury, *store*, 636
Arms, *blazon*, 550
  scutcheon, 877
  war, 722
  weapon, 727
  See Arm
Army, *troops*, 726
  multitude, 102
  collection, 72
Aroma, *fragrance*, 400
Around, *circumjacent*, 227
Arouse, *motive*, 615
Arpeggio, *music*, 415
Arquebus, *arms*, 727
Arraign, *accuse*, 938
  indict, 969
Arrange, *order*, 60
  plan, 626
  to prepare, 673
  to settle, 723
Arrangement, *order*, 58
  music, 415
Arrant, *greatness*, 31
Arras, *ornament*, 847
Array, *order*, 58
  series, 69
  dress, 225
  prepare, 673
  beauty, 845
  multitude, 102
  assemblage, 72
Arrears, *debt*, 806
Arrest, *stop*, 142, 265
  seize, 789
  imprison, 751
  commit, 969
* Arrière-pensée, *plan*, 626
  sequel, 65
Arrive, *reach*, 292
  approach, 286
  happen, 151
  complete, 729
Arrogant, *insolent*, 885
  severe, 739
  proud, 878
Arrogate, *assume*, 885
  claim, 922
* Arrondissement, *region*, 181
Arrow, *swift*, 274
  missile, 284
  arms, 727
Arrow-headed, *angular*, 244
Arrowy, *sharp*, 253

Arsenal, *store*, 636
  military, 727
Arson, *calefaction*, 384
Art, *skill*, 698
  cunning, 702
  deception, 545
  representation, 554
  business, 625
Artemis, *goddess*, 979
Arterialize, *to aerate*, 338
Artery, *conduit*, 350
Artesian well, *conduit*, 348
Artful, *cunning*, 702
  deceitful, 544
Article, *thing*, 3, 316
  goods, 798
  part, 51
  conditions, 770
  dissertation, 595
Articles, *belief*, 484, 983
Articulation, *speech*, 580
  junction, 43
Artifice, *cunning*, 702
  plan, 626
  deception, 545
Artificer, *agent*, 690
Artificial, *cunning*, 702
  fictitious, 544
  style, 579
Artillery, *arms*, 727
  corps of, 726
  explosion, 404
Artisan, *agent*, 690
Artist, *contriver*, 626
  producer, 164
  painter, 559
  agent, 690
Artiste, *the drama*, 599
Artistic, *skilful*, 698
  beautiful, 845
  tasteful, 850
Artless, *natural*, 703
  veracious, 543
  plain, 576
As, *motive*, 615
Ascend, *ascent*, 305
Ascendancy, *power*, 157, 175
  success, 731
Ascent, *rise*, 305
  acclivity, 217
  glory, 873
Ascertain, *find out*, 480A
Asceticism, *asceticism*, 955
  temperance, 953
Ascribable, *effect*, 154
Ascribe, *attribution*, 155
Asepsis, *cleanness*, 652
Ash colour, *grey*, 432
Ashamed, *shame*, 874
  humility, 879
  modest, 881

Ashes, *residue*, 40
 corpse, 362
Ashore, *land*, 342
Ashy, *colourless*. 429
Aside, *laterally*, 236
 privately, 528
 soliloquy, 589
Aside (to put), *relinquish*,
 624
 disuse, 678
Asinine, *imbecile*, 499
Ask, *inquire*, 461
 request, 765
 as price, 812
 supplicate, 990
Askance, *obliquity*, 217
 doubt, 485
Askew, *oblique*, 217
 distorted, 243
Aslant, *obliquity*, 217
Asleep, *inactivity*, 683
Aslope, *obliquity*, 217
Aspect, *appearance*, 448
 state, 7
 feature, 5
 situation, 183
 relation, 9
 of thought, 453
Asperge, *sprinkle*, 337
Aspergillum, *spray*, 348
Asperity, *roughness*, 256
 tartness, 895
 anger, 900
Asperse, *detraction*, 934
Aspersorium, *spray*, 348
Asphalt, *semiliquid*, 352
Asphyxiate, *killing*, 361
Aspirant, *petitioner*, 767
Aspirate, *voice*, 580
Aspire, *rise*, 305
 desire, 865
 hope, 858
 project, 620
Ass, *beast of burden*, 271
 fool, 501
Assagai, *arms*, 727
Assail, *attack*, 716
 plain, 830
Assailant, *opponent*, 710
 attacker, 716, 726
Assassinate, *killing*, 361
Assault, *attack*, 716
Assay, *experiment*, 463
Assemble, *assemblage*, 72
Assembly-room, *sociality*,
 892
Assent, *agree*, 488
 consent, 762
Assert, *affirm*, 535
 claim as a right, 924
Assess, *measure*, 466
 judge, 480

Assess, *price*, 812
Assessor, *adviser*, 695
Assets, *property*, 780
 money, 800
Asseverate, *affirm*, 535
Assiduous, *activity*, 682
Assign, *attribute*, 155
 transfer, 783
 give, 784
 commission, 755
 allot, 786
 duty, 926
Assignat, *money*, 800
Assignation, *sociality*, 892
Assignee, *receive*, 785
Assignment, *allotment*, 786
 business, 625
 commission, 755
Assimilate, *resemble*, 17, 144
 imitate, 19
 agree, 23
Assist, *aid*, 707
 benefit, 906
Assistant, *auxiliary*, 711
Assize, *measure*, 466
 tribunal, 966
Associate, *accompany*, 88
 concur, 178
 unite, 43
 mixture, 41
 assemble, 72
 friend, 890
 society, 892
Association, *relation*, 9
 intuition, 477
Assoil, *free*, 750
 acquit, 970
Assonance, *similarity*, 17
 poetry, 597
Assort, *arrange*, 60
Assortment, *class*, 75
 collection, 72
Assuage, *physically*, 174
 morally, 826
 relieve, 834
Assume, *suppose*, 514
 evidence, 467
 hope, 858
 right, 924
 insolence, 739, 885
 pride, 878
 falsehood, 544
Assumption, *qualification*,
 469
 severity, 739
Assurance, *assertion*, 535
 promise, 768
 certainty, 474
 belief, 484
 hope, 858
 insolence, 885
Assuredly, *positively*, 31

Assuredly, *assert*, 488
 safety, 664
Asterisk, *indication*, 550
 expletive, 908
Astern, *rear*, 235
Asteroid, *world*, 318
Asteroth, *deity*, 979
Asthenia, *weakness*, 160
Astigmatism, *dim-sighted-
 ness*, 443
Astonish, *wonder*, 870
Astonishing, *great*, 31
Astound, *surprise*, 870
 excite, 824
Astraea, *right*, 922
Astral, *world*, 318
 immaterial, 317
Astray, *deviation*, 279
Astriction, *junction*, 43
Astride, *support*, 215
Astringent, *contraction*, 195
Astrology, *prediction*, 511
Astronaut, *navigator*, 269
Astronautics, *navigation*,
Astronomy, *world*, 318 [267
Astrophysics, *world*, 318
Astute, *wisdom*, 498
Asunder, *separate*, 44
 distant, 196
 disjunction, 44
Asylum, *retreat*, 666
 hospital, 662
 defence, 717
Asymmetry, *disorder*, 59,
 243
Asymptote, *converge*, 290
At-home, *sociality*, 892
At once, *transientness*, 111
At the end of the day,
 finally, 67
Ataraxia, *insensibility*, 823
Atavism, *reversion*, 145
Atelier, *workshop*, 691
Atheism, *irreligion*, 989
 unbelief, 485
Athena, *goddess*, 979
Athirst, *desire*, 865
Athletic, *strength*, 159
Athletics, *training*, 673
 contention, 720
Athwart, *oblique*, 217
 crossing, 219
 opposing, 708
Atlantis, *visionary*, 515
Atlas, *support*, 215
 strength, 159; *maps*, 554
Atmosphere, *air*, 338
 circumstances, 227
Atoll, *island*, 346
Atom, *small in degree*, 32
 in size, 193
 particle, 330

Atomic bomb, *arms*, 727
Atomizer, *spray*, 348
Atonality, *melody*, 413
Atonement, *atonement*, 952
 religious, 976
 reward, 973
Atony, *weakness*, 160
Atrabilious, *dejection*, 837
Atrocious, *vice*, 945
 guilt, 947
 malevolence, 907
Atrophy, *shrinking*, 195
 disease, 655
 decay, 659
Attaboy, *approval*, 931
Attach, *join*, 43
 love, 897
 legal, 969
Attaché, *servant*, 746
 consignee, 758
Attaché-case, *receptacle*, 191
Attachment, *see* Attach
Attack, *attack*, 716
 disease, 655
Attain, *arrive*, 292
 succeed, 731
Attainable, *possible*, 470
 easy, 705
Attainder, *condemnation*, 971
Attainment, *learning*, 539
 knowledge, 490
 skill, 698
Attar, *fragrance*, 400
Attemper, *mix*, 41
 moderate, 174
Attempt, *undertaking*, 676
 try, 675
Attend, *accompany*, 88
 follow, 281
 treat, 662
 apply the mind, 457
 frequent, 136
 be present, 186
Attendant, *servant*, 746
Attention, *attention*, 451, 457
 respect, 928
Attentions, *courtesy*, 894
 courtship, 902
 kindness, 906
Attenuate, *lessen*, 36
 rarefy, 322
 contract, 195
 narrow, 203
Attest, *bear testimony*, 467
 indicate, 550
 adjure, 768
Attestation, *record*, 551
Attic, *garret*, 191
 high, 206

Attic, *elegant*, 578
 wit, 842
 taste, 850
Atticism, *wit*, 842
Attila, *evildoer*, 913
Attire, *vestment*, 225
Attitude, *posture*, 183, 240
 circumstance, 8
Attitudinize, *affectation*, 855
 ostentation, 882
Attorney, *consignee*, 758, 769
 in law, 968
Attract, *bring towards*, 288,
 please, 829
 allure, 865
Attractability, *motive*, 615
Attractive, *beautiful*, 845
 pleasing, 829
 lovely, 897
 alluring, 615
Attrahent, *attraction*, 288
Attributable, *effect*, 154
Attribute, *power*, 157
Attribution, *attribution*, 155
Attrition, *friction*, 331
* Attroupement, *assemb-
 lage*, 72
Attune, *music*, 415
 prepare, 673
* Au courant, *knowledge*, 490
* Au fait, *knowledge*, 490
* Au fond, *truth*, 494
 inbeing, 5
* Au pied de la lettre, *truth*, 494
 meaning, 516
* Au revoir, *departure*, 293
Aubade, *music*, 415
Auburn, *brown*, 433
Auction, *sale*, 796
Auctorial, *book*, 593
Audacity, *courage*, 861
 insolence, 863, 885
* Audi alteram partem, *evi-
 dence*, 468
 right, 922
Audible, *sound*, 402
Audience, *hearing*, 418
 conversation, 588
Audiometer, *hearing*, 418
Audiphone, *hearing*, 418
Audit, *accounts*, 811
 numeration, 85
Audition, *hearing*, 418
Auditor, *hearer*, 418
 accounts, 811
Auditorium, *amusement*, 840

Auditory, *hearing*, 418
* Auf wiedersehen, *depart-
 ure*, 293
Auger, *perforation*, 262
Augment, *to increase*, 35
 thing added, 39
Augmentation, *expansion*, 194
Augur, *predict*, 507, 511
 soothsayer, 513
Augury, *prediction*, 511, 512
August, *repute*, 873
Augustine, *clergy*, 996
Aura, *touch*, 380
 emanation, 295
Aureate, *yellowness*, 436
Aureole, *light*, 420
Aureolin, *orange*, 439
Auricular, *hearing*, 418
Aurist, *doctor*, 662
Aurora, *light*, 423
 dawn, 125
Auroral, *rosy*, 434
Auscultation, *hearing*, 418
Auspices, *patronage*, 175
 prediction, 511
Auspicious, *hopeful*, 858
 prosperous, 734
 expedient, 646
 opportune, 134
Auster, *wind*, 349
Austere, *harsh taste*, 395
 severe, 739
 discourteous, 895
 ascetic, 955
Austerity, *economy*, 817
Authentic, *truth*, 494
 certain, 474
 existence, 1
Authenticate, *record*, 551
 evidence, 467
 security, 771
Author, *producer*, 164
 cause, 153
 writer, 590
Authoritative, *certain*, 474
 peremptory, 741
Authority, *power*, 157, 737
 command, 741
 right, 924
 permission, 760
 testimony, 467
 sign, 500
* Auto da fé, *burning*, 384
 execution, 972
* Autobahn, *way*, 627
Autobiography, *description*, 594
Autobus, *vehicle*, 272
Autocar, *vehicle*, 272
Autochrome, *photograph*, 556

Baptize, *name*, 564
Bar, *hindrance*, 706
　line, 200
　to exclude, 55
　close, 261
　enclosure, 232
　prison, 752
　prohibition, 761
　tribunal, 966
　legal profession, 968
　drink, 298
* Baragouin, *absurdity*, 497
Barb, *spike*, 253
　horse, 271
Barbarian, *evildoer*, 913
Barbarism, *discourtesy*, 895
　solecism, 568
Barbarous, *maleficent*, 907
　vulgar, 851
　rude, 876
　style, 579
Barbette, *defence*, 717
Barbican, *defence*, 717
Bard, *poetry*, 597
Bare, *mere*, 32
　nude, 226
　scanty, 640
　exposed to view, 446
Barefaced, *visible*, 446
　shameless, 885
　insolent, 886
Barefoot, *divest*, 226
Bareheaded, *divest*, 226
　respect, 928
Barely, *smallness*, 32
Bargain, *compact*, 769
　barter, 794
　promise, 768
　cheap, 813, 815
Bargain, into the, *addition*,
　37
Barge, *ship*, 273
Bargee, *mariner*, 269
Baritone, *deep-toned*, 408
Bark, *rind*, 223
　ship, 273
　to yelp, 412
　to censure, 932
Barker, *interpreter*, 524
　publicity, 531
Barm, *yeast*, 353
Barmy, *foolish*, 499
Barn, *abode*, 189
Barnacles, *spectacles*, 445
Barometer, *measurement*,
　466
　air, 338
Baron, *nobility*, 875
　master, 745
Baronet, *nobility*, 875
Baronetage, *list*, 86
Baronetcy, *title*, 877

Baroque, *ridiculous*, 853
Barque, *ship*, 273
Barquentine, *ship*, 273
Barrack, *abode*, 189
Barrage, *obstacle*, 706
Barred, *crossed*, 219
　striped, 440
Barrel, *vessel*, 191
　cylinder, 249
Barren, *sterile*, 169
　useless, 645
Barricade, *fence*, 232
　prison, 752
　obstacle, 706
Barrier, *fence*, 232
　obstacle, 706
Barring, *except*, 83
　save, 38
Barrister, *lawyer*, 968
Barrow, *vehicle*, 272
　grave, 363
Barter, *exchange*, 794
* Bas bleu, *affectation*, 855
Bascule, *instrument*, 633
Base, *lowest part*, 211
　support, 215
　bad, 649
　dishonourable, 940
　shameful, 874
　vicious, 945
　cowardly, 862
　plebeian, 876
Base-minded, *improbity*,
　940
Baseless, *unreal*, 2
　erroneous, 495
Basement, *base*, 211
Bashaw, *ruler*, 745
Bashful, *modesty*, 881
Basic, *support*, 215
Basic English, *language*,
　560
Basilica, *temple*, 1000
Basilisk, *serpent*, 949
　monster, 83
　evil eye, 441
Basin, *hollow*, 252
　vessel, 191
　plain, 344
　dock, 189
Basis, *preparation*, 673
　foundation, 215
Bask, *warmth*, 382
　physical enjoyment, 377
　moral enjoyment, 827
　prosperity, 734
Basket, *receptacle*, 191
Basket-work, *plaiting*, 219
Basketry, *plaiting*, 219
Bas-relief, *convexity*, 250
Bass, *deep-sounding*, 408,
　413

Bass-viol, *musical instru-
　ment*, 417
Bassinette, *vehicle*, 272
* Basso rilievo, *convexity*,
　250
　sculpture, 557
Bassoon, *musical instru-
　ment*, 417
Bastard, *spurious*, 544, 925
　erroneous, 495
Bastardy, *illegitimacy*, 964
Baste, *beat*, 276
　punish, 972
Bastille, *prison*, 752
Bastinado, *punishment*, 972
Bastion, *defence*, 717
Bat, *club*, 727, 633
　spree, 840
Batch, *assemblage*, 72
　quantity, 25
Bate, *diminish*, 36, 38
　reduce price, 813
Bath, *immersion*, 300
　water, 337
Bath-chair, *vehicle*, 272
Bath-room, *room*, 191
Bathe, *immersion*, 300
　plunge, 310
Bathing-suit, *dress*, 225
Bathos, *depth*, 208
　anticlimax, 497
　ridiculous, 853
Bathymetry, *depth*, 208
Bathysphere, *depth*, 208
Baton, *sceptre*, 747
　impact, 276
Bats, *insane*, 503
Battalion, *troop*, 726
　assemblage, 72
Batten, *feed*, 296
Batter, *beat*, 276
　destroy, 162
Battered, *imperfect*, 651
Battering-ram, *weapon*,
　276, 727
Battery, *instrument*, 633
Battle, *contention*, 720
Battle array, *warfare*, 722
　arrangement, 60
Battle-axe, *arms*, 727
Battle-bowler, *defence*, 717
Battle-cruiser, *ship*, 273
Battle-dress, *dress*, 225
Battle-field, *arena*, 728
Battlement, *bulwark*, 666
　defence, 717
　enclosure, 232
　embrasure, 257
Battleship, *ship*, 273
Battue, *pursuit*, 622
　killing, 361
Batty, *insane*, 503

Bauble, *trifle*, 643
  toy, 840
Baulk; *see* Balk
* Bavardage, *absurdity*, 497
Bawbee, *money*, 800
Bawd, *libertine*, 962
Bawdy, *impurity*, 961
Bawl, *cry*, 411, 839
Bay, *gulf*, 343
  brown, 433
  to howl, 412
Bay, at, *defence*, 717
Bayadère, *dancer*, 599
Bayard, *carrier*, 271
  perfection, 650
Bayonet, *arms*, 727
  attack, 716
  kill, 361
Bays, *trophy*, 733
  reward, 973
Bazaar, *mart*, 799
Bazooka, *gun*, 727
Be, *existence*, 1
Be of, *inclusion*, 76
Be off, *departure*, 293
  ejection, 297
Beach, *land*, 342
Beacon, *sign*, 423, 550
  warning, 668
Bead-roll, *list*, 86
Beadle, *janitor*, 263
  officer, 745
  law officer, 965
  church, 996
Beads, *rite*, 998
Beak, *front*, 234
  nose, 250
  judge, 967
Beaker, *receptacle*, 191
Beam, *support*, 215
  of a balance, 466
  of light, 420
  beauty, 845
Beamless, *darkness*, 421
Bean-feast, *pleasure*, 827,
                              840
  meal, 298
Bear, *sustain*, 215
  produce, 161
  carry, 270
  suffer, 821
  admit, 470
  brute, 895
Bear down upon, *attack*, 716
Bear-garden, *arena*, 728
  brawl, 713
Bear-leader, *teacher*, 540
Bear off, *taking*, 789
Bear out, *confirm*, 467
  vindicate, 937
Bear up, *cheerfulness*, 836
Bear upon, *influence*, 175

Bear upon, *evidence*, 467
  to relate to, 9
Bear with, *indulge*, 740
Bearable, *tolerable*, 651
Beard, *spike*, 253
  rough, 256
  to defy, 715
  courage, 861
  insolence, 885
Beardless, *youth*, 127
Bearer, *carrier*, 271
Bearing, *support*, 215
  direction, 278
  meaning, 516
  appearance, 448
  demeanour, 692
  circumstance, 8
  situation, 183
Bearish, *discourtesy*, 895
Beast, *animal*, 366
  blackguard, 895
Beastly, *uncleanness*, 653
Beat, *strike*, 716, 972
  surpass, 33, 303
  periodic, 138
  oscillation, 314
  agitation, 315
  crush, 330; *sound*, 407
  succeed, 731
  line of pursuit, 625
  news, 532
Beat down, *chaffer*, 794
  insolent, 885
Beat hollow, *superiority*, 33
Beat it, *go away*, 293, 287
  escape, 671
Beat off, *defence*, 717
Beat time, *chronometry*, 114
Beat up for, *seek*, 461
Beatify, *enrapture*, 829
  honour, 873
  sanctify, 987, 995
Beating, *impulse*, 276
Beatnik, *hippy*, 183
Beatitude, *pleasure*, 827
Beau, *fop*, 854
  man, 373; *admirer*, 897
* Beau idéal, *beauty*, 845
  perfection, 650
* Beau monde, *fashion*, 852
  nobility, 875
* Beau sabreur, *hero*, 861
Beauty, *beauty*, 845
  ornament, 847
  symmetry, 242
Beaver, *hat*, 225
Bebop, *melody*, 413
Becalm, *quiescence*, 265
Because, *attribution*, 155
  reasoning, 476
  motive, 615

Bechance, *eventuality*, 151
Beck, *rill*, 348
  signal, 550
  mandate, 741
Beckon, *signal*, 550
Becloud, *darkness*, 421
Become, *change to*, 144
  behove, 926
Become of, *event*, 151
Becoming, *proper*, 646
  beautiful, 845
  just, 922
  apt, 23
Bed, *layer*, 204
  support, 215
  lodgment, 191
Bed-maker, *servant*, 746
Bedabble, *splash*, 337
Bedarken, *darkness*, 421
Bedaub, *cover*, 222
  dirt, 653
  deface, 846
Bedazzle, *light*, 420
Bedeck, *beauty*, 845
  ornament, 847
Bedevil, *derange*, 61
  bewitch, 992
Bedew, *moisture*, 339
Bedfellow, *friend*, 890
Bedight, *beauty*, 845
Bedim, *darkness*, 421
Bedizen, *beautify*, 845
  ornament, 851
Bedlam, *insanity*, 503
Bedlamite, *madman*, 504
Bedraggle, *soil*, 653
Bedridden, *disease*, 655
Bedstead, *support*, 215
Bedtime, *evening*, 126
Bee, *active*, 682
  party, 892
Bee-line, *direction*, 278
Bee-witted, *folly*, 499
Beef, *complain*, 839
Beefy, *corpulent*, 192
Beelzebub, *Satan*, 978
Beery, *drunken*, 959
Beeswax, *oil*, 356
Beetle, *high*, 206
  projecting, 250
  impact, 276
Befall, *eventuality*, 151
Befit, *agree*, 23
Befitting, *right*, 926
  expedient, 646
Befool, *deceive*, 503, 545
  baffle, 732
Before, *precedence*, 62
Before Christ, *period*, 108
Beforehand, *prior*, 116, 132
Befoul, *uncleanness*, 653
Beg, *request*, 765

Bijou, *gem*, 650
  little, 193
Bijouterie, *ornament*, 847
Bike, *bicycle*, 266
Bikini, *dress*, 225
Bilateral, *duplication*, 90
  side, 236
Bilbo, *arms*, 727
Bilboes, *prison*, 752
Bile, *resentment*, 900
Bilge, *trash*, 645
Bilge-water, *dirt*, 653
Bilious, *dejection*, 837
Bilk, *deception*, 545
  swindle, 791
  disappointment, 509
Bill, *money, account*, 811
  charge, 812
  money-order, 800
  security, 771
  in law, 969
  placard, 531
  ticket, 550
  instrument, 633
  weapon, 727
  sharpness, 253
Bill of fare, *food*, 298
  list, 86
  plan, 626
Billabong, *river*, 348
Billet, *epistle*, 592
  ticket, 550
  to apportion, 786
  to locate, 184
* Billet-doux, *epistle*, 592
  endearment, 902
Billiard-table, *level*, 213
Billingsgate, *scolding*, 932
  imprecatory, 908
Billion, *numbers*, 98
Billow, *wave*, 348
Billycock, *hat*, 225
Bimetallism, *money*, 800
Bimonthly, *periodical*, 138
Bin, *receptacle*, 191
Binary, *duality*, 89
Bind, *connect*, 43
  compel, 744
  obligation, 926
  condition, 770
Binge, *amusement*, 840
Bingle, *clip*, 201
Binoculars, *lens*, 445
Binomial, *duplication*, 90
Bint, *girl*, 374
Biograph, *spectacle*, 448
Biographer, *recorder*, 553
Biography, *description*, 594
Biology, *organization*, 357
  life, 359
Bioscope, *spectacle*, 448
Bipartition, *duplication*, 91

Biplane, *aircraft*, 273A
Birch, *scourge*, 975
  to punish, 972
Bird, *animal*, 366
Bird of passage, *traveller*,
  268
Bird-fancier, *collector*, 775
Bird-lime, *vinculum*, 45
Bird's-eye, *tobacco*, 298A
  general, 78
Bird's-eye view, *sight*, 448
Birds of a feather, *inclusion,*
  conformity, 82   [76
Bireme, *ship*, 273
Biretta, *cap*, 225
  vestments, 999
Biro, *pen*, 590
Birth, *beginning*, 66
  production, 161
  nobility, 875
Birthday, *anniversary*, 138
Birthmark, *blemish*, 848
Birthplace, *origin*, 153
Birthright, *dueness*, 924
* Bis, *duplication*, 89
  repetition, 104
* Bise, *wind*, 349
Bisection, *duality*, 91
Bishop, *clergy*, 996
Bishopric, *churchdom*, 995
Bissextile, *period*, 108
Bistoury, *sharpness*, 253
Bistre, *brown*, 433
Bisulcate, *fold*, 258, 259
Bit, *part*, 51
  mixture, 41
  small quantity, 32
  money, 800; *curb*, 752
Bit by bit, *part*, 51
  degree, 26
Bitch, *bad woman*, 949
Bite, *pain*, 378
  painful, 830
  cheat, 545
Biting, *cold*, 383
  pungent, 392
  painful, 830
Bitter, *taste*, 395
  cold, 383
  animosity, 898
  wrath, 900
  malevolence, 907
  regret, 833
  painful, 830
Bitumen, *semiliquid*, 352
Bivouac, *repose*, 265
  to encamp, 186
  camp, 189; *watch*, 664
Bizarre, *ridiculous*, 853
  unconformity, 83
Blab, *disclosure*, 529

Black, *colour*, 431
  crime, 945
  copy, 590
Black-and-white, *colourless*,
  429
Black art, *sorcery*, 992
Black hole, *prison*, 752
Black-letter, *printing*, 591
Black looks, *discourtesy*, 598
Black market, *illegality*, 964
  theft, 791
Black-out, *darkness*, 421
Black out, *obliterate*, 552
Black sheep, *bad man*, 949
Blackamoor, *blackness*, 431
Blackball, *exclude*, 55
  reject, 610
  seclude, 893
  disapprove, 932
Blacken, *disapprobation*,
  932
Blackguard, *rude*, 895
  vulgar, 851
  vagabond, 949
  evildoer, 913
  to revile, 932
Blackleg, *sharper*, 548
  thief, 792
  traitor, 941
Blacklist, *disapprove*, 932
Blackmail, *theft*, 791
  booty, 793
Bladder, *receptacle*, 191
Blade, *instrument*, 633
  sharpness, 253
  man, 372
  fop, 854
* Blague, *humbug*, 545
  boast, 884
Blah, *nonsense*, 497
Blain, *swelling*, 250
Blamable, *vice*, 945
Blame, *disapprobation*, 932
Blameless, *innocence*, 946
Blameworthy, *vice*, 945
  disapproval, 932
Blanch, *whiteness*, 430
Bland, *courteous*, 894
  mild, 174
Blandiloquence, *flattery*,
  933
Blandishment, *flattery*, 902,
  933
  motive, 615
Blank, *insubstantiality*, 2, 4
  simple, 42
  vacant, 187
  verse, 597
Blare, *loudness*, 404
Blarney, *flattery*, 933
  plea, 617
Blasé, *weariness*, 841

Blasé, *satiety*, 869
Blasphemy, *impiety*, 988
  malediction, 908
Blast, *wind*, 349
  sound, 404
  evil, 619
  curse, 908
  explosion, 173
  destroy, 162
Blast-furnace, *furnace*, 386
Blatant, *cry*, 412
  loud, 404
  silly, 499
Blatherskite, *chatter*, 584
Blaze, *light*, 420
  heat, 382
Blaze abroad, *publish*, 531
Blazon, *publication*, 531
Blazonry, *colour*, 428
Bleach, *discolour*, 429
  whiten, 430
Bleak, *cold*, 383
  dreary, 830
Blear-eyed, *dim-sighted*, 443
Bleat, *animal cry*, 412
Bleb, *swelling*, 250
  bubble, 353
Bleed, *physical pain*, 378
  moral pain, 828
  overcharge, 814
  despoil, 789
Bleeding, *excretion*, 299
Blemish, *ugly*, 846
  defect, 651, 848
Blench, *avoid*, 623
  fear, 860
Blend, *mix*, 41
  combine, 48
Bless, *approbation*, 931
Blessed, *happy*, 827
Blessing, *good*, 618
Blether, *nonsense*, 497, 499
  loquacity, 584
Blight, *evil*, 619
  adversity, 735
  decay, 659
Blighter, *knave*, 949
Blighty, *home*, 189
Blimp, *balloon*, 273A
  die-hard, 606
Blimpish, *prejudiced*, 481
  foolish, 499
Blind, *blindness*, 442
  ignorant, 491
  screen, 424
  falsehood, 546
  deception, 545
  concealment, 528
  necessity, 601
  heedless, 458
  pretext, 617
  imperforate, 261

Blind alley, *closure*, 261
Blind side, *obstinacy*, 606
  prejudice, 481
Blindfold, *sightless*, 442
  ignorant, 491
Blink, *wink*, 442
  neglect, 460
  overlook, 458
  shirk, 623
Blinkard, *dim-sighted*, 443
Blinkers, *mask*, 530
Bliss, *pleasure*, 827
Blister, *swelling*, 250
Blithe, *cheerfulness*, 836
Blitz, *attack*, 716
Blizzard, *wind*, 349
Bloated, *swollen*, 194
Block, *mass*, 192
  dense, 321
  fool, 501
  execution, 975
Block-buster, *bomb*, 727
Block in, *sketch*, 556
Block out, *form*, 240
Block up, *plug*, 261
  impede, 706
Blockade, *closure*, 261
  hindrance, 706
  restraint, 751
Blockhead, *fool*, 501
Blockhouse, *defence*, 716
Blockish, *folly*, 499
Bloke, *man*, 373
Blonde, *whiteness*, 430
Blood, *relation*, 11
  killing, 361
  fluid, 333
  affections, 820
  nobility, 875
  fop, 854
Blood-guilty, *killing*, 361
Blood-letting, *ejection*, 297
Blood-red, *redness*, 434
Blood-stained, *murderous*,
      361
  maleficent, 907
Bloodhound, *evil-doer*, 913
  detective, 461
Bloodless, *weak*, 160
  peaceful, 721
Bloodshed, *killing*, 361
Bloodsucker, *evildoer*, 913
Bloodthirsty, *malevolence*,
      907
Bloody, *malevolence*, 907
  killing, 361
Bloom, *youth*, 127
  prosperity, 734
  success, 731
  blueness, 438
Bloomer, *error*, 495
  dress, 225

Blooming, *beauty*, 845
  health, 654
Blossom, *plant*, 367
  success, 731
  prosperity, 734
Blot, *obliterate*, 552
  dry up, 340
  darken, 431
  disappear, 449
  discoloration, 429
  forget, 506
  ugly, 846
  blemish, 848
  disgrace, 874
  dishonour, 940
  guilt, 947
Blotch, *blackness*, 431
  blemish, 848
Blotto, *drunk*, 959
Blouse, *dress*, 225
Blow, *wind*, 349
  boast, 884
  knock, 276
  action, 680
  evil, 619
  expletive, 908
  pain, 828
  disappointment, 732
  inexpectation, 508
  mishap, 830
  to prosper, 734
Blow down, *destruction*, 162
Blow-hole, *air-pipe*, 351
Blow out, *extinguish*, 385,
      421
  gluttony, 957
Blow over, *preterition*, 122
  cessation, 142
Blow up, *fan*, 615
  wind, 349
  inflame, 194
  eruption, 173
  objurgation, 932
Blow upon, *censure*, 934
Blower, *signal*, 550
Blown, *fatigued*, 688
Blowpipe, *wind*, 349
Blowzy, *red*, 434
  sluttish, 653
Blubber, *cry*, 839
  fat, 356
Bludgeon, *club*, 276
  weapon, 727
Blue, *colour*, 438
  learned, 490
Blue-book, *record*, 551
Blue devils, *dejection*, 837
Blue lights, *firework*, 423
Blue-pencil, *expletive*, 908
Blue-print, *model*, 22
  plan, 626
Blue ruin, *drunkenness*, 959

Bowdlerize, *expurgate*, 652
Bowels, *interior*, 221
   of *compassion*, 914
Bower, *alcove*, 189
   chamber, 191
Bowie-knife, *arms*, 727
   sharpness, 253
Bowl, *vessel*, 191
   hollow, 252
   to *propel*, 284
Bowler, *hat*, 225'
Bowling-green, *horizontality*
   213
Bowshot, *nearness*, 197
Bowstring, *scourge*, 975
Box, *chest*, 191
   house, 189
   theatre, 599
   to *strike*, 972
   to *fight*, 720
Boxer, *combatant*, 726
Boxing, *contention*, 720
Boy, *infant*, 129
Boy friend, *love*, 897
Boycott, *exclude*, 893
   eject, 297
Boyhood, *youth*, 127
Bra, *dress*, 225
Brace, to *tie*, 43
   fastening, 45
   two, 89
   to *refresh*, 689
   to *strengthen*, 159
Brace and bit, *perforator*, 262
Bracelet, *ornament*, 847
   circularity, 247
Bracer, *remedy*, 662
Brachygraphy, *writing*, 590
Bracing, *strengthening*, 159
   refreshing, 689
Bracket, *tie*, 43
   support, 215
   vinculum, 45
   couple, 89
Brackish, *pungent*, 392
Brad, *vinculum*, 45
Bradawl, *perforator*, 262
Brae, *height*, 206
Brag, *boasting*, 884
Braggadocio, *boasting*, 884
Braggart, *boasting*, 884
   bully, 887
Brahma, *god*, 979
Brahmin, *clergy*, 996
   religious, 984
Braid, to *tie*, 43
   ligature, 45
   intersection, 219
Braille, *printing*, 591
Brain, *intellect*, 450
   skill, 498
Brain-sick, *giddy*, 460

Brain-storm, *excitability*,
   825
Brainless, *imbecile*, 499
Brains trust, *council*, 696
Brainwash, *teach*, 537
Brake, *copse*, 367
   curb, 752
   vehicle, 272
Bramble, *thorn*, 253
   painful, 830
Bran, *pulverulence*, 330
Bran-new, see Brand-new
Branch, *member*, 51
   plant, 367
   duality, 91
   posterity, 167
   ramification, 256
Branch off, *divergence*, 291
Branch out, *style*, 573
   divide, 91
Brand, to *burn*, 384
   fuel, 388
   to *stigmatize*, 932
   mark, 550
   to *accuse*, 938
   reproach, 874
Brand-new, *new*, 123
Brander, *roast*, 384
Brandish, *oscillate*, 314
   flourish, 315
* Bras croisés, *inactive*, 683
Brasier, *furnace*, 386
Brass, *insolence*, 885
   colour, 439
Brass up, *pay*, 809
Brassed off, *bored*, 641
   sated, 869
Brasserie, *food*, 298
Brassière, *dress*, 225
Brassy, *club*, 276
Brat, *infant*, 129
Bravado, *boasting*, 884
Brave, *courage*, 861
   to *defy*, 715
Bravery, *courage*, 861
   ornament, 847
Bravo, *assassin*, 361
   applause, 931
* Bravura, *music*, 415
Braw, *handsome*, 845
Brawl, *cry*, 411
   discord, 713
   contention, 720
Brawny, *strong*, 159
   stout, 192
Bray, *cry*, 412
   to *grind*, 330
Brazen-faced, *insolent*, 885
Breach, *crack*, 44
   quarrel, 713
   violation, 925
   exception, 83

Bread, *food*, 298
Breadstuffs, *food*, 298
Breadth, *thickness*, 202
   of *mind*, 498
Break, *fracture*, 44
   shatter, 162
   incompleteness, 53
   interval, 70, 106, 198
   opportunity, 134
   luck, 621, 731
   crumble, 328
   violation, 773
   bankruptcy, 808
   to *infringe*, 927
   to *disclose*, 529
   to *tame*, 749
   to *decline*, 659
   to *swerve*, 311
Break down, *fail*, 158, 732
Break ground, *undertaking*,
   676
Break in, *teach*, 537
   train, 370, 673
Break loose, *escape*, 671
   liberate, 750
Break off, a *habit*, 614
   leave off, 142
   abrogate, 756
Break out, *fly out*, 825
Break the ranks, *derange-*
   ment, 61
Break the record, *superior-*
   ity, 33
Break up, *destroy*, 162
   deteriorate, 659
   decompose, 49
Break with, *discord*, 713
Breaker, *wave*, 348
   danger, 667
Breakfast, *food*, 298
Breakneck, *perilous*, 665
   precipitous, 217
Breakwater, *refuge*, 666
   enclosure, 232
Breast, *interior*, 221
   convexity, 250
   mind, 450
   will, 600
   soul, 820
   to *oppose*, 708
Breastplate, *defence*, 717
Breastwork, *defence*, 717
Breath, *air*, 349
   sound, 405
   life, 359, 364
Breathe, *exist*, 1
   live, 359
   blow, 349
   mean, 516
   utter, 580, 582
   repose, 687
Breather, *preparation*, 673

Bruise, *hurt*, 619
  to *injure*, 649
  pound, 330
Bruiser, *fighter*, 726
Bruit, *publication*, 531
  news, 532
Brumal, *cold*, 383
  evening, 126
Brummagem, *spurious*, 544
Brumous, *foggy*, 422
Brunette, *brown*, 433
Brunt, *impulse*, 276
  attack, 716
Brush, *rapid motion*, 274
  to *clean*, 652
  painting, 559
  fight, 720
  rough, 256
Brush up, *memory*, 505
Brushwood, *plant*, 367
Brusque, *discourteous*, 895
  inelegant, 579
  rough, 173
Brutal, *vicious*, 945
  ill-bred, 895
  savage, 907
Brutalize, *harden*, 823, 895
Brute, *animal*, 366
  rude, 895
  maleficent, 913
Brute force, *illegality*, 964
Brute matter, *materiality*,
    316
  inanimate matter, 358
Brutish, *vulgar*, 851, 876
  intemperate, 954
* Brutum fulmen, *impotence*, 158
  laxity, 738
Bubble, *air*, 353
  light, 320
  trifle, 643
  error, 495
  vision, 515
  deceit, 545
  excitement, 824
  flow, 348
Buccaneer, *thief*, 792
Buck, *leap*, 309
  to *wash*, 652
  fop, 854
  money, 800
Buck up, *hasten*, 274
  stimulate, 615
  cheer, 836
Bucket, *receptacle*, 191
Bucketful, *quantity*, 25
Buckle, *to tie*, 43
  vinculum, 45
  distort, 243
Buckle to, *apply oneself*, 682
Buckle with, *grapple*, 720

Buckler, *defence*, 666, 717
Buckram, *hardness*, 323
  affectation, 855
Buckshee, *superfluous*, 641
Bucolic, *domestication*, 370
  poem, 597
Bud, *beginning*, 66
  to *expand*, 194
  effect, 154
  graft, 300
Buddha, *deity*, 979
  religious founder, 986
Buddhism, *religions*, 984
Buddy, *friend*, 891
  associate, 88
Budge, *move*, 264
Budget, *heap*, 72
  store, 636
  news, 532
  accounts, 811
Buff, *yellow*, 436
  grindstone, 331
Buffer, *defence*, 717
  fellow, 373
Buffet, *cupboard*, 191
  beat, 276, 972
Buffet car, *vehicle*, 272
* Buffo, *the drama*, 599
Buffoon, *humorist*, 844
  butt, 857
  actor, 599
Buffoonery, *amusement*, 840
  ridiculous, 856
Bugaboo, *fear*, 860
Bugbear, *fear*, 860
  alarm, 669
  imaginary, 515
Buggy, *vehicle*, 272
Bughouse, *insane*, 503
Bugle, *instrument*, 417
  war-cry, 722
Bugs, *insane*, 503
Buhl, *variegation*, 440
Build, *construct*, 161
  compose, 54
Build-up, *display*, 882
Build upon, *expect*, 507, 858
  count upon, 484
Builder, *producer*, 164
Building, *abode*, 189
Bulb, *knob*, 249, 250
Bulbous, *swollen*, 194
  rotund, 249
Bulge, *convexity*, 250
Bulimia, *desire*, 865
Bulk, *whole*, 50
  size, 192
Bulkhead, *hindrance*, 706
Bulky, *size*, 192
Bull, *absurdity*, 497, 853
  error, 495
  solecism, 568

Bull, *nonsense*, 497, 517
  law, 963
  ordinance, 741
  police, 664
Bull-calf, *fool*, 501
Bulldog, *courage*, 861
  resolution, 604
Bullet, *ball*, 249
  missile, 284
  arms, 727
  swiftness, 274
Bullet-proof, *defence*, 717
Bulletin, *message*, 532
Bullion, *money*, 800
Bull's-eye, *middle*, 68
Bully, *bluster*, 885
  blusterer, 887
  fight, 726
  domineer, 739
  frighten, 860
  good, 648
Bulrush, *unimportance*, 643
Bulwark, *defence*, 717
  refuge, 666
Bum, *tramp*, 268, 876
  loafer, 683
  pauper, 804
  rascal, 949
Bumbledom, *authority*, 737
Bumboat, *ship*, 273
  provision, 637
Bumboatman, *trader*, 797
Bump, *projection*, 250
  thump, 276
Bump off, *kill*, 361
Bumper, *sufficiency*, 639
  fullness, 52
Bumpkin, *commonalty*, 876
Bumptious, *insolent*, 885
Bun-fight, *party*, 892
Bunce, *profit*, 618
Bunch, *protuberance*, 250
  collection, 72
Bundle, *packet*, 72
  to *move*, 275
Bung, *stopper*, 263
  throw, 284
Bung-ho, *departure*, 293
Bungalow, *abode*, 189
Bungle, *unskilfulness*, 699
  failure, 732
Bungler, *unskilful*, 701
Bunion, *swelling*, 250
Bunk, *bed*, 191, 215
  escape, 671
Bunker, *receptacle*, 191
  obstruction, 706
Bunkie, *friend*, 891
Bunkum, *humbug*, 545
  nonsense, 497
Bunt, *inversion*, 218
  deviate, 279

Campanologist, *musician*, 416
Campus, *field*, 344
  arena, 728
Can, *power*, 157
  mug, 191
  to preserve, 670
* Canaille, *commonalty*, 876
  rabble, 949
Canal, *opening*, 260
  way, 627
Canard, *deception*, 545
  news, 532
Can-can, *dance*, 840
Cancel, *obliterate*, 552, 773
  abrogate, 756
Cancellated, *crossing*, 219
* Cancelli, *lattice*, 219
Cancer, *disease*, 655
  swelling, 250
  foulness, 653
  painful, 830
Candelabra, *luminary*, 423
Candescence, *heat*, 382
Candid, *sincere*, 543
  ingenuous, 703
  honourable, 939
Candidate, *petitioner*, 767,
  865
Candidature, *offer*, 763
  solicitation, 765
Candied, *flattering*, 933
Candle, *luminary*, 423
Candle-ends, *remainder*, 40
Candle-holder, *auxiliary*,
  711
Candle-light, *dimness*, 422
Candlestick, *luminary*, 423
Candour, *veracity*, 543
  artlessness, 703
  honour, 939
Candy, *sweetness*, 396
Cane, *scourge*, 975
  to beat, 276
  punish, 972
Cangue, *shackle*, 752
  stocks, 975
Canicular, *heat*, 382
Canister, *receptacle*, 191
Canker, *disease*, 655
  bane, 663
  deterioration, 659
  pain, 830
Cankering, *badness*, 649
Canned, *drunk*, 959
Cannibal, *sinner*, 949
Cannibalize, *repair*, 658
Cannon, *arms*, 727
  collision, 276
Cannonade, *attack*, 716
Cannoneer, *combatant*, 726
Canny, *cautious*, 459, 864

Canny, *cunning*, 702
  intelligent, 498
  thrifty, 817
Canoe, *ship*, 273
Canon, *rule*, 80
  music, 415
  precept, 697
  priest, 996
Canonical, *orthodox*, 983A
Canonicals, *holy orders*, 999
Canonize, *rites*, 995, 998
  honour, 873
Canoodle, *endearment*, 902
Canopy, *height*, 206
  roof, 210
  covering, 222
Canorous, *resonant*, 402
  melodious, 415
Cant, *neology*, 563
  language, 560
  oblique, 217
  hypocrisy, 544, 988
Cantankerous, *discourtesy*,
  895
Cantata, *music*, 415
* Cantatrice, *musician*, 416
Canted, *obliquity*, 217
Canteen, *receptacle*, 191
  feeding, 298
Canter, *move*, 266
  gallop, 274
Canticle, *music*, 415
Cantilever, *support*, 215
Cantle, *part*, 51
Canto, *poetry*, 597
Canton, *region*, 181
Cantonment, *location*, 184
  abode, 189
Canty, *cheerfulness*, 836
Canvas, *sail*, 267
Canvass, *investigate*, 461
  treat of, 595
  solicit, 765
Canyon, *ravine*, 198
Canzonet, *song*, 415
  poem, 597
Caoutchouc, *elasticity*, 325
Cap, *hat*, 225
  height, 206
  to be superior, 33, 194
  counter, 718
  to salute, 894
Cap-à-pie, *preparation*, 673
  length, 200
Capability, *power*, 157
  strength, 159
  skill, 698
  facility, 705
  endowment, 5
Capacity, *space*, 180
  size, 192
  endowment, 5

Capacity, *power*, 157
  intellect, 450
  aptitude, 539
  talent, 698
  wisdom, 498
  utility, 644
  office, 625
Caparison, *vestment*, 225
Cape, *land*, 342
  projection, 250
  height, 206
  cloak, 225
Caper, *leap*, 309
  dance, 840
Capillary, *thinness*, 203, 205
Capital, *excellent*, 648
  important, 642
  summit, 210
  money, 800; *wealth*, 803
Capitalist, *wealth*, 803
Capitation, *numeration*, 85
Capitol, *defence*, 717
Capitular, *clergy*, 996
Capitulate, *submission*, 725
Capote, *vestment*, 224
* Capriccio, *caprice*, 608
Caprice, *chance*, 608
  irresolution, 605
  music, 415
Capricious, *irregular*, 139
  changeable, 149
  whimsical, 608
Capriole, *leap*, 309
Capsize, *inversion*, 218
  wreck, 731
Capsized, *failure*, 732
Capstan, *instrument*, 633
Capsule, *vessel*, 191
  tunicle, 222
Captain, *master*, 745
  of industry, 745
Caption, *indication*, 550
Captious, *capricious*, 608
  censorious, 932
  discourteous, 795
Captivated, *fascinated*, 827,
  induced, 615   [897
Captivating, *pleasing*, 829
  lovely, 897
Captive, *prisoner*, 754
Captivity, *restraint*, 751
Capture, *taking*, 789
Capuchin, *clergy*, 996
* Caput mortuum, *remain-
  der*, 40
  unclean, 653
Car, *vehicle*, 272
Carabineer, *combatant*, 726
Caracole, *leap*, 309
  journey, 266
Carafe, *receptacle*, 191

Chorus, *voices*, 411
musicians, 416
unanimity, 488
* Chose jugée, *judgment*, 480
* Chota hazri, *food*, 298
Chouse, *deception*, 545
Chrism, *rite*, 998
CHRIST, *Deity*, 976
Christen, *nomenclature*, 564
Christendom, *Christianity*, 983A
Christian, *piety*, 987
Christianity, 983A
Christianity, *Christian religion*, 983A
Christmas box, *gift*, 784
Chromatic, *colour*, 428
musical scale, 413
Chromatrope, *optical instrument*, 445
Chromolithograph, *engraving*, 558
Chronic, *diuturnity*, 110
Chronicle, *annals*, 551
measure of time, 114
account, 594
Chronicler, *recorder*, 553
* Chronique scandaleuse, *gossip*, 532, 588
Chronology, *time measurement*, 114
Chronometry, *time measurement*, 114
Chrysalis, *youth*, 127, 129
Chubby, *size*, 192
Chuck, *throw*, 284
desist, 142
cry, 412
food, 298
Chuck out, *expel*, 297
Chuck up, *abandon*, 624
Chucker-out, *doorkeeper*, 263
Chuckle, *laugh*, 838
exult, 884
Chuckle-head, *fool*, 501
Chum, *friend*, 890
Chummy, *friendly*, 888
Chunk, *size*, 192
part, 51
Chunky, *short*, 201
broad, 202
Church, *Christian religion*, 983A
temple, 1000
Churchdom, *churchdom*, 995
Churchman, *clergy*, 996
Churchwarden, *clergy*, 996
tobacco-pipe, 298A
Churchy, *bigoted*, 988
Churchyard, *interment*, 363
Churl, *boor*, 876

Churl, *rude*, 895
irascible, 901
niggard, 819
Churn, *agitation*, 315, 352
Chute, *obliquity*, 217
Chutney, *condiment*, 393
Chyle, *fluid*, 333
Chyme, *semiliquid*, 352
Cicatrize, *improvement*, 658
Cicerone, *teacher*, 540
director, 694
* Cicisbeo, *love*, 897
* Ci-devant, *preterition*, 122
Cigar, *tobacco*, 298A
Cigar-case, *receptacle*, 191
Cigar-shaped, *rotund*, 249
Cigarette, *tobacco*, 298A
Cigarette-case, *receptacle*, 191
Ciliated, *roughness*, 256
Cimmerian, *darkness*, 421
Cinch, *grip*, 781
connection, 45
easy, 705
Cincture, *circularity*, 247
Cinders, *remainder*, 40
Cine-camera, *lens*, 445
Cinema, *theatre*, 599A
amusement, 840
Cinemaddict, *cinema*, 599A
Cinematograph, *show*, 448
Cinerary, *burial*, 363
Cineration, *calefaction*, 384
Cinerator, *furnace*, 386
Cinereous, *grey*, 432
Cingulum, *belt*, 229
Cinnabar, *red*, 434
Cinque, *numbers*, 98
Cipher, *zero*, 101
number, 84
to compute, 85
secret, 533
mark, 550
writing, 590
unimportant, 643
Circe, *seductor*, 615
sensuality, 954
Circle, *form*, 247
curvature, 245
space, 181
theatre, 599
party, 712
social, 892
Circuit, *deviation*, 279
indirect path, 629
winding, 248
turn, 311
tour, 266
space, 181
Circuitous, *devious*, 279
turning, 311
indirect, 629

Circular, *round*, 247
curved, 245
advertisement, 531
letter, 592
Circulate, *rotate*, 312
publish, 531
Circumambient, *circumjacence*, 227
Circumambulate, *move*, 266
wind, 311
Circumbendibus, *winding*, 248
circuit, 629
circuition, 311
Circumference, *outline*, 229
Circumfluent, *circuition*, 311
Circumfuse, *dispersion*, 73
Circumgyration, *rotation*, 312
Circumjacence, *surrounding*, 227
Circumlocution, *phrase*, 566, 573
Circumnavigation, *navigation*, 267
circuition, 311
Circumrotation, *rotation*, 312
Circumscribe, *surround*, 231
limit, 761
Circumspect, *attentive*, 457
careful, 459
cautious, 864
Circumstance, *phrase*, 8
event, 151
Circumstantial, *diffuse*, 573
evidence, 472
Circumvallation, *enclosure*, 232
defence, 717
Circumvent, *cheat*, 545
defeat, 731
cunning, 702
Circumvolution, *rotation*, 312
Circus, *arena*, 728
amusement, 840
edifice, 189
Cistern, *receptacle*, 191
store, 636
Citadel, *fort*, 666
defence, 717
Cite, *quote as example*, 82, 564
as evidence, 467
summon, 741
accuse, 938
arraign, 969
Cithern, *musical instrument*, 417
Citizen, *inhabitant*, 188

Citizen, *man*, 373
Citrine, *yellow*, 436
City, *abode*, 189
Civet, *fragrance*, 400
Civic, *urban*, 189
  public, 372
Civicism, *patriotism*, 910
Civil, *courteous*, 894
  laity, 997
Civilian, *lawyer*, 968
  non-combatant, 726A
Civilization, *courtesy*, 894
  mankind, 372
Civvies, *dress*, 225
Clachan, *village*, 189
Clack, *talk*, 588
  snap, 406
  animal cry, 412
Clad, *dressed*, 225
Claim, *demand*, 741, 765
  property, 780
  right, 924
Claimant, *dueness*, 924
  petitioner, 767
Clairvoyance, *occult arts*, 992
  insight, 490
  foresight, 510
Clam, *taciturn*, 585
Clamant, *cry*, 411
Clamber, *ascent*, 305
Clammy, *semiliquid*, 352
Clamour, *loudness*, 404, 411
Clamp, *to fasten*, 43
  fastening, 45
Clan, *class*, 75
  kindred, 11
  clique, 892
Clandestine, *concealment*, 528
  secret, 534
Clang, *loudness*, 404
  resonance, 408
Clanger, *error*, 495, 732
  solecism, 568
Clank, *harsh sound*, 410
Clannishness, *prejudice*, 481
  co-operation, 709
Clap, *explosion*, 406
  to applaud, 931
Clap on, *addition*, 37
Clap up, *restraint*, 751
Clapperclaw, *beat*, 972
Claptrap, *plea*, 617
  pretence, 546
  sophistry, 477
  nonsense, 492
* Claqueur, *flatterer*, 935
Clarence, *vehicle*, 272
Clarify, *cleanness*, 652
Clarinet, *musical instru-
  ment*, 417

Clarion, *musical instrument*, 417
Clarity, *transparency*, 425
  perspicuity, 570
Clart, *mud*, 352
  dirt, 653
Clash, *oppose*, 708
  disagree, 24
  discord, 713
  contest, 720
  concussion, 276
  sound, 406
  chatter, 584
Clasp, *to unite*, 43
  fastening, 45
  entrance, 903
  come close, 197
Clasp-knife, *sharpness*, 253
Class, *category*, 75
  to arrange, 60
  learner, 541
Classic, *masterpiece*, 650
  symmetry, 242
  ancient, 124
Classical, *taste*, 578, 580
Classify, *arrangement*, 60
  class, 75
Clatter, *roll*, 407
  din, 404
Clause, *part*, 51
  passage, 593
  condition, 770
Claustral, *secluded*, 893
Claustrophobia, *dislike*, 867
  seclusion, 893
Clavichord, *musical*, 417
Claw, *hook*, 633
  to grasp, 789
Clay, *earth*, 342
  corpse, 362
  tobacco-pipe, 298A
Clay-cold, *cold*, 383
Claymore, *arms*, 727
Clean, *unstained*, 652
  entirely, 31
Clean-handed, *innocence*, 946
Cleanse, *purge*, 652
Clear, *transparent*, 425
  light, 420
  visible, 446
  intelligible, 518
  perspicuous style, 570
  to prepare, 673
  to free, 750
  to vindicate, 937
  to acquit, 970
  innocent, 946
  simple, 42
  easy, 705
  to pay, 807
  to pass, 302

Clear decks, *prepare*, 673
Clear of, *distant*, 196
Clear out, *eject*, 297
  depart, 203
Clear-sighted, *vision*, 441
  shrewd, 498
Clear up, *interpret*, 518, 522
Clearance, *payment*, 807
Clearway, *way*, 627
Cleave, *adhere*, 46
  sunder, 44, 91
Cleek, *club*, 276
Clef, *music*, 413
Cleft, *chink*, 198
Clem, *starve*, 956
Clement, *lenient*, 740
  kind, 906
  pitiful, 914
Clench, *see* Clinch
Clepsydra, *chronometry*, 114
Clergy, *clergy*, 996
Clerical, *churchdom*, 995
Clerihew, *drollery*, 853
  absurdity, 497
Clerk, *scholar*, 492
  recorder, 553
  writer, 590
  servant, 746
  agent, 758
  church, 996
Clerkship, *commission*, 755
Clever, *skill*, 698
Cliché, *platitude*, 497
Click, *snap*, 406
Client, *dependant*, 746
  buyer, 795
  frequenter, 136
Clientship, *subjection*, 749
Cliff, *height*, 206
  verticality, 212, 217
Climacteric, *age*, 128
Climate, *region*, 181
  weather, 338
Climax, *summit*, 210
  completion, 729
  increase, 35
  in degree, 33
Climb, *ascent*, 305
Clime, *region*, 181
Clinch, *snatch*, 789
  fasten, 43
  close, 261
  an argument, 474, 478
Cling, *cohere*, 46
Clinic, *medicine*, 662
Clink, *resonance*, 408
  prison, 752
Clinker, *concretion*, 321
  dirt, 653
Clinometer, *angularity*, 244
Clinquant, *ornament*, 847

Colourless, *achromatism*, 429
Colours, *standard*, 550
 decoration, 877
Colporteur, *agent*, 758
Colt, *fool*, 501
 horse, 271
Column, *series*, 69
 height, 206
 monument, 551
 cylinder, 249
 procession, 266
 troop, 726
Colure, *universe*, 318
Coma, *insensibility*, 376, 823
 inactivity, 683
Comb, *sharpness*, 253
Combat, *contention*, 720, 722
Combatant, *contention*, 726
Comber, *wave*, 348
Combination, *union*, 48
Combinations, *arithmetical*, 84
 dress, 225
Combine, *join*, 48
 co-operate, 709
 union, 712
 syndicate, 778
Combustible, *heating*, 384
 fuel, 388
Come, *arrive*, 292
 approach, 286
 happen, 151
Come about, *eventuality*, 151
Come after, *sequence*, 63
Come-at-able, *accessible*, 705
Come away, *recession*, 287
Come-back, *retort*, 462, 479, 842
 retaliation, 718
Come before, *precedence*, 62
Come by, *acquisition*, 775
Come down, *descend*, 306
 cheapness, 815
 pay, 809
Come-down, *adversity*, 735
Come forth, *existence*, 1
Come from, *effect*, 154
Come in for, *obtain*, 775
Come near, *approach*, 286
Come off, *disjunction*, 44
 take place, 151
Come on, *follow*, 63
 defy, 715
 prosper, 731
Come out, *egress*, 294
Come over, *induce*, 615
Come to, *whole*, 50

Come up to, *equal*, 27
Come up with, *arrival*, 292
Come upon, *arrival*, 292
Comedian, *the drama*, 599
 humorist, 844
Comedy, *drama*, 599
 ridicule, 856
Comely, *beauty*, 845
Comestible, *food*, 298
Comet, *wanderer*, 268
 universe, 318
Comfit, *sweetness*, 396
Comfort, *pleasure*, 377, 827
 content, 831
 relief, 834
Comfort station, *toilet*, 191, 653
Comfortable, *pleased*, 827
 pleasing, 829
Comforter, *deity*, 976
 dress, 225
Comfortless, *unhappy*, 828
 painful, 830
 dejected, 837
Comic, *witty*, 842
 ridiculous, 853
Comintern, *council*, 696
* Comitium, *assemblage*, 72
 council, 696
Comity, *courtesy*, 894
Comma, *stop*, 142
Command, *order*, 741
 authority, 737
Commandeer, *impress*, 744
 take, 789
Commander, *master*, 745
Commanding, *dignified*, 873
Commando, *combatant*, 726
* Comme il faut, *taste*, 850
 fashion, 852
Commemorate, *celebration*, 883
 record, 551
 memory, 505
Commence, *beginning*, 66
Commend, *approbation*, 931
Commendable, *virtuous*, 944
Commensurate, *accord*, 23
 adequate, 639
Comment, *reason*, 476
 interpret, 522
 dissertation, 595
Commerce, *intercourse*, 588
 business, 625
 barter, 794
Commercialese, *verbiage*, 573
Commination, *threat*, 909
Commingle, *mixture*, 41
Comminute, *pulverulence*, 330
 disjunction, 44
 incoherence, 47

Commiserate, *pity*, 914
Commissariat, *provision*, 298, 637
Commissary, *consignee*, 758
 deputy, 759
Commission, *business*, 625
 consignee, 755
 fee, 809
Commissionaire, *agent*, 690
 door-keeper, 263
Commissioner, *consignee*, 758
Commissure, *junction*, 43
Commit, *act*, 680
 delegate, 755
 imprison, 751
 arrest, 969
Committee, *council*, 696
 assemblage, 72
Commix, *mixture*, 41
Commodious, *spacious*, 180
 expedience, 646
Commodity, *merchandise*, 798
Commodore, *master*, 745
Common, *ordinary*, 82
 low, 876
 unimportant, 643
 general, 78
 reciprocal, 12
 frequent, 136
 plain, 344
Common-room, *sociality*, 892
Common sense, *intellect*, 450
 wisdom, 498
Commonalty, *common*, 876
 people, 372
Commoner, *commonalty*, 876
Commonplace, *unimportant*, 643
 habitual, 613
 dull, 843
Commons, *commonalty*, 876
 food, 298
Commonwealth, *man*, 373
Commotion, *agitation*, 315
Commune, *muse*, 451
 converse, 588
 territorial division, 181
Communicant, *worship*, 990
Communicate, *tell*, 527
 participate, 778
 join, 43
Communication, *information*, 527, 532
 connection, 43
Communion, *society*, 712
 participation, 778
 sacrament, 998

* Con amore, *willing*, 602
Con man, *cheat*, 548
* Con moto, *music*, 415
Conation, *will*, 600
Concatenation, *junction*, 43
  continuity, 69
Concave, *concavity*, 252
Conceal, *hide*, 528
  invisible, 447
Concede, *consent*, 762
  admit, 467, 529
  give, 784
  assent, 488
  permit, 760
Conceit, *idea*, 453
  belief, 484
  supposition, 514
  imagination, 515
  affectation, 855
  vanity, 880
  wit, 842
Conceited, *folly*, 499
Conceivable, *possible*, 470
Conceive, *believe*, 484
  imagine, 515
  produce, 161, 168
Concent, *melody*, 413
Concentrate, *assemble*, 72
  compress, 321
  converge, 290
Concentric, *centrality*, 223
Concept, *idea*, 453
Conception, *intellect*, 450
  idea, 453
  belief, 484
  knowledge, 490
  imagination, 515
  beginning, 66
Conceptual, *thought*, 451
Concern, *relation*, 9
  grief, 828
  importance, 642
  business, 625
  firm, 797
Concerning, *relation*, 9
Concert, *music*, 415
  plan, 626
  co-operation, 709
  agreement 23
Concert-hall, *amusement*,
  840
Concertina, *musical*, 417
Concerto, *music*, 415
Concession, *grant*, 762, 784
  assent, 488
  permit, 760
* Concetto, *wit*, 842
Conchoid, *curvature*, 245
Conchy, *non-combatant*,
  726A
* Concierge, *keeper*, 263,
  753

Conciliate, *talk over*, 615
  satisfy, 831
  atone, 952
  courtesy, 894
Conciliation, *concord*, 714
  pacification, 723
  mediation, 724
Concinnity, *style*, 578
  beauty, 845
Concise, *conciseness*, 572
Conclave, *assembly*, 72
  council, 696
  church, 995
Conclude, *end*, 67
  infer, 476
  opine, 480, 484
  complete, 729
  determine, 604
Conclusions (to try), *conten-*
  tion, 720
Conclusive, *demonstration*,
  478
Concoct, *prepare*, 673
  falsify, 544
  plan, 626
Concomitant, *synchronous*,
  120
  concurring, 178
  accompanying, 88
Concord, *agreement*, 23
  in music, 413
  assent, 488
  harmony, 714
  amity, 888
Concordance, *dictionary*,
  562
Concordat, *compact*, 769
* Concours, *contention*, 720
Concourse, *assemblage*, 72
  convergence, 290
Concrete, *mass*, 46
  material, 3, 316
  density, 321
Concubine, *libertine*, 962
Concupiscence, *desire*, 865
  impurity, 961
Concur, *co-operate*, 178
  in concert, 709
  converge, 290
  assent, 488
Concurrence, *agreement*, 23
  coexistence, 120
Concussion, *impulse*, 276
Condemn, *censure*, 932
  convict, 971
Condense, *contraction*, 195
  density, 321
  style, 572
Condescend, *humility*, 879
Condescending, *patronizing*,
  878
Condign, *dueness*, 922, 924

Condiment, *condiment*, 393
Condition, *state*, 7
  rank, 873
  term, 770
  modification, 469
  sensitiveness, 375
  teach, 537
  habit, 613
Conditional, *circumstance*, 8
Condole, *condolence*, 915
Condonation, *forgiveness*,
  918
* Condottiere, *master*, 745
Conduce, *tend*, 176
  concur, 178
  avail, 644
  contribute, 153
Conduct, *lead*, 693
  transfer, 270
  procedure, 692
  music, 415
Conductor, *guard*, 666
  director, 694
  interpreter, 524
  musician, 416
  conveyor, 271
Conduit, *conduit*, 350
Condyle, *convexity*, 250
Cone, *round*, 249
  pointed, 253
Confabulation, *interlocu-*
  tion, 588
Confection, *sweetness*, 396
Confederacy, *party*, 712
  co-operation, 709
Confederate, *auxiliary*, 711
Confer, *give*, 784
  converse, 588
  advise, 695
Confess, *avow*, 529, 535
  assert, 488
  penitence, 950
  rite, 998
Confessedly, *affirmation*,
  535
  admission, 467
Confessional, *temple*, 1000
Confidant, *auxiliary*, 711
  friend, 890
Confide, *trust*, 484
  credulity, 486
  hope, 858
Confidence, *courage*, 861
Confidence man, *cheat*, 548
Confidential, *concealment*,
  528
Configuration, *form*, 240
Confine, *limit*, 233
  imprison, 751
  circumscribe, 231
  frontier, 199
Confined, *ailing*, 655

Confirm, *corroborate*, 467
consent, 762
rites, 998
Confirmed, *fixed*, 150
Confiscate, *condemn*, 971
take, 789
Conflagration, *calefaction*,
384
Conflation, *combination*, 48
Conflict, *contention*, 720
disagreement, 24
Conflicting, *opposing*, 14,
179, 708
Confluence, *convergence*,
290
Conflux, *assemblage*, 72
Conform, *assent*, 488
accustom, 613
concur, 178
agree, 646
Conformation, *form*, 240
frame, 7
Conformity, *to rule*, 16, 82
Confound, *disorder*, 61
injure, 649
perplex, 475
baffle, 731
confuse, 519
astonish, 870
indiscriminate, 465A
expletive, 908
Confoundedly, *greatness*, 31
Confraternity, *friendship*,
888
* Confrère, *friend*, 890
Confront, *face*, 234
compare, 467
resist, 719
Confucianism, *religion*, 984
Confucius, *religious founder*,
986
Confuse, *derange*, 61
indiscriminate, 465A
obscure, 519
perplex, 458, 475
abash, 874
style, 571
Confusion, *disorder*, 59
shame, 874
Confutation, *disproof*, 479
Confute, *deny*, 536
* Congé, *dismissal*, 756
Congeal, *cold*, 385
Congealed, *dense*, 321
Congener, *consanguinity*, 11
similar, 17
included, 76
Congenial, *agreeing*, 23, 714
expedient, 646
Congenital, *intrinsic*, 5
habitual, 613
Congeries, *assemblage*, 72

Congestion, *collection*, 72
redundance, 641
disease, 655
Conglobation, *assemblage*,
72
Conglomerate, *assemblage*,
72
density, 321
Conglutinate, *coherence*, 46
Congratulate, *congratula-
tion*, 896
Congregate, *assemblage*, 72
Congregation, *laity*, 997
worship, 990
Congress, *assemblage*, 72,
290
council, 696
Congruous, *agreeing*, 23
expedient, 646
Conical, *round*, 249
pointed, 253
Conjecture, *supposition*,
514
Conjoin, *junction*, 43
concur, 178
Conjointly, *together*, 37, 43
Conjugal, *marriage*, 903
Conjugate, *word*, 562
Conjugation, *junction*, 43
pair, 89
phase, 144
grammar, 567
Conjunct, *junction*, 43
Conjunction, *vinculum*, 45
Conjuncture, *contingency*, 8
occasion, 134
Conjuration, *deception*, 545
sorcery, 992
Conjure, *entreat*, 765
exorcise, 992
Conjure up, *imagine*, 515
Conjurer, *sorcerer*, 994
adept, 700
Connate, *cause*, 153
intrinsic, 5
Connatural, *uniform*, 16
similar, 17
Connect, *relate*, 9
link, 43
Connection, *kindred*, 11
link, 45
Connective, *link*, 45
Connive, *overlook*, 460
concur, 178
allow, 760
Connoisseur, *taste*, 850
judge, 480
proficient, 700
Connotation, *indication*,
550
Connubial, *marriage*, 903
Conquer, *success*, 731

Conquered, *failure*, 732
Conquest, *success*, 731
Consanguinity, *kindred*, 11
Conscience, *moral sense*, 926
knowledge, 490
Conscience-smitten, *peni-
tence*, 950
Conscientious, *virtuous*, 944
scrupulous, 726A, 939
true, 494
Consciousness, *intuition*,
450
knowledge, 490
Conscript, *soldier*, 726
Conscription, *compulsion*,
744
Consecrate, *dedicate*, 873
sanctify, 987, 995, 998
Consectary, *corollary*, 480
Consecution, *sequence*, 63
Consecutive, *following*, 63
continuous, 69
Consecutively, *gradually*,
144
Consensus, *agreement*, 23
assent, 488
Consent, *grant*, 762
concur, 178
assent, 488
agreement, 23
Consentaneous, *agreeing*, 23
expedient, 646
Consequence, *effect*, 154
event, 151
importance, 642
Consequent, *sequence*, 63
Consequential, *arrogant*, 878
deducible, 467, 478
Consequently, *reasoning*,
154, 476
Conservation, *preservation*,
670
Conservative, *permanence*,
141
Conservatoire, *school*, 542
Conservatory, *store*, 636
hothouse, 386
Conserve, *sweet*, 396
Consider, *think*, 451
attend to, 457
inquire, 461
Considerable, *in degree*, 31
in size, 192
important, 642
Considerate, *judicious*, 498
benevolent, 906
respectful, 928
Consideration, *motive*, 615
qualification, 469
importance, 642
requital, 973
respect, 928

Contradict, *oppose*, 708
 dissent, 489
Contradiction, *contrariety*, 14
Contradistinction, *difference*, 15
Contralto, *melody*, 413
 low note, 408
Contraposition, *reversion*, 237
 inversion, 218
Contraption, *instrument*, 633
Contrapuntal, *melody*, 413
Contrapuntist, *music*, 415
Contrary, *opposite*, 14, 179
 opposing, 708
 capricious, 608
Contrast, *contrariety*, 14
 comparison, 464
Contravallation, *defence*, 717
Contravene, *counteract*, 179
 oppose, 14, 708
 hinder, 706
 counter-evidence, 468
 argue, 476
 deny, 536
 violate, 927
* Contrétemps, *difficulty*, 704
 check, 706
 intempestivity, 135
Contribute, *tend*, 176
 concur, 178
 give, 784
 cause, 153
Contribution, *giving*, 784
 expenses, 809
Contrition, *abrasion*, 331
 penitence, 950
Contrive, *plan*, 616, 702
 succeed, 731
 produce, 161
Contriving, *artful*, 702
Control, *poser*, 157
 authority, 737
 restraint, 751
 norm, 80, 643, 467
 to regulate, 693
 to check, 179, 708
Controller, *director*, 694
Controversialist, *combatant*, 736
Controversy, *debate*, 476
 dispute, 713
Controvert, *deny*, 536
 oppose, 708
Controvertible, *dubious*, 475
Contumacy, *obstinacy*, 606
 disobedience, 742

Contumely, *disrespect*, 929
 arrogance, 885
 rudeness, 895
 scorn, 930
 reproach, 932
Contund, *pulverize*, 330
Contuse, *pulverize*, 330
Conundrum, *secret*, 533
 pun, 563
 wit, 842
 problem, 461
Conurbation, *abode*, 189
Convalescence, *improvement*, 658
 health, 654
Convection, *transference*, 270
* Convenances, *rule*, 80
Convene, *assemblage*, 72
Convenience, *room*, 191
 lavatory, 653
 means, 632
Convenient, *expedient*, 646
Convent, *temple*, 1000
 assembly, 72
 council, 696
Convention, *compact*, 769
 treaty of peace, 723
 assembly, 72
 council, 696
 rule, 80; taste, 850
Conventional, *uniform*, 82
 fashionable, 852
 banal, 575
Conventual, *clergy*, 996
Converge, *convergence*, 290
 assemblage, 72
Conversable, *sociable*, 588, 892
Conversant, *knowing*, 490
 skilful, 698
Conversation, *interlocution*, 588
Conversazione, *meeting*, 72
 chat, 588; sociality, 892
Converse, *reverse*, 14
 talk, 588
Conversion, *change*, 144
 religious, 987
Convert, *opinion*, 484
 learner, 541
 piety, 987
 to change to, 144
 to use, 677
Convertible, *identical*, 13
 equal, 27
Convex, *convexity*, 250
Convey, *transfer*, 270, 783
Conveyance, *vehicle*, 272
Conveyancer, *lawyer*, 968

Convict, *condemn*, 971
 to convince, 537
 prisoner, 754
 condemned, 949
Conviction, *belief*, 484
Convince, *teaching*, 537
Convincement, *belief*, 484
Convivial, *social*, 892
Convocation, *council*, 696, 995
Convoke, *assemblage*, 72
Convolution, *coil*, 248
 rotation, 312
 crossing, 219
Convoy, *transfer*, 270
 guard, 664, 753
Convulse, *violent*, 173
 agitate, 315
 pain, 378
 torture, 830
Coo, *animal cry*, 412
Cook, *heat*, 384
 prepare, 673
 falsify, 544
 accounts, 811
Cool, *cold*, 383
 to refrigerate, 385
 judicious, 498
 to moderate, 174
 to dissuade, 616
 to allay, 826
 indifferent, 866
 torpid, 826
Cool-headed, *torpid*, 826
 judicious, 498
Cooler, *refrigerator*, 387
 prison, 752
Coolie, *carrier*, 271
Coombe, *valley*, 252
Coon, *black*, 431
Coop, *confine*, 752
 restrain, 751
 abode, 189
Co-operate, *physically*, 178
 voluntarily, 709
Co-operation, *agreement*, 23
Co-operator, *auxiliary*, 711
Co-ordinate, *equality*, 27
 arrange, 60
Cop, *police*, 664
Copal, *semiliquid*, 352
Copartner, *participator*, 778
 associate, 892
 accompanying, 88
Cope, *contend*, 720
 equal, 27
 canonicals, 999
* Copia verborum, *diffuseness*, 573
 speech, 582
Coping-stone, *completion*, 729

Creation, *universe*, 318
Creationism, *causation*, 153
Creative, *productive*, 168
Creator, *deity*, 976
  producer, 164
Creature, *animal*, 366
  thing, 3
  effect, 154
Creature comforts, *food*, 298
Crèche, *nursery*, 542
Credence, *belief*, 484
Credential, *evidence*, 467
Credible, *probable*, 472, 484
  possible, 470
Credit, *belief*, 484
  authority, 737
  pecuniary, 805
  account, 811
  influence, 737
  hope, 858
  repute, 873
  desert, 944
Creditor, *credit*, 805
Credo, *belief*, 484
Credulity, *belief*, 486
  superstition, 984A
Creed, *belief*, 484, 496
  tenet, 983
Creek, *gulf*, 343
Creep, *crawl*, 275
  bad man, 949
Creeper, *plant*, 367
Creeping, *sensation*, 380
Creepy, *fearsome*, 860
Cremation, *burning*, 384
  of corpses, 363
* Crème de la crème, *goodness*, 648
Cremona, *musical instrument*, 417
Crenated, *notch*, 257
Crenelated, *notched*, 257
Crepitate, *snap*, 406
Crepuscule, *dawn*, 125
  dimness, 422
Crescendo, *increase*, 35
  music, 415
Crescent, *curve*, 245
  street, 189
Cresset, *torch*, 423
Crest, *summit*, 210
  tuft, 256
  armorial, 550, 877
Crestfallen, *dejected*, 837
  humiliated, 881, 879
Cretin, *fool*, 501
Crevasse, *interval*, 198
Crevice, *interval*, 198
  opening, 260
Crew, *assemblage*, 72
  party, 712
  inhabitants, 188

Crib, *bed*, 215
  to steal, 791
  interpretation, 522
Crick, *pain*, 378
Crier, *messenger*, 534
Crime, *guilt*, 947
Criminal, *culprit*, 949
  vicious, 945
Criminality, *guilt*, 947
Criminate, *accusation*, 938
Criminology, *crime*, 947
Crimp, *curl*, 248
  fold, 258
  to steal, 791
Crimson, *red*, 434
Cringe, *submit*, 725, 743
  servility, 886
  fear, 860
Crinkle, *fold*, 258
  angle, 244
Crinoline, *dress*, 225
Cripple, *weaken*, 160
  disable, 158
  injure, 649, 659
  disease, 655
Crisis, *conjuncture*, 8
  event, 151
  difficulty, 704
  opportunity, 134
Crisp, *brittle*, 328
  rough, 256
  rumpled, 248
  concise, 572
Criss-cross-row, *letter*, 561
Criterion, *trial*, 463
  evidence, 467
Critic, *taste*, 850
  judge, 480
  reviewer, 590
  dissertation, 595
  detractor, 936
Critical, *opportune*, 134
  important, 642
  difficult, 704
  dangerous, 665
Criticism, *disapprobation*,
  932
  dissertation, 595
Criticize, *taste*, 850
Critique, *discrimination*,
  465
  dissertation, 595
  disapprobation, 932
Croak, *cry*, 412
  stammer, 583
  complain, 839
  discontent, 832
  predict, 511
Croceate, *yellow*, 436
Crochet, *knit*, 43
Crock, *weakness*, 160
Crock up, *failure*, 732

Crocodile tears, *falsehood*,
  544
Croesus, *wealth*, 803
Croft, *hut*, 189
Crofter, *peasant*, 876
Cromlech, *interment*, 363
Crone, *veteran*, 130
Crony, *friend*, 890
Crook, *curvature*, 245
  evildoer, 913
  swindler, 792
  ill, 655
Crooked, *angular*, 244
  distorted, 243, 846
  sloping, 217
  dishonourable, 940
Croon, *to hum*, 405, 415
Crop, *stomach*, 191
  to shorten, 201
  to gather, 775
  to take, 789
  to eat, 297
  harvest, 154
Crop up, *inexpectation*, 508
  event, 151
  appear, 446
Cropper, *fall*, 306
Crosier, *canonicals*, 999
Cross, *intersection*, 219
  passage, 302
  swindle, 545
  opposition, 179, 708
  refusal, 572
  vexation, 828
  vexatiousness, 830
  ill-tempered, 895
  fretful, 901
  failure, 732
  mixture, 41
  decoration, 877
  reward, 973
  rites, 998
Cross-breed, *unconformity*,
  83
Cross-cut, *method*, 627
Cross-examine, *inquiry*, 461
Cross-grained, *obstinate*, 606
  ill-tempered, 895, 901
Cross-purposes, *error*, 495
  misinterpretation, 523
Cross-question, *inquiry*, 461
Cross-reading, *misinterpretation*, 523
Cross-road, *way*, 627
Crossbow, *arms*, 727
Crossing, *crossing*, 219
Crosspatch, *ill-tempered*, 895
Crossword, *puzzle*, 461, 533
Crotch, *angularity*, 244
Crotchet, *music*, 413
  prejudice, 481
  caprice, 608

Curable, *improvement*, 658
Curacy, *churchdom*, 995
Curate, *clergy*, 996
Curative, *remedial*, 834
Curator, *consignee*, 758
Curb, *restrain*, 751
  hinder, 706
  shackle, 752
  moderate, 174
  check, 826
  dissuade, 616
  counteract, 179
  slacken, 275
Curd, *mass*, 46
  density, 321
  pulp, 354
Curdle, *condense*, 321
  coagulate, 46, 352
Cure, *remedy*, 662, 834
  reinstate, 660
  religious, 995
  preserve, 670
  improve, 656
* Curé, *priest*, 996
Curfew, *evening*, 126
Curio, *toy*, 643
* Curiosa felicitas, *elegance*, 578
Curiosity, *curiosity*, 455
  phenomenon, 872
Curious, *true*, 494
  exceptional, 83
Curl, *bend*, 245, 248
  cockle up, 258
Curlicue, *convolution*, 248
Curliewurlie, *convolution*, 248
Curmudgeon, *parsimony*, 819
Currency, *publicity*, 531
  money, 800
Current, *existing*, 1
  present, 118
  happening, 151
  stream, 347
  river, 348
  wind, 349
  course, 109
  danger, 667
  opinion, 484
  public, 531
  prevailing, 82
* Currente calamo, *diffuseness*, 573
Curricle, *vehicle*, 272
Curriculum, *teaching*, 537
Curry, *condiment*, 393
  rub, 331
Curry favour, *flattery*, 933
Curse, *malediction*, 908
  bane, 663
  evil, 619

Curse, *adversity*, 735
  badness, 649
  painfulness, 830
Cursive, *writing*, 590
Cursory, *transient*, 111
  inattentive, 458
  neglecting, 460
  hasty, 684
Curst, *perverse*, 895
Curt, *short*, 201
  taciturn, 585
  concise, 572
Curtail, *shorten*, 201, 572
  retrench, 38
  decrease, 36
  deprive, 789
Curtain, *shade*, 424
  ambush, 530
Curtain lecture, *speech*, 582
Curtain-raiser, *play*, 599
Curtsy, *obeisance*, 743, 894
  submission, 725
  stoop, 308
Curule, *council*, 696
Curve, *curvature*, 245
Curvet, *leap*, 309
  oscillate, 314
  agitate, 315
Cushion, *pillow*, 215
  softness, 324
  to frustrate, 706
  relief, 834
Cushy, *easy*, 705
Cusp, *point*, 253
  angle, 244
Cussedness, *obstinacy*, 606
Custodian, *keeper*, 753
Custody, *captivity*, 664, 751, 781
  captive, 754
Custom, *rule*, 80
  habit, 613
  fashion, 852
  sale, 796
  barter, 794
  tax, 812
Custom-house, *mart*, 799
Customer, *purchaser*, 795
Cut, *divide*, 44
  bit, 51
  interval, 70, 198
  sculpture, 557
  curtail, 201
  cultivate, 371
  layer, 204
  notch, 257
  form, 240
  road, 627
  print, 558
  attach, 716
  pain, 828
  to give pain, 830

Cut, *affect*, 824
  ignore, 460, 893, 895
  neglect, 773
  state, 7; *cold*, 385
Cut across, *passage*, 302
Cut along, *velocity*, 274
Cut and dried, *ready*, 673
  trite, 82
Cut and run, *escape*, 671
Cut capers, *leap*, 309
  dance, 840
Cut down, *diminish*, 36
  destroy, 162
  shorten, 201
  lower, 308
  kill, 361
Cut down to size, *humiliate*, 879
Cut off, *kill*, 361
  subduct, 38
  impede, 706
  disjunction, 44
Cut out, *surpass*, 33
  retrench, 38; *plan*, 626
  supplant, 147
Cut short, *shorten*, 201, 572
  stop, 142; *decrease*, 36
  contract, 195
Cut-throat, *killing*, 361
  sinner, 913, 949
Cut up, *divide*, 44
  destroy, 162
  censure, 932
  unhappy, 828, 837
Cutaneous, *covering*, 222
Cuthbert, *pacifist*, 726A
Cuticle, *covering*, 222
Cutie, *sweetheart*, 897
Cutlass, *arms*, 727
Cutlery, *sharpness*, 253
Cutpurse, *thief*, 792
Cutter, *ship*, 273
Cutting, *cold*, 383
  affecting, 821
  censorious, 932
  extract, 596, 609
Cutty, *tobacco*, 298A
Cybernetics, *statecraft*, 693
Cycle, *period*, 138
  duration, 106
  circle, 247; *travel*, 266
Cycloid, *circularity*, 247
Cyclone, *violence*, 173
  rotation, 312
  agitation, 315
  wind, 349
Cyclopaedia, *knowledge*, 490
Cyclopean, *huge*, 192
Cyclops, *monster*, 83
Cylinder, *rotundity*, 249

Dig, *cultivate*, 371
 deepen, 208
 poke, 276
 understand, 518
Dig up, *past*, 122
Digamy, *marriage*, 903
Digest, *arrange*, 60, 826
 think, 451
 plan, 626
 book, 593
 compendium, 596
Diggings, *abode*, 189
Dight, *dressed*, 225
Digit, *number*, 84
Digitated, *pointed*, 253
Dignify, *honour*, 873
Dignitary, *cleric*, 996
 personage, 875
Dignity, *glory*, 873
 pride, 878
 honour, 939
Digress, *deviate*, 279
 style, 573
Digs, *abode*, 189
Dike, *ditch*, 198, 232
 defence, 666, 717
Dilaceration, *disjunction*, 44
Dilapidation, *wreck*, 162
 deterioration, 659
Dilate, *increase*, 35
 swell, 194
 lengthen, 202
 rarefy, 322
 style, 573
 discourse, 584
Dilatory, *slow*, 275
 inactive, 683
Dilemma, *difficulty*, 704
 logic, 476
 doubt, 475, 485
Dilettante, *ignoramus*, 493
 taste, 850
 idler, 683
Diligence, *coach*, 272
 activity, 682
Dilly-dally, *irresolution*, 605
 lateness, 133
Dilution, *weakness*, 160
 tenuity, 322
 water, 337
Diluvian, *old*, 124
Dim, *dark*, 421
 obscure, 422
 invisible, 447
Dim-out, *dim*, 422
Dim - sighted, *imperfect vision*, 443
 foolish, 499
Dime, *trifle*, 643
Dimension, *size*, 192
Dimidiation, *bisection*, 91

Diminish, *lessen*, 32, 36
 contract, 195
* Diminuendo, *music*, 415
Diminutive, *in degree*, 32
 in size, 193
Dimness, *dimness*, 422
Dimple, *concavity*, 252
 notch, 257
Din, *noise*, 404
 repetition, 104
 loquacity, 584
Dine, *to feed*, 297
Diner, *vehicle*, 272
Ding-dong, *noise*, 407
Dinghy, *boat*, 273
Dingle, *hollow*, 252
Dingus, *euphemism*, 565
Dingy, *dark*, 421, 431
 dim, 422
 colourless, 429
 grey, 432
Dining-car, *vehicle*, 272
Dinner, *food*, 298
Dinner-jacket, *dress*, 225
Dint, *power*, 157
 instrumentality, 631
 dent, 257
Diocesan, *clergy*, 996
Diocese, *churchdom*, 995
Diorama, *view*, 448
 painting, 556
Dip, *plunge*, 310
 direction, 278
 slope, 217
 depth, 208
 insert, 300
 immerse, 337
 thief, 792
Dip into, *examine*, 457
 investigate, 461
Diphthong, *letter*, 561
Diploma, *commission*, 755
 document, 551
Diplomacy, *mediation*, 724
 artfulness, 702
 courtesy, 894
 negotiation, 769
Diplomatic, *artful*, 544, 702
 tactful, 498, 698
Diplomat(ist), *messenger*,
 emissary, 758   [534
Dippy, *insane*, 503
Dipsomania, *drunkenness*, 959
 insanity, 503, 504
 craving, 865
Dire, *fearful*, 860
 grievous, 830
 hateful, 649
Direct, *straight*, 246, 278,
 to order, 737   [628

Direct, *to command*, 741
 to teach, 537
 artless, 703
Direction, *tendency*, 278
 course, 622
 place, 183
 management, 693
 precept, 697
Directly, *soon*, 111
 towards, 278
Director, *manager*, 694
 master, 745
 teacher, 540
Directorship, *authority*, 737
Directory, *council*, 696
 list, 86
Dirge, *song*, 415
 lament, 839
 funeral, 363
Dirigible, *airship*, 273A
Dirk, *arms*, 727
Dirt, *uncleanness*, 653
 trifle, 643
 ugly, 846
 blemish, 848
Dirt-cheap, *cheap*, 815
Dirt-track, *arena*, 728
Dirty, *dishonourable*, 940
Disability, *impotence*, 158
 fault, 651
 unskilfulness, 698
Disable, *weaken*, 158, 160, 674
Disabuse, *disclosure*, 529
Disadvantage, *evil*, 649
 inexpedience, 647
 badness, 649
Disaffection, *hate*, 898
 disobedience, 742
 disloyalty, 940
Disagreeable, *unpleasant*, 830
 disliked, 867
Disagreement, *incongruity*, 24
 difference, 15
 discord, 713
 dissent, 489
Disallow, *prohibit*, 761
Disannul, *abrogate*, 756
Disapparel, *divest*, 226
Disappear, *vanish*, 2, 449
Disappoint, *discontent*, 832
 fail, 732
 baulk, 509
Disapprobation, *blame*, 932
 disrepute, 874
Disarm, *incapacitate*, 158
 weaken, 160
 conciliate, 831
 propitiate, 914
Disarrange, *derange*, 61

Enigma, *secret*, 533
  question, 461
Enigmatic, *concealed*, 528
  obscure, 519
  uncertain, 475
Enjambement, *transcur-*
  sion, 303
Enjoin, *command*, 741
  induce, 615
  enact, 963
Enjoy, *physically*, 377
  morally, 827
  possess, 777
Enkindle, *induce*, 615
Enlace, *surround*, 227
  entwine, 219, 248
  join, 43
Enlarge, *increase*, 35
  swell, 194
  liberate, 750
  in writing, 573
Enlighten, *illuminate*, 420
  inform, 527
  instruct, 537
Enlightened, *wise*, 498
Enlightenment, *knowledge*,
  490
Enlist, *commission*, 755
  engage, 615
Enliven, *amuse*, 840
  cheer, 836
  delight, 829
Enmesh, *entwine*, 219
Enmity, *hostility*, 889
  hate, 898
  discord, 713
Ennead, *nine*, 98
Enneagon, *nine*, 98
Ennoble, *glorify*, 873
Ennui, *weariness*, 841
Enormity, *crime*, 947
Enormous, *in degree*, 31
  in size, 192
Enough, *much*, 31
  sufficient, 639
  satiety, 869
Enquiry, *see* Inquiry
Enrage, *incense*, 900
  provoke, 830
Enrapture, *excite*, 824
  beatify, 829
  love, 897
Enravish, *beatify*, 829
Enrich, *wealth*, 803
  ornament, 847
Enrobe, *invest*, 225
Enrol, *record*, 551
  appoint, 755
Enrolment, *list*, 86
Ens, *essence*, 1
Ensanguined, *red*, 434
  murderous, 361

Ensconce, *settle*, 184
  render safe, 664
  conceal, 528
* Ensemble, *whole*, 50
Enshrine, *memory*, 505, 873
  sanctify, 987
Enshroud, *conceal*, 528
Ensiform, *sharpness*, 253
Ensign, *standard*, 550
  officer, 726
  master, 745
Enslave, *subjection*, 749
Ensnare, *cheat*, 545
Ensue, *follow*, 63, 117
  happen, 151
Ensure, *certainty*, 474
Entablature, *summit*, 210
Entail, *cause*, 153
  involve, 467
  impose, 741
Entangle, *derange*, 61
  entwine, 219
  disorder, 59
  embroil, 713
  perplex, 528
  mixture, 41
* Entente cordiale, *friend-*
  ship, 888
  concord, 714
Enter, *go in*, 294
  note, 551
  accounts, 811
Enter in, *converge*, 290
Enter into, *component*, 56
Enter upon, *begin*, 66
Enterprise, *pursuit*, 622
  attempt, 676
Enterprising, *active*, 682
  energetic, 171
  courageous, 861
Entertain, *amuse*, 840
  support, 707
  sociality, 892
  an idea, 451, 484
Entertainment, *repast*, 298
* Entêté, *obstinate*, 606
  prejudiced, 481
Enthral, *subdue*, 749
  delight, 829
Enthrone, *repute*, 873
Enthusiasm, *feeling*, 821
  imagination, 515
  love, 897
  hope, 850, 858
Enthusiast, *game*, 840
  zealot, 606
Enthusiastic, *sensibility*,
  822
  excitability, 825
Enthymeme, *reasoning*, 476
Entice, *motive*, 615
Enticing, *pleasure*, 829

Entire, *whole*, 50
  complete, 52
Entirely, *greatness*, 31
Entitle, *name*, 564
  give a right, 924
Entity, *existence*, 1
Entomb, *inter*, 231, 363
  imprison, 751
* Entourage, *environment*,
  227
  retinue, 746
* Entr'acte, *interval*, 106
Entrails, *interior*, 221
Entrain, *depart*, 293
Entrance, *beginning*, 66
  ingress, 294
  fee, 809
  to enrapture, 824, 829
  to conjure, 992
Entrap, *deceive*, 545
* Entre nous, *concealment*,
  528
Entreat, *request*, 765
* Entrechat, *leap*, 309
Entrée, *ingress*, 294
* Entremet, *food*, 298
Entrench, *defence*, 717
* Entrepôt, *store*, 636
  mart, 799
* Entrepreneur, *organizer*,
  626
* Entresol, *interjacence*, 228
Entrust, *consign*, 784
  lend, 787
  charge with, 755
Entry, *ingress*, 294
  beginning, 66
  record, 551
  evidence, 467
Entwine, *join*, 43
  intersect, 219
  convolve, 248
Enumerate, *number*, 85
Enunciate, *publish*, 531
  inform, 527
  affirm, 535
  voice, 580
Envelop, *invest*, 225
  conceal, 528
Envelope, *covering*, 222
  enclosure, 232
Envenom, *poison*, 649
  deprave, 659
  exasperate, 835, 898
Environs, *nearness*, 197
  circumjacence, 227
Envisage, *view*, 441
  confront, 234
  intuition, 477
Envoy, *messenger*, 534
  postscript, 39
Envy, *jealousy*, 921

Enwrap, *invest*, 225
Eolith, *oldness*, 124
Epaulet, *badge*, 550
  decoration, 877
  ornament, 847
* Éperdu, *excited*, 824
Ephemeral, *transient*, 111
  changeable 149
Ephemeris, *calendar*, 114
  record, 551
  book, 593
Epic, *poem*, 597
Epicedium, *interment*, 363
Epicene, *exceptional*, 83
  multiform, 81
Epicure, *sensual*, 954
  glutton, 957
  fastidious, 868
Epicycle, *circularity*, 247
Epicycloid, *circularity*, 247
Epidemic, *disease*, 655
  dispersed, 73
  general, 78
Epidermis, *covering*, 222
Epidiascope, *spectacle*, 448
Epigram, *wit*, 842
Epigrammatic, *pithy*, 516
  concise, 572
Epigrammatist, *humorist*,
  844
Epigraph, *indication*, 550
Epilepsy, *convulsion*, 315
Epilogue, *sequel*, 65
  drama, 599
Episcopal, *clergy*, 995
Episode, *event*, 151
  interjacence, 228
  interruption, 70
Episodic, *unrelated*, 10
  style, 573
Epistle, *letter*, 592
Epitaph, *interment*, 363
Epithalamium, *marriage*,
  903
Epithem, *remedy*, 662
Epithet, *nomenclature*, 564
Epitome, *compendium*, 596
  conciseness, 572
  miniature, 193
Epizootic, *insalubrity*, 657
Epoch, *time*, 113
  duration, 106
  period, 114
Epode, *poetry*, 597
Epopee, *poetry*, 597
* Épris, *love*, 897
Equable, *right*, 922
Equal, *equality*, 27
  equitable, 922
Equanimity, *inexcitability*,
  826
Equate, *equality*, 27

Equations, *numeration*, 85
Equator, *middle*, 68
Equerry, *servant*, 746
Equestrian, *traveller*, 268
Equidistant, *middle*, 68
Equilibrium, *equality*, 27
  steadiness, 265
Equip, *dress*, 225
  prepare, 673
Equipage, *vehicle*, 272
  instrument, 633
  materials, 635
Equipoise, *equal*, 27
Equipollent, *equal*, 27
  identical, 13
Equiponderant, *equal*, 27
Equitable, *just*, 922
  fair, 480, 939
  due, 924
Equitation, *journey*, 266
Equity, *justice*, 922
  law, 963
  honour, 939
Equivalence, *equal*, 27
Equivalent, *identity*, 13
  compensation, 30
  synonymous, 516
Equivocal, *dubious*, 475
  double meaning, 520, 961
Equivocate, *pervert*, 477
  prevaricate, 520
Equivoque, *equivocal*, 520
  uncertainty, 475
  impurity, 961
  error, 495
Era, *duration*, 106
  chronology, 114
Eradicate, *destroy*, 162
  extract, 301
Erase, *efface*, 162, 499, 552
Ere, *priority*, 116
Ere long, *earliness*, 132
Erebus, *dark*, 421
  hell, 982
Erect, *raise*, 307
  build, 161
  vertical, 212
Erection, *house*, 189
Erewhile, *preterition*, 122
  priority, 116
Ergatocracy, *rule*, 737
* Ergo, *reasoning*, 476
Ergotism, *reasoning*, 476
Eriometer, *optical*, 445
Erk, *fighter*, 726
Ermine, *badge of authority*
  747
Erode, *destroy*, 162
  injure, 659
Erotic, *amorous*, 897
  impure, 961
Eroticism, *pleasantness*, 829

Err, *in opinion*, 495
  morally, 945
Errand, *commission*, 755
  business, 625
  message, 532
Erratic, *capricious*, 149, 608
  wandering, 264, 279
Erratum, *error*, 495
  misprint, 555
Error, *false opinion*, 495
  failure, 732
  vice, 945
  guilt, 947
Erst, *preterition*, 122
Erubescence, *redness*, 434
Eructate, *eject*, 297
Erudite, *scholar*, 492
Erudition, *knowledge*, 490
Eruption, *egress*, 295
  violence, 173
  disease, 655
Escalade, *mount*, 305
  attack, 716
Escalator, *way*, 627
  lift, 307
Escallop, *convolution*, 248
Escapade, *freak*, 608
  prank, 840
  vagary, 856
Escape, *flight*, 671
  liberate, 750
  evade, 927
  forget, 506
Escarpment, *slope*, 217
Eschatology, *intention*, 620
  end, 67
Escheat, *penalty*, 974
Eschew, *avoid*, 623
  dislike, 867
Escort, *to accompany*, 88
  safeguard, 664
  keeper, 753
Escritoire, *desk*, 191
Esculent, *food*, 298
Escutcheon, *indication*, 550
Esoteric, *private*, 79
  concealed, 528
Espalier, *agriculture*, 371
Especial, *private*, 79
Esperanto, *language*, 560
Espial, *vision*, 441
* Espièglerie, *wit*, 842
Espionage, *inquiry*, 461
Esplanade, *flat*, 213
  plain, 344
Espousal, *marriage*, 903
* Esprit, *shrewdness*, 498
  wit, 842
* Esprit de corps, *party*, 712
  misjudgment, 781
  belief, 484
  sociality, 892

Exhaust, *drain*, 638, 789
  fatigue, 688
  weaken, 160
  misemploy, 679
  squander, 818
  complete, 52, 729
  tube, 351
Exhaustless, *infinite*, 105
  plentiful, 639
Exhibit, *show*, 525
  display, 882
Exhilarate, *cheer*, 836
Exhort, *advise*, 695
  induce, 615
  preach, 998
Exhume, *interment*, 363
  past, 122
Exigency, *crisis*, 8
  chance, 621
  difficulty, 704
  requirement, 630
  need, 865
  dearth, 640
Exigent, *severe*, 640
  exacting, 832
Exiguous, *little*, 193
Exile, *displace*, 185
  send out, 297
  seclude, 893
  punish, 972
Exility, *thinness*, 203
Existence, *being*, 1
  life, 359
  thing, 3
  in time, 118
  in space, 186
Exit, *departure*, 293
  egress, 295
  escape, 671
Exodus, *departure*, 293
  egress, 295
Exogamy, *marriage*, 903
Exonerate, *exempt*, 927
  vindicate, 937
  forgive, 918
  acquit, 970
  disburden, 705
  absolve, 760
  release, 756
Exorbitant, *enormous*, 31
  redundant, 641
  dear, 814
Exorcise, *conjure*, 992
Exorcism, *theology*, 993
Exorcist, *heterodoxy*, 994
Exordium, *beginning*, 66
Exosmosis, *passage*, 302
Exoteric, *disclosed*, 531
  public, 529
Exotic, *alien*, 10
  exceptional, 83
Expand, *swell*, 194

Expand, *increase*, 35
  in breadth, 202
  rarefy, 322
  in writing, 573
Expanse, *space*, 180, 202
  size, 192
Expansion, *space*, 180
Expatiate, *in writing*, 573
  in discourse, 582, 584
Expatriate, *deport*, 295
  displace, 185
  exclude, 55, 893
Expect, *look for*, 121, 507
  not wonder, 871
  hope, 858
Expectorant, *remedy*, 662
Expectorate, *eject*, 296
Expedience, *utility*, 646
Expedient, *means*, 632
  substitute, 634
  plan, 626
Expedite, *accelerate*, 274
  earliness, 132
  aid, 707
Expedition, *speed*, 274
  activity, 682
  warfare, 722
  march, 266
Expel, *displace*, 185
  eject, 297
  drive from, 289
  punish, 972
Expend, *use*, 677
  waste, 638
  pay, 809
Expense, *price*, 812
Expensive, *dear*, 814
Experience, *knowledge*, 490
  undergo, 821
  event, 151
Experienced, *skilled*, 698
Experiment, *trial*, 463
  endeavour, 675
* Experimentum crucis,
  demonstration, 478
Expert, *skill*, 698
  adept, 700
* Experto crede, *knowledge*,
  490
Expiate, *atonement*, 952
Expire, *death*, 360
  end, 67
  breathe out, 349
Explain, *expound*, 522
  inform, 527
  teach, 537
  answer, 462
Explain away, *misinterpret*,
  523
Expletive, *redundance*, 573,
  641
  malediction, 908

Explication, *interpret*, 522
Explicit, *distinct*, 516, 518,
  535
Explode, *burst*, 173
  sound, 406
  refute, 479
  passion, 825
  anger, 900
Exploit, *action*, 680
  to use, 677
Explore, *investigate*, 461
  experiment, 463
Explosion, *see* Explode
Exponent, *index*, 550
  numerical, 84
  interpreter, 522
Export, *transfer*, 270
  send out, 297
  thing sent, 295
* Exposé, *account*, 596
  disclosure, 529
Expose, *show*, 525
  interpret, 522
  confute, 479
  denude, 226
  endanger, 665
Exposition, *answer*, 462
  disclosure, 529
Expositor, *interpreter*, 524
  teacher, 540
Expository, *information*,
  527, 595
Expostulate, *deprecate*, 766
  reprehend, 932
  dissuade, 616
  advise, 695
Exposure, *disclosure*, 529
Exposure meter, *optical instrument*, 445
Exposure to, *liability*, 177
Expound, *interpret*, 522
  teach, 537
  answer, 462
Expounder, *interpreter*, 524
Express, *voluntary*, 600
  intentional, 620
  declare, 525
  mean, 516
  inform, 527
  phrase, 566
  intelligible, 518
  name, 564
  squeeze out, 301
  rapid, 274
Expression, *aspect*, 448
Expressive, *style*, 574
Exprobation, *disapproval*,
  932
Exprobration, *accusation*,
  938
Expropriate, *take*, 789
Expulsion, *see* Expel

Falsify, *misinterpret*, 523
  accounts, 811
  deceive, 495
  lie, 544
Falstaffian, *fat*, 192
Falter, *stammer*, 583
  hesitate, 605
  demur, 603
  slowness, 275
Fame, *renown*, 873
  rumour, 531
  news, 532
Familiar, *common*, 82
  habit, 613
  known, 490
  friendly, 888
  affable, 894, 892
  spirit, 979
Family, *class* 75
  consanguinity, 11
  paternity, 166
  posterity, 167
Famine, *insufficiency*, 640
Famished, *fasting*, 956
Famous, *repute*, 873
  greatness, 31
Fan, *blow*, 349
  excite, 615
  enthusiast, 840, 865
  frequenter 136
Fanatic, *extravagant*, 515
Fanatical, *feeling*, 821
Fanaticism, *folly*, 499
  obstinacy, 606
  religious, 984A
Fanciful, *capricious*, 608
  imaginative, 515
  mistaken, 495
  unreal, 2
Fancy, *think*, 451
  believe, 484
  wit, 842
  idea, 453
  suppose, 514
  imagine, 515
  caprice, 608
  choice, 609
  desire, 865
  like, 394
  love, 897
  pugilism, 726
Fandango, *dance*, 840
Fane, *temple*, 1000
Fanfare, *loudness*, 404
  ostentation, 882
Fanfaronade, *boasting*, 884
Fang, *bane*, 663
Fanlight, *opening*, 260
Fantasia, *music*, 415
  imagination, 515
Fantastic, *odd*, 83
  imaginary, 515

Fantastic, *capricious*, 608
  ridiculous, 853
Fantasy, *caprice*, 608
  imagination, 515
  idea, 453
* Fantoccini, *marionettes*,
          554, 599
Far, *distant*, 196
Far-fetched, *irrelation*, 10
  irrelevant, 24
  irrational, 477
  obscure, 519
Far from it, *dissimilarity*, 18
Far-seeing, *foresight*, 510
Farce, *drama*, 599
  ridiculous, 856
* Farceur, *humorist*, 844
Farcical, *ridiculous*, 856
  witty, 842
  trifling, 643
Fardel, *assemblage*, 72
Fare, *circumstance*, 8
  event, 151
  to eat, 296
  food, 298
  price, 812
Farewell, *departure*, 293
Farm, *house*, 189
  property, 780
  to rent, 788, 795
Farrago, *mixture*, 41
  confusion, 59
Farthing, *coin*, 800
  worthless, 643
Farthingale, *dress*, 225
Fasces, *sceptre*, 747
Fascia, *band*, 205
  circle, 247
Fascicle, *assemblage*, 72
Fascinate, *please*, 829
  excite, 824, 825
  astonish, 870
  love, 897
  conjure, 992
Fascination, *spell*, 993
  motive, 615
  occult arts, 992
Fash, *worry*, 830
Fashion, *form*, 144, 240
  custom, 613
  mould, 140
  mode, 627, 852
  nobility, 875
Fast, *rapid*, 274
  steadfast, 150
  stuck, 265
  joined, 43
  dissolute, 954
  not to eat, 640, 956
Fast and loose, *false*, 544
  changeful, 607

Fasten, *join*, 45, 214
  fix, 150
  restrain, 751
Fastener, *hanging*, 214
Fastening, *vinculum*, 45
Fastidious, *dainty*, 868
  squeamish, 932
Fasting, *abstinence*, 956
  atonement, 952
  insufficient 640
Fastness, *asylum*, 666
  defence, 717
Fat, *oleaginous*, 356
  unctuous, 355
  broad, 202
  big, 192
Fat-head, *fool*, 501
Fat-witted, *folly*, 499
* Fata morgana, *phantasm*,
          4
  dim sight, 443
  imagination, 515
Fatal, *lethal*, 361
  pernicious, 649
Fatalism, *destiny*, 152
  necessity, 601
Fatality, *killing*, 361
Fate, *necessity*, 601
  chance, 152, 621
  end, 67, 360
Father, *paternity*, 166
  priest, 996
  theologian, 983
Father upon, *attribute*, 155
Fatherland, *home*, 189
Fatherless,*unsustained*,160
Fathom, *measure*, 466
  investigate, 461
  answer, 462
Fathomless, *depth*, 208
Fatidical, *prediction*, 511
Fatigue, *lassitude*, 688
  weariness, 841
* Fatras,*unimportance*,643
Fatten on, *feeding*, 296
Fatuity, *folly*, 499
* Faubourg, *suburb*, 227
Fauces, *beginning*, 66
Faucet, *opening*, 260
  channel, 350
  outlet, 295
Faugh! *dislike*, 867
Fault, *imperfection*, 651
  blemish, 848
  break, 70
  vice, 945
  guilt, 947
  error, 495
  failure, 732
  ignorance, 491
Faultless, *perfect*, 650
  innocent, 946

Fauna, *animal*, 366
* Faute de mieux, *shift*, 147
  626
* Fauteuil, *support*, 215
* Faux pas, *failure*, 732
  error, 495
  vice, 945
Favour, *aid*, 707
  permit, 760
  friendship, 888
  partiality, 923
  gift, 784
  letter, 592
  to resemble, 17
Favourable, *good*, 648
  willing, 602
  friendly, 707, 888
  co-operating, 709
Favourite, *pleasing*, 829
  beloved, 897, 899
Favouritism, *wrong*, 923
Fawn, *colour*, 433
  cringe, 886
  flatter, 933
Fay, *fairy*, 979
Faze, *worry*, 830
  discompose, 458
  perplex, 704
Fealty, *duty*, 926
  respect, 928
  obedience, 743
Fear, *fear*, 860
  cowardice, 862
Fearful, *great*, 31
Fearless, *hopeful*, 858
  courageous, 861
Feasible, *possible*, 470
  easy, 705
Feast, *repast*, 298
  to devour, 296
  gluttony, 957
  revel, 840
  enjoyment, 827
  celebration, 883
  anniversary, 138
Feast on, *enjoy*, 377
Feat, *action*, 680
Feather, *tuft*, 256
  lightness, 320
  trifle, 643
  class, 75
  ornament, 847
  decoration, 877
Feather-bed, *softness*, 324
Feathery, *roughness*, 256
Feature, *character*, 5
  form, 240
  appearance, 448
  lineament, 550
  component, 56
  to resemble, 17
  cinema, 599A

Febrifuge, *remedy*, 662
* Fecit, *painting*, 556
Feckless, *feeble*, 160
  improvident, 674
  useless, 645
Feculence, *uncleanness*, 653
Fecund, *productive*, 168
Fecundation, *production*,
  161
Fed up, *weariness*, 841
  dislike, 867
  satiety, 869
Federation, *co-operation*,
  709
  party, 712
Fee, *expenditure*, 795, 809
Fee simple, *property*, 780
Feeble, *weak*, 160
  imperfect, 651
  scanty, 32
  silly, 477
  style, 575
Feeble-minded, *foolish*, 499
  irresolute, 605
Feed, *eat*, 296
  supply, 637
  meal, 298
Feel, *touch*, 379
  sensibility, 375
  moral, 821
Feel for, *seek*, 461
  sympathize, 914
Feeler, *inquiry*, 461
Feet, *journey*, 266
Feign, *falsehood*, 544
Feint, *deception*, 545
Felicitate, *congratulate*, 896
Felicitous, *expedient*, 646
  favourable, 648
  skilful, 698
  successful, 731
  happy, 827
  elegant, 578
  apt, 23
Felicity, *happiness*, 827
  prosperity, 734
  skill, 698
Feline, *stealthy*, 528
  sly, 702
Fell, *mountain*, 206
  cut down, 308
  knock down, 213
  dire, 162
  wicked, 907
Fellah, *commonalty*, 876
Fellow, *similar*, 17
  equal, 27
  companion, 88
  man, 373
  dual, 89
Fellow creature, *man*, 372,
  373

Fellow-feeling, *love*, 897
  friendship, 888
  sympathy, 906, 914
Fellowship, *sociality*, 892
  partnership, 712
  friendship, 888
Felo-de-se, *killing*, 361
Felon, *sinner*, 949
Felonious, *vice*, 945
Felony, *guilt*, 947
Felt, *matted*, 219
Felucca, *ship*, 273
Female, *woman*, 374
Feminality, *feebleness*, 160
Feminine, *woman*, 374
Feminism, *rights*, 924
* Femme couverte, *mar-
  riage*, 903
* Femme de chambre, *ser-
  vant*, 746
Fen, *marsh*, 345
Fence, *circumscribe*, 231
  enclose, 232
  defence, 717
  fight, 720, 722
  safety, 664
  refuge, 666
  prison, 752
  to evade, 544
Fencible, *combatant*, 726
Fend, *defence*, 717
  provision, 637
Fenestrated, *windowed*,
  260
Feoff, *property*, 780
Ferine, *malevolence*, 907
Ferment, *disorder*, 59
  energy, 171
  violence, 173
  agitation, 315
  effervesce, 353
Fern, *plant*, 367
Ferocity, *brutality*, 907
  violence, 173
Ferret, *tape*, 45
Ferret out, *inquiry*, 461
  discover, 480A
Ferry, *transference*, 270
  way, 627
Fertile, *productive*, 168
  abundant, 639
Ferule, *scourge*, 975
Fervent, *devout*, 990
Fervour, *heat*, 382
  animation, 821
  desire, 865
  love, 897
Fester, *disease*, 655
  corruption, 653
* Festina lente, *haste*, 684
Festival, *celebration*, 883
  anniversary, 138

Float, *sound*, 405
  vehicle, 272
Floater, *error*, 495, 732
  solecism, 568
Flocculent, *soft*, 324
  pulverulent, 330
Flock, *herd*, 366
  assemblage, 72, 102
  laity, 997
Flog, *punishment*, 972
  steal, 791
Flong, *engraving*, 558
Flood, *water*, 348
  abundance, 639
  multitude, 72
  superfluity, 641
  increase, 35
  of light, 420
Floodgate, *conduit*, 350
Floor, *base*, 221
  level, 23
  horizontal, 213
  support, 215
  to puzzle, 485, 704
  to overthrow, 731
Floosy, *girl*, 374
Flop, *flutter*, 315
  failure, 732
Flora, *plant*, 367, 379
Florid, *colour*, 428
  red, 434
  health, 654
  style, 577
Flotilla, *ship*, 273
Flotsam, *fragments*, 51
  little, 643
Flounce, *quick motion*, 274
  agitation, 315
  trimming, 230
  fold, 258
Flounder, *toss*, 315
  waver, 314
  mistake, 495
  to blunder, 499, 699, 732
  struggle, 704
Flourish, *brandish*, 314
  succeed, 731, 734
  display, 873, 882
  boast, 884
  exaggerate, 549
  of speech, 577, 582
Flout, *mock*, 856, 929
  sneer, 929
Flow, *stream*, 347
  motion, 264
  course, 109
  result from, 154
Flow out, *egress*, 295
Flow over, *run over*, 348
  abound, 641
Flower, *plant*, 367
  beauty, 845

Flower, *perfection*, 648, 650
  prosper, 734
  produce, 161
  of life, 127
  of speech, 577
  honour, 873
Flowing, *style*, 573
  sound, 405
  abundant, 639
Fluctuate, *oscillate*, 314
  wavering, 605
Flue, *air-pipe*, 351
  egress, 295
  opening, 260
  down, 320
  dross, 643, 653
Fluent, *speech*, 584
  style, 573
  flowing, 348
  skilful, 698
Fluff, *lightness*, 320
Fluid, *liquidity*, 333
Fluke, *angularity*, 244
  chance, 621
Flummery, *vain*, 643
  flattery, 933
  absurd, 497
Flummox, *bewilder*, 458
Flunk, *break down*, 158
Flunkey, *lackey*, 746
  toady, 886
  flatterer, 935
Fluorescence, *light*, 420
Flurry, *hurry*, 684
  discompose, 458
  agitation, 821, 825
Flush, *flat*, 251
  flood, 348
  heat, 382
  light, 420
  redness, 434
  abundance, 639
  feeling, 821
  passion, 825
  series, 69
  flock, 72
  rich, 803
  in liquor, 959
Flushed, *elated*, 836, 884
  vain, 880
  proud, 878
Fluster, *excitement*, 824
  fuss, 682
  discompose, 458
Flustered, *tipsy*, 959
Flute, *musical*, 417
Fluted, *furrow*, 259
Flutter, *move*, 315
  fear, 860
  feeling, 821, 824, 825
Fluviatile, *river*, 348
Flux, *flow*, 109, 348

Flux, *excretion*, 299
  motion, 264
  oscillation, 314
  changes, 140
Fly, *depart*, 293
  take wing, 287
  speed, 274
  escape, 671
  recede, 287
  shun, 623
  run away, 862
  lose colour, 429
  minute, 193
  time, 109, 111
  burst, 173, 328
  vehicle, 272
  clever, 498
  cunning, 702
Fly at, *attack*, 716
Fly back, *recoil*, 277
  elastic, 325
Fly-down, *unclean*, 653
Fly-leaf, *insertion*, 228
  book, 593
Fly out, *burst*, 173
  passion, 825
  anger, 900
Fly-boat, *ship*, 273
Flying boat, *aircraft*, 273A
Flying bomb, *arms*, 727
Flying fortress, *aircraft*, 273A
Flying wing, *aircraft*, 273A
Flyover, *way*, 627
Flyte, *curse*, 908
Flywheel, *instrument*, 633
  rotation, 312
Foal, *young*, 129
  carrier, 271
Foam, *spray*, 353
  passion, 173, 900
Fob, *pocket*, 191
  to cheat, 545
  evade, 773
Focus, *reunion*, 74
  centre, 223
Fodder, *food*, 298
Foe, *antagonist*, 710
  enemy, 891
Foetid, see Fetid
Foetus, *infant*, 129
Fog, *cloud*, 353
  dimness, 422
Foggy, *obscure*, 447
  shaded, 426
Fogy, *veteran*, 130
* Föhn, *wind*, 349
Foible, *vice*, 945
Foil, *contrast*, 14
  success, 731
Foiled, *failure*, 732
Foist in, *insert*, 228, 300

Forge, *produce*, 161
 furnace, 386
 workshop, 691
 trump up, 544
Forge ahead, *advance*, 282
Forgery, *untruth*, 546
 imitation, 19
Forget, *oblivion*, 506
Forgive, *forgiveness*, 918
Forgo, *relinquish*, 624, 782
 renounce, 757
Forgotten, *unremembered*,
 506
 ingratitude, 917
Fork, *angularity*, 244
 bisection, 91
Fork out, *give*, 784
 expend, 809
Forlorn, *abandoned*, 893
 dejected, 837
 woebegone, 828
Forlorn hope, *hopeless*, 859
 danger, 665
Form, *shape*, 240
 state, 7
 arrange, 60
 rule, 80
 to make up, 54
 produce, 161
 educate, 537
 habituate, 613
 bench, 215
 part, 569
 fashion, 852
 etiquette, 882
 law, 963
 rite, 998
 fours, 58
 manner, 627
 beauty, 845
 likeness, 21
 pupils, 541
Formal, *regular*, 82
 affected, 855
 positive, 535
Formalism, *hypocrisy*, 988
Formality, *ceremony*, 852
 parade, 882
 law, 963
Format, *style*, 7
Formation, *production*, 161
 shape, 240
Formed of, *composition*, 54
Former, *in order*, 62
 in time, 122
Formication, *itching*, 380
Formidable, *fear*, 860
 difficult, 704
 great, 31
Formless, *amorphism*, 241
Formula, *rule*, 80
 precept, 697

Formula, *law*, 963
 number, 84
Fornication, *impurity*, 961
Fornicator, *libertine*, 962
Forsake, *relinquish*, 624
Forsooth, *truth*, 494
Forswear, *renounce*, 624
 retract, 607
 refuse, 764
 perjure, 544, 940
 violate, 927
Fort, *defence*, 717
 refuge, 666
Forte, *excellence*, 698
* Forte, *loudness*, 404
Forth, *progression*, 282
Forthcoming, *futurity*, 121,
 673
Forthwith, *transient*, 111
Fortification, *defence*, 717
 refuge, 666
Fortify, *strength*, 159
Fortitude, *courage*, 861
 endurance, 826
Fortnight, *period*, 108, 138
Fortress, *defence*, 716
 prison, 752
Fortuitous, *chance*, 156,
 621
Fortunate, *opportune*, 134
 prosperous, 734
Fortune, *chance*, 156
 accident, 621
 wealth, 803
Fortune-teller, *oracle*, 513
Fortune-telling, *prediction*,
 511
Forum, *tribunal*, 966
 school, 542
Forward, *early*, 132
 to advance, 282
 to help, 707
 active, 682
 willing, 602
 vain, 880
 impertinent, 885
Fosse, *furrow*, 259
 gap, 198
 defence, 717
 enclosure, 232
Fossick, *inquiry*, 461
Fossil, *antiquated*, 851
 old, 124
 bore, 841
Foster, *aid*, 707
Fou, *drunken*, 959
Foul, *bad*, 649
 corrupt, 653
 odour, 401
 offensive, 830
 ugly, 846
 vicious, 945

Foul-mouthed, *malevolent*,
 907
Foul-tongued, *scurrilous*,
 934
Found, *cause*, 153
 prepare, 673
Foundation, *base*, 211
 support, 215
Founder, *originator*, 164
 sink, 310, 732
Foundling, *outcast*, 893
Fount, *origin*, 153
 spring, 348
 type, 591
Fountain, *cause*, 153
 river, 348
 store, 636
Fountain-pen, *writing*, 590
Four, *number*, 95
Four-square, *number*, 95
Fourfold, *number*, 96
Fourscore, *number*, 98
Fourth, *number*, 97
Fowl, *animal*, 366
Fowling-piece, *arms*, 727
Fox, *cunning*, 702
Fox-trot, *dance*, 840
Foxhole, *refuge*, 666
 defence, 717
Foxhound, *chase*, 622
Foyer, *room*, 191
Fracas, *contention*, 720
 brawl, 713
Fraction, *part*, 51
 numerical, 84
Fractious, *irascibility*, 901
Fracture, *disjunction*, 44
 discontinuity, 70, 198
 to break, 328
Fragile, *brittle*, 328
 frail, 149, 160
Fragment, *part*, 51
Fragrant, *fragrant*, 400
'Fraid-cat, *coward*, 862
Frail, *brittle*, 328
 mutable, 149
 weak, 160
 irresolute, 605
 imperfect, 651
 unchaste, 961
 failing, 945
Frame, *condition*, 7
 support, 215
 texture, 329
 form, 240
 substance, 316
 to construct, 161
 border, 230
* Franc-tireur, *fighter*, 726
Franchise, *right*, 924
 freedom, 748
 exemption, 927

Ground, *arena*, 728
  teach, 537
Ground swell, *surge*, 348
  agitation, 315
Grounded, *knowing*, 490
  wrecked, 732
Groundless, *erroneous*, 495
  sophistical, 477
Groundling, *commonalty*,
                                876
Grounds, *lees*, 653
Groundwork, *basis*, 211
  support, 215
  cause, 153
  precursor, 64
  preparation, 673
Group, *cluster*, 72
  troop, 726
  to marshal, 58
Group-captain, *master*, 745
Grouse, *grumble*, 832, 839
Grout, *vinculum*, 45
Grove, *wood*, 367
  house, 189
Grovel, *move slowly*, 275
  be low, 207
  cringe, 886
  base, 940
Grow, *increase*, 35
  expand, 194
Grow from, *effect*, 154
Growl, *cry*, 412
  complain, 839
  threaten, 909
  be rude, 895
  anger, 900
Growler, *vehicle*, 272
Growth, *in degree*, 35
  in size, 194
Groyne, *refuge*, 666
Grub, *little*, 193
  food, 298
Grub up, *extract*, 301
  destroy, 162
  discover, 480A
Grudge, *hate*, 898
  stingy, 640, 819
  unwilling, 603
Gruelling, *punishment*, 972
Gruesome, *ugly*, 846
Gruff, *morose*, 895
  sound, 410
Grumble, *sound*, 411
  complain, 832, 839
Grumous, *dense*, 321
  pulpy, 354
Grumpy, *discourteous*, 895
  bad-tempered, 901
Grundyism, *prudery*, 855
Grunt, *cry*, 412
  complain, 839
Guano, *manure*, 653

Guarantee, *security*, 771
  evidence, 467
  promise, 768
Guard, *defend*, 717
  safety, 664
Guard-room, *prison*, 752
Guarded, *circumspect*, 459
  conditional, 770
Guardian, *safety*, 664, 717
  keeper, 753
Guardless, *danger*, 665
Guardsman, *combatant*, 726
Gubernatorial, *directing*,
                                693
  authority, 737
Gudgeon, *dupe*, 547
Guerdon, *reward*, 973
Guerrilla, *combatant*, 726
Guess, *suppose*, 514
Guest, *friend*, 890
  arrival, 292
* Guet-apens, *untruth*, 546
  ambush, 530
Guffaw, *laughter*, 834
Guggle, *see* Gurgle
Guide, *direct*, 693
  director, 694
  advice, 695
  teach, 537
  teacher, 540
  road-book, 266
Guide-post, *indicator*, 550
  warning, 668
Guideless, *danger*, 665
Guild, *corporation*, 712
  tribunal, 966
  partnership, 797
Guildhall, *mart*, 799
Guile, *cunning*, 702
  deceit, 545
Guileless, *artless*, 703
  sincere, 543
Guillotine, *engine*, 975
  to decapitate, 972
Guilt, *crime*, 947
  vice, 945
Guiltless, *innocence*, 946
* Guindé, *conciseness*, 572
Guise, *state*, 7
  appearance, 448
  manner, 627
  plea, 617
Guiser, *the drama*, 599
Guitar, *music*, 417
Gulch, *gap*, 198
Gules, *redness*, 434
Gulf, *sea*, 343
  depth, 208
Gull, *dupe*, 547
  credulous, 486
Gullet, *throat*, 260
  rivulet, 348

Gullible, *credulity*, 486
Gully, *conduit*, 350
  opening, 260
  hollow, 252
  ravine, 198
Gulosity, *gluttony*, 957
Gulp, *swallow*, 297
  believe, 484
Gum, *fastening*, 45
  coherence, 46
  semiliquid, 352
Gum-boot, *dress*, 225
Gumption, *capacity*, 498
Gumshoe, *prowl*, 528
Gun, *arms*, 727
  fighter, 726
Gun-cotton, *arms*, 727
Gunboat, *ship*, 273
Gunman, *bad man*, 949
Gunner, *combatant*, 726
Gurgitation, *rotation*, 312
Gurgle, *sound*, 405, 408
  bubble, 353
Gurkha, *soldier*, 726
Guru, *priest*, 996
Gush, *flow*, 295
  flood, 348
  feeling, 821
  affectation, 855
Gusset, *angularity*, 244
Gust, *wind*, 349
  physical taste, 390
  enjoyment, 826
  moral taste, 850
Gustatory, *taste*, 390
Gusto, *relish*, 827
  taste, 850
Gut, *opening*, 260
  to sack, 789
  vitals, 221
Guts, *courage*, 861
  resolution, 604
Gutter, *conduit*, 350
  groove, 259
Guttersnipe, *commonalty*,
                                876
  vulgarity, 851
Guttle, *devour*, 296
Guttural, *stammer*, 583
  letter, 561
Guy, *rope*, 45
  ugliness, 846
  man, 373
  to ridicule, 842, 856
  deride, 929
Guzzle, *drink*, 296
  tipple, 959
  gluttony, 957
Gymkhana, *contention*, 720
Gymnasium, *school*, 542
  training, 673
Gymnast, *strength*, 159

Gymnastic, *exertion*, 686
  contention, 720
  teaching, 537
Gymnosophist, *heathen*,
        984
  temperance, 953
Gynaecocracy, *rule*, 737
Gynaecology, *remedy*, 662
Gyp, *servant*, 746
Gypsy, *see* Gipsy
Gyration, *rotation*, 312
Gyre, *rotation*, 312
Gyroscope, *rotation*, 312
Gyve, *chain*, 45
  shackle, 752

H

Haberdashery, *dress*, 225
Habergeon, *defence*, 717
Habiliment, *dress*, 225
Habilitation, *skill*, 698
Habit, *intrinsic*, 5
  custom, 613
  coat, 225
Habitat, *abode*, 189
Habitation, *abode*, 189
  location, 184
Habitual, *regular*, 82, 613
Habituate, *accustom*, 613
  train, 673
Habitude, *state*, 7
  relation, 9
  habit, 613
* Habitué, *guest*, 891
  frequenter, 136
* Hacienda, *property*, 780
Hack, *cut*, 44
  shorten, 201
  horse, 271
  drudge, 690
  writer, 590
Hackle, *cut*, 44
Hackneyed, *regular*, 82
  trite, 496
  habitual, 613
  experienced, 698
Hades, *hell*, 982
Hadji, *clergy*, 996
  pilgrim, 268
Haecceity, *speciality*, 79
Haemorrhage, *excretion*,
        299
Haft, *instrument*, 633
Hag, *ugly*, 846
  veteran, 130
  wretch, 913
  bad woman, 949
Haggard, *ugly*, 846
  wild, 824
  insane, 503

Haggle, *bargain*, 769, 794
Hagiography, *theology*, 983
Ha-ha, *ditch*, 198
  defence, 717
Haik, *dress*, 225
Hail, *call*, 586
  ice, 383
Hair, *thread*, 45
  filament, 205
  roughness, 256
Hair-oil, *ornament*, 847
Hair-raising, *fear*, 860
Hair's breadth, *thin*, 203
Halberd, *arms*, 727
Halberdier, *combatant*, 726
Halcyon, *prosperous*,
        734, 829
  joyful, 827
  calm, 174
Hale, *health*, 654
Half, *bisection*, 91
Half a dozen, *six*, 98
Half and half, *mixture*, 41
Half-baked, *incomplete*, 53
  witless, 499
Half-blood, *unconformity*,
        83
Half-breed, *unconformity*,
        83
Half-caste, *mixture*, 41
  unconformity, 83
Half-hearted, *indifferent*,
        866
  irresolute, 605
  timorous, 862
Half-moon, *curvature*, 245
Half-pint, *little*, 193
Half-seas-over, *drunk*, 959
Half-track, *vehicle*, 272
Half-way, *middle*, 68
Half-wit, *fool*, 501
Half-witted, *folly*, 499
Hall, *chamber*, 189
  receptacle, 191
  mart, 799
Hall-marked, *genuine*, 494
Hallelujah, *worship*, 990
Hallo! *call*, 586
  wonder, 870
  arrival, 292
Halloo, *cry*, 411
Hallow, *sanctify*, 987
Hallowed, *venerated*, 928
  Deity, 976
Hallucination, *error*, 495
  delusion, 503
Halo, *light*, 420
  glory, 873
Halt, *stop*, 142, 265
  flag, 655
  rest, 685, 687
  limp, 275

Halter, *rope*, 45
  fetter, 752
  punishment, 975
Halting, *lame*, 160
Halve, *bisect*, 91
Halyard, *rope*, 45
Hamadryad, *nymph*, 979
Hamlet, *abode*, 189
* Hammal, *carrier*, 271
Hammam, *furnace*, 386
Hammer, *to knock*, 276
  instrument, 633
  auction, 796
  repetition, 104
  bankrupt, 808
Hammer at, *thought*, 583
  action, 682
Hammock, *support*, 215
Hamper, *basket*, 191
  obstruct, 706
Hamstring, *injure*, 649
  weaken, 160
  incapacitate, 158
Hand, *instrument*, 633
  indicator, 550
  agent, 690
  side, 236
  writing, 590
  to give, 784
  agency, 170
Hand-barrow, *vehicle*, 272
Hand-gallop, *velocity*, 274
Hand in hand, *accompaniment*, 88
Hand over, *transfer*, 270
Handbook, *advice*, 695
Handcuff, *tie together*, 43
  manacle, 751, 752
Handfast, *marriage*, 903
Handful, *quantity*, 25, 103
  smallness, 32
Handicap, *inequality*, 28
  disadvantage, 651
Handicraft, *action*, 680
Handicraftsman, *agent*, 690
Handiwork, *action*, 680
  effect, 154
Handkerchief, *dress*, 225
  clean, 652
Handle, *instrument*, 633
  plea, 617
  touch, 379
  use, 677
  describe, 594
  dissert, 595
  work, 680
Handling, *treatment*, 692
Handmaid, *servant*, 746
  instrumentality, 631
Hands off! *resist*, 719
  prohibit, 761
Handsel, *security*, 771

Heteroclite, *incongruity,* 83
Heterodox, *heresy,* 984A
Heterogeneous, *mixed,* 10,
    15, 41
  multiform, 81
  exceptional, 83
Heteromorphic, *difference,*
    15
Heuristic, *inquiry,* 461
Hew, *cut,* 44
  shorten, 201
  fashion, 240
Hexachord, *melody,* 413
Hexad, *six,* 98
Hexagon, *numbers,* 98
  angularity, 244
Hexahedron, *angularity,*
    244
  six, 98
Hey, *attention,* 547
  accost, 586
Heyday, *wonder,* 870
  success, 731
  exultation, 836, 838
  youth, 127
Hiatus, *interval,* 198
  opening, 260
  unsubstantiality, 4
  discontinuity, 70
Hibernal, *cold,* 383
Hibernate, *sleep,* 683
Hibernicism, *absurdity,* 497
* Hic jacet, *burial,* 363
Hiccup, *cough,* 349
Hick, *peasant,* 876
Hid, *invisible,* 447
  concealed, 528
Hidalgo, *master,* 875
Hide, *conceal,* 528
  ambush, 530
  skin, 222
Hide-bound, *intolerant,* 481
  obstinate, 606
  strait-laced, 751
Hideous, *ugly,* 846
Hiding-place, *refuge,* 666
  ambush, 530
Hie, *go,* 264, 266, 274
Hiemal, *cold,* 383
  evening, 126
Hierarchy, *churchdom,* 995
  order, 58
Hieroglyphic, *letter,* 561
  writing, 590
  representation, 554
  unintelligible, 519
Hierogram, *revelation,* 985
Hierography, *theology,* 983
Hierophant, *churchman,*
    996
Higgle, *chaffer,* 794
  bargain, 769

Higgledy-piggledy, *dis-*
  order, 59
Higgler, *merchant,* 797
High, *lofty,* 206
  pungent, 392
  stinking, 401
  proud, 878
  magnanimous, 942
  drunk, 959
High-born, *master,* 875
High-brow, *scholar,* 492
  sage, 500
High-falutin, *bombast,* 549
  affected, 855
  florid, 577
High-flier, *imagination,* 515
  pride, 878
High-flown, *proud,* 878, 880
  insolent, 885
  exaggerated, 549
High-handed, *insolent,* 885
High-hat, *affected,* 855
High jinks, *festivity,* 840
High life, *fashion,* 852
  nobility, 875
High-mettled, *spirited,* 861
  proud, 878
High-minded, *proud,* 878
  generous, 942
  honourable, 940
High-powered, *power,* 157
High-priced, *dear,* 814
High-seasoned, *pungent,* 932
  obscene, 961
High-spirited, *brave,* 861
High-strung, *excitable,* 825
High-wrought, *perfect,* 650
  finished, 729
  excited, 825
Highball, *intoxicant,* 959
Higher, *superiority,* 33
Highland, *land,* 342
Highly, *great,* 31
Highness, *title,* 877
  prince, 745
Hight, *nomenclature,* 564
Highway, *road,* 627
Highwayman, *thief,* 792
Hijack, *rob,* 791, 792
Hike, *journey,* 266
Hiker, *traveller,* 268
Hilarity, *cheerfulness,* 836
Hill, *height,* 206
Hillock, *height,* 206
Hilt, *instrument,* 633
Hind, *back,* 235
  clown, 876
Hinder, *back,* 235
  end, 67
  to impede, 179
  obstruct, 706
  prohibit, 761

Hindrance, *obstruction,* 706
Hindsight, *thought,* 451
  memory, 505
Hinduism, *religions,* 984
Hinge, *depend upon,* 154
  cause, 153; *rotate,* 312
  fastening, 43, 45
Hinny, *beast of burden,* 271
Hint, *suggest,* 505
  inform, 527
  suppose, 514
Hinterland, *interior,* 221
Hip, *side,* 236
Hipped, *dejection,* 837
Hippocentaur, *oddity,* 83
Hippodrome, *arena,* 728
  amusement, 840
Hippogriff, *incongruity,* 83
Hippophagous, *eat,* 296
Hippy, *unconformity,* 83
Hire, *commission,* 755
  fare, 812
  purchase, 795
  borrow, 788
Hire purchase, *buy,* 795
Hireling, *servant,* 746
Hirsute, *rough,* 256
Hispid, *rough,* 256
Hiss, *sound,* 409
  disrespect, 929, 932
Histology, *texture,* 329
Historian, *recorder,* 553, 594
Historic, *indication,* 550
History, *record,* 551
  narrative, 594
Histrionic, *the drama,* 599
  ostentation, 882
Hit, *strike,* 276
  impress, 824
  punish, 972
  succeed, 731
  chance, 156, 621
  reach, 292; *agree,* 23
Hit off, *imitate,* 19, 554
Hit-or-miss, *chance,* 621
Hit upon, *find,* 480A
Hitch, *difficulty,* 704
  impediment, 135
  jerk, 315
  hang, 43, 214
Hitch-hike, *travel,* 266
Hither, *arrival,* 292
Hitherto, *preterition,* 122
Hive, *workshop,* 691
  multitude, 102
  dwelling, 186
Hive-off, *distribute,* 73
Hoar, *white,* 430; *aged,* 128
Hoar-frost, *cold,* 383
Hoard, *store,* 636
  assemblage, 72

Hoarding, *screen*, 530
Hoarse, *sound*, 405, 410
   voice, 581
Hoary, *white*, 430
   aged, 128
Hoax, *deception*, 545
Hob, *support*, 215
   fire, 386
Hobble, *limp*, 275
   difficulty, 704
   lame, 732
   tether, 751
   bond, 752
   awkward, 699
Hobbledehoy, *youth*, 129
Hobby, *pursuit*, 622
   desire, 865
Hobgoblin, *demon*, 980
Hobnob, *courtesy*, 894
Hobo, *traveller*, 268
   tramp, 876
Hobson's choice, *necessity*,
            601
   absence of choice, 610
Hock, *pawn*, 787
Hocus, *deceive*, 545
   stupefy, 376
Hocus-pocus, *cheat*, 545
   conjuration, 992
Hod, *receptacle*, 191
   vehicle, 272
Hodge, *clown*, 876
Hodge-podge, *mixture*, 41
   confusion, 59
Hog, *sensuality*, 954
   gluttony, 957
   selfishness, 943
Hog-wash, *uncleanness*,
            653
Hoist, *elevate*, 307
   lift, 627
Hoity-toity! *wonder*, 870
Hokum, *humbug*, 497
   deception, 545
Hold, *possess*, 777
   believe, 484
   retain, 781
   cohere, 46
   fix, 150
   stop, 265
   discontinue, 142
   continue, 141, 143
   refrain, 623
   contain, 54
   influence, 175
   prison, 752
   in a ship, 207
   term, 71
Hold forth, *declaim*, 582
   teach, 537
Hold good, *truth*, 494
Hold in, *moderation*, 174

Hold on, *move*, 264
   continue, 141, 143
   determination, 604
Hold out, *resist*, 718
   offer, 763
Hold the tongue, *silence*,
          403, 585
Hold together, *junction*, 43
Hold up, *sustain*, 707
   continue, 143
   delay, 133; *plunder*, 791
Holder, *possessor*, 779
Holdfast, *vinculum*, 45
Holding, *property*, 780
Hole, *opening*, 260
   place, 182; *den*, 189
   receptacle, 191
   ambush, 530
   difficulty, 704
Hole-and-corner, *concealment*, 528
Holiday, *amusement*, 840
   repose, 687
   leisure, 685; *time*, 134
Holiness, *Deity*, 976
Hollow, *concavity*, 252
   depth, 208
   incomplete, 53
   false, 544; *sound*, 408
   specious, 477
   unsubstantial, 4
Holm, *island*, 346
Holocaust, *idolatry*, 991
   killing, 361
Holograph, *writing*, 590
Holt, *plant*, 367
Holy, *Deity*, 976
   piety, 987
HOLY GHOST, *Deity*, 976
Holy Writ, *revelation*, 985
   truth, 494
Homage, *reverence*, 928
   submission, 725
   approbation, 931
   fealty, 743
   worship, 990
Home, *habitation*, 189
   interior, 221
   focus, 74; *near*, 197
   arrival, 292
Home and dry, *successful*,
           731
Home-felt, *feeling*, 821
Home Guard, *combatant*,
           726
Homeless, *outcast*, 893
   displaced, 185
Homeliness, *ugliness*, 846
   simplicity, 849
   style, 576

Homeric, *poetry*, 597
Homespun, *simple*, 849
   ugly, 846
   vulgar, 851
   low, 876
   coarse, 329
   style, 576
Homestead, *abode*, 189
Homicide, *killing*, 361
Homily, *advice*, 595
   speech, 582
   sermon, 998
Homoeopathic, *littleness*,
         32, 193
Homogeneity, *relation*, 9
   uniformity, 16
   simplicity, 42
Homologate, *concede*, 467,
          762
Homology, *relation*, 9
   uniformity, 16
Homonym, *word*, 562
   equivocal, 520
* Homunculus, *littleness*,
         193
Hone, *sharpener*, 253
   grind, 331
Honest, *pure*, 960
   true, 543
   candid, 703
   honour, 939
Honey, *sweetness*, 396
   darling, 899
Honeycomb, *concavity*, 252
   opening, 260
Honeydew, *tobacco*, 298A
Honeyed, *flattering*, 933
Honeymoon, *wedding*, 903
   happiness, 827
Honorarium, *expenditure*,
         809
Honorary, *gratuitous*, 815
Honour, *probity*, 939
   glory, 873
   title, 877
   respect, 928
   to pay, 807
Hood, *cowl*, 999
   cap, 225
Hoodlum, *evildoer*, 913, 949
Hoodoo, *sorcery*, 992
   spell, 993
Hoodwink, *blind*, 442
   conceal, 528
   ignore, 491
Hooey, *nonsense*, 497
   trash, 643
Hoof, *to kick*, 276
Hoof it, *walking*, 266
Hoof out, *eject*, 297
Hook, *to fasten*, 43
   fastening, 45

Hook, *grip*, 781
 hang, 214
 curvature, 245
 deviation, 279
 take, 789
Hook-up, *junction*, 43
Hookah, *tobacco-pipe*, 298A
Hooker, *ship*, 273
Hooligan, *ruffian*, 913, 949
Hooliganism, *brutality*, 907
Hoop, *circle*, 247
Hoot, *cry*, 411
 deride, 929, 930, 932
 drink, 298
Hooter, *indication*, 550
Hoots, *contempt*, 930
Hop, *leap*, 309
 dance, 840
Hop it, *go away*, 293, 287
 escape, 671
Hop the twig, *die*, 360
Hope, *hope*, 858
 probability, 472
Hopeful, *probable*, 472
Hopeless, *desperate*, 859
 impossible, 471
Hophead, *intemperance*,
  954
Horde, *assemblage*, 72
Horizon, *distance*, 196
 view, 441
 prospect, 507
 futurity, 121
Horizontal, *horizontality*,
  213
Horn, *sharpness*, 253
 musical, 417
 alarm, 669
Horn-mad, *jealousy*, 920
Horn of plenty, *sufficient*,
  639
Hornbook, *school*, 542
Hornet, *bane*, 663, 830
Hornpipe, *dance*, 840
Hornswoggle, *deceive*, 545
Horny, *hard*, 323
Horology, *chronometry*, 114
Horoscope, *prediction*, 511
Horrible, *great*, 31
 fearful, 860
Horrid, *noxious*, 649
 ugly, 846
 dire, 830
 vulgar, 851
 fearful, 860
 hateful, 898
Horripilation, *cold*, 383
 terror, 860
Horrisonous, *strident*, 410
Horror, *dislike*, 867
 hate, 898
 fear, 860

* Hors de combat, *impotence*, 158
 disease, 655
* Hors-d'œuvre, *food*, 298
Horse, *animal*, 271
 cavalry, 726
 stand, 215
Horse-box, *vehicle*, 272
Horse-laugh, *laugh*, 838
Horse-power, *measure*, 466
Horse-sense, *wisdom*, 498
Horse-shoe, *curvature*, 245
Horseman, *traveller*, 268
Horseplay, *violence*, 173
Horsewhip, *punishment*,
  972
Hortation, *advice*, 615, 695
Horticulture, *agriculture*,
  371
* Hortus siccus, *botany*, 369
Hosanna, *worship*, 990
Hose, *dress*, 225
 conduit, 350
Hospice, *abode*, 189
Hospitable, *social*, 892
 liberal, 816
Hospital, *remedy*, 662
Hospodar, *master*, 745
Host, *multitude*, 100
 collection, 72
 friend, 890
 religious, 999
Hostage, *security*, 771
Hostel, *inn*, 189
Hostile, *adverse*, 708
Hostilities, *warfare*, 722
Hostility, *enmity*, 889
Hot, *warm*, 382
 pungent, 392
 irascible, 901
 rhythm, 413
 contraband, 964
Hot air, *sophistry*, 477
Hot-bed, *workshop*, 691
 cause, 153
Hot-blooded, *rash*, 863
Hot-brained, *rash*, 863
 excited, 825
Hot-headed, *rash*, 863
 excited, 825
Hot-plate, *heater*, 386
Hot water, *difficulty*, 704
Hot-water bottle, *heater*,
  386
Hotchpotch, *mixture*, 41
 confusion, 59
Hotel, *inn*, 189
Hothouse, *conservatory*, 386
 workshop, 691
Hotspur, *rashness*, 863
 courage, 861
Hottentot, *boor*, 876

Hough, *maltreat*, 649
Hound, *pursue*, 281, 622
 oppress, 907
 wretch, 949
Hour, *period*, 108
Hour-glass, *time*, 114
 form, 203
Houri, *beauty*, 845
Hourly, *routine*, 138
House, *abode*, 189
 to locate, 184
 safety, 664
 party, 712
 senate, 696
 partnership, 797
House-warming, *sociality*,
  892
Houseboat, *abode*, 189
Housebreaker, *thief*, 792
Household, *abode*, 189
 conformity, 82
 plain, 849
 property, 780
Housekeeper, *director*, 694
 servant, 746
Housekeeping, *conduct*, 692
Houseless, *displaced*, 185
Housemaid, *servant*, 746
Housewifery, *conduct*, 692
 economy, 817
Housing, *lodging*, 189
Hovel, *abode*, 189
Hover, *soar*, 267
 rise, 305
 high, 206
Hoverplane, *aircraft*, 273A
How, *in what way*, 627
 by what means, 632
How-d'ye-do, *difficulty*, 704
Howbeit, *counteraction*, 179
Howdah, *seat*, 215
However, *except*, 83
 notwithstanding, 179
 degree, 23
 compensation, 30
Howff, *resort*, 74
Howitzer, *arms*, 727
Howl, *ululation*, 411, 412,
  839
Howler, *error*, 495
 solecism, 568
Howsoever, *degree*, 26
Hoy, *ship*, 273
 salutation, 586
Hoyden, *vulgarity*, 851
Hub, *centre*, 223
 middle, 68
Hubble-bubble, *tobacco-pipe*, 298A
Hubbub, *din*, 404
 discord, 713
 agitation, 315

Huckster, *merchant*, 797
Huddle, *mix*, 41
  disorder, 59
  derange, 61
  collect, 72
  don, 225
  nearness, 197
Hue, *colour*, 428
Hue and cry, *noise*, 404
  outcry, 931
  alarm, 669
  proclamation, 531
Hueless, *achromatism*, 429
Huff, *anger*, 900
  insolence, 885
Huffiness, *irascibility*, 901
Hug, *cohere*, 46
  retain, 781
  endearment, 894, 902
Hug oneself, *rejoice*, 838
Hug the shore, *approach*,
    286
Huge, *in degree*, 31
  in size, 192
Hugger-mugger, *confusion*,
    59
Hulk, *whole*, 50
  ship, 273
Hulking, *big*, 192
  awkward, 853
  ugly, 846
Hull, *whole*, 50
Hullabaloo, *noise*, 404
  cry, 411
Hullo, *see* Hallo
Hum, *faint sound*, 405
  continued sound, 407,
    412
  to sing, 415
  deceive, 545
  stink, 401
Hum and ha, *hesitate*, 583
  demur, 605
Hum-note, *melody*, 413
Human, *mankind*, 372
Humane, *benevolent*, 906
  philanthropic, 910
Humanism, *knowledge*, 490
Humanist, *scholar*, 492
Humanitarian, *philanthropist*, 906
Humanities, *letters*, 560
Humanity, *human nature*,
    372
  benevolence, 906
Humanize, *courtesy*, 894
Humble, *meek*, 879
  modest, 881
  to abash, 874
  pious, 987
Humbug, *deception*, 545
  falsehood, 544

Humdrum, *dull*, 843
Humectate, *moisten*, 339
Humid, *moist*, 339
Humiliate, *humble*, 879
  shame, 874
  worship, 990
Humility, *piety*, 987
Humming-top, *musical*, 417
Hummock, *height*, 206, 250
Humoresque, *music*, 415
Humorist, *humorist*, 844
Humour, *essence*, 5
  liquid, 333
  disposition, 602
  tendency, 176
  caprice, 608
  indulge, 760
  affections, 820
  to please, 829
  wit, 842
Humoursome, *capricious*,
    608
  discourteous, 895
Hump, *convexity*, 250
Hump bluey, *journey*, 266
Hump yourself, *activity*,
    682
Humpbacked, *distortion*,
    243
  ugliness, 846
Humph! *wonder*, 870
Humus, *soil*, 342
Hun, *evildoer*, 913
Hunch, *convexity*, 250
Hundred, *number*, 99
  region, 181
Hunger, *desire*, 865
Hunks, *parsimony*, 819
Hunnish, *malevolent*, 907
Hunt, *follow*, 281
  pursue, 622
  inquire, 461
Hunter, *carrier*, 271
Hunting grounds, *heaven*,
    981
Hurdle, *fence*, 232
Hurdy-gurdy, *musical*, 417
Hurl, *propel*, 284
Hurly-burly, *confusion*, 59
  turmoil, 315
Hurrah! *cheerfulness*, 836
  rejoicing, 838
Hurricane, *tempest*, 349
  violence, 173
Hurried, *excitability*, 825
Hurry, *haste*, 684
  swiftness, 274
  earliness, 132
  to urge, 615
  to excite, 824
Hurst, *plant*, 367
Hurt, *evil*, 619

Hurt, *physical pain*, 378
  moral pain, 828
  to injure, 649, 907
  to molest, 830
Hurtful, *badness*, 649
Hurtle, *impulse*, 276
Husband, *spouse*, 903
  to store, 636
Husbandman, *agriculture*,
    371
Husbandry, *agriculture*, 371
  conduct, 692
  economy, 817
Hush, *silence*, 403
  latent, 526
  moderate, 174
  assuage, 826
  pacify, 723
Hush-hush, *secret*, 534
Hush-money, *bribe*, 809
  compensation, 30
Hush up, *conceal*, 526, 528
Husk, *covering*, 222
  to strip, 226
Husky, *dry*, 340
  big, 192
  strong, 159
  faint sound, 405, 501
Hussar, *combatant*, 726
Hussy, *libertine*, 962
  bad woman, 949
  impertinent, 887
Hustings, *tribunal*, 966
  platform, 542
Hustle, *push*, 276
  disarrange, 61
  agitate, 315
  bustle, 171, 682
  haste, 684
Hut, *abode*, 189
Hutch, *abode*, 189
Huzza! *cheerfulness*, 836
Hyaline, *transparency*, 425
Hybrid, *mixture*, 41
  nondescript, 83
Hydra, *unconformity*, 83
Hydra-headed, *reproduction*, 163
Hydrant, *spray*, 348
Hydraulics, *fluids*, 348
Hydrogen bomb, *arms*, 727
Hydrographic, *sea*, 341
Hydrology, *water*, 333
Hydromel, *sweetness*, 396
Hydrometer, *density*, 321
Hydropathic, *salubrity*, 656
  remedy, 662
Hydropathy, *remedy*, 662
Hydrophobia, *dislike*, 867
Hydroplane, *aircraft*, 273A
Hydroponics, *agriculture*,
    371

Impulsive, *motiveless*, 616
  rash, 863
Impunity, *acquittal*, 970
Impure, *foul*, 653
  licentious, 961
Imputation, *disrepute*, 874
Impute, *ascribe*, 155
  accuse, 938
* In esse, *existence*, 1
* In extenso, *whole*, 50
  diffuse, 573
* In extremis, *death*, 360
In fine, *end*, 67
In hand, *possession*, 777
  business, 625
* In limine, *beginning*, 66
* In loco, *agreement*, 23
* In mediis rebus, *middle*,
                    68
* In nubibus, *inexistence*, 2
  incogitancy, 452
  imagination, 515
  unintelligibility, 519
* In propria persona, *spec-
  iality*, 79
* In puris naturalibus, *di-
  vestment*, 226
* In re, *relation*, 9
* In saecula saeculorum,
  perpetuity, 112
* In statu pupillari, *youth*,
                    127
  learner, 541
* In statu quo, *permanence*,
                    141
  restoration, 660
* In terrorem, *threat*, 909
* In toto, *whole*, 50
  greatness, 31
* In transitu, *transient*, 111
  conversion, 144
  motion, 264
  transference, 270
  method, 627
Inability, *want of power*, 158
  want of skill, 699
Inaccessible, *distance*, 196
  impossible, 471
Inaccurate, *error*, 495, 568
Inaction, *inaction*, 681
Inactivity, *inactivity*, 172,
                    683
Inadaptability, *disagreement*, 24
Inadequate, *insufficient*,
                    640, 645
  imperfect, 651
  weak, 158, 160
Inadmissible, *inexpedient*,
                    647
  incongruous, 24
  excluded, 55

Inadvertence, *inattention*,
                    458
  unintentional, 621
Inalienable, *right*, 924
  possession, 777
  retention, 781
* Inamorata, *love*, 897
Inane, *trivial*, 643
  useless, 645
  void, 4
Inanimate, *dead*, 360
  inorganic, 358
Inanition, *insufficiency*, 640
Inanity, *inutility*, 645
  absence of thought, 452
  absence of meaning, 517
  insignificance, 643
Inappetence, *indifference*,
                    866
Inapplicable, *irrelation*, 10
  disagree, 24
Inapposite, *disagree*, 24
  irrelevant, 10
Inappreciable, *in size*, 193
  in degree, 32
  unimportant, 643
Inappreciative, *ungrateful*,
                    917
Inapprehensible, *unknow-
  able*, 519
Inappropriate, *discordant*,
                    24
  inexpedient, 647
Inapt, *inexpedient*, 647
  incongruous, 24
Inaptitude, *impotence*, 158
Inarticulate, *stammering*,
                    583
Inartificial, *artlessness*, 703
Inartistic, *unskilled*, 699
  imperfect, 651
Inattention, *indifference*,
                    458
Inaudible, *silent*, 403, 405
  mute, 581
Inaugurate, *begin*, 66
  precedence, 62
  celebrate, 883
Inauguration, *commission*,
                    755
Inauspicious, *hopeless*, 859
  untimely, 135
  untoward, 649
Inbeing, *intrinsicality*, 5
Inborn, *intrinsic*, 5, 820
  habitual, 613
Inbred, *intrinsic*, 5, 820
Inca, *master*, 745
Incalculable, *infinite*, 105
  much, 31
Incalescence, *heat*, 382
Incandescence, *heat*, 382

Incandescence, *light*, 420
Incantation, *invocation*, 765
  spell, 993
Incapable, *weak*, 16(
  unable, 158
Incapacity, *impotence*, 158
  weakness, 160
  stupidity, 499
  indocility, 538
Incarcerate, *imprison*, 751
  surround, 231
Incarnadine, *red*, 434
Incarnate, *materialize*, 316
Incarnation, *intrinsic*, 5
  Deity, 976
Incautious, *neglectful*, 460
  rash, 863
Incendiary, *evildoer*, 913
  destructive, 162
Incense, *fragrance*, 400
  to provoke, 900
  hatred, 898
  flattery, 933
  worship, 990
Incentive, *motive*, 615
Inception, *beginning*, 66
Inceptor, *learner*, 541
Incertitude, *uncertain*, 475
Incessant, *perpetual*, 112
  frequency, 136
Incest, *impurity*, 961
Inch, *littleness*, 193
  slowness, 275
  island, 346
Inch by inch, *degree*, 26
Inchoate, *amorphous*, 241
Inchoation, *beginning*, 66
Incidence, *direction*, 278
Incident, *event*, 151
Incidental, *extrinsic*, 6, 8
  irrelative, 10
  liable, 177
  casual, 156, 621
Incinerate, *calefaction*, 384
Incipient, *beginning*, 66
  style, 574
Incision, *cut*, 44
Incisive, *style*, 574
  feeling, 821
Incite, *urge*, 615
  exasperate, 173
Incivility, *rudeness*, 895
Incivism, *misanthropy*, 911
Inclement, *cold*, 383
  severe, 739
Incline, *slope*, 217
  direction, 278
  tendency, 176
  willing, 602
  desire, 865
  love, 897
  induce, 615

Inextinguishable, *immut-*
able, 150
uncontrollable, 825
energetic, 157
Inextricable, *difficult,* 704
impossible, 471
disorder, 59
coherence, 46
Infallible, *certainty,* 474
perfect, 650
Infamy, *dishonour,* 940
shame, 874
vice, 945
Infancy, *beginning,* 66
youth, 127
Infant, *infant,* 129
Infanta, *master,* 745
Infanticide, *killing,* 361
Infantile, *puerile,* 643
foolish, 499
Infantry, *combatant,* 726
Infatuation, *folly,* 499
misjudgment, 481
obstinacy, 606
credulity, 486
passion, 825
love, 897
Infeasible, *impossible,* 471
difficult, 704
Infect, *mix,* 41
Infection, *disease,* 655
contamination, 659
excitation, 824
Infectious, *insalubrity,* 657
Infecund, *unproductiveness,*
169
Infelicity, *unhappiness,*
828
inexpertness, 699
Infer, *judgment,* 480
Inference, *judgment,* 480
interpretation, 522
Inferential, *deducible,* 478
Inferior, *less,* 34
imperfect, 651
Infernal, *bad,* 649
wicked, 945
malevolent, 907
Infertility, *unproductive-*
ness, 169
Infest, *annoy,* 649, 830
frequent, 136
Infibulation, *junction,* 43
Infidel, *heathen,* 984
Infidelity, *dishonour,* 940
irreligion, 989
Infiltrate, *intervene,* 228
influence, 175
imbue, 339
teach, 537
mixture, 41
Infiltration, *ingress,* 294

Infiltration, *passage,* 302
presence, 186
Infinite, *in quantity,* 105
in degree, 31
in size, 192
Infinitesimal, *in degree,* 32
in quantity, 193
Infinity, *infinitude,* 105
space, 180
Infirm, *weak,* 160
irresolute, 605
vicious, 945
Infirmary, *remedy,* 662
Infirmity, *weakness,* 160
disease, 655
failing, 945
Infix, *teaching,* 537
Inflame, *burn,* 384
stir up, 173
incense, 900
incite, 615
Inflammation, *disease,* 655
Inflate, *expend,* 194
rarefy, 322
blow, 349
style, 573, 577
ridiculous, 853
vanity, 880
Inflect, *curvature,* 245
grammar, 567
Inflexible, *hard,* 323
resolved, 604
obstinate, 606
stern, 739
Inflexion, *curvature,* 245
change, 140
appendage, 39
grammar, 567
Inflict, *condemn,* 971
act upon, 680
give pain, 830
Infliction, *pain,* 828
Influence, *physical,* 175
authority, 737
inducement, 615
importance, 642
Influential, *important,* 642
Influx, *ingress,* 294
Inform, *information,* 527
Inform against, *accusation,*
938
Informal, *irregular,* 83
lawless, 964
Information, *knowledge,*
490
communication, 527
Informer, *witness,* 467
* *Infra, posterior,* 117
* *Infra dignitatem, disre-*
pute, 874
Infra-microscopic, *little,*
193

Infraction, *non-observance,*
773
unconformity, 83
exemption, 927
disobedience, 742
violation, 614
Infrangible, *coherence,* 46,
321
Infrastructure, *base,* 211
Infrequency, *infrequency,*
137
fewness, 103
Infringe, *transgress,* 303
violate, 742, 773, 925,
927
break through, 614
Infundibular, *concavity,* 252
Infuriate, *wrathful,* 900
excite, 824
violent, 173
Infuse, *mix,* 41
insert, 300
teach, 537
Infusible, *solid,* 321
Ingeminate, *duplication,* 90
Ingenious, *skill,* 698
* Ingénue, *actress,* 599
Ingenuous, *artless,* 703
sincere, 543
guileless, 939
Ingest, *absorb,* 296
Ingle, *fuel,* 388
Inglorious, *disrepute,* 874
base, 940
Ingoing, *ingress,* 294
Ingot, *money,* 800
Ingraft, *see* Engraft
Ingrate, *ingratitude,* 917
Ingratiate, *love,* 897
Ingratitude, *ingratitude,*
917
Ingredient, *component,* 56
Ingress, *ingress,* 294
Ingrowing, *insertion,* 300
Ingurgitate, *reception,* 296
Inhabile, *unskilfulness,* 699
Inhabit, *presence,* 186
Inhabitant, *inhabitant,* 188
Inhale, *reception,* 296
sniff, 398
Inharmonious, *discordant,*
414
incongruity, 24
Inherence, *intrinsicality,* 5
Inherit, *acquire,* 775
possess, 777
Inheritance, *property,* 780
Inhesion, *intrinsicality,* 5
Inhibit, *prohibit,* 761
not think of, 452
dissuade, 616
hinder, 706

Instalment, *portion,* 51
  payment, 807
Instance, *example,* 82
  solicitation, 765
  motive, 615
Instancy, *urgency,* 642
Instant, *moment,* 113
  present, 118
  future, 121
Instanter, *earlier,* 132
  instantaneity, 113
Instauration, *restoration,*
  600
Instead, *substitution,* 147
Instigate, *motive,* 615
Instil, *insert,* 300
  teach, 537
  mix, 41
Instinct, *intellect,* 450
  intuition, 477
  impulse, 601
  innate, 5
Instinctive, *habitual,* 613
  impulsive, 612
Institute, *school,* 542
  beginning, 66
  cause, 153
  organize, 161
Institution, *legality,* 963
  poorhouse, 804
Institutor, *teacher,* 540
Instruct, *teach,* 537
  advise, 695
  precept, 697
  command, 741
Instructor, *teacher,* 540
Instrument, *implement,* 633
  record, 551
  security, 771
Instrumental, *means,* 632
  music, 415
  subservient, 631
Instrumentality, *medium,*
  631
Insubordinate, *disobedience,*
  742
  anarchy, 738
Insubstantiality, *nothingness,* 4
Insufferable, *painfulness,*
  830
Insufficient, *insufficiency,*
  640
  shortcoming, 304
Insufflation, *wind,* 349
Insular, *island,* 346
  detach, 44
  single, 87
Insulate, *separate,* 44
Insult, *rudeness,* 895
  disrespect, 929
  offence, 900

Insuperable, *difficulty,* 704
  impossible, 471
Insupportable, *painfulness,*
  830
Insuppressible, *violence,*
  173
Insurance, *promise,* 768
  security, 771
  precaution, 664
Insurgent, *disobedience,* 742
Insurmountable, *difficulty,*
  704
  impossible, 471
Insurrection, *disobedience,*
  742
  resistance, 719
Insusceptible, *insensibility,*
  823
Intact, *permanence,* 141
  preserve, 669
Intaglio, *concavity,* 252
  sculpture, 557
Intake, *inlet,* 260
Intangible, *numbness,* 381
  immaterial, 317
Integer, *whole,* 50
Integral calculus, *number,*
  84
Integral part, *component*
  56
Integrate, *consolidate,* 50
  complete, 52
Integration, *number,* 84
Integrity, *whole,* 50
  virtue, 944
  probity, 939
Integument, *covering,* 222
Intellect, *intellect,* 450
Intelligence, *mind,* 450
  news, 532
  wisdom, 498
Intelligible, *intelligibility,*
  518, 570
Intemperate, *intemperance,*
  954
  drunkenness, 957
Intempestivity, *unseason-
  ableness,* 135
Intend, *design,* 620
Intendant, *director,* 694
Intended, *will,* 600
Intensify, *energize,* 171
  aggravate, 835
Intensity, *degree,* 26
  greatness, 31
  energy, 171
Intent, *active,* 682
  thoughtful, 451, 457
Intention, *design,* 620
Intentional, *will,* 600
Intentness, *attention,* 457
  thought, 451

Inter, *bury,* 363
  insert, 300
* Inter alia, *conformity,* 82
Interaction, *reciprocal,* 12
Interblend, *mix,* 41
Interbreed, *mix,* 41
Intercalate, *insert,* 300
  intervene, 228
Intercede, *mediate,* 724
  deprecate, 766
Intercept, *hinder,* 706
  take, 789
Intercession, *deprecation,*
  766
Interchange, *interchange,*
  148
  reciprocate, 12
  barter, 794
  transfer, 783
Intercipient, *hinder,* 706
Interclude, *hindrance,* 706
Intercom, *hearing,* 418
Intercommunicate, *inter-
  locution,* 588
  information, 527
Intercommunion, *society,*
  892
Intercostal, *interiority,* 221
Intercourse, *converse,* 588
Intercross, *mix,* 41
Intercurrence, *passage,* 302
Interdict, *prohibition,* 761
Interdigitate, *intervene,* 228
  intersect, 219
Interest, *advantage,* 618
  concern, 9
  importance, 642
  curiosity, 455
  attention, 457
  aid, 707
  to please, 829
  debt, 806
Interested, *selfish,* 943
Interesting, *style,* 574
Interfere, *intervene,* 228
  meddle, 682
  disagree, 24
  counteract, 179
  thwart, 706
  mediate, 724
  activity, 682
Interglossa, *language,* 560
Interim, *duration,* 106
  synchronism, 120
Interior, *interiority,* 221
Interjacence, *coming be-
  tween,* 228
  middle, 68
Interject, *insert,* 300
  interpose, 228
Interlace, *twine,* 219
  join, 43

Irremovable, *quiescence*, 265
Irreparable, *loss*, 776
  bad, 649
  hopeless, 859
Irrepentance, *impenitence*,
    951
Irreplaceable, *indispens-*
  able, 630
Irrepressible, *violent*, 173
  excitement, 825
  free, 778
Irreproachable, *innocence*,
    946
Irresistible, *strength*, 159
  compulsory, 601
  evidence, 467
Irresolute, *irresolution*,
    149, 605
Irresolvable, *unity*, 87
Irrespective, *irrelation*, 10
Irresponsible, *exempt*, 927A
  arbitrary, 964
  silly, 499
Irretrievable, *lost*, 776
Irreverence, *disrespect*, 929
  impiety, 988
Irreversible, *past*, 122
  immutable, 150
Irrevocable, *immutable*,
    150, 601, 604
  hopeless, 859
Irrigate, *water*, 337
Irritable, *excitable*, 825
  irascible, 901
Irritate, *provoke*, 898
  incense, 900
  fret, 828
  pain, 830
Irruption, *ingress*, 294
  invasion, 716
Ishmael, *enemy*, 891
Isis, *deity*, 979
Islam, *religions*, 984
Island, *island*, 346
Isobar, *air*, 338
Isocheimal, *cold*, 383
Isochimenal, *cold*, 383
Isochronous, *synchronism*,
    120
Isolation, *singleness*, 87
  seclusion, 893
  safety, 644
  detachment, 44
  irrelation, 10
Isomeric, *part*, 51
Isomorphism, *form*, 240
Isothermal, *heat*, 382
Issue, *effect*, 154
  event, 151
  end, 67
  posterity, 121, 167
  disease, 655

Issue, *kindred*, 11
  depart, 293
  egress, 295
  stream, 347
  distribute, 73
  money, 800
Issueless, *unproductive*, 169
Isthmus, *narrowness*, 203
  land, 342
  connection, 45
It, *charm*, 829
Italicize, *emphasize*, 642
Italics, *indication*, 550
  type, 591
Itch, *desire*, 865
  titillation, 380
Item, *addition*, 37
  speciality, 79
  adjunct, 39
  part, 51
Iteration, *repetition*, 90, 104
Itinerant, *moving*, 266
  traveller, 268
Itinerary, *description*, 594
  guide, 695
Ivory, *whiteness*, 430
Ivory-skulled, *stupid*, 499
Ivory tower, *retirement*, 893

J

Jab, *stab*, 260
  poke, 276
Jabber, *chatter*, 584
  nonsense, 517
  stammer, 583
Jabot, *frill*, 230
Jacent, *horizontal*, 213
Jack, *instrument*, 633
  raise, 307
  ensign, 550
  money, 800
Jack-a-dandy, *fop*, 854
Jack-in-office, *blusterer*, 887
Jack-o'-lantern, *vision*, 515
  light, 423
Jack-pot, *stake*, 771
Jack-pudding, *buffoon*, 844
Jackal, *provision*, 637
  mediate, 631
Jackanapes, *fop*, 854
  bluster, 887
Jackass, *carrier*, 271
Jacket, *dress*, 225
Jacquerie, *tumult*, 719
Jactitation, *tossing*, 315
Jade, *to fatigue*, 688, 841
  woman, 374
  bad woman, 949
  courtesan, 962
  horse, 271
Jag, *spree*, 954

Jagged, *angular*, 244
  notched, 257
  pointed, 253
Jail, *prison*, 752
Jail-bird, *prisoner*, 754
Jailer, *keeper*, 753
Jake, *good*, 648
Jakes, *privy*, 653
Jalopy, *vehicle*, 272
Jam, *to squeeze*, 43
  confection, 396
Jamb, *support*, 215
Jangle, *sound*, 410
  discord, 713
Janitor, *stopper*, 263
Janizary, *combatant*, 726
Janus, *deceiver*, 548
Janus-headed, *duality*, 89
Japan, *varnish*, 222
  beautify, 845
  ornament, 847
Jape, *jest*, 842
Jar, *vessel*, 191
  stridor, 410
  discord, 414, 713
  agitation, 315
  shock, 824
  pain, 830
  clash, 24
Jargon, *unmeaning*, 519
  absurdity, 497
Jasper-coloured, *green*, 435
Jaundiced, *prejudiced*, 481
  jealous, 920
  dejected, 837
  yellow, 436
Jaunt, *journey*, 266
Jaunting-car, *vehicle*, 272
Jaunty, *fashionable*, 852
  pretty, 845
  showy, 882
Javelin, *arms*, 727
Jaw, *mouth*, 230
  loquacity, 584
  to scold, 932
Jaw-breaker, *neology*, 563
Jay, *loquacity*, 584
Jazz, *melody*, 413
* Je ne sais quoi, *euphem-*
  ism, 565
Jealousy, *envy*, 920
Jeans, *dress*, 225
Jeep, *vehicle*, 272
Jeer, *gibe*, 856, 929
  joke, 842
Jehovah, *Deity*, 976
Jehu, *director*, 694
Jejune, *scanty*, 640
  style, 575
Jell, *set*, 321
Jelly, *pulpiness*, 354
  sweet, 396

Jellyfish, *weakness*, 160
Jennet, *carrier*, 271
Jeopardy, *danger*, 665
Jeremiad, *invective*, 932, 938
    lamentations, 839
Jerk, *throw*, 146, 284
    draw, 285
    agitate, 315
    bad man, 949
Jerry, *flimsy*, 643
Jerry-built, *fragile*, 328
Jersey, *dress*, 225
Jest, *wit*, 842
    trifle, 643
Jester, *humorist*, 844
    buffoon, 857
Jesuit, *clergy*, 996
Jesuitry, *deception*, 544
    sophistry, 477
Jesus, *Deity*, 976
Jet, *water*, 347
    stream, 348
    aircraft, 273A
    blackness, 431
Jetsam, *fragments*, 51
    little, 643
Jettison, *abandon*, 782
Jetty, *convexity*, 250
* Jeu d'esprit, *wit*, 842
* Jeu de mots, *neology*, 563
* Jeu de théâtre, *appearance*, 448
* Jeune fille, *girl*, 129
Jew, *religions*, 984
Jewel, *gem*, 650
    ornament, 847
    goodness, 648
    favourite, 899
Jew's harp, *musical*, 417
Jezebel, *wretch*, 949
    courtesan, 962
Jib, *deviation*, 279
    demur, 603
Jibe, *accord*, 23
Jiffy, *instant*, 113
Jig, *dance*, 840
Jilt, *deception*, 545
    lovelorn, 898
Jimjams, *insanity*, 503
Jingle, *resonance*, 408
    vehicle, 272
Jingo, *warlike*, 722
    boasting, 884
    blusterer, 887
Jinnee, *demon*, 980
Jinx, *spell*, 993
Jitters, *fear*, 860
Jiu-jitsu, *contention*, 720
Jive, *rhythm*, 413
Job, *business*, 625
    action, 680
    unfairness, 940

Jobation, *upbraiding*, 932
Jobber, *merchant*, 797
    agent, 690
    trickster, 943
Jobbernowl, *fool*, 501
Jobbery, *cunning*, 702
Jobbing, *skill*, 698
    barter, 794
Jockey, *horseman*, 268
    servant, 746
    to deceive, 545
    deceiver, 548
Jocose, *witty*, 836, 840, 842
Jocular, *gay*, 836
    amusing, 840
Jocund, *cheerful*, 836
Joe Soap, *fool*, 501
    dupe, 547
Jog, *push*, 276
    shake, 315
Jog on, *advance*, 282
    slowness, 275
    trudge, 266
Jog-trot, *routine*, 613
Joggle, *agitation*, 315
Johnsonian, *style*, 577
Join, *junction*, 43
    contiguity, 199
Joint, *part*, 44, 51
    junction, 43
    flexure, 258
    accompanying, 88
Joint stock, *share*, 778
Jointly, *addition*, 37
Jointress, *widow*, 905
Jointure, *receipt*, 810
    property, 780
Joist, *support*, 215
Joke, *wit*, 842
    trifle, 643
Jollification, *spree*, 954
Jollity, *amusement*, 480
Jolly, *gay*, 836
    conviviality, 892
    pleasing, 829
    plump, 192
    joke, 842
    flatter, 933
Jolly-boat, *ship*, 273
Jolt, *impulse*, 276
    agitation, 315
    shock, 824
Jonathan Wild, *thief*, 792
Jorum, *receptacle*, 191
Josh, *tease*, 830
    joke, 842
    ridicule, 856
Joskin, *clown*, 876
Joss, *idolatry*, 991
Joss-house, *temple*, 1000
Jostle, *clash*, 24
    push, 276

Jostle, *agitate*, 315
Jot, *small quantity*, 32
    particle, 193
    to record, 551
Jotting, *writing*, 590
Jounce, *agitation*, 315
Journal, *annals*, 114
    record, 551
    description, 594
    book, 593
Journalism, *publication*, 531
Journalist, *recorder*, 553
    writer, 590
Journey, *journey*, 266
    progression, 282
Journeyman, *agent*, 690
    servant, 746
Joust, *contention*, 720
Jove, *god*, 979
Jovial, *gay*, 836
    convivial, 892
    amusement, 840
Jowl, *laterality*, 236
Joy, *pleasure*, 827
Joy-ride, *journey*, 266
Joyful, *cheerful*, 836
Joyless, *dejection*, 830, 837
Joyous, *cheerful*, 836
Jubilant, *joyous*, 836
    boastful, 884
Jubilation, *celebration*, 882
Jubilee, *rejoicing*, 836, 838
    festival, 840
    anniversary, 138
    celebration, 883
Judaism, *religions*, 984
Judge, *arbitrator*, 967
    master, 745
    taste, 850
Judgmatic, *wisdom*, 498
Judgment, *decision*, 480
    intellect, 450
    belief, 484
    wisdom, 498
    sentence, 969
Judgment-seat, *tribunal*, 966
Judicature, *law*, 965
Judicial, *discriminative*, 465
    impartial, 922
Judicious, *wisdom*, 498
    expedient, 646
Jug, *receptacle*, 191
    prison, 752
Juggernaut, *idol*, 991
Juggle, *deception*, 545
Juice, *liquid*, 333
Juicy, *moist*, 339
    style, 574
Ju-ju, *idol*, 991

Jujube, *sweet*, 396
Juke box, *mechanical in-strument*, 417
Julep, *sweet*, 396
Jumble, *confusion*, 59
  derangement, 61
  mixture, 41
Jump, *leap*, 309, 146
  dance, 840
Jump at, *seize*, 789
  pursue, 622
  desire, 865
  conclusion, 480
Jump over, *neglect*, 460
Jumper, *dress*, 225
Jumpy, *fear*, 860
Junction, *join*, 43
Juncture, *period*, 134
  circumstance, 8
  junction, 43
Jungle, *plant*, 367
  disorder, 59
Junior, *youth*, 127
Junk, *ship*, 273
  trumpery, 643, 645
Junket, *merry-making*, 840
  dish, 298
Junkie, *addict*, 613
Juno, *goddess*, 979
Junta, *party*, 712
  council, 696
Jupiter, *god*, 979
* Jure divino, *dueness*,
                                624
Jurisconsult, *lawyer*, 958
Jurisdiction, *law*, 965
  authority, 737
Jurisprudence, *law*, 963
Jurist, *lawyer*, 968
Jury, *judge*, 967
Jury-mast, *resource*, 666
* Jus gentium, *law*, 963
Just, *accurate*, 494
  reasonable, 476
  right, 922
  equitable, 939
Just as, *similarity*, 17
Just so, *assent*, 488
* Juste milieu, *mean*, 29
Justice, *right*, 922
  legality, 963
  magistrate, 967
Justiciar, *judge*, 967
Justification, *religious*, 987
  vindication, 937
Justify, *deity*, 976
Jut out, *convexity*, 250
Juvenescence, *youth*, 127
Juvenile, *youth*, 127
Juxtaposition, *contiguity*,
                                199

K

K.C., *lawyer*, 968
K.O., *end*, 67
Kadi, *judge*, 967
Kaleidoscope, *optical*, 445
  changeable, 149
* Kaput, *done for*, 360
Karma, *destiny*, 152
Katabolism, *dissolution*,
                                360
Kavass, *authority*, 745
  jurisdiction, 965
Keck, *ejection*, 297
Kedge, *anchor*, 666
  ship, 273
Keel, *base*, 211
Keelhaul, *punish*, 972
Keen, *sharp*, 253
  cold, 383
  energetic, 171
  poignant, 821
  desirous, 865
  lament, 363, 839
Keen-witted, *wisdom*, 498
Keep, *retain*, 781
  custody, 751
  prison, 752
  refuge, 666
  to observe, 772
  to celebrate, 883
  to continue, 141, 143
  food, 298
  provision, 637
  preserve, 670
Keep back, *conceal*, 528
  disuse, 678
  dissuade, 616
Keep from, *refrain*, 603
Keep off, *distance*, 196
Keep on, *continue*, 143
Keep pace with, *equality*, 27
Keep under, *restrain*, 751
Keep up, *continue*, 143
Keeper, *keep*, 753
Keeping, *congruity*, 23
Keepsake, *memory*, 505
Keg, *receptacle*, 191
Kelpie, *fabulous being*, 979
Ken, *knowledge*, 490
Kennel, *ditch*, 259
  conduit, 350
  hovel, 189
Kenspeckle, *eminent*, 873
Kerb, *edge*, 230
Kerchief, *dress*, 225
Kermess, *amusement*, 840
Kern, *commonalty*, 876
Kernel, *central*, 223
  importance, 642
Ketch, *ship*, 273
Kettle, *vessel*, 191

Kettle, *cauldron*, 386
Kettle-drum, *musical*, 417
Key, *interpretation*, 522
  answer, 462
  music, 413
  cause, 153
  opener, 260
  instrument, 631
  insignia, 747
Key up, *stimulate*, 615
Keyhole, *opening*, 260
Keynote, *music*, 413
  model, 22
  rule, 80
Keystone, *support*, 215
Kgotla, *council*, 696
Khaki, *brown*, 433
Khan, *master*, 745
Khedive, *master*, 745
Khidmutgar, *servant*, 746
Kibitka, *vehicle*, 272
Kibitz, *meddle*, 682
Kibosh, *defeat*, 731
Kick, *strike*, 276
  attack, 716
  recoil, 277
  disobey, 742
  resist, 719
  punish, 972
  feeling, 821
  pleasure, 827
Kickshaw, *trifle*, 643
  food, 298
Kid, *child*, 129
  to hoax, 545
  chaff, 842
Kidnap, *stealing*, 789, 791
Kidney, *class*, 75
Kilderkin, *receptacle*, 191
Kill, *kill*, 361
Kill-joy, *dejection*, 837
Killing, *charming*, 829
  funny, 842
Kiln, *furnace*, 386
Kilt, *dress*, 225
Kimono, *dress*, 225
Kin, *class*, 75
Kind, *class*, 75
  benevolent, 906
Kindle, *set fire to*, 384
  cause, 153
  quicken, 171
  incite, 615
  excite, 824
  incense, 900
Kindly, *request*, 765
Kindred, *consanguinity*, 11
Kinematics, *motion*, 264
Kinematograph, *see* Cine-matograph
King, *master*, 745
Kingcraft, *authority*, 737

Libel, *detraction* 934
  censure, 932
  lawsuit, 969
Liberal, *generous*, 816
  disinterested, 942
  ample, 639
  giving, 784
Liberate, *release*, 672, 750
  disjoin, 44
Libertarianism, *will*, 600
Libertinage, *impurity*, 961
Libertine, *libertine*, 962
Libertinism, *impurity*, 961
Liberty, *freedom*, 748
  right, 924
  exemption, 927A
  permission, 760
Libidinous, *impurity*, 961
Libido, *desire*, 865
Library, *book*, 593
  room, 191
Librate, *oscillation*, 314
Libretto, *poetry*, 597
Licence, *permission*, 760
  laxity, 738
  right, 924
  exemption, 927
  toleration, 750
License, *permit*, 760
  exempt, 927A
Licentiate, *scholar*, 492
Licentious, *dissolute*, 954
  debauched, 961
Lich-gate, *see* Lych-gate
Lichen, *plant*, 367
Licit, *dueness*, 924
Lick, *beat*, 972
Lickerish, *fastidious*, 868
  greedy, 865
  licentious, 961
Lickspittle, *flatterer*, 935
  servile, 886
Lictor, *law*, 965
Lid, *cover*, 263
  integument, 22
Lie, *place*, 186
  position, 183
  exist, 1
  recline, 213, 215
  descend, 306
  to deceive, 545
  untruth, 546
  contradict, 489
Lie by, *inaction*, 681
Lie doggo, *conceal*, 528
Lie in wait, *ambush*, 530
Lie low, *lowness*, 207
  concealment, 528
Lie over, *postpone*, 133
  future, 121
Lie to, *quiescence*, 265
* Lied, *music*, 415

Lief, *willingness*, 602
Liege, *master*, 745
Lien, *dueness*, 924
  security, 771
  credit, 805
Lieutenant, *officer*, 745
  deputy, 759
Life, *vitality*, 359
  activity, 682
  existence, 1
  events, 151
Life and death, *important*,
                              642
Life-preserver, *impact*, 276
Lifeblood, *life*, 359
  inbeing, 5
Lifeboat, *boat*, 273
  safety, 666
Lifeless, *dead*, 360
  inert, 172
Lifelike, *similarity*, 17
Lift, *raise*, 307
  way, 627
  aid, 707
  steal, 791
Ligament, *vinculum*, 45
Ligation, *junction*, 43
Ligature, *vinculum*, 45
Light, *luminosity*, 420
  opening, 260
  levity, 320
  colour, 428
  to kindle, 384
  luminary, 423
  small, 32
  trifling, 643
  gay, 836
  idea, 453
  knowledge, 490
  descent, 306
  to arrive, 292
  loose, 961
Light-fingered, *stealing*, 791
Light-footed, *swift*, 274
  active, 682
Light-headed, *delirious*, 503
  foolish, 499
Light-hearted, *cheerful*, 836
Light-legged, *velocity*, 274
Light-minded, *irresolution*,
                              605
Light up, *illuminate*, 420
  cheer, 836
  awaken, 615
Light upon, *find*, 480A
  arrive, 292
Lighten, *render easy*, 705
Lighter, *ship*, 273
  fuel, 388
Lighterman, *mariner*, 269
Lighthouse, *beacon*, 668
  luminary, 423

Lightness, *see* Light
Lightning, *velocity*, 274
  luminousness, 420
Lightship, *light*, 423
  warning, 668
Lightsome, *cheerful*, 836
  fickle, 605
Likable, *attractive*, 829
Like, *similar*, 17
  to relish, 394
  will, 600
  enjoy, 827
Likely, *probable*, 472
Likeness, *similitude*, 17
  copy, 21
  representation, 554
  portrait, 556
Likewise, *addition*, 37
Liking, *love*, 897
  desire, 865
Lilac, *purple*, 437
Lilliputian, *little*, 193
  low, 207
Lilt, *music*, 415
  rhythm, 138
  cheerful, 836
Lily, *whiteness*, 430
  beauty, 845
Limature, *pulverulence*, 330,
                              331
Limb, *member*, 51
  component, 56
  instrument, 633
Limber, *flexible*, 324
Limbo, *incarceration*, 751
  purgatory, 982
Lime, *deception*, 545
Limelight, *publicity*, 531
Limerick, *absurdity*, 497
Limit, *boundary*, 233
  end, 67
  to circumscribe, 231
  qualify, 469
  prohibit, 761
Limitless, *infinity*, 105
  space, 180
Limn, *painting*, 556
Limner, *artist*, 559
Limousine, *vehicle*, 272
Limp, *halt*, 275
  fail, 732
  weak, 160
  inert, 172, 683
  soft, 324
Limpid, *transparent*, 425
Lincture, *remedy*, 662
Line, *length*, 200
  filament, 205
  to coat, 224
  band, 45
  order, 58
  contour, 229

Love, *attachment*, 897
　favourite, 899
　nothing, 4
Love-nest, *love*, 897
Lovelorn, *love-sick*, 897
　rejected, 898
Lovely, *dear*, 897
　pleasing, 829
　beautiful, 845
Lover, *love*, 897
Low, *depressed*, 207
　debased, 940
　vulgar, 876
　cry, 412
　price, 815
　bad, 649
　sound, 403
　smallness, 32
Low-bred, *commonalty*, 876
Low-brow, *ignoramus*, 493
　fool, 501
Low-down, *information*,
Low-lying, *low*, 207　[527
Low-thoughted, *improbity*,
　　　　　　　　940
Lowboy, *receptacle*, 191
Lower, *depress*, 308
　decrease, 36
　inferior, 34
Lowering, *unhealthy*, 657
Lowlands, *lowness*, 207
Lowly, *humility*, 879
Lowness, *see* Low
Loyal, *probity*, 939
　obedient, 743
Lozenge, *angularity*, 244
　sweet, 396
Lubber, *slow*, 683
　awkward, 699
　fool, 501
　big, 192
Lubricate, *smooth*, 255, 332
　facilitate, 705
Lubricity, *slippery*, 255
　impurity, 961
Lucid, *luminous*, 420
　intelligible, 518
　style, 570
　sane, 502
Lucifer, *Satan*, 978
　match, 388
Luck, *chance*, 156, 621
　good, 618
　success, 731
　prosperity, 734
Luckless, *failure*, 732
　adversity, 735
　distressed, 828
Lucky, *prosper*, 134, 734
Lucrative, *receipt*, 810
　useful, 644
　profitable, 775

Lucre, *gain*, 775
　wealth, 803
Lucubration, *thought*, 451
Luculent, *light*, 420
Ludicrous, *laughable*, 838
　ridiculous, 853
　witty, 842
Lug, *traction*, 285
Luggage, *baggage*, 635, 780
Lugger, *ship*, 273
Lugubrious, *dejection*, 837
Lukewarm, *temperate*, 382
　unwilling, 603
　indifferent, 866
　torpid, 823
Lull, *assuage*, 174
　mitigate, 826
　silence, 403
　quiescence, 142, 265
Lullaby, *soothing*, 174
　sleep, 683
　song, 415
　relief, 834
Lum, *funnel*, *chimney*, 351
Lumber, *useless*, 645
　slow, 275
　trash, 643
　disorder, 59
　hindrance, 647, 706
Lumber-room, *receptacle*,
　　　　　　191, 636
Lumbering, *ugly*, 846
Lumberjacket, *dress*, 225
Luminary, *light*, 423
　sage, 500
Luminous, *light*, 420
Lump, *mass*, 192
　density, 321
　concrete, 46
　totality, 50
　to amass, 72
Lumpish, *heavy*, 319
　massive, 192
　sluggish, 683
　awkward, 853
Lunacy, *insanity*, 503
Lunar, *world*, 318
Lunatic, *madman*, 504
Lunation, *period*, 108
Luncheon, *food*, 298
Lunette, *curvature*, 245
Lunge, *impulse*, 276
　attack, 716
Lunik, *space ship*, 273A
Lurch, *sink*, 306
　difficulty, 704
　deception, 545
　oscillation, 314
　slope, 217
Lure, *entice*, 615
　allurement, 865
　deception, 545

Lurid, *dim*, 422
　dark, 421
　yellow, 436
　sensational, 549
Lurk, *latent*, 526
　concealed, 528
　hide, 530
　unseen, 447
Luscious, *savoury*, 394, 396
　grateful, 829
　style, 577
Lush, *succulent*, 333
　vegetation, 365
　luxuriant, 639
Lushy, *drunkenness*, 959
Lust, *desire*, 865
　concupiscence, 961
Lustily, *exertion*, 686
Lustration, *purification*,
　　　　　　　　652
　atonement, 952
Lustre, *brightness*, 420
　chandelier, 423
Lustrum, *period*, 108
Lusty, *size*, 192
　strong, 159
* Lusus naturae, *uncon-
　formity*, 83
Lute, *cement*, 45
　to cement, 46
　guitar, 417
Luxation, *disjunction*, 44
Luxuriant, *sufficiency*, 639
　vegetation, 365
Luxuriate, *pleasure*, 827
Luxurious, *pleasurableness*,
　　　　　　　　829
Luxury, *physical*, 377
　enjoyment, 827
　sensuality, 954
Lyceum, *school*, 542
Lych-gate, *opening*, 260
Lyddite, *arms*, 727
Lying, *decumbent*, 213
　deceptive, 546
Lyke-wake, *interment*, 363
Lymph, *water*, 337
Lymphatic, *inert*, 172
　soft, 324
Lynch, *punish*, 972
　kill, 361
Lynch law, *illegality*, 964
Lynx-eyed, *vision*, 441
Lyre, *musical instrument*,
　　　　　　　　417
Lyrics, *poetry*, 597

M

M.C., *director*, 694
Ma, *mother*, 166

Mab, *fairy*, 979
Macabre, *gruesome*, 846
Macadam, *smoothness*, 255
Macaroni, *fop*, 854
Macaronic, *poetry*, 597
Mace, *club*, 633
  weapon, 727
  sceptre, 747
Mace-bearer, *jurisprudence*,
  965
Macerate, *water*, 337
Maceration, *asceticism*, 955
  atonement, 952
Machiavellian, *falsehood*,
  544
Machiavellism, *cunning*,
  702
Machicolation, *embrasure*,
  257
Machination, *plan*, 626
Machine, *instrument*, 633
Machinist, *agent*, 690
Mackerel sky, *cloud*, 353
Mackintosh, *dress*, 225
Macrobiotic, *lasting*, 110
Macrocosm, *world*, 318
  greatness, 31
Macrology, *diffuseness*, 573
Mactation, *idolatry*, 991
Macula, *blemish*, 848
Maculated, *variegation*, 440
Maculation, *ugliness*, 846
Mad, *insane*, 503
  violent, 173
Madcap, *caprice*, 608
  rash, 863
  excitable, 825
Madden, *excite*, 824
Madder, *red*, 434
Made of, *composition*, 54
Madefaction, *moisture*, 339
Madhouse, *hospital*, 662
Madman, *madman*, 504
Madness, *insanity*, 503
Madrigal, *poetry*, 597
Maelstrom, *whirlpool*,
  312, 348
  turmoil, 59
Maenad, *violence*, 173
Maffick, *make merry*, 836
Magazine, *store*, 636
  record, 551
  book, 593
Magdalen, *penitent*, 950
Mage, *sorcerer*, 994
Magenta, *purple*, 437
Maggot, *whim*, 608
  desire, 865
Maggoty, *uncleanness*, 653
Magi, *sage*, 500
  saint, 948
Magic, *sorcery*, 992

Magic lantern, *optical*, 445
  spectacle, 448
Magician, *sorcerer*, 994
Magisterial, *pride*, 878
Magistracy, *authority*, 737
  jurisdiction, 965
Magistrate, *justiciary*, 967
  ruler, 745
Magistrature, *authority*,
  737
Magma, *mixture*, 41
Magnanimity, *disinterestedness*, 942
Magnate, *nobility*, 875
Magnet, *attraction*, 288, 829
  desire, 865
  motive, 615
* Magnificat, *worship*, 990
Magnificent, *grand*, 882
  fine, 845
  magnanimous, 942
Magnifico, *nobility*, 875
Magnifier, *optical instru-
  ment*, 445
Magnify, *increase*, 35
  enlarge, 194
  exaggerate, 549
  praise, 990
  approve, 931
Magniloquent, *ornament*,
  577
  extravagant, 549
  speech, 582
Magnitude, *quantity*, 25
  size, 192
Magpie, *loquacity*, 584
Magsman, *thief*, 792
Magus, *heathen*, 984
Maharajah, *master*, 745
  noble, 875
Maharanee, *noble*, 875
  chief, 745
Mahatma, *sorcerer*, 994
Mahogany colour, *brown*,
  433
Mahomet, *religious founder*,
  986
Mahometanism, *religions*,
  984
Maid of honour, *marriage*,
  903
Maiden, *girl*, 129, 374
  servant, 746
  spinster, 904
  purity, 960
  guillotine, 975
  first, 66
Mail, *letters*, 592
  news, 532
  defence, 717
  armoury, 727
Mail-cart, *vehicle*, 272

Maim, *injure*, 649, 659
  weaken, 160
Main, *whole*, 50
  tunnel, 260
  conduit, 350
  ocean, 341
  principal, 642
Mainland, *land*, 342
Mainly, *greatness*, 31
Mainspring, *cause*, 153
  motive, 615
Mainstay, *instrument*, 631
  refuge, 666
  hope, 858
Maintain, *continue*, 141, 143
  preserve, 670
  sustain, 170
  assert, 535
* Maison de santé, *remedy*,
  662
* Maître, *expert*, 700
Majestic, *repute*, 873
Majesty, *king*, 745
  rank, 873
  Deity, 976
Major, *greater*, 33
  officer, 745
Majordomo, *director*, 694
  commissary, 746
Majority, *age*, 131
  greater number, 102
  dead, 362
Majuscules, *printing*, 591
Make, *produce*, 161
  constitute, 54
  form, 240
  arrive at, 292
  price, 812
Make-believe, *untruth*, 546
Make fast, *vinculum*, 43
Make for, *tend*, 176
Make good, *compensation*,
  30
  substantiate, 467
Make it up, *forgive*, 918
Make known, *information*,
  527
Make loose, *incoherence*, 47
Make out, *decipher*, 522
  understand, 518
  discover, 480A
Make over, *transfer*, 783
Make up, *complete*, 52
  compose, 54
  imagine, 515
  invent, 544
  improvise, 612
Make up for, *compensate*, 30
Make up to, *accost*, 586
  approach, 286
Make way, *progress*, 282
  improve, 658

Materials, *materials*, 635
Maternity, *paternity*, 166
Mathematical. *exact*, 494
Mathematics, *quantity*, 25
Matinée, *drama*, 599
Matins, *rite*, 990, 998
  morning, 125
Matriarchy, *authority*, 737
Matricide, *killing*, 361
Matriculation, *learner*, 541
Matrimony, *wedlock*, 903
  mixture, 41
Matrix, *mould*, 22
  engraving, 558
  workshop, 691
Matron, *woman*, 374
  wife, 903
  old, 130
  adolescent, 131
  superintendent, 694
Matt, *rough*, 256
Matted, *crossing*, 219
Matter, *substance*, 3
  material world, 316
  topic, 454
  business, 625
  meaning, 516
  importance, 642
  pus, 653
Matter of course, *conformity*,
  82
Matter of fact, *being*, 1
Matter-of-fact, *prosaic*, 843
Matting, *plaiting*, 219
Mattock, *instrument*, 633
  sharpness, 253
Mattress, *support*, 215
Mature, *ripe*, 144, 673
  scheme, 626
  old, 124
  adolescent, 131
Matutinal, *early*, 125, 132
Maudlin, *drunk*, 959
  sensitive, 822
Maugre, *counteraction*, 179
Maul, *maltreat*, 649
  impact, 276
Maunder, *digress*, 573
Mausoleum, *interment*, 363
* Mauvais sujet, *bad man*,
  949
* Mauvaise honte, *modesty*,
  881
  affectation, 855
* Mauvaise plaisanterie,
  vulgarity, 852
Mauve, *purple*, 437
Maw, *receptacle*, 191
Mawkish, *insipid*, 391
  indifferent, 866
Maxim, *maxim*, 496, 697
  gun, 727

Maximum, *greatness*, 33
Maxixe, *dance*, 840
May, *possible*, 470
  chance, 156
  supposition, 514
* Maya, *illusion*, 495
Maybe, *possible*, 470
  chance, 156
  supposition, 514
Mayhap, *possible*, 470
  chance, 156
  supposition, 514
Mayhem, *evil*, 619
Mayor, *master*, 745
Maypole, *height*, 206
Mazarine, *blue*, 438
Maze, *convolution*, 248
  bewilderment, 491
  enigma, 533
Mazuma, *money*, 800
Mazurka, *dance*, 840
  music, 415
Me, *personality*, 317
* Me judice, *belief*, 484
* Mea culpa, *penitence*, 950
Mead, *plain*, 344
  sweet, 396
Meadow, *plain*, 344
Meagre, *thin*, 193
  narrow, 203
  scanty, 640
  style, 575
Meal, *powder*, 330
  repast, 298
Mealy-mouthed, *false*, 544
  servile, 886
Mean, *average*, 29
  middle, 68, 628
  small, 32
  contemptible, 643
  shabby, 874
  base, 940
  humble, 879
  sneaking, 886
  selfish, 943
  stingy, 819
  intend, 620
  to signify, 516
Meander, *circuition*, 311
  convolution, 248
  river, 348
  wander, 279, 629
Meaningless, *nonsense*, 517
Means, *appliances*, 632
  fortune, 803
  property, 780
Meantime, *period*, 106, 120
Meanwhile, *duration*, 106,
  120
Measure, *extent*, 25
  degree, 26
  moderation, 174, 639

Measure, *to compute*, 466
  proceeding, 626, 680
  to apportion, 786
  in music, 413
  in poetry, 597
Measure, in a great, *greatness*, 31
Measure for measure, *compensation*, 30
Meat, *food*, 298
Meaty, *savoury*, 394
Mechanic, *agent*, 690
Mechanical, *automatic*, 601
  style, 575
  imitative, 19
Mechanics, *force*, 159
  machinery, 632
Mechanism, *means*, 632
Medal, *reward*, 973
  record, 551
  palm, 733
  decoration, 877
Medallion, *sculpture*, 557
Meddle, *interpose*, 682
  act, 680
Meddlesome, *interpose*, 682
Medial, *middle*, 68
Median, *mean*, 29
Mediation, *mediation*, 724
  deprecation, 766
Mediator, *Saviour*, 976
Medicament, *remedy*, 662
Medicaster. *deceiver*, 548
Medicate, *heal*, 660
  compound, 41
Medicine, *remedy*, 662
Medieval, *oldness*, 124
  past, 122
Mediocrity, *moderate*, 32
  mean, 29
  of fortune, 736
  imperfect, 648, 651
Meditate, *think*, 451
  purpose, 620
Mediterranean, *middle*, 68
  interjacent, 228
Medium, *mean*, 29
  pigment, 428
  instrument, 631
  spiritualist, 994
Medley, *mixture*, 41
Meed, *reward*, 973
  gift, 784
  share, 786
  praise, 931
Meek, *humble*, 879
  gentle, 826
Meerschaum, *tobacco-pipe*,
  298A
Meet, *contact*, 199, 292
  agreement, 23
  converge, 290

Meteorology, *air*, 338
Methinks, *belief*, 484
Method, *order*, 58
　way, 627
Methodize, *arrange*, 60
Meticulous, *careful*, 459
Metonymy, *metaphor*, 521
　substitution, 147
Metre, *poetry*, 597
Metrical, *measurement*, 466
Metropolis, *abode*, 189
Mettle, *spirit*, 820
　courage, 861
Mettlesome, *excitable*, 822,
　　　　　825
　brave, 861
Mew, *enclose*, 231
　restrain, 751
　divest, 226
　complain, 839
Mewl, *ululation*, 412
* Mezzo-rilievo, *sculpture*,
　　　　　557
Mezzo-soprano, *melody*, 413
* Mezzo termine, *middle*, 68
　mid-course, 628
Mezzotint, *engraving*, 558
Miasma, *bane*, 663
Miasmal, *morbific*, 649
Micawber, *careless*, 460
Microbe, *bane*, 663
　insalubrity, 657
Microcosm, *little*, 32, 193
Microfilm, *copy*, 21
Microphone, *loudness*, 404
　hearing, 418
Microscope, *optical*, 445
Microscopic, *little*, 193
Mid, *middle*, 68
Mid-course, *middle*, 628
Midas, *wealth*, 803
Midday, *course*, 125
Midden, *uncleanness*, 653
Middle, *in order*, 68
　in degree, 29
　in space, 223
Middleman, *agent*, 690
　go-between, 631
　salesman, 797
Middling, *imperfect*, 651
　mean, 29
Midge, *littleness*, 193
Midget, *dwarf*, 193
Midland, *land*, 342
Midnight, *evening*, 126
　darkness, 421
Midriff, *interjacence*, 228
Midshipman, *master*, 745
Midst, *central*, 223
Midsummer, *morning*, 125
Midway, *middle*, 68
Midwife, *doctor*, 662

Mien, *appearance*, 448
　conduct, 692
Miff, *resentment*, 900
Might, *power*, 157
　degree, 26
　violence, 173
Mighty, *much*, 31
　large, 192
　powerful, 159
　haughty, 878
Migrate, *journey*, 266
Mikado, *master*, 745
Mike, *loudness*, 404
　hearing, 418
Milch cow, *store*, 636
Mild, *moderate*, 174
　insipid, 391
　lenient, 740
　calm, 826
　courteous, 894
　warm, 382
Mildew, *unclean*, 653
Mileage, *measurement*, 466
Militant, *contention*, 720
Militarism, *warfare*, 722
　authority, 737
Military, *combatant*, 726
Militate, *opposition*, 179, 608
Militia, *combatant*, 726
Milk, *to despoil*, 789
Milk-and-water, *imperfect*,
　　　　　651
Milk-white, *whiteness*, 430
Milksop, *coward*, 862
Milky, *semitransparent*, 427
　emulsive, 252
Milky Way, *world*, 318
Mill, *machine*, 330, 633
　workshop, 691
Mill-pond, *store*, 636
Millenary, *celebration*, 883
Millennium, *period*, 108
　thousand, 98
　futurity, 121
　Utopia, 515
　hope, 858
Millesimal, *thousand*, 98
Millet-seed, *littleness*, 193
Milliner, *dress*, 225
Million, *number*, 98
Millionaire, *wealth*, 803
Millstone, *incubus*, 706
　weight, 319
Miltonic, *sublime*, 574
　poetry, 597
Mime, *player*, 599
　buffoon, 856
Mimeograph, *imitation*, 19
Mimesis, *imitation*, 19
Mimic, *imitation*, 19
　repeat, 104
Minacity, *threat*, 909

Minaret, *height*, 206
Minatory, *threatening*, 909
　dangerous, 665
* Minaudérie, *affected*, 855
Mince, *disjoin*, 44
　stammer, 583
Mincing, *slow*, 275
　affected, 855
Mind, *intellect*, 450
　will, 600
　desire, 865
　dislike, 867
　purpose, 620
　to attend to, 457
　believe, 484
　remember, 505
Minded, *willing*, 602
Mindful, *attentive*, 457
　remembering, 505
Mindless, *inattentive*, 458
　forgetful, 506
Mine, *store*, 636
　abundance, 639
　to hollow, 252
　open, 260; *snare*, 545
　sap, 162
　damage, 659
Mine-layer, *ship*, 273
Mine-sweeper, *ship*, 273
Mineral, *inorganic*, 358
Mineralogy, *inorganic*, 358
Minerva, *goddess*, 979
Mingle, *mix*, 41
Mingy, *parsimony*, 819
Mini, *small*, 193
Miniature, *portrait*, 556
　small, 193
Minikin, *small*, 193
Minim, *small*, 32, 193
Minimize, *moderate*, 174
　underestimate, 483
Minimum, *small*, 32, 193
Mining, *opening*, 260
Minion, *favourite*, 899
Minister, *deputy*, 759
　instrumentality, 631
　director, 694
　to aid, 707
　rites, 998
Ministry, *direction*, 693
　church, 995
Minnow, *littleness*, 193
Minor, *inferior*, 34
　infant, 129
Minority, *fewness*, 103
Minotaur, *unconformity*, 83
Minster, *temple*, 1000
Minstrel, *music*, 416
Minstrelsy, *musician*, 415
Mint, *workshop*, 691
　mould, 22
　wealth, 803

Minuend, *deduction*, 38
Minuet, *dance*, 840
   music, 415
Minus, *less*, 38
   in debt, 806
   deficient, 304
Minuscules, *printing*, 591
Minute, *in quantity*, 32
   in size, 193
   of time, 108
   instant, 113
   compendium, 596
   record, 551
   in style, 573
Minutest, *inferior*, 34
Minutiae, *small*, 32
   little, 193
   unimportant, 643
Minx, *impertinent*, 887
   bad woman, 949
* Mirabile dictu, *wonder*, 870
Miracle, *prodigy*, 872
Miraculous, *wonder*, 870
Mirage, *dim sight*, 443
   appearance, 448
   shadow, 4
Mire, *uncleanness*, 653
Mirk, *darkness*, 421
Mirror, *reflector*, 445
   perfection, 650
   saint, 948
   imitate, 19
Mirth, *cheerful*, 836
Mirthless, *dejected*, 837
Misadventure, *failure*, 732
   adversity, 735
   misfortune, 830
Misalliance, *marriage*, 903
Misanthrope, *recluse*, 893,
         911
Misapply, *misuse*, 679
   misinterpret, 523
   mismanage, 699
Misapprehend, *mistake*, 495
   misinterpret, 523
Misappropriate, *misuse*, 679
Misarrange, *derange*, 61
Misbecome, *vice*, 945
Misbegotten, *vice*, 945
Misbehaviour, *discourtesy*,
         895
   vulgarity, 852
   guilt, 947
Misbelief, *doubt*, 495
Miscalculate, *sophistry*, 477
   disappoint, 509
Miscall, *misnomer*, 565
Miscarriage, *failure*, 732
Miscegenation, *mixture*, 41
Miscellany, *mixture*, 41
   collection, 72
   generality, 78

Mischance, *misfortune*, 830
   adversity, 735
   failure, 732
Mischief, *evil*, 619
Mischievous, *badness*, 649
Miscible, *mix*, 41
Miscompute, *mistake*, 495
Misconceive, *mistake*, 495
   misinterpret, 481, 523
Misconduct, *guilt*, 947
   bungling, 699
Misconstrue, *misinterpret*,
         523
Miscount, *error*, 495
Miscreant, *wretch*, 949
   apostate, 941
Miscreated, *vice*, 945
Miscue, *unskilfulness*, 699
Misdate, *anachronism*, 115
Misdeed, *guilt*, 947
Misdeem, *misinterpret*, 523
Misdemean, *vice*, 945
Misdevotion, *impiety*, 988
Misdirect, *misteaching*, 538
   bungle, 699
Misdoing, *guilt*, 947
* Mise en scène, *appearance*,
         448
Misemploy, *misuse*, 679
Miser, *parsimony*, 819
Miserable, *contemptible*,
         643
   unhappy, 828
   pitiable, 914
   small, 32
Miserly, *parsimony*, 819
Misery, *pain*, 828
Misestimate, *error*, 495
Misfit, *disparity*, 24
Misfortune, *evil*, 619
   failure, 732
   adversity, 735
   unhappiness, 830
Misgiving, *fear*, 860
   doubt, 485
Misgovern, *unskilful*, 699
Misguide, *misteaching*, 538
Misguided, *foolish*, 699
Mishandle, *maltreat*, 649
Mishap, *evil*, 619
   failure, 732
   adversity, 735
   disaster, 830
Mishmash, *mixture*, 41
Misinform, *misteach*, 538
   ignorance, 491
   error, 495
Misintelligence, *misteach*,
         538
Misinterpret, *misinterpret*,
         523
Misjoined, *disagreement*, 24

Misjudge, *err*, 495
   sophistry, 477
Mislay, *lose*, 776
   derange, 61
Mislead, *deceive*, 477, 545
   misteach, 538
   error, 495
Mislike, *dislike*, 867
Mismanage, *unskilful*, 699
Mismatch, *difference*, 15
Mismatched, *disagreement*,
         24
Misname, *misnomer*, 565
Misnomer, *misnomer*, 565
Misogamy, *celibacy*, 904
Misogynist, *celibacy*, 904
Misplace, *disorder*, 59
   unconformity, 83
Misplaced, *unsuitable*, 24
Misprint, *error*, 495
Mispronounce, *speech*, 583
Misproportioned, *ugliness*,
         846
Misquote, *misinterpret*, 523
   false, 544
Misreckon, *error*, 495
Misrelate, *error*, 495
Misremember, *error*, 495
Misreport, *err*, 495
   falsify, 544
Misrepresent, *untruth*, 546
Misrepresentation, *perver-*
   sion, 523
   falsehood, 544
   caricature, 555
Misrule, *misconduct*, 699
   laxity, 738
Miss, *lose*, 776
   fail, 732
   inattention, 458, 460
   want, 865
   girl, 374
Missal, *rite*, 998
Missay, *stammer*, 583
   misnomer, 565
Misshapen, *ugliness*, 846
   distortion, 243
Missile, *thing thrown*, 284
   arms, 727
Missing, *absence*, 187
Mission, *commission*, 755
   undertaking, 676
   business, 625
   warfare, 722
Missionary, *clergy*, 996
Missive, *correspond*, 592
Misspell, *misinterpret*, 523
Misspend, *prodigal*, 818
Misstate, *misinterpret*, 523
   falsify, 544
Misstatement, *error*, 495
   falsehood, 544

Misstatement, *untruth*, 546
　perversion, 523
Mist, *dimness*, 422
Mistake, *error*, 495
　failure, 732
　mismanagement, 699
　misconstrue, 523
Misteach, *misteach*, 538
Misterm, *misnomer*, 565
Misthink, *error*, 495
Mistime, *intempestivity*, 135
Mistral, *wind*, 349
Mistranslate, *misinterpret*,
　　　　　　　　　523
Mistress, *lady*, 374
　sweetheart, 897
　concubine, 962
Mistrust, *doubt*, 485
Misty, *opaque*, 426
　dim, 422
　invisible, 447
Misunderstanding, *error*,
　　　　　　　　　495
　misinterpretation, 523
　discord, 713
Misuse, *misuse*, 679
　waste, 638
Mite, *small*, 193
　bit, 32
　money, 800
Mitigate, *abate*, 36, 174
　relieve, 834
　calm, 826
　improve, 658
　extenuate, 937
* Mitrailleuse, *gun*, 727
Mitre, *canonicals*, 999
　joint, 43
Mitten, *dress*, 225
Mittimus, *command*, 741
Mix, *mix*, 41
Mixed, *disorder*, 59
Mixture, *mix*, 41
Mizzle, *rain*, 348
Mnemonics, *memory*, 505
Mnemosyne, *memory*, 505
Moan, *lamentation*, 839, 411
Moat, *enclosure*, 232
　ditch, 350
　defence, 717
Mob, *crowd*, 72, 31
　multitude, 102
　troop, 726
　plenty, 639
　vulgar, 876
　to scold, 932
Mob law, *illegal*, 964
Mobile, *movable*, 264
　sensible, 822
　inconstant, 607
Mobilization, *warfare*, 722
　move, 264

Mobility, *commonalty*, 876
Mobocracy, *authority*, 737
Mobsman, *thief*, 792
Moccasin, *dress*, 225
Mock, *imitate*, 17
　repeat, 104
　erroneous, 495
　false, 544
　to ridicule, 483, 856
　laugh at, 838
Mock-heroic, *ridiculous*,
　　　　　　　　　853
Modal, *extrinsic*, 6
　state, 7
　circumstance, 8
Mode, *fashion*, 852
　method, 627
Model, *prototype*, 22
　to change, 140, 144
　rule, 80
　example, 82
　to copy, 19
　sculpture, 557
　perfection, 650
　saint, 948
Modeller, *artist*, 559
Moderate, *small*, 32
　to allay, 174
　to assuage, 826
　temperate, 953
　cheap, 815
Moderation, *temperateness*,
　　　　　　　　　174
　mediocrity, 736
* Moderato, *music*, 415
Moderator, *master*, 745
　director, 694
Modern, *newness*, 123
Modernize, *change*, 140
Modesty, *humility*, 881
　purity, 960
Modicum, *little*, 33
　allotment, 786
Modification, *difference*, 15
　variation, 20
　change, 140
　qualification, 469
Modify, *convert*, 144
Modish, *fashion*, 852
Modulation, *change*, 140
　harmony, 413
* Modus operandi, *method*,
　　　　　　　　　627
　conduct, 692
* Modus vivendi, *arrange-
　ment*, 723
　compromise, 774
Mogul, *master*, 745
Mohammed, *religious
　founder*, 986
Mohammedanism, *religions*,
　　　　　　　　　984

Mohock, *roisterer*, 949
Moider, *bewilder*, 475
　inattention, 458
Moiety, *bisection*, 91
Moil, *action*, 680
　work, 686
Moist, *wet*, 337
　humid, 339
Moke, *carrier*, 271
Molasses, *sweetness*, 396
Mole, *mound*, 206
　defence, 717
　refuge, 666
Molecule, *small*, 32, 193
Molehill, *lowness*, 207
　trifling, 643
Molestation, *evil*, 619
　damage, 649
　malevolence, 907
Mollify, *allay*, 174
　soften, 324
　conciliate, 918
　assuage, 826
Mollusc, *animal*, 366
Mollycoddle, *cowardice*,
　　　　　　　　　862
Moloch, *tyranny*, 739
　divinity, 979
　idol, 986
Molten, *liquid*, 335
Moment, *of time*, 113
　importance, 642
Momentary, *transient*, 111
Momentum, *impulse*, 276
Momus, *rejoicing*, 838
Monachism, *church*, 995
Monad, *littleness*, 193
　unity, 87
Monarch, *master*, 745
Monarchy, *authority*, 737
Monastery, *temple*, 1000
Monastic, *churchdom*, 995
Monetary, *money*, 800
Money, *money*, 800
Money-bag, *treasury*, 802
Money-changer, *merchant*,
　　　　　　　　　797
Money-grubber, *miser*, 819
　acquisition, 775
Moneyed, *wealth*, 803
Moneyer, *treasurer*, 801
Moneyless, *poverty*, 804
Monger, *merchant*, 797
Mongrel, *mixture*, 41
　anomalous, 83
Moniker, *name*, 564
Moniliform, *circular*, 247
Monism, *unity*, 87
Monition, *advice*, 695
　warning, 668
　information, 527
　omen, 512

Monitor, *teacher*, 540
  director, 694
  master, 745
  ship, 723
Monitory, *prediction*, 511
  warning, 668
Monk, *clergy*, 996
Monkery, *churchdom*, 995
Monkey, *imitative*, 19
  engine, 276
  ridiculous, 856
  laughing-stock, 857
  to play the fool, 499
  money, 800
Monkey-shines, *prank*, 840
  foolery, 497
  caprice, 608
Monkish, *clergy*, 995
Monochord, *musical*, 417
Monochrome, *colourless*, 429
Monocular, *lens*, 445
Monody, *lamentation*, 839
Monogamy, *marriage*, 903
Monogram, *sign*, 550
  cipher, 533
  diagram, 554
Monograph, *dissertation*,
              595
Monolith, *record*, 551
Monologue, *soliloquy*, 589
Monomania, *insanity*, 503
  error, 495
  obstinacy, 606
Monomaniac, *madman*, 504
Monometallism, *money*, 800
Monoplane, *aircraft*, 273A
Monopolize, *possess*, 777
  engross, 457
Monopoly, *syndicate*, 778
Monosyllable, *letter*, 561
Monotheism, *theology*, 983
Monotonous, *unchanging*,
              141
Monotony, *identity*, 13
  uniformity, 16
  repetition, 104, 141
  in style, 575
  weariness, 841
Monotype, *printing*, 591
* Monsieur, *title*, 877
Monsoon, *wind*, 349
Monster, *exception*, 83
  prodigy, 872
  size, 192
  ugly, 846
  evildoer, 913
  ruffian, 949
Monstrous, *greatness*, 31
  huge, 192
  wonderful, 870
  ugly, 846
  ridiculous, 853

* Mont de piété, *lending*, 787
Montgolfier, *balloon*, 273A
Month, *period*, 108
Monthly, *periodical*, 138
Monticule, *height*, 206
Monument, *record*, 551
  interment, 363
  tallness, 206
Monumental, *great*, 31
Mood, *nature*, 5
  state, 7
  temper, 820
  will, 600
  tendency, 176
  disposition, 602
  affections, 820
  variations, 20
  change, 140
Moody, *sullen*, 895
  fretful, 900
  furious, 825
Moon, *inaction*, 681
  changeable, 149
Moon-eyed, *dim sight*, 443
Moonbeam, *light*, 420
  dimness, 422
Mooncalf, *fool*, 501
Moonless, *dark*, 421
Moonlight, *light*, 420
Moonshine, *nonsense*,
              497, 517
  excuse, 617
  trumpery, 643
  dimness, 422
Moonstruck, *insanity*, 503
Moony, *dreamy*, 458
  foolish, 499
  listless, 683
Moor, *open space*, 180
  plain, 344
  locate, 184
  join, 43; *rest*, 265
Moorland, *space*, 180
  plain, 344
Moot, *inquire*, 461
  argue, 476
  conjecture, 514
Moot point, *topic*, 454, 461
Mop, *clean*, 652
Mope, *dejection*, 837
Mope-eyed, *dim sight*, 443
Moped, *vehicle*, 272
Moppet, *darling*, 899
Moraine, *debris*, 330
Moral, *right*, 922
  duty, 926
  virtuous, 944
  maxim, 496
Moral fibre, *courage*, 861
Morale, *state*, 7
Moralize, *reason*, 476
  teach, 537

Morality, *drama*, 599
Morass, *marsh*, 345
Moratorium, *delay*, 133
Morbid, *bad*, 649
  diseased, 655
  noxious, 657
Morbific, *bad*, 649
  diseased, 655
  noxious, 657
Mordacity, *malevolence*, 907
Mordant, *pungent*, 392
  vigorous, 574
  sarcastic, 932
Mordent, *grace-note*, 415
More, *addition*, 37
  superiority, 33
More or less, *smallness*, 32
  equality, 27
* More suo, *conformity*, 82
Moreover, *addition*, 37
  accompaniment, 88
Morganatic, *marriage*, 903
* Morgue, *pride*, 878
  dead-house, 363
Moribund, *dying*, 360
  sick, 655
Mormon, *polygamist*, 903
Morning, *morning*, 125
Moron, *fool*, 501
Morose, *discourtesy*, 895
Morphia, *anaesthetic*, 376
Morphology, *form*, 240
Morris-dance, *dance*, 840
Morrison, *shelter*, 717
Morrow, *futurity*, 121
  morning, 125
Morsel, *small quantity*, 32
  portion, 51
Mortal, *man*, 373
  fatal, 361
  bad, 649
  weariness, 841
Mortality, *death*, 360
  evanescence, 111
  mankind, 372
Mortar, *cement*, 45
  artillery, 727
  pulverization, 330
Mortgage, *sale*, 796
  lend, 787
  security, 771
  credit, 805
Mortgagee, *credit*, 805
Mortgagor, *debt*, 806
Mortice, *see* Mortise
Mortician, *interment*, 363
Mortify, *pain*, 828
  to vex, 830
  to discontent, 832
  to humiliate, 874, 879
  disease, 655
  asceticism, 955

Mortise, *unite*, 43
   insert, 300
   intersect, 219
Mortuary, *interment*, 363
Mosaic, *mixture*, 41
   variegation, 440
   painting, 556
Moslem, *religions*, 984
Mosque, *temple*, 1000
Moss, *marsh*, 345
   tuft, 256
Moss-grown, *deterioration*, 65
Moss-trooper, *thief*, 792
Most, *greatness*, 31
Most part, for the, *general*, 78
   conformity, 82
* Mot, *maxim*, 496
Mote, *particle*, 193
   smallness, 32
   blemish, 848
   light, 320
Motel, *inn*, 189
Motet, *music*, 415
   worship, 990
Moth, *decay*, 659
Moth-eaten, *imperfect*, 651
Mother, *parent*, 166
   mould, 653
   nun, 997
Mother-of-pearl, *variegation*, 440
Mother tongue, *language*, 560
Mother wit, *wisdom*, 498
Motherland, *abode*, 189
Motherly, *love*, 897
Motif, *music*, 415
   theme, 454
Motion, *change of place*, 264
   proposition, 514
   topic, 454
   request, 765
   offer, 763
Motion picture, *drama*, 599
Motionless, *quiescence*, 265
Motive, *reason*, 615
   music, 415
Motiveless, *absence of motive*, 616
Motley, *multiform*, 81
   mixed, 41
   variegated, 440
Motor, *machine*, 633
   vehicle, 272
Motor-boat, *ship*, 273
Motor-bus, *vehicle*, 272
Motor-car, *vehicle*, 272
Motor-coach, *vehicle*, 272
Motor-cycle, *vehicle*, 272
Motor-van, *vehicle*, 272

Motorize, *move*, 264
Motorman, *director*, 694
Mottled, *variegated*, 440
Motto, *device*, 550
   maxim, 496
   phrase, 566
Mouch, *inactivity*, 688
Mould, *form*, 240, 329
   condition, 7
   earth, 342
   mildew, 653
   to model, 554
   carve, 557
   matrix, 22
Moulder, *deterioration*, 659
Moulding, *ornament*, 847
Mouldy, *decayed*, 653
   fetid, 401
Moult, *divestment*, 226
Mound, *defence*, 717
   hillock, 206
Mount, *to rise*, 305
   hill, 206, 250
   support, 215
   to prepare, 673
Mountain, *hill*, 206
   size, 192
   weight, 319
Mountaineer, *climber*, 305
Mountebank, *quack*, 548
   ignoramus, 493
   buffoon, 844, 857
Mourn, *grieve*, 828
   lament, 839
Mournful, *sad*, 837
   afflicting, 830
Mouse, *little*, 193
   to search, 461
Mouse-coloured, *grey*, 432
Mouse-hole, *opening*, 260
* Mousseux, *bubble*, 353
Moustache, *hair*, 256
Mouth, *entrance*, 66
   opening, 260
   brink, 230
   voice, 580
   stammer, 583
Mouth-honour, *flattery*, 933
Mouth-watering, *desire*, 865
Mouthful, *portion*, 51, 193
Mouthpiece, *speaker*, 524, 540
   speech, 582
Mouthy, *style*, 577
Movable, *transference*, 270
Movables, *property*, 780
Move, *be in motion*, 264
   induce, 615
   excite, 824
   act, 680
   undertaking, 676
   propose, 514

Move off, *recede*, 287
   depart, 293
Move on, *progression*, 282
Moved, *impressed*, 827
Moveless, *quiescence*, 265
Movement, *motion*, 264
   stir, 682
Movie, *cinema*, 599A
Mow, *cultivate*, 371
   destruction, 162
Mr., *title*, 877
Much, *greatness*, 31
Mucilage, *semiliquid*, 352
   adhesive, 45
Muck, *uncleanness*, 653
Muckle, *greatness*, 31
Muckworm, *miser*, 819
   baseborn, 876
Mucronate, *sharpness*, 253
Mucus, *semiliquid*, 352
Mud, *unclean*, 653
Muddle, *disorder*, 59
   derange, 61
   bungle, 699
Muddled, *confused*, 458
   tipsy, 959
   foolish, 499
Muddy, *opaque*, 426
Mudlark, *commonalty*, 876
Muezzin, *clergy*, 996
Muff, *bungler*, 701
   to bungle, 699
Muffle, *silent*, 403, 581
   conceal, 528
   taciturn, 585
   wrap, 225
Muffler, *dress*, 225
Mufti, *clergy*, 996
   judge, 966
   dress, 225
Mug, *receptacle*, 191
   fool, 501
   face, 448
   to study, 539
Muggy, *dim*, 422
   moist, 339
Mulatto, *unconformity*, 83
   mixture, 41
Mulct, *penalty*, 974
Mule, *beast*, 271
   mongrel, 83
   obstinate, 606
   fool, 499
   slipper, 225
Muleteer, *director*, 694
Muliebrity, *woman*, 374
Mull, *cape*, 250
   sweeten, 396
Mull over, *think*, 451
Mullah, *judge*, 967
   priest, 996
Mulligrubs, *depression*, 837

Mullion, *support*, 215
Multifarious, *multiform*, 81
 various, 15
Multifid, *divided*, 51
Multifold, *multiform*,
 16A, 81
Multiform, *diversified*,
 16A, 81
Multigenerous, *multiform*,
 81
Multilateral, *side*, 236
Multipartite, *disjunction*, 44
Multiple, *numerous*, 102
 product, 84
Multiplicand, *number*, 84
Multiplication, *arithmetical*,
 85
 reproduction, 163
Multiplicator, *number*, 84
Multiplicity, *multitude*, 102
Multiplier, *number*, 84
Multisonous, *loud*, 404
Multitude, *number*, 102
 greatness, 31
 assemblage, 72
 mob, 876
Multitudinous, *multitude*,
 102
* Multum in parvo, *contrac-
 tion*, 195
 conciseness, 572
Mum, *silence*, 403
 aphony, 581
 mother, 166
Mumble, *eat*, 296
 mutter, 405, 583
Mumbo Jumbo, *idol*, 991
Mumchance, *silent*, 403
 mute, 581
Mummer, *the drama*, 599
Mummery, *absurdity*, 497
 ridicule, 856
 parade, 882
 imposture, 545
 masquerade, 840
Mummify, *preserve*, 670
 bury, 363
Mummy, *corpse*, 362
 dryness, 340
 mother, 166
Mump, *dejection*, 837
Mumper, *beggar*, 767
Mumps, *sullenness*, 895
Munch, *eat*, 296
Munchausen, *exaggerate*,
 549
Mundane, *world*, 318
 selfishness, 943
 irreligion, 989
Munerary, *reward*, 973
Municipal, *law*, 965
 distinct, 189

Munificent, *liberality*, 816
 giving, 784
Muniment, *record*, 551
 defence, 717
 refuge, 666
Munition, *material*, 635
Murder, *killing*, 361
 to bungle, 699
Murex, *purple*, 437
Muricate, *sharpness*, 253
Murky, *darkness*, 421
Murmur, *sound*, 405
 complaint, 839
 flow, 348
Murrain, *disease*, 655
Murrey, *redness*, 434
Muscle, *strength*, 159
Muse, *to reflect*, 451
 poetry, 597
 language, 560
Musette, *musical instru-
 ment*, 415
Museum, *store*, 636
 collection, 72
 focus, 74
Mushroom, *small*, 193
 newness, 123
 low-born, 876
 upstart, 734
Music, *music*, 415
Music-hall, *theatre*, 599
 amusement, 840
Musical, *melodious*, 413
Musician, *musician*, 416
Musk, *fragrance*, 400
Musket, *arms*, 727
Musketeer, *combatant*, 726
Muslin, *semitransparent*, 427
Muss, *dishevel*, 61
Mussulman, *religions*, 984
Must, *mucor*, 653
 necessity, 152
 obligation, 926
 compulsion, 744
 essential, 630
Mustard, *condiment*, 393
 yellow, 436
Mustard-seed, *little*, 193
Muster, *collect*, 72
 numeration, 85
Muster-roll, *record*, 551
 list, 86
Musty, *foul*, 653
 rank, 401
Mutable, *changeable*, 149
 irresolute, 605
Mutation, *change*, 140
* Mutatis mutandis, *recipro-
 calness*, 12
 substitution, 147
* Mutato nomine, *substitution*, 147

Mute, *silent*, 403
 letter, 561
 silencer, 417
 speechless, 581
 taciturn, 585
 interment, 363
Mutilate, *retrench*, 38
 deform, 241
 garble, 651
 incomplete, 53
 injure, 649, 659
 spoliation, 619
Mutineer, *disobey*, 742
Mutiny, *disobey*, 742
 misrule, 738
 revolt, 719
Mutt, *fool*, 501
Mutter, *speak*, 583
 murmur, 405
 threaten, 909
Mutual, *reciprocal*, 12, 148
Muzzle, *opening*, 260
 edge, 230
 to silence, 403, 581
 taciturn, 585
 to incapacitate, 158
 restrain, 751
 imprison, 752
Muzzle-loader, *gun*, 727
Muzzy, *confused*, 458
 in liquor, 959
Myopic, *dim sight*, 443
Myriad, *number*, 98
 multitude, 102
Myrmidon, *troop*, 726
Myrrh, *fragrance*, 400
Myrtle, *love*, 897
Mysterious, *concealed*, 528
 obscure, 519
Mystery, *secret*, 533
 latency, 526
 concealment, 528
 craft, 625
 drama, 599
Mystery-ship, *deception*, 545
Mystic, *concealed*, 528
 obscure, 519
Mystify, *to deceive*, 545
 hide, 528
 falsify, 477
 misteach, 538
Myth, *imagination*, 515
Mythological, *god*, 979
 imaginary, 515

N

N.B., *attention*, 457
N or M., *generality*, 78
Na, *dissent*, 489
Nab, *seize*, 789
Nabob, *wealth*, 803

Negro, *black*, 431
Neigh, *cry*, 412
Neighbour, *friend*, 890
Neighbourhood, *nearness*, 197
Neighbourly, *social*, 892
   friendly, 707, 888
Neither, *rejection*, 610
* Nem. con., *assent*, 488
Nemesis, *revenge*, 919
* Nemine contradicente, *assent*, 488
* Nemo, *zero*, 101
* Nenia, *dirge*, 415
Neolithic, *oldness*, 124
Neology, *language*, 563
Neon lighting, *light*, 423
Neophyte, *learner*, 541
   novice, 674
Neoteric, *newness*, 123
Nepenthe, *remedy*, 662
Nephelology, *clouds*, 353
Nepotism, *relation*, 11
   sociality, 892
Neptune, *god*, 979
   ocean, 341
Nereid, *ocean*, 341
   goddess, 979
Nerve, *strength*, 159
   courage, 861
Nerveless, *weakness*, 160
Nervous, *weak*, 160
   timid, 860
   powerful, 157
   concise style, 572
   vigorous style, 574
Nescience, *ignorance*, 491
Ness, *cape*, 250
Nest, *lodging*, 189
   cradle, 153
Nest-egg, *store*, 636
Nested, *layer*, 204
Nestle, *lodge*, 186
   safety, 664
   endearment, 902
Nestling, *infant*, 129
Nestor, *veteran*, 130
Net, *intersection*, 219
   snare, 667, 702
   to capture, 789
   difficulty, 704
   remainder, 40
Nether, *lowness*, 207
Nettle, *to sting*, 830
   incense, 900
Network, *crossing*, 219
   disorder, 59
Neurasthenia, *weakness*, 160
Neurosis, *insanity*, 503
Neurotic, *sensitive physically*, 375
   morally, 822

Neutral, *mean*, 29, 628
   indifferent, 610, 866
   non-interference, 681
Neutral tint, *grey*, 432
Neutralize, *counteract*, 179
   compensate, 30
Never, *neverness*, 107
Never-ending, *long*, 200
Never-never, *purchase*, 795
   debt, 806
Nevertheless, *counter*, 179
   compensation, 30
New, *newness*, 123
New-born, *newness*, 123
New-fashioned, *new*, 123
Newcomer, *extraneous*, 57
Newfangled, *new*, 123
   strange, 83
   barbarous, 851
News, *news*, 532
Newscast, *radio*, 599B
Newspaper, *record*, 551
Next, *after*, 63, 117
Nib, *point*, 253
   summit, 210
   disjunction, 44
   end, 67
Nibble, *carp at*, 932
   eat, 296
Niblick, *club*, 276
Nice, *savoury*, 394
   good, 648
   exact, 494
   pleasing, 829
   honourable, 939
   fastidious, 868
Nicely, *greatness*, 31
Nicety, *taste*, 850, 868
   discrimination, 465
   exactness, 494
Niche, *recess*, 182
   receptacle, 191
* Nichevo, *indifference*, 460,
Nick, *notch*, 257   [823
   mark, 550
   deceive, 545
   of time, 134
   prison, 752
Nickelodeon, *juke box*, 417
Nicker, *animal sound*, 412
Nickname, *misnomer*, 565
Nicotian, *tobacco*, 298A
Nictitate, *blind*, 442
   dim sight, 443
Nidification, *abode*, 189
Nidus, *nest*, 189
   cradle, 153
Niff, *stink*, 401
Niggard, *parsimony*, 819
Nigger, *blackness*, 431
Niggle, *trifle*, 643
   depreciate, 483

Nigh, *nearness*, 197
Night, *darkness*, 421
Night-glass, *lens*, 445
Nightfall, *evening*, 126
Nightgown, *dress*, 225
Nightingale, *music*, 416
Nightmare, *pain*, 378, 828
   imagination, 515
   hindrance, 706
Nightshade, *bane*, 663
Nightshirt, *dress*, 225
Nigrification, *black*, 431
Nihilism, *non-existence*, 1
   scepticism, 487
   anarchism, 738
Nihilist, *evildoer*, 913
Nihility, *unsubstantiality*, 4
* Nil admirari, *expectance*, 871
* Nil desperandum, *hope*, 858
* Nil ultra, *superiority*, 33
Nimble, *swift*, 274
   active, 682
   skilful, 698
Nimbus, *cloud*, 353
   light, 420
Nimiety, *redundance*, 641
Niminy-piminy, *affectation*, 855
* N'importe, *unimportance*, 643
Nimrod, *chase*, 622
Nincompoop, *fool*, 501
Nine, *number*, 98
Nine days' wonder, *transientness*, 111
Ninny, *fool*, 501
Ninnyhammer, *fool*, 501
Niobe, *lament*, 839
Nip, *cut*, 44
   destroy, 162
   smallness, 32
Nip up, *taking*, 789
Nipper, *youngster*, 129
Nipping, *cold*, 383
Nipple, *convexity*, 250
Nirvana, *extinction*, 2
   happiness, 827
   heaven, 979
Nit, *dissent*, 489
Nitrous oxide, *anaesthetic*, 379
Niveous, *white*, 430
Nix, *nothing*, 4
Nixie, *fairy*, 980
Nizam, *master*, 745
No, *dissent*, 489
   negation, 536
No go, *impossible*, 471
Nob, *summit*, 210
   nobility, 875

INDEX

Overweight, *overrate*, 482
  exceed, 33
  influence, 175
Overwhelm, *destroy*, 162
  affect, 824
Overwhelming, *excitability*,
  825
Overwork, *fatigue*, 688
Overwrought, *excited*, 825
Ovoid, *rotundity*, 249
Ovule, *circularity*, 247
Owe, *debt*, 806
Owing to, *attribution*, 155
Owl-light, *dimness*, 422
Own, *assent*, 488, 535
  divulge, 529
  possess, 777
Owner, *possessor*, 779
Ownership, *property*, 780
Oxygenate, *air*, 338
Oy, *attention*, 457
Oyez, *hearing*, 418
Oyster, *taciturnity*, 585

P

P.A.Y.E., *tax*, 812
P.B.I., *soldier*, 725
p.m., *evening*, 126
P.O.P., *photograph*, 556
P.O.W., *prisoner*, 754
p.p., *commission*, 755
P.T., *teaching*, 537
  exertion, 686
Pa, *father*, 166
Pabulum, *food*, 298
Pace, *speed*, 274
  step, 266
  measure, 466
Pachydermatous, *insen-
  sible*, 376, 823
Pacific, *concord*, 714, 721
Pacifism, *pacification*, 723
Pacifist, *non-combatant*,
  726A
Pacify, *allay*, 174
  compose, 826
  give peace, 723
  forgive, 918
Pack, *to join*, 43
  arrange, 60
  bring close, 197
  locate, 184
  assemblage, 72
Pack-horse, *carrier*, 271
Pack off, *depart*, 293
  recede, 287
  decamp, 671
Pack up, *circumscribe*, 231
  fail, 732
Package, *parcel*, 72

Packet, *parcel*, 72
  ship, 273
Packing-case, *receptacle*,
  191
Packthread, *vinculum*, 45
Pact, *agreement*, 769
Pactolus, *wealth*, 803
Pad, *carrier*, 271
  line, 224
  expand, 194
  diffuse, 573
Padding, *softness*, 324
Paddle, *oar*, 267, 633
  to bathe, 337
Paddle-steamer, *ship*, 273
Paddle-wheel, *navigation*,
  267
Paddock, *arena*, 181
  enclosure, 232, 752
Padlock, *fastening*, 45
  fetter, 752
Padre, *clergy*, 996
Paean, *thanks*, 916
  rejoicing, 836
  worship, 990
Paediatrics, *remedy*, 662
Paeon, *verse*, 597
Paganism, *heathen*, 984, 996
Page, *attendant*, 746
  of a book, 593
Pageant, *spectacle*, 448
  the drama, 599
  show, 882
Pagoda, *temple*, 1000
Pail, *receptacle*, 191
Pailful, *quantity*, 25
* Paillard, *libertine*, 962
Pain, *physical*, 378
  moral, 828
  penalty, 974
Painful, *painfulness*, 830
Pains, *exertion*, 686
Painstaking, *active*, 682
  laborious, 686
Paint, *coat*, 222
  colour, 428
  adorn, 847
  delineate, 556
  describe, 594
Painter, *artist*, 559
  rope, 45
Painting, *painting*, 556
Pair, *couple*, 89
  similar, 17
Pair off, *average*, 29
Pal, *friend*, 890
Palace, *abode*, 189
Paladin, *courage*, 861
Palaeography, *interpreta-
  tion*, 522
Palaeolithic, *oldness*, 142
Palaeology, *preterition*, 122

Palaeontology, *zoology*, 368
  past, 122
Palaestra, *school*, 542
  arena, 728
  training, 673
Palaestric, *exertion*, 686
Palanquin, *vehicle*, 272
Palatable, *savoury*, 394
  pleasant, 829
Palatal, *letter*, 561
Palate, *taste*, 390
Palatine, *master*, 745
Palaver, *speech*, 582
  colloquy, 588
  council, 696
  nonsense, 497, 517
  loquacity, 584
Pale, *dim*, 422
  colourless, 429
  enclosure, 232
Palfrey, *carrier*, 271
Palimpsest, *substitution*, 147
  writing, 590
Palindrome, *neology*, 563
  inversion, 218
Paling, *prison*, 752
  enclosure, 232
Palingenesis, *restore*, 660
Palinode, *denial*, 536
  recantation, 607
Palisade, *prison*, 752
  enclosure, 232
Pall, *funeral*, 363
  disgust, 395, 867
  satiate, 869
Palladium, *defence*, 664, 717
Pallet, *support*, 215
Palliasse, *support*, 215
Palliate, *mend*, 658
  relieve, 834
  moderate, 174
  extenuate, 937
Palliative, *remedy*, 662
Pallid, *achromatism*, 429
Palling, *unsavouriness*, 395
Pallium, *dress*, 225
  canonicals, 999
Pally, *friendship*, 888
Palm, *trophy*, 733
  glory, 873
  laurel, 877
  deceive, 545
  impose upon, 486
Palmer, *traveller*, 268
Palmist, *fortune-teller*, 513
Palmistry, *prediction*, 511
Palmy, *prosperous*, 734
  halcyon, 827, 829
Palpable, *tactile*, 379
  tangible, 316
  obvious, 446, 525
  intelligible, 518

Palpitate, *tremble*, 315
  emotion, 821
  fear, 860
Palsy, *disease*, 655
  weakness, 160
  incapacity, 158
  insensibility, 376, 823
Palter, *falsehood*, 544
  shift, 605
  elude, 773
Paltry, *mean*, 940
  despicable, 643, 930
  little, 32
Paludal, *marsh*, 345
Pampas, *plain*, 344
Pamper, *indulge*, 954
  gorge, 957
Pampero, *wind*, 349
Pamphlet, *book*, 593
Pamphleteer, *writing*, 590
  dissertation, 595
Pan, *receptacle*, 191
  face, 234, 448
Panacea, *remedy*, 662
* Panache, *plume*, 256
  ornament, 847
Pandect, *code*, 963
  compendium, 596
  erudition, 490
Pandemic, *insalubrity*, 657
Pandemonium, *hell*, 982
  disorder, 59
Pander, *flatter*, 933
  indulge, 954
  mediate, 631
  help, 707
Pandora, *evil*, 619
Paned, *variegation*, 440
Panegyric, *approbation*, 931
Panel, *list*, 86
  partition, 228
  accused, 938
  legal, 967
* Panem et circenses, *giving*,
    784
Pang, *physical*, 378
  moral, 828
Panhandler, *tramp*, 876
Panic, *fear*, 860
Pannier, *receptacle*, 191
Panoply, *defence*, 717
Panopticon, *prison*, 752
Panorama, *view*, 448
  painting, 556
Panoramic, *general*, 78
Pansophy, *knowledge*, 490
Pansy, *effeminate*, 374
Pant, *breathless*, 688
  desire, 865
  agitation, 821
Pantaloon, *buffoon*, 844
  dress, 225

Pantechnicon, *vehicle*, 272
Pantheism, *heathen*, 984
Pantheon, *temple*, 1000
Pantograph, *imitation*, 19
Pantomime, *sign*, 550
  language, 560
  drama, 599
Pantry, *receptacle*, 191
Pap, *pulp*, 354
  teat, 250
Papa, *father*, 166
Papacy, *churchdom*, 995
Paper, *writing*, 590
  book, 593
  record, 551
  white, 430
Paperback, *book*, 593
Papilla, *convexity*, 250
Papoose, *infant*, 129
Pappy, *semiliquidity*, 352
Par, *equality*, 27
Parable, *metaphor*, 521
  analogy, 464
  story, 594
Parabolic, *metaphor*, 521
  curve, 245
Parachronism, *anachron-ism*, 115
Parachute, *refuge*, 666
Paraclete, *Deity*, 976
Parade, *walk*, 189
  ostentation, 882
Paradigm, *prototype*, 22
  example, 80
Paradise, *heaven*, 981
  bliss, 827
Paradox, *obscurity*, 519
  absurdity, 497
  mystery, 528
  enigma, 533
Paragon, *perfection*, 650
  saint, 948
  glory, 873
Paragraph, *phrase*, 566
  part, 51
  article, 593
Paralipsis, *neglect*, 460
Parallax, *distance*, 196
Parallel, *position*, 216
  similarity, 17
  to imitate, 19
  agreement, 23
  comparison, 464
Parallelepiped, *angularity*,
    244
Parallelogram, *angularity*,
    244
Paralogism, *sophistry*, 477
Paralyse, *weaken*, 160
  benumb, 381
  deaden, 823
  insensibility, 376

Paralyse, *impassivity*, 823
  stillness, 265
  disqualify, 158
  disease, 655
Paramount, *essential*, 642
  in degree, 33
  authority, 737
Paramour, *love*, 897
Paranoia, *insanity*, 503,
    504
Parapet, *defence*, 717
Paraph, *writing*, 590
Paraphernalia, *machinery*,
    633
  materials, 635
  property, 780
Paraphrase, *interpretation*,
    522, 524
  phrase, 566
  imitation, 19, 21
Paraplectic, *disease*, 655
Parapsychology, *occult*, 992
Parasite, *flatterer*, 935
  servile, 886
  follow, 88
Parasol, *shade*, 424
Paratrooper, *fighter*, 726
Paravane, *defence*, 717
Parboil, *calefaction*, 384
Parcel, *group*, 72
  portion, 51
Parcel out, *arrange*, 60
  allot, 786
Parch, *dry*, 340
  heat, 382
  bake, 384
Parchment, *manuscript*,
    590
  record, 551
Pardon, *forgiveness*, 918
Pardonable, *vindication*,
    937
Pare, *scrape*, 38, 226, 331
  shorten, 201
  decrease, 36
Paregoric, *salubrity*, 656
Parenchyma, *texture*, 329
Parent, *paternity*, 166
Parentage, *kindred*, 11
Parenthesis, *interjacence*,
    228
  discontinue, 70
Parenthetical, *irrelation*, 10
  occasion, 134
* Par excellence, *greatness*,
    31
  superiority, 33
* Pari passu, *equality*, 27
Pariah, *commonalty*, 876
  outcast, 892
Paring, *part*, 51
  smallness, 32

Parish, *region*, 181
Parishioner, *laity*, 997
Parity, *equality*, 27
Park, *plain*, 344
  vegetation, 367
  amusement, 840
  artillery, 727
  locate, 184
Parlance, *speech*, 582
* Parlementaire, *messenger*,
  534
Parley, *talk*, 588
  mediation, 724
Parliament, *council*, 696
Parlour, *room*, 191
Parlour-car, *vehicle*, 272
P rlourmaid, *servant*, 746
P rnassus, *poetry*, 597
P rochial, *regional*, 181
  ignoble, 876
Parody, *imitation*, 19
  copy, 21
  travesty, 856
  misinterpret, 523
Parole, *promise*, 768
Paronomasia, *pun*, 563
Paronymous, *word*, 562
Paroxysm, *violence*, 173
  emotion, 825
  anger, 900
Parquetry, *variegation*, 44c
Parricide, *killing*, 361
Parrot, *imitation*, 19
  loquacity, 584
  repetition, 104
Parry, *avert*, 623
  confute, 479
  defend, 717
Parse, *grammar*, 567
Parsee, *religions*, 984
Parsimony, *parsimony*, 81ς
Parson, *clergy*, 996
Parsonage, *temple*, 1000
Part, *portion*, 51
  component, 56
  to diverge, 291
  to divide, 44
  business, 625
  function, 644
Part with, *relinquish*, 782
  give, 784
Partake, *participation*, 778
Parterre, *agriculture*, 371
* Parti, *adolescence*, 131
* Parti pris, *prejudgment*,
  481
  predetermination, 611
Partial, *unequal*, 28
  special, 79
  one-sided, 481
  unjust, 923
  love, 897

Partial, *friendship*, 888
  desire, 865
  erroneous, 495
  smallness, 32
  harmonic, 413
* Particeps criminis, *auxil
  iary*, 711
  bad man, 949
Participation, *participation*,
  77ᶜ
  co-operation, 709
Particle, *quantity*, 32
  size, 193
Particoloured, *variegation*,
  44ᴄ
Particular, *special*, 79
  event, 151
  careful, 459
  capricious, 608
  fastidious, 868
  item, 51
  detail, 79
  description, 594
Particularly, *greatness*, 31
Parting, *disjunction*, 44
Partisan, *auxiliary*, 711
  friend, 891
  fighter, 726
Partition, *allot*, 51, 786
  wall, 228
Partner, *auxiliary*, 711
Partnership, *participation*,
  778
  company, 797
  companionship, 88
Parts, *intellect*, 450
  wisdom, 498
  talents, 698
Party, *assemblage*, 72
  association, 712
  society, 892
  merry-making, 840
  special, 79
Party-wall, *interjacence*,
  228
Parvenu, *upstart*, 876
  intruder, 57
  successful, 734
* Pas, *rank*, 873
  precedence, 62
  term, 71
Pash, *love*, 897
Pasha, *master*, 745
  noble, 875
Pasquinade, *satire*, 932
Pass, *move*, 264
  move out, 295
  move through, 302
  exceed, 303
  be superior, 33
  happen, 151
  lapse, 122

Pass, *vanish*, 449
  passage, 260
  gap, 198
  defile, 203
  way, 627
  difficulty, 704
  conjuncture, 8
  forgive, 918
  thrust, 716
  passport, 760
  time, 106
Pass away, *cease*, 2, 142
Pass-book, *accounts*, 811
Pass by, *disregard*, 929
Pass for, *falsehood*, 544
Pass in the mind, *thought*,
  451
Pass over, *disregard*, 458
  neglect, 460
  forgive, 918
  exclude, 55
  exempt, 927A
  traverse, 302
Pass the time, *duration*, 106
Pass through, *experience*,
  151
Passable, *imperfection*, 651
  tolerable, 736
Passage, *passage*, 302
  motion, 264
  opening, 260
  eventuality, 151
  method, 627
  transfer, 270
  text, 593
  part, 50
  act, 680
  assault, 720
* Passage d'armes, *contention*, 720
* Passé, *age*, 128
  deterioration, 659
Passe-partout, 462
  instrumentality, 631
Passenger, *traveller*, 268
  hindrance, 706
* Passim, *dispersion*, 73
  situation, 183
Passing, *exceeding*, 33
  transient, 111
  greatness, 31
Passion, *emotion*, 820, 821
  desire, 865
  love, 879
  anger, 900
Passionate, *warm*, 825
  irascible, 901
Passionless, *insensibility*,
  823
Passive, *inert*, 172
  inactive, 681
  submissive, 743

Pneumatology, *intellect*, 450
Poach, *steal*, 791, 964
Poacher, *thief*, 792
Poachy, *marsh*, 345
Pocket, *pouch*, 191
　to place, 184
　take, 789
　receive, 785
　endure, 826
　receipts, 810
　treasury, 802
　diminutive, 193
Pococurante, *indifferent*,
603
Pod, *receptacle*, 191
Podgy, *broad*, 202
　short, 200
Poem, *poetry*, 597
Poet, *poetry*, 597
　writer, 593
Poetic, *metrical*, 597
Poignant, *physical*, 171
　moral, 821
　vigorous, 574
Point, *condition*, 8
　degree, 26
　term, 71
　place, 182
　question, 461
　topic, 454
　prominence, 250
　mark, 550
　intention, 620
　wit, 842
　style, 574
　punctilio, 939
　speck, 193
　poignancy, 171
　sharp, 253
Point-blank, *direction*, 278
* Point d'appui, *influence*,
175
Point of view, *aspect*, 441
　idea, 453
　relation, 9
Point to, *indicate*, 550
　show, 525
　mean, 516
　predict, 511
Point-to-point, *direction*,
278
　chase, 622
Pointed, *explicit*, 535
　great, 31
Pointer, *index*, 550
　hint, 527
Pointillism, *variegation*,
440
Pointillist, *artist*, 559
Pointless, *dullness*, 843
　motiveless, 616
Poise, *balance*, 27

Poise, *measure*, 466
　composure, 826
Poison, *bane*, 663
　to injure, 659
Poisonous, *deleterious*, 657
　injurious, 649
Poke, *push*, 276
　project, 250
　pocket, 191
Poker, *stiff*, 323
Polacca, *ship*, 273
Polar, *summit*, 210
Polariscope, *optical*, 445
Polarity, *duality*, 89
　antagonism, 179, 237
Polder, *land*, 342
Pole, *lever*, 633
　axis, 223
　summit, 210
　tallness, 206
Pole-axe, *arms*, 727
Pole-star, *indication*, 550
　sharpness, 253
Polecat, *fetor*, 401
Polemarch, *master*, 745
Polemics, *discussion*, 476
　discord, 713
Polemoscope, *optical*, 445
Police, *jurisdiction*, 965
　safety, 664
Policy, *plan*, 626
　conduct, 692
　skill, 698
Polish, *smooth*, 255
　to rub, 331
　urbanity, 894
　furbish, 658
　beauty, 845
　ornament, 847
　taste, 850
Politburo, *council*, 696
Politeness, *manners*, 852
　urbanity, 894
　respect, 928
Politic, *wise*, 498
　expedient, 646
　skilful, 698
　cautious, 864
　cunning, 702
Politician, *statesman*, 745
Politics, *government*, 693
Polity, *plan*, 626
　conduct, 692
　community, 372
Polka, *dance*, 840
Poll, *count*, 85
　choice, 609
　crop, 201
　parrot, 584
Pollard, *clip*, 201
Pollute, *corrupt*, 659
　soil, 653

Pollute, *disgrace*, 874
　dishonour, 940
Pollution, *vice*, 945
　disease, 655
Poltergeist, *demon*, 980
Poltroon, *cowardice*, 862
Polychord, *musical*, 417
Polychromatic, *variegation*,
440
Polygamy, *marriage*, 903
Polyglot, *word*, 562
　interpretation, 522
Polygon, *figure*, 244
　building, 189
Polygraphy, *writing*, 590
Polygyny, *marriage*, 903
Polymorphic, *multiform*, 81
Polyp, *convexity*, 250
Polyphonism, *voice*, 580
Polyphony, *melody*, 413
Polysyllable, *letter*, 561
Polytechnic, *school*, 542
Polytheism, *heathen*, 984
Pomade, *oil*, 356
Pomatum, *oil*, 356
Pommel, *rotundity*, 249
Pommy, *stranger*, 57
　greenhorn, 674
Pomp, *ostentation*, 882
Pom-pom, *gun*, 727
Pomposity, *pride*, 878
　style, 577
Ponce, *libertine*, 962
Poncho, *dress*, 225
Pond, *lake*, 343
Ponder, *thought*, 451
Ponderation, *judgment*, 480
Ponderous, *gravity*, 319
　style, 577
Pong, *stink*, 501
Poniard, *arms*, 727
* Pons asinorum, *difficulty*,
704
Pontiff, *clergy*, 996
Pontifical, *churchdom*, 995
Pontificals, *dress*, 225
Pony, *carrier*, 271
　money, 800
Pooh-pooh, *trifle*, 643
　contempt, 930
　to make light of, 483
Pool, *lake*, 343
　participation, 778
Poop, *rear*, 235
　fool, 501
Poor, *indigent*, 804
　afflicted, 828
　weak, 160
　insufficient, 640
　trifling, 643
　contemptible, 930
　style, 575

Poor-spirited, *cowardice*, 862

Poorly, *disease*, 655

Pop, *noise*, 406
  unexpected, 508
  pawn, 787

Pop upon, *arrive*, 292
  find, 480

Pope, *clergy*, 996

Popgun, *snap*, 406

Popinjay, *fop*, 854

Popsy, *girl*, 374

Populace, *commonalty*, 876

Popular, *current*, 484
  favourite, 897
  celebrated, 873

Popularize, *facilitate*, 705

Populate, *to stock*, 184

Population, *mankind*, 373
  inhabitants 188

Populous, *crowded*, 72

Porch, *entrance*, 66
  opening, 260
  mouth, 230
  way, 627
  receptacle, 191

Porcupine, *sharpness*, 253

Pore, *opening*, 260
  conduit, 350
  look, 441
  learn, 539
  apply the mind, 457

Porism, *corollary*, 480

Pornography, *impurity*, 961

Porous, *foraminous*, 260
  concavity, 252
  light, 322

Porpoise, *size*, 192

Porringer, *receptacle*, 191

Port, *harbour*, 666
  gait, 264
  resting-place, 265
  arrival, 292
  carriage, 448
  demeanour, 852

Port-hole, *opening*, 260

Portable, *movable*, 268, 270
  light, 320
  little, 193

Portage, *transference*, 270

Portal, *entrance*, 66
  mouth, 230
  opening, 260
  way, 627

Portative, *transference*, 270
  small, 193

Portcullis, *defence*, 706, 717

* Porte-monnaie, *purse*, 802

Portend, *prediction*, 511

Portent, *omen*, 512
  prodigy, 872

Portentous, *prophetic*, 511
  fearful, 860

Porter, *carrier*, 271
  janitor, 263

Porterage, *transference*, 270

Portfolio, *record*, 551
  miscellany, 72
  receptacle, 191
  badge, 747
  direction, 693

Portico, *entrance*, 66
  room, 191

Portion, *piece*, 51, 41
  allotment, 786

Portland, *prison*, 752

Portly, *size*, 192

Portmanteau, *receptacle*, 191

Portmanteau word, *conciseness*, 572

Portrait, *painting*, 556
  copy, 21

Portray, *describe*, 594
  represent, 554
  paint, 556

Pose, *puzzle*, 485
  hide, 528
  difficulty, 704
  affirm, 535
  embarrassment, 491
  attitude, 240
  affectation, 855

Poseidon, *god*, 979

Poser, *secret*, 533

* Poseur, *affectation*, 855

Posh, *fashion*, 852

Posit, *locate*, 184
  assume, 467, 514
  affirm, 535

Position, *circumstance*, 7
  situation, 183
  assertion, 535
  degree, 26

Positive, *certain*, 474
  real, 1
  true, 494
  unequivocal, 518
  absolute, 739
  obstinate, 481, 606
  assertion, 535
  quantity, 84

Positively, *great*, 31

Positivism, *materiality*, 316
  irreligion, 989

Posse, *party*, 712
  jurisdiction, 965

Possess, *have*, 777
  feel, 821

Possessed, *insane*, 503

Possession, *property*, 780

Possessor, *possessor*, 779

Possible, *feasible*, 470, 705
  casual, 156, 177, 621

Post, *support*, 215
  place, 184
  beacon, 550
  swift, 274
  employment, 625
  office, 926
  to record, 551
  accounts, 811
  mail, 592
  news, 532
  inform, 527

Post-chaise, *vehicle*, 272

Post-classical, *posterior*, 117

Post-date, *anachronism*, 115

Post-diluvian, *posterity*, 117

Post-existence, *futurity*, 121

Post-haste, *fast*, 274

* Post hoc, *sophistry*, 477

Post-impressionist, *artist*, 559

Post-mortem, *death*, 360
  disinter, 363

Post-obit, *death*, 360

Postcard, *news*, 532
  epistle, 592

Poster, *notice*, 531

Posterior, *in time*, 117
  in order, 63
  in space, 235

Posterity, *in time*, 117, 121
  descendants, 167

Postern, *back*, 235
  portal, 66
  opening, 260

Postfix, *appendage*, 39

Posthumous, *late*, 133
  subsequent, 117

Postiche, *artificial*, 544

Postilion, *director*, 694

Postlude, *music*, 415
  posterior, 117

Postman, *messenger*, 534

Postpone, *lateness*, 133

Postscript, *sequel*, 65
  appendix, 39

Postulant, *petitioner*, 767
  request, 765
  nun, 997

Postulate, *supposition*, 514
  evidence, 467
  reasoning, 476

Postulation, *request*, 765

Posture, *circumstance*, 8
  attitude, 240
  display, 882

Posy, *motto*, 550
  poem, 597
  flowers, 847

Pot, *mug*, 191
  stove, 386
  greatness, 31
  ruin, 732

Pot-companion, *friend*, 890
Pot-hooks, *writing*, 590
Pot-hunting, *acquisition*,
   775
Pot-luck, *food*, 298
Pot-pourri, *mixture*, 41
  fragrance, 400
  music, 415
Pot-valiant, *drunk*, 959
Potable, *drinkable*, 298
Potation, *drink*, 296
Potency, *power*, 157
Potentate, *master*, 745
Potential, *virtual*, 2
  possible, 470
  power, 157
Pother, *to worry*, 830
  fuss, 682
  confusion, 59
Pottage, *food*, 298
Potter, *idle*, 683
Pottle, *receptacle*, 191
Potty, *mad*, 503
* Pou sto, *influence*, 175
Pouch, *receptacle*, 191
  insert, 184
  receive, 785
  take, 789
  acquire, 775
Pouffe, *support*, 215
Poultice, *soft*, 354
  remedy, 662
Pounce upon, *taking*, 789
Pound, *bruise*, 330
  mix, 41
  enclose, 232
  imprison, 752
Poundage, *discount*, 813
Pounds, *money*, 800
Pour, *egress*, 295
Pour out, *eject*, 185, 297, 248
* Pour rire, *ridicule*, 853
* Pourboire, *giving*, 784
  expenditure, 809
* Pourparler, *discussion*,
  476
Pout, *sullen*, 895
  sad, 837
Poverty, *indigence*, 804
  scantiness, 640
  trifle, 643
Powder, *pulverulence*, 330
  ornament, 845, 847
Powder-box, *receptacle*, 191
Power, *efficacy*, 157
  physical energy, 171
  authority, 737
  spirit, 977
  much, 31
  multitude, 102
  numerical, 84
  of style, 574

Powerful, *strength*, 159
Powerless, *weakness*, 160
Pow-wow, *conference*, 588
Pox, *disease*, 655
  expletive, 908
Praam, *ship*, 273
Practicable, *possible*, 470
  easy, 705
Practical, *activity*, 672
  agency, 170
Practice, *act*, 680
  conduct, 692
  use, 677
  habit, 613
  teaching, 537
  rule, 80
  proceeding, 626
Practise, *deceive*, 645
Practised, *skill*, 698
Practitioner, *agent*, 690
* Praecognita, *evidence*, 467
Praenomen, *name*, 564
Praetor, *master*, 745
Pragmatical, *pedantic*, 855
  vain, 880
Prairie, *plain*, 344
  plaint, 367
Praise, *commendation*, 931
  thanks, 916
  worship, 990
Praiseworthy, *commendable*,
  931
  virtuous, 944
Prance, *dance*, 315
  swagger, 878
  move, 266
Prang, *bomb*, 162, 716, 732
Prank, *caprice*, 608
  amusement, 840
  vagary, 856
  to adorn, 845
Prate, *babble*, 584, 588
Prattle, *talk*, 582, 588
Pravity, *badness*, 649
Pray, *request*, 765
Prayer, *request*, 765
  worship, 990
Preach, *teach*, 537
  speech, 582
  predication, 998
Preacher, *clergy*, 996
Preachify, *speech*, 582
Preamble, *precursor*, 64
  speech, 582
Preapprehension, *misjudg-
ment*, 481
Prebendary, *clergy*, 996
Prebendaryship, *church-
dom*, 995
Precarious, *uncertain*, 475
  perilous, 665
Precatory, *request*, 764

Precaution, *care*, 459
  expedient, 626
  preparation, 673
Precede, *in order*, 62
  in time, 116
  lead, 280
Precedence, *rank*, 873
Precedent, *rule*, 80
  verdict, 969
Precentor, *clergy*, 996
  director, 694
Precept, *maxim*, 697
  order, 741
  rule, 80
  permit, 760
  decree, 963
Preceptor, *teacher*, 540
Precession, *in oder*, 62
  in motion, 280
* Précieuse ridicule, *affectation*, 855
  style, 577
Precincts, *environs*, 227
  boundary, 233
  region, 181
  place, 182
Preciosity, *affectation*, 855
Precious, *excellent*, 648
  valuable, 814
  beloved, 897
Precipice, *slope*, 217
  vertical, 212
  danger, 667
Precipitancy, *haste*, 274, 684
Precipitate, *rash*, 863
  impulse, 612
  early, 132
  transient, 111
  to sink, 308
  refuse, 653
  consolidate, 321
  swift, 274
Precipitous, *obliquity*, 217
Précis, *compendium*, 596
Precise, *exact*, 494
  definite, 518
Precisely, *assent*, 488
Precisian, *formalist*, 855
  taste, 850
Preclude, *hindrance*, 706
Precocious, *early*, 132
  immature, 674
Precognition, *foresight*, 510
  knowledge, 490
Preconception, *misjudg-
ment*, 481
Preconcert, *preparation*, 673
  predetermine, 611
Preconcerted, *will*, 600
Precursor, *forerunner*, 64
  precession, 280
  harbinger, 512

Prismatic, *colour*, 428, 440
  changeable, 149
Prison, *prison*, 752
  restraint, 751
Prisoner, *captive*, 754
  defendant, 967
Pristine, *preterition*, 122
Prithee, *request*, 765
Prittle-prattle, *interlocu-
tion*, 588
Privacy, *secrecy*, 526
  concealment, 528
  seclusion, 893
Private, *special*, 79
Private eye, *inquiry agent*,
461
Privateer, *combatant*, 726
Privation, *loss*, 776
  poverty, 804
Privative, *taking*, 789
Privilege, *dueness*, 924
Privity, *knowledge*, 490
Privy, *concealed*, 528
Prize, *booty*, 793
  reward, 973
  success, 731
  palm, 733
  good, 618
  love, 897
  approve, 931
Prize-fighter, *combatant*,
726
Pro and con, *reasoning*, 476
* Pro bono publico, *utility*,
644
  philanthropy, 910
* Pro forma, *habit*, 613
* Pro hac vice, *present*, 118
* Pro more, *conformity*, 62
  habit, 613
* Pro rata, *relation*, 9
* Pro re nata, *circumstance*,
8
  occasion, 134
* Pro tanto, *greatness*, 31
  smallness, 32
Proa, *ship*, 273
Probable, *probability*, 472
  chance, 156
Probate, *evidence*, 467
Probation, *trial*, 463
  essay, 675
  demonstration, 478
Probationer, *learner*, 541
Probe, *stiletto*, 262
  measure, 466
  depth, 208
  investigate, 461
Probity, *virtue*, 944
  right, 922
  integrity, 939
Problem, *enigma*, 533

Problem, *inquiry*, 461
Problematical, *uncertain*,
475
  hidden, 528
Proboscis, *convexity*, 250
Procedure, *conduct*, 692
  action, 680
  plan, 626
Proceed, *advance*, 282
  from, 154
  elapse, 109
  happen, 151
Proceeding, *action*, 680
  event, 151
  plan, 626
  incomplete, 53
Proceeds, *money*, 800
  receipts, 810
  gain, 775
Procerity, *height*, 206
* Procès-verbal, *compen-
dium*, 596
Process, *projection*, 250
  plan, 626
  action, 680
  conduct, 692
  engraving, 558
  time, 109
Procession, *train*, 69
  ceremony, 882
Prochronism, *anachronism*,
115
Proclaim, *publication*, 531
Proclivity, *disposition*, 602
  proneness, 176, 820
Proconsul, *deputy*, 759
  master, 745
Proconsulship, *authority*,
737
Procrastination, *delay*, 133,
683
Procreant, *productiveness*,
168
Procreate, *production*, 161
Procreator, *paternity*, 166
Proctor, *officer*, 694
  law, 968
Proctorship, *direction*, 693
Procumbent, *horizontality*,
213
Procuration, *commission*,
755
  pimping, 961
Procurator, *director*, 694
Procure, *get*, 775
  cause, 153
  buy, 795
  pimp, 962
Prod, *poke*, 276
Prodigal, *extravagant*, 818
  lavish, 641
  penitent, 950

Prodigious, *wonderful*, 870
  much, 31
Prodigy, *prodigy*, 872
Prodromal, *precedence*, 62
Prodrome, *precursor*, 64
Produce, *cause*, 153
  create, 161
  prolong, 200
  show, 525, 599
  evidence, 467
  result, 154
  fruit, 775
  ware, 798
Product, *effect*, 154
  acquisition, 775
  multiple, 84
Productive, *productiveness*,
168
Proem, *precursor*, 64
Proemial, *preceding*, *in
order*; 62
  in time, 106
  beginning, 66
Profane, *impious*, 988
  pagan, 986
  desecrate, 679
  laical, 997
Profess, *affirmation*, 535
Profession, *business*, 625
  promise, 768
Professor, *teacher*, 540
Proffer, *offer*, 763
Proficiency, *skill*, 698
Proficient, *adept*, 700
  knowledge, 490
  skilful, 698
Profile, *lateral*, 236
  outline, 229
  appearance, 448
Profit, *acquisition*, 775
  advantage, 618
Profitable, *useful*, 644
  gainful, 810
Profiteer, *acquisition*, 775
  upstart, 734
Profitless, *inutility*, 645
Profligacy, *vice*, 945
Profluent, *advancing*, 282
  flowing, 348
Profound, *deep*, 208
  sagacity, 702
  feeling, 821
  thought, 451
Profoundly, *great*, 31
Profuse, *prodigal*, 818
  lavish, 641
Prog, *food*, 298
Progenitor, *paternity*, 166
Progeny, *posterity*, 121, 167
Prognostic, *omen*, 512
Prognosticate, *prediction*,
511

Prosector, *anatomist*, 44
Prosecute, *pursue*, 622
  accuse, 938
  arraign, 969
  action, 680
Prosecutor, *judge*, 967
Proselyte, *learner*, 541
  convert, 484
Proselytism, *teaching*, 537
  belief, 484
Prosit, *drink*, 959
Prosody, *poetry*, 597
Prosopopoeia, *metaphor*,
                521
Prospect, *view*, 448
  probability, 472
  futurity, 121, 507
Prospectus, *scheme*, 626
  compendium, 596
  programme, 86
Prosperity, *success*, 731, 734
Prostitute, *to corrupt*, 659
  misuse, 679
  dishonour, 961, 962
Prostrate, *low*, 207
  level, 213
  to depress, 308
  weak, 160
  exhausted, 688
  laid up, 655
  dejected, 837
  heart-broken, 830
Prostration, *ruin*, 619
  disease, 655
  servility, 886
  obeisance, 725, 743, 928
  worship, 990
Prosy, *diffuse*, 573
  dull, 575, 843
Prosyllogism, *reasoning*,
                476
Protagonist, *leader*, 745
  champion, 711
  proficient, 700
Protasis, *precursor*, 64
Protean, *mutable*, 149, 605
Protect, *shield*, 664
  defend, 717
Protection, *influence*, 175
Protector, *master*, 745
Protectorate, *region*, 181
  authority, 737
Protégé, *servant*, 746
  friend, 890
Protein, *living beings*, 357
Protervity, *petulance*, 901
Protest, *dissent*, 489
  denial, 536
  affirmation, 535
  refusal, 764
  deprecate, 766
  censure, 932

Protest, *non-observance*, 773
  non-payment, 808
Protestant, *Christian religion*, 983A
Proteus, *change*, 149
Prothonotary, *recorder*, 553
Protocol, *document*, 551
  compact, 769
  warrant, 771
  etiquette, 613
  ceremony, 882
Protoplasm, *substance*, 3
  living beings, 357
Protoplast, *prototype*, 22
Prototype, *thing copied*, 22
Protract, *time*, 110, 133
  length, 200
Protractor, *angularity*, 244
Protrude, *convexity*, 250
Protuberance, *convexity*,
                250
Proud, *lofty*, 878
  dignified, 873
Prove, *demonstrate*, 85, 478
  try, 463
  turn out, 151
  affect, 821
Provenance, *cause*, 153
Provender, *food*, 298
  materials, 635
  provision, 637
Proverb, *maxim*, 496
Proverbial, *knowledge*, 490
Provide, *furnish*, 637
  prepare, 673
Provided, *qualification*, 469
  condition, 770
  conditionally, 8
Providence, *foresight*, 510
  divine government, 976
Provident, *careful*, 459
  foresight, 510
  wise, 498
  prepared, 673
Providential, *opportune*,
                134
Province, *region*, 181
  department, 75
  office, 625
  duty, 926
Provincialism, *language*,
                560
  vulgarity, 851, 876
Provision, *supply*, 637
  materials, 635
  preparation, 673
  wealth, 803
  food, 298
Provisional, *preparing*, 673
  substituted, 147
  temporary, 111
  conditional, 8

Proviso, *qualification*, 469
  condition, 770
Provoke, *incite*, 615
  cause, 153
  excite, 824
  vex, 830
  hatred, 898
  anger, 900
Provoking, *difficult*, 704
Provost, *master*, 745
Prow, *front*, 234
Prowess, *courage*, 861
Prowl, *journey*, 266
  conceal, 528
Proximity, *nearness*, 197
  contiguity, 199
Proximo, *futurity*, 121
  posterior, 117
Proxy, *deputy*, 759
  substitute, 634
Prude, *affectation*, 855
Prudent, *cautious*, 864
  foresight, 510
  careful, 459
  wise, 498
  discreet, 698
Prudery, *affectation*, 855
Prune, *shorten*, 201
  correct, 658
  purple, 437
Prunella, *unimportance*, 643
Prurient, *desire*, 865
  lust, 961
Pry, *inquire*, 461
  curiosity, 455
  look, 441
Psalm, *worship*, 990
Psalmody, *music*, 415
Psalter, *rite*, 998
Pseudo, *spurious*, 495
  sham, 544
Pseudonym, *misnomer*, 565
Pseudoscope, *optical*, 445
Pshaw, *contempt*, 930
Psst, *accost*, 586
Psyche, *soul*, 450
Psychiatrist, *mind*, 450
  remedy, 662
Psychical, *immaterial*, 317
  intellectual, 450
Psycho-analysis, *remedy*,
                662
Psychokinesis, *occult*, 992
Psychology, *intellect*, 450
Psychomancy, *divination*,
                992
Psychopath, *madman*, 504
Psychosis, *insanity*, 503
Psycho-therapist, *intellect*,
                450
  remedy, 662
Ptisan, *remedy*, 662

INDEX

Quod, *prison*, 752
Quodlibet, *sophism*, 477
　subtle point, 454
　enigma, 461
　wit, 842
Quondam, *preterition*, 122
Quorum, *assembly*, 72
Quota, *apportionment*, 786
Quotation, *imitation*, 19
　citation, 82
　price, 812
Quote, *cite*, 82, 467
　bargain, 794
Quotidian, *period*, 108, 138
Quotient, *number*, 84

R

R.A., *artist*, 559
R.I.P., *burial*, 363
Rabbet, *junction*, 43
Rabbi, *clergy*, 996
Rabble, *mob*, 876
　bad man, 949
　assemblage, 72
Rabelaisian, *coarse*, 961
Rabid, *insanity*, 503
　headstrong, 606
　angry, 900
　feeling, 821
Race, *to run*, 274
　contest, 720
　course, 622
　career, 625
　torrent, 348
　lineage, 11, 69
　kind, 75
　people, 372
Racehorse, *horse*, 271
　fleetness, 274
Racer, *horse*, 271
　fleetness, 274
Racial, *ethnic*, 372
Rack, *frame*, 215
　physical pain, 378
　moral pain, 828
　to torture, 830
　punish, 975
　purify, 652
　refine, 658
　cloud, 353
Racket, *noise*, 402, 404
　brawl, 713
　roll, 407
　bat, 633
　plan, 626
　* Raconteur, *narrator*, 594
Racy, *strong*, 171
　pungent, 392
　feeling, 821
　style, 574

Radar, *direction*, 693
Raddle, *weave*, 219
　red, 434
Radiant, *diverging*, 291
　light, 420, 423
　beauty, 845
　glory, 873
Radiator, *fire*, 386
Radical, *cause*, 153
　algebraic root, 84
　complete, 52
　intrinsic, 5
　reformer, 658
　revolution, 146
Radically, *thorough*, 31
Radio, *hearing*, 418
　publication, 531
　news, 532
　wireless, 599B
Radioactivity, *light*, 420
Radiogram, *hearing*, 418
　news, 532
Radioscopy, *light*, 420
Radiotherapy, *light*, 420
Radius, *length*, 200
　degree, 26
Radix, *cause*, 153
Raff, *refuse*, 653
　rabble, 876
Raffia, *tape*, 45
Raffish, *vulgar*, 851
Raffle, *chance*, 156, 621
Raft, *ship*, 273
Rafter, *support*, 215
Rag, *shred*, 51
　clothes, 225
　escapade, 497
　to tease, 830
　joke, 842
　deride, 929
　revile, 932
Ragamuffin, *rabble*, 876
Rage, *violence*, 173
　fury, 825
　wrath, 900
　desire, 865
　fashion, 852
Ragged, *bare*, 226
Ragout, *food*, 298
Ragtag, *commonalty*, 876
　bad man, 949
Raid, *attack*, 716
　robbery, 791
Rail, *enclosure*, 232
　fence, 666
　imprison, 752
Rail at, *disapprove*, 932
Rail-car, *vehicle*, 272
Rail in, *circumscribe*, 231
Raillery, *ridicule*, 856
Railroad, *way*, 627
Railway, *road*, 627

Raiment, *dress*, 225
Rain, *river*, 348
Rainbow, *variegation*, 440
Raise, *elevate*, 307
　increase, 35
　produce, 161
　excite, 824
　* Raison d'être, *cause* 153
　motive, 615, 620
Raj, *authority*, 737
Rajah, *master*, 745
Rake, *cultivate*, 371
Rake-off, *payment*, 809
Rake up, *collect*, 72
　extract, 301
　recall, 504
　excite, 824
Rakehell, *intemperate*, 954
Rakish, *intemperate*, 954
　licentious, 961
Rally, *ridicule*, 856
　joke, 842
　recover, 658
　stand by, 707
　pluck up courage, 861
Ram, *impel*, 276
　press in, 261
　insert, 300
Ram down, *condense*, 321
　fill up, 261
Ramadan, *fasting*, 956
Ramble, *stroll*, 266
　wander, 279
　diffuse, 572
　delirium, 503
　folly, 499
Rambler, *traveller*, 268
Ramification, *branch*, 51,
　　　　　256
　divergence, 291
　posterity, 167
Rammer, *plug*, 263
　impeller, 276
Ramp, *rise up*, 307
　slope, 217
Rampage, *violence*, 173
　excitement, 825
Rampant, *violent*, 173
　vehement, 825
　licentious, 961
　free, 748
　rearing, 307
Rampart, *defence*, 717
Ramrod, *stopper*, 263
Ramshackle, *imperfect*, 651
Ranch, *farm*, 780
Rancid, *fetid*, 401
　rotten, 653
Rancour, *malevolence*, 907
　revenge, 919
Randem, *row*, 69
Random, *casual*, 156, 621

Rejuvenate, *restore*, 660
Rekindle, *ignite*, 384
   motive, 615
Relapse, *reversion*, 145
   retrogression, 661
Relate, *narrate*, 594
   refer, 9
Relation, *relation*, 9
Relative, *consanguinity*, 11
Relax, *weaken*, 160
   soften, 324
   slacken, 275
   unbend the mind, 452
   repose, 687
   leisure, 685
   amuse, 840
   lounge, 683
   loose, 47
   misrule, 738
   relent, 914
Relaxing, *unhealthy*, 657
Relay, *materials*, 635
Release, *liberate*, 750
   deliver, 672
   discharge, 970
   restore, 790
   exempt, 927A
   repay, 807
   death, 360
Relegate, *transfer*, 270
   remove, 185
   banish, 55
Relent, *moderate*, 174
   pity, 914
   relax, 324
Relentless, *malevolent*, 907
   wrathful, 900
   revengeful, 919
   flagitious, 945
   impenitent, 951
Relevancy, *pertinence*, 9
   congruity, 23
Reliable, *believable*, 484
   trustworthy, 939
Reliance, *confidence*, 484
   hope, 858
Relic, *remainder*, 40
   reminiscence, 505
   token, 551
   sacred, 998
Relict, *widow*, 905
Relief, *sculpture*, 557
   convexity, 250
   aid, 707
Relieve, *comfort*, 834
   refresh, 689
   help, 707
   improve, 658
Religion, *theology*, 983
   belief, 484
   piety, 987
Religiosity, *sanctimony*, 988

Religious, *exact*, 494
   pious, 987
Relinquish, *a purpose*, 607, 624
   property, 782
   to discontinue, 142
Reliquary, *rite*, 998
Relish, *like*, 377, 827
   taste, 390
   savoury, 394
   desire, 865
Relucent, *luminous*, 420
   transparent, 425
Reluct, *resist*, 719
Reluctance, *dislike*, 867
   unwillingness, 603
   dissuasion, 616
Reluctation, *resistance*, 719
Relume, *light*, 384
Rely, *confidence*, 484
   expectation, 507
   hope, 858
Remain, *endure*, 106, 110
   exist, 1
   to be left, 40
   rest, 265
   continue, 141
Remainder, *left*, 40
   property, 780
Remains, *corpse*, 362
   vestige, 551
Remand, *restraint*, 751
   delay, 133
Remark, *observe*, 457
   assert, 535
Remarkable, *important*, 642
Remarkably, *greatness*, 31
Remedy, *cure*, 662
   salubrious, 656
   to restore, 660, 834
Remember, *recollect*, 505
Remembrance, *compliment*, 894
Remembrancer, *recorder*, 553
Remigration, *egress*, 295
Remind, *recollect*, 505
Reminiscence, *remember*, 505
Remiss, *neglectful*, 460
   idle, 683
   reluctant, 603
   laxity, 738
Remission, *see* Remit
Remit, *relax*, 174
   forgive, 918
   restore, 790
   discontinue, 142
   pay, 807
Remnant, *remainder*, 40
Remodel, *conversion*, 140, 144

Remodel, *improve*, 658
Remonstrate, *dissuade*, 616
   expostulate, 932
Remorse, *penitence*, 950
Remorseless, *resentment*, 900
   revenge, 919
Remote, *distant*, 196
   not related, 10
Remotion, *see* Remove
Remove, *displace*, 185
   retrench, 38
   depart, 293
   recede, 287
   transfer, 270
   extract, 301
   term, 71
Removed, *distant*, 196
Remunerate, *reward*, 973
   pay, 810
Renaissance, *revival*, 660
Renascent, *reproduction*, 163
Rencontre, *see* Rencounter
Rencounter, *fight*, 720
   meeting, 197, 292
Rend, *disjoin*, 44
Render, *give*, 784
   restore, 790
   interpret, 522
   music, 415
Rendezvous, *focus*, 74
   assemblage, 72
Rending, *loud*, 404
   painful, 830
Rendition, *surrender*, 782
   interpretation, 522
Renegade, *apostate*, 742, 941
   turncoat, 144, 607
Renew, *repeat*, 104
   reproduce, 163
   frequent, 136
   newness, 123
   repair, 658
   restore, 660
Reniform, *curvature*, 245
Renounce, *relinquish*, 624
   property, 782
   recant, 607
   resign, 757
   deny, 536
   repudiate, 927
   exempt, 927A
Renovate, *reproduce*, 163
   newness, 123
   restore, 660
Renown, *repute*, 873
Rent, *fissure*, 44, 198
   hire, 788, 794
   receipt, 810
Renter, *possessor*, 779

Resignation, *abdication*, 757
 humility, 743, 879
 renunciation, 872
Resilient, *elasticity*, 325
 rebound, 283
Resin, *semiliquid*, 352
Resist, *withstand*, 719
 disobey, 742
 refuse, 764
 oppose, 179
 tenacity, 327
Resistant, *tough*, 327
Resistless, *strength*, 159
Resolute, *determined*, 604
 brave, 861
Resolution, *decomposition*,
 49
 investigation, 461
 solution, 462
 topic, 454
 determination, 604
 courage, 861
Resolve, *purpose*, 620
 to *liquefy*, 335
 decompose, 49
 investigate, 461
 discover, 480A
 interpret, 522
Resonant, *sonorous*, 402
 ringing, 408
Resorb, *reception*, 296
Resort, *employ*, 677
 converge, 290
 focus, 74
 assemble, 72
 frequent, 136
 move, 266
 dwell, 189
Resound, *be loud*, 402, 404
 ring, 408
 praises, 931
Resourceful, *skill*, 698
Resourceless, *inactive*, 683
Resources, *means*, 632, 780
 wealth, 803
Respect, *deference*, 928
 fame, 873
 salutation, 894
 observe, 772
 reference, 9
Respectable, *repute*, 873
 upright, 939
 tolerable, 651
Respecting, *relation*, 9
Respective, *speciality*, 79
 apportio::ment, 786
Respectless, *inattention*,
 458
Respire, *breathe*, 359
 repose, 687
Respite, *pause*, 265
 intermission, 106

Respite, *rest*, 142, 685, 687
 escape, 671, 672
 reprieve, 970
Resplendent, *luminous*, 420
 splendid, 845
Respond, *agree*, 23
 sensibility, 375, 822
Respondent, *accused*, 938
Response, *answer*, 462
 verbal, 587
 rites, 998
Responsible, *duty*, 926
 liable, 177
Responsive, *see* Respond
Rest, *quiescence*, 265
 repose, 687
 leisure, 685
 remainder, 40
 remain, 141
 pause, 142
 satisfaction, 831
 recumbence, 215
Rest-house, *inn*, 189
Rest on, *support*, 215
Restaurant, *food*, 298
Restaurant-car, *vehicle*, 272
* Restaurateur, *provision*,
 637
Restful, *soothing*, 174
Resting-place, *support*, 215
 quiescence, 165
 arrival, 292
Restitution, *restitution*, 790
Restive, *obstinate*, 606
 disobedient, 742
 refusing, 764
 impatient, 825
 bad-tempered, 901
Restless, *moving*, 264
 agitated, 315
 active, 682
 excited, 825
 fearful, 860
Restorative, *remedial*, 662
 salubrious, 656
 relieving, 834
Restore, *reinstate*, 145, 660
 newness, 123
 improve, 658
 refresh, 689
 return, 790
 meaning, 522
Restrain, *moderate*, 174
 emotion, 826
 check, 706
 curb, 751
 prohibit, 761
 circumscribe, 231
 dissuade, 616
Restrict, *moderate*, 174
 emotion, 826
 check, 706

Restrict, *curb*, 751
 prohibit, 761
 circumscribe, 231
 dissuade, 616
Result, *effect*, 154, 476
 remainder, 40
Resultant, *combination*, 48
Resume, *taking*, 789
 restore, 660
Résumé, *compendium*, 596
Resurgence, *reproduction*,
 163
Resurrection, *reproduction*,
 163
Resuscitate, *reanimate*, 163
 reinstate, 660
Retail, *sell*, 796
 particularize, 594
Retailer, *merchant*, 797
Retain, *keep in place*, 150
 keep possession, 781
 enlist, 615
Retainer, *servant*, 746
Retaliate, *retort*, 718
 revenge, 919
Retard, *hinder*, 706
 slacken, 275
Retch, *rejection*, 297
Retention, *keeping*, 781
 in the memory, 505
Retentive, *retention*, 781
Reticence, *latency*, 526
 taciturnity, 585
 concealment, 528
Reticle, *crossing*, 219
Reticulate, *crossing*, 219
Reticule, *receptacle*, 191
Retiform, *crossing*, 219
Retinue, *followers*, 65
 suite, 69
 servants, 746
Retire, *recede*, 283, 287
 depart, 293
 avoid, 623
 resign, 757
Retirement, *seclusion*, 893
 privacy, 526
Retort, *answer*, 462
 confutation, 479
 retaliation, 718
 wit, 842
 vessel, 191
 vaporizer, 336
Retouch, *improve*, 658
 restore, 660
Retrace, *memory*, 505
Retrace steps, *recede*, 283
Retract, *deny*, 536
 recant, 607
 abjure, 757
 annul, 756
 violate, 773

Retreat, *recede*, 287, 283
  surrender, 725
  abode, 189
  asylum, 666
  escape, 671
  hiding-place, 530
Retrench, *subduct*, 38
  shorten, 201
  lose, 789
  economize, 817
Retribution, *retaliation*, 718
  payment, 807
  punishment, 972
Retrieval, *acquisition*, 775
Retrieve, *restore*, 660
Retroaction, *recoil*, 277
  regression, 283
  counteraction, 179
Retrocession, *recession*, 287
Retrocognition, *thought*, 451
Retrograde, *motion*, 283
  declension, 659
  relapse, 661
  reversion, 145
Retrogression, *see* Retrograde
Retrospect, *memory*, 505
  thought, 451
  past, 122
Retroversion, *inversion*, 218
Return, *regression*, 283
  arrival, 292
  frequency, 136
  to restore, 790
  reward, 973
  report, 551; *list*, 86
  appoint, 755
  profit, 775; *proceeds*, 810
Reunion, *junction*, 43
  assemblage, 72
  party, 892
Revanchist, *revenge*, 919
Reveal, *disclosure*, 529
Reveille, *signal*, 550
Revel, *enjoy*, 827
  amuse, 840
  dissipation, 954
Revelation, *disclosure*, 529
  theological, 985
Revelry, *cheerful*, 836
* Revenant, *ghost*, 980
Revendication, *claim*, 765
  recovery, 660
Revenge, *revenge*, 919
Revenue, *wealth*, 803
  receipts, 810
Reverberate, *sound*, 408
  recoil, 277
Reverberatory, *fire*, 386
Reverence, *respect*, 928
  salutation, 894

Reverence, *piety*, 987
  worship, 990
  title, 877
Reverend, *clergy*, 996
Reverie, *train of thought*,
  451
  imagination, 515
Reversal, *inversion*, 218
Reverse, *antiposition*, 237
  contrary, 14
  change, 140
  cancel, 756
  evolution, 313
  inversion, 218
  misfortune, 830
  adversity, 735
Reversion, *possession*, 777
  property, 780
  transfer, 783
Revert, *recur*, 104, 136
  go back, 283
  deteriorate, 659
Review, *consider*, 457
  memory, 505
  judge, 480
  criticism, 595
  rectify, 658
  display, 882
Reviewer, *writer*, 590
Revile, *abuse*, 932
  blaspheme, 988
Revise, *consider*, 457
  improve, 658
  restore, 660
  proof, 21, 591
Revisit, *presence*, 186
Revitalize, *restore*, 660
Revival, *worship*, 990
Revivalist, *clergy*, 996
Revive, *live*, 359
  restore, 660
  refresh, 689
Revivify, *reproduction*, 163
  restore, 660
Revoke, *recant*, 607
  deny, 536
  cancel, 756
  refuse, 754
Revolt, *resist*, 719
  revolution, 146
  disobey, 742
  shock, 830, 932
Revolting, *vulgar*, 851
Revolution, *rotation*, 312
  change, 140, 146
  periodicity, 138
Revolve, *meditate*, 451
Revolver, *arms*, 727
Revue, *drama*, 599
Revulsion, *recoil*, 277
Reward, *reward*, 973
Rhadamanthine, *severe*, 739

Rhapsody, *discontinuity*, 70
  nonsense, 497
  fancy, 515
  music, 415
Rhetoric, *speech*, 582
Rhetorical, *ornament*, 577
Rheum, *humour*, 333
  water, 337
Rhine, *ditch*, 350
Rhino, *money*, 800
Rhomb, *angularity*, 244
Rhombohedron, *angularity*,
  244
Rhomboid, *angularity*, 244
Rhombus, *angularity*, 244
Rhumb, *direction*, 278
Rhyme, *poetry*, 597
  similarity, 17
Rhymeless, *prose*, 598
Rhythm, *harmony*, 413
  regularity, 138
  poetry, 597
Rib, *ridge*, 250
  banter, 256
  wife, 903
Ribald, *vile*, 874, 961
  vulgar, 851
  maledictory, 908
  impious, 988
  abuse, 932
Ribbed, *furrow*, 259
Ribbon, *filament*, 205
  tie, 45
  trophy, 733
  decoration, 877
Rich, *wealthy*, 803
  abundant, 639
  savoury, 394
  adorned, 847
  style, 577
Richly, *great*, 31
Rick, *store*, 636
  accumulation, 72
Rickety, *weak*, 160
  imperfect, 651
  ugly, 846
Rickshaw, *vehicle*, 272
Ricochet, *recoil*, 277
  reversion, 145
Rid, *loss*, 776
  relinquish, 782
  abandon, 624
  deliver, 672
Riddle, *enigma*, 533
  obscurity, 519
  question, 461
  confute, 479
  sieve, 260
  arrange, 60
Ride, *move*, 266
  get above, 206
  road, 627

Roll, *fillet*, 205
   record, 551
   list, 86
Roll-call, *number*, 85
Roll in, *abound*, 639
Roller, *rotundity*, 249
Rollicking, *frolicsome*, 836
   blustering, 885
Rolling-stock, *vehicle*, 292
Rolling stone, *traveller*, 268
Roly-poly, *size*, 192
Roman, *type*, 591
Roman Catholic, *Christian religion*, 983A
Romance, *fiction*, 515
   falsehood, 544
   absurdity, 497
   fable, 594
   love, 897
Romantic, *sentimental*, 822
Romp, *leap*, 309
Rompers, *dress*, 225
Rondeau, *poem*, 597
Rondo, *music*, 415
Roof, *summit*, 210
   height, 206
   cover, 222
   house, 189
Roofless, *divestment*, 226
Rook, *deceiver*, 548
   swindle, 791
Rookery, *abode*, 189
Room, *space*, 180
   occasion, 124
   chamber, 191
Roommate, *friend*, 891
Roomy, *space*, 180
Roost, *abode*, 186, 189
Root, *cause*, 153
   base, 211
   word, 562
   algebraic, 84
   to place, 184
Root for, *commend*, 931
Root out, *destroy*, 162
   displace, 185
   eject, 301
   discover, 480A
Rooted, *fixed*, 265
   permanent, 141
   old, 124
   habitual, 613
Rope, *cord*, 205
   fastening, 45
Ropy, *semiliquidity*, 352
Roral, *moisture*, 339
Rosary, *rite*, 998
   garden, 371
Roscid, *moisture*, 339
Roscius, *actor*, 599
Rose, *redness*, 434
   beauty, 845

Rose, *spout*, 350
Rosette, *cluster*, 72
   ornament, 847
Rosicrucian, *heathen*, 984
Rosin, *semiliquid*, 352
Roster, *list*, 86
   record, 551
Rostrum, *beak*, 234
   pulpit, 542
Rosy, *red*, 434
   auspicious, 858
Rot, *disease*, 655
   decay, 659
   decompose, 48
   putrefy, 653
   nonsense, 497, 517
   to banter, 856
Rota, *periodicity*, 138
   list, 86
   record, 551
Rotate, *rotation*, 312
Rote, *memory*, 505
Rotor, *navigation*, 267
   ship, 273
Rotten, *foul*, 653
   fetid, 401
Rotter, *knave*, 949
Rotund, *fat*, 192
   round, 249
Rotunda, *abode*, 189
Rotundity, *roundness*, 249
* Roturier, *commonalty*, 876
* Roué, *scoundrel*, 949
   sensualist, 954
   libertine, 962
Rouge, *red*, 434
   ornament, 847
* Rouge-et-noir, *chance*, 156, 621
Rough, *uneven*, 256
   shapeless, 241
   pungent, 392
   sour, 397
   austere, 395
   violent, 173
   windy, 349
   sound, 410
   unprepared, 674
   ugly, 846
   churlish, 895
   brute, 913
   bad man, 949
   to fag, 686
Rough and ready, *transient*, 111
   provisional, 673
Rough-grained, *texture*, 329
Rough-hewn, *rugged*, 256
   unprepared, 674
Rough-house, *disorder*, 59
Roughcast, *unprepared*, 674
Roughly, *near*, 197

Roughneck, *ruffian*, 949
Rouleau, *cyclinder*, 249
   money, 800
Roulette, *engraving*, 558
   gambling, 621
Round, *circular*, 247
   rotund, 249
   assertion, 535
   periodicity, 138
   song, 415
   fight, 720
   rung, 71
   work, 625
Round-house, *prison*, 752
Round on, *attack*, 716
   peach, 529
Round robin, *record*, 551
   request, 765
Round-shot, *arms*, 727
Round-shouldered, *distorted*, 243
Round up, *assemblage*, 72
   capture, 789
Roundabout, *circuitous*, 31
   way, 629
   circumlocutory, 566, 573
Roundelay, *poetry*, 597
Roundlet, *circular*, 247
Roundly, *exertion*, 686
Roup, *sale*, 796
Rouse, *stimulate*, 615
   passion, 824
Roustabout, *labourer*, 690
Rout, *discomfort*, 732
   assembly, 892
   rabble, 876
Rout out, *destruction*, 162
Route, *method*, 627
   direction, 278
Route march, *journey*, 266
Routine, *order*, 58
   uniformity, 16
   cycle, 138; *rule*, 60
   custom, 613
   work, 625
Rove, *wander*, 266, 279
Rover, *traveller*, 268
Row, *series*, 69
   navigate, 267
   violence, 173
   brawl, 713
   riot, 720; *din*, 404
Rowdy, *violent*, 173
   vulgar, 851
Rowel, *sharpness*, 253
   stimulus, 615
Royalty, *authority*, 737
   receipt, 810
Rozzer, *police*, 664
Rub, *friction*, 331
   difficulty, 703

Sands, *pitfall*, 667
Sandwich, *interpose*, 228
Sandy, *pulverulence*, 330
Sane, *intelligent*, 498
  rational, 502
Sang-froid, *insensibility*,
                              823
  inexcitability, 826
  caution, 864
Sanguinary, *brutal*, 907
Sanguine, *expectant*, 507
  hopeful, 858
Sanhedrim, *tribunal*, 696
Sanies, *fluidity*, 333
Sanitary, *salubrity*, 656
Sanity, *rationality*, 502
  health, 654
Sans, *absence*, 187
* Sans cérémonie, *modesty*,
                              881
  sociality, 892
  friendship, 888
* Sans façon, *modesty*, 881
  sociality, 892
* Sans pareil, *superiority*, 33
* Sans phrase, *frankness*,
                           543, 566
* Sans souci, *pleasure*, 827
  content, 831
Sansculotte, *rebel*, 742
  commonalty, 876
Santon, *hermit*, 893
  priest, 996
Sap, *juice*, 333
  inbeing, 5
  to destroy, 162
  damage, 659
  fool, 501
Sapid, *tasty*, 390
Sapient, *wisdom*, 498
Sapless, *dry*, 340
Sapling, *youth*, 129
Saponaceous, *soapy*, 355
Sapor, *flavour*, 390
Sapphire, *ornament*, 847
Sappy, *juicy*, 333
  foolish, 499
Saraband, *dance*, 840
Sarcasm, *satire*, 932
  disrespect, 929
Sarcastic, *irascible*, 901
  derisory, 856
Sarcoma, *disease*, 655
Sarcophagus, *interment*, 363
Sardonic, *contempt*, 838
Sartorial, *dress*, 225
Sash, *central*, 247
Satan, *devil*, 978
Satanic, *evil*, 649
  hellish, 982
  vicious, 945
Satchel, *bag*, 191

Sate, *see* Satiate
Satellite, *follower*, 281
  companion, 88
  space ship, 273A
Satiate, *sufficient*, 639
  redundant, 641
  cloy, 869
Satiety, *see* Satiate
Satin, *smooth*, 255
Satire, *ridicule*, 856
  censure, 932
Satirist, *detractor*, 936
Satisfaction, *duel*, 720
  reward, 973
Satisfactorily, *well*, 618
Satisfy, *content*, 831
  gratify, 827, 829
  convince, 484
  fulfil a duty, 926
  an obligation, 772
  reward, 973
  pay, 807; *suffice*, 639
  satiate, 869
  grant, 762
Satrap, *ruler*, 745
  deputy, 759
Satrapy, *province*, 181
Saturate, *fill*, 52, 639
  soak, 337
  moisten, 339
  satiate, 869
Saturated, *greatness*, 31
Saturnalia, *amusement*, 840
  intemperance, 954
  disorder, 59
Saturnian, *halcyon*, 734,
Saturnine, *grim*, 837 [829
Satyr, *ugly*, 846
  demon, 980
  rake, 961
Sauce, *mixture*, 41
  adjunct, 39
  abuse, 832
Sauce-box, *impudence*, 887
Saucepan, *stove*, 386
Saucer, *receptacle*, 191
Saucy, *insolent*, 885
  flippant, 895
  cheerful, 836
Saunter, *ramble*, 266
  dawdle, 275
* Sauve qui peut, *speed*, 274
  recession, 287
  avoidance, 623
  escape, 671
  cowardice, 862
Savage, *violent*, 173
  brutal, 876; *angry*, 900
  malevolent, 907
  a wretch, 913

Savanna, *plain*, 344
Savant, *scholar*, 492
  wisdom, 500
Save, *except*, 38, 55, 83
  to preserve, 670
  deliver, 672
  lay by, 636
  economize, 817
Savings certificates,
  treasury, 802
Saviour, *Deity*, 976
  benefactor, 912
* Savoir faire, *tact*, 698
  manners, 852
* Savoir vivre, *sociality*, 892
  breeding, 852
Savour, *taste*, 390
  fragrance, 400
Savour of, *similarity*, 17
Savourless, *insipid*, 391
Savoury, *palatable*, 394
  delectable, 829
Savvy, *know*, 490
Saw, *jagged*, 257
  saying, 496
Sawder, *flattery*, 933
Sawdust, *pulverulence*, 330
Sawney, *fool*, 501
Saxophone, *musical instru-
  ment*, 417
Say, *speak*, 582
  assert, 535
  attention, 457
  about, 32
Saying, *assertion*, 535
  maxim, 496
* Sayonara, *departure*, 293
Scab, *traitor*, 941
Scabbard, *receptacle*, 191,
                              222
Scabby, *improbity*, 940
Scabrous, *rough*, 256
  indelicate, 961
Scaffold, *frame*, 215
  preparation, 673
  way, 627
  execution, 975
Scald, *burn*, 384
  poet, 597
Scalding, *hot*, 382
  burning, 384
Scale, *slice*, 204
  skin, 222
  order, 58
  measure, 466
  weight, 319
  series, 69
  gamut, 413
  to mount, 305
  attack, 716
Scale, on a large, *greatness*,
                              31

Scotch, *maltreat*, 649
  stop, 706
  notch, 257
Scotch mist, *rain*, 348
Scotomy, *dim-sightedness*,
                          443
Scotticism, *language*, 560
Scoundrel, *vice*, 949
  evildoer, 913
Scour, *rub*, 331
  run, 274
  clean, 652
Scourge, *whip*, 972, 975
  bane, 663
  painful, 830
  bad, 649
Scourings, *refuse*, 643
Scout, *messenger*, 534
  servant, 746
  watch, 664
  to disdain, 930
  deride, 643
Scowl, *frown*, 895
  complain, 839
  anger, 900
Scrabble, *fumble*, 379
  nonsense, 517
Scraggy, *narrow*, 203
  ugly, 846
Scram, *go away*, 293, 287
  escape, 671
  repel, 289
  ejection, 297
Scramble, *confusion*, 59
  haste, 684
  difficulty, 704
  mount, 305
Scrannel, *stridulous*, 410
  meagre, 643
Scrap, *piece*, 51
  small portion, 32, 193
  disuse, 678
  contention, 720
  to fight, 722
Scrap-book, *collection*, 596
Scrape, *difficulty*, 704
  mischance, 732
  abrade, 330, 331
  bow, 894
  save, 817
Scrape together, *collect*, 72
  get, 775
Scratch, *groove*, 259
  mark, 550
  write, 590
  daub, 555
  abrade, 331
  hurt, 619
  to wound, 649
Scratch out, *obliteration*,
                          552
Scrawl, *write*, 590

Scrawny, *lean*, 193, 203
Scream, *cry*, 410
  complain, 839
Screech, *cry*, 410
  complain, 839
Screech-owl, *noise*, 412
Screed, *speech*, 582
Screen, *concealment*, 528
  asylum, 666, 717
  ambush, 530
  to shield, 664
  sieve, 260
  sift, 652
  inquire, 461
  discriminate, 465
  sort, 42, 60
  exclude, 55
  shade, 424
  cinema, 599A
Screened, *safe*, 664
  invisible, 447
Screever, *artist*, 559
Screw, *fasten*, 43
  joining, 45
  instrument, 267, 633
  rotation, 312
  salary, 809
  miser, 819
Screw-steamer, *ship*, 273
Screw up, *strengthen*, 159
Screwball, *madman*, 504
Screwed, *drunk*, 959
Scribble, *write*, 590
  unmeaning, 517
Scribe, *writer*, 553, 590
  priest, 996
Scrimp, *shorten*, 201
  stint, 640
  save, 817
Scrip, *receptacle*, 191
Script, *writing*, 590
  radio, 599D
Scriptural, *Christian*, 983A
Scripture, *revelation*, 985
  certain, 474
Scrivener, *writing*, 590
Scroll, *record*, 551
  convolution, 248
Scrounge, *steal*, 791
Scrub, *clean*, 652
  plant, 367
Scrubby, *vulgar*, 876
  shabby, 940
  bad, 649
  trifling, 643
  small, 193
  rough, 256
Scrumptious, *pleasing*, 829
Scrunch, *pulverulence*, 330
Scruple, *doubt*, 485
  dissuasion, 616
  smallness, 32

Scrupulous, *careful*, 459
  incredulous, 487
  exact, 494
  reluctant, 603
  punctilious, 939
  virtuous, 944
Scrutator, *inquiry*, 461
Scrutinize, *examine*, 457,
                          461
Scud, *speed*, 274
  sail, 267
  shower, 348
  haze, 353
Scuffle, *contention*, 720
Scull, *navigation*, 267
Scullery, *room*, 191
Scullion, *servant*, 746
Sculp, *produce*, 161
Sculptor, *artist*, 559
Sculpture, *carving*, 557
  form, 240
Scum, *dregs*, 643, 653
Scunner, *disgust*, 395
Scupper, *conduit*, 350
Scurf, *uncleanness*, 653
Scurrility, *ridicule*, 856
  malediction, 908
  detraction, 934
  disrespect, 929
Scurry, *hasten*, 274, 684
Scurvy, *bad*, 649
  bass, 940, 945
Scut, *tail*, 235
Scutcheon, *standard*, 550
  honour, 877
Scuttle, *tray*, 191
  opening, 260
  to destroy, 162
  hasten, 274, 684
Scythe, *angularity*, 244
  sharpness, 253
Sea, *water*, 341
  blue, 438
Sea-nymph, *sea*, 341
Seaboard, *edge*, 342
Seal, *to close*, 67, 261
  sigil, 550
  mould, 22
  evidence, 467
  record, 551
  compact, 769
  security, 771
  authority, 747
Seal up, *shut up*, 231, 751
Seam, *junction*, 43
Seaman, *mariner*, 269
Seamanship, *conduct*, 603
Seamstress, *see* Sempstress
Séance, *council*, 696
Seaplane, *aircraft*, 273A
Sear, *burn*, 384
  deaden, 823

Sermon, *dissertation*, 595
  lesson, 537
  speech, 582
  pastoral, 998
Serosity, *fluidity*, 333
Serpent, *tortuous*, 248
  Satan, 978
  deceiver, 548
  cunning, 702
  evil, 663
Serpentine, *convolution*, 248
Serrated, *angular*, 244
  notched, 257
Serried, *crowded*, 72
  dense, 321
Serum, *lymph*, 333
  water, 337
Servant, *servant*, 711, 746
Serve, *aid*, 707
  obey, 743, 749
  work, 625, 680
  suffice, 639
Serve out, *apportion*, 786
  punish, 972
Service, *good*, 618
  use, 677
  utility, 644
  worship, 990
  servitude, 749
  warfare, 722
Serviceable, *useful*, 644
  good, 648
Servile, *obsequious*, 886
  flattery, 933
Servitor, *servant*, 746
Servitude, *subjection*, 749
Sesqui-, *number*, 87
* Sesquipedalia verba, *ornament*, 577
Sesquipedalian, *long*, 200
Sessions, *legal*, 966
  council, 696
Sestina, *poetry*, 597
Set, *condition*, 7
  group, 72
  class, 75
  firm, 43
  to place, 184
  establish, 150
  prepare, 673
  sharpen, 253
  solidify, 321
  leaning, 278
  gang, 712
  lease, 796
  habitual, 613
Set about, *begin*, 676
Set apart, *disjoin*, 55
Set aside, *disregard*, 460
  annul, 756
  release, 927A
Set-back, *hindrance*, 706

Set-back, *adversity*, 735
  relapse, 661
Set down, *humiliate*, 879
  censure, 932
  slight, 929
  rebuff, 732
Set fire to, *burn*, 384
Set foot in, *ingress*, 294
Set forth, *publish*, 531
  tell, 527
  show, 525
  assert, 535
  describe, 594
Set forward, *depart*, 293
Set in, *begin*, 66
  tide, 348
  approach, 286
Set off, *depart*, 293
  compensate, 30
  adorn, 845
Set-off, *foil*, 14
Set on, *attack*, 615
Set out, *begin*, 66
  depart, 293
  decorate, 845
Set right, *reinstate*, 660
Set sail, *depart*, 293
Set-square, *angularity*, 244
Set-to, *combat*, 720
Set to work, *begin*, 676
Set up, *raise*, 307
  prosperous, 734
Set-up, *state*, 7
  structure, 329
  plan, 626
Set upon, *attack*, 716
  desire, 865
  willing, 602
  determined, 604, 620
Setaceous, *rough*, 256
Settee, *support*, 215
Setting, *surroundings*, 227
Settle, *decide*, 480
  be fixed, 141
  be stationary, 265
  place, 184
  dwell, 186
  sink, 306
  arrange, 60
  pacify, 723
  defeat, 731
  consent, 762
  pay, 807
  give, 784
  bench, 215
Settlement, *location*, 184
  colony, 188
  dregs, 653
  compact, 762, 769
  property, 780
Settler, *inhabitant*, 188
Seven, *number*, 98

Seventy-four, *ship*, 273
Sever, *disjoin*, 44
Several, *repetition*, 102
  special, 79
Severally, *one by one*, 44, 79
  sharing, 786
Severe, *harsh*, 739
  energetic, 171
  painful, 830
  unadorned, 576, 849
  critical, 932
  greatness, 31
Sew, *join*, 43
Sewer, *drain*, 295, 350
  cloaca, 653
Sex, *kind*, 75
  women, 374
Sex-appeal, *charm*, 829
Sexagesimal, *sixty*, 98
Sexcentenary, *celebration*,
                            883
Sext, *worship*, 990
Sextant, *angularity*, 244
  roundness, 247
Sextet, *number*, 98
Sextodecimo, *book*, 593
Sexton, *church*, 996
  interment, 363
Sextuple, *number*, 98
* Sforzando, *music*, 415
Sgraffito, *see* Graffito
Shabby, *mean*, 819, 874
  bad, 649
  disgraceful, 940
  trifling, 643
  smallness, 32
Shack, *abode*, 189
Shackle, *to tie*, 43
  hinder, 706
  restrain, 751
  fetter, 752
Shade, *darkness*, 421
  shadow, 424
  colour, 428
  degree, 26
  difference, 15, 41
  small quantity, 32
  screen, 530
  manes, 362
  ghost, 980
  decrease, 36
Shaded, *invisible*, 447
Shades, *hell*, 982
Shading off, *degree*, 26
Shadow, *darkness*, 421
  shade, 424
  error, 495
  phantom, 4
  little, 193, 203
  small in degree, 32
  part, 51
  sequence, 281

Shadow forth, *show*, 525
  indicate, 550
  adumbrate, 521
  describe, 594
Shadow of doubt, *unbelief*,
                    485
Shadow out, *represent*, 554
Shadowy, *imaginary*, 2
  invisible, 447
  erroneous, 495
Shady, *umbrageous*, 424
  dishonest, 544
  disreputable, 945
Shaft, *pit*, 260
  air-pipe, 351
  deep, 208
  frame, 215
  missile, 284.
  shank, 633
  weapon, 727
Shag, *roughness*, 256
  tobacco, 298A
Shaggy, *hirsute*, 256
Shah, *master*, 745
Shake, *agitate*, 315
  fluctuate, 149
  trill, 314, 407
  musical, 415
  dissuade, 616
  injure, 659
  impress, 821
  flutter, 824
  shiver, 383
Shake-down, *bed*, 215
Shake off, *ejection*, 297
Shake up, *agitation*, 315
Shaken, *weak*, 160
Shakespearian, *poetry*, 597
Shaky, *in danger*, 665
  frail, 149
Shallop, *ship*, 273
Shallow, *not deep*, 209
  ignorant, 491
  foolish, 499
Shallow-brained, *foolish*,
                    499
Shallow-pated, *foolish*, 499
Shallows, *dangers*, 667
Sham, *humbug*, 544
  deceive, 545
Shamble, *shuffle*, 275, 315
Shambles, *butchery*, 361
Shame, *disgrace*, 874
  humiliation, 879
Shamefaced, *abashed*, 881
Shameful, *disgraceful*, 874
  profligate, 945
Shameless, *profligate*, 945
  impudent, 885
Shampoo, *friction*, 331
  cleanness, 652
Shandrydan, *vehicle*, 272

Shanghai, *kidnap*, 789
Shangri-la, *fancy*, 515
  retirement, 893
Shank, *shaft*, 633
Shape, *form*, 240
  condition, 7
  to fashion, 144
  aspect, 448
Shape well, *hopeful*, 858
Shapeless, *amorphous*, 241
  ugly, 846
Shapely, *comely*, 845
  symmetrical, 242
Share, *part*, 51
  participate, 778
  allotted portion, 786
Shark, *thief*, 792
  cheat, 548
Sharp, *acute*, 253, 376
  musical tone, 410
  pungent, 392, 821
  energetic, 171
  violent, 173
  intelligent, 498
  clever, 698
  cunning, 702
  active, 682
  rude, 895
  censorious, 932
Sharper, *cheat*, 548
  thief, 792
  knave, 941
Sharp-sighted, *vision*, 441
Sharpshooter, *combatant*,
                    726
Shatter, *destroy*, 162
  weaken, 160
Shave, *cut*, 203
Shaving, *layer*, 204
  filament, 205
  small part, 32, 51
Shawl, *dress*, 225
Sheaf, *assemblage*, 72
Shear, *subduction*, 38
  take, 789
Shears, *sharpness*, 253
Sheath, *receptacle*, 191
  envelope, 222
Shed, *building*, 189
  to emit, 297
  scatter, 73
  diverge, 291
Shed tears, *weep*, 839
Sheen, *light*, 420
Sheepfold, *enclosure*, 232
Sheepish, *foolish*, 881
Sheep's eyes, *ogle*, 902
Sheer, *vertical*, 212
  simple, 42
  complete, 52
  smallness, 32
Sheer off, *departure*, 293

Sheet, *layer*, 204
  paper, 593
Sheet-anchor, *refuge*, 666
Sheik, *ruler*, 745
  priest, 996
  philanderer, 902
Shelf, *support*, 215
Shell, *cover*, 222
  arms, 727; *attack*, 716
Shell out, *expend*, 809
Shelter, *refuge*, 666, 717
  safety, 664
Shelty, *horse*, 271
Shelve, *slope*, 217
  locate, 184
  neglect, 460
  relinquish, 624
  disuse, 678
Shemozzle, *row*, 713
  contention, 720
Shenanigans, *caprice*, 608
Shepherd, *director*, 694
  pastor, 996
Sheriff, *jurisdiction*, 965
Sherlock Holmes, *inquiry*,
                    461
Shibboleth, *indication*, 550
  criterion, 467
Shield, *defend*, 717
  safety, 664
  buckler, 666
Shift, *move*, 264
  change, 140, 144
  substitute, 147
  transfer, 270
  expedient, 626, 634
  evasion, 546
  plea, 617
  difficulty, 704
  dress, 225
Shifting, *transient*, 111
  moving, 270
Shiftless, *unprepared*, 674
  inhabile, 699, 951
Shifty, *dishonest*, 544
Shikar, *pursuit*, 622
Shillelagh, *club*, 727
  impact, 276
Shilly-shally, *irresolution*,
                    605
Shilpit, *weak*, 160
Shimmer, *lustre*, 420
Shin, *climb*, 305
  kick, 276
Shindig, *prank*, 840
Shindy, *violence*, 173
  contention, 720
  din, 404
Shine, *to emit light*, 420
  glory, 873
  beauty, 845
Shintoism, *religions*, 984

Ship, *vessel*, 273
  to deliver, 270
Shipload, *cargo*, 31
  abundance, 639
Shipment, *transference*, 270
Shipshape, *order*, 58
  conformity, 82
Shipwreck, *failure*, 732
  to defeat, 731
Shire, *county*, 181
Shirk, *avoid*, 623
  disobey, 742
Shirt, *dress*, 225
Shirt-waist, *dress*, 225
Shirty, *angry*, 900
Shivaree, *uproar*, 404
Shiver, *shake*, 315
  cold, 385
  layer, 204
  fragment, 51
  filament, 205
  to divide, 44
  destroy, 162
Shoal, *shallow*, 209
  assemblage, 72, 102
  danger, 667
Shock, *concussion*, 276
  violence, 173
  sheaf, 72
  contest, 720
  affect, 821
  move, 824
  pain, 830
  inexpectation, 508
  dislike, 867
  hate, 898
  scandalize, 932
Shocking, *ugly*, 846
  vulgar, 851
  fearful, 860
  painful, 830
  considerable, 31
Shoe, *dress*, 225
Shogun, *master*, 745
Shoogle, *oscillate*, 314
Shoot, *propel*, 284
  dart, 274
  kill, 361
  grow, 194
  attack, 716
  pain, 378
  offspring, 167
Shoot up, *increase*, 35
  ascend, 305
  prominent, 250
Shop, *mart*, 799
  buy, 795
  workshop, 691
Shopkeeper, *merchant*, 797
Shoplifting, *stealing*, 791
Shopman, *merchant*, 797
Shopwalker, *director*, 694

Shore, *support*, 215
  land, 342; *edge*, 230
  sewer, 653
Shoreless, *space*, 180
Shorn, *deprived*, 776
  reduced, 36
Short, *not long*, 201
  concise, 572
  incomplete, 53
  unaccomplished, 730
  insufficient, 640
  brittle, 328; *uncivil*, 895
Shortfall, *deficit*, 204
Short-lived, *youth*, 111
Short of, *inferiority*, 34
Short-sighted, *myopic*, 443
  foolish, 499
Short-tempered, *irascible*,
          901
Short-witted, *foolish*, 499
Shortage, *insufficiency*, 640
Shortcoming, *failing*, 304
  fault, 651
Shorten, *diminish*, 36
Shorthand, *write*, 590
Shortly, *soon*, 132
Shorts, *dress*, 225
Shot, *missile*, 284
  weapon, 727
  variegated, 440
  changeable, 149
  guess, 514
Shoulder, *projection*, 250
  support, 215
  to shove, 276
Shout, *loudness*, 404
  cry, 411
  voice, 580
Shove, *impulse*, 276
Shovel, *vehicle*, 272
  to transfer, 270
  receptacle, 191
Show, *manifest*, 525
  appear, 446, 448
  evince, 467
  demonstrate, 478
  parade, 852, 882
  drama, 599
Show-down, *disclosure*, 529
  opportunity, 134
Show of, *similarity*, 17
Show up, *accuse*, 938, 874
  appear, 446
Shower, *rain*, 348
  abundance, 639
  liberality, 816
  assemblage, 72
Showman, *interpreter*, 524
Showy, *coloured*, 428
  gaudy, 847, 882
  vulgar, 851

Shrapnel, *arms*, 727
Shred, *bit*, 51
  filament, 205
Shrew, *vixen*, 901
Shrewd, *intelligent*, 498
  wise, 490
  clever, 698
  cunning, 702
Shriek, *cry*, 410, 411
Shrill, *noise*, 410
Shrimp, *little*, 193
Shrine, *altar*, 1000
  interment, 363
Shrink, *shrivel*, 195
  narrow, 203
  decrease, 36
  small, 32
  recoil, 287, 898
  avoid, 623
  unwilling, 603
Shrive, *penitence*, 950
  atonement, 952
Shrivel, *decrease*, 36
  shrink, 195
  small, 193
Shroud, *funeral*, 363
  shelter, 666
  safety, 664
  hide, 528
Shrub, *plant*, 367
Shrubbery, *agriculture*, 371
Shrug, *hint*, 527, 550
  dissent, 489
Shrunken, *little*, 193
Shucks, *contempt*, 643, 930
Shudder, *fear*, 860
  aversion, 867
  hate, 898
  cold, 383
Shuffle, *mix*, 41
  disorder, 59
  derange, 61
  interchange, 148
  agitate, 315
  toddle, 266, 275
  evasion, 544, 546
  cunning, 702
  irresolution, 605
  disgrace, 940
Shuffler, *deceiver*, 548
Shun, *avoid*, 623
  dislike, 867
Shunt, *turn aside*, 279
  shelve, 460, 678
Shut, *close*, 261
Shut down, *cease*, 142
Shut off, *disconnect*, 44
Shut out, *exclude*, 55
  prohibit, 761
Shut up, *enclose*, 231
  imprison, 751
  close, 261

Shut up, *confute*, 479
Shutter, *shade*, 424
Shuttlecock, *irresolute*, 605
Shy, *avoid*, 623
  suspicious, 485
  unwilling, 603
  modest, 881
  fearful, 862
  propel, 276, 284
Shylock, *usurer*, 805
Shyster, *knave*, 941
Sib, *relation*, 11
Sibilant, *hiss*, 409
Sibilation, *decry*, 929
  censure, 932
Sibling, *relation*, 11
Sibyl, *oracle*, 513
  ugly, 846
Sibylline, *prediction*, 511
* Sic, *imitation*, 19
  word, 562
Sick, *ill*, 655
  tired, 841
Sicken, *weary*, 841
  nauseate, 395
  fall ill, 655
  disgust, 830, 867
  hate, 898
Sickle, *instrument*, 244
  sharpness, 253
Sickly, *ill*, 655
  weak, 160
Sickness, *disease*, 655
Side, *laterality*, 236
  party, 712
  affectation, 855
  insolence, 878, 885
Side-car, *vehicle*, 272
Side-kick, *friend*, 890
  associate, 88
  partner, 711
Side-slip, *deviation*, 279
Side-track, *set aside*, 678
Side with, *aid*, 707
Sideboard, *receptacle*, 191
  whisker, 256
Sideburns, *whiskers*, 256
Sidelight, *interpretation*, 522
Sidelong, *lateral*, 236
Sidereal, *world*, 318
Sideways, *oblique*, 217
  lateral, 236
Sidle, *oblique*, 217
  deviate, 279, 291
  lateral, 236
Siege, *attack*, 716
Siesta, *inactivity*, 683
Sieve, *perforation*, 260
  to sort, 60
Sift, *to sort*, 60
  winnow, 42
  clean, 652

Sift, *inquire*, 461
  discriminate, 465
Sigh, *lament*, 839
Sigh for, *desire*, 865
Sight, *vision*, 441
  spectacle, 448
  prodigy, 872
  large quantity, 31
Sightless, *blind*, 442
  invisible, 447
Sightly, *beauty*, 845
Sightseer, *spectator*, 444
Sigil, *seal*, 550
  evidence, 467
Sigmoidal, *convolution*, 248
Sign, *indication*, 550
  omen, 512
  record, 551
  write, 590
  prodigy, 872
  evidence, 467
  compact, 769
Sign manual, *sign*, 550
Signal, *sign*, 550
  manifest, 525
  important, 642
  greatness, 31
Signalize, *celebrate*, 883
  glory, 873
Signally, *great*, 31
Signature, *mark*, 550
  writing, 590
Signboard, *indication*, 550
Signet, *evidence*, 467
  signature, 550
  sign of authority, 747
Significant, *meaning*, 516,
                             527
  clear, 518
  foreboding, 511
  important, 642
Signify, *mean*, 516
  inform, 527
  forebode, 511
* Signor, *title*, 877
Silence, *no sound*, 403
  aphony, 581
  confute, 479
  taciturn, 585
  to check, 731
Silhouette, *portrait*, 556
  outline, 229
Silk, *smooth*, 255
Silk hat, *dress*, 225
Siller, *money*, 800
Silly, *irrational*, 477
  credulous, 486
  foolish, 499
Silt, *dirt*, 653
  dregs, 50
Silver, *money*, 800
Silver-toned, *harmony*, 413

Silver wedding, *celebration*,
                             883
  anniversary, 138
Silversmith, *artist*, 559
Silvery, *colour*, 430
  voice, 580
Similar, *relation*, 9
  resembling, 17
  comparison, 464
Simile, Similitude, *see*
  Similar
Simmer, *heat*, 382, 384
  excitement, 824
Simoleons, *money*, 800
Simon Stylites, *hermit*,
                             893
Simony, *churchdom*, 995
Simoon, *blast*, 349
  heat, 382
Simp, *fool*, 501
Simper, *smile*, 838
  affectation, 855
Simple, *unmixed*, 42
  unadorned, 576, 849
  small, 32
  credulous, 486
  silly, 499
  true, 543
Simpleton, *fool*, 501
Simplify, *meaning*, 518
Simulate, *resemble*, 17
  imitate, 19
  cheat, 544
Simultaneous, *contempor-*
  ary, 120
Sin, *guilt*, 947
  vice, 945
Sin-offering, *atonement*, 952
Since, *in order*, 8, 63
  in time, 117
  because, 155, 476, 615
Sincere, *veracious*, 543
  ingenuous, 703
Sinecure, *receipt*, 810
* Sine die, *neverness*, 107
  long duration, 110
* Sine qua non, *condition*,
                             770
  importance, 642
  requirement, 630
Sinewy, *strong*, 159
  tough, 327
* Sinfonietta, *music*, 415
Sinful, *evil*, 947
Sing, *music*, 415
  poetry, 597
  cheerful, 836
  rejoice, 838
Sing out, *cry*, 411
Sing-song, *untuneful*, 414
  concert, 415
  repetition, 104

Singe, *burn*, 384
Singer, *musician*, 416
Single, *unit*, 87
   unmixed, 42
   secluded, 893
   unmarried, 904
Single-handed, *unaided*,
       708
Single-minded, *honest*, 543
Single out, *select*, 609
Singlet, *dress*, 225
Sing Sing, *prison*, 752
* Singspiel, *drama*, 599
Singular, *exceptional*, 79, 83
   one, 87
   remarkable, 31
Sinister, *left*, 239
   bad, 649
   discourtesy, 895
   menacing, 909
   vicious, 945
Sink, *descend*, 306
   lower, 308
   submerge, 310
   deep, 208
   fail, 732
   destroy, 162
   decay, 659
   fatigue, 688
   cloaca, 653
   depressed, 837
   droop, 828
   conceal, 528
   neglect, 460
   in the memory, 505
Sinless, *good*, 946
Sinner, *sinner*, 949
   impiety, 988
Sinuous, *curved*, 245
   convoluted, 248
Sinus, *concavity*, 252
Sip, *drink*, 296
   smallness, 32
Siphon, *conduit*, 350
Sir, *respect*, 877
Sirdar, *master*, 745
Sire, *elder*, 166
Siren, *musician*, 416
   indication, 550
   alarm, 669
   seducing, 615
   sea, 341
   demon, 980
   evildoer, 913
Sirocco, *wind*, 349
   heat, 382
Sissy, *weakness*, 160
Sister, *kindred*, 11
   likeness, 17
Sisterhood, *assembly*, 72
   party, 712
Sisyphean, *difficulty*, 704

Sit, *repose*, 215
   lie, 213
   lowering, 308
Site, *situation*, 183
Sitting, *consultation*, 696
Situate, *location*, 184
Situation, *circumstances*, 8
   place, 183
   business, 625
Siva, *deity*, 979
Six, *number*, 98
Six-shooter, *gun*, 727
Sixth sense, *intuition*, 477
Size, *magnitude*, 31, 192
   grade, 60
   glue, 45, 352
   quantity, 25
Size up, *measure*, 466
   estimate, 480
   scrutinize, 457
Sizy, *sticky*, 350
Sjambok, *scourge*, 975
Skate, *locomotion*, 266
Skean, *arms*, 727
Skedaddle, *escape*, 671
   go away, 293, 287
Skein, *knot*, 219
   disorder, 59
Skeleton, *corpse*, 362
   frame, 626
   small, 193
   lean, 203
   imperfect, 651
   essential part, 50
Skelp, *impact*, 276
   punishment, 972
Sketch, *painting*, 556
   description, 594
   plan, 626
Sketcher, *artist*, 559
Sketchy, *imperfect*, 53, 651
Skew, *obliquity*, 217
Skew-whiff, *oblique*, 217
Skewbald, *variegation*, 440
Skewer, *vinculum*, 45
Ski, *locomotion*, 266
Skid, *deviation*, 279
   hindrance, 706
Skiff, *boat*, 273
Skiffle, *melody*, 413
Skill, *ability*, 450, 698
Skim, *move*, 266
   rapid, 274
   attend lightly, 458, 460
Skimp, *shorten*, 201
   stint, 640
   save, 817
Skin, *tegument*, 222
   to peel, 226
Skin-deep, *shallow*, 220
Skinflint, *miser*, 819
Skinful, *fullness*, 52

Skinny, *small*, 193
   slender, 203
   tegumentary, 222
Skip, *jump*, 309
   neglect, 460
   omit, 773
   escape, 671
   dance, 840
Skipjack, *upstart*, 734, 876
Skipper, *master*, 745
Skirl, *shriek*, 410, 411
   lamentation, 839
Skirmish, *fight*, 720, 722
Skirt, *edge*, 230
   appendix, 39
   pendent, 214
   circumjacent, 227
   woman, 374
Skirting-board, *base*, 211
Skit, *parody*, 856
   satire, 932
Skite, *boast*, 884
Skittish, *capricious*, 608
   bashful, 881
   excitable, 825
   timid, 862
Skivvy, *servant*, 746
* Skoal, *drink*, 959
Skulk, *hide*, 447, 528
   coward, 860
   flock, 72
Skull, *head*, 450
Skunk, *fetid*, 401
   bad man, 949
Sky, *world*, 318
   air, 338
   summit, 210
Sky-line, *outline*, 229
Sky-rocket, *ascent*, 350
Skylark, *frolic*, 840
Skylight, *opening*, 260
Skymaster, *aircraft*, 273A
Skyscraper, *height*, 206
Slab, *layer*, 204
   flatness, 251
   record, 551
Slabber, *ejection*, 297
Slack, *loose*, 47
   weak, 160
   slow, 275
   inert, 172
   inactive, 683
   unwilling, 603
   laxity, 738
   to moderate, 174
   retard, 706
   calm, 826
Slacken, *relax*, 687
Slacker, *evasion*, 623
Slacks, *dress*, 225
Slag, *refuse*, 40
   dirt, 653

INDEX

Spring tide, *flow*, 348
 abundance, 639
Spring up, *grow*, 194
Springe, *snare*, 667
 deception, 545
Sprinkle, *mix*, 41
 disperse, 73, 291
 omit, 297
 wet, 337
Sprinkler, *spray*, 348
Sprinkling, *smallness*, 32
 little, 193
Sprint, *velocity*, 274
Sprite, *ghost*, 890
Sprocket, *tooth*, 257
Sprog, *recruit*, 674
Sprout, *grow*, 35
 expand, 194
 arise from, 154
 offspring, 167
Spruce, *neat*, 652
 beautiful, 845
Spry, *active*, 682
 healthy, 654
 clever, 698
 cheerful, 836
Spume, *foam*, 353
Spunk, *courage*, 861
Spur, *sharp*, 253
 incite, 615
 ridge, 250
Spurious, *false*, 544
 erroneous, 495
 illegitimate, 925
Spurn, *disdain*, 866, 930
 refuse, 764
Spurt, *impulse*, 612
 haste, 684
 swift, 274
 gush, 348
Sputnik, *space ship*, 273A
Sputter, *emit*, 297
 stammer, 583
Spy, *see*, 441
 spectator, 444
 emissary, 534
Spy-glass, *optical instru-ment*, 445
Squab, *large*, 192
 short, 201
 broad, 202
 recumbent, 215
Squabble, *quarrel*, 713
Squabby, *broad*, 202
 short, 201
Squad, *assembly*, 72
Squadron, *navy*, 273
 army, 726
 assemblage, 72
Squadron-leader, *master*, 745
Squalid, *dirty*, 653

Squalid, *unattractive*, 846
Squall, *cry*, 411
 win, 349
 violence, 173
Squalor, *see* Squalid
Squamous, *scaly*, 204
 covering, 222
Squander, *waste*, 638, 818
Squandermania, *waste*, 818
Square, *number*, 95
 buildings, 189
 congruity, 23
 expedience, 646
 justice, 924
 honour, 939
 form, 244
 prig, 855
 to equalize, 27
 to bribe, 784, 795
Square-toes, *butt*, 857
Squash, *destroy*, 162
 check, 706
 throw, 276
 soft, 324
 water, 337
Squashy, *pulpy*, 352
Squat, *to encamp*, 186
 sit, 308
 short, 201
 broad, 202
 flat, 213
 ugly, 846
Squatter, *inhabitant*, 188
Squatting, *horizontal*, 213
Squaw, *marriage*, 903
Squawk, *cry*, 411, 412
 complain, 839
Squeak, *cry*, 411, 412
 complain, 839
Squeal, *cry*, 410, 411, 412
 blab, 529
 complain, 839
Squeamish, *fastidious*, 868
 censorious, 932
Squeeze, *contract*, 195
 narrow, 203
 condense, 321
 extort, 789
 copy, 21
Squeeze out, *extraction*, 301
Squelch, *squash*, 162
Squib, *sound*, 406
 lampoon, 932
Squiffy, *drunk*, 959
Squiggle, *convolution*, 248
Squint, *dim-sighted*, 443
 look, 441
Squire, *gentry*, 875
 possessor, 779
 attendant, 746
Squirm, *wriggle*, 315
Squirrel, *velocity*, 274

Squirt, *eject*, 297
 spurt, 348
Stab, *pierce*, 260
 attack, 716
 kill, 361
 injure, 649, 659
Stable, *house*, 189
 at rest, 265
 immutable, 150
 resolute, 604
Stable-boy, *servant*, 746
* Staccato, *music*, 415
Stack, *assembly*, 72
Stadtholder, *master*, 745
Staff, *support*, 215
 instrument, 633
 weapon, 727
 impact, 276
 sceptre, 747
 retinue, 746
 party, 712
 hope, 858
Stage, *degree*, 26
 term, 71
 step, 58
 layer, 204
 forum, 542
 vehicle, 272
 arena, 728
 drama, 599
Stage effect, *drama*, 599
 ostentation, 882
Stage-play, *the drama*, 599
Stager, *old*, *proficient*, 700
Stagger, *totter*, 314
 slow, 275
 agitate, 315
 doubt, 485
 dissuade, 616
 affect, 824
 astonish, 508, 870
Stagnant, *quiescent*, 265
 unchanging, 141
 insert, 172
 inactive, 683
Stagy, *affected*, 855
 ostentatious, 882
Staid, *steady*, 604
 calm, 826
 wise, 498
 grave, 837
Stain, *colour*, 428
 adorn, 847
 deface, 846
 blemish, 848
 spoil, 659
 disgrace, 874
 dishonour, 940
Stainless, *clean*, 652
 innocent, 946
Stair, *way*, 627
Stake, *wager*, 621

Status, *standing*, 8, 71
  situation, 183
  order, 58
  rank, 873
* Status quo, *reversion*, 145
Statute, *law*, 697, 963
Staunch, *spirited*, 604
  trusty, 939
  healthy, 654
Stave, *verse*, 597
Stave in, *open*, 260
  concavity, 252
Stave off, *defer*, 133
Stay, *wait*, 133
  continue, 141
  exist, 1; *support*, 215
  refuge, 666
  rest, 265; *prevent*, 706
  dissuade, 616
  corset, 225
Stead, *utility*, 644
Steadfast, *resolved*, 604
  stable, 150
  quiescent, 265
  thought, 451
Steading, *farm*, 189
Steady, *resolved*, 604
  cautious, 864
  still, 265
  constant, 138, 150
  normal, 82
Steady as she goes, *caution*,
Steal, *rob*, 791   [864
  creep, 275, 528
Steal away, *evade*, 671
Stealth, *concealment*, 528
Steam, *vapour*, 334, 353
  to sail, 267
Steamboat, *ship*, 273
Steamer, *ship*, 273
Steam-roller, *compel*, 744
Stearic, *unctuous*, 355
Stearin, *fat*, 356
Steed, *horse*, 271
Steek, *close*, 261
Steel, *strength*, 159
  sharpener, 253
  inure, 823
Steel-cut, *engraving*, 558
Steeled, *resolved*, 604
Steelyard, *scale*, 466
  weight, 319
Steep, *slope*, 217
  height, 206; *immerse*, 300
  soak, 337; *clean*, 652
Steeple, *spire*, 253
  high, 206
Steeplechase, *race*, 274
  pursuit, 282, 622
Steer, *guide*, 693

Steer for, *direction*, 278
Steersman, *director*, 694
Steganography, *writing*, 590
Stegophilist, *climber*, 305
Stele, *record*, 551
Stellar, *heavens*, 318
Stem, *origin*, 153
  result, 154
  front, 234
  to oppose, 708
  to resist, 718
Sten, *gun*, 727
Stench, *fetor*, 401
Stencil, *copy*, 556
Stenographer, *secretary*, 553
Stenography, *writing*, 590
Stentorian, *loud*, 404
Step, *degree*, 26
  station, 58
  term, 71
  near, 197
  support, 215
  motion, 264, 266
  measure, 466
  expedient, 626
  means, 632
  action, 680
Steppe, *plain*, 344
Stepping-stone, *link*, 45
  way, 627
  preparation, 763
  resource, 666
Stercoraceous, *unclean*, 653
Stereoscope, *optical*, 445
Stereoscopic, *visible*, 446
Stereotype, *printing*, 591
  engraving, 558
Stereotyped, *ordinary*, 82
  habitual, 613
  fixed, 141, 150
Sterile, *unproductive*, 169
  useless, 645
  clean, 652
Sterling, *true*, 494
  good, 648
  virtuous, 944
  money, 800
Stern, *back*, 235
  severe, 739
  forbidding, 895
Stern-wheeler, *ship*, 273
Sternutation, *sneeze*, 349
  sound, 409
Sternway, *navigation*, 267
Stertorous, *sound*, 411
* Stet, *unchanged*, 150
Stetson, *hat*, 225
Stevedore, *doer*, 271, 690
Stew, *confusion*, 59
  fluster, 821
  difficulty, 704
  heat, 382

Stew, *cook*, 384
  perplex, 828
  bagnio, 961
Steward, *director*, 694
  agent, 690
  treasurer, 801
Stewardship, *charge*, 693
  conduct, 692
Stick, *adhere*, 46
  stop, 142
  continue, 143
  staff, 215
  to stab, 260, 830
  pierce, 302
  difficulty, 704
  fool, 501
  scourge, 975
Stick at, *demur*, 603
Stick in, *insert*, 300
  locate, 184
Stick-in-the-mud,   *in-*
  activity, 683
Stick out, *project*, 250
  erect, 212
Stick up, *project*, 250
  erect, 212, 307
  rob, 791
Stickit, *failure*, 732
Stickle, *haggle*, 769
  barter, 794
  reluctant, 603
Stickler, *obstinacy*, 606
  severity, 739
Sticky, *cohering*, 46
  semiliquid, 352
Stiff, *rigid*, 323
  resolute, 604
  difficult, 704
  restrained, 751
  severe, 739
  dear, 814
  affected, 855
  haughty, 878
  pompous, 882
  ugly, 846
  style, 572, 579
Stiff-necked, *obstinate*, 606
  resolute, 604
Stifle, *silence*, 403
  conceal, 528
  destroy, 162
  kill, 361
  sound, 405
Stigma, *disgrace*, 874
  blame, 932
Stigmatize, *accuse*, 938
Stile, *way*, 627
Stiletto, *piercer*, 262
  dagger, 727
Still, *ever*, 112
  silent, 403
  quiet, 174

INDEX

Temper, *to moderate*, 174
  soften, 324, 826
  prepare, 673
  irascibility, 901
Temperament, *nature*, 5
  tendency, 176
  disposition, 820
  music, 413
Temperance, *moderation*,
      953
Temperate, *moderate*, 174
  mild, 826
Temperature, *heat*, 382
Tempest, *violence*, 173
  wind, 349; *agitation*, 315
  excitement, 825
Tempestivity, *occasion*, 134
Temple, *church*, 1000
  side, 236
* Tempo, *melody*, 413
Temporal, *transient*, 111
  material, 316
  laical, 997
Temporary, *transient*, 111
Temporize, *cunning*, 702
  policy, 698
  diuturnity, 110
  delay, 133
  opportunity, 134
Tempt, *entice*, 615
  desire, 865; *try*, 676
Ten, *number*, 98
Tenable, *probable*, 472
Tenacious, *retentive*, 781
  avaricious, 819
  resolved, 604
  obstinate, 606
  prejudiced, 481
Tenacity, *toughness*, 327
Tenancy, *possession*, 777
Tenant, *occupier*, 188
  possessor, 779
  present, 186
Tenantless, *empty*, 187
  solitary, 893
Tend, *aid*, 107
  train, 370
  contribute, 153
  conduce, 176
  direct to, 278
Tendentious, *misjudgment*,
Tender, *soft*, 324   [481
  susceptible, 822
  loving, 897
  compassionate, 914
  to offer, 763; *ship*, 273
  vehicle, 272
Tenderfoot, *stranger*, 57
  learner, 541
Tendon, *fastening*, 45

Tendril, *infant*, 129
  filament, 205
  fastening, 45
Tenebrific, *darkness*, 421
Tenement, *house*, 189
  property, 780
Tenet, *belief*, 484
  creed, 983
Tenner, *money*, 800
Tennysonian, *poetry*, 597
Tenon, *dovetail*, 300
Tenor, *course*, 7
  degree, 26
  direction, 278
  meaning, 516
  musical, 413
Tense, *hard*, 323
Tensile, *elasticity*, 325
Tension, *strength*, 159
  length, 200
  hardness, 323
  strain, 686
Tent, *receptacle*, 189
  covering, 222
Tentacle, *instrument*, 633
  grip, 781
Tentative, *experimental*,
      463
  essaying, 675
Tenterhooks, *expectation*,
      507
Tenuity, *rarity*, 322
  thinness, 203
  smallness, 32
Tenure, *dueness*, 924
  possession, 777
Tepefaction, *heating*, 384
Tepid, *warm*, 382
  passionless, 823
Terce, *worship*, 990
Tercentenary, *period*, 138
  celebration, 883
Terebration, *opening*, 260
  piercing, 302
Tergiversation, *change*, 140,
      607
  equivocation, 520
Term, *place in series*, 71
  end, 67
  limit, 233
  period of time, 106
  property, 780
  word, 562
  name, 564
Termagant, *irascibility*, 901
  fury, 173
Terminal, *end*, 67
Terminate, *completion*, 729
Terminology, *word*, 562
Terminus, *end*, 67
Termless, *infinity*, 105
Terms, *conditions*, 770

Terms, *circumstances*, 8
  reasoning, 476
Ternary, *number*, 92, 93
Terpsichore, *music*, 415
Terpsichorean, *leap*, 309
Terrace, *plain*, 344
  level, 213
  buildings, 189
Terra firma, *support*, 215
* Terra incognita, *ignorance*, 491
Terraqueous, *land*, 342
  world, 318
Terrene, *land*, 342
  world, 318
Terrestrial, *land*, 342
  world, 318
Terrible, *fearful*, 860
  great, 31
Terrier, *list*, 86
Terrific, *frightful*, 830
  great, 31
Terrify, *affright*, 860
Territory, *region*, 181
  realm, 780
Terror, *fear*, 860
Terrorist, *enemy*, 891
  evildoer, 913
Terse, *concise*, 572
Tertian, *periodicity*, 138
Tertiary, *triality*, 92
* Tertium quid, *difference*,
      15
  mixture, 41
  three, 92
* Terza rima, *poetry*, 597
Tessara, *four*, 95
Tessellated, *variegation*, 440
Test, *experiment*, 463
Test-tube, *receptacle*, 191
Testament, *revelation*, 985
Tester, *support*, 215
Testify, *evidence*, 467, 560
Testimonial, *record*, 551
  gift, 784
Testimony, *evidence*, 467
Testy, *irascible*, 901
  rude, 895
Tetchy, *irascible*, 901
Tête-à-tête, *duality*, 89
  chat, 588
Tether, *fasten*, 43
  moor, 265
  restrain, 751
Tetrad, *number*, 95
Tetragon, *four*, 95
Tetrahedron, *angularity*,
      244
  four, 95
Tetralogy, *four*, 95
Tetrarch, *master*, 745
Text, *meaning*, 516

Trooper, *combatant*, 726
  ship, 273
Trope, *metaphor*, 521
Trophy, *triumph*, 733
  record, 551
Tropical, *heat*, 382
  metaphor, 520
Tropology, *metaphor*, 520
Tropopause, *air*, 338
Troposphere, *air*, 338
Trot, *run*, 266
  velocity, 274
Trot out, *manifestation*, 525
Troth, *truth*, 494
  promise, 768
  belief, 484
Trothless, *faithless*, 940
  false, 544
Troubadour, *musician*, 416
Trouble, *derange*, 61
  evil, 619, 649
  adversity, 735
  pain, 828, 830
  exertion, 686
Troubleshooter, *mediator*, 724
Troublesome, *difficulty*, 704
Troublous, *disorder*, 59
Trough, *conduit*, 250
  trench, 259
  hollow, 252
Trounce, *censure*, 932
  punish, 972
Trousers, *dress*, 225
Trousseau, *dress*, 225
Trow, *think*, 451, 484
  know, 490
Trowel, *instrument*, 191
Truant, *absent*, 187
  fugitive, 623
  idle, 683
Truce, *pacification*, 723
  suspension, 141, 142
Truck, *vehicle*, 272
  barter, 794
  summit, 210
Truckle to, *submission*, 725
Truculent, *malevolence*, 907
Trudge, *slowness*, 275
True, *real*, 1, 3
  veracious, 543
  good, 648
  faithful, 772
  orthodox, 983A
True-love, *love*, 897
Truepenny, *probity*, 939
Truism, *absurdity*, 497
Trull, *impurity*, 962
Truly, *really*, 31
  assent, 488
  verily, 494, 543
Trump, *good man*, 939, 948

Trump card, *device*, 626
  success, 731
Trump up, *falsehood*, 544
Trumpery, *unimportance*, 643
  nonsense, 517
Trumpet, *musical instru-ment*, 417
  to publish, 531
  roar, 412
  war-cry, 722
Trumpet-tongued, *publica-tion*, 531
Trumpeter, *messenger*, 534
Truncate, *shorten*, 201
  incomplete, 53
  subduct, 38
Truncheon, *club*, 727
  staff of office, 747
  mace, 633
Trundle, *roll*, 312
  propel, 284
Trunk, *whole*, 50
  origin, 153
  paternity, 166
  box, 191
Truss, *join*, 43
  support, 215
  packet, 72
Trust, *credit*, 805
  belief, 484
  credulity, 486
  hope, 858
Trustee, *consignee*, 758
  treasurer, 801
Trustless, *improbity*, 940
Trustworthy, *probity*, 939
  certainty, 474
Trusty, *probity*, 939
Truth, *truth*, 494
Truthful, *veracity*, 543
Truthless, *falsehood*, 544
Try, *experiment*, 463
  endeavour, 675
  use, 677
  annoy, 830
  judge, 967
Try-out, *trial*, 463
Trying, *difficult*, 704
Tryst, *party*, 892
Tsar, *see* Czar
* Tu quoque, *retaliation*, 718
Tub, *vessel*, 191
  to bathe, 337
Tub-thumper, *ranter*, 584
Tuba, *wind instrument*, 417
Tubby, *corpulent*, 192
Tube, *opening*, 260
  way, 627
Tubercle, *convexity*, 250
Tuberosity, *convexity*, 250
Tubular, *opening*, 260

Tuck, *fold*, 258
  dagger, 727
Tuck in, *insert*, 300
  eat, 296
  locate, 184
Tuft, *rough*, 256
  collection, 72
Tuft-hunter, *sycophant*, 886
  flatterer, 935
  time-server, 943
Tug, *pull*, 285
  effort, 686
  ship, 273
Tuition, *teaching*, 537
Tulip, *variegation*, 440
Tumble, *fall*, 306
  derange, 61
  spoil, 659
  fail, 732
  agitate, 315
Tumbledown, *deterioration*, 659
Tumbler, *glass*, 191
  buffoon, 844
Tumbrel, *vehicle*, 272
Tumefaction, *expansion*, 194
Tumid, *swollen*, 194
  bombastic, 549, 577
Tumour, *swelling*, 194
  convexity, 250
Tumult, *disorder*, 59
  violence, 173
  agitation, 315, 825
  resistance, 719
  revolt, 742
  emotion, 825
Tumultuous, *disorder*, 59
Tumulus, *interment*, 363
Tun, *large*, 192
  drunkard, 959
Tunable, *harmony*, 413
Tundra, *space*, 180
  plain, 344
Tune, *music*, 415
  melody, 413
  to prepare, 673
Tune, out of, *irrelation*, 10
  disagreement, 24
Tuneful, *harmony*, 413
Tuneless, *discord*, 414
Tunic, *cover*, 222
  dress, 225
Tuning-fork, *musical*, 417
Tunnage, *size*, 192
Tunnel, *opening*, 260
  way, 627
Turban, *dress*, 225
Turbid, *opaque*, 416
  foul, 653
Turbinate, *convolution*, 248
  rotation, 312

Ukase, *order*, 741
  law, 963
Ukelele, *stringed instrument*,
  417
Ulcer, *disease*, 655
  care, 830
Ulema, *judge*, 967
Ullage, *deficiency*, 53
Ulster, *coat*, 225
Ulterior, *in space*, 196
  in time, 121
Ultimate, *end*, 67
Ultimatum, *conditions*, 770
Ultimo, *priority*, 116
Ultimogeniture, *descent*, 167
Ultra, *superiority*, 33
  greatness, 31
  extremist, 604
Ultramarine, *blueness*, 438
Ultramontane, *authority*,
  737
  alien, 57
Ululation, *cry*, 412
Ulysses, *cunning*, 702
Umber, *brown*, 433
Umbilical, *centrality*, 223
Umbra, *darkness*, 421
Umbrage, *shade*, 424
  darkness, 421
  offence, 900
  enmity, 889
  grudge, 898
Umbrella, *shelter*, 666
Umpire, *judge*, 480, 967
Umpteen, *plurality*, 100
Unabashed, *bold*, 861
  haughty, 873, 878
  insolent, 885
  conceited, 880
Unabated, *great*, 31
Unable, *impotence*, 158
Unacceptable, *painfulness*,
  830
Unaccommodating, *dis-
  agreeing*, 24
  uncivil, 895
  disobliging, 907
Unaccompanied, *alone*, 87
Unaccomplished, *incom-
  plete*, 730
Unaccountable, *obscure*, 519
  wonderful, 870
  arbitrary, 964
  irresponsible, 927A
Unaccustomed, *unused*, 614
  unskilled, 699
  unusual, 83
Unachievable, *difficult*, 704
  impossible, 471
Unacknowledged, *ignored*,
  489
  unrequited, 917

Unacquainted, *ignorant*,
  491
Unactuated, *unmoved*, 616
Unadmonished, *unwarned*,
  665
Unadorned, *simple*, 849
  style, 575
Unadulterated, *simple*, 42
  genuine, 494, 648
Unadventurous, *quiet*, 864
Unadvisable, *inexpedient*,
  647
Unadvised, *unwarned*, 665
  foolish, 699
Unaffected, *callous*, 376
  genuine, 494
  sincere, 543
  simple, 576, 849
  elegant, 578
  in good taste, 850
Unafflicted, *serene*, 831
Unaided, *weak*, 160
Unalarmed, *courage*, 861
Unalienable, *dueness*, 924
Unallayed, *strength*, 159
Unallied, *irrelative*, 10
Unallowable, *wrong*, 923
Unalluring, *indifference*, 866
Unalterable, *identical*, 13
  unchanged, 141
  unchangeable, 150
Unamazed, *expectance*, 871
Unambiguous, *intelligi-
  bility*, 518
Unambitious, *indifference*,
  866
Unamiable, *ill-natured*, 907
Unanimity, *accord*, 714
  assent, 488
Unannexed, *disjoined*, 44
Unannounced, *inexpecta-
  tion*, 508
Unanswerable, *demonstra-
  tive*, 478
  certain, 474
  irresponsible, 927A
  arbitrary, 964
Unappalled, *courage*, 861
Unapparent, *invisible*, 447
  latent, 526
Unappeasable, *violence*, 173
Unapplied, *disuse*, 678
Unapprehended, *unknown*,
  491
Unapprehensive, *courage*,
  861
Unapprised, *ignorance*, 491
Unapproachable, *distant*,
  196
  great, 31
Unapproved, *disapproba-
  tion*, 932

Unapt, *incongruous*, 24
  inexpedient, 647
  unskilful, 699
Unarmed, *weak*, 158, 160
Unarranged, *in disorder*, 59
  unprepared, 674
Unarrayed, *simplicity*, 849
Unascertained, *ignorance*,
  491
Unasked, *voluntary*, 602
Unaspiring, *indifferent*, 866
  modest, 881
Unassailable, *safety*, 664
Unassailed, *freedom*, 748
Unassembled, *non-assem-
  blage*, 73
Unassociated, *disjunction*,
  44
Unassuming, *modesty*, 881
Unatoned, *impenitence*, 951
Unattached, *disjunction*, 44
Unattackable, *safety*, 664
Unattainable, *difficult*, 704
  impossible, 471
Unattained, *failure*, 732
Unattempted, *avoidance*,
  623
Unattended, *alone*, 87
Unattended to, *neglect*, 460
Unattested, *counter-evi-
  dence*, 468
  unrecorded, 552
Unattracted, *dissuasion*,
  616
Unattractive, *indifference*,
  866
Unauthentic, *uncertainty*,
  475
Unauthenticated, *counter-
  evidence*, 468
  erroneous, 495
Unauthorized, *undue*, 738,
  925
  wrong, 923
  lawless, 964
  prohibited, 761
Unavailing, *useless*, 645
  failure, 732
Unavoidable, *necessary*, 601
  certain, 474
Unavowed, *dissent*, 489
Unawakened, *inactivity*,
  683
Unaware, *ignorant*, 491
  unexpecting, 508
  impulsive, 601
Unawed, *courage*, 861
Unbalanced, *inequality*, 28
Unballasted, *mutable*, 149
  foolish, 499
Unbar, *liberate*, 750
Unbearable, *pain*, 830

Unbeaten, *success*, 731
Unbecoming, *undue*, 925
　disgraceful, 874, 940
　incongruous, 24
Unbefitting, *undue*, 925
　disgraceful, 940
　incongruous, 24
Unbegotten, *inexistence*, 2
Unbeguile, *disclosure*, 529
Unbegun, *unprepared*, 674
Unbeheld, *invisibility*, 447
Unbelief, *doubt*, 485
　infidelity, 989
　incredulity, 487
Unbelievable, *improbable*,
　　　　　　　　473
Unbeliever, *heathen*, 984
Unbeloved, *hate*, 898
Unbend, *straighten*, 246
　repose, 687
　the mind, 452
Unbending, *hard*, 323
　resolute, 604
Unbeseeming, *base*, 940
Unbesought, *willingness*,
　　　　　　　　602
　deprecation, 766
Unbewailed, *disapproba-
tion*, 932
Unbiased, *wise*, 498
　impartial, 480
　spontaneous, 602
　uninfluenced, 616
　free, 748
Unbidden, *spontaneous*, 600
　disobedient, 742
Unbind, *detach*, 44
　release, 750
Unblameable, *innocence*,
　　　　　　　　946
Unblemished, *innocence*,
　　　　　　　　946
Unblenching, *courage*, 861
Unblended, *unmixed*, 42
Unblest, *unhappy*, 838 ✓
　unapproved, 932
Unblown, *non-preparation*,
　　　　　　　　674
Unblushing, *impudent*, 885
　proud, 878
　vain, 880
Unboastful, *modest*, 881
Unbodied, *immateriality*,
　　　　　　　　317
Unbolt, *liberate*, 750
Unbonnet, *divestment*, 226
Unborn, *future*, 121
　not existing, 2
Unborrowed, *lending*, 787
Unbosom, *disclosure*, 529
Unbound, *free*, 748
　exempt, 927A

Unbounded, *great*, 31
　large, 192
　infinite, 105
　space, 180
Unbrace, *relax*, 655
　weaken, 160
Unbreathed, *latent*, 526
Unbribed, *disinterested*, 942
Unbridled, *lax*, 738
　violent, 173
　free, 748
Unbroken, *entire*, 50
　continuous, 69
　unviolated, 939
Unbruised, *whole*, 50
Unbuckle, *disjunction*, 44
Unbusiness-like, *inactivity*,
　　　　　　　　683
Unbutton, *unfasten*, 44
Unbuttoned, *freedom*, 748
Uncage, *liberation*, 750
Uncalled-for, *useless*, 645
　superfluous, 641
　not used, 678
Uncandid, *morose*, 907
　insincere, 544
Uncanny, *strange*, 83
　wonderful, 870
　supernatural, 980
Uncanonical, *heterodox*,
　　　　　　　　984A
Uncared-for, *indifferent*,
　　　　　　　　866
　hated, 898
Uncase, *divestment*, 226
Uncaught, *freedom*, 748
Uncaused, *chance*, 156
Unceasing, *perpetuity*, 112
Uncensured, *approbation*,
　　　　　　　　931
Unceremonious, *rude*, 895
Uncertain, *uncertainty*, 475
　irresolute, 605
　irregular, 139
Unchain, *unfasten*, 44
　liberate, 750
　free, 748
Unchallenged, *dueness*, 924
　assent, 488
Unchangeable, *immutable*,
　　　　　　　　150
　firm, 604
Unchanged, *permanent*, 141
Uncharitable, *malevolent*,
　　　　　　　　907
Uncharted, *unknown*, 491
Unchartered, *unauthorized*,
　　　　　　　　925
　illegal, 964
Unchaste, *impure*, 961
Unchastized, *acquittal*, 970
Unchecked, *freedom*, 748

Unchristian, *irreligion*, 989
Uncial, *writing*, 590
Uncircumscribed, *spacious*,
　　　　　　　　180
Uncivil, *rude*, 895
　vulgar, 851
Unclad, *naked*, 226
Unclaimed, *freedom*, 748
Unclasp, *loosen*, 44
Unclassed, *disorder*, 59
Unclassical, *vulgarity*, 851
Unclassified, *disorder*, 59
Uncle, *relative*, 11
　pawnbroker, 787
Unclean, *uncleanness*, 653
　impurity, 961
Unclinch, *disjunction*, 44
Unclipped, *whole*, 50
Unclog, *liberate*, 705, 750
Unclose, *opening*, 260
Unclothe, *divestment*, 226
Unclouded, *light*, 420
　joyful, 827
Unclubbable, *unsociable*,
　　　　　　　　893
Uncoif, *divestment*, 226
Uncoil, *straighten*, 246
　evolve, 313
Uncollected,　　*non-assem-
blage*, 73
Uncoloured, *achromatism*,
　　　　　　　　429
Uncombed, *vulgarity*, 851
Uncombined, *single*, 47
Un-come-at-able, *difficult*,
　　　　　　　　704
Uncomely, *ugliness*, 846
Uncomfortable, *annoyed*,
　　　　　　　　828
　annoying, 830
　in pain, 378
Uncommendable, *bad*, 945
　blamable, 932
Uncommon, *unconformity*,
　　　　　　　　83
　greatness, 31
　infrequency, 137
Uncommunicative, *close*,
　　　　　　　　585
　concealing, 528
Uncompact, *rarity*, 322
Uncompelled, *voluntary*,
　　　　　　　　600
　free, 748
Uncomplaisant, *discourtesy*,
　　　　　　　　895
Uncomplying, *refusing*, 764
　disobedient, 742
Uncompounded,　*simple-
ness*, 42
Uncompressed, *light*, 320
　rare, 322

Unguarded, *neglected*, 460
  improvident, 674
  dangerous, 665
  spontaneous, 612
Unguent, *oil*, 356
Unguided, *ignorant*, 491
  unskilful, 699
Unhackneyed, *desuetude*,
  614
Unhallowed, *irreligion*, 989
  profane, 988
Unhand, *liberation*, 750
Unhandsome, *ugly*, 940
Unhandy, *unskilfulness*,
  699
Unhappy, *pain*, 828
Unhardened, *tender*, 914
  penitent, 950
  innocent, 946
Unharmed, *safety*, 664
Unharness, *disjoin*, 44
  liberate, 750
Unhatched, *non-prepara-
  tion*, 674
Unhazarded, *safety*, 664
Unhealthy, *ill*, 655
  unwholesome, 657
Unheard-of, *ignorant*, 491
  exceptional, 83, 137
  impossible, 471
  improbable, 473
  wonderful, 870
Unheeded, *neglected*, 460
Unheralded, *inexpectation*,
  507
Unheroic, *cowardly*, 862
Unhesitating, *resolution*,
  604
Unhewn, *formless*, 241
  unprepared, 674
Unhindered, *free*, 748
Unhinge, *weaken*, 169
  derange, 61
Unhinged, *unsettled*, 605
  insane, 503
Unholy, *evil*, 989
Unhonoured, *disrespect*, 874
Unhook, *disjoin*, 44
Unhoped, *unexpected*, 508
Unhouse, *displace*, 185
Unhurt, *uninjured*, 670
Unicorn, *monster*, 83
  prodigy, 872
Unidea'd, *unthinking*, 452
Unideal, *true*, 494
  existing, 1
Uniform, *homogeneous*, 16
  simple, 42
  orderly, 58
  regular, 82
  symmetrical, 242
  livery, 225

Uniform, *insignia*, 550
  uniformity, 23
Unify, *combine*, 48
  make one, 87
Unilluminated, *dark*, 421
  ignorant, 491
Unimaginable, *inconceiv-
  able*, 519
Unimaginative, *dull*, 843
Unimagined, *truth*, 494
Unimitated, *original*, 20
Unimpaired, *preserved*, 670
  sound, 648
Unimpassioned, *inexcitable*,
  826
Unimpeachable, *innocent*,
  946
  irrefutable, 474, 478
  inalienable, 924
  perfect, 650
Unimpeded, *facility*, 705
Unimpelled, *uninduced*, 616
Unimportant, *insignificant*,
  643
Unimpressionable, *insen-
  sible*, 823
Unimproved, *deterioration*,
  659
Uninfluenced, *unbiased*, 616
  obstinate, 606
Uninfluential, *inert*, 172
Uninformed, *ignorance*, 491
Uninhabited, *empty*, 187
  solitary, 893
Uninitiated, *unschooled*, 699
Uninjured, *good*, 648
  preserved, 670
  healthy, 644
Uninquisitive, *indifferent*,
  456
Uninspired, *unexcited*, 823
  unactuated, 616
Uninstructed, *ignorant*, 491
Unintellectual, *ignorant*,
  452
  imbecile, 499
Unintelligent, *foolish*, 499
Unintelligible, *difficult*, 519
  style, 571
Unintentional, *change*, 621
Uninterested, *incurious*, 456
  inattentive, 458
  indifferent, 823
  weary, 841
Uninteresting, *wearisome*,
  841
  dull, 843
Unintermitting, *unbroken*,
  69
  durable, 110
  continuing, 143
  active, 682

Uninterrupted, *continuous*,
  69
  unremitting, 143
Uninvestigated, *unknown*,
  491
Uninvited, *exclusion*, 893
Uninviting, *unattractive*,
  866
  unpleasant, 830
Union, *junction*, 43
  combination, 48
  concord, 23, 714
  concurrence, 178
  marriage, 903
Union Jack, *flag*, 550
Unique, *special*, 79
  alone, 87
  exceptional, 83
  dissimilarity, 18
  non-imitation, 20
Unison, *agreement*, 23
  concord, 714
  uniformity, 16
  melody, 413
Unisonant, *harmony*, 413
Unit, *number*, 87
  troop, 726
Unitarian, *heterodoxy*, 984A
Unite, *join*, 43
  agree, 23
  concur, 178
  assemble, 72
  converge, 290
  league, 712
Unity, *singleness*, 87
  integrity, 50
  concord, 714
Universal, *general*, 78
Universe, *world*, 318
University, *school*, 542
Unjust, *wrong*, 923
Unjustified, *undue*, 925
Unkempt, *careless*, 653
  slovenly, 851
Unkennel, *turn out*, 185
  disclose, 529
Unkind, *malevolent*, 907
Unknit, *disjoin*, 44
Unknowable, *concealment*,
  528
Unknown, *ignorant*, 491
  latent, 526
  to fame, 874
Unlaboured, *unprepared*,
  674
  style, 578
Unlace, *disjoin*, 44
Unlade, *ejection*, 297
Unladylike, *vulgar*, 851
  rude, 895
Unlamented, *disliked*, 898
  unapproved, 932

Unstirred, *unmoved*, 826
   calm, 265
Unstitch, *disjoin*, 44
Unstopped, *open*, 260
   continuing, 143
Unstored, *unprovided*, 640
Unstrained, *unexerted*, 172
   relaxed, 687
   turbid, 653
Unstrengthened, *weak*, 160
Unstrung, *weak*, 160
Unsubdued, *free*, 748
Unsubjugated, *free*, 748
Unsubmissive, *disobedient*,
   742
Unsubstantial, *unsubstanti-*
   ality, 4
   rare, 322
   texture, 329
   imaginary, 515
   erroneous, 495
Unsubstantiated, *erroneous*,
   495
Unsuccessful, *failure*, 732
Unsuccessive, *discontinu-*
   ous, 70
Unsuitable, *incongruous*, 24
   inexpedient, 647
   time, 135
Unsuited, *see* Unsuitable
Unsullied, *clean*, 652
   honourable, 939
   guiltless, 946
Unsummed, *infinity*, 105
Unsummoned, *voluntary*,
   600
Unsung, *untold*, 526
Unsunned, *dark*, 421
Unsupplied, *insufficiency*,
   640
Unsupported, *weak*, 160
Unsuppressed, *persisting*,
   141
Unsurpassed, *great*, 31
   superior, 33
Unsusceptible, *unfeeling*,
   823
Unsuspected, *latent*, 526
Unsuspicious, *credulous*,
   484, 486
   hopeful, 858
Unsustained, *weak*, 160
Unswayed, *uninfluenced*,
   616
Unsweetened, *unsavoury*,
   395
Unswept, *dirty*, 653
Unswerving, *straight*, 246
   direct, 278
   determined, 604
Unsymmetrical, *disorder*, 59
   distortion, 243

Unsympathetic, *unfriendly*,
   907
Unsystematic, *disorder*, 59
Untack, *disjoin*, 44
Untainted, *healthy*, 654
   pure, 652
   honourable, 939
Untalented, *unskilled*, 699
Untalked-of, *latency*, 526
Untamed, *rude*, 851
   ferocious, 907
Untangled, *order*, 58
Untarnished, *probity*, 939
   innocence, 946
Untasted, *taste*, 391
Untaught, *ignorant*, 491
Untaxed, *cheap*, 815
Unteach, *misteach*, 538
Unteachable, *unskilled*, 699
Untempered, *greatness*, 31
Untempted, *uninfluenced*,
   616
Untenable, *weak*, 160
   undefended, 725
   sophistical, 477
Untenanted, *empty*, 187
Untended, *neglected*, 460
Untested, *neglected*, 460
Unthanked, *ingratitude*, 917
Unthankful, *ungrateful*, 917
Unthawed, *solid*, 321
   cold, 383
Unthinkable, *impossible*,
   471
Unthinking, *thoughtless*, 452
Unthought-of, *neglected*,
   460
   unconsidered, 452
Unthoughtful, *neglectful*,
   460
Unthreatened, *safe*, 664
Unthrifty, *prodigal*, 818
   unprepared, 674
Unthrone, *dismiss*, 756
Unthwarted, *unhindered*,
   748
Untidy, *in disorder*, 59
   slovenly, 653
Untie, *loose*, 44
   liberate, 750
Until, *time*, 106, 108
Untilled, *unprepared*, 674
Untimely, *ill-timed*, 135
Untinged, *simple*, 42
   uncoloured, 429
Untired, *refreshed*, 689
Untiring, *active*, 682
Untitled, *commonalty*, 876
Untold, *secret*, 526, 528
   countless, 105
Untouched, *disused*, 678
   insensible, 376, 823

Untoward, *bad*, 649
   inopportune, 135
   unprosperous, 735
   unpleasant, 830
Untraced, *latency*, 526
Untracked, *latency*, 526
Untrained, *unskilled*, 699
   unprepared, 674
   unaccustomed, 614
Untrammelled, *free*, 705,
   748
Untranslated, *misinterpre-*
   tation, 523
Untravelled, *quiescent*, 265
   unknown, 491
Untreasured, *unstored*, 640
Untried, *undetermined*, 461
Untrimmed, *simple*, 849
   unprepared, 674
Untrodden, *new*, 123
   not used, 678
   impervious, 261
Untroubled, *calm*, 174, 721
Untrue, *false*, 544
Untrustworthy, *dishonest*,
   940
   erroneous, 495
   uncertain, 475
   dangerous, 665
Untruth, *falsehood*, 544,
   546
Untunable, *discord*, 414
Unturned, *straight*, 246
Ununtutored, *ignorant*, 491
Untwine, *unfold*, 313
Untwist, *straighten*, 246
   evolve, 313
   separate, 44, 47
Unurged, *spontaneous*, 600
Unused, *unaccustomed*, 614,
   699
   untouched, 678
Unusual, *unconformity*, 83
   greatness, 31
Unutilized, *disuse*, 678
Unutterable, *wonderful*, 870
   great, 31
Unvalued, *depreciated*, 483
   undesired, 866
   disliked, 898
Unvanquished, *free*, 748
Unvaried, *permanent*, 141
   continued, 143
   monotonous, 576
Unvarnished, *truth*, 494
Unvarying, *uniform*, 16
Unveil, *manifest*, 525
   disclose, 529
Unventilated, *close*, 261
Unveracious, *false*, 544
Unverified, *indiscrimina-*
   tion, 465A

Unversed, *unconversant*, 491
  unskilled, 699
Unvexed, *content*, 831
Unviolated, *probity*, 939
Unvisited, *exclusion*, 893
Unvitiated, *unspoiled*, 648
Unvouched-for, *unattested*, 468
Unwakened, *dormant*, 683
Unwanted, *unnecessary*, 645
Unwarlike, *cowardly*, 862
Unwarmed, *cold*, 383
Unwarned, *danger*, 665
Unwarped, *unprejudiced*, 480
Unwarranted, *unjustifiable*, 923, 925
  inconclusive, 477
Unwary, *heedless*, 460
Unwashed, *unclean*, 653
  vulgar, 851
Unwasted, *unexhausted*, 639
Unwatched, *neglected*, 460
Unwatchful, *inattentive*, 458
Unwatered, *dry*, 340
  undiluted, 159
Unwavering, *resolute*, 604
Unweakened, *strong*, 159
Unwearied, *indefatigable*, 682
  refreshed, 689
Unwedded, *celibacy*, 904
Unweeded, *neglected*, 460
Unweighed, *neglected*, 460
Unwelcome, *disagreeable*, 830
Unwell, *ill*, 655
Unwept, *hate*, 898
Unwholesome, *insalubrious*, 657
Unwieldy, *large*, 192
  heavy, 319
  difficult, 704
  cumbersome, 647
Unwilling, *unwillingness*, 603
  dissent, 489
Unwind, *evolve*, 313
  straighten, 246
Unwinking, *vigilant*, 457
Unwiped, *unclean*, 653
Unwise, *fool*, 499
Unwished, *undesirable*, 866
Unwithered, *strong*, 159
Unwitnessed, *unseen*, 526
Unwitting, *ignorant*, 491
  involuntary, 601
Unwomanly, *unbecoming*, 940

Unwonted, *unaccustomed*, *unusual*, 83 [614
Unworkmanlike, *unskilful*, 699
Unworldly, *disinterested*, *pious*, 987 [943
Unworn, *unused*, 159
Unworthy, *vicious*, 945
  base, 940
  shameful, 874
Unwrap, *straighten*, 246
Unwreathe, *straighten*, 246
Unwrinkled, *smooth*, 255
Unwritten, *untold*, 526
Unwrought, *unprepared*, 674
Unyielding, *tough*, 323
  resolute, 604
  severe, 739
  obstinate, 606
  resisting, 719
Unyoke, *disjoin*, 44
Up, *fizzy*, 353
Up in arms, *resist*, 719
Up-country, *interiority*, 221
Upanishads, *sacred books*, 986
Upbear, *support*, 215
Upbraid, *disapprove*, 932
Upbringing, *teaching*, 537
Upcast, *elevation*, 307
Upgrow, *height*, 206
Upgrowth, *ascent*, 305
Upheave, *elevation*, 307
Uphill, *activity*, 217
  ascent, 305
  difficult, 704
Uphold, *support*, 215
  evidence, 467
  aid, 707
  continue, 143
Upholster, *cover*, 222
  furnish, 637
Upkeep, *preservation*, 670
Uplands, *height*, 206
Uplift, *elevation*, 307
Upper, *height*, 206
Upper hand, *authority*, 737
  success, 731
Upper storey, *brain*, 450
Uppermost, *height*, 206, 210
Uppish, *self-assertive*, 885
Upraise, *elevation*, 307
Uprear, *elevation*, 307
Upright, *vertical*, 212
  honest, 939
  virtuous, 944
Uprise, *ascent*, 305
Uproar, *noise*, 404
  turmoil, 173

Uproar, *disorder*, 59
Uproot, *destruction*, 162
  extraction, 301
Upset, *throw down*, 308
  disorder, 59
  derange, 61
  change, 140
  invert, 218
  destroy, 162
Upshot, *end*, 66
  total, 50
Upside-down, *inversion*, 218
Upstage, *affected*, 855
  supercilious, 930
  proud, 878
Upstairs, *height*, 207
Upstart, *plebeian*, 876
  prosperous, 734
Upturn, *inversion*, 218
Upwards, *height*, 206
Uranology, *world*, 318
Urban, *abode*, 189
Urbane, *courtesy*, 894
Urchin, *small*, 193
  child, 129
  wretch, 949
Urge, *impel*, 276
  incite, 615
  solicit, 765
  hasten, 684
  accelerate, 274
  violence, 173
Urgent, *important*, 642
  required, 630
Uriah Heep, *servility*, 886
Urinal, *room*, 191
  privy, 653
Urinate, *excrete*, 299
Urn, *vase*, 191
  funereal, 363
  kettle, 386
Usage, *custom*, 613
  rule, 80
  use, 677
Usance, *debt*, 806
Use, *employment*, 677
  waste, 638
  utility, 644
  habit, 613
  rule, 80
Used up, *worn*, 651
  surfeited, 869
Useful, *use*, 644
Useless, *misuse*, 645
Usher, *teacher*, 540
  servant, 746
  announce, 511
  receive, 296, 894
  begin, 66
  precede, 62, 280
  prior, 116
Ustulation, *heating*, 384

ORIGINAL INTRODUCTION

By Peter Roget

THE present work is intended to supply, with respect to the English language, a desideratum hitherto unsupplied in any language; namely, a collection of the words it contains and of the idiomatic combinations peculiar to it, arranged, not in alphabetical order, as they are in a dictionary, but according to the *ideas* which they express.[1] The purpose of an ordinary dictionary is simply to explain the meaning of words; and the problem of which it professes to furnish the solution may be stated thus: The word being given, to find its signification, or the idea it is intended to convey. The object aimed at in the present undertaking is exactly the converse of this; namely, the idea being given, to find the word, or words, by which that idea may be most fitly and aptly expressed. For this purpose, the words and phrases of the language are here classed, not according to their sound or their orthography, but strictly according to their *signification*.

The communication of our thoughts by means of language, whether spoken or written, like every other object of mental exertion, constitutes a peculiar art, which, like other parts, cannot be acquired in any perfection but by long and continued practice. Some, indeed, there are, more highly gifted than others with a facility of expression, and naturally endowed with the power of eloquence; but to none is it at all times an easy process to embody in exact and appropriate language the various trains of ideas that are passing through the mind, or to depict in their true colours and proportions the diversified and nicer shades of feeling which accompany them. To those who are unpractised in the art of composition, or unused to extempore speaking, these difficulties present themselves in their most formidable aspect. However distinct may be our views, however vivid our conceptions, or however fervent our emotions, we cannot but be often conscious that the phraseology we have at our command is inadequate to do them justice. We seek in vain the words we need, and strive ineffectually to devise forms of expression which shall faithfully portray our thoughts and sentiments. The appropriate terms, notwithstanding our utmost efforts, cannot be conjured up at will. Like 'spirits from the vasty deep,' they come not when we call; and we are driven to the employment of a set of words and phrases either too general or too limited, too strong or too feeble, which suit not the occasion, which hit not the mark we aim at; and the result of our prolonged exertion is a style at once laboured and obscure, vapid and redundant, or vitiated by the still graver faults of affectation or ambiguity.

[1] See note on p. 571.

It is to those who are thus painfully groping their way and struggling with the difficulties of composition, that this work professes to hold out a helping hand. The assistance it gives is that of furnishing on every topic a copious store of words and phrases, adapted to express all the recognizable shades and modifications of the general idea under which those words and phrases are arranged. The inquirer can readily select, out of the ample collection spread out before his eyes in the following pages, those expressions which are best suited to his purpose, and which might not have occurred to him without such assistance. In order to make this selection, he scarcely ever need engage in any elaborate or critical study of the subtle distinctions existing between synonymous terms; for if the materials set before him be sufficiently abundant, an instinctive tact will rarely fail to lead him to the proper choice. Even while glancing over the columns of this work, his eye may chance to light upon a particular term, which may save the cost of a clumsy paraphrase, or spare the labour of a tortuous circumlocution. Some felicitous turn of expression thus introduced will frequently open to the mind of the reader a whole vista of collateral ideas, which could not, without an extended and obtrusive episode, have been unfolded to his view; and often will the judicious insertion of a happy epithet, like a beam of sunshine in a landscape, illumine and adorn the subject which touches it, imparting new grace, and giving life and spirit to the picture.

Every workman in the exercise of his art should be provided with proper implements. For the fabrication of complicated and curious pieces of mechanism the artisan requires a corresponding assortment of various tools and instruments. For giving proper effect to the fictions of the drama, the actor should have at his disposal a well-furnished wardrobe, supplying the costumes best suited to the personage he is to represent. For the perfect delineation of the beauties of nature, the painter should have within reach of his pencil every variety and combination of hues and tints. Now the writer, as well as the orator, employs for the accomplishment of his purposes the instrumentality of words; it is in words that he clothes his thoughts; it is by means of words that he depicts his feelings. It is therefore essential to his success that he be provided with a copious vocabulary, and that he possess an entire command of all the resources and appliances of his language. To the acquisition of this power no procedure appears more directly conducive than the study of a methodized system such as that now offered to his use.

The utility of the present work will be appreciated more especially by those who are engaged in the arduous process of translating into English a work written in another language. Simple as the operation may appear, on a superficial view, of rendering into English each of its sentences, the task of transfusing, with perfect exactness, the sense of the original, preserving at the same time the style and character of its composition, and reflecting with fidelity the mind and the spirit of the author, is a task of extreme difficulty. The cultivation of this useful department of literature was in ancient times strongly recommended both by Cicero and by Quintilian as essential to the formation of a good writer and accomplished orator. Regarded simply as a mental exercise, the practice of translation is the best training for the attainment of that mastery of language and felicity of diction which are the sources of the highest oratory and are requisite for the possession of a graceful and persuasive eloquence. By rendering ourselves the faithful interpreters of the thoughts and feelings of others, we are rewarded with the acquisition of greater readiness and facility in correctly expressing our own; as he who has best learned to execute the orders of a commander becomes himself best qualified to command.

In the earliest periods of civilization, translations have been the agents for propagating knowledge from nation to nation, and the value of their labours has been inestimable; but, in the present age, when so many different languages have become the depositories of the vast treasures of literature and of science which have been accumulating for centuries, the utility of accurate translations has greatly increased, and it has become a more important object to attain perfection in the art.

The use of language is not confined to its being the medium through which we communicate our ideas to one another; it fulfils a no less important function as an *instrument of thought*, not being merely its vehicle, but giving it wings for flight. Metaphysicians are agreed that scarcely any of our intellectual operations could be carried on to any considerable extent without the agency of words. None but those who are conversant with the philosophy of mental phenomena can be aware of the immense influence that is exercised by language in promoting the development of our ideas, in fixing them in the mind, and detaining them for steady contemplation. In every process of reasoning, language enters as an essential element. Words are the instruments by which we form all our abstractions, by which we fashion and embody our ideas, and by which we are enabled to glide along a series of premises and conclusions with a rapidity so great as to leave in the memory no trace of the successive steps of the process; and we remain unconscious how much we owe to this potent auxiliary of the reasoning faculty. It is on this ground, also, that the present work founds a claim to utility. The review of a catalogue of words of analogous signification will often suggest by association other trains of thought, which, presenting the subject under new and varied aspects, will vastly expand the sphere of our mental vision. Amidst the many objects thus brought within the range of our contemplation, some striking similitude or appropriate image, some excursive flight or brilliant conception, may flash on the mind, giving point and force to our arguments, awakening a responsive chord in the imagination or sensibility of the reader, and procuring for our reasonings a more ready access both to his understanding and to his heart.

It is of the utmost consequence that strict accuracy should regulate our use of language, and that every one should acquire the power and the habit of expressing his thoughts with perspicuity and correctness. Few, indeed, can appreciate the real extent and importance of that influence which language has always exercised on human affairs, or can be aware how often these are determined by causes much slighter than are apparent to a superficial observer. False logic, disguised under specious phraseology, too often gains the assent of the unthinking multitude, disseminating far and wide the seeds of prejudice and error. Truisms pass current, and wear the semblance of profound wisdom, when dressed up in the tinsel garb of antithetical phrases, or set off by an imposing pomp of paradox. By a confused jargon of involved and mystical sentences, the imagination is easily inveigled into a transcendental region of clouds, and the understanding beguiled into the belief that it is acquiring knowledge and approaching truth. A misapplied or misapprehended term is sufficient to give rise to fierce and interminable disputes: a misnomer has turned the tide of popular opinion; a verbal sophism has decided a party question; an artful watchword, thrown among combustible materials, has kindled the flames of deadly warfare, and changed the destiny of an empire.

In constructing the following system of classification of the ideas which are expressible by language, my chief aim has been to obtain the greatest amount of practical utility. I have accordingly adopted such principles of arrangement as appeared to me to be the simplest and most natural, and which would not require, either for their comprehension or application, any disciplined acumen, or depth of metaphysical or antiquarian lore. Eschewing all needless refinements and subtleties, I have taken as my guide the more obvious characters of the ideas for which expressions were to be tabulated, arranging them under such classes and categories as reflection and experience had taught me would conduct the inquirer most readily and quickly to the object of his search. Commencing with the ideas expressing mere abstract relations, I proceed to those which relate to the phenomena of the material world, and lastly to those in which the mind is concerned, and which comprehend intellect, volition, and feeling; thus establishing six primary Classes of Categories.

1. The first of these classes comprehends ideas derived from the more general and ABSTRACT RELATIONS among things, such as *Existence, Resemblance, Quantity, Order, Number, Time, Power*.

2. The second class refers to SPACE and its various relations, including *Motion*, or change of place.

3. The third class includes all ideas that relate to the MATERIAL WORLD; namely, the *Properties of Matter*, such as *Solidity, Fluidity, Heat, Sound, Light*, and the *Phenomena* they present, as well as the simple *Perceptions* to which they give rise.

4. The fourth class embraces all ideas of phenomena relating to the INTELLECT and its operations, comprising the *Acquisition*, the *Retention*, and the *Communication of Ideas*.

5. The fifth class includes the ideas derived from the exercise of VOLITION, embracing the phenomena and results of our *Voluntary and Active Powers*, such as *Choice, Intention, Utility, Action, Antagonism, Authority, Compact, Property*, etc.

6. The sixth and last class comprehends all ideas derived from the operation of our SENTIENT AND MORAL POWERS, including our *Feelings, Emotions, Passions*, and *Moral and Religious Sentiments*.[1]

The object I have proposed to myself in this work would have been but imperfectly attained if I had confined myself to a mere catalogue of words, and had omitted the numerous phrases and forms of expression, composed of several words, which are of such frequent use as to entitle them to rank among the constituent parts of the language.[2] Very few of these verbal combinations, so essential to the knowledge of our native tongue, and so profusely abounding in its daily use, are to be met with in ordinary dictionaries. These phrases and forms of expression I have endeavoured diligently to collect and to insert in their proper places, under the general ideas they are designed to convey. Some of these conventional forms, indeed, partake of the nature of proverbial expressions; but actual proverbs, as such, being wholly of a didactic character, do not come within the scope of the present work, and the reader must therefore not expect to find them here inserted.

For the purpose of exhibiting with greater distinctness the relations

[1] It must necessarily happen in every system of classification framed with this view, that ideas and expressions arranged under one class must include also ideas relating to another class; for the operations of the *Intellect* generally involve also those of the *Will*, and vice versa; and our *Affections* and *Emotions*, in like manner, generally imply the agency both of the *Intellect* and the *Will*. All that can be effected, therefore, is to arrange the words according to the principal or dominant idea they convey. *Teaching*, for example, although a Voluntary act, relates primarily to the Communication of Ideas, and is accordingly placed at No. 537, under Class IV, Division II. On the other hand, *Choice, Conduct, Skill*, etc., although implying the co-operation of Voluntary with Intellectual acts, relate principally to the former, and are therefore arranged under Class V.

It often happens that the same word admits of various applications, or may be used in different senses. In consulting the Index the reader will be guided to the number of the heading under which that word, in each particular acceptation, will be found, by means of *supplementary words*, printed in italics; which words, however, are not to be understood as explaining the meaning of the word to which they are annexed, but only assisting in the required reference. I have also, for shortness' sake, generally omitted words immediately derived from the primary one inserted, which sufficiently represents the whole group of correlative words referable to the same heading. Thus the number affixed to *Beauty* applies to all its derivatives, such as *Beautiful, Beauteous, Beautify, Beautifulness, Beautifully*, etc., the insertion of which was therefore needless.

[2] For example: To take time by the forelock; to turn over a new leaf; to show the white feather; to have a finger in the pie; to let the cat out of the bag; to take care of number one; to kill two birds with one stone, etc.

between words expressing opposite and correlative ideas, I have, whenever the subject admitted of such an arrangement, placed them in two parallel columns in the same page, so that each group of expressions may be readily contrasted with those which occupy the adjacent column, and constitute their antitheses. By carrying the eye from the one to the other, the inquirer may often discover forms of expression of which he may avail himself advantageously to diversify and infuse vigour into his phraseology. Rhetoricians, indeed, are well aware of the power derived from the skilful introduction of antitheses in giving point to an argument, and imparting force and brilliancy to the diction. A too frequent and indiscreet employment of this figure of rhetoric may, it is true, give rise to a vicious and affected style; but it is unreasonable to condemn indiscriminately the occasional and moderate use of a practice on account of its possible abuse.

The study of correlative terms existing in a particular language may often throw valuable light on the manners and customs of the nations using it. Thus Hume has drawn important inferences with regard to the state of society among the ancient Romans, from certain deficiencies which he remarked in the Latin language.[1]

In many cases, two ideas, which are completely opposed to each other, admit of an intermediate or neutral idea, equidistant from both: all these being expressible by corresponding definite terms. Thus, in the following examples, the words in the first and third columns,

[1] 'It is an universal observation,' he remarks, 'which we may form upon language, that where two related parts of a whole bear any proportion to each other, in numbers, rank, or consideration, there are always correlative terms invented which answer to both the parts and express their mutual relation. If they bear no proportion to each other, the term is only invented for the less, and marks its distinction from the whole. Thus *man* and *woman*, *master* and *servant*, *father* and *son*, *prince* and *subject*, *stranger* and *citizen*, are correlative terms. But the words *seaman*, *carpenter*, *smith*, *tailor*, etc., have no correspondent terms which express those who are no seamen, no carpenters, etc. Languages differ very much with regard to the particular words where this distinction obtains; and may thence afford very strong inferences concerning the manners and customs of different nations. The military government of the Roman emperors had exalted the soldiery so high, that they balanced all the other orders of the state: hence *miles* and *paganus* became relative terms; a thing, till then, unknown to ancient, and still so to modern, languages.' 'The term for a slave, born and bred in the family, was *verna*. As *servus* was the name of the genus, and *verna* of the species without any correlative, this forms a strong presumption that the latter were by far the least numerous: and from the same principles I infer that if the number of slaves brought by the Romans from foreign countries had not extremely exceeded those which were bred at home, *verna* would have had a correlative, which would have expressed the former species of slaves. But these, it would seem, composed the main body of the ancient slaves, and the latter were but a few exceptions.'—Hume, *Essay on the Populousness of Ancient Nations.*

The warlike propensity of the same nation may in a like manner be inferred from the use of the word *hostis* to denote both a *foreigner* and an *enemy*.

which express opposite ideas, admit of the intermediate terms contained in the middle column having a neutral sense with reference to the former:

Identity	Difference	Contrariety
Beginning	Middle	End
Past	Present	Future

In other cases, the intermediate word is simply the negative to each of two opposite positions; as, for example:

Convexity	Flatness	Concavity
Desire	Indifference	Aversion

Sometimes the intermediate word is properly the standard with which each of the extremes is compared; as in the case of

Insufficiency	Sufficiency	Redundance

For here the middle term, *Sufficiency*, is equally opposed on the one hand to *Insufficiency* and on the other to *Redundance*.

These forms of correlative expressions would suggest the use of triple, instead of double, columns for tabulating this threefold order of words; but the practical inconvenience attending such an arrangement would probably overbalance its advantages.

It often happens that the same word has several correlative terms, according to the different relations in which it is considered. Thus to the word *Giving* are opposed both *Receiving* and *Taking*; the former correlation having reference to the *persons* concerned in the transfer, while the latter relates to the *mode* of transfer. *Old* has for opposite both *New* and *Young*, according as it is applied to *things* or to *living beings*. *Attack* and *Defence* are correlative terms, as are also *Attack* and *Resistance*. *Resistance*, again, has for its other correlative *Submission*. *Truth in the abstract* is opposed to *Error*, but the opposite of *Truth communicated* is *Falsehood*. *Acquisition* is contrasted both with *Deprivation* and with *Loss*. *Refusal* is the counterpart both of *Offer* and of *Consent*. *Disuse* and *Misuse* may either of them be considered as the correlative of *Use*. *Teaching*, with reference to what is taught, is opposed to *Misteaching*, but with reference to the act itself, its proper reciprocal is *Learning*.

Words contrasted in form do not always bear the same contrast in their meaning. The word *Malefactor*, for example, would, from its derivation, appear to be exactly the opposite of *Benefactor*, but the ideas attached to these two words are far from being directly opposed; for while the latter expresses one who confers a benefit, the former denotes one who has violated the laws.

Independently of the immediate practical uses derivable from the arrangement of words in double columns, many considerations, interesting in a philosophical point of view, are presented by the study of correlative expressions. It will be found, on strict examination, that there seldom exists an exact opposition between two words which may at first sight appear to be the counterparts of one another; for, in general, the one will be found to possess in reality more force or extent of meaning than the other with which it is contrasted. The correlative term sometimes assumes the form of a mere negative, although it is really endowed with a considerable positive force. Thus *Disrespect* is not merely the absence of *Respect*; its signification trenches on the opposite idea, namely, *Contempt*. In like manner, *Untruth* is not merely the negative of *Truth*; it involves a degree of *Falsehood*. *Irreligion*, which is properly *the want of Religion*, is understood as being nearly synonymous with *Impiety*. For these reasons, the reader must not expect that all the words which stand side by side in the two columns shall be the precise correlatives of each other; for the nature of the subject, as well as the imperfections of language, renders it impossible always to preserve such an exactness of correlation.

There exist comparatively few words of a general character to which no correlative term, either of negation or of opposition, can be assigned, and which therefore require no corresponding second column. The correlative idea, especially that which constitutes a sense negative to the primary one, may, indeed, be formed or conceived; but, from its occurring rarely, no word has been framed to represent it; for in language, as in other matters, the supply fails when there is no probability of a demand. Occasionally we find this deficiency provided for by the contrivance of prefixing the syllable *non*; as, for instance, the negatives of *existence*, *performance*, *payment*, etc., are expressed by the compound words, *non-existence*, *non-performance*, *non-payment*, etc. Functions of a similar kind are performed by the prefixes *dis-*,[1] *anti-*, *contra-*, *mis-*, *in-*, and *un*.[2] With respect to all these, and especially the last, great latitude is allowed according to the necessities of the case, a latitude which is limited only by the taste and discretion of the author.

On the other hand, it is hardly possible to find two words having in all respects the same meaning, and being therefore interchangeable; that is, admitted of being employed indiscriminately, the one or the other, in all their applications. The investigation of the distinctions to be drawn between words apparently synonymous forms a separate branch of inquiry which I have not presumed here to enter upon; for the subject has already occupied the attention of much abler critics than myself, and its complete exhaustion would require the devotion of a whole life. The purpose of this work, it must be borne in mind, is not to explain the signification of words, but simply to classify and arrange them according to the sense in which they are now used, and which I presume to be already known to the reader. I enter into no inquiry into the changes of meaning they may have undergone in the

---

[1] The word *disannul*, however, had the same meaning as *annul*.

[2] In the case of adjectives, the addition to a substantive of the terminal syllable *less*, gives it a negative meaning: as *taste, tasteless*; *care, careless*; *hope, hopeless*; *friend, friendless*; *fault, faultless*, etc.

course of time.[1] I am content to accept them at the value of their present currency, and have no concern with their etymologies, or with the history of their transformations; far less do I venture to thrid the mazes of the vast labyrinth into which I should be led by any attempt at a general discrimination of synonyms. The difficulties I have had to contend with have already been sufficiently great without this addition to my labours.

The most cursory glance over the pages of a dictionary will show that a great number of words are used in various senses, sometimes distinguished by slight shades of difference, but often diverging widely from their primary signification, and even, in some cases, bearing to it no perceptible relation. It may even happen that the very same word has two significations quite opposite to one another. This is the case with the verb *to cleave*, which means *to adhere tenaciously*, and also *to separate by a blow*. *To propugn* sometimes expresses *to attack*; at other times, *to defend*. *To ravel* means both *to entangle* and *to disentangle*. The alphabetical index at the end of this work sufficiently shows the multiplicity of uses to which, by the elasticity of language, the meaning of words has been stretched so as to adapt them to a great variety of modified significations in subservience to the nicer shades of thought which, under peculiarity of circumstances, require corresponding expression. Words thus admitting of different meanings have therefore to be arranged under each of the respective heads corresponding to these various acceptations. There are many words, again, which express ideas compounded of two elementary ideas belonging to different classes. It is therefore necessary to place these words respectively under each of the generic heads to which they relate. The necessity of these repetitions is increased by the circumstance that ideas included under one class are often connected by relations of the same kind as the ideas which belong to another class. Thus we find the same relations of *order* and of *quantity* existing among the ideas of *Time* as well as those of *Space*. Sequence in the one is denoted by the same terms as sequence in the other, and the measures of time also express the measures of space. The cause and the effect are often designated by the same word. The word *Sound*, for instance, denotes both the impression made upon the ear by sonorous vibrations, and also the vibrations themselves, which are the cause or source of that impression. *Mixture* is used for the act of mixing, as well as for the product of that operation. *Taste* and *Smell* express both the sensations and the

---

[1] Such changes are innumerable; for instance, the words *tyrant, parasite, sophist, churl, knave, villain,* anciently conveyed no 'opprobrious meaning. *Impertinent* merely expressed *irrelative,* and implied neither *rudeness* nor *intrusion,* as it does at present. *Indifferent* originally meant *impartial; extravagant* was simply *digressive;* and *to prevent* was properly to *precede* and *assist.* The old translations of the Scriptures furnish many striking examples of the alterations which time has brought in the signification of words. Much curious information on this subject is contained in Trench's *Lectures on the Study of Words.*

qualities of material bodies giving rise to them. *Thought* is the act of thinking, but the same word denotes also the idea resulting from that act. *Judgment* is the act of deciding, and also the decision come to. *Purchase* is the acquisition of a thing by payment, as well as the thing itself so acquired. *Speech* is both the act of speaking and the words spoken; and so on with regard to an endless multiplicity of words. Mind is essentially distinct from Matter, and yet, in all languages, the attributes of the one are metaphorically transferred to those of the other. Matter, in all its forms, is endowed by the figurative genius of every language with the functions which pertain to intellect; and we perpetually talk of its phenomena and of its powers as if they resulted from the voluntary influence of one body on another, acting and reacting, impelling and being impelled, controlling and being controlled, as if animated by spontaneous energies and guided by specific intentions. On the other hand, expressions of which the primary signification refers exclusively to the properties and actions of matter are metaphorically applied to the phenomena of thought and volition, and even to the feelings and passions of the soul; and in speaking of a *ray of hope*, a *shade of doubt*, a *flight of fancy*, a *flash of wit*, the *warmth of emotion*, or the *ebullitions of anger*, we are scarcely conscious that we are employing metaphors which have this material origin.

As a general rule, I have deemed it incumbent on me to place words and phrases which appertain more especially to one head also under the other heads to which they have a relation, whenever it appeared to me that this repetition would suit the convenience of the inquirer, and spare him the trouble of turning to other parts of the work; for I have always preferred to subject myself to the imputation of redundance, rather than incur the reproach of insufficiency.[1] When, however, the divergence of the associated from the primary idea is sufficiently marked, I have contented myself with making a reference to the place where the modified signification will be found. But in order to prevent needless extension, I have, in general, omitted *conjugate words* [2] which are so obviously derivable from those that are given in the same place, that the reader may safely be left to form them for himself. This is the

---

[1] Frequent repetitions of the same series of expressions, accordingly, will be met with under various headings. For example, the word *Relinquishment*, with its synonyms, occurs as a heading at No. 624, where it applies to *intention*, and also at No. 782, where it refers to *property*. The word *Chance* has two significations, distinct from one another: the one implying the *absence of an assignable* cause, in which case it comes under the category of the relation of Causation, and occupies the No. 156; the other, the *absence of design*, in which latter sense it ranks under the operations of the Will, and has assigned to it the place No. 621. I have, in like manner, distinguished *Sensibility, Pleasure, Pain, Taste*, etc., according as they relate to *Physical* or to *Moral Affections*; the former being found at Nos. 375, 377, 378, 390, etc., and the latter at Nos. 822, 827, 828, 850, etc.

[2] By '*conjugate* or *paronymous* words is meant, correctly speaking, different parts of speech from the same root, which exactly correspond in point of meaning.'—*A Selection of English Synonyms*, edited by Archbishop Whately.

case with adverbs derived from adjectives by the simple addition of the terminal syllable -*ly*, such as *closely, carefully, safely,* etc., from *close, careful, safe,* etc., and also with adjectives or participles immediately derived from the verbs which are already given. In all such cases, an 'etc.' indicates that reference is understood to be made to these roots. I have observed the same rule in compiling the index, retaining only the primary or more simple word, and omitting the conjugate words obviously derived from them. Thus I assume the word *short* as the representative of its immediate derivatives *shortness, shorten, shortening, shortened, shorter, shortly,* which would have had the same references, and which the reader can readily supply.

The same verb is frequently used indiscriminately either in the active or transitive, or in the neuter or intransitive sense. In these cases I have generally not thought it worth while to increase the bulk of the work by the needless repetition of that word, for the reader, whom I suppose to understand the use of the words, must also be presumed to be competent to apply them correctly.

There are a multitude of words of a specific character, which although they properly occupy places in the columns of a dictionary, yet, having no relation to general ideas, do not come within the scope of this compilation, and are consequently omitted. The names of objects in Natural History, and technical terms belonging exclusively to Science or to Art, or relating to particular operations, and of which the signification is restricted to those specific objects, come under this category. Exceptions must, however, be made in favour of such words as admit of metaphorical application to general subjects with which custom has associated them, and of which they may be cited as being typical or illustrative. Thus the word *Lion* will find a place under the head of *Courage,* of which it is regarded as the type. *Anchor,* being emblematic of *Hope,* is introduced among the words expressing that emotion; and, in like manner, *butterfly* and *weathercock,* which are suggestive of fickleness, are included in the category of *Irresolution.*

With regard to the admission of many words and expressions which the classical reader might be disposed to condemn as vulgarisms, or which he, perhaps, might stigmatize as pertaining rather to the slang than to the legitimate language of the day, I would beg to observe that, having due regard to the uses to which this work was to be adapted, I did not feel myself justified in excluding them solely on that ground, if they possessed an acknowledged currency in general intercourse. It is obvious that, with respect to degrees of conventionality, I could not have attempted to draw any strict lines of demarcation, and far less could I have presumed to erect any absolute standard of purity. My object, be it remembered, is not to regulate the use of words, but simply to supply and to suggest such as may be wanted on occasion, leaving the proper selection entirely to the discretion and taste of the employer. If a novelist or a dramatist, for example, proposed to delineate some vulgar personage, he would wish to have the power of putting into the mouth of the speaker expressions that would

accord with his character, just as the actor, to revert to a former comparison, who had to personate a peasant, would choose for his attire
the most homely garb, and would have just reason to complain if the
theatrical wardrobe furnished him with no suitable costume.

Words which have, in process of time, become obsolete, are, of course,
rejected from this collection. On the other hand, I have admitted a
considerable number of words and phrases borrowed from other languages, chiefly the French and Latin, some of which may be considered
as already naturalized; while others, though avowedly foreign, are
frequently introduced in English composition, particularly in familiar
style, on account of their being peculiarly expressive, and because we
have no corresponding words of equal force in our own language.[1]
The rapid advances which are being made in scientific knowledge, and
consequent improvement in all the arts of life, and the extension of
those arts and sciences to so many new purposes and objects, create a
continual demand for the formation of new terms to express new
agencies, new wants, and new combinations. Such terms, from being
at first merely technical, are rendered, by more general use, familiar
to the multitude, and having a well-defined acceptation, are eventually
incorporated into the language, which they contribute to enlarge and
to enrich. *Neologies* of this kind are perfectly legitimate, and highly
advantageous; and they necessarily introduce those gradual and progressive changes which every language is destined to undergo.[2] Some
modern writers, however, have indulged in a habit of arbitrarily
fabricating new words and a new-fangled phraseology without any
necessity, and with manifest injury to the purity of the language.
This vicious practice, the offspring of indolence or conceit, implies an
ignorance or neglect of the riches in which the English language already
abounds, and which would have supplied them with words of recognized
legitimacy, conveying precisely the same meaning as those they so
recklessly coin in the illegal mint of their own fancy.

A work constructed on the plan of classification I have proposed
might, if ably executed, be of great value in tending to limit the
fluctuations to which language has always been subject, by establishing
an authoritative standard for its regulation. Future historians, philo-
logists, and lexicographers, when investigating the period when new
words were introduced, or discussing the import given at the present
time to the old, might find their labours lightened by being enabled to
appeal to such a standard, instead of having to search for data among

---

[1] All these words and phrases are printed in italics.

[2] Thus in framing the present classification I have frequently felt the want
of substantive terms corresponding to abstract qualities or ideas denoted
by certain adjectives, and have been tempted to invent words that might
express these abstractions; but I have yielded to this temptation only in
the four following instances: having framed from the adjectives *irrelative*,
amorphous, *sinistral*, and *gaseous* the abstract nouns *irrelation*, *amorphism*,
sinistrality, and *gaseity*. I have ventured also to introduce the adjective
intersocial to express the active voluntary relations between man and man.

the scattered writings of the age. Nor would its utility be confined to a single language, for the principles of its construction are universally applicable to all languages, whether living or dead. On the same plan of classification there might be formed a French, a German, a Latin, or a Greek Thesaurus, possessing, in their respective spheres, the same advantages as those of the English model. Still more useful would be a conjunction of these methodized compilations in two languages, the French and the English, for instance; the columns of each being placed in parallel juxtaposition. No means yet devised would so greatly facilitate the acquisition of the one language by those who are acquainted with the other: none would afford such ample assistance to the translator in either language; and none would supply such ready and effectual means of instituting an accurate comparison between them, and of fairly appreciating their respective merits and defects. In a still higher degree would all those advantages be combined and multiplied in a *Polyglot Lexicon* constructed on this system.

Metaphysicians engaged in the more profound investigation of the Philosophy of Language will be materially assisted by having the ground thus prepared for them in a previous analysis and classification of our ideas, for such classification of ideas is the true basis on which words, which are their symbols, should be classified.[1] It is by such

[1] The principle by which I have been guided in framing my verbal classification is the same as that which is employed in the various departments of natural history. Thus the sectional divisions I have formed correspond to natural families in botany and zoology, and the filiation of words presents a network analogous to the natural filiation of plants or animals.

The following are the only publications that have come to my knowledge in which any attempt has been made to construct a systematic arrangement of Ideas with a view to their expression. The earliest of these, supposed to be at least nine hundred years old, is the AMERA CÓSHA, or *Vocabulary of the Sanscrit Language*, by Amera Sinha, of which an English translation, by the late Henry T. Colebrooke, was printed at Serampoor in the year 1808. The classification of words is there, as might be expected, exceedingly imperfect and confused, especially in all that relates to abstract Ideas or mental operations. This will be apparent from the very title of the first section, which comprehends '*Heaven, Gods, Demons, Fire, Air, Velocity, Eternity, Much*'; while *Sin, Virtue, Happiness, Destiny, Cause, Nature, Intellect, Reasoning, Knowledge, Senses, Tastes, Odours, Colours*, are all included and jumbled together in the fourth section. A more logical order, however, pervades the sections relating to natural objects, such as *Seas, Earth, Towns, Plants*, and *Animals*, which form separate classes, exhibiting a remarkable effort at analysis at so remote a period of Indian literature.

The well-known work of Bishop Wilkins, entitled *An Essay towards a Real Character and a Philosophical Language*, published in 1668, had for its object the formation of a system of symbols which might serve as a universal language. It professed to be founded on a 'scheme of analysis of the things or notions to which names were to be assigned'; but notwithstanding the immense labour and ingenuity expended in the construction of this system, it was soon found to be far too abstruse and recondite for practical application.

In the year 1797 there appeared in Paris an anonymous work, entitled *Pasigraphie, ou Premiers Éléments du nouvel Art-Science d'écrire et d'imprimer*

analysis alone that we can arrive at a clear perception of the relation which these symbols bear to their corresponding ideas, or can obtain a correct knowledge of the elements which enter into the formation of compound ideas, and of the exclusions by which we arrive at the abstractions so perpetually resorted to in the process of reasoning and in the communication of our thoughts.

Lastly, such analyses alone can determine the principles on which a strictly *Philosophical Language* might be constructed. The probable result of the construction of such a language would be its eventual adoption by every civilized nation, thus realizing that splendid aspiration of philanthropists—the establishment of a Universal Language. However Utopian such a project may appear to the present generation, and however abortive may have been the former endeavours of Bishop Wilkins and others to realize it,[1] its accomplishment is surely not beset with greater difficulties than have impeded the progress to many other beneficial objects which in former times appeared to be no less visionary, and which yet were successfully achieved, in later ages, by the continued and persevering exertions of the human intellect. Is there at the present day, then, any ground for despair that, at some future stage of that higher civilization to which we trust the world is gradually tending, some new and bolder effort of genius towards the solution of this great problem may be crowned with success, and compass an object of such vast and paramount utility? Nothing, indeed, would conduce more directly to bring about a golden age of union and harmony among the several nations and races of mankind than the removal of that barrier to the interchange of thought and mutual good understanding between man and man which is now interposed by the diversity of their respective languages.

---

une langue de manière à être lu et entendu dans toute autre langue sans traduction, of which an edition in German was also published. It contains a great number of tabular schemes of categories, all of which appear to be excessively arbitrary and artificial, and extremely difficult of application, as well as of apprehension.

[1] 'The languages,' observes Horne Tooke, 'which are commonly used throughout the world, are much more simple and easy, convenient and philosophical, than Wilkins's scheme for a *real character*; or than any other scheme that has been at any other time imagined or proposed for the purpose.' —Ἔπεα Πτερόεντα, p. 125.

Pan study aids

selected titles published in the Brodie's Notes series

Jane Austen Emma Mansfield Park Northanger Abbey Persuasion
Pride and Prejudice

Anthologies of Poetry Ten Twentieth Century Poets The Poet's Tale

Robert Bolt A Man for All Seasons

Charlotte Brontë Jane Eyre

Emily Brontë Wuthering Heights

Geoffrey Chaucer The Knight's Tale The Nun's Priest's Tale
The Pardoner's Tale The Prologue to the Canterbury Tales
(parallel text editions) The Franklin's Tale The Miller's Tale

John Clare Selected Poetry and Prose

Joseph Conrad The Nigger of the Narcissus & Youth The Secret Agent

Charles Dickens Bleak House David Copperfield Great Expectations
Hard Times Oliver Twist Tale of Two Cities

George Eliot Middlemarch The Mill on the Floss Silas Marner

T. S. Eliot Murder in the Cathedral

Henry Fielding Joseph Andrews

F. Scott Fitzgerald The Great Gatsby

E. M. Forster A Passage to India Where Angels Fear to Tread

William Golding Lord of the Flies The Spire

Oliver Goldsmith Two Plays of Goldsmith: She Stoops to Conquer;
The Good Natured Man

Grahame Green The Power and the Glory

Thomas Hardy Chosen Poems of Thomas Hardy
Far from the Madding Crowd Jude the Obscure
The Mayor of Casterbridge Return of the Native
Tess of the d'Urbervilles The Trumpet-Major

L. P. Hartley The Go-Between The Shrimp and the Anemone

Joseph Heller Catch-22

Ernest Hemingway For Whom the Bell Tolls
The Old Man and the Sea

Barry Hines A Kestrel for a Knave

Gerard Manley Hopkins Poetry and Prose of Gerard Manley Hopkins

Aldous Huxley Brave New World

James Joyce A Portrait of the Artist as a Young Man

Ken Kesey One Flew over the Cuckoo's Nest

Rudyard Kipling Kim

D. H. Lawrence Selected Tales Sons and Lovers

Harper Lee To Kill a Mocking-Bird

Laurie Lee As I Walked out One Midsummer Morning
Cider With Rosie

Thomas Mann Death in Venice & Tonio Kröger

Christopher Marlowe Dr Faustus

W. Somerset Maugham Of Human Bondage

Arthur Miller The Crucible Death of a Salesman

John Milton A Choice of Milton's Verse Paradise Lost I, II

George Orwell Animal Farm 1984

Peter Shaffer The Royal Hunt of the Sun

William Shakespeare Antony and Cleopatra As You Like It
Coriolanus Hamlet Henry IV (Part I) Henry IV (Part II)
Henry V Julius Caesar King Lear King Richard III
Love's Labour's Lost Macbeth Measure for Measure
The Merchant of Venice A Midsummer-Night's Dream
Much Ado about Nothing Othello Richard II Romeo and Juliet
The Taming of the Shrew The Tempest Twelfth Night
The Winter's Tale

G. B. Shaw Androcles and the Lion Arms and the Man
Caesar and Cleopatra Pygmalion Saint Joan

Richard Sheridan Plays of Sheridan: The Rivals; The Critic;
The School for Scandal

John Steinbeck The Grapes of Wrath Of Mice and Men & The Pearl

J. M. Synge The Playboy of the Western World

Jonathan Swift Gulliver's Travels

William Thackeray Vanity Fair

Dylan Thomas Under Milk Wood

Mark Twain Huckleberry Finn

Keith Waterhouse Billy Liar

H. G. Wells The History of Mr Polly

Oscar Wilde The Importance of Being Earnest

William Wordsworth The Prelude (Books 1, 2) Wordsworth Selections
W. B. Yeats Selected Poetry

Australian titles
George Johnston My Brother Jack
Thomas Keneally The Chant of Jimmie Blacksmith
Ray Lawler Summer of the Seventeenth Doll
Henry Lawson The Bush Undertaker & Selected Short Stories
Ronald McKie The Mango Tree
Kenneth Slesor Selected Poems
Randolph Stow The Merry-Go-Round in the Sea To the Islands
Patrick White The Tree of Man
David Willi The Removalists

Robin Hyman
A Dictionary of Famous Quotations £1.25

This collection took over five years to compile. Its exceptionally clear and attractive presentation makes it a delight to read, and the lively selection of quotations encourages the browser as well as the seeker of specific references. The comprehensive index, with over 25,000 entries, enables one to trace a partly-remembered quotation with maximum speed.

edited by A. M. Macdonald
Chambers Essential English Dictionary £1.25

A dictionary of the words essential to daily life, with clear, precise and informative examples of usage, and idiomatic expressions.

This is outstanding among small dictionaries for legibility and ease of reference. And although the background of our language makes up the body of the book, it fully reflects modern developments in words, meanings and outlook.

Ronald Ridout and Clifford Witting
The Facts of English £1.00

An invaluable new edition of an established work of reference that gives the linguistic and literary facts of the English language from adverbs to zeugma.

Thoroughly revised and expanded by Ronald Ridout and Anthony Hern, this edition has been brought up to date with current cultural and commercial usage.

Over 1,000 entries, fully cross-referenced, explained and illustrated with suitable examples, and ranging from the elementary to the specialized, make this an ideal guide for student and expert alike.

G. H. Vallins
Good English 60p

Words 'have enabled us to rise above the brutes and often sink to the level of the demons' ALDOUS HUXLEY

Can you always write exactly what you mean? Are you sometimes at a loss for the right word?

G. H. Vallins states clearly and simply the main principles of current English usage, outlines the basic conventions, and deals entertainingly with jargon, idiom and cliché. It is a perfect guide on how to achieve a good simple style for business and everyday usage.

Better English 60p

This fascinating sequel to *Good English* leaves the world of accidence and syntax for that of idiom, figure, the logical expression of thought and the niceties of language . . . Introducing examples of unsound sentences from a variety of books, magazines and newspapers G. H. Vallins shows how they can be reconstructed far more effectively.

The Best English 60p

Believing that English is a rich and living language, G. H. Vallins takes the reader on an exciting exploration of literature. Dealing with the techniques of composition – in poetry, drama and prose – he shows how words, properly used, can communicate directly with the minds and emotions of others.

Harry Maddox
How to Study 70p

Successful study depends not only on ability and industry but on effective methods of working. This invaluable and comprehensive handbook tells you how to obtain the greatest benefit from your studies for the least expenditure of energy and effort. Using the author's methods you can speed up your reading rate, better your ability to memorize and take accurate notes, improve your written English and understand elementary mathematics. Whatever you may be studying, the author will help you to work without supervision and realize your full potential.

Clifford Allen
Passing Examinations 50p

This invaluable book for students of all ages explains the techniques of study which are afforded by modern psychology and advises how these can be applied to both written and oral examinations.

'Refreshingly down to earth' BIRMINGHAM POST

C. L. Barber
The Story of Language 80p

In the first half of this book more general topics such as the nature of language, its origins, the causes of linguistic changes and language families, are gone into – the second half is, in effect, a history of the English language.

from the Pan Management Series

Peter F. Drucker
The Practice of Management £1.50

'A "key" book on the subject, A "tour de force", brilliantly and admirably
carried out. It is original, stimulating, and full of wisdom'
THE TIMES REVIEW OF INDUSTRY

'His penetrating accounts of the Ford Company, the retail enterprise of
Sears Roebuck, and, most interesting of all, the International Business
Machines concern, are worth a library of formal business histories'
NEW STATESMAN

Ray Willsmer
Directing the Marketing Effort £1.50

Based on a series of seminars given by Ray Willsmer for the BIM, the book
successfully bridges the credibility gap between the theory and practice of
consumer and industrial marketing.

'. . . Perhaps the greatest benefit to be gained, even by the most practised of
marketing men, is the critical self-analysis to which readers will subject
themselves, their peers and their organizations. All students of marketing
would benefit from reading this book' MARKETING

John W. Humble
Improving Business Results 75p

The outstandingly successful basic text on Management by Objectives.

'It is as sure as anything can be in the world of management that a company
which adopted the techniques suggested would improve its results and often
by a substantial margin' THE TIMES BUSINESS NEWS

'John Humble's feet are firmly planted in reality . . . a veritable gold-mine of
distilled wisdom and experience which fully lends itself to practical
application' INDUSTRIAL RELATIONS JOURNAL

edited by S. E. Stiegeler BSc and Glyn Thomas BSc Econ
A Dictionary of Economics and Commerce £1.50

An authoritative A–Z of the terms used internationally in the overlapping
fields of theoretical economics and practical commerce.

A team of expert contributors provides a formal definition of each word or
term, followed by an explanation of its underlying concepts and
accompanied by appropriate illustrations. Special attention is paid to such
new and rapidly expanding subjects as cost-benefit analysis and welfare
economics. And the vocabularies of banking, accounting, insurance, stock
exchanges, commodity dealing, shipping, transport and commercial law
are all included.

Derek French and Heather Saward
Dictionary of Management £1.50

A handy reference work providing definitions for nearly 4,000 terms,
abbreviations and techniques current in general and functional management,
and in such areas as government, law and economics that affect the
manager's work.

Definitions are based on how managers and writers on management
actually use the words and phrases selected. The vocabulary ranges from
established terms to contemporary jargon and there is extensive
cross-reference.

You can buy these and other Pan books from booksellers and
newsagents; or direct from the following address:
Pan Books, Sales Office, Cavaye Place, London SW10 9PG
Send purchase price plus 20p for the first book and 10p for
each additional book, to allow for postage and packing
Prices quoted are applicable in the UK

While every effort is made to keep prices low, it is sometimes
necessary to increase prices at short notice. Pan Books reserve the
right to show on covers and charge new retail prices which may differ
from those advertised in the text or elsewhere